Where the classroom comes to life!

From watching actual classroom video footage of teachers and students interacting to building standards-based lessons and web-based portfolios . . . from a robust resource library of the "What Every Teacher Should Know About" series to complete instruction on writing an effective research paper . . . **MyLabSchool** brings together an amazing collection of resources for future teachers. This website gives you a wealth of videos, print and simulated cases, career advice, and much more.

Use **MyLabSchool** with this Allyn and Bacon Education text, and you will have everything you need to succeed in your course. Assignment IDs have also been incorporated into many Allyn and Bacon Education texts to link to the online material in **MyLabSchool** . . . connecting the teachers of tomorrow to the information they need today.

VISIT www.mylabschool.com **to learn more about this invaluable resource and Take a Tour!**

Here's what you'll find in mylabschool™

Where the classroom comes to life!

VideoLab ▶

Access hundreds of video clips of actual classroom situations from a variety of grade levels and school settings. These 3- to 5-minute closed-captioned video clips illustrate real teacher–student interaction, and are organized both topically *and* by discipline. Students can test their knowledge of classroom concepts with integrated observation questions.

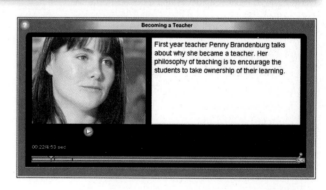

Becoming a Teacher

First year teacher Penny Brandenburg talks about why she became a teacher. Her philosophy of teaching is to encourage the students to take ownership of their learning.

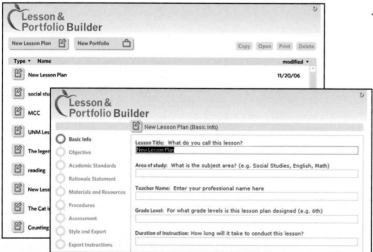

◀ Lesson & Portfolio Builder

This feature enables students to create, maintain, update, and share online portfolios and standards-based lesson plans. The Lesson Planner walks students, step-by-step, through the process of creating a complete lesson plan, including verifiable objectives, assessments, and related state standards. Upon completion, the lesson plan can be printed, saved, e-mailed, or uploaded to a website.

Here's what you'll find in **mylabschool**™

Simulations ▶

This area of MyLabSchool contains interactive tools designed to better prepare future teachers to provide an appropriate education to students with special needs. To achieve this goal, the IRIS (IDEA and Research for Inclusive Settings) Center at Vanderbilt University has created course enhancement materials. These resources include online interactive modules, case study units, information briefs, student activities, an online dictionary, and a searchable directory of disability-related web sites.

◀ Resource Library

MyLabSchool includes a collection of PDF files on crucial and timely topics within education. Each topic is applicable to any education class, and these documents are ideal resources to prepare students for the challenges they will face in the classroom. This resource can be used to reinforce a central topic of the course, or to enhance coverage of a topic you need to explore in more depth.

Research Navigator ▶

This comprehensive research tool gives users access to four exclusive databases of authoritative and reliable source material. It offers a comprehensive, step-by-step walk-through of the research process. In addition, students can view sample research papers and consult guidelines on how to prepare endnotes and bibliographies. The latest release also features a new bibliography-maker program—AutoCite.

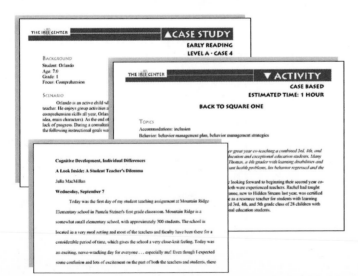

◀ Case Archive

This collection of print and simulated cases can be easily accessed by topic and subject area, and can be integrated into your course. The cases are drawn from Allyn & Bacon's best-selling books, and represent the complete range of disciplines and student ages. It's an ideal way to consider and react to real classroom scenarios. The possibilities for using these high-quality cases within the course are endless.

About the Authors

In combination, the three authors of this text represent well over 100 years of experience in schools, teacher education, and education research. Each brings a special perspective about teacher education and complementary views of the importance of teachers in the context of today's schools. Each author is professionally involved and regularly engaged with teacher education candidates, teacher education faculty, and teachers in schools.

Gene E. Hall is a professor of Educational Leadership at the University of Nevada, Las Vegas. He also is Director of the Partnerships for Excellence in Teacher Education (PETE) Project, which is housed at the American Association of Colleges of Teacher Education in Washington, D.C. The PETE project provides assistance to teacher education institutions seeking national accreditation. Dr. Hall is a national and internationally recognized scholar for his research on the change process in organizations. He is coauthor of *Implementing Change: Patterns, Principles, and Potholes* (2nd Edition), and *Introduction to the Foundations of American Education* (14th Edition).

Linda F. Quinn, professor of curriculum and instruction at the University of Nevada, Las Vegas, is an experienced classroom teacher who has practiced extensively both within the United States and abroad, including in Italy, Iran, and Japan. She earned a doctorate in curriculum and instruction at the University of Houston and also served as the director of professional development for classroom teachers at the University of Northern Iowa. Dr. Quinn works frequently with teacher education candidates and doctoral students who are considering careers in education and has published numerous articles in leading educational journals.

Donna M. Gollnick is senior vice president of the National Council for Accreditation of Teacher Education (NCATE) where she oversees the accreditation of over 700 colleges and universities. She is the coauthor of the textbooks, *Multicultural Education in a Pluralistic Society* and *Introduction to the Foundations of American Education*. She also has been promoting and writing about multicultural education and equity in teacher education and schools since the 1970s and is past president of the National Association for Multicultural Education (NAME).

The Joy of Teaching

Making a Difference in Student Learning

Gene E. Hall
University of Nevada, Las Vegas

Linda F. Quinn
University of Nevada, Las Vegas

Donna M. Gollnick
National Council for Accreditation of Teacher Education (NCATE)

PEARSON

Boston • New York • San Francisco
Mexico City • Montreal • Toronto • London • Madrid • Munich • Paris
Hong Kong • Singapore • Tokyo • Cape Town • Sydney

Executive Editor and Publisher: Stephen D. Dragin
Series Editorial Assistant: Katie Heimsoth
Developmental Editor: Alicia Reilly
Marketing Manager: Weslie Sellinger
Production Editor: Annette Joseph
Editorial Production Service: Modern Graphics, Inc.
Composition Buyer: Linda Cox
Manufacturing Buyer: Megan Cochran
Electronic Composition: Modern Graphics, Inc.
Interior Design: Denise Hoffman
Photo Researchers: Annie Pickert and Naomi Rudov
Cover Administrator: Linda Knowles
Cover Designer: Studio Nine

For related titles and support materials, visit our online catalog at www.ablongman.com.

Between the time website information is gathered and then published, it is not unusual for some sites to have closed. Also, the transcription of URLs can result in typographical errors. The publisher would appreciate notification where these errors occur so that they may be corrected in subsequent editions.

Library of Congress Cataloging-in-Publication Data

Hall, Gene E.,
   The joy of teaching : making a difference in student learning / Gene E. Hall, Linda F. Quinn,
Donna M. Gollnick.
      p. cm.
   Includes bibliographical references (p.) and indexes.
   ISBN 0-205-40559-2
     1. Teaching—United States—Textbooks. I. Quinn, Linda F. II. Gollnick, Donna M. III. Title.

LB1025.3.H34 2007
371.102—dc22

2006051513

978-0-205-40559-6

Printed in the United States of America

10 9 8 7 6 5 4 3 2 1 [RRD-OH] 11 10 09 08 07

Credits appear on page 619, which constitutes an extension of the copyright page.

The authors dedicate this book to all the great teachers we have known—from early childhood teachers to research university professors. We have great memories of their deep knowledge and skillful teaching, their helpfulness, and cheerful willingness to offer guidance. They taught us to learn and laugh at the same time. They brought true joy to our learning. We thank each and every one of them.

Brief Contents

Contents

Chapter 2   Today's Students   44

Part Two. **Today's Schools**

Chapter **3** Families and Communities   90

Part Three The Foundations of Education

Part Four Teaching Today

Chapter *10* Integrating Technology and Teaching   364

Chapter 11   Assessing Student Learning and Results   398

Chapter 12

Managing the Classroom and Student Behavior   436

Part Five **Education for Tomorrow**

Features at a Glance

Teachers and the Law

Understanding & USING EVIDENCE

Teachers' Lounge

Preface

Why did we decide to develop another "introduction to teaching" text when there are so many available already? Today's schools have changed dramatically over the past decade, and we believed that there was a need for a book that truly reflected these changes. Today's students and parents are different, certainly in terms of their ethnic diversity, but also within a broader context of family, community, and society.

A dramatic paradigm change is occurring in schools and affecting the content of teacher education. There are many reasons for this shift, including the accountability movement, the last twenty plus years of research on learning coming out of the educational psychology field, research on teacher effectiveness, and the fact that national and state program accreditation has moved to looking at outcomes, rather than counting the number of books in the library. We no longer think about teaching in terms of inputs ("What I teach"). Educators now view teaching in terms of outputs ("What are my students learning?" "What evidence do I have that my students are learning?"). Teachers' work is now more than ever focused on making a difference in student learning. All that we do as teachers must have some connection to what our students do as learners. For this reason, we've framed our discussions about teaching around its connection to student learning. The decisions that we make as educators must be informed—always, first and foremost—by the learning needs of our students.

Teachers' jobs are more challenging and complex than they used to be, with new external pressures such as those brought about by high-stakes testing and the increasing role of the federal government in the daily activities of teachers. These challenges could lead one to conclude that teaching can no longer be satisfying and fun. This was another important reason we wanted to write this text, emphasizing that there is joy in teaching! An unfortunate reality for today's teacher candidates is that they've been exposed to so much criticism of schools, teachers, and the education profession. Nowadays this is practically a spectator sport! We decided it was high time to remind ourselves of the good that teachers do and of the many, many rewards that a career in teaching still brings. Yes, teaching is hard work, but it is still one of the most satisfying and personally fulfilling careers one can choose, not to mention one of the most vital to the future of our world. Throughout this text you'll hear from real teachers—from first-year teachers to seasoned masters of the profession—who have shared their stories with us. We learn how they get things done every day, of course, but also how they make a difference for their students, and how in doing so they find wonder, inspiration, and joy.

Plan of the Book

We've organized the parts and chapters of the text in order to answer the questions that aspiring teachers ask: What does it take to become a teacher? What are schools and students really like? What will I be expected to teach? Is teaching the right career choice for me? Part I, *Today's Teachers and Students*, includes two chapters that describe what is entailed in becoming a qualified teacher and what today's students are like. Part II, *Today's Schools*, describes the way schools are structured and how things work day to day for teachers and students. This section also addresses the increasing importance of understanding families. Part III, *The Foundations of Education*, describes the historical, social, and philosophical roots of education and schooling. Part IV, *Teaching Today*, addresses the nuts and bolts of teaching, stressing the importance of student learning in terms of standards and benchmarks, often referred to as the "output" of teaching. This section includes chapters devoted to usable teaching strategies, tips for classroom management, ideas for integrating technology in the classroom, and, more central than ever, information about assessing student learning. Finally, Part V, *Education for Tomorrow*, addresses the need for schools to continue to improve, discussing schoolwide reforms and the innovations that today's teachers are implementing. The final chapter explores the future: obtaining a first teaching position, the importance of teacher leadership, and anticipating the career options that are open to high quality teachers.

Five Major Themes

- **Student Learning as "Output":** Until very recently, quality was defined in terms of what teachers did. Now the framework is dramatically different. Teacher quality has come to be defined in terms of the impacts, the results, and the differences each teacher makes in student learning. Our text continually makes this connection with sections and features throughout that reinforce the relationship between teaching and learning.

- **Joy:** As educators ourselves, we are very aware of how hard today's teachers work, but we want aspiring teachers to look for the joy that comes from being an excellent teacher. We've tried to infuse our text with examples of experienced teachers and how they've discovered joy in their teaching careers.

- **Excellence:** In this time of increasing standards it is more important than ever that future teachers set high expectations for themselves and for the students that they teach. We've filled our text with tools and information to help teachers teach with confidence and in ways that are always professional and informed by research.

- **Real Schools:** We take pride in knowing that every word of this text is grounded in the reality of today's schools. The workplace of today's schools is intense and complex. Today's students are diverse. Today's schools have a range of technology resources. We believe that every page of this text "lives" in these new realities.

- **Real People:** Our text is full of them! Teachers, students, and principals come from all walks of life. They teach and learn in all kinds of settings ranging from inner cities, to the suburbs, to rural communities. We've taken every opportunity to introduce you to the experiences and stories of real students, teachers, and school leaders. We believe you'll find their stories interesting and helpful as you approach the beginning of your own teaching career.

Special Text Features

Several features are included in each chapter of this text, each designed with a specific purpose, and all designed to support your understanding of and engagement in the material we present. These features include:

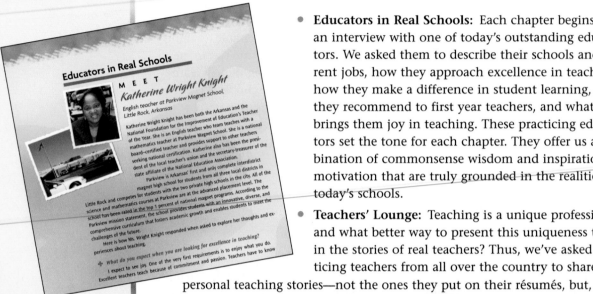

- **Educators in Real Schools:** Each chapter begins with an interview with one of today's outstanding educators. We asked them to describe their schools and current jobs, how they approach excellence in teaching, how they make a difference in student learning, what they recommend to first year teachers, and what brings them joy in teaching. These practicing educators set the tone for each chapter. They offer us a combination of commonsense wisdom and inspirational motivation that are truly grounded in the realities of today's schools.

- **Teachers' Lounge:** Teaching is a unique profession, and what better way to present this uniqueness than in the stories of real teachers? Thus, we've asked practicing teachers from all over the country to share their personal teaching stories—not the ones they put on their résumés, but, rather, the ones that may matter even more. Each chapter includes one of their accounts and reflections about a day, a moment, or a particular student or colleague—but always about laughter, inspiration, and joy.

Teachers' Lounge

Why I Became a 1st-Grade Teacher
One of my colleagues once asked his graduate education students to introduce themselves to one another by talking about why they wanted to stay in teaching. An elderly blonde teacher slowly walked to the podium. During a recent back-to-school night, one of her student's parents arrived just as she was turning off the lights. The teacher, feeling badly that the parents missed the event, asked if their daughter had given them the invitation with the correct time and place. The parents replied yes and in addition said that their daughter had added one other piece of information. She told them that her teacher had yellow hair and was the prettiest teacher at the school. The teacher said, with a tear in her eye, that is why she is a 1st-grade teacher.

● Dawn Yonally, Ph.D.
Northeastern
State University

- **Classroom Teaching Vignettes:** Every chapter section in this text begins with an authentic teaching story that provides real-world context for the material that you'll read about in the upcoming section. Revisiting sections conclude each section with follow-up information on the opening stories in light of the material that you'll just have read.

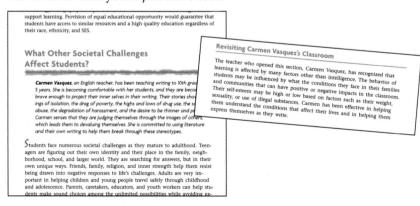

support learning. Provision of equal educational opportunity would guarantee that students have access to similar resources and a high quality education regardless of their race, ethnicity, and SES.

What Other Societal Challenges Affect Students?

Carmen Vasquez, an English teacher, has been teaching writing to 10th grade for 5 years. She is becoming comfortable with her students, and they are becoming brave enough to project their inner selves in their writing. Their stories show feelings of isolation, the drag of poverty, the highs and lows of drug use, the sting of abuse, the degradation of harassment, and the desire to be thinner and prettier. Carmen senses that they are judging themselves through the images of others, which leads them to devaluing themselves. She is committed to using literature and their own writing to help them break through these stereotypes.

Students face numerous societal challenges as they mature to adulthood. Teenagers are figuring out their own identity and their place in the family, neighborhood, school, and larger world. They are searching for answers, but in their own unique ways. Friends, family, religion, and inner strength help them resist being drawn into negative responses to life's challenges. Adults are very important in helping children and young people travel safely through childhood and adolescence. Parents, caretakers, educators, and youth workers can help students make sound choices among the unlimited possibilities while avoiding ex-

Revisiting Carmen Vasquez's Classroom

The teacher who opened this section, Carmen Vasquez, has recognized that learning is affected by many factors other than intelligence. The behavior of students may be influenced by what the conditions they face in their families and communities that can have positive or negative impacts in the classroom. Their self-esteem may be high or low based on factors such as their weight, sexuality, or use of illegal substances. Carmen has been effective in helping them understand the conditions that affect their lives and in helping them express themselves as they write.

- **Teachers and the Law:** Informed teachers must know about the legal aspects of education. Rather than presenting a separate chapter that dryly summarizes the legal aspects of education in an abstract fashion, we wanted to make the law more relevant to specific chapter content and to the questions students and teachers have asked us. Thus, each chapter includes this feature that addresses the real needs and concerns of today's teachers.

- **Challenging Assumptions: Findings from Research:** In many cases the principles set forth by educators may sound ridiculously obvious: "Everybody knows that!" However, research findings often are counterintuitive and do not conform to what most people might see as common sense. Thus, we've provided examples of surprising research information that we hope will encourage you to question the obvious, and to become more discerning in your selection of teaching strategies and more demanding of your own teaching practices.

- **Understanding and Using Evidence:** Today's teachers need to be able to use research data and evidence as never before. Thus, we've included in each chapter a feature that presents a set of research findings or data. You are asked to form an understanding of the information and to attempt your own analysis. Follow-up information and sample answers or analyses for each are provided in the *Understanding and Using Evidence* Appendix at the end of the text.

Teachers and the Law

TRACKING STUDENTS

Can students be grouped by ability or achievement?

Yes, unless the practice results in discrimination against a group of students. In the most publicized case, Hobson v. Hansen, parents in Washington, D.C., in 1967 argued that their children were assigned to lower tracks with limited curriculum and little chance for moving to higher levels. The court found that the testing methods used by the school district discriminated against students of color. Testing instruments used to make decisions about placement must be reliable, valid, and unbiased. They cannot be racially biased or administered in discriminatory ways. They must be administered in the student's native language and with appropriate accommodations for students with disabilities.

STUDENTS' FREEDOM OF EXPRESSION

Can students criticize governmental policies or practices in school?

Yes, as long as the action is not disruptive. The 1965 Tinker decision is the basis of most decisions related to students' freedom of expression. In this case, three students were sent home for wearing black armbands to protest the United States' involvement in Vietnam. The Supreme Court ruled that students are allowed to express their views in an orderly way.

The First Amendment allows both students and adults the right to express themselves and the right to be silent. For example, students cannot be forced to salute the American flag or say the Pledge of Allegiance. However, some student expression is not covered by the First Amendment. School officials can take action against a student whose written or oral language is defamatory, shaming, or ridiculing others. The Supreme Court in 1986 ruled in Bethel School District v. Fraser that school officials could censor lewd, vulgar, and indecent student behavior. Courts have also upheld schools' rights to discipline students for inflammatory expression such as threatening other students or teachers.

REPORTING CHILD ABUSE

Can teachers be held liable for not reporting suspected child abuse?

Yes. Teachers are among the professionals who are required to report signs of child abuse. Penalties for not reporting include fines and/or prison terms. School districts may also impose disciplinary action. For example, the Seventh Circuit upheld the suspension and demotion of a teacher-psychologist who did not promptly report suspected abuse in Pesce v. J. Sterling Morton High School District 201, Cook County, Illinois, in 1987. School districts usually have procedures for reporting suspected abuse, including to whom the abuse should be reported. In 1998, the Kentucky Supreme Court ruled that once the abuse is reported to a supervisor, the supervisor has the responsibility for reporting it to the appropriate authority. However, teachers should check to ensure that the appropriate agency has been notified.

Sources: Cambron-McCabe, N. H., McCarthy, M. M., & Thomas, S. B. (2004). Public school law: Teachers' and students' rights (5th ed.). Boston: Allyn and Bacon; Essex, N. L. (2005). School law and the public schools: A practical guide for educational leaders. Boston: Allyn and Bacon.

Challenging Assumptions
FINDINGS FROM RESEARCH

In small-group instruction, should teachers call on students randomly or in turn?

The Assumption: A frequently used teaching tactic is to organize students in small groups for instruction. This tactic is used heavily for reading and mathematics instruction in elementary schools. Researchers have identified a number of principles that make for success including: (a) the difficulty of teacher questions should be such that the lesson can move right along; (b) the teacher should aim for 80 percent of student's answers being correct; (c) students should have frequent opportunity to respond; and (d) the teacher should provide clear feedback about the correctness of student responses. A critical assumption has to do with whether the teacher should call on the students in small-group instruction randomly or in turn.

Study Design and Methods: One of the early major studies that examined teacher behaviors in relation to student achievement was the Texas Teacher Effectiveness Study. In this study, 4 years of student achievement data were available for 165 2nd and 3rd-grade teachers. A sample of these teachers (n = 31) were observed for 10 hours in the first year of the study and 30 hours in the second year of the study. Their teaching behaviors were correlated with student achievement. Much to the researcher's surprise, "patterned turns" in small groups was positively correlated with student achievement. In other words, teachers who called on students in sequence had greater gains than those who called on students randomly or called on students who volunteered.

Implications: Contrary to the logic that calling on students randomly will keep them attending to the lesson, the findings from this research indicates that calling on students in turn ensures that all students participate and in equal proportions. The study findings apply to high- as well as low-SES classes. In high-SES classes, it helps students focus on the content of the lesson, rather than trying to get the teacher to call on them. In low-SES classes, it provides a structure and predictability that may help more anxious students participate.

With the findings from this research in mind, in your next practicum experiences, observe small-group instruction. Find situations where students are called on in-turn and where they are called on randomly. What differences do you see in terms of student participation and achievement?

Source: Brophy, J., & Evertson, C. (1976). Learning from teaching: A developmental perspective. Boston: Allyn and Bacon.

Understanding & USING EVIDENCE

Each state sets the qualifying or cut-off score that a test taker must achieve before they can receive a license to teach in the state. These scores differ across selected states as shown here.

Test	AR	CT	LA	MS	NV	OH	PA	VA
Biology: Content Knowledge	—	152	150	135	154	148	147	155
Elementary Education: Curriculum, Instruction, & Assessment	—	163	—	135	158	—	168	—
Elementary Education: Content Knowledge	—	—	150	—	—	—	—	143
English Language, Literature, & Composition: Content Knowledge	159	172	160	157	150	167	160	172
Mathematics: Content Knowledge	116	137	125	123	144	139	136	147
Social Studies: Content Knowledge	155	162	149	143	152	157	157	161

Your Task: Just because you have passed the licensure test in the state in which you have completed a teacher education program does not mean that you have met the qualifying score in another state. You should be aware of the qualifying scores in the state in which you would like to work.

1. What do you know about requirements in the states listed in the table above?
2. What does this table tell you about becoming qualified in these eight states?
3. Why are scores not indicated for some states?
4. Why do some states require higher scores than others?

Source: Educational Testing Service. Retrieved June 15, 2006, from www.ets.org/praxis/prxstate.html.

Refer to the Understanding & Using Evidence Appendix at the end of the text for answers and information related to these activities.

Connecting TO THE CLASSROOM

This chapter has provided some basic information about the need for qualified teachers, where the jobs are, how to become licensed, and some of the circumstances you might encounter during your first few years of teaching. The following are some key principles for applying the information in this chapter to the classroom.

1. Effective teachers make a difference in student learning.
2. Professional teachers are responsible for the well-being of their clients (students).
3. Mentoring of new teachers is a critical factor in the retention of teachers in the profession.
4. A school's curriculum is guided by the state or school district's standards for students.
5. Teacher standards identify the key knowledge, skills, and disposition that teachers should demonstrate in the classroom.
6. The collection of your work in a portfolio provides evidence that you have met standards and that you can help students in your classroom learn.

- **Connecting to the Classroom:** Ideas, examples, and recommendations for teachers are included throughout the body of each chapter. In addition, each chapter concludes with this convenient summary or "punch list" of suggestions for best teaching practice.

Aids to Understanding

Each chapter includes a number of elements designed to facilitate your comprehension, guide your reading, stimulate class discussions, and encourage critical thinking and reflection.

- **Focus Questions:** Each chapter begins with questions to guide your reading and thinking about the upcoming chapter material. These questions serve as a "pre-summary" of the main topics to be covered.

- **Margin Glossary:** Like any other profession, teaching has a professional vocabulary. When key terms are introduced within each chapter, their definitions are provided in the adjacent margin. We hope this will enhance your reading of the text and also provide a useful reference when it comes time to review the material. Key terms are also provided in an alphabetical list in the Glossary.

- **Summary:** Each chapter concludes with a few brief paragraphs touching on the chapter's main ideas, highlighting in broad-brush fashion its most important topics, which we hope will be highly useful to you in your reviewing and test preparation.

- **Class Discussion Questions:** Each chapter concludes with questions written to stimulate conversations about ways in which the chapter relates to your ideas about becoming a teacher.

- **Field Guide for School Observations:** Most of today's teacher education candidates will have opportunities to visit and participate in real classrooms. This feature proposes suggestions for taking the best advantage of these opportunities.

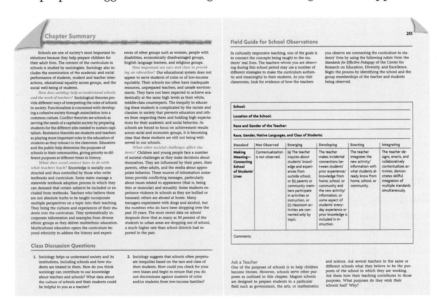

- **Ask a Teacher or Principal:** When there is an opportunity, aspiring teachers can learn a lot from those who are already working in schools. This feature suggests interview questions that can be useful for delving deeper into what today's teachers and principals do and think.

- **Journaling: Becoming a Thoughtful Teacher:** Taking a few minutes each day or week to jot down notes about your current thoughts and ideas should be part of your routine as a teacher. Over time these notes provide a personal record of how your ideas and thoughts have developed and how you can become more personally involved in the work of teachers in real schools. This feature provides suggestions for getting you started.

- **Portfolio Task:** As you progress through your teacher education preparation program it is important that you record your progress. The tasks suggested in this feature support this activity and also anticipate the more formal portfolio that will be required at the completion of your program and when you apply for a teaching position.

- **Self-Assessments: What Am I Learning?** Short assessment tasks for review and reflection are presented at the end of each chapter. These items mimic some of the testing formats that you may find when you take your state's licensure exam.

- **Using the Web:** The Web is a rich and invaluable resource for teachers—from undergraduates in teacher education programs, to veterans and master teachers. Each chapter concludes with a small sample of what we've found to be particularly useful websites.

- **Your Professional Library:** It's never too early to begin developing your own professional library. Here we provide an annotated list of key books and journal articles to get you started.

Supplements

Supplements for the Instructor

To help you get the most out of using *The Joy of Teaching*, we have provided a number of useful supplements for instructors:

- **Instructor's Manual.** The Instructor's Manual includes a wealth of interesting ideas and activities designed to help instructors teach the course. Each chapter includes outline and lecture notes, discussion questions, Web activities, and additional resources.

- **Test Bank.** The Test Bank includes hundreds of questions, including multiple choice items, true/false items, essay questions, case studies, and authentic assessments, plus text page references and answer feedback.

- **Computerized Test Bank.** The printed Test Bank is also available electronically through the Allyn & Bacon computerized testing system, TestGen EQ. Instructors can use TestGen EQ to create exams in just minutes by selecting from the existing database of questions, editing questions, and/or writing original questions.

- **PowerPoint™ Presentation.** Ideal for lecture presentations or student handouts, the PowerPoint™ Presentation created for this text provides dozens of ready-to-use graphic and text images.

- **Allyn & Bacon Transparencies for Foundations of Education and Introduction to Teaching.** A set of 100 acetate transparencies related to topics in the text.

- **MyLabSchool** **(mylabschool** Available as a value-package item with student copies of *The Joy of Teaching*, MyLabSchool is a collection of online tools for student success in the course, in licensure exams, and the teaching career. Visit www.mylabschool.com to access the following: **video clips** from real classrooms, with opportunities for students to reflect on the videos and offer their own thoughts and suggestions for applying theory to practice; an extensive archive of **text and multimedia cases** that provide valuable perspectives on real classrooms and real teaching challenges; Allyn & Bacon's **Lesson and Portfolio Builder** application, which includes an integrated state standards correlation tool; help with research papers using **Research Navigator™**, which provides access to three exclusive databases of credible and reliable source material including EBSCO's ContentSelect Academic Journal Database, *New York Times* Search by Subject Archive, and "Best of the Web" Link Library. MyLabSchool also includes a **Career Center** with resources for Praxis exams and licensure preparation, professional portfolio development, job search, and interview techniques.

- **VideoWorkshop for Foundations/Introduction to Teaching, Version 2.0.**
An easy way to bring video into your course for maximized learning! This total
teaching and learning system includes quality video footage on an easy-to-use
CD-ROM plus a Student Learning Guide and an Instructor's Teaching Guide—
both with textbook-specific Correlation Grids. The result? A program that
brings textbook concepts to life with ease and that helps students understand,
analyze, and apply the objectives of the course. VideoWorkshop is available for
students as a value-pack option with this textbook.

Supplements for the Student

To help you get the most of using *The Joy of Teaching*, we have provided a number
of useful supplements for students:

- **Companion Website.** An exciting array of tools and activities that will help
students study more effectively and can take them beyond the book. It includes focus questions, practice tests, Web links, and flash cards. The website
also features an interactive timeline and selected New York Times articles.
Visit www.ablongman.com/hall1e.

- **MyLabSchool mylabschool.** Available as a value-package item with student copies of *The Joy of Teaching*, MyLabSchool is a collection of online tools
for student success in the course, in licensure exams, and the teaching career.
Visit www.mylabschool.com to access the following: **video clips** from real
classrooms, with opportunities for students to reflect on the videos and offer
their own thoughts and suggestions for applying theory to practice; an extensive archive of **text and multimedia cases** that provide valuable perspectives
on real classrooms and real teaching challenges; Allyn & Bacon's **Lesson and
Portfolio Builder** application, which includes an integrated state standards
correlation tool; help with research papers using **Research Navigator™**,
which provides access to three exclusive databases of credible and reliable
source material including EBSCO's ContentSelect Academic Journal Database,
New York Times Search by Subject Archive, and "Best of the Web" Link Library.
MyLabSchool also includes a **Career Center** with resources for Praxis exams
and licensure preparation, professional portfolio development, job search,
and interview techniques.

- **Course Management.** Powered by Blackboard and hosted nationally, Allyn
& Bacon's own course management system, CourseCompass, helps you
manage all aspects of teaching your course. For colleges and universities
with WebCT™ and Blackboard™ licenses, special course management packages can be requested in these formats as well, and the Test Item file for
this text can be prepared in the appropriate format for porting into your
system. Allyn & Bacon is proud to offer premium content for Special
Education in these platforms.

- Allyn & Bacon CourseCompass for Introduction to Teaching/Foundations of Education (Access code required)
- Allyn & Bacon WebCT for Introduction to Teaching and Foundations of Education, Version 3.0 (Access code required)
- Allyn & Bacon Blackboard for Introduction to Teaching/Foundations of Education (Access code required)

Acknowledgments

The development of this text would not have been possible without the ideas and opportunities to learn about today's schools, teachers, and students that have been provided by the many outstanding teachers, education leaders, and academic colleagues we have known. Their willingness to share about their successes, joys, and challenges has been instrumental in our decision to collaborate in the writing of this text. We thank each and every one of them for their willingness to share what it is really like, as well as their direct (we might even say blunt) feedback on earlier drafts of our manuscript.

We also wish to express our deep appreciation for the contributions of the many talented people at Allyn and Bacon. First and foremost Steve Dragin not only made the strategic decision to develop this project, but also maintained close contact with us authors throughout the writing and production processes. He had many good suggestions that have significantly improved the final product. Alicia Reilly, our developmental editor, not only has guided the project from its inception, she also has made many substantive contributions and been a constant enthusiastic supporter of our efforts. There are many other A&B people who have been a significant part of this effort including Annette Joseph, Katie Heimsoth, Martha White Tenney, and Weslie Sellinger. It has been a pleasure and an honor to collaborate with so many talented professionals.

We are grateful to the following reviewers for their thoughtful reading and commentary at all stages of the development of this book. Their reasoned and constructive input—on everything from that very first book outline, pedagogy plan, and sample features proposal to the various stages of draft manuscript were instrumental in shaping the tone of the book and ensuring its accuracy and relevance.

Dwight Allen, Old Dominion University
Ramona M. Bartee, Creighton University
Jody S. Britten, Ball State University
Susan H. Christian, Patrick Henry Community College
Marta Cronin, Indian River Community College
Bill Estes, Lee University
Cornelia J. Glenn, Owensboro Community and Technical College
Linda Gronberg-Quinn, Community College of Baltimore County

Judy A. Smith, California State University, Fullerton
Dale N. Titus, Kutztown University
Diana Wagner, Salisbury University
Vincent Walencik, Montclair State University
Merrill K. Watrous, Lane Community College
Joan Rudel Weinreich, Manhattanville College
Carlise E. Womack, Bainbridge College
LaDonna R. Young, Southwest Tennessee Community College

GEH
LFQ
DMG
September, 2006

Becoming a Teacher

Educators in Real Schools

M E E T

Michele Clarke

Inclusion Assistant, Pointers Run Elementary School

Michele has worked for 4 years. She is working with students with disabilities in the 1st and 4th grades. Michele has a bachelor's degree in psychology and has been taking required courses in reading and assessment to become eligible for a license to teach preschool special education. She already has passed a basic skills test and content tests in special education and early childhood education. She hopes to be a fully qualified, licensed teacher when school opens in the fall.

Pointers Run Elementary School serves 800 students in preschool through the 5th grade in the middle of Howard County, which is located between Washington, D.C., and Baltimore. Middle-class and upper-middle-class families populate this community where most parents are actively involved in their children's education. The student population is diverse. Twenty-two percent of the students are Asian American, 6 percent African American, 2 percent Latino, and 70 percent European American. A number of students' families are recent immigrants from Asia, Eastern Europe, India, and Russia. Four percent of the students are English language learners. Three- and 4-year-olds with speech and language delays and multiple intense needs attend the Regional Early Childhood Center (RECC) at Pointers Run. These preschool inclusion classes include students without disabilities whose parents have voluntarily enrolled them in the program. Students who are gifted and talented and students with learning disabilities, autism, emotional disabilities, Down syndrome, mental retardation, attention deficit/hyperactivity disorder (ADHD), physical disabilities, and vision disabilities attend classes with their peers

without special needs. Pointers Run is staffed by 45 teachers, eight instructional assistants, eight inclusion assistants, and seven assistants as well as other education professionals such as a school psychologist, a guidance counselor, and reading specialists. During her tenure at Pointers Run, Michele has worked with preschool, kindergarten, 1st grade, and 4th grade teachers in inclusion classrooms. She reports that all teachers have strengths and weaknesses in their teaching, but some are more effective than others. Michele is often exhausted at the end of a day, especially when the 4th grader with Down syndrome has had a bad day, usually leading to his removal from the regular classroom. When asked whether she is sure she wants to teach, she enthusiastically responds in the affirmative.

❖ *Why do you want to teach?*

I enjoy working with children and passing on the knowledge I have. It is fun to see them learning for the first time and a challenge to figure out ways to help them learn.

❖ *What do you expect when you are looking for excellence in teaching?*

I am very impressed with the general education 4th grade teacher. She uses a variety of activities to keep the children engaged. The class includes children with learning disabilities and ADHD, but she incorporates hands-on experiences in which they actively participate along with their peers without disabilities. All of the students learn through experimentation, especially in science and math. The teacher uses group activities such as the jigsaw strategy very effectively. In health education, she divides the class into groups to develop posters that then become the center of their presentations to the class. The students are encouraged to be creative and they gain experience in speaking to a

group. Her lessons incorporate technology as students work in the computer lab, using the Internet to explore planets and other science topics. She helps students learn the keyboard through a software package with games interspersed in the lessons. The students really enjoy learning to type.

The teacher treats students equitably. Instead of ability groups, she uses heterogeneous groupings that mix students with disabilities and students without disabilities, helping them learn to accept each other. The children read to the student who has visual problems. The students without disabilities are reaching out to assist those with disabilities.

❖ *How do you know you have made a difference in student learning?*

Students are excited about what they are learning. They are not bored and are talking about the subject. In addition, the assessments, including the required tests, show that they are achieving at higher levels.

❖ *What brings you joy in teaching?*

I love watching students grow. At the beginning of the school year, the child with autism does not look at you. During the year, he begins to look at you and even remembers your name. It is a preschooler beginning to place letters in the right order. You see a student grow as a person. It is thrilling to see the 4th grade students without disabilities interacting positively with students with special needs, and, conversely, the special education students interacting with others.

Questions to Consider

1. What are the benefits of having special needs and gifted and talented students placed in regular classrooms with their peers?

2. Some teachers are expert at finding ways to engage all students in learning. What are some of the ways that teachers can organize information and activities so that all students are involved in lessons?

3. What are some ways that a teacher can keep track of student growth throughout the year so that the teacher, the students, and the families of the students have some tangible record of the ways in which students have grown?

▶ **Profession.** A career that requires specialized knowledge and advanced college preparation often beyond the baccalaureate.

So you are thinking about teaching as a career. Teaching is a joyful **profession** because teachers see students complete simple and complex tasks, learn new concepts, win a competition, and graduate. Teaching is also a demanding profession that requires leaders who can make multiple decisions during a school day, manage 20 to 40 students hour after hour, analyze data about learning, and interact with parents and colleagues. Understanding how to help each student learn is complex because students have different learning styles, come from different cultural backgrounds, and have different learning needs. High levels of energy, effort, and motivation are required.

Is teaching the right choice for you? Some candidates in teaching start along this career path because it is a profession with which they are very familiar. Although we spend much of our lives in classrooms, it is different on the other side of the desk. This book will help you explore whether teaching is the right profession for you. We will look at the diversity of students, communities, and schools in the United States; introduce the theoretical foundations supporting the profession; and identify the basic skills needed to manage the classroom and help students learn. Throughout these chapters, we will discuss realities that teachers face today such as student testing, inclusion of students with disabilities, and discipline.

Focus QUESTIONS

After reading this chapter, you should be able to answer the following questions:

1 Why do most teachers select teaching as a career?

2 Why do many educators consider teaching a profession similar to law and medicine?

3 How do teacher shortages affect the teaching job market?

4 What support services should be available to new teachers to increase their effectiveness and likelihood that they will remain in the profession beyond 5 years?

5 What steps will you have to complete to earn a teaching license?

6 How can you begin now to develop patterns of behavior that will contribute to a successful career as a teacher?

Why Teach?

Darnell Jackson loves teaching U.S. history to high school sophomores. One of his goals is to get students as excited about history as he is. His favorite project requires students to select an ethnic group other than their own and to conduct research about their involvement in civil rights from 1950 to 1975 and the impact of the civil rights movement on the group. He helps the students look for resources in the library and on the Internet. He encourages them to interview older members of the group who live in the community and remember the struggles of that period. After their initial gathering of information on their own, he groups students with others who have chosen the same ethnic group to share their findings, write a paper, and present their findings to the class. Over the years, students have used drama, music, and art as well as the more common speeches and PowerPoint presentations to make their points. The project always results in students learning much more about another ethnic group and becoming engaged in the issues of equity, discrimination, and racism.

Mr. Jackson's love of history and social studies does not stop in the classroom. He plans his summer vacations to visit a historical landmark he has not yet seen. He can't be in any part of the country without visiting the local historical society or local history museum. He volunteers to teach at his city's history camp for 2 weeks each summer. He is always learning more about the subject he loves.

What interests you about a career in teaching? Most teachers say they want to teach because they care about children and youth and believe they can make a difference in the lives of their students. In a survey of teachers by the National Education Association (2003), over half of the teachers indicate that they originally chose teaching because of the value of education to society. Many secondary teachers like Mr. Jackson report they chose teaching because they love the subject they are teaching.

This idealistic art teacher inspired her female college students to reach for high academic and career goals in the film, *Mona Lisa Smile*. Most students can identify at least one teacher who made a difference in their lives.

Many people have wanted to teach for as long as they can remember. Few indicate they fell into teaching because nothing else was available. Over half of the new teachers in surveys by the Public Agenda indicate they would be satisfied with a job that involves the work they love to do, allows enough time to be with family, contributes to society and helps others, provides the supervision and support they need, has job security, and gives the sense that they are respected and appreciated (Farkas, Johnson, & Foleno, 2000). Salary and opportunities for advancement were less important (Farkas et al., 2000). Figure 1.1 shows how those teachers rate their current teaching positions against the characteristics they value.

Teaching is one of the most important careers in a democratic society because it can prepare students to be productive citizens who can think crucially about society and their own lives. Public perceptions of the importance of teaching have improved over the past 15 years. In fact, the public is placing teaching first by more than a three-to-one margin over physicians, nursing, business persons, lawyers, journalists, politicians, and accountants (Recruiting New Teachers, 2003).

Rewards of Teaching

The rewards of teaching vary from teacher to teacher. The best teachers enjoy working with

Figure 1.1 Why new teachers choose to teach

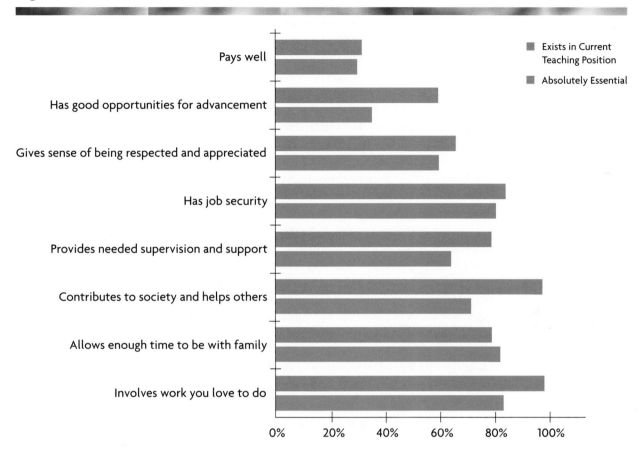

Source: Adapted from Farkas, S., Johnson, J., & Foleno, T. (2000). *A sense of calling: Who teaches and why*. New York: Public Agenda, p. 10.

children and youth. They find a challenge in ensuring that underserved students learn at high levels and take joy in the academic success of their students. Sandra McBrayer, the 1994 Teacher of the Year, taught homeless children in a storefront school in San Diego, encouraging them not only to finish high school, but also college. The 2002 Teacher of the Year, Chauncey Veatch, is a retired U.S. Army colonel who works with secondary English language learners, students with disabilities, and students from low-income families in southern California. The majority of students in his classes have entered college, in great part because he believed they could learn and challenged them to do so (CCSSO, 2006). Mathematics teacher Jaime Escalante prepared Latino students from low-income families in Los Angeles to pass the advanced placement test in calculus—a story that was made into the movie, *Stand and Deliver*. These teachers and many others not only believe that all students can learn, they take the challenge of ensuring that they do.

Intrinsic Rewards It's the little things that count: the joy you feel when you see a student making progress in your classroom; the joy you feel when a student finally "gets it." Some students, for example, are very successful in everything they pursue. You are proud of their accomplishments and try to enrich their experiences as you engage them in the learning process. Other students move through the year regularly attending class and completing assignments, but are not actively engaged in discussions or projects; you have to draw them into the activity. Another group of students seem to resist learning. They may be late to class, skip class, and disrupt the class when they are there. Rather than making excuses for these students not participating, successful teachers figure out ways for them to participate. At the beginning, it may be managing the class so that those who had not been participating begin to be involved. You see a difference that could lead to greater involvement with the subject you are teaching. Your strategy for engaging more students has worked.

At the beginning of this section, Ms. Clarke found joy in a student with autism remembering her name. The student was not an award winner nor was he even ready to be promoted to the next level, but he had grown over time. Most teachers experience **intrinsic rewards** when a student grasps the concept or task they have been teaching. Of course, not all students learn at the same rate. When a teacher discovers a way to help that last student complete a mathematical problem correctly, he knows he is being an effective teacher.

Helping Students Learn One of the most joyful aspects of teaching is to see students achieve at high levels. This achievement could be physical, social, or creative as well as intellectual. All are important in the development of the whole child or person. During your teacher education program, you learn how to develop **lesson plans** and deliver instruction. You will be expected to be creative in developing rigorous and engaging instructional strategies that draw on the cultural backgrounds and prior experiences of students. Your success will depend on students learning the concepts you are trying to teach.

How will you know that students are learning at the expected levels? One of the most superficial measures will be performance on standardized tests, which are required annually in most schools. Of course, you will want students to perform well on those tests, but they measure only a narrow slice of the knowledge that students should be developing. Teachers also help students develop skills to use the knowledge in real-life situations. They provide the skills for students to analyze and think critically about the subject. They help students develop **dispositions**—attitudes and behaviors—that will show they value learning. Evidence of student learning can be seen in a student's interaction with the subject during discussions and activities, writing assignments, **portfolio** entries, and other student projects. Joy is seeing examples of student learning in multiple forms that convince you a student is ready for the next grade. The challenge is to ensure that all students in the classroom meet appropriate **benchmarks** or levels of performance that show they have met standards.

▶ **Intrinsic rewards.** Importance due to internal satisfaction such as helping a child learn rather than external incentives such as salary or prestige.

▶ **Lesson plans.** A teacher's detailed guide for classroom instruction.

▶ **Dispositions.** The values, commitments, professional ethics, and behaviors that influence beliefs, attitudes, and behaviors.

▶ **Portfolio.** A compilation of works, records, and accomplishments that a student prepares for a specific purpose in order to demonstrate his/her learnings, performances, and contributions.

▶ **Benchmarks.** A description of performances required to meet a standard at an expected level (for example, unacceptable, acceptable, and target).

Ed Lines

"In a truly national society, the best of us would be teachers, and the rest would have to settle for something else." *Lee Iaccoca*

Teachers Make a Difference

Can you think of a teacher who made a difference in your life? It may be one who really cared about you, one who convinced you to apply for college, one who challenged you to learn, or one who helped you develop self-esteem. Professional athletes, presidents of companies, and national leaders often attribute their success to a teacher. The teacher may not know until years after the student has left her classroom that she had such an impact.

Parents believe that teachers make a difference in their children's lives, especially when it comes to learning. Many parents know who the good teachers are in their schools and do everything they can to ensure their children are in those teachers' classrooms. Research validates these parents' beliefs; effective teachers do make a difference in student learning. In the 1990s, Sanders and Rivers (1996) and their colleagues at the University of Tennessee compiled achievement data from standardized tests for students in Tennessee schools and followed the data through successive years of school. They found that two students who performed at the same level in the 2nd grade could be separated by as many as 50 percentile points by the 5th grade if one of them had an effective teacher and the other an ineffective teacher for the next 3 years. Other researchers have found that the influence of teachers on student achievement is greater than any other observable factor such as small class sizes (for example, Darling-Hammond, 1999; Rivkin, Hanushek, & Kain, 1998).

Revisiting Darnell Jackson, History Teacher

Darnell Jackson, the teacher at the beginning of this section, doesn't just teach history, he brings it alive for his students by letting them work collaboratively on projects that allow them to use multiple resources and to involve people from the community. Darnell's love of history also takes him on professional development journeys that increase his knowledge of the subject he loves and enables him to include new information and materials in his lessons. Excellent teachers hardly ever stop thinking about the subjects they teach. When you discover a subject that you love, the best way to enjoy it for the rest of your life is to teach it to others.

What Makes Teaching a Profession?

*Lucy Chu is back in her classroom after spending the past 5 days at a university in Seattle. She had been part of a national **accreditation** team that included another teacher and four professors. They worked together from Saturday through Wednesday to determine whether the university's college of education met national standards. Lucy was exhausted, but knew that she could not afford to be*

Accreditation. Recognition by members of a profession that an educational institution meets standards.

Ed Lines

"[National board certification] is probably the most important professional development tool that has come along in the last century." *Sharon Draper, 1997 National Teacher of the Year*

away from her students any longer. She did not know the substitute teacher who replaced her and worried that she might have to spend more time than she would like refocusing her students on learning again.

Most teachers consider themselves professionals. However, until recently, teaching was identified by many as a semiprofession as compared to the profession of law, medicine, architecture, engineering, or accountancy. One reason is that teaching has not provided the same monetary advantages or prestige as the traditional professional fields. Another reason is that teachers seem to have relatively little control over their work. Other professionals or policy makers select the curriculum, set rules, and develop learning standards. Most teachers have limited access to an office, telephone, computer, and a secretary. The structure of their day leaves little time to interact with colleagues to plan or challenge each other intellectually. Nevertheless, changes over the past 15 years have moved teaching to behave more like the other professions.

Definition of a Profession

A *profession* is defined as "a calling requiring specialized knowledge and often long and intensive academic preparation" (Merriam-Webster, 2004). All states require at least a bachelor's degree to be eligible for an initial license to teach. Traditionally states have required some specialized preparation in education that includes student teaching or an internship. A growing number of universities require teacher candidates to have a bachelor's degree in the subject to be taught before they begin graduate work in education. Thus, over time a larger number of teachers are receiving their specialized preparation for teaching at the graduate level. Most teachers today have a master's degree and continue to participate in professional development activities throughout their careers.

A number of new teachers are entering the profession through alternate routes that allow them to begin teaching without any specialized preparation in teaching and learning or field experiences in schools. Other professions such as medicine and engineering never would allow a person to work in the field without proper preparation and supervised experiences with professionals in the field. Opening the entry to teaching to anyone with a bachelor's degree challenges the status of a profession because no specialized training is required. However, most states require alternate-route teachers to take education courses and be mentored by experienced teachers.

Characteristics of a Profession

A profession sets standards for entry into it. In addition, its members apply standards and codes of ethics to themselves and others, disciplining one another when necessary by removing licenses from offenders. Professionals provide services to clients. Their work is intellectual, requiring specialized knowledge and skills. They are bound by an ethical code that guides their relationships with clients and colleagues. They also have an obligation to practice their profession in ways the public would find acceptable (as explored further in the Challenging Assumptions on page 12).

Setting and Upholding Standards   Throughout the past decade, teachers have worked with professors, parents, and public members to set standards for students and teachers in their school districts, states, and national organizations. In 10 states, teachers have the majority control of professional standards boards that have the responsibility for developing licensure standards for teachers and other school professionals. When necessary, these boards withdraw licenses from teachers whose behaviors have led to malpractice. In states without professional standards boards, these functions are usually provided by a state board of education whose members have been elected or appointed by the governor.

Accreditation   Both schools and teacher education programs are held to professional standards. Teachers like Ms. Chu apply these standards when they conduct an accreditation review. Most other professions require their members to graduate from an accredited program before they can take the state licensure examination. However, this is not the case for teachers. Only a few states require teacher education programs to be nationally accredited by the National Council for Accreditation of Teacher Education (NCATE) or the Teacher Education Accreditation Council (TEAC). If you are in a program hosting a visit by an accreditation visiting team, you may be asked to talk about your program and field experiences. The team may ask you about your portfolio and what you have learned about working with students from diverse populations. They may ask how you know that students are learning. They are also likely to ask you about the quality of teaching at the university and particularly by education faculty members. When you are teaching, you are likely to be involved every few years in an accreditation visit by the state and/or regional accrediting agency.

Licensure   To teach in a public school, teachers must be licensed by a state agency to teach a specific subject (for example, mathematics or social studies) at the middle or high school levels. Early childhood, elementary, special education, physical education, music, and art teachers are licensed to teach children in specific grades such as preschool, primary, K–6, or K–12. If you graduate from a state-approved program, which is often connected to national accreditation, you have usually met the state requirements for a state license. You also will be required to pass a state licensure test in most states. Most states grant a provisional license that allows you to teach for 3 to 5 years. Several years of successful practice and completion of a master's degree is normally required for a professional license to continue teaching.

Requirements may be different when you apply for a license in a state other than the one in which you graduated. The second state may have additional requirements that you must meet and may have a higher cut-off (or qualifying) score on the required licensure tests. If you plan to move to a different state to teach, check the requirements for a license so that you can take the appropriate courses during your program. A teacher is usually allowed to meet the additional requirements of a state during their first years of teaching on a provisional or similar license.

National Board Certification   Teachers with 3 years of experience are eligible to apply for national certification by the **National Board for Professional Teaching Standards (NBPTS)**. Applicants provide evidence in the collection of documents

National Board for Professional Teaching Standards (NBPTS). The organization that has developed standards for accomplished teachers and a process for determining whether teachers meet the standards.

Challenging Assumptions
FINDINGS FROM RESEARCH

Can anyone teach?

The Myth: Many states allow some teachers to enter their first teaching job with little or no coursework related to teaching and learning and no field experiences in a school setting. Is it really not important for teacher candidates to understand the professional and pedagogical knowledge that provide the foundation for teaching? Are there any teacher characteristics that influence achievement gains of students?

Study Design and Method: Andrew J. Wayne and Peter Youngs of SRI International and Stanford University, respectively, reviewed studies that examined teachers' characteristics and the standardized test scores of their students. The data reviewed were collected in the United States and accounted for students' prior achievement and socioeconomic status.

Study Findings: The researchers found that a relationship exists between college ratings and student achievement gains. This relationship implies that factors beyond licensure tests should be used by states in determining who should teach. Institutional quality as determined by accreditation is a factor that should be considered. Studies indicated that (Wayne and Youngs, 2003):

- students learn more from teachers with higher test scores (p. 100)

- high school students learn more mathematics when their mathematics teachers have additional degrees or coursework in mathematics (p. 103)

- mathematics students learn more when their teachers have standard mathematics certification (pp. 105–106)

In the report of the National Commission on Teaching and America's Future, *Solving the Dilemmas of Teacher Supply, Demand, and Standards* (2000), Linda Darling-Hammond stated that

> One recent analysis found that, after controlling for student characteristics like poverty and language status, the strongest predictor of state-level student achievement in reading and mathematics on the NAEP [National Assessment of Educational Progress] was each state's proportion of well-qualified teachers (as defined by the proportion with full certification and a major in the field they teach). . . . A strong negative predictor of student achievement was the proportion of teachers on emergency certificates. (p. 15)

Implications: Teacher licensure or certification requirements, which Darling-Hammond and others have found to be critical to student achievement, outline the content, professional, and pedagogical knowledge and skills expected of teachers in the state. These are the proficiencies that teacher candidates should develop in their teacher education programs.

Sources: Wayne, A. J., & Youngs, P. (2003 Spring). Teacher characteristics and student achievement gains: A review. *Review of Educational Research 73*(1): 89–122; and Darling-Hammond, L. (2000). *Solving the dilemmas of teacher supply, demand, and standards: How we can ensure a competent, caring, and qualified teacher for every child*. Washington, DC: National Commission on Teaching and America's Future.

▶ **Reflections.** Self-assessments of one's thoughts, feelings, and teaching practice.

that are compiled in a portfolio to demonstrate meeting standards for their subject area at a specific age level. The portfolio must include a videotape of the teacher teaching a lesson, his or her **reflections** on his or her teaching, and an analysis of student work. In addition, the teacher must complete assessment exercises at a testing center. Teaching performance is judged by experienced teachers using

rubrics aligned with standards. Many states and school districts cover the costs for teachers to participate in this process, which could be $2,300 or more.

What are the advantages of seeking national board certification? Most applicants report that the process helped improve their teaching and the performance of their students. They learned to reflect on their practice and make changes to improve student learning. A 2004 research study (Goldhaber & Anthony, 2004) of student test scores in North Carolina supports the perceptions of these teachers. The study found that the students of national board–certified teachers are more likely to improve their scores on state tests than students of nonnational board–certified teachers. In addition, many national board–certified teachers receive annual bonuses or increments.

Specialized Knowledge Teachers must know the subjects they will be teaching. The knowledge and related skills for teaching the subject are described in the standards of the national organizations that represent teachers in that field. These include the National Council of Teachers of Mathematics (NCTM), Council for Exceptional Children (CEC), National Association for the Education of Young Children (NAEYC), and others. You will be expected to understand the subject well enough to help young people know it and apply it to the world in which they live. If students are not learning a concept or skills, teachers must be able to relate the content to the experiences of students to provide meaning and purpose.

The professional and pedagogical knowledge needed by teachers is outlined in the widely accepted principles of the Interstate New Teacher Assessment and Support Consortium, which have been adapted by most states. To receive a license, you should be able to demonstrate in a portfolio and field experiences that you:

1. understand the central concepts, tools of inquiry, and structures of the discipline(s) you will teach and can create learning experiences that make these aspects of subject matter meaningful for students.

2. understand how children learn and develop and can provide learning opportunities that support their intellectual, social, and personal development.

3. understand how students differ in their approaches to learning and can create instructional opportunities that are adapted to diverse learners.

4. understand and can use a variety of instructional strategies to encourage students' development of critical-thinking, problem-solving, and performance skills.

5. understand individual and group motivation and behavior and can create a learning environment that encourages positive social interaction, active engagement in learning, and self-motivation.

6. can use knowledge of effective verbal, nonverbal, and media communication techniques to foster active inquiry, collaboration, and supportive interaction in the classroom.

7. can plan instruction based on knowledge of the subject matter, students, the community, and curriculum goals.

Rubrics. Criteria for judging a person's performance against standards that include descriptions of performance at levels such as inadequate, proficient, and beyond expectations.

8. understand and can use formal and informal assessment strategies to evaluate and ensure the continuous intellectual, social, and physical development of the learner.

9. are a reflective practitioner who continually evaluates the effects of your choices and actions on others (students, parents, and other professionals in the learning community) and who actively seeks out opportunities to grow professionally.

10. can foster relationships with school colleagues, parents, and agencies in the larger community to support students' learning and well-being (Interstate New Teacher Assessment and Support Consortium, 1992).

Code of Ethics Like other professions, teachers as a group have developed a code of ethics to guide their work and relationships with students and colleagues. Professional standards boards and other state bodies investigate teachers for infractions against the code of ethics adopted by the state. Ethics statements address issues such as discrimination against students, restraint of students, protecting students from harm, personal relationships with students, and misrepresenting one's credentials. The Teachers and the Law on page 15 explores the legal ramifications of this issue.

Obligation to Practice in Acceptable Ways Being a member of the teaching profession is more than showing up for work by 7:30 and leaving by 3:30. The parents of students in your classroom expect that you help their children learn. They expect their children to score at acceptable or better levels on achievement tests. They are counting on you to contribute to their child's literacy and to push them beyond minimal standards. Good teachers manage their classrooms so that students can focus on learning. The public and parents become extremely concerned when classrooms and schools appear out of control. As a teacher, it will be your obligation to model acceptable behavior based on the norms of the profession.

Participation in the Profession

In other professions, standards and rules for their profession are set by the professionals themselves. School administrators, members of the school board, and state legislators usually set teaching standards and rules. This practice is not likely to change unless teachers become involved in the teaching profession beyond their own classrooms. Teacher unions provide an opportunity for teachers to negotiate contracts that outline salary and working conditions. Teacher organizations in most states conduct annual or semiannual statewide meetings for their members. These meetings provide professional development opportunities, a chance to network with other teachers, and a mechanism for becoming involved at the state level. You can stay engaged with your subject area and other educational interests by joining national organizations such as the National Association for Multicultural Education (NAME) or the National Council of Teachers of English (NCTE). Many of the national organizations have state affiliates in which you could be a member or become a leader. Through teacher organizations,

Teachers and the Law

COPYING MATERIALS FOR CLASSROOM USE

Are teachers, and teacher education students, exempt from copyright laws?

No. All intellectual products, whether they be writings, drawings, digital, or musical are protected by copyright laws. There are rules and procedures that protect the creators of new ideas and products. Within these laws is the doctrine of "fair use," which teachers will often use to rationalize their making multiple copies of copyrighted material. Making a single copy for preparing a lesson is permissible. However, there are clear restrictions on the conditions under which teachers can make multiple copies. These restrictions address *brevity* (e.g., a poem of not more than 250 words), *spontaneity* (e.g., an inspiration close to class time), and *cumulative effect* (e.g., the copying is for one class only).

IMMORALITY AND UNPROFESSIONAL CONDUCT

Can teachers lose their jobs for immoral behavior or unprofessional conduct?

Yes. These are the cases that make the news, but they are also among those most often used to fire teachers. The courts define *immorality* broadly as "unacceptable conduct that affects a teacher's fitness" (Cambron-McCabe, McCarthy, & Thomas, 2004, 413). It includes sexual relations between a teacher and student, but is not limited to them. In 1998, the West Virginia high court upheld the termination of a teacher for repeated sexual comments to students after he had been warned to stop. In 1983, the Missouri Supreme Court supported the dismissal of a teacher for sexually harassing a female student and permitting male students in the class to harass her. Other acts of immorality that courts have accepted as reason for a teacher's termination include dishonest, criminal, and drug-related conduct.

Unprofessional conduct is defined by most courts as conduct that breaches "the rules or ethical code of a profession or [is] 'unbecoming to a member in good standing of a profession'" (Cambron-McCabe et al., 2004, 420). Teachers have been terminated for hurting students, humiliating students in front of other students, allowing students to kick or hit each other, sexual harassment, and showing a sexually explicit film to students. The courts often require that teachers be warned that their misconduct could lead to dismissal before they are actually fired.

MALPRACTICE FOR STUDENTS NOT LEARNING

Are teachers or school districts liable when students do not learn?

No. Former students in California and New York claimed their school districts had not provided them an adequate education. The California student could barely read and write by the time he graduated from high school. The judge in this case said that

> The science of pedagogy itself is fraught with different and conflicting theories . . . and any layman might—and commonly does—have his own emphatic viewpoints on the subject. . . . The achievement of literacy in the schools, or its failure, is influenced by a host of factors from outside the formal teaching process, and beyond the course of its ministries. (*Peter W. v. San Francisco Unified School District*, 1976)

The judge in New York said, "The failure to learn does not bespeak a failure to teach" (*Donahue v. Copiogue Union Free School District*, 1978).

Schools today are being held accountable for student learning through the No Child Left Behind Act. Some principals and teachers have lost their jobs because students have not performed at expected levels on required tests. Students are allowed to move to a higher performing school if their own school does not make adequate yearly progress for several years in a row. With the continuing emphasis on accountability for student learning, malpractice cases are likely to reappear.

Source: Cambron-McCabe, N. H., McCarthy, M. M., & Thomas, S. B. (2004). *Public school law: Teachers' and students' rights* (5th ed.). Boston: Allyn and Bacon.

One of the opportunities teachers have for serving the profession is participation in their teacher union to help negotiate contracts with school districts.

teachers can serve on accreditation teams that evaluate schools and universities in their state or across the country. A sign of a professional is active and continued involvement in professional organizations at local, state, and national levels.

Salaries

Teachers do not select teaching because they expect to receive a high salary. However, three of four new teachers tell Public Agenda (Farkas et al., 2000) they are seriously underpaid, especially considering the talent and hard work that teaching requires. The average teacher salary in the United States was $47,808 in school year 2004–2005 (NEA, 2006). The highest and lowest average teacher salaries are shown in Table 1.1. According to the NEA (2006), Connecticut tops the list with $58,688; at the other end of the scale is South Dakota with $34,040. Salaries in most northeastern states are higher than in other parts of the country. Connecticut and school districts such as Rochester, New York, view teachers as professionals, have high expectations for them, support them through mentoring and professional development, use multiple assessments to determine teacher effectiveness, and pay salaries commensurate with other professionals. Salaries in the Plains states west of the Mississippi River fall disproportionately in the bottom 20 percent.

Most teacher contracts are for less than 12 months, but over 60 percent of the teachers earn additional income within the school or in summer or second jobs outside the school. Teachers report earning supplemental income above their contract by doing the following activities related to schools or their education:

▶ **Mentor.** An experienced teacher who coaches and guides new teachers through their first years of practice.

- Serving as a **mentor** or staff developer
- Achieving additional teaching licenses or certifications
- Becoming national board certified

Table 1.1 Average Teacher Salaries in 2004–2005

	Top Ten		Bottom Ten
$58,688	Connecticut	$39,175	Kansas
$58,456	District of Columbia	$38,971	Missouri
$55,876	California	$38,880	Louisiana
$56,973	Michigan	$38,485	Montana
$56,682	New Jersey	$38,360	West Virginia
$56,200	New York	$38,186	Alabama
$55,629	Illinois	$37,879	Oklahoma
$54,325	Massachusetts	$36,590	Mississippi
$53,473	Rhode Island	$36,449	North Dakota
$53,258	Pennsylvania	$34,040	South Dakota

Source: National Education Association. (2006). Fall 2005 update to *NEA rankings and estimates: Rankings of the states 2004 and estimates of school statistics 2005* (NEA Research, Estimates Databank). Washington, DC: Author. Retrieved August 31, 2006, from www.nea.org/edstats/index.html Reprinted with permission of the National Education Association © 2005. All rights reserved.

- Teaching in a subject area where there is a teacher shortage
- Improving student performance
- Working in a school more challenging to staff than other schools in the district
- Developing new skills/knowledge in nonuniversity settings (NEA, 2003, 80)

Teachers also may receive supplemental income for chairing departments, being team leaders, sponsoring extracurricular activities, and coaching.

Even with the supplemental income that many teachers earn, their income is less than their counterparts in other professions. Teachers between 22 and 28 years old earned an average $7,894 less in 1998 than other college-educated adults of the same age. By age 44 to 50, they earned $23,655 less than their counterparts in other occupations. The difference is even greater between teachers with master's degrees and others with a master's degree; these teachers earned $43,313 as compared to $75,824 by nonteachers (Who Should Teach, 2000). Forty-seven percent of recent college graduates who were interested in teaching, but were not teaching, indicated they would be more likely to consider teaching if the salary was higher (Farkas et al., 2000).

Revisiting Lucy Chu and Professional Work Beyond the Classroom

Like Lucy Chu at the beginning of this section, many classroom teachers engage in professional activities not associated with teaching students in classrooms. Many teachers believe their professional roles extend beyond the classroom and the school. Teachers with a commitment to the profession often volunteer their time to serve on committees to determine state and national guidelines for teacher effectiveness. As teachers serve on committees or teams with other teachers, school administrators, and university professors, they learn more about the world of teaching and improving their profession.

Where Are the Jobs?

Cindy Johnson moved away from home to study elementary education in the public university about 70 miles from where she grew up, but she planned to move back home to teach after she finished college. It is August 1 and she still has not heard from any of the three school districts near the town in which her parents live. She is starting to panic because she did not apply to other school districts. She was told by the personnel office in each of the three districts that teachers sometimes decide to leave during the summer, and jobs often become available as the fall semester begins. They also said that her chances would be better if she had a second license or endorsement in special education or English as a second language. Nevertheless, she was an optimist and planned to wait it out.

Teaching jobs become available as current teachers retire, move to other schools, or leave the profession. By 2012 around 700,000 teachers—almost one of four current teachers—are projected to retire. Teachers leave the profession and move from school to school for a variety of reasons as shown in Figure 1.2. The primary reasons for moving are layoffs, school closings, and other organizational changes in a school or district. Personal reasons include pregnancy, child-rearing responsibilities, moving to a new location, and health problems (Ingersoll, 2003). One in five entry-level teachers are gone within the first 3 years.

Around 25 percent of the teachers who leave the profession or change schools indicate they are dissatisfied with their jobs. This dissatisfaction varies across the types of schools in which they work. Teachers in small private schools leave primarily because of low salaries, followed by inadequate administrative support. Teachers in urban high-poverty schools say they are most dissatisfied with the lack of student motivation, followed closely by poor pay. Discipline problems and unsafe environments are also cited by the urban teachers much more often than private school teachers (Ingersoll, 2003).

The teacher turnover rate in urban high-poverty schools is almost one-third higher than in other schools (National Commission, 2003), but the largest turnover rate is in small private schools. The rate of teachers leaving large private schools is fairly low, but small private schools suffer from a turnover that is often one-fourth of the staff annually. Although teachers in private schools report greater satisfaction and that their environments

© Scott Arthur Masear.

Figure 1.2 Reasons for teacher turnover

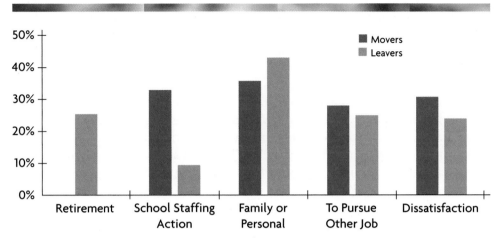

Source: Data from Ingersoll, R. M. (2003). *Is there really a teacher shortage?* Philadelphia, PA: The Consortium for Policy Research in Education, The University of Pennsylvania and Seattle, WA: Center for the Study of Teaching and Policy, University of Washington, p. 16.

are more positive than public schools, they are much more likely to transfer to a public school than their public school counterparts to transfer to a private school (Ingersoll, 2003).

Teacher Shortages

The nation does not have a shortage of licensed teachers. The problem is that over 40 percent of the people who complete a teacher education program do not teach in the first 5 years after they graduate (Ingersoll, 2003). They find other jobs, are in graduate school, or are staying at home to raise children. Others teach for a short time, leaving to take care of personal needs or moving to a nonteaching job. Thus, not all new hires in a school district are recent graduates. About half of them are teachers returning to the classroom or moving from another district. A growing number of new teachers are not recent college graduates. They are military retirees or people switching from business or other careers. They often complete alternative pathways into teaching in school-based graduate programs that build on their prior experiences.

You may not be able to find a teaching job in the community in which you grew up or near the university you are attending because these schools often have few openings. However, jobs do exist if you are willing to move to a part of the country where there are shortages because of high turnover, a growing student population, or there is a move to reduce the teacher-to-student ratio in classes.

The demographics of the teaching force do not match the population at large. The majority of teachers are white female. The profession has a shortage of men and teachers of color. Other shortages exist in some areas of the country and for some teaching fields as described later. To attract teachers to areas with teaching shortages, some school districts offer signing bonuses, pay moving expenses, and assist teachers in purchasing homes.

Location of Jobs

Wealthy school systems usually have a surplus of teachers who are applying for jobs. Some new teachers are willing to substitute in these school systems for a year or more until a job becomes available. Others such as Ms. Clarke, whose story opened the chapter, are willing to work as a teaching assistant while waiting for a full-time teaching position. Opportunities are greater in urban high-poverty areas where high turnover exists. Generally, urban and rural areas have more openings than suburban areas although acute shortages exist in high-poverty suburban areas as well. If you are willing to move to another state, your job opportunities will grow. Alaska and the western and southern states are actively recruiting new teachers to staff schools for a growing school-age population (National Commission, 2003). California, Texas, Nevada, North Carolina, and Florida are experiencing growth in their student populations, increasing the need for teachers.

Shortage Fields

Have you decided what subjects you would like to teach? Urban and rural schools are likely to have openings for all subjects from elementary through high school. However, not enough teachers are being prepared or retained in schools to teach mathematics and science, English language learners, and students with disabilities. Your chances of finding a job improve if you meet one of these high-need areas.

Many secondary schools report they have had to hire teachers who did not major in mathematics or science to teach these courses. These **out-of-field teachers** sometimes have not even minored in these subjects and lack the knowledge and skills to help students learn these core subjects. The lack of qualified mathematics and science teachers in urban high schools has contributed to not offering advanced placement classes in these subjects and to the poor test performance of students in these schools. The organization Recruiting New Teachers (RNT) reports that over 95 percent of the largest urban school districts have an immediate need for qualified teachers of mathematics and science (RNT, 2000).

School districts report a shortage of culturally and linguistically diverse educators, especially in areas of the country with large numbers of Latino and immigrant students. Over the past decade, the schools with these needs have expanded from the Southwest, California, Florida, and large urban areas to smaller cities and communities in the Midwest and South where immigrants are employed and migrant workers have settled. Knowledge and skills in **English as a Second Language (ESL)** and **bilingual education** will give a new teacher an advantage in many urban and rural areas today. Seventy-three percent of the large urban school districts in the RNT survey indicated they had an immediate need for ESL bilingual teachers (2000).

Another major shortage area is special education teachers who are needed from preschool through high school. These teachers may work with a classroom of special education students, but often work as a resource teacher with regular teach-

Out-of-field teachers. Educators assigned to teach a subject in which they did not major in college, nor have been licensed to teach.

English as a Second Language (ESL). An education strategy for teaching English to speakers of other languages without the use of the native language for instruction.

Bilingual education. An education strategy that uses both English and the native language of students in classroom instruction.

Ed Lines

"You can't teach what you don't know any more than you can come back from where you ain't been." *Will Rogers*

ers in inclusive classrooms. They teach students with mental, behavioral, sensory, physical, and learning disabilities. These jobs are usually very demanding—sometimes physically—but can lead to a great deal of joy as students become academically successful or learn to be independent. RNT reported that 98 percent of the large urban schools had an immediate need for special education teachers (2000).

More teaching jobs are usually available in urban areas. However, fewer teachers feel comfortable working in these areas because of less-than-desirable working conditions in the schools and locations in neighborhoods that are economically depressed.

Revisiting Cindy Johnson and her First Teaching Job

Cindy Johnson wants to teach in the community where she grew up and went to school. This is not an uncommon desire among beginning teachers. However, the types of communities that most beginning teachers have grown up in are not always the places that need the most teachers. If you want to assure beginning your teaching career when you graduate, you must go where the jobs are. Highly qualified teachers are always in demand.

What Should You Know about Your First Year?

John Whitehorse began his first teaching job in a middle school in an urban area in the upper Midwest. He accepted this job because he hoped to be able to transfer eventually to the magnet Indian school in the district and wanted to get his foot in the door. His first teaching assignment was in a school with a large number of English language learners from Russia, Iraq, and Laos. He knew none of these languages and had no preparation in ESL. During the orientation for new teachers, he learned that he would have a mentor—an experienced teacher who had an excellent record at helping English language learners be successful in her classes. He could hardly wait to ask her for suggestions.

There is so much you need to know before you enter the classroom that first day. You will begin to become acquainted with some of these critical points in this book. In this section, we want to explore some steps you could take to make the first year a successful one for you and your students.

Ed Lines

"To be successful, the first thing to do is fall in love with your work." *Sister Mary Lauretta*

Teachers' Lounge

Why I Became a 1st Grade Teacher
One of my colleagues once asked his graduate education students to introduce themselves to one another by talking about why they wanted to stay in teaching. An elderly blonde teacher slowly walked to the podium. During a recent back-to-school night, one of her students' parents arrived just as she was turning off the lights. The teacher, feeling badly that the parents missed the event, asked if their daughter had given them the invitation with the correct time and place. The parents replied yes and in addition said that their daughter had added one other piece of information. She told them that her teacher had yellow hair and was the prettiest teacher at the school. The teacher said, with a tear in her eye, that is why she is a 1st grade teacher.

● Dawn Yonally, Ph.D.
Northeastern
State University

Unfortunately, many new teachers are assigned the most challenging schools and students during their first year. The best experienced teachers are recruited to schools serving children whose families are at a higher socioeconomic status (SES) level, leaving few openings for new teachers. Teachers in challenging schools choose to transfer to another school, often at better pay, when the opportunity arises. Therefore, many more openings exist in these hard-to-staff schools. In these situations, new teachers may be asked to teach a course for which they have little or no preparation, but no one else will teach it. You may want a job or need a job so badly that you feel you can't turn down the offer. Of course, you may be lucky enough to find the job you have always dreamed of. Or you may choose to accept the challenge of working with students who have a great number of needs. The joy will come in turning around students who may have started down a destructive path.

Novice and Experienced Teachers

We become better at our jobs with experience, and teachers are no exception to this rule. It is for good reason that the National Board for Professional Teaching Standards does not allow teachers to seek national certification before they have 3 years of teaching experience. Teachers who serve as cooperating teachers or internship supervisors when you are student teaching usually have spent at least 3 years in the classroom. If we are to be effective teachers, we learn as we practice. We test theories and strategies, expanding our repertoire of ways to help students learn. With time, we become more familiar with the subjects we teach and the students with whom we work. We become more comfortable in the classroom as we under-

stand the bureaucratic requirements of a school and become a
better manager of the classroom
and learning.

As a new or novice teacher,
learn from the effective experienced teachers in your school. You
will hear students, parents, other
teachers, and administrators refer
to effective teachers. Ask if you can
visit their class during your planning period to observe their interactions with the subject matter and
with students. Join teacher groups
in which teachers discuss teaching
and learning issues and develop
strategies for serving students with
the greatest needs. Take advantage
of the expertise that can be gained

Mentoring programs provide support for new teachers during their first
years of practice. New teachers who are mentored are more likely to
continue to teach than other new teachers.

from the experienced teachers in your school. When you visit schools as part of
your field experience requirements, note effective teaching practices that you
could incorporate into your own repertoire as you student teach and later have
your own classroom.

Mentoring

Other professions such as medicine and architecture require new graduates to
practice as an intern under the tutelage of experienced doctors or architects during
their first years of practice. Unfortunately, most new teachers are left on their own
to learn how to make critical decisions related to learning and discipline. Sharing
what works with colleagues and having them react and provide advice is not part
of the culture in many schools. However, some school districts are assigning mentors to work with new teachers. When you apply for your first teaching job, look
for school districts that provide mentoring or **induction** for their new teachers.
Researchers have found that new teachers who have been mentored for the first 1
or 2 years in the classroom are more likely to be satisfied with their jobs and to remain in the profession for longer than 5 years (National Commission, 2003). Forty
percent of the teachers who did not participate in mentoring or induction programs during their first year of teaching left that school or the profession after the
first year as compared to 18 percent of those who had mentors or were in an induction program (Smith & Ingersoll, 2003).

Mentor teachers are usually a wonderful resource for a new teacher. They visit
your classroom and give feedback on your teaching. You can discuss problems you
are having and ask them for advice. They should be able to direct you to helpful
resources on the Web and professional development activities to improve your
knowledge and skills. They may arrange meetings of new teachers to improve net-
working and support for each other.

Induction. School district
and state programs de-
signed to provide support
for new teachers through-
out the first one or two
years of practice.

Change is hard and it is hardest for those who are least prepared. John took a job with a school district in hopes that eventually he would end up in the position he truly desired. In the meantime, he will have to do well in a position he feels inadequately prepared for in order to make a favorable impression on the administrators who may eventually make it possible for him to switch schools. Most of us have probably experienced the same sort of "catch-up" situation as John. What we normally do in such a situation is to turn to an on-the-job expert who can show us the ropes and help us be successful while we are quickly learning new skills. John might also decide to enroll in some graduate classes at the local college or look into becoming certified in a critical area of teaching. Whatever John does decide to do, he needs to do it well. He has his foot in the door, but any aspiring door-to-door salesperson will tell you that a foot isn't enough.

How Can You Become a Highly Qualified Teacher?

José Garcia has been teaching science for 3 years in the local middle school. His degree was in sociology, and he took the courses required to be licensed to teach sociology. When he started to look for teaching jobs, most school districts had very few openings in history or social studies. One personnel office said they could hire him if he would be willing to teach science until a job in his field became available. He liked science and had taken the required science courses when he was a college freshman and sophomore. He thought he could read up on science and should be able to keep ahead of the students because they were only 6th and 7th graders.

   The first year was difficult. He didn't know as much as he thought he did, but he read and used the Internet to find interesting activities for his students. He even found that he liked science at this level. The school district indicated that he would have to take some science courses to retain his license to teach out of field. Now he has learned that the No Child Left Behind Act requires that he become fully qualified to teach science by the end of the next school year. The letter from the state board of education says that he must have majored in science or pass the state licensure test in science.

The No Child Left Behind Act has defined the minimal qualifications that a teacher must meet to be hired by a school district. In the past, not all teachers have been even minimally prepared to teach before they took charge of a classroom. Over a fourth of newly hired teachers are not qualified for the beginning license to teach. Some new hires do not have a license; others have a temporary, provisional, or emergency license.

   The pattern of urban and rural schools hiring unqualified teachers to ensure a teacher in every classroom is changing. The 2002 federal elementary and secondary education act, No Child Left Behind (NCLB), required most public schools to be fully staffed by qualified teachers no later than the end of the 2005–2006 school year. The legislation allows states to determine the criteria for fully qualified teachers, but it outlines general requirements that new and current teachers must meet to be hired in the future. The requirements for new, fully qualified elementary, middle level, and high school teachers are shown in Figure 1.3. The 34 percent of the teachers who do not currently hold a regular license must meet these qualifications to retain their teaching jobs.

State departments of education and professional standards boards set the scores for passing tests. They may also require teacher candidates to complete portfolio assessments or take courses in human relations or technology. In almost all cases, the state expects new teachers to know the state standards, pass assessments, pass state licensure tests, complete a teacher education program, and spend time in schools. Each of these is described in the next section.

Know the Standards

You may feel overwhelmed with standards, but if you can't talk about standards during your job interview, you will not be the top candidate for the job. Most schools have adopted a **standards-based curriculum**. It is not only the standards for the students you will be teaching that affect your work. The teacher education program in which you are enrolled should be standards based. Your program should be preparing you to meet Interstate New Teacher Assessment and Support Consortium (INTASC) standards, and professional standards for your field (for example, mathematics or early childhood education). Are you familiar with any of these standards?

Standards-based curriculum. A course of study designed to help students meet the proficiencies identified in standards adopted by a school or state.

Figure 1.3 The No Child Left Behind Act requires highly qualified new teachers to

Hold a minimum of a bachelor's degree

Hold a teaching license that fully meets state requirements

Demonstrate subject matter knowledge in the core academic subjects they will teach by:

Elementary School Teachers	Middle Level and Secondary School Teachers
Passing a state test on teaching skills and the elementary curriculum	Passing a subject knowledge test
	Successfully completing an academic major or equivalency of a graduate degree in each of the academic subjects being taught

Source: Coble, C. R. (2004). Highly qualified teachers: A national imperative. Presentation at No Child Left Behind workshop. Retrieved August 31, 2006, from www.ed.gov/teachers/how/tools/initiative/summerworkshop/coble/coble.pdf.

With the emphasis on standards today, teachers must make sure that their students are acquiring the knowledge and skills necessary to meet state and local student standards.

Student Standards   New teachers should know the student standards for the subject they will be teaching or the students with whom they will be working. All states have developed student standards that indicate what students at different grade levels should know and be able to do in a subject area. The tests that students are required to take annually in mathematics, reading, science, and social studies are based on the state standards. Many of the state standards have been adapted from the standards of national organizations such as the National Council of Teachers of Mathematics (NCTM), International Reading Association (IRA), National Council of Social Studies (NCSS), and American Association for the Advancement of Science (AAAS). These standards should provide the guide for what you should be teaching in those core curriculum areas. They can be used to develop your own **performance assessments** to determine what students are learning. The state tests also provide feedback, although limited, on what students have learned. State standards can be accessed on the website of your state department of education.

▶ Performance assessments. Evaluations of teachers' or students' abilities to meet standards as demonstrated in their accomplishments in a real situation such as teaching or a project.

Teacher Standards   National professional standards also have been developed that describe what teachers should know and be able to do to teach a specific group of students (for example, English language learners or students with disabilities) or a specific subject such as English language arts or physical education. If teachers meet these standards, they should be able to help students meet the student standards.

After you teach for 3 or more years, you may decide to apply for national board certification. The NBPTS standards expect accomplished teachers to

1. be committed to students and their learning
2. know the subjects they teach and how to teach those subjects to students
3. be responsible for managing and monitoring student learning
4. think systematically about their practice and learn from experience
5. be members of learning communities (NBPTS, 1987)*

In addition to these general expectations, the NBPTS has standards for teaching each subject area for specific age levels such as early childhood, middle childhood, early adolescence, and young adulthood. Your teacher education program should be helping you develop the foundation to meet these standards later in your career. A number of colleges and universities have re-designed their master's degrees to reflect these standards and help teachers be-come nationally certified.

Pass Assessments

It is no longer enough to sit through the courses in a teacher education program to be eligible for a license to teach. You will be required to show evidence that you meet professional and state standards through a number of performance assess-ments throughout your program that demonstrate that you know your subject matter and can teach. These assessments are usually administered at admission to the program, before you can student teach, at completion of student teaching, and on completion of the program. The assessments include standardized paper-and-pencil tests, portfolios, case studies, your student teaching or internship, com-prehensive examinations at the end of the program, and projects. You will also be expected to show that you can help students (that is, preschoolers, special educa-tion students, or high schoolers) learn.

Completing the assessment alone is not enough to determine if you have de-veloped the necessary **proficiencies**. Your professors and **field-based supervisors** will evaluate your performance on the assessment using a scoring guide or rubric that describes the level that you must reach to meet the standards. When you re-ceive the feedback from the scoring guide, you should know areas that you need to improve to meet the standards.

Assessment of Knowledge
Knowledge is one of the easier areas to assess. The most popular assessment of knowledge is a standardized pencil-and-paper test, which now is often completed on a computer. Teacher-developed quizzes and tests provide information on what is known or understood. Grades and your perfor-mance on papers, projects, presentations, and case studies contribute to the over-all evaluation of the knowledge needed to teach.

Assessment of Skills
Skills or performances are usually demonstrated as you collaborate with your peers, interact with your professors, and work with teachers and students in schools. Your skills can be observed and measured by how success-ful you are in helping students achieve at acceptable levels on tests and other as-sessments. Field experiences and student teaching provide opportunities for you to apply your knowledge about a subject and pedagogy. You and others will assess your effectiveness in these settings. Although standardized assessments exist, they are relatively expensive to implement.

A few states require beginning teachers to complete Praxis III in which trained assessors evaluate their performance as a first-year teacher against standards using a scoring rubric. Teacher education programs in those states emphasize the devel-opment of the skills assessed by Praxis III. National board assessments are also standardized and employ trained assessors. Other states such as Connecticut require their new teachers to submit a portfolio after their first years of teaching as evidence they are meeting state standards.

Proficiencies. Knowledge, skills, or dispositions that students are expected to acquire to meet a set of standards.

Field-based supervisors. The teacher or other pro-fessional school personnel who provide support for teacher candidates when they observe and work in schools.

Assessment of Dispositions   The teacher education program at your institution may have identified the dispositions that you should demonstrate before you become a teacher. They might include proficiencies such as:

- The belief that all children can learn at high levels, which requires persistence in helping all children achieve success
- Appreciating and valuing human diversity, showing respect for students' varied talents and perspectives, and commitment to the pursuit of individually configured excellence
- Respecting students as individuals with differing personal and family backgrounds and various skills, talents, and interests (INTASC, 1992)

These proficiencies cannot be easily measured on a test. They come across in the papers that you write, the presentations that you make, the lessons you teach, and your interactions with students and parents in schools. Over time and in multiple ways, your dispositions are demonstrated and assessed (see the Understanding & Using Evidence on page 31).

Assessment of Student Learning   In your teacher education program, you should expect to learn how to assess student learning and how to respond when a student is not learning. You could be required to collect data on student learning as you teach a lesson in student teaching, analyze those data, and determine the follow-up steps if one or more students are not learning. Figure 1.4 provides an example of an assessment exercise you may be asked to complete during student teaching. See Figure 1.5 for an example of a rubric that accompanies the student learning assessment.

You might be asked to design an assessment that will help you know whether students are learning. You might be given a sample of student work and asked to analyze it and describe any concerns raised by the student's work. By the time you finish your program, you should be familiar with a number of assessments besides a test. You should also know that students learn in different ways, requiring that you teach using various strategies that build on their prior experiences and cultures.

Pass Licensure Tests

Potential teachers in most states must pass one or more licensure tests to be eligible for a license to teach. States either develop their own licensure tests or contract with a major test company such as the Educational Testing Service (ETS) or National Evaluation Systems (NES). A state board of education or standards board determines the cut-off score, or qualifying score, that test takers must achieve to pass the test. The score required to pass the same or similar tests varies from state to state. Your score could be high enough to be licensed in one state, but not in another. Ohio, Virginia, and Connecticut have set higher cut-off scores than other states as part of their effort to raise the quality of teachers in the state. Check with the state in

Ed Lines

"There is but one secret to success—never give up!" *Ben Nighthorse Campbell*

Figure 1.4 Assessment for the analysis of student learning in a teacher work sample

Teacher Work Sample Standard: *The teacher candidate uses assessment data to profile student learning and communicate information about student progress and achievement.*

Task. Analyze your assessment data, including pre- and postassessments and formative assessments to determine students' progress related to the unit learning goals. Use visual representations and narrative to communicate the performance of the whole class, subgroups, and two individual students. Conclusions drawn from this analysis should be provided in the "Reflection and Self-Evaluation" section.

Prompt. In this section, you will analyze data to explain progress and achievement toward learning goals demonstrated by your whole class, subgroups of students, and individual students.

> **Whole class.** To analyze the progress of your whole class, create a table that shows pre- and postassessment data on every student on every learning goal. Then, create a graphic summary that shows the extent to which your students made progress (from pre- to post-) toward the

learning criterion that you identified for each learning goal (identified in your Assessment Plan section). Summarize what the graph tells you about your students' learning in this unit (i.e., the number of students who met the criterion).

Subgroups. Select a group characteristic (e.g., gender, performance level, socioeconomic status, language proficiency) to analyze in terms of *one learning goal*. Provide a rationale for your selection of this characteristic to form subgroups (e.g., girls vs. boys; high vs. middle vs. low performers). Create a graphic representation that compares pre- and postassessment results for the subgroups on this learning goal. Summarize what these data show about student learning.

Individuals. Select two students who demonstrated different levels of performance. Explain why it is important to understand the learning of these particular students. Use preformative, and postassessment data with examples of the students' work to draw conclusions about the extent to which these students attained the two learning goals. Graphic representations are not necessary for this subsection.

Source: Elliott, E. (2003). *Assessing education candidate performance: A look at changing practices.* Washington, DC: National Council for Accreditation of Teacher Education, p. 48.

which you plan to work to determine the tests you will be required to pass before you receive a license (see the Understanding & Using Evidence feature).

Basic Skills Tests Teacher candidates are usually required to pass a basic skills test before they are admitted to a teacher education program. These tests are designed to determine that future teachers have the basic knowledge and skills in reading, writing, and computing.

Content Tests Content tests assess candidates' knowledge of the subject or subjects they will be teaching or the field in which they will be working (for example, English as a second language or special education). These tests generally assess the knowledge outlined in the state and professional standards for the field, which is another reason to be familiar with the standards. You should develop the knowledge bases for your field in the courses you have taken in the sciences, humanities, arts, psychology, and social sciences. Secondary and middle-level teacher

Ed Lines

"All labor that uplifts humanity has dignity and importance and should be undertaken with painstaking excellence." *Martin Luther King, Jr.*

Figure 1.5 A scoring guide to assess student learning

Teacher Work Sample Standard: *The teacher candidate uses assessment data to profile student learning and communicate information about student progress and achievement.*

Indicator	Rating 1 — Indicator Not Met	Rating 2 — Indicator Partially Met	Rating 3 — Indicator Met	Score
Clarity and Accuracy of Presentation	Presentation is not clear and accurate; it does not accurately reflect the data.	Presentation is understandable and contains few errors.	Presentation is easy to understand and contains no errors of representation.	
Evidence of Impact on Student Learning	Analysis of student learning fails to include evidence of impact on student learning in terms of numbers of students who achieved and made progress toward learning goals.	Analysis of student learning includes incomplete evidence of the impact on student learning in terms of numbers of students who achieved and made progress toward learning goals.	Analysis of student learning includes evidence of the impact on student learning in terms of numbers of students who achieved and made progress toward each learning goal.	

Source: Elliott, E. (2003). *Assessing education candidate performance: A look at changing practices.* Washington, DC: National Council for Accreditation of Teacher Education, p. 49.

candidates often major in the academic discipline they plan to teach. Some states require elementary teacher candidates to major or have a concentration in one or more academic fields such as social sciences, mathematics, science, a foreign language, or English. Are you required to have an academic, rather than education, major to be licensed in your state?

Most states require new teachers to pass content tests before they receive the first license to teach. Many institutions require candidates to pass this test before they are eligible to student teach.

Pedagogical and Professional Knowledge Tests Some states also require new teachers to pass another test that assesses general pedagogical and professional knowledge that teachers should have to manage instruction and students. This information is taught in courses such as educational foundations, educational psychology, multicultural education, tests and measurement, methods, and the course that requires you to read this book. Your specialized knowledge about teaching and learning is assessed in this group of tests. They require you to know theories in education, the critical research that guides how to teach your subject, instructional strategies, the impact of diversity on learning, and the use of technology in teaching.

Understanding & USING EVIDENCE

LICENSURE TEST SCORES

Each state sets the qualifying or cut-off score that a test taker must achieve before they can receive a license to teach in the state. These scores differ across selected states as shown here.

Test	AR	CT	LA	MS	NV	OH	PA	VA
Biology: Content Knowledge	—	152	150	135	154	148	147	155
Elementary Education: Curriculum, Instruction, & Assessment	—	163	—	135	158	—	168	—
Elementary Education: Content Knowledge	—	—	150	—	—	—	—	143
English Language, Literature, & Composition: Content Knowledge	159	172	160	157	150	167	160	172
Mathematics: Content Knowledge	116	137	125	123	144	139	136	147
Social Studies: Content Knowledge	155	162	149	143	152	157	157	161

Your Task: Just because you have passed the licensure test in the state in which you have completed a teacher education program does not mean that you have met the qualifying score in another state. You should be aware of the qualifying scores in the state in which you would like to work.

1. What do you know about requirements in the states listed in the table above?

2. What does this table tell you about becoming qualified in these eight states?

3. Why are scores not indicated for some states?

4. Why do some states require higher scores than others?

Refer to the Understanding & Using Evidence Appendix at the end of the text for answers and information related to these activities.

Source: Educational Testing Service. Retrieved June 15, 2006, from www.ets.org/praxis/prxstate.html.

Complete a Teacher Education Program

You can study to become a teacher through many routes. Programs are delivered in college classrooms and schools with faculty in the room or are available online. Some programs can be completed via distance learning without stepping on a campus. A growing number of candidates begin exploring teaching as a career in community colleges, initially developing portfolios and working with children and youth in schools and community projects. In the past, the majority of new teachers completed a bachelor's program that led to a teaching license. A number of college graduates who majored in an academic discipline, but did not take education courses, enter full-time internships in schools as a part of a postbaccalaureate program. In most cases, these interns must take required education courses while they are teaching. School districts sometimes "grow" their own teachers by supporting teacher aides and assistants, who usually live in the school's community, in obtaining their bachelor's degrees and licenses. Professionals who have worked in business, engineering, retail, and other fields enter nontraditional programs designed for career changers. Institutions often work collaboratively with school districts to prepare retired military personnel and returning Peace Corps workers as teachers.

Most colleges and universities offer a number of pathways for becoming a teacher. You will need to decide which program best meets your needs. Beware of programs that require few assignments and field experiences; completion of such programs is likely not to be recognized by the state for a license.

Traditional Undergraduate Programs   The majority of teachers have completed bachelor's programs that prepared them for a license to teach. Most often, they began their preparation soon after high school. Although some education courses may be taken in the first 2 years of college, candidates are usually not admitted to education programs until they are juniors. Many education courses require candidates to complete field experiences in schools as a component of the course. Some programs require candidates to be observing and working in schools for several days a week, even offering the education courses at the school. Candidates student teach under the supervision of a teacher and college supervisor during the final year of their bachelor's program.

Postbaccalaureate Programs   Some teacher education programs are 5-year programs that begin at the undergraduate level and end with a master's degree or eligibility for a license after completing a sequence of graduate courses. These programs allow more time for candidates' in-depth study of teaching and learning. They sometimes require a year-long internship in schools, allowing candidates to practice under the guidance of professionals who provide feedback and support throughout the internship.

College graduates who decide after they have completed their bachelor's degree that they want to teach have several options for pursuing a teaching career. They could choose a master of arts in teaching (MAT) program that provides in-depth study and an internship. Many colleges and universities have certificate or licensure programs in which candidates can complete the courses and student teaching required for a state license. These courses often can be used toward a master's degree, but check with a college advisor to ensure this is the case.

Alternate Routes   In the past decade, a number of nontraditional or alternate routes to teaching careers have emerged. Many of these programs are designed for adults beyond the traditional college age of 18–24. They build on the experience

Ed Lines

"**Be the change that you want to see in the world.**" *Mahatma Gandhi*

and background of candidates who often have worked for a number of years in a nonteaching field. These programs may be similar to traditional undergraduate and graduate programs, but offer greater flexibility in scheduling courses and field experiences. Many candidates in these programs are working full-time in schools or other jobs.

Military personnel may participate in Troops to Teachers, a program to assist men and women who have completed their military service in becoming teachers. Other programs help professionals in nonteaching fields become teachers. These programs often place candidates in classrooms to complete their coursework and field experiences.

Not all teachers complete programs at colleges and universities. School districts, state departments of education, and other organizations are also preparing teachers. Alternate route programs such as Teach for America bring candidates with bachelor's degrees together for a few weeks of intensive training before they begin teaching in a school with a high density of students who have traditionally been underserved. A number of states support similar alternate route programs in which college graduates are prepared for a few weeks during the summer before they begin teaching in the fall.

Spend Time in Schools

Most teacher education programs require candidates to observe and work in schools, often beginning with the first education course. You want to make sure you really like working with young children if you are planning to teach at the primary level or older adolescents if you are planning to teach high school. You can also learn whether you have the temperament to work with 30 students at a time or to maintain a schedule that requires you to be in a classroom with students for hours at a time without talking on your cell phone or having a snack. Field experiences confirm for most candidates that they really do want to teach. Others discover that teaching is not the job for them.

Student Teaching   Unless you are in an alternate route program that places you in the classroom as the teacher almost immediately, you will be required to practice teach in a real classroom before you complete your program. Student teaching is usually at least 10 weeks long and often a semester in length. An internship may be as long as a year. During clinical practice, you work directly with one or more experienced teachers. At the beginning, you observe the teacher and begin to teach some lessons and work with groups of students. Gradually, you assume responsibility for the full teaching load. The school-based teacher should provide you regular feedback on your performance, helping you think about what works and doesn't work as you interact with students, other teachers, and administrators in the schools. The supervisor from your college should visit you periodically, providing support as needed and evaluating your performance. At different points during your clinical practice, your supervisors should be evaluating your

Ed Lines

"**A life isn't significant except for its impact on other lives.**" *Jackie Robinson*

performance against the state and professional standards you are expected to meet. They should share their evaluations with you and indicate areas in which you need to improve.

Professional Development Schools You may be assigned to a professional development school (PDS) for your field experiences and clinical practice. Teachers, teacher candidates, and college professors in a PDS work together to support student learning. They may team teach and take turns teaching, planning together, and supporting each other. After a few weeks of working together, students and parents often are not able to distinguish between the teacher, professor, and teacher candidate. One or more professors may spend most of their time in a PDS, working with the teacher and candidate in the classroom and providing professional development for faculty as needed.

Revisiting José Garcia's Dilemma

Knowledge of the subject you teach and how you teach it may seem like the same side of a coin, but they are truly quite different. It is possible to be an expert in a field and not be able to help a group of students understand it. To continue to teach science, José Garcia must either pass a licensure test in science or return to college to complete courses for a science major. He would rather work on a master's degree in social studies education. Maybe the school district will have an opening for a social studies teacher by the time the next school year begins, or he will need to move to another school district.

How Do You Get Off to a Good Start?

After teaching for 4 years, **Lisa Nowinski** decided she was ready to seek national board certification. Two teachers in her high school already had been recognized as accomplished teachers by the NBPTS and, as a result, were receiving an extra $7,000 annually from the school district. The students in her English and literature courses were writing well, and a few of them had been finalists in district essay contests. A number of students entered her basic English courses with limited writing skills, but she worked diligently with them over the school year. She always received glowing evaluations from her department head and principal. She considered herself an effective teacher and the process of becoming a national board–certified teacher would make her even better.

In reviewing the information on the NBPTS website, Lisa discovered that applicants spent 200–400 hours preparing their portfolios. The portfolio for English language arts would require entries to show that she could use assessment, scaffold learning, facilitate interactions in small groups, and contribute to student learning. Her portfolio would have to include two videotapes of her teaching and interacting with students, samples of the work of students in her classes, and documentation of her work with families and communities. She would have 12 months *to complete the portfolio after she applied. "My portfolio at the end of student teaching received rave reviews from my professors," she thought. "I can do this."*

There is no time like now to start down the path toward successful teaching. Take advantage of the assignments and experiences you are required to complete, always thinking about how they relate to the subject or students you will be teaching next week or in a few years. In the activities at the end of each chapter in this book, you are provided opportunities to apply your knowledge to the realities of classrooms and schools. These activities can be incorporated into a portfolio of your work that will show your growth as you learn how to teach over the next year or two and can be used later during your interview for a job. This section addresses some of these starting points.

Begin a Portfolio

A *portfolio* is a collection of your work, including papers, projects, lesson plans, and assessments. It serves many purposes. During your program, the **artifacts** (that is, the documents and presentations) in your portfolio show your growth as a teacher from the first education course you took to completion of the program. Your written papers may have been submitted as part of your coursework or are written reflections of your experiences working with students. They show that you understand a particular topic in your field and have the ability to analyze issues and classroom situations as well as your writing skills.

Artifacts. The documents and presentations included in a teacher's portfolio.

Lesson plans, which you will develop later in the program as a detailed guide for your instruction of a topic, show that you understand the subject you are teaching and that you can select appropriate instructional strategies for helping students learn the lesson. Evaluations of your field experiences and student teaching by your school and university supervisors provide evidence of your effectiveness in the classroom. Samples of student work related to the lessons you teach along with your analysis of the student work, and reflections on how effective your teaching was and what you would do differently the next time, provide evidence that you have the knowledge, skills, and dispositions critical to a teacher's work.

The artifacts in your portfolio can serve as evidence that you meet the state and professional standards discussed earlier in this

Many teacher education programs require teacher candidates to show that they meet national and state standards by presenting their work in a portfolio. The entries in the portfolio are assessed by faculty and can be included in a portfolio that is later presented when seeking a teaching position.

chapter. This connection is most clear when the scoring guides or rubrics used by faculty to assess your work are aligned with the standards. A lesson plan, for example, could show that you have drawn on the prior experiences and cultures of your students and used technology effectively to help students learn. It could also show that you know how to plan a lesson and assess student learning. The lesson plan and the scoring guide completed by faculty should be included in your portfolio along with other related documents that you have compiled for that lesson, such as your reflections on your teaching of the lesson and samples of student work. The portfolio could include videotapes of you teaching a lesson accompanied by your reflections on meeting your objectives for the lesson. You could select your best artifacts for a portfolio that serves as a final step to convince faculty that you have met a particular set of standards.

Like architects and artists, new teachers select examples of their best work for portfolios to be presented at job interviews. These portfolios also should include demographic information that present your credentials: a résumé, transcripts, child-abuse clearance, criminal-background clearance, and teaching license (Netterville, 2002). Any awards or honors that you receive should be added to this portfolio. Letters of recommendation from faculty or your supervising teacher should be included along with any letters of appreciation or commendations from parents or students. This portfolio should be well organized and very professional in appearance to present yourself as the professional teacher the school district wants to hire.

You may not be asked to present a portfolio until you are further along in your program. However, the task of compiling a portfolio will be much easier if you begin now to collect and organize your papers, projects, evaluations, and student work. You may be surprised to see your own growth over time. Some of the projects that you develop in your teacher education program can be used in your own classroom later. You will select different information and artifacts to include in the portfolio, depending on its purpose. The portfolio for your capstone project at the end of the program will include different information than the one you use to seek your first job or national certification after you have taught a few years.

Because portfolios and all of the artifacts that could be placed in a portfolio could fill a number of file cabinets or storage boxes, candidates may want to consider an electronic portfolio. Professors and school districts usually find it much easier to review your portfolio on a CD than in a notebook, but check with them before spending time developing the CD and then discovering they preferred a paper version. Your institution may require you to use a specific software package for the portfolio that allows you and the faculty to track your projects and the related assessments to standards. One advantage to the electronic portfolio is that it provides you the opportunity to highlight your technology skills—one of the requirements in standards. To assist you in beginning your portfolio, each chapter in this book will suggest one or two tasks for that purpose.

Reflect on Your Observations and Practice in Schools

Reflection, a valued skill in teaching, allows you to think about the effects of your choices and actions on students, parents, and other professionals in the learning community. National board–certified teachers must present evidence to show they reflect on their teaching and make changes as necessary to support learning.

Portfolios may include papers in which teacher candidates reflect on their practice in the classroom. The papers show that candidates think about what works and what doesn't in the classroom. Reflective teachers can articulate why they chose one instructional method over another, analyze the effectiveness of the approach when they use it, and choose another approach for a student who did not learn.

Early in your program, you will be observing teachers and working with small groups of students rather than teaching. However, you can begin to develop your reflection skills in both these school settings and activities in your college classroom. One popular process is the maintenance of **journals** in which you summarize your thoughts about and reactions to the major things you observed or experienced in a class or school. Journal entries should be brief, candid, and personal. You should record how you were affected by the events and why. You may be surprised, angry, puzzled, delighted, or apathetic. You may not believe what you are reading or seeing. You may want to step in and change something. You may have learned a new strategy for accommodating the needs of a student with disabilities. The journal allows you to regularly record (usually daily or weekly) your reflections on what you are learning. As you read your journal later, you will see how your thoughtful reflections helped you define your own teaching. The section at the end of each chapter, "Journaling: Becoming a Thoughtful Teacher," provides suggestions for topics you could address in journal entries related to the chapter.

Journals. Documents in which teacher candidates record their thoughts about a topic or their reflections on the teaching of a lesson, student behavior, and other classroom events.

Begin Collaborating

One way to help determine whether you want to teach is to talk and work with teachers and other school professionals. You will begin to get a better sense of what it is like to be a teacher rather than a student. Ask them why they chose a particular lesson, responded to one student differently than all of the others, and used a particular assessment. Be helpful to the teachers you are observing when they ask for assistance.

You should begin to develop your collaborative skills as you work with other candidates and professors on campus. You are likely to be assigned to work with your peers on group activities. These activities provide you the opportunity to be a leader in planning and delivering papers and presentations. To be successful, you will have to work with people with whom you have many common experiences and others with whom you have little in common. You may have to assist others and sometimes do some of their work for the good of the team. When you are in the classroom, you will find similar dilemmas as you work with other teachers. You may also have a better understanding of the group dynamics of students when you assign them to group work in the classroom. It is wise to begin now to learn to collaborate with professional colleagues.

Revisiting Lisa Nowinski's Journey to National Board Certification

Both you and Lisa Nowinski can do this. Lisa first created a portfolio during her teacher education program and added a few artifacts to it from her first years of teaching. She decided to continue documenting her professional growth through

Connecting
TO THE CLASSROOM

This chapter has provided some basic information about the need for qualified teachers, where the jobs are, how to become licensed, and some of the circumstances you might encounter during your first few years of teaching. The following are some key principles for applying the information in this chapter to the classroom.

1. Effective teachers make a difference in student learning.
2. Professional teachers are responsible for the well-being of their clients (students).
3. Mentoring of new teachers is a critical factor in the retention of teachers in the profession.
4. A school's curriculum is guided by the state or school district's standards for students.
5. Teacher standards identify the key knowledge, skills, and disposition that teachers should demonstrate in the classroom.
6. The collection of your work in a portfolio provides evidence that you have met standards and that you can help students in your classroom learn.

journals and a portfolio. She signed up at the local university for a national board support program for advice and assistance as she prepares her evidence for becoming a national board–certified teacher. In a year or two or three, you will be amazed at where your journey to become a teacher has taken you. You are also likely to be thinking about national certification.

Chapter Summary

As prospective teachers explore the teaching profession as their career goal, they consider the demands of working in schools and the possible rewards teaching will bring them. Not everyone can teach. It is a challenging profession that requires its members to be extremely knowledgeable of the subjects they teach, how students learn, the importance of culture in helping students learn, and instructional strategies that work.

Why teach? Teachers are committed to their work with students. They care for children and youth and view education as a way to make a difference in the lives of students. They experience intrinsic rewards in seeing students learn and develop under their tutelage. Research studies show that effective teachers make a great deal of difference in student achievement.

What makes teaching a profession? Teaching is in a period of defining itself as a profession. It has a number of characteristics of other professions, but does not yet have the same prestige, especially as reflected in comparable salaries. Teaching usually requires advanced study beyond the bachelor's degree to maintain a teaching license, and a growing number of new teachers have completed a postbaccalaureate or master's program before they begin teaching. Teachers are integrally involved in setting the standards and ethics for teachers and their practice at the state and national levels. Professional standards boards, of which teachers comprise the majority of the members, develop standards for state licenses and revoke the licenses of teachers who do not uphold professional standards.

Where are the jobs? Teacher shortages are projected over the next decade as baby boomers retire from teaching. However, retirements account for less than one-third of the teachers who leave the profession annually. Jobs also open up in schools as teachers move to other schools with better working conditions and better pay. Teaching positions are more prevalent in the South and West where student populations are growing. Urban and rural schools also have more openings than most suburban schools. Many school districts report that they cannot find enough qualified teachers in mathematics, science, bilingual education, English as a second language, and special education.

What should you know about your first year? One of five new teachers is not teaching after 3 years often because they are not satisfied with the job. New teachers who have had a mentor or participated in an induction program during their first year are more likely to remain in the classroom than those who do not. Effective teachers build on the knowledge and skills they learned in their teacher education programs and learn from their hands-on experiences during their early years of teaching.

How can you become a highly qualified teacher? Because both teacher education programs and P–12 schools are likely to be standards based, teacher candidates need to become familiar with standards for P–12 students and teachers. The knowledge, skills, and dispositions of prospective teachers are assessed from admission into a teacher education program to completion. Most states require teachers to pass one or more licensure tests before they are granted a teaching license. Teacher candidates can prepare for a teaching license as part of a bachelor's degree or at the postbaccalaureate level, master's degree, or other alternate route program. All programs require work in schools, but candidates are teaching as they learn to teach in some of the alternate route programs.

How do you get off to a good start? As teacher candidates visit schools and observe teachers in field experiences that occur early in their preparation program, they learn whether teaching is really the career they want to pursue. Activities that contribute to a teacher's development include the initiation of a portfolio, reflection on one's practice, and collaboration with colleagues.

Class Discussion Questions

1. Some policy makers are attacking teachers as standing in the way of reforming schools. They argue that teachers do not want to be held accountable for student learning. Some teachers argue that the state and federal governments do not provide them adequate resources to make it possible for them to help children achieve academically and learn the skills they will need to be successful and productive citizens. Who do you think is to blame for students not learning? How accountable do you think teachers should be for student learning? How should teachers be held accountable?

2. This chapter suggests that new teachers should be able to show evidence that they meet the INTASC standards. Why should teachers have the knowledge, skills, and dispositions identified in these standards? Which of the INTASC standards do you personally find most important? Why?

Both teachers and students are expected to meet standards in today's schools. The NBPTS states that teachers should be committed to students and their learning, know the subjects they teach and how to teach those subjects, be responsible for managing and monitoring student learning, think systematically about their practice and learn from experience, and be members of learning communities. For one of your next visits to a school, select one of these five expectations and record evidence that you see of teachers in the school demonstrating that expectation.

Ask a Teacher

Ask one new and one experienced teacher to recall their first year of teaching. If they could start over, what would they do differently? What had they been well prepared to handle when they first entered the classroom? What were their greatest challenges? What recommendations do they have for making your first year successful?

Journaling *Becoming a Thoughtful Teacher*

Begin an entry in your journal about why you want to teach. Why do you want to teach a specific subject? Why do you want to teach at the preschool, elementary, middle, or high school level? Where would you like to teach when you complete your program? Why do you want to teach in a specific location? What adult, if any, had an influence on your decision to teach? As you observe and work in schools over the next few years, you may want to revisit your reasons for teaching and update them based on your new experiences.

Portfolio Tasks

1. Many people report that a teacher has made a great difference in their lives. Write a short paper on the influence one or more teachers made on your life. Describe what the teacher did in the classroom that impressed you. Begin to develop a list of characteristics of teachers who made a difference. Later you can return to this paper to determine if you are developing the same characteristics in yourself as the teachers you admire.

2. Learn the standards for teaching in your state. Make a list of the proficiencies related to knowledge, skills, and dispositions that you are expected to demonstrate in the classroom. When, during your field experiences, you achieve one of these standards, place a check mark by the standard and indicate how you know that you had achieved the proficiency (for example, the assessment used and your score). As you progress through your teacher education program, continue to add check marks until all the standards are met. This exercise will help you become familiar with the standards and will also be tangible proof of how much you have learned.

Self-Assessment *What Am I Learning?*

Using the professional standards for the field that you plan to teach from the following list, make a list of areas in the standards that you think you already meet and those that you know little about at this time. You might use a table similar to the one that follows:

Standard	Have little or no knowledge or experience	Have studied this area, but need more information and experience	Am already proficient

Standards for Professional Education Fields

American Alliance for Health, Physical Education, Recreation, and Dance (AAHPERD)	www.aahperd.org
American Association of Physics Teachers (AAPT)	www.aapt.org
American Council on the Teaching of Foreign Languages (ACTFL)	www.actfl.org
Association for Advancement of Health Education (AAHE)	www.aahperd.org/aahe
Association for Childhood Education International (ACEI)	www.acei.org
Association for Education in Journalism and Mass Communications (AEJMC)	www.ukans.edu/~acejmc/ STUDENT/PROGLIST.HTML
Association for Educational Communications and Technology (AECT)	www.aect.org
Council for Exceptional Children (CEC)	www.cec.sped.org
International Reading Association (IRA)	www.reading.org
International Technology Education Association (ITEA)	www.itea.org
International Society for Technology Education (ISTE)	www.iste.org
Modern Language Association of America (MLA)	www.mla.org
Music Teachers National Association (MTNA)	www.mtna.org
National Art Education Association (NAEA)	www.naea-reston.org
National Association of Biology Teachers (NABT)	www.nabt.org
National Association for Bilingual Education (NABE)	www.nabe.org
National Association for the Education of Young Children (NAEYC)	www.naeyc.org
National Association for Gifted Children (NAGC)	www.nagc.org
National Association for Multicultural Education (NAME)	www.inform.umd.edu/name
National Association for Sports and Physical Education (NASPE)	www.aahperd.org/naspe

(continued)

National Business Education Association (NBEA)	www.nbea.org
National Council for the Social Studies (NCSS)	www.ncss.org
National Council of Teachers of English (NCTE)	www.ncte.org
National Council of Teachers of Mathematics (NCTM)	www.nctm.org
National Middle Schools Association (NMSA)	www.nmsa.org
National Science Teachers Association (NSTA)	www.nsta.org
Teachers of English to Speakers of Other Languages (TESOL)	www.tesol.org

Using the Web

1. You can see examples of National Teachers of the Year at **www.ccsso.org/projects/National_Teacher_of_the_Year/National_Teachers/**.

2. For other reports of effective teachers, visit the website of Recruiting New Teachers at **www.rnt.org/channels/clearinghouse/whyteach/default.htm**.

3. State licensure requirements can be accessed from the state agency in which you are interested at the Recruiting New Teachers website at **www.rnt.org/channels/clearinghouse/deptedu.asp**.

4. See the website of the National Education Association for an example of a code of ethics at **www.nea.org/code.html**. You should become familiar with the code of ethics in your state and school district.

5. If you are not familiar with the standards that you must meet in your teaching field, you can access them at **www.ncate.org/institutions/programstandards.asp?ch=4** or the website of your professional association.

6. For more information on the NBPTS standards for becoming a national board–certified teacher, visit the standards at **www.nbpts.org/the_standards/standards_by_cert**.

7. For additional information on the licensure tests and study guides, visit the websites of the two major testing companies at **www.ets.org** or **www.nesinc.com**. You will need to check with your state to determine the tests you will be required to pass.

Your Professional Library

Ayers, W. (2004). *Teaching toward freedom.* Boston: Beacon Press.

Drawing on his own teaching and popular culture of film, poetry, and novels, the author discusses how and why we teach. Making students visible and heard in their education is the central message of this book as teachers engage students in their own learning.

Nieto, S. (2005). *Why we teach.* New York: Teachers College Press.

Experienced and new teachers share the reasons they find purpose and value in teaching. They discuss the kinds of learning that really matter and the kinds of lessons students can take with them for their entire lives. This inspirational book focuses on the quintessential values of teaching and challenges current issues of accountability and testing.

Nieto, S. (2003). *What keeps teachers going?* New York: Teachers College Press.

Veteran urban teachers who are effective at working with students of diverse cultural and linguistical backgrounds provide advice on solving the everyday challenges of student learning. Their stories provide vision of what's important in teaching and learning.

Rethinking Schools. (2004). *The new teacher book: Finding purpose, balance, and hope during your first years in the classroom.* Milwaukee, WI: Author.

New and experienced teachers offer practical guidance for beginning a teaching career in this collection of writings. They reflect on classroom management, curriculum, discipline, and the students.

Thomas-El, S., & Murphey, C. (2003). *I choose to stay: A black teacher refuses to desert the inner city.* New York: Kensington.

A teacher at Roberts Vaux Middle School in Philadelphia discusses why he has continued to teach in the inner city. This dedicated educator believes in the potential of all students, making a difference in the lives of students who may have otherwise become statistics without his intervention.

Companion Website

To access chapter objectives, practice tests, weblinks, and flashcards, visit the Companion Website at **www.ablongman.com/hall1e**

(mylabschool

Where the classroom comes to life!

Log on to Allyn & Bacon's MyLabSchool (**www.mylabschool.com**). Enter Assignment ID **FDV1** in the **Assignment Finder** and view the clip, *Becoming a Teacher*. Then enter Assignment **FDV9**, and view the clip, *Teaching Fifth Grade Instruction*. The teachers in these clips, Penny Brandenburg and Lora Dorn, talk about their reasons for becoming teachers, and in Lora's case for choosing a particular grade level. Consider the information in Chapter 1 about choos-

ing teaching as a profession and the reasons Penny and Lora offer. Then consider your own reasons for wanting to become a teacher by responding to the following questions:

1. What characteristics do you believe you have that would make you an effective teacher?
2. What experiences did you have as a student that made you want to become a teacher?
3. What grade level would you choose to teach? Why?

Today's Students

Educators in Real Schools

M E E T

Katherine Wright Knight

*English teacher at Parkview Magnet School,
Little Rock, Arkansas*

Katherine Wright Knight has been both the Arkansas and the National Foundation for the Improvement of Education's Teacher of the Year. She is an English teacher who team teaches with a mathematics teacher at Parkview Magnet School. She is a national board–certified teacher and provides support to other teachers seeking national certification. Katherine also has been the president of the local teacher's union and the secretary-treasurer of the state affiliate of the National Education Association.

Parkview is Arkansas' first and only complete interdistrict magnet high school for students from all three local districts in Little Rock and competes for students with the two private high schools in the city. All of the science and mathematics courses at Parkview are at the advanced placement level. The school has been rated in the top 1 percent of national magnet programs. According to the Parkview mission statement, the school provides students with an innovative, diverse, and comprehensive curriculum that fosters academic growth and enables students to meet the challenges of the future.

Here is how Ms. Wright Knight responded when asked to explore her thoughts and experiences about teaching.

❖ *What do you expect when you are looking for excellence in teaching?*

I expect to see joy. One of the very first requirements is to enjoy what you do. Excellent teachers teach because of commitment and passion. Teachers have to know

Chapter 2

what they are teaching, but that's not all. They have to establish rapport with students, peers, and parents. Teachers must be able to talk about the importance of education to the students and to themselves. Teachers must be involved in their own personal development. I had to accept the fact that I had to go to professional development courses after I started teaching and attend these courses with the right attitude; I could always learn something. Excellent teachers seek out learning. They find things to make their classes interesting. Teachers must be familiar with what their kids are doing. They need to be able to laugh and cry with students. Teachers can show emotions. They can talk about characters in books they read as though they are real. Good teachers know the trends in their field. Most of all, teachers must be relevant to kids in their classroom and know how to assess kids at their level of knowledge.

❖ *How do you know you have made a difference in student learning?*

You know by students' responses. You can see it in their eyes, their attentiveness, their response to you, and their efforts to go beyond the requirements. They light up and know when you light up, too. When they start asking questions beyond what you are doing that day and building on the past, seeing future possibilities, then you know they are learning.

❖ *What brings you joy in teaching?*

I love it. I love the literature. I like the 10th grade because it includes diverse literature from multicultural works. I love the excitement of having children openly discuss their learning. I see innovative ideas in student presentations as well as in their development of skills to collaborate, work with each other, make decisions about what to cover, and assess knowledge they taught with their own quizzes. One of the joys is having kids get excited about books they probably wouldn't read on their own.

I had a student who is a medical doctor now. His parents are extremely well educated; his mother was a well-respected English teacher. Julian was very shy and had the worst handwriting of any I have ever seen. I would put the worst handwritten papers on the bottom of the papers I had to read. His paper was the best written piece in the group, but it took so long to read because of the poor handwriting. I could have refused to read the paper because it was so difficult to read, but it was brilliant. I could have missed that message. Teachers really need to read what students are writing.

Students sometimes come back after they have gone to college to say they didn't like me when they were in my class. However, they report they were the only ones in their freshman composition course who could write a paper and read a book. I love to run into parents who introduce me as their children's teacher and say that I had an impact on them. A lot of former students send me notes. I like running into them in the grocery store. Some still call several times a year.

❖ *Who are the students in your school?*

Of the nearly 1,200 students enrolled at Parkview, the majority are African American (52%), with a slightly smaller number of white students (48%). A few Latino, East Indian, and biracial students are also enrolled at Parkview. Students come from families with low-income and higher incomes due to the professional status of their parents. Parents are very involved in the school and push their children to make good grades.

Questions to Consider

1. How would you describe the diversity of students in the schools that you attended in kindergarten through twelfth grade?

2. How do Ms. Wright Knight's classes differ from schools with which you are familiar?

3. What impresses you most about Ms. Wright Knight's comments about her classes?

▶ **Socioeconomic status (SES).** Composite of the economic status of families or persons on the basis of occupation, educational attainment, and income.

▶ **Disability.** A long-standing physical, mental, or emotional condition that can make it difficult for a person to perform activities such as walking, climbing stairs, dressing, bathing, learning, or remembering.

The students you will be teaching may be very similar to you, coming from the same racial and ethnic group, from families with the same **socioeconomic status (SES)** as your own family, attending the same church and speaking the same language. Or they may be very different from you, coming from a different racial and ethnic group, speaking a different language, and practicing a religion different from your own. Very few schools are segregated by gender so it is likely that not all of your students will be the same sex as you. You are likely to have one or more students in the classroom with a **disability** that you have not experienced. Many new teachers often find their first jobs in schools with students from groups and **cultures** with which they have little or no firsthand experience.

Students represent many different groups in society. They develop their identity based on their **race**, **ethnicity**, gender, socioeconomic status, language, religion, **sexual orientation**, disability, and age. Being a member of one group impacts on how we see ourselves in another group. Religion, for instance, may have a great influence on how girls and boys act. In our society, race defines power relationships. Our identities are also determined by others who define us based on our age or discriminate against us for one reason or another.

One of the keys to being a successful teacher is to care about the students in your classroom. A part of caring is to know the students, their families, and the realities of their everyday lives. This task is much easier in a close-knit community in which most families know one another because they attend the same church, synagogue, temple, or mosque. It is more challenging in large urban and suburban areas in which the histories and experiences of families differ greatly. At the same time, learning to value the diversity of students and communities can be one of the joyful parts of teaching. This chapter will introduce you to the student diversity you may encounter as you prepare to be a teacher and in your subsequent jobs.

Cultures. Socially transmitted ways of thinking, believing, feeling, and acting within a group. These patterns are transmitted from one generation to the next.

Race. A social category that groups people by the skin color of their ancestors.

Ethnicity. Membership based on one's national origin or the national origin of one's ancestors when they immigrated to the United States.

Sexual orientation. One's sexual attraction to persons of the same or opposite sex or both.

Focus QUESTIONS

After reading this chapter, you should be able to answer the following questions:

1. Who are the students in the nation's schools?
2. How do race and ethnicity impact student identity?
3. How does poverty affect student learning?
4. What impact has immigration and language diversity had on the composition of schools and the programs offered?
5. How are students with disabilities changing classroom contexts?

How Racially and Ethnically Diverse Are Our Schools?

John Lin taught 9th grade algebra for a number of years in an inner city school with low-income African American and Southeast Asian students. He was surprised, and somewhat skeptical, when he was asked to begin teaching algebra to 8th graders. He had found that many of his 9th grade students did not have the mathematical background necessary to be successful in algebra as 9th graders. How could they do it even earlier? Fortunately, his school district was willing to send him and several other teachers to a workshop on the Algebra Project, which was developed by Robert Moses, a mathematician who was also a 1960s civil rights leader. John learned that he needed to connect algebra to the students' own experiences in the community. He also learned that African American students and *other low-income students are performing at high levels when they are appropriately engaged in the subject by connecting it to their own cultures and experiences. John is now a member of a community of mathematics teachers in his district who have taken on the challenge of teaching algebra to inner-city school children. He is beginning to believe that he can get his students interested in algebra and improve their performance on the state achievement test.*

*E*thnicity is determined by the country or countries from which families or ancestors have come. *Race*, on the other hand, is a term that groups people by biological traits of color and texture of hair, color of skin and eyes, and body stature. In the United States, white has been the dominant and privileged race. Persons of color historically have faced discrimination no matter their ethnic heritage or socioeconomic status.

We often are asked to identify our group membership on applications and surveys. The U.S. Census Bureau places the population into six **pan-ethnic** and racial groups: African American or black, American Indian and Native Alaskan, Asian American, Latino, Native Hawaiian and Pacific Islander, and white. People now can choose the category, "Two or More Races," to indicate that their parents or ancestors are from different races. Still a number of students find it difficult to classify themselves into one of these groups because they do not see themselves as a member of any of them.

The U.S. population is predominantly white (68%), but less so every year as shown in the projections through 2050 in Figure 2.1. According to the U.S.

▶ **Pan-ethnic.** Ethnic membership based on national origin from a large geographic region that includes numerous countries; examples are African or Asian American.

Figure 2.1 Projected diversity of the United States

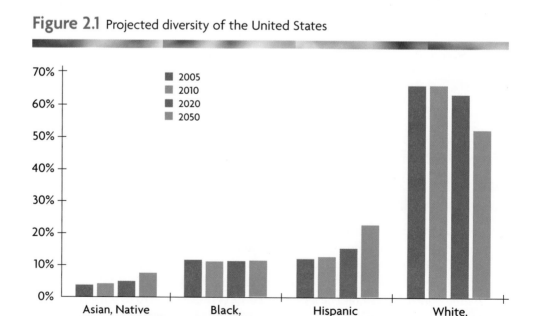

Sources: 2005 data are from the U.S. Census Bureau. (2006). *Statistical abstract of the United States: 2006* (125th ed.). Washington, DC: U.S. Government Printing Office. Projections were retrieved on December 19, 2004, from www.census.gov/population/projections/nation/summary/np-t5-c.txt, www.census.gov/population/projections/nation/summary/np-t5-e.txt, and www.census.gov/population/projections/nation/summary/np-t5-g.txt.

Census Bureau, by 2050, whites will be just over 50 percent of the population. The number of Latino or Hispanic persons surpassed African Americans at the beginning of the twenty-first century and will continue to grow. Asian Americans comprise only 4 percent of the population today, but are currently the fastest growing group (U.S. Census Bureau, 2006).

The school population reflects this growing diversity because a large number of immigrants are Latino or Asian, and the average age of those groups is younger than whites. In 1986 students of color comprised 30 percent of the student population (U.S. Department of Education, 2003); by 2010 they will comprise 43 percent (U.S. Census Bureau, 2004c) as shown in Figure 2.2. The African American and American Indian student population will remain about the same while the number of Latino and Asian American students will continue to grow (U.S. Census Bureau, 2004c).

The largest concentration of students of color is in the western part of the United States; the least diverse part of the country is the Midwest (U.S. Census Bureau, 2004c). California, Hawaii, New Mexico, and the District of Columbia are home to the greatest percentage of students of color who represent over 60 percent of the student population (U.S. Census Bureau, 2004c). Over half of the student population in Texas, Louisiana, and Mississippi are students of color, and more than 40 percent of the student population in Arizona, Georgia, Maryland, New York, and South Carolina are students of color (U.S. Department of Education, 2002). The highest concentration (25%) of African American students is in the South; Latinos

Figure 2.2 The changing diversity of the school-age population (5–17-year-olds)

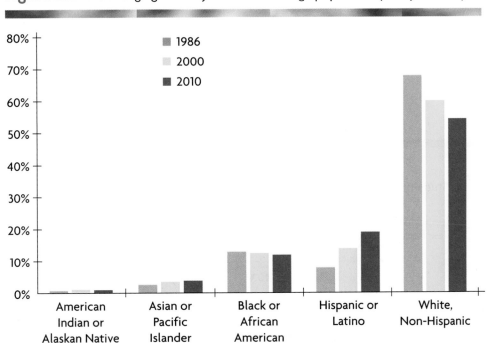

Sources: 1986 data are from National Center for Education Statistics. (June 2003). *Digest of education statistics 2002*. Washington, DC: U.S. Department of Education. 2000 and 2010 data are from U.S. Census Bureau. (2004). *Statistical abstract of the United States: 2004–2005* (124th ed.). Washington, DC: U.S. Government Printing Office.

make up 32 percent of the students in the West (U.S. Department of Education, 2002). Three of four students in the nation's largest school districts are students of color (Council of Great City Schools, 2006).

As shown in Figure 2.3, the diversity of teachers in the nation's schools does not match the ethnic and racial diversity of the student population. Nearly 85 percent of public school teachers are white and nearly three of four are women (U.S. Census Bureau, 2006). Many teachers do not understand their students' cultures and have no or limited experience in them. In these cases, teachers and students may misunderstand the cultural cues of the other. Teachers may **stereotype** students from ethnic and racial groups with whom they have no experience. Students and parents may come to believe that the teacher does not respect or accept their cultures. They feel that the only way to be successful in school is to adopt the teacher's culture, which may lead to the denigration of their own culture. Some adolescents of color resist the dominant culture of schools, labeling students who are academically successful as "acting white." The incongruence between students' and teachers' cultures may contribute to students not participating in school in meaningful ways. More students of color than white students are not actively engaged in their school work, too often dropping out of school, in part, because they don't see the payoff in completing high school.

To help all students learn, regardless of their ethnic or racial identity, teachers should learn as much as possible about groups other than their own before they begin teaching. Learning about other groups can be very enlightening and should become a lifelong learning experience. This chapter provides a brief introduction to different ethnic and racial groups, but further study of this topic is strongly recommended for anyone planning to be an effective teacher.

▶ **Stereotype.** Exaggerated, and usually biased views about a group.

African Americans

African Americans have developed their own culture out of their different African, European, and Native American heritages and their unique experiences in this

Figure 2.3 Diversity of teachers and students

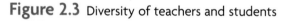
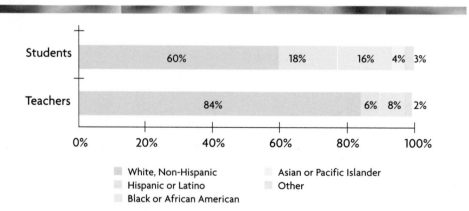

Source: U.S. Census Bureau. (2006). *Statistical abstract of the United States: 2006* (125th ed.). Washington, DC: U.S. Government Printing Office.

country. Unlike most other ethnic groups in the United States, persons of African ancestry have been in this country for nearly four centuries. For the most part, they were involuntary immigrants who were forced to leave their homelands under a system of slavery to serve the growing economy in the eighteenth and nineteenth centuries. Not all African American students come from families who have been in the United States for generations. Four percent of the students identified as black are foreign born and 14 percent have at least one foreign-born parent from Africa or the Caribbean (U.S. Census Bureau, 2006).

African Americans are the majority population in many counties in the South. They also comprise the majority population in a number of large cities and the first ring of suburbs around them (U.S. Census Bureau, 2000). African American students make up between 23 percent and 51 percent of the student population in the southeastern states and 84 percent of the students in the District of Columbia (U.S. Department of Education, 2005b). One in five students in Illinois and New York are African American (U.S. Census Bureau, 2004c). Most African American students are greatly influenced by their group membership. They know about their sordid treatment as a group in the United States. By middle school, they have experienced **racism** firsthand or know families or friends who have. Many African American students attend segregated schools. Others attend suburban or rural schools where they may be the only students of color.

Identity The recognition of racism and one's acceptance of being black or African American is key to a student's identity. Researchers (Cross, 1992; Jackson, 2001, Tatum, 1997) have identified stages that African Americans go through as they develop their identities. Students exhibit these stages as they mature and move into college and adulthood. These stages may help explain why they respond to the teacher and their peers in certain ways as they clarify their own identities.

According to Jackson (2001), Black Identity Development begins with a naïve stage in early childhood when African American children are aware of physical and some cultural differences among people, but they "generally do not feel fearful or hostile, inferior or superior" (p. 19). In the acceptance stage, young students internalize the **dominant group**'s ideology of racial superiority and generally conform to standards of the dominant group. By middle or high school, most African American students have been the victims of racial incidents or have known people who have. In this resistance stage, they begin to understand racism and how it impacts their daily lives. They may become actively hostile to racism as they gain a sense of personal power with an understanding of who African Americans are. They begin to develop their own identity as African Americans and no longer feel the need to act like members of the dominant group.

Young people are concerned with defining themselves in the redefinition stage. During this period, they tend to limit their interactions to other African American students. They appear to choose segregation and are not interested in integrating with other ethnic groups. They develop pride in being African American as they reclaim their heritage. In the final stage, internalization, young people or adults "no longer feel a need to explain, defend, or protect their Black identity, although they may recognize that it is important to nurture this sense of self" (Jackson, 2001, p. 25). Some African Americans "adopt a multicultural perspective, which bring

Racism. The belief that one race is inherently superior to all others and thereby has the right to dominance.

Dominant group. The group with power in society. In the United States the group with the most power is white, heterosexual, Christian, English speaking, middle class, able bodied, and male.

together worldviews from as many compatible cultural perspectives as possible"
(Jackson, 2001, p. 26).

Educational Experiences   Education has been very important to African
Americans from the days when they were not allowed to read or attend school.
They always have found ways to learn and even established schools when they were
illegal (Anderson, 1988). Before schools were integrated in the 1950s and 1960s,
many African American students were pushed by their parents and teachers to
achieve at high academic levels, finish high school, and attend college. This enthusiasm about education has not changed. However, parents also have high expectations for teachers and schools. They hold teachers responsible for helping their
children learn. Parents believe that it's the teacher's job to make students study, engage their children in learning, and teach them so that they perform at high levels.

The academic achievement gap, which is measured by test scores, has affected
African American students more than any other group (Education Trust, 2003).
They receive the lowest test scores, in part because they are more likely to be from
low-income families and have attended schools with inadequately prepared teachers. African American males are also more likely not to be at school because they
have been suspended from classes at higher rates than other groups. Eighty-one
percent of all African Americans over 25 years old have completed high school
as compared to 86 percent of whites, 87 percent of Asian Americans, and 58 percent of Latinos. Eighteen percent have graduated from college as compared to 28
percent of whites, 49 percent of Asians, and 12 percent of Latinos (U.S. Census
Bureau, 2006). Although African American students comprise 13 percent of high
school students, they make up only 6 percent of the students who take advanced
placement tests (Samuels, 2005). See the Challenging Assumptions on page 54.

American Indians and Alaska Natives

Indigenous. Population
that is native to a country
or region. In the United
States, Native Americans,
Hawaiians, and Alaska
Natives are the indige-
nous populations.

American Indians and Alaska Natives are the **indigenous**, or original, people who
inhabited North America. The United Nations (2002) estimates that 300 million
people in at least 5,000 groups around the world are indigenous. Many indigenous
people are often connected closely to the environments in which they live. They
try to maintain their traditional cultures, religions, and ways of life within countries in which they are not the majority and have little voice in state and national
policies and practices.

Today, 2.8 million citizens identify themselves as solely American Indian or
Alaska Native. Another 1.6 million indicate they are partially Native American
or Alaska Native (U.S. Census Bureau, 2006). The American Indian population
identifies with one or more of the 562 tribal governments recognized by the federal government (Bureau of Indian Affairs, 2005). Some identify with a tribe that
is not recognized. More than half of the Native American population belongs
to one of six tribes, each with over 100,000 members: Cherokee, Navajo, Latin
American Indian, Choctaw, Sioux (that is, Dakota, Lakota, and Nakota peoples),
and Chippewa. Other tribes with between 50,000 and 100,000 members include
Apache, Blackfeet, Iroquois, Pueblo, Creek, Lumbee, and Eskimo (U.S. Census
Bureau, 2006). American Indians or Alaska Natives comprise over 10 percent of

the population in five states as shown in Figure 2.4. Unlike the stereotype that many people have, the majority of them do not live on reservations. Six of 10 American Indians and Alaska Natives live in urban areas; the other 40 percent live in rural areas, most often in small towns (U.S. Census, 2004a).

One of the struggles for indigenous groups is the maintenance or recapturing of their native languages and traditions. Many of the languages traditionally have been transmitted orally and not captured as a written language. Many have been lost as children attended schools that used only English. Today, 28 percent of American Indian and Alaska Natives speak a language other than English at home (U.S. Census Bureau, 2004a). However, 98 percent of all American Indians and Alaska Natives speak English very well (U.S. Census Bureau, 2004a).

Identity American Indians identify foremost with their tribal affiliation (Horse, 2001). "Identity development begins with the family, extended family, kinship, or clan affiliations. Then it extends to the tribal group, and then to identification with the general Indian populace" (Horse, 2001, p. 94). They identify strongly with home and community. Learning the language, customs, traditions, and beliefs of their community is an important part of being Indian. The need for balance and harmony in life is a rather common worldview of American Indians (Horse, 2001).

An important part of American Indian identity is the validity of one's genealogical heritage. A number of people declare themselves as American Indian, but they have not grown up in the native way and cannot verify their Indian heritage. An important part of one's identity is knowing the native language and culture, especially the old traditions and native worldview. Another part of American Indian identity is being officially recognized as a member of a tribe by the tribal government (Horse, 2001).

Figure 2.4 States with the largest American Indian or Alaska Native student population

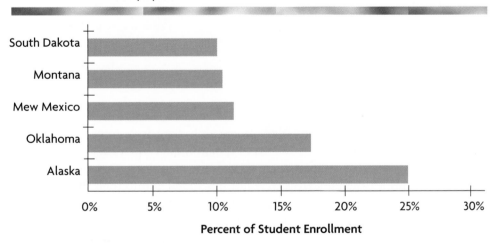

Source: Snyder, T. D., Tan, A. G., & Hoffman, C. M. (2004). *Digest of education statistics 2003* (NCES 2005-025), U.S. Department of Education, National Center for Education Statistics. Washington, DC: Government Printing Office.

Challenging Assumptions
FINDINGS FROM RESEARCH

Should teachers be colorblind as they interact with students of different races?

The Assumption: Many teachers say they are color-blind and do not see the race of their students and treat all students equally regardless of their race or SES. They believe that equality is treating all students the same way.

Study Design and Method: Drawing on 20 years of fieldwork in 11 elementary classrooms in the Midwest and South, a researcher traced the origins of school experiences for students of different races and gender. She also explored the implications of how teachers and students interacted based on their race, gender, and status.

Study Findings: White girls had the most positive interactions with teachers. They received frequent praise from teachers for their good behavior and academic work. In addition, teachers chatted with them about personal issues. For the most part, white girls understood the classroom routine and rules, followed the rules, and focused on the teachers.

Black males, on the other hand, had limited interactions with teachers, which were almost always negative and initiated by the teacher, not themselves. Teachers tended to monitor or criticize their behavior or academic work. Black boys were much more likely to interact with their peers than their teachers. White boys and black girls had a more balanced ratio of interactions with teachers and peers. Their relationships with teachers were cordial, but not as close as those of white girls.

The researcher concluded that schools do more to enhance than to diminish gender and race differences among African American girls, white girls, African American boys, and white boys. Although teachers do not appear consciously to intend to support white girls more than other students, such practices help ensure inequality in a classroom.

Implications: Many teachers think they are treating students equally, but they are responding to students through their own cultural lenses. Those students who share the same culture, especially the same race, gender, and SES as the teacher, generally have positive interactions with the teacher. Other students feel left out, in part, because they do not understand the teacher's culture and what they need to do to be accepted. The teacher, on the other hand, reads their behavior as inappropriate and unacceptable rather than different. Students of color and male students conclude that the teacher favors the white girls. Thus, teachers need to monitor their interactions with students to determine whether they are actually favoring some students over others and providing one group of students more academic support than others.

Source: Grant, L. (2004). Everyday schooling and the elaboration of race-gender stratification. In J. H. Ballantine & J. Z. Spade, *Schools and society: A sociological approach to education* (2nd ed.) (pp. 296–307). Belmont, CA: Wadsworth/Thomson.

Educational Experiences Many older American Indians were forced to attend boarding schools operated by the Bureau of Indian Affairs when they were young. One of the goals of these early boarding schools was to unlearn their Indian ways. Their native cultures and languages were not incorporated into their formal education, and, in fact, were often denigrated. Even today, tribal traditions, history, and native languages are not valued in most schools. The exceptions are native-centric schools in which the American Indian culture is centered in the curriculum. The Bureau of Indian Affairs still provides education services to approximately 48,000 American Indian students and 31 American Indian nations have tribal colleges to serve their communities (Bureau of Indian Affairs, 2005).

Asian Americans, Native Hawaiians, and Pacific Islanders

The pan-ethnic classification of Asian and Pacific Islander Americans includes both individuals whose families have been here for generations and those who are first-generation immigrants. Many do not have much more in common than that their countries of origin are part of the same continent. They are "Bangladeshi, Bhutanese, Bornean, Burmese, Cambodian, Celbesian, Cernan, Chamorro, Chinese, East Indian, Filipino, Hawaiian, Hmong, Indonesian, Japanese, Korean, Laotian, Okinawan, Samoan, Sikkimese, Singaporean, Sri Lankan, and Vietnamese" (Young & Pang, 1995, p. 5). Native Hawaiians are indigenous to the Hawaiian islands and face many of the struggles of other indigenous groups such as American Indians; they have been an oppressed people in their own homeland.

For the most part, Asians first came to the United States to fill labor needs in Hawaii and on the West Coast. The Chinese were recruited to work the plantations in Hawaii; Chinese, Japanese, and Filipinos provided the labor needed on the West Coast for mining gold and building railroads in the nineteenth century. During this early period, the immigrants were almost always men who planned to earn money to send back to their families. Early Asian immigrants were often seen as a threat to the dominant population, leading to severe restrictions on their immigration. The Chinese Exclusion Act of 1882 eliminated immigration from China for decades. Japanese Americans were interned during World War II, and immigration from Japan was stopped. Not until the Immigration Act of 1965 were Asian Americans allowed to immigrate in any significant numbers. Today, they comprise only 4 percent of the population, but are projected to more than double to 9 percent by 2050 (U.S. Census Bureau, 2004c).

Before 1970, the Asian American population was primarily Japanese, Chinese, and Filipino. Chinese Americans comprise the largest Asian ethnic group in the United States today with 2.8 million, followed by Filipinos with 2.4 million. Ethnic groups with more than a million people include Indians, Koreans, Vietnamese, and Japanese (Lee & Zhou, 2004). Since 1990, immigration has been predominantly from India, China, the Philippines, and Vietnam (U.S. Census Bureau, 2006). Native Hawaiians and other Pacific Islanders comprise 0.2 percent of the U.S. population with nearly half a million.

California is home to the largest number of Asian Americans, followed by New York (U.S. Census Bureau, 2006). Vietnamese Americans are more likely to live in Texas than in any other state. The majority of Japanese Americans live in California, Hawaii, and Washington. More Filipinos live in California and Illinois than in other states; New Jersey is home to many Indian and Korean families. Asian Americans are most likely to live in urban areas and are the majority population in Honolulu and Daly City, California. Native Hawaiians and other Pacific Islanders live primarily in California (29%) and Hawaii (23%). You may think of Asian Americans living in Chinatown or Little Saigon, but only 15 percent of Asian Americans live in such ethnic enclaves. The only exception is the Cam-bodian community in Los Angeles (Lee & Zhou, 2004).

Asian Americans comprise 72 percent of the students in Hawaii schools and 11 percent of the students in California schools. They make up 6 percent to 7 percent of the student population in the states of Washington, New Jersey, New York, Nevada, and Alaska (U.S. Census Bureau, 2004c). Asian American students are more likely to be foreign born (23%) or have one or more foreign born parents (91%) than any other pan-ethnic group (U.S. Census Bureau, 2006).

Identity   Although Asian American students have roots in different countries, they generally share some cultural expectations such as obligation to obey elders; obligation to repay parental sacrifices; high parental expectations for education and occupational achievement; and pressure for children to succeed academically. Their identity is defined, in part, by when their families immigrated and the way racism affects them. Sometimes conflict arises between native-born Asian Americans and recent immigrants (for example, what sounds fine to a new immigrant may be perceived as racist to a native-born person). The two groups often hold contradictory views about "individualism, civil liberties, labor rights, and ultimately, the ideology of **assimilation**" (Lee & Zhou, 2004, 14).

▶ Assimilation. Process by which groups adopt or change the dominant culture.

Asian Americans' self-identity is primarily influenced by external messages from their social environment, especially the impact of racism on them. Kim's Asian American Identity Development Model (2001) has five stages. The first is the ethnic awareness that children develop before entering school, which is based on their interactions with family and relatives. If they live in predominantly Asian communities, they will have more awareness of their Asian identity than those children growing up in predominantly white neighborhoods

In elementary and middle school, Asian American students develop an identification in which they try to fit into white society. They develop a strong sense of being different and believe that being different is bad; they can be alienated from other Asian Americans. As they begin to awaken to a social political consciousness, they become aware of racism. Whites are no longer their reference group and they overcome their negative experiences of blaming themselves for being different. In the fourth stage, they redirect themselves to an Asian American consciousness, becoming immersed in the Asian American experience. They show anger and outrage toward whites as they develop racial pride and a positive self-concept as Asian Americans. In the last stage, incorporation, they develop confidence in their Asian American identity.

Asian American adolescents are as confused as other adolescents about their identity, struggling with determining their identity into adulthood. One of the confusing issues is a feeling of invisibility in society, in part because they do not often see themselves in magazines, on the television, or in the movies. Instead, they see whites and blacks as the media stars on the screen and in music videos (Kim, 2001).

Educational Experiences   Many Asian American children are raised in affluent suburbs, maintaining little contact with Asians in ethnic enclaves and urban schools. Generally, their parents look for strong public schools and demand a rigorous curriculum from school officials. They often send their children to private after-school programs to ensure high academic achievement (Lee & Zhou, 2004).

Ed Lines

"I am very much aware of my black heritage, . . . And I think sometimes it bothers people [who want me to say] that I'm black and that's it. . . . When people ask, I say I'm black, Venezuelan, and Irish because that's who I am." *Mariah Carey*

Overall, they have a higher educational attainment than all other ethnic and racial groups (U.S. Census Bureau, 2006). For example, the number of Asian American students who take the advanced placement tests is nearly double their representation in schools (Samuels, 2005). Eighty-seven percent of all Asian Americans who are 25 years old or older have graduated from high school—a rate higher than any other group (U.S. Census Bureau, 2006). They finish college at about double the rate of whites; half of the Asian American population have college degrees (U.S. Census Bureau, 2006). They are also enrolled in professional degree programs at nearly twice the rate of whites (U.S. Census Bureau, 2006).

Their high educational attainment rates have led some writers to refer to Asian Americans as *model minorities*. They appear to have taken advantage of the opportunities that many believe American society offers. One benefit of this stereotype is that most teachers have high academic expectations for their Asian American students. However, many Asian American young people resent the label (Lee & Zhou, 2004). They feel that it constrains them with a "superhuman" mold that they are all expected to model. It limits their being recognized for who they really are with similar frustrations and struggles as other students of color. The label prevents recognition that not all Asian American groups are achieving at a high level. Many students from southeast Asia live in low-income families in urban areas and suffer from high dropout rates and low academic performance. Some advocates worry that the needs of these children and young people are being overlooked.

European Americans

Many whites do not think about themselves as either white or European American unless they or their families are recent immigrants. They often see themselves as simply American because their families have been in the United States for many generations. At the same time, many maintain a **symbolic ethnicity**, participating in ethnic celebrations and clubs when they choose. Over half of the population indicated their European heritages in the 2000 census. The **national origins** identified most often were German (17%), Irish (12%), Italian (6%), Polish (3%), and French except Basque (3%) (U.S. Census Bureau, 2006). Many Arab Americans classify themselves as white as well on census forms. Multiple ancestries were reported by 22 percent of the population who can trace their roots to two or more national origins (U.S. Census Bureau, 2003).

Europeans from northern and western European countries comprised the major portion of immigrants to the United States in the first three centuries after Columbus arrived in the Americas. This pattern began to change in the 1800s. Between 1815 and 1920, 5.5 million Irish came to the United States (Takaki, 1993). Later in the century, Jews came from Russia and Eastern Europe. By the beginning of World War I, one-third of all Jews in those countries had emigrated with a large proportion of them coming to the United States (Takaki, 1993). With

Symbolic ethnicity. Conscious identification with one's ethnic group through ethnic clubs or celebrations rather than primary relationships with other members of the ethnic group.

National origins. Country or area of the world where one's ancestors lived.

Ed Lines

"What you do speaks so loudly that I cannot hear what you say." *Ralph Waldo Emerson*

the growing need for labor at the beginning of the twentieth century, companies recruited workers from southern and eastern Europe. More recently, the largest number of immigrants has come from the eastern European countries that were part of the former Soviet Union. The largest percentage of European immigrants in the twenty-first century has come from Bosnia and Herzegovina, Russia, Ukraine, and the United Kingdom (U.S. Bureau of Census, 2006). Many of these immigrants faced discrimination when they first arrived in the United States and competed for jobs with the Europeans whose families had been in the country for generations. Although assimilation into the dominant society may have taken several generations, most European immigrants have been able to join the dominant group because they were white and, for the most part, gave up their native languages, customs, and cultures.

The highest concentration of European American or white students is in the Midwest and Northeast with 76 percent and 68 percent of the population respectively (U.S. Department of Education, 2002). With the exception of Michigan and Washington, the northernmost states are home to the largest percentages of European American students (U.S. Department of Education, 2003). Although only 5 percent of the nation's white students are foreign born, nearly one in five has at least one foreign-born parent (U.S. Census Bureau, 2006).

Identity   Most of the research on European American identity has focused on the understanding of their race with respect to racial privilege. Many whites do not move through all six of the identity statuses identified by Helms (1995). Until they have some direct experience with racism, they often are not able to move into the higher status levels. In the first status, whites are oblivious to racism; they do not believe racism exists. As they become aware of racism and white privilege, they feel guilt and shame about the role whites have played in perpetuating racism. They begin to accept that they contribute to society's racial ideology. In the next stage, they regress to an intolerance of other races. In the fifth stage, they become more aware of the existence of institutional racism. They often feel guilty about their "whiteness." In the last stage, they confront racism and work toward its elimination while accepting their own identification as a white person.

In the development of their European identity, many whites move from denying that racism exists to feeling guilt and shame about white privilege. Some youth and adults eventually move to the stage in which they fight against racism.

Educational Experiences   Schools in the United States primarily reflect the culture of middle-class whites. With the exception of some white students from low-income families, white students perform better in schools than all other groups except Asian Americans. For example, 65 percent of them take advanced placement tests, slightly less than their percentage of the student population (68%). Next to Asian Americans, whites have the highest high school graduation rate. Eighty-five percent of all whites over 25 years of age have finished high school, while 28 percent has a bachelor's or higher degree (U.S. Census Bureau, 2006).

Latinos

Mexican Americans played a key role in the formation of the United States. In the sixteenth century, Spanish explorers began to exploit Mexico and Central America for their gold and other resources. Over the centuries, a new population evolved in Mexico and the southwest United States with roots in the indigenous tribes of the area, Europe, and Africa. Many of the Latinos in U.S. schools come from a similar Spanish and Indian heritage even though they come from Puerto Rica, Cuba, Honduras, Mexico, Ecuador, or Argentina.

Latinos represent different racial groups and mixtures of racial groups, as well as distinct ethnic groups from the Caribbean, Spain, and Central and South American countries. They don't usually identify themselves with a race such as black and white, but see their color as spanning a continuum from light to dark. When Latinos were asked to declare their race in the 2000 census, many rejected the classification and declared their race as Hispanic.

Nearly half of the Latinos in the United States live in two states: California (30%) and Texas (19%) (U.S. Census Bureau, 2006). However, Latino students also comprise over 20 percent of the student population in Florida, New Mexico, Arizona, Nevada, and Colorado (U.S. Department of Education, 2005). The Northeast is home to the majority of the Puerto Rican population in the U.S. (U.S. Census Bureau, 2006). New Jersey, Rhode Island, and Illinois also have a significant percentage of Latino students (U.S. Department of Education, 2005). Due in large part to the movement of families from Mexico into the southwest United States, nearly one of five Latino students is foreign born. However, nearly two-thirds of them have one or more foreign-born parents (U.S. Census Bureau, 2006).

Identity   Although Latinos come from many different nations, the Spanish language, interest in maintaining their culture, a focus on the family, and religious traditions appear to be common across groups. Another link is a sociopolitical connection to fight racism as a group (Ferdman & Gallegos, 2001).

Six orientations have been recognized in the identity development of Latinos (Ferdman & Gallegos, 2001); the first is Latino-integrated when their "sense of themselves [is] based on a philosophy of 'both/and' rather than 'either/or' " (p. 50). In this orientation, they see themselves as members of one of many groups in the United States. They also see both the positive and negative sides of their group. As they grow older, they identify themselves as Latino, placing their Latino culture, history, and traditions at the center of their lives. In the third orientation, they begin to identify themselves not just as Latino, but by their ethnic group (for example, Cuban, El Salvadoran, or Mexican American).

How Does Socioeconomic Status (SES) Affect Students?

*In her 4th and 5th grade classes in a multiracial and multilingual school, **Katherine Johnson** wanted to help her students develop their knowledge and skills related to geography, language arts, writing, and speaking within a social justice context. A unit of child labor was the means that she chose. She began with a "label hunt." Students worked in pairs to identify the countries of origin for their shoes and their shirts and Katherine made a list of the countries where the clothes were manufactured. As a class, they tallied the number of articles made in each country. Most of the clothing was manufactured throughout Southeast Asia; the shoes primarily came from China. Then students were given world maps and asked to highlight all the countries from the class list. Students followed up by reading about child labor in a number of resources, including short biographies of child laborers. They spent a number of days debating whether child labor should be abolished or regulated, developing and refining their arguments, and making formal presentations that met the state benchmark for speeches. Finally, their oral arguments evolved into persuasive essays, which they all wrote from the notes they had accumulated in their research and debates. Interestingly, the students' interest in the topic did not terminate when the unit was complete. They displayed their essays on the bulletin board outside of their classroom to help educate the school community about child labor in the world. They became activists. They decided to make magnets to sell for donations to the Rugmark Group, which operates schools for former and current child laborers (Johnson, 2004).*

Schools are often described by the *socioeconomic status (SES)* of their students and their families. Students are distinguished by their family's income and wealth which lead to differential economic, social, and political resources. Even within a school, students are sometimes classified and sorted by their economic conditions, giving the advantage to students in higher income families.

Low-Income Students

Family members in the low-income group may be unemployed or working at low wages. Some are temporarily in poverty because of a job loss or family illness. A very small portion (2.2%) of the population is persistently poor as measured by living in poverty for at least 8 of the last 10 years (Rose, 2000). Other members of this group are the working poor. They often work more than one job at the minimum wage, but can't pull themselves out of poverty. Work in minimum wage jobs can be sporadic and unemployment is unpredictably affected by the economy. Fringe benefits are often not available, leaving many of these workers without health insurance or vacation time.

Poverty differs by age, race, and ethnicity as shown in Figure 2.5. Although the number of whites in poverty is larger than any other group, the percentage of whites in poverty is much less than Latinos and African Americans. A larger percentage of American Indians suffers from poverty than any other group (U.S.

Figure 2.5 Persons in poverty

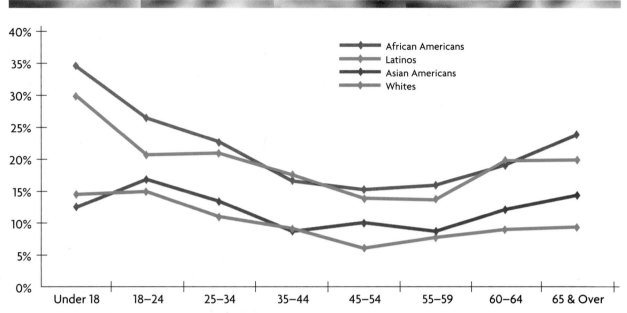

Source: U.S. Census Bureau. (2006). *Statistical abstract of the United States: 2006* (125th ed.). Washington, DC: U.S. Government Printing Office.

Census Bureau, 2004a), followed by African Americans and Latinos. The poverty rate for Asian Americans is near that of whites, but differs by ethnic group. Thirty-two percent of the Vietnamese and 52 percent of other Southeast Asian children are in poverty. Children under 18 are more likely to be in poverty than any other age group, ranging from 12 percent of Asian American children to 32 percent of African American children.

Some of the children in poverty are homeless. Children and families comprise 41 percent and youth 5 percent of the homeless population (U.S. Conference of Mayors, 2002). Between 2.3 and 3.5 million people are homeless at some time during a year; 900,000 to 1.4 million of them are children (National Association for the Education of Homeless Children and Youth, 2004). Homeless people are not always unemployed; some work at such low wages they are unable to afford housing. Others have lost their jobs or have become estranged from their families. Homeless women may have left home to escape violent relationships. Homeless teenagers often have left home to avoid abuse and other family problems.

Most homeless students are in school and regularly attend classes (Urban Institute, 2000); however, some do not attend school for extended periods of time. Many have not received childhood immunizations and experience higher rates of asthma, ear infections, stomach problems, and speech problems than other children (Books & Polakow, 2001).

Public schools must provide educational rights to homeless children and youth. The **McKinney-Vento Homeless Assistance Act** requires school districts to provide transportation for homeless students to stay in their schools of origin if their parents request it. Enrollment cannot be denied because homeless students

McKinney-Vento Homeless Assistance Act. The federal legislation that outlined the education rights and protections for homeless children and youth.

Teachers' Lounge

The Liberty Bell

One of the most difficult, but most rewarding, classes I've taught was during the year I was assigned a language arts/social studies block of 15 of the lowest-achieving, least-motivated 8th graders in the middle school. I worked hard to reach these students and sometimes wondered if I was succeeding. On the day before winter break, I saw two of my students in the corner of the classroom working hard on something that was not an activity I had prepared for them. I put on my best "teacher face" and walked over. As I approached, they turned around and offered up a small, plastic bell that they had purposely broken. They grinned and exclaimed "Merry Christmas! Do you know what this is?" I choked up as I recognized the Liberty Bell from our social studies' lessons. It was only later that I learned they had stolen the bell from the holiday tree at the entrance to the school! This bell is still one of my prized holiday decorations.

● Lorae Roukema, Ed.D.
Campbell University

do not have their school records, immunization records, proof of residency, or other documents. The school district's liaison for homeless students is expected to be an advocate for them, helping them access available services in the school system and community.

Schools determine students from low-income families by the criteria that make them eligible to participate in the free or reduced lunch program. To be eligible for a free lunch, family income must fall below 130 percent of the federal poverty level or $24,343 for a family of four. For a subsidized lunch, family income must fall between 130 and 185 percent of the federal poverty level or between $24,344 and $34,641 for a family of four (U.S. Department of Education, 2004). In 2003, 43 percent of all K–12 students lived in these low-income families. The percentage of students eligible for free or reduced school lunches ranges greatly from state to state. Eighteen percent of the students in New Hampshire were eligible as compared to over 60 percent of the students in Louisiana, Mississippi, and the District of Columbia (College Participation Rates, 2004).

Because families of color often earn less than white families (U.S. Census Bureau, 2006), their children are more likely to be in the low-income bracket. Of the 4th graders eligible for free or reduced-price lunches in 2003, 70 percent of the African American, 71 percent of the Latino, and 23 percent of the white students were eligible (U.S. Department of Education, 2004). African American and Latino students were also more likely to attend schools with large numbers of students in poverty (U.S. Department of Education, 2004).

What does living in a low-income family mean for children and teenagers? For one, they are more likely to be in poorer health than students in higher income families. They have a greater incidence of vision and hearing problems, especially ear infections. They often lack dental care, leading to toothaches. They have greater exposure to lead in water pipes, which affects their cognitive functioning and behavior. They are more likely to have asthma, especially when living in densely populated neighborhoods. They are less likely to have regular medical care and usually lack health insurance. Their nutrition is often poor. The lack of affordable housing results in their families moving from one school district to another. All of these factors affect school attendance and their ability to concentrate and attend carefully to their work when they are in school (Rothstein, 2004).

Students in low-income families are less likely to graduate from high school and less likely to attend college. However, the chances of attending college vary by state from 7.7 percent in Alaska to 43.7 percent in New Jersey. Attendance rates are higher in the Northeast and the uppermost states in the middle region of the country (College Participation Rates, 2004).

Students from low-income families are concentrated in cities and rural areas but they can be found almost anywhere (U.S. Department of Education, 2004). When children from low-income families are the majority of the students in a school, they are more likely to have low test scores, unsafe and unattractive schools, and less-than-stimulating school work that has little to do with their lives (Rothstein, 2004). Teachers should be careful not to stereotype students because their families are low income or to have low academic expectations for them. From the beginning of their school career, they are too often not expected to go to college.

Middle Class

Many Americans identify themselves as middle class. It is an amorphous category that often includes everyone who works steadily and who is not accepted as a member of the upper class. It ranges from well-paid professionals to service workers. Most white-collar workers, no matter their salary, see themselves as middle class.

Middle-class families generally earn yearly incomes between $30,000 and $80,000 (Rose, 2000), 44 percent of those submitting tax returns in 2003. However, many live from paycheck to paycheck, not earning enough to accumulate wealth. Both parents often work to make ends meet. This group includes white-col-

Many students identify themselves as middle class, which generally means that one or both of their parents are working and their family owns a home.

lar workers who work in offices as secretaries, administrative assistants, and managers. It also includes many blue-collar workers who are involved in manual labor and have incomes in this range. Middle-class workers generally have greater job security and better fringe benefits than low-income workers.

The number of African Americans and Latinos who are middle class has increased since the 1950s as their incomes have become closer to those of whites. However, whites and Asian Americans continue to be more likely to be in the middle class, continuing to earn the higher incomes (U.S. Census Bureau, 2006). The middle class usually has high educational expectations for their children, expecting them to attend college or receive training after they finish high school. The parents are more likely to be involved with schools and their children's education than low-income families.

Upper Middle Class

The elite of the middle class are professionals, managers, and administrators. Their income level allows them to lead fairly affluent lives. The members of this group usually hold professional or advanced degrees and credentials to practice their professions. Judges, lawyers, physicians, college professors, teachers, and scientists are the professionals. Excluding teachers, most professionals earn far more than the **median income** of $46,644 reported for this category (U.S. Census Bureau, 2006). Managers and administrators, who make up 16 percent of the employed population, are members of this class (U.S. Census Bureau, 2006). The incomes and opportunities to accumulate wealth are higher for the upper middle class than for the bulk of the population. Many of them are active in civic and voluntary organizations. They are politically active and as a result, the major recipients of public benefits.

Families with higher incomes could choose to send their children to private schools or contribute to school funds that can pay for art, music, and additional teachers. They not only have computers, but have high-speed access to the Internet (U.S. Census Bureau, 2006). When their children are not learning at the level expected, they hire tutors. Their children participate in enrichment activities such as academic summer camps when they are not in school. Income provides the advantages to ensure that the children in higher income families are able to achieve at high academic levels and attend college.

▶ **Median income.** An equal number of persons, families, or households earn below as above the number.

Revisiting Katherine Johnson's Child Labor Project

Ms. Johnson, whose project on child labor opened this section, found a way to help her students understand how some societies treat students from low-income families. Many children in the United States never study low-income families or the inequities that exist among families with wealth and power and those without. Projects like Ms. Johnson's help students have a better understanding of the conditions in which many low-income students live.

Ed Lines

"**If you don't like the way the world is, you change it. You have an obligation to change it.**"
Marian Wright Edelman

How Does Gender Influence Students?

*It has become clear to **Ted Kowalski** that sophomore and junior girls in Middle-brook High School have little or no interest in his computer science course. Less than one in five of the students in his class are female even though half of the high school students are female. He thinks that the girls who are doing well in mathematics should be perfect candidates for computer science. When he asks them why they don't enroll in computer science, he finds that the girls think it is a subject for geeks who don't like social interactions. They see the boys who are into computers spending all of their free time in front of a screen, often playing violent video games. They say it's just not their thing. Ted knows that college graduates in computer science receive higher beginning salaries than most other fields. These girls won't choose that career path unless he can interest them in computer science in high school.*

Sex is the term used to identify an individual as male or female based on biological differences while **gender** is the behavioral, cultural, and psychological traits typically associated with one sex. Females and males are sometimes segregated by sex in schools or school activities. The Teachers and the Law feature on page 73 explores the legal ramifications of sports for girls and boys. They often segregate themselves at social gatherings and participate in gender-specific leisure activities. They often have stereotypical perceptions about themselves and the other sex. They disproportionately enter different occupations and have access to different financial opportunities.

Gender. The behavioral, cultural, or psychological traits typically associated with one sex.

Differences between Females and Males

Physical differences between men and women can usually be determined by appearance alone. Before age 8, boys and girls have similar hormonal levels and similar physical development. During puberty, hormonal levels of estrogen and testosterone, which control the physical development of the two sexes, change. Physical differences between the two contribute to a female's lower endurance for heavy labor, greater difficulty in running or over-arm throwing, and a better ability to float in water. However, these physical differences can be altered with good nutrition, physical activity, practice, and different behavioral expectations.

Intelligence tests show no differences in the general intelligence between the sexes, but many studies have found some gender differences in mathematical, verbal, and spatial skills. These differences are sometimes attributed to biology. Spatial relations are controlled by the right hemisphere of the cerebral cortex. The left hemisphere controls language and other sequential skills. Females favor the left hemisphere associated with speaking, reading, and writing. Males tend to have greater right-hemisphere specialization, which leads to better performance on tests

Ed Lines

"All of us [blacks worldwide] are bound to Mother Africa by invisible but tenacious bonds."
Archbishop Desmond Tutu

of spatial visualization and higher achievement in mathematics and science. However, not all boys and not all girls exhibit the inclination usually identified with their sex. Some girls achieve high scores in mathematics and science, while some boys achieve high scores in language, reading, and writing (Gurian, 2001). Therefore, educators cannot predetermine ability in these academic areas based on a student's sex.

The Role of Biology   Proponents of brain-based differences based on sex argue that teachers who know these hemispheric differences have a better understanding of why boys behave the way they do in classrooms. As a result, these teachers are able to develop more appropriate instruction for both girls and boys. For instance, Gurian (2001) reports that boys and girls generally conceptualize differently. Boys are more likely to be **deductive**, thinking about the general and then moving to the details. Girls, on the other hand, are more likely to be **inductive**, beginning with the details to figure out the general. Gurian (2001) documented that boys are more easily bored in classrooms. They are stimulated by movement, requiring more physical space. Movement also helps them manage and relieve impulsive behavior. Girls, on the other hand, are more social and prefer working together on a learning project.

> ▶ **Deductive.** A way of thinking and reasoning that begins with the general and moves to the details.
>
> ▶ **Inductive.** A way of thinking and reasoning that begins with the details to figure out the general.
>
> ▶ **Socialization.** Process of learning the social norms and expectations of the culture.

Other researchers attribute most male and female differences to **socialization** patterns learned from their parents, relatives, teachers, and peers. They argue that girls and boys are socialized to use the skills associated with one gender or the other that are attributed to the right and left hemispheres of their brains. These debates focus on whether nature or nurturing is most important in determining the differences between the sexes. A balanced view gives credit to the interaction of both nature and nurture. Girls and boys can learn to use the hemisphere of the brain that is not being fully utilized. Gender-sensitive instruction helps boys and girls develop the knowledge, skills, and dispositions that may come more naturally to one than the other.

Some researchers believe that the differences between boys and girls are grounded in biology and that boys naturally behave differently than girls in the classroom.

The Role of Culture   Schools generally reinforce culture's view of gender. Girls are expected to be feminine. In school they are expected to be quiet and well behaved. As adults, they usually work, but do not always see themselves as eligible for the same jobs as their male peers. However, girls are encouraged to break out of their stereotypical modes more often than boys. Many parents and schools have told them they can be whatever they want. Today's girls can play on sports teams, are the leaders in many school activities, and attend college at higher rates than boys (U.S. Census Bureau, 2006). A new stereotype is that females can be the feminine women of the past while they work full-time, raise children, and take care of their husbands. In reality, women and girls are trying to develop a balance between their femininity and their participation in a masculine world.

Young men are encouraged to be independent, assertive, leaders, self-reliant, and emotionally stable. The focus on these masculine characteristics by families, peers, and teachers ignores their inner lives and feelings (Flood, 2001; Kindlon & Thompson, 2000). Boys are pushed toward these characteristics, in part, to prevent them from being labeled gay or a sissy, which could lead to harassment by others (Flood, 2001). As a result, they sometimes go overboard in proving their masculinity.

"YOU'RE FREE RANGE, SON. THE SKY'S THE LIMIT."

© Scott Arthur Masear.

Some males do not fit the masculine stereotype because they have the feminine characteristics of empathy and caring. Some critics of **feminism** worry that boys are being harmed by classroom practices that encourage them to develop traits traditionally associated with women. Some young men are not adjusting well in society as shown in the statistics indicating "climbing suicide rate, binge drinking, steroid use, undiagnosed depression, academic underachievement, and the disproportionate representation of boys among car crash victims" (Kindlon & Thompson, 2000). Psychologists do not always agree on the reasons that a number of boys and young men seem to be at risk today. Kindlon and Thompson (2000), for example, find that boys have not learned to be **emotionally literate**, believing that boys are not encouraged to be themselves. Too often, says the researchers, boys are programmed for a culturally determined identity with little room for divergence.

Feminism. Movement that actively supports the rights of women.

Emotionally literate. The ability to read and understand our emotions and those of others (Klindlon & Thompson, 2000, 4).

Teachers are expected to treat all individuals equally and encourage academic excellence in all of their students. Whether a student exhibits masculine or feminine characteristics regardless of their gender, it is a teacher's responsibility to exhibit unconditional positive regard for all students, to recognize their special talents and needs and to provide a learning environment that fosters acceptance and understanding.

Revisiting Ted Kowalski's Dilemma

Ted, the teacher at the beginning of this section, knows that girls can do well in the field of computer science and that all boys who are interested in technology are not geeks. He knows that it is his duty as a teacher to find ways to make the curriculum come alive for all students and to provide them with learning opportunities that will improve their status as individuals and bring them self-actualization as productive members of society. Having a clear understanding of the developmental process of his students as well as understanding the power of peer pressure and the labels society creates for differences in gender will help Ted find the necessary instructional tools to interest them in exploring new and different ideas.

What Should Teachers Know About English Language Learners?

Carmen Garcia is an experienced bilingual teacher, having taught primarily Latino elementary students in a school that also includes white and African American students. Up to this point, she has worked almost exclusively with Latino students and families. The school principal asks her if she would be interested in developing a bilingual program that includes students from all three groups. The Latino students would be using Spanish and learning English while the other students would be using English and learning Spanish. She is excited about English-speaking students learning Spanish at this young age. She thinks that the community would be better served if everyone could converse in both languages.

Over 48 million residents of the United States speak a language other than English at home (U.S. Census Bureau, 2006). Most of them are recent immigrants from countries around the world and many of their children will be learning English in school. You may have students in your classroom who are immigrants themselves or the children of immigrants. They may speak no English, limited English, or be fluent in English. Your concern will be helping them improve their English while learning the academic subject being taught. There is a danger that they will fall behind their native-born classmates in academic achievement during the years that it takes for them to function effectively in English.

Immigration

The U.S. Congress establishes the criteria for immigrants and sets a limit for the number of immigrants allowed from different parts of the world. At times Congress has prohibited or limited the immigration of different national or ethnic groups, sometimes based on the racist ideology of citizens whose families immigrated many generations earlier. For instance, Pennsylvania passed a statute in 1729 that increased the head tax on foreigners in that colony. The Chinese Exclusion Act of 1882 stopped immigration from China. The Johnson-Reed Act of 1924 established annual immigration quotas that favored immigrants from western European countries and stopped all immigration from Japan. When the Johnson-Reed Act was abolished in 1965, a new quota system dramatically increased the number of immi-

Ed Lines

"I have never been disabled in my dreams." *Christopher Reeve*

grants who could come from the eastern hemisphere. Immigrants have come to the United States for different reasons: to escape political oppression, famine, or economic hardships in their homelands. At other times, immigrants have come for the promise of jobs or to join family members who were already here.

National Origins   The immigration rate during the past decade has been nearly 1 million per year (U.S. Census Bureau, 2006). The foreign-born population is concentrated in six states: California, New York, Texas, Florida, Illinois, and New Jersey (U.S. Census Bureau, 2006) with 40 percent of them living in the western United States (Briggs, 2000). Most (94%) foreign-born persons settle in the central cities and suburbs of metropolitan areas (Rumbaut & Portes, 2001). New York City; Los Angeles/Long Beach; Chicago; Miami; the Washington, D.C. area; San Francisco; Orange County (California); Oakland (California); Houston; and the Boston area are home to 65 percent of today's immigrants (Olson, 2000). Immigration to nonmetropolitan areas is often dependent on job availability and the perceived quality of life. As a result, schools in Arkansas, Iowa, Nebraska, Montana, North Dakota, and Wisconsin include students from different cultures and with languages other than English.

The nations contributing the largest number of legal immigrants in 1960 were Mexico, Germany, Canada, the United Kingdom, and Italy. In 2004, the largest number of immigrants came from other North American countries (36%), followed by Asia (35%), Europe (13%), South America (8%), and Africa (7%). Nineteen percent of the immigrants were from Mexico—almost twice the number from the Caribbean (9%), which was next highest contributor of immigrants. Other countries with a significant number of immigrants include India (7%), the Philippines (6%), China (5%), Vietnam (3%), and El Salvador (3%) (U.S. Census Bureau, 2004c).

Another group of immigrants are **refugees** who have been recognized by the federal government as being persecuted or legitimately bearing persecution in their home country because of race, religion, nationality, or membership in a specific social or political group. Over a million immigrants were admitted as refugees between 1991 and 2000. Vietnamese represented the largest number of refugees, followed by refugees from Cuba, Ukraine, the Soviet Union, Russia, Bosnia and Herzegovina, and Laos (U.S. Census Bureau, 2006).

Refugees. Persons recognized by the U.S. government as being persecuted or legitimately bearing persecution in their home country because of race, religion, nationality, or membership in a specific social or political group.

Another group of immigrants is the approximately seven million unauthorized immigrants (U.S. Census Bureau, 2006). Many of these people are eligible to have their status reclassified as legal when they meet the requirements for employment-based visas, refugees, or being sponsored by a family. Amnesty programs also periodically allow them to become legal immigrants. Just over two-thirds of the illegal immigrants are from Mexico; only 5 percent are from outside the western hemisphere (U.S. Census Bureau, 2006). California is home to the largest number, with 32 percent of the undocumented population (U.S. Census Bureau, 2006). Because the Mexican and U.S. border is the entry point for many undocumented workers, border patrols regularly search for persons who are trying to enter the United States illegally, which sometimes results in Latino citizens being stopped and harassed as well.

Ed Lines

"If we can put the names of our faiths aside for a moment and look at principles, we will find a common thread running through all the great religious expressions." *Louis Farrakhan*

Educational Experiences Immigrants come to the United States with different levels of education. Twenty-two percent of the foreign-born population hold bachelor's degrees or above as compared to 17 percent of the native population (U.S. Census Bureau, 2006). At the same time, over one of four foreign-born adults does not have a high school degree—almost four times as many as the native-born population (U.S. Census Bureau, 2006). Immigrants come from different socioeconomic levels, entering the country with limited economic resources or resources to invest or begin a business. Those who assimilate fairly easily into the middle class have high SES and educational credentials. Their educational credentials and economic status in their home countries give them the social and **cultural capital** that makes them acceptable to dominant society (Portes & Rumbaut, 2001).

▶ **Cultural capital.** Endowments such as academic competence, language competence, and wealth that provide an advantage to an individual, family, or group.

The children of immigrants also have different educational experiences. Some have never been in school and know no English. Others have strong educational backgrounds and are fluent in English. School districts with large numbers of immigrant families may have established special programs or schools for immigrant students to help them learn English and adjust to U.S. culture. Children of undocumented parents will be in schools as well as discussed in the Teachers and the Law feature on the facing page. Parents cannot be asked for their immigration status. They cannot be asked for social security numbers or other documentation that might expose their status.

More and more classrooms across the country include students who are foreign born or have one or more foreign-born parents. A large number of foreign-born students are Latino or Asian American.

Language Diversity

Language diversity is valued in most countries of the world. The population of many European, Middle Eastern, and African countries are bilingual or multilingual. In today's global world in which many companies operate internationally, employees who know more than one language and culture can be an asset to the company, especially in its interactions with other nations in the areas of commerce, defense, education, science, and technology. Bilingualism is also an asset for jobs such as hotel clerks, airline attendants, social workers, nurses, teachers, and police officers who come into contact with individuals who speak little or no English.

The children and grandchildren of immigrant adults learn English in school. Between 30 and 40 percent of the population in California, New Mexico, and Texas speak a language other than English at home (U.S. Census Bureau, 2006) as shown in Figure 2.6. Other than Florida, most southern states have few non-English language speakers. Some families work hard to retain the native language from one generation to another, using their native language at home or sending

GIRLS' SPORTS

Can separate playing seasons be scheduled for girls' and boys' teams that are playing the same sport?

No. This practice violates the equal protection clauses of federal and state constitutions. Some school districts argue that they do not have the facilities or coaches for both teams to practice and compete during the same season. The courts in Michigan and West Virginia ruled that if the two teams cannot play during the same season, the burden of playing during the off-season must be shared. For example, the boys' team would have to play during the "off" season in alternating years.

UNDOCUMENTED STUDENTS

Can the undocumented children of foreign-born parents be denied a public school education?

No. In 1975, the Texas legislature decided to withhold funds from local school districts for children who were not "legally admitted" into the United States. The act also empowered school districts to deny enrollment to undocumented children. In *Plyer v. Doe* (1982), the Supreme Court was asked to determine the constitutionality of the Texas statute. The Equal Protection Clause of the Fourteenth Amendment, which says that "No State shall . . . deprive any person of life, liberty, or property, without due process of law; nor deny to any person within its jurisdiction the equal protection of the laws," does not limit protection to citizens.

The court found that although public education is not a right granted by the Constitution, it is not merely a governmental "benefit" indistinguishable from other forms of social welfare. Education was found to be important in both maintaining U.S. basic institutions and having a lasting impact on the life of the child. In sum, education has a fundamental role in maintaining the fabric of society. The significant social costs borne by the nation cannot be ignored when select groups are denied an education. Illiteracy is an enduring disability. Paradoxically, by depriving the children of any disfavored group of an education, society forecloses the means by which that group might raise the level of esteem in which it is held by the majority.

Source: Cambron-McCabe, N. H., McCarthy, M. M., & Thomas, S. B. (2004). *Public school law: Teachers' and students' rights* (5th ed.). Boston: Allyn and Bacon.

their children to classes to learn their language and culture. They are helped in this process when they live in communities that value bilingualism.

Revisiting Carmen Garcia's New Assignment

As the population of the United States becomes more and more diverse with larger numbers of people speaking languages other than English, the expertise of classroom teachers will need to include knowledge of how to teach English

Figure 2.6 Percentage of population speaking a language other than English at home in 2000

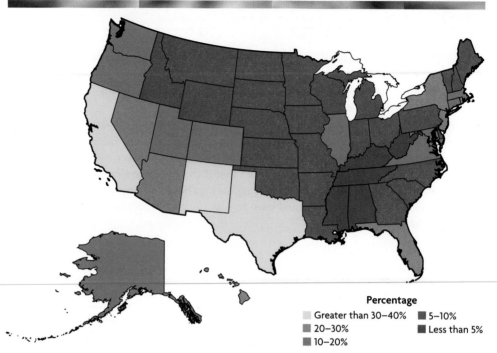

Percentage

Greater than 30–40% ■ 5–10%
■ 20–30% ■ Less than 5%
■ 10–20%

Source: U.S. Census Bureau. (2006). *Statistical abstract of the United States: 2006* (125th ed.). Washington, DC: U.S. Government Printing Office.

language learners. Carmen, the experienced bilingual teacher at the beginning of this section, knows firsthand the value of helping language learners maintain the use of their native language while learning English. She also recognizes the value of language diversity and hopes all of her students will soon be able to communicate and learn in more than one language.

What Are the Religions of Students?

Dale Weiss had been a political activist through college, participating in a number of civil rights rallies and volunteering as a tutor for homeless children. When he began teaching 1st grade in a suburban school that was part of a large metropolitan area, he bonded well with the other teachers who had worked for the system for many years. They provided advice and helped him understand the students and the culture of the school. As Dale planned lessons, he was very conscious about incorporating diversity. When Thanksgiving approached, he introduced his students to a number of ways that the December holidays were celebrated such as Christmas, Hanukkah, and Kwanzaa. He also wanted them to understand that some people do not celebrate these holidays.

When Dale returned to school after Thanksgiving, two of the girls in his class asked if they were going to put up Christmas decorations. He said "No," not wanting to privilege one way of celebrating over others and being conscious of the one Jehovah's Witness student in class who did not celebrate Christmas. Not long afterwards, he discovered that a Christmas tree had appeared in the library and that most classrooms had Christmas decorations. At the faculty meeting that week, he expressed his surprise at all of the Christmas decorations and suggested that the presentations be more diverse. The next day the librarian removed the Christmas tree and placed a Kwanza book in the same location. Other teachers began to pull down their decorations. Some told Dale that he did not understand the community and had no right to intervene in their traditions. He even found a note in his mailbox saying "What's next? Gay rights?" Teachers stopped talking to him, and his enthusiasm for going to school every day diminished over the next semester (Weiss, 2004).

Religion has a great influence on the values and lifestyles of families and plays an important role in the socialization of children and young people. Religious doctrines and practices guide how and when one worships, but they also guide beliefs about many aspects of daily life, including the roles of men and women, birth control, child rearing, friendships, and political attitudes. A religious doctrine can dictate a family's expectations for teachers and schools. When the religious perspectives and school expectations differ, numerous challenges arise for educators.

Eighty-six percent of the U.S. population identify with a religion (U.S. Census Bureau, 2006). However, only 44 percent of adults attend a church, synagogue, mosque, or temple in an average week (Gallup Organization, 2005). Regular attendance is higher in the United States than in much of western Europe where it has dwindled to 8 percent in England and 4 percent in Sweden. Nevertheless, religious beliefs and self-identification remain high in Europe as well as the United States (Gallup Organization, 2005; Woodhead, 2005).

Religious Diversity

The United States historically has had strong Judeo-Christian roots. Some fundamentalist Christians believe that God led the European founders to establish this country as a Christian nation (Hutchison, 2003). With the increase of immigrants from Asia and the Middle East since the 1960s, other religious traditions have been introduced. Fourteen percent of the adults do not participate in any organized religion, some declaring themselves as **atheist** or **agnostic** (U.S. Census Bureau, 2006). Within all of these religious groups are liberal, moderate, and conservative or fundamentalist sects. The fundamentalist groups believe that their holy documents (for example, the Bible, Qur'an, and Torah) are the actual word of their god that must be followed to the letter of the law. Liberal religions, on the other hand, accept the validity of diverse perspectives that have evolved from different historical experiences. Although religious differences have led to intergroup conflicts and wars throughout world history, most religions endorse the virtues of social justice, love, and compassion (Orfield & Lebowitz, 1999).

Just over 3 of 4 Americans identify themselves as Christian (U.S. Census Bureau, 2006). Protestants have long dominated the U.S. population, currently

Atheist. A person who does not believe in the existence of a god.

Agnostic. A person who is not sure of the existence of a god, and does not commit to believing that God exists or not.

▶ **Born-again.** Individuals who have had a religious experience that led them to recommit themselves to God and Jesus Christ as an evangelic.

▶ **Evangelical.** Identification with Christian groups who believe the Bible is the actual word of God.

representing 48 percent of the population (Gallup Organization, 2005). Catholicism grew greatly over the past century as southern and eastern Europeans immigrated to the United States, now comprising one-fourth of the population (U.S. Census, 2006). Forty-four percent describe themselves as **born-again** or **evangelical**, which is referred to as fundamentalist in the discussions that follow (Gallup Poll, 2005). The affiliations of the remaining fourth of the population are shown in Figure 2.7. About one of three of the world's population believes in Christianity; 20 percent are believers of Islam; 16 percent are nonreligious or atheists; and 13 percent are believers of Hinduism (Partridge, 2005). The fastest growing religion worldwide is Islam, followed by Christianity, Hinduism, and Sikhism (Partridge, 2005). Most religions in the United States, especially Protestants, see the United States as God's country (Hutchison, 2003), often displaying the American flag in their places of worship.

Muslims have been in the United States for several centuries. Nearly one-third of the African slaves were Muslim when they arrived in this country (Haque, 2004). Like other immigrants, Muslims came at different periods of time in the nineteenth and twentieth centuries. The first wave immigrated from Middle Eastern countries between 1875 and 1912 primarily because of poor economic conditions in their native countries. More recently, Muslims have immigrated from South Asian countries with large Islamic populations. The Nation of Islam with primarily African American followers was established in the United States in 1930 by Wallace Ford, who was succeeded by Elijah Muhammad. By 1965, prominent figures within the Nation of Islam such as Malcolm X had moved to the

Figure 2.7 Religious preferences among Americans, 2003

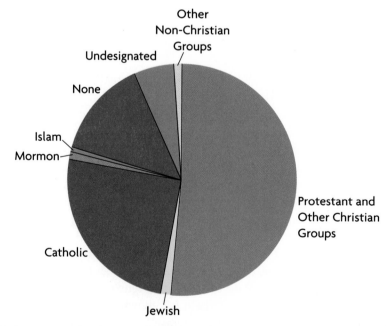

Source: U.S. Census Bureau. (2006). *Statistical abstract of the United States: 2006* (125th ed.). Washington, DC: U.S. Government Printing Office.

American families
practice many differ-
ent religions, includ-
ing Islam. Educators
should be sure that
their practices do
not discriminate
against students
whose families prac-
tice a religion differ-
ent than their own.

more traditional Sunni Islam teachings of the Qur'an. Today, 22 percent of the Muslims in the United States were born here. Twenty-four percent of all the Muslims in this country are African American, 27 percent are from the Middle East, and 24 percent are from South Asia (Haque, 2004).

Although Jews, Protestants, and Catholics once were expected to intermarry with members of their faith, marriage across those three groups is fairly common today. Some religious groups such as the Amish and Hutterites continue to seek group cohesiveness by establishing their own communities and schools. Mormons promote primary relationships with other Mormons, often living in communities in which social activities and politics are linked to their religion.

Religion in the Schools   If you teach in an urban or metropolitan area, you can expect to have students from a number of different religious groups. Even smaller midwestern and western towns have had an influx of Asian, African, or Middle Eastern immigrants who are bringing their cultural version of Christianity, Islam, Hinduism, and Buddhism to communities that previously had only a few Christian denominations. Schools should recognize that accommodations will be needed to respect the religious diversity in the community. Christian holidays are acknowledged through school holidays and the singing of Christian songs at some school convocations. Jewish students will not attend school during Rosh Hashanah and Yom Kippur. Islamic students will fast during the month of Ramadhan and are expected to have daily prayers. Policies that prevent the wearing of head scarves and yarmulkes discriminate against Muslim women and Jewish men. School officials should involve the parents of their religious communities in providing professional development about their religious traditions and cultures for educators and providing advice for guaranteeing that the civil rights of their children are not violated.

Religion is very important to some families and of little or no importance to others. In many communities, religion plays a major role in the lives of families, requiring attendance not only on Saturday or Sunday, but at services and activities throughout the week. Religious stories reinforce the values of the religion in Sunday school, Bible classes, and other organized religious education programs. Parents in these communities may expect schools to reflect those same values, sometimes enrolling their children in private Catholic, Jewish, Islamic, or Christian schools that reinforce their values and teach their religious doctrine. They may decide to home-school their children to ensure they are not exposed to values they disapprove of such as lack of respect for teachers, swearing by students, lack of discipline, and exposure to multiple perspectives.

Recent immigration from Asia and the Middle East has led to mosques and temples being built in communities that were formerly all Christian. Most urban and suburban areas are home to numerous religious groups and beliefs. Metropolitan areas may have a number of megachurches with thousands of members and their own schools. Students whose religious beliefs differ from the majority in the community may be ostracized in school and social settings. Jews, atheists, Jehovah's Witnesses, Pentecostals, Muslims, and Sikhs are among the groups whose members are sometimes shunned and suffer discrimination. Educators must be careful that their own religious beliefs do not interfere with their ability to provide equal educational opportunities to students whose families are members of other religious groups.

Revisiting Dale Weiss's Introduction of Diversity to the Holidays

When the teacher highlighted at the beginning of this section suggested to the other teachers in his school that they should make the holidays more diverse, he did not intend for them not to observe Christmas as they had in the past. He wanted them to acknowledge that not all people are Christians and not even all Christians observe the holiday in the same way. However, the teachers were Christians and had always decorated their classrooms to reflect their holiday. Among themselves, they asked: Who did this new Jewish teacher think he was, coming into our school and telling us that we are wrong to celebrate Christmas with our students? Mr. Weiss misread the faculty and had not considered the importance of Christianity in the community. They took his comments as criticisms of their religion and teaching. Helping colleagues incorporate other cultures is not an easy task and can quickly lead to misunderstandings. Dale wishes that he had approached the other teachers on an individual basis rather than at a faculty meeting.

How Are Students with Disabilities Integrating Schools?

Cindy Wilkins has two children with individualized education programs (IEPs) in her social studies class. One girl is hearing impaired. Although she speaks with sign lan-

guage, she can also read lips. One boy has attention deficit hyperactivity disorder (ADHD). His academic skills are 2 years below grade level, and his attention span is limited during periods of instruction. A few other students are reading below grade level. Although these children are obviously having difficulties with reading, writing, and spelling, they do not currently qualify for special education services. Cindy works with a special education resource teacher who has been assigned to work with the students with IEPs, but her time is split with the other social studies and English teachers so she is lucky to have her assistance on a daily basis.

Thirteen percent of the school population has a *disability* (U.S. Census Bureau, 2006), which is defined as a long-lasting condition such as visual or hearing impairment or a condition that substantially limits basic physical, emotional, or mental activities. The nation's Individuals with Disabilities Education Act (IDEA), originally enacted by Congress in 1975 as the Education for All Handicapped Children Act, was established to make sure that children with disabilities had the opportunity to receive a free appropriate public education. The law has been revised over the years with the most recent amendments passed by Congress in December 2004. IDEA requires that students with disabilities be educated with students without disabilities whenever possible and in as normal an environment as possible. IDEA guides how states and school districts provide special education and related services to more than six million eligible children and youth (U.S. Census Bureau, 2006).

All teachers are expected to implement **individual education programs** (IEP) for students with disabilities in their classrooms. The IEP is developed by parents, teachers, special educators, and other specialists such as a school psychologist or occupational therapist and indicates the accommodations and special services that must be provided to that student. Providing services to these students usually involves a team of professionals and assistants, depending on the severity of the disability. The special educator may team teach a class with a classroom teacher or serve as a resource teacher who works with students on the development of skills. Students with severe disabilities such as autism or physical conditions that require feeding tubes should be assigned a teaching or health assistant to help provide the necessary accommodations.

Individual education program (IEP). A document that describes the classroom accommodations and activities needed to meet the unique needs of a student with disabilities.

Students with disabilities should have an IEP (individual education program) that has been developed collaboratively by their parents, teachers, and other specialists to identify the accommodations necessary to help them learn.

Disability Categories

School professionals categorize children with disabilities to determine the most appropriate services for students. Figure 2.8 on page 80 shows the number of students

Figure 2.8 Children and youth with disabilities in special education programs

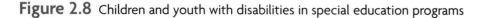

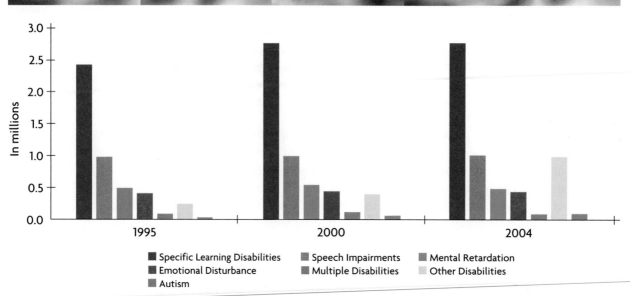

Source: U.S. Census Bureau. (2006). *Statistical abstract of the United States: 2006* (125th ed.). Washington, DC: U.S. Government Printing Office.

being served for different disabilities. Nearly half of the students receiving special education services have a learning disability (U.S. Census Bureau, 2006), which makes it difficult for them to read, write, or compute. The number of students with speech impairments is nearly double the disability categories other than learning disabilities (U.S. Census Bureau, 2006). This section provides a brief introduction to the categories with the largest number of students. You should take at least one course during your teacher-preparation program to provide an overview of these disabilities and understand the accommodations necessary to help students with disabilities learn.

Learning Disabilities   Students with learning disabilities usually comprehend the material being studied at the same rate as students without disabilities. The problem is that they can't decode text or they may have dyslexia, which prevents them from reading. These students are in regular classrooms with accommodations that might include a teaching assistant who reads to them or writes for them. Their IEPs will include strategies such as reading or writing for the student, especially in testing situations. In mathematics, it may allow students to use a calculator. Student work might be modified with fewer questions or a shorter reading assignment. Extra time may be required to complete an assignment or a computer used to type out an assignment.

Students with learning disabilities are discovered when teachers or parents realize these students are not learning to read or compute at the same level as other students. Their ability to answer questions exceeds their performance on reading or mathematical tasks. They can verbally respond, but are not able to put their responses in writing. Many learning disabilities are identified in the 3rd grade when students are expected to do more writing.

Speech Impairment   *Speech impairment* is a communication disorder; a person might stutter or cannot produce certain words or sounds. Some students cannot process language (that is, they can hear directions, but cannot repeat them), preventing them from following the teacher's directions for an assignment. Students may be able to comprehend at the same levels as other students, but are not able to put their thoughts into words due to difficulties with word retrieval and recall. They may have trouble understanding directional prepositions such as "under" and "above." These students should be receiving support from a speech pathologist. In the regular classroom, teachers will need to allow additional wait time for the student to process the question and respond to it. Just because these students take extra time for processing or speaking does not mean that they do not comprehend and will not perform well academically.

Mental Retardation   Students with mental retardation have significant problems in intellectual functioning and in using socially appropriate behaviors for their age. The most severe of these students participate in life-skills classes to prepare them to function independently as adults. The majority of these students are classified as mildly mentally retarded and should spend most of their school time in regular classrooms. The IEPs for these students require work modified to skill level, more repetition of work, and shorter time periods for work with breaks built into their schedule (Council for Exceptional Children, 2006).

Students with mental retardation are disproportionately males from low-income families living in environments where they may have been exposed to lead poisoning or other toxins. Their mothers are more likely to have had little or poor prenatal care. African Americans are also overly represented in this category; they represent 16 percent of total school population, but 33 percent of mentally retarded students (U.S. Department of Education, 2005a). A number of researchers and student advocates charge that the disproportionate referral and placement of African Americans in this category is the result of prejudice of professional educators.

Emotionally Disturbed   Students who are emotionally disturbed exhibit behaviors that impact their ability to learn and cannot be explained by other intellectual, sensory, or health factors. They have trouble maintaining appropriate interpersonal relationships with their classmates and teachers. They may always be unhappy or depressed. They may develop physical symptoms and fears associated with personal or school problems. These behaviors may be diagnosed by professionals. The behaviors sometimes manifest themselves in outbursts in the classroom. They may indicate the need for therapy for abuse, family problems, or another traumatic incident that has affected their behavior. Students with severe behavior problems that interfere with their learning and the learning of their classmates may be removed from classrooms until they are stabilized.

African American students are also overrepresented in the emotionally disturbed category (U.S. Department of Education, 2005b). Again, one could question the reasons for students being labeled as emotionally disturbed. Some critics believe that teachers are referring a disproportionate number of African American boys to remove them from the classroom because they are sometimes disruptive. They suggest that many of these teachers simply do not know how to handle these students and find it easier to have them removed.

Other Disabilities   As shown in Figure 2.8, the number of students in this category has tripled since 1995. This growth may be due to the greater move toward inclusion of all students with disabilities in regular classrooms, and the increased knowledge and research that has led to increased diagnoses of many disabilities, especially ADHD. This other disabilities category includes students who are blind, deaf, autistic, or have ADHD, physical impairments, seizure disorders, or cerebral palsy. It also includes students who were crack babies, students with feeding tubes, and students with severe disabilities. The goal is for these students to be a part of the regular classroom as much as possible. Students with the most severe disabilities may receive much of their instruction in a special education classroom, but join students without disabilities at lunch and during specials such as music, art, and physical education.

The multiple disabilities included in this group are determined by medical evidence. They are not as subjective as the categories previously discussed. As a result, the number of students with these disabilities is proportionate to their representation in the student population (Viadero, 2004).

School Experiences

Students with disabilities will be in your classroom. A critical factor in working with them effectively is to remember that they are more like regular students than unlike them. However, you are likely to have to make accommodations to promote their learning. The school should have special educators available to advise you on the implementation of students' IEPs. One of the problems is that most schools have not been designed for some of the needed accommodations. Chalkboards are too high and desks too low for students in wheelchairs; ramps are not always available. However, computers, amplification devices, books in Braille, and other educational resources will provide students with disabilities the opportunity to learn at the same level as other students.

Students with disabilities are less likely to graduate from high school and attend college than their able-bodied peers. Only 72 percent of persons with disabilities have a high school diploma; 11 percent have college degrees (U.S. Census Bureau, 2002). They drop out of high school at twice the rate of other students. Adults with disabilities are very underrepresented in the workforce; less than one in four are employed (U.S. Census Bureau, 2004c). Sometimes their disability prevents them from working, but more often the necessary accommodations for them to work do not exist in the workplace.

▶ **Inclusion.** The integration of all students, regardless of their background or abilities, in all aspects of the educational process.

Inclusion   **Inclusion** is the integration of students with disabilities into the regular classroom. The goal is to have students with disabilities in regular education as much as possible with as much interaction with the classroom teacher as possible. Students with and without disabilities are in the same class, but they do not always do the same work, depending on the nature and severity of the disability.

Teaching and medical assistants may be assigned to work on skills development and accommodations with the students with disabilities in the classroom. Special educators may provide special services to the students at defined times during the school day.

In full inclusion, students with disabilities and other special needs receive all of their education in the regular classroom; they are never found in segregated settings with only other students with disabilities. However, one of five students with disabilities spends more than 60 percent of his or her class time outside of regular classrooms (Olson, 2004), receiving special instruction or services from special educators, a speech language pathologist, a school nurse, or school psychologist. They should not be pulled out of the regular classroom during language arts and mathematics lessons. Because music, art, and physical education classes also provide the opportunity to develop social skills with students without disabilities, students with disabilities are almost always integrated into these classes. The students who are able to remain in the general education classroom have higher scores than those students in pull-out classes (Olson, 2004). In the process of inclusion, students without disabilities become more tolerant of their peers who are disabled and learn to appreciate diversity and be more responsive to others' needs (Lipskey & Gartner, 1996).

Many general education teachers do not feel prepared to work effectively with students with disabilities. They do not always know the appropriate accommodations. They sometimes are concerned that the students with disabilities will require so much of their time that other students will not receive the necessary attention. They worry that students without disabilities will not accept students with disabilities. They also worry that the school district will not provide the necessary resources to adequately serve both groups of students (Gollnick & Chinn, 2005).

Parental Involvement   Parents of students with disabilities must be involved with school personnel in the process of determining the best treatment for their children. Some teachers and administrators find that parents of students with disabilities are unrealistically demanding of services and attention for their children. These parents are in the minority. Most parents report that it is often difficult to access information from school personnel about available special education services. Once their children are in the program, they report finding caring and knowledgeable teachers and give high ratings to the quality of the services. At the same time, they are not sure that their school has sufficient resources to support special education (Johnson, Duffett, Farkas, & Wilson, 2002).

In a survey of parents of special education students, parents indicated that their children were in regular classrooms most of the day. They strongly believed that their children were best served by being in a regular classroom to develop academic and social skills rather than being segregated with other students with disabilities. Parents believe that the social stigma attached to special education is declining. However, they do feel that parents of students without disabilities resent the special services and attention their children receive (Johnson et al., 2002).

Disproportionate Placement   Students classified as having mental retardation, emotional disturbance, or a specific learning disability are disproportionately male, African American, Latino, American Indian, English language learners, or

Understanding & USING EVIDENCE

DIVERSITY IN SCHOOL DISTRICTS

You are nearly finished with your teacher education program and are beginning to look for a teaching job. You think you would like to work in an urban area and are interested in knowing whether your diversity knowledge and skills fit with the population in the school districts you are considering. You find the following table that describes the diversity of the student population in the areas you are considering.

Area of Country	Enrollment	Black (%)	Latino (%)	White (%)	Other (%)	FRPL* (%)	IEP (%)	ELL** (%)
Albuquerque, NM	87,201	3.8	50.6	38.9	6.7	42.3	19.9	17.7
Baltimore, MD	98,817	88.0	0.9	10.2	0.9	67.4	16.7	1.3
Dayton, OH	21,547	72.4	1.0	27.5	0.5	73.7	20.1	0.0
Des Moines, IA	32,010	15.3	9.8	69.6	5.2	44.5	17.4	9.8
Houston, TX	21,950	31.3	56.1	9.6	3.1	72.7	9.9	28.4
Norfolk, VA	37,006	67.4	2.4	28.0	2.2	59.8	13.1	0.2
Providence, RI	27,159	22.6	51.6	16.3	9.6	79.6	19.1	20.6
Salt Lake City, UT	25,161	4.1	30.3	53.9	11.8	52.9	12.9	33.5
San Francisco, CA	59,566	15.2	21.3	10.3	51.7	54.5	11.9	30.8
Seattle, WA	47,449	23.1	10.8	40.1	26.0	39.6	12.6	11.7

*FRPL = free or reduced price lunch
** = English language learners

Your Task: The diversity of cities in different areas of the country differs greatly. If you are fluent in Spanish as well as English, you may want to work in a city in southwestern United States. If you want to work with students who are economically impoverished, you might like the challenge of a school in an inner city. Look at the chart above and determine the cities with different types of diverse students.

1. What city has the greatest balance of ethnic and racial diversity?
2. What city has the fewest students from low-income families?
3. What city has the largest percentage of students with disabilities?
4. Which city has the largest percentage of English language learners?
5. Which city best matches your knowledge and skills in diversity? Why?

Refer to the **Understanding & Using Evidence Appendix** *at the end of the text for answers and information related to these activities.*

whites from low-income families. For example, 11 percent of all African American students are in special education as compared to 3 percent of Asian American students (U.S. Department of Education, 2005a). White and Asian American students are overrepresented in gifted classes. Educators should monitor their referrals of students to be tested for placement in these classes to ensure that equity in the delivery of education services is being provided.

A number of factors contribute to the disproportionate placements of students in special education and gifted education. Placement tests may be biased

Should schools be charged with ensuring that the children of low-income families achieve at the same level as middle-class students? Why or why not?

2. Over one in five students has one or more foreign-born parents, many who speak a language other than English at home. Because many of these students speak little or limited English when they begin school in the United States, schools must ensure that they are learning academic subjects at the same time they are learning language. Schools generally use bilingual education or English as a second language to transition students into English-only classrooms. Which strategy do you think more effectively serves the need of students and families? Which strategy is more cost effective for school districts?

Field Guide for School Observations

Students with disabilities are supposed to spend as much of their school day as possible in regular classrooms. In your next visit to a school, observe a classroom that includes students with disabilities. Who are the students with disabilities? (You may need to ask the teacher which students have a disability and the nature of the disability.) What kinds of accommodations are being made to assist their learning? Are any of these students removed from the regular classroom for special services? Describe these services. How are the students with disabilities interacting with the other students in the classroom?

Ask a Teacher

Your future classroom is likely to include a diverse group of students. Ask one or more of the teachers in the schools you are observing how they adapt their instruction to serve students from different ethnic, racial, socioeconomic, and language groups. What are their greatest concerns about providing equity across groups? What do they suggest that you do to prepare to work in a school with diverse student populations?

Journaling _Becoming a Thoughtful Teacher_

This chapter indicates that some students are being better served by schools than others as measured by achievement on the standardized tests required by No Child Left Behind. In your journal, write why you think African American, American Indian, and Latino students do not perform as well on these tests. What difference do you think teachers can make in improving the achievement of these students on standardized tests?

Portfolio Tasks

1. The degree of diversity at a school differs greatly across the country. Choose a school in the community in which your university is located or in which you grew up and describe the cultural make-up of the community and student population in the school, including their ethnicity, socioeconomic, religious, and language backgrounds.

2. The religions practiced in a community can influence what is taught in schools. Write a brief paper on the importance of understanding diverse religions when teaching in an urban area. Indicate the knowledge and skills that you need to develop to teach students from diverse religious backgrounds.

Self-Assessment *What Am I Learning?*

Thinking about the diversity groups introduced in this chapter, assess your knowledge and experiences with each, using the following table:

Group	Am a member of this group	Have personal experiences with the group (summarize experiences)	Have studied this group in one or more courses (list courses)	My plan for increasing my knowledge
African American				
American Indian				
Asian American				
Latino				
Native Hawaiian and Pacific Islander				
Whites				
Families in Poverty				
Females				
Males				
English Language Learners				
Students with Disabilities				

Using the Web

1. To hear students talk about their experiences in schools, go to **www.pbs.org/merrow/listenup/**.

2. For a checklist for addressing harassment in schools prepared by the U.S. Office of Civil Rights, visit **www.ed.gov/about/offices/list/ocr/checklist.html**.

3. Information about Title IX and women's equity issues, including links to additional resources, can be found at **www2.edc.org/Womens Equity/resource/title9/**.

4. Resources and updates for ending bias against gays in schools and society from the website of the Gay, Lesbian, and Straight Education Network (GLSEN) are available at **www.glsen .org/cgi-bin/iowa/home.html**.

5. Resources for preventing the behavioral health risks of lesbian, gay, and bisexual students can be found at **www.apa.org/ed/hlgb/**.

6. For statistics on the status of children and policies and practices for improving the conditions of students, visit the Children's Defense Fund at **www.childrensdefense .org/**.

7. For assistance on educational strategies for English language learners, check the website of the Center for Applied Linguistics at **www.cal.org/**.

Your Professional Library

Educating language learners. (2005, January). *Educational Leadership, 62*(4).

This issue of a popular educators' magazine focuses on teaching English language learners. It addresses teaching content areas, bilingual education, testing issues, different instructional strategies, and the experiences of other nations.

Hale, J. E. (2001). *Learning while black: Creating educational excellence for African American children.* Baltimore, MD: Johns Hopkins Press.

Helping African American students learn requires educators to develop a culturally appropriate pedagogy and to work with the community to monitor educational performance and extracurricular activities for each child.

Kozol, J. (2005). *The shame of the nation: The restoration of apartheid schooling in America.* New York: Crown.

This former teacher and public school activist found in his visits to 60 schools that the nation's schools have been resegregated. Students of color and low-income students are attending schools with deplorably inadequate resources and low expectations for their academic and economic success. He believes that a new civil rights movement will be required to provide an adequate education for these students.

Thompson, G. L. (2004). *Through ebony eyes: What teachers need to know but are afraid to ask about African American students.* San Francisco: Jossey Bass.

This book tackles the issues that many teachers face as they work with African American students with the goal of increasing teachers' effectiveness at helping students achieve academically.

Thompson, G. L. (2003). *What African American parents want educators to know.* Westport, CT: Praeger.

This study of African American parents and guardians found that the majority of these adults believe that a good education can help their children have a better life. They are willing to work with educators to achieve this goal.

 To access chapter objectives, practice tests, weblinks, and flashcards, visit the Companion Website at **www.ablongman.com/hall1e**

mylabschool

Log on to Allyn & Bacon's MyLabSchool (**www. mylabschool.com**). Enter Assignment ID **FDRN** in the **Assignment Finder** and launch Research Navigator. Go to the Link Library and search by the subject History—U.S. History. Find the links for Middle Class (under "M") and read "Black Middle Class." Consider the information about the black middle class and what you have read about class in this chapter and answer the following questions.

1. Why should teachers understand the influence class may have on the learning opportunities students have?

2. In your opinion could the category of middle class be defined by criteria other than income?

3. Do you anticipate that the students of color in your future classrooms will come from the middle class? Explain your answer.

Families and Communities

Educators in Real Schools

MEET
Blanca Estela Carbajal Rodriguez

4th grade bilingual teacher
Frederick Elementary School in Colorado

Blanca Estela Carbajal Rodriguez, a 4th grade bilingual education teacher, has been teaching for 25 years. She teaches at Frederick Elementary School, a rural elementary school that serves both the towns of Frederick and Dacono in Colorado. The Title I school has 525 preschool through 5th grade students who are from low-income families with parents who are generally unskilled laborers. Spanish is the native language of all the English language learners except one whose native language is Italian. Thirty percent of the students are Hispanic, nearly 70 percent are white; a few African Americans, American Indians, and Asian Americans also attend the school. One bilingual teacher is assigned to each grade level. For the most part, English language learners are segregated in classes with a few white students.

English language learners are supposed to transition into English by 4th grade. However, Mrs. Rodriguez finds that most of her students have some basic knowledge of English at the 4th grade, but they are not ready for transition into English-only classrooms. One of four of her students is still Spanish dominant. Some of her students were born in the United States, but their parents speak only Spanish. Some lack the confidence to transition to English, in part, because their peers ridicule them when they mess up. Blanca's class is bilingual in the morning with only English language learners. In the afternoon, her instruction is in English. Once a week she teaches an enrichment class in Spanish for English-only students.

from the community. These are schools in which it feels that no one cares about the children who attend them. They do not provide pleasant or engaging environments; they too often are not safe havens for the students who attend them. Many of their teachers are not fully qualified or may not appear to care about their students' social, psychological, or academic growth. In some cases, it may seem that the community has given up on its schools and their inhabitants. In this chapter, we will explore the involvement of families, communities, and educators in making schools work for students.

Focus QUESTIONS

After reading this chapter, you should be able to answer the following questions:

1   What does the public think about schools and teachers?

2   Of what importance is a student's family structure on learning?

3   What influence does culture have on the way students behave in schools?

4   In what ways can schools and teachers work effectively with parents and communities?

How Does the Public View Schools?

*Teachers at **Charles Beckum**'s school are abuzz about the latest poll reported in today's local newspaper. A large portion of the community is complaining that students at his high school are disruptive both in school and in the community after school. They think that many of the students are using drugs, joining gangs, and not being disciplined by their teachers. Some community leaders are pressuring the school district to crack down on students with stricter discipline standards and teach character education. Charles and most of his colleagues find that most of the students are well-behaved. Of course, a few students are disruptive, but they are usually served detention or are suspended. They can't understand why people outside the school have developed a different perception of their students and their behavior.*

Public Attitudes

Almost everyone has an opinion about schools and how they could be improved. Public attitudes about schools can influence educational policies and practices. Public attitudes also can cause educators to make changes reluctantly. When the public is upset with the quality of schools, politicians may respond with demands on teachers and school administrators for reform.

The most common way to determine what the public thinks is the conduct of surveys by pollsters. Educators and policy makers use survey results to determine agreement or disagreement with current and proposed policies and practices. "They provide clues to what people value and what they understand. They can be an early warning system about policies that may unnerve or alienate people. But in the end, they are a starting point for dialogue, not a substitute for it" (Johnson & Duffett, 2003b, p. 7). In this section, we will examine some of the public's, educators', and parents' views of education that may impact your work in schools.

Attitudes about Schools   The quality of schools is important to families when they choose the community in which they want to raise their children. Nearly 50 percent of the respondents to the annual Phi Delta Kappa/Gallup Poll grade their community schools as an A or B, just slightly higher than 10 years earlier. Parents grade their community schools higher than the general public, with 69 percent of them giving the school of their oldest child an "A" or "B" as shown in Figure 3.1 (Rose & Gallup, 2005). However, Latino and African American parents are not as satisfied with schools. Only 3 of 10 African American parents (Black America's Political Action Committee, 2004) and half of the Latino parents (Latino Coalition, 2004) rate their community schools as excellent or good. Interestingly, the public believes that their community schools are better than other schools in the United States with only 24 percent of them grading the nation's schools as an A or B (Rose & Gallup, 2005).

Employers and college professors are not as positive about the quality of schools as most parents and teachers. An independent public interest group, Public Agenda, found that 73 percent of the parents and 93 percent of the teachers surveyed rated schools as excellent or good, but less than half of employers and professors felt the same (Public Agenda, 2005). Employers and professors do not believe that high school graduates have the skills to succeed in college or the work world. They are concerned about the basic writing, speaking, and math skills of high school graduates. They also find that many graduates are not organized, not on time, and not as motivated and conscientious as they should be. They do report, however, that graduates have good or excellent computer skills.

Figure 3.1 Percentage awarding A's and B's to the public schools

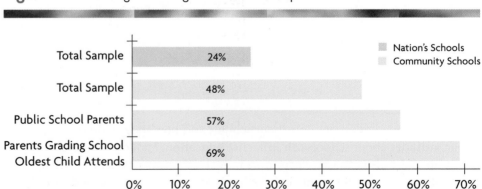

Source: Policy implications of the 37th annual Phi Delta Kappa/Gallup poll. *Phi Delta Kappan, 87*(1), 54.

Attitudes about Teachers The quality of schools is measured, in great part, by the quality of the teachers in the schools. Parents and students know who the effective teachers are. A number of parents do everything possible to ensure their children are in those teachers' classes. At the same time, they know the teachers who do not help students learn and steer their children into other classes if at all possible. They clearly know the value of an effective teacher to the potential academic success of their children. Public Agenda found that "the vast majority of parents say their child's teachers are qualified and caring" (Johnson & Duffett, 2003, p. 9).

The public now ranks teaching as one of the most prestigious in society. Public perceptions of the importance of teaching have improved over the past 27 years since the Harris Poll first began asking the question (HarrisInteractive, 2004b). In fact, teaching wins by more than a three-to-one margin over entertainers, journalists, stockbrokers, and accountants. The only occupations that respondents ranked as "very great prestige" above teaching were doctors and scientists (HarrisInteractive, 2004b).

Perspectives on School Improvement

Many reports on the quality of schools decry the low academic achievement of students, particularly when compared to the students of other nations. You may have seen television commentators discussing what they perceive as the poor state of affairs. These reports sometimes lead to local, state, and federal policies for improving U.S. students' performance on international tests and closing the achievement gap between groups of students. Schools respond by adding more days to the school year, hiring only highly qualified teachers, and providing tutoring for students. How do parents and the public perceive these problems?

Standards The majority of parents, teachers, and principals believe that all children should meet high standards (Johnson & Duffett, 2003). The public agrees. Nearly 8 of 10 believe the high school curriculum should be more rigorous, and 66 percent would increase the mandatory age for attending school to 18 (Rose & Gallup, 2004). Although most states have adopted standards for every subject and grade level, employers and college professors think that schools have not set high enough expectations for meeting the standards. They would like schools to push students harder. African American parents also believe that schools should raise academic standards and achievement for their children (Johnson & Duffett, 2003).

The majority of parents today believe that their children should seek a college degree, but a larger percentage of Latino parents (78%) holds this

© Michael Sieron.

Parents and the public in general have different perspectives on the effectiveness of schools. They usually think that their children's schools are better than the schools of other people's children.

aspiration as compared to African Americans (67%), and whites (57%) (Immerwahr & Foleno, 2000). However, African American and Latino parents do not think their children are as likely to get a good education as white children (HarrisInteractive, 2004a). Although parents have high expectations for their own children, they are not necessarily so optimistic for other people's children (Johnson & Duffett, 2003).

Accountability Over 7 of 10 adults believe that teachers and schools should be held accountable for student learning (Educational Testing Service, 2002). What do they mean by accountability? One part of determining accountability is the testing of teachers and students. However, the majority do not approve of using a single test to determine whether a school is making adequate progress in helping students learn. They worry that testing only English and mathematics skills is limiting attention to art, music, history, and other subjects. They are evenly divided on whether standardized tests should be used for high-stakes purposes such as high school graduation. Half of the respondents believe that tests should be only one of the measures used to determine the quality of their schools (Rose & Gallup, 2004). When their schools are not performing as well as expected, two of three respondents prefer to reform their schools rather than sending students to alternative schools. Only 38 percent of the respondents support using public funds for vouchers to allow students and families to choose a private instead of a public school (Rose and Gallup, 2005).

One of the major public concerns is the achievement gap among groups of students (Rose and Gallup, 2004). Respondents believe that the achievement gap is due to the lack of parental involvement (90%), poor home life and upbringing (87%), lack of student interest (80%), poor community environment (66%), racism (42%), and low family income (26%) (Rose & Gallup, 2004). Even though they do not blame schools for the achievement gap, nearly 9 of 10 respondents expect schools to close it by encouraging greater parent involvement, providing more instructional time for low-performing students, and strengthening remedial programs (Rose & Gallup, 2004). They also propose closing the gap by providing free breakfasts and lunches to students, using state funds to support preschool programs, and providing in-school health clinics (Rose & Gallup, 2004).

Ed Lines

"Let us put our minds together and see what life we can make for our children." *Sitting Bull*

Problems   A number of surveys have identified the lack of parental involvement as a major problem faced by schools. The majority of teachers complain that parents do not set limits and create structures at home, do not hold their children accountable for academic performance, and are not involved in the school (Johnson & Duffett, 2003). Three of 10 new teachers report that communications with and involving parents are their greatest challenge (MetLife, 2005). Other problems identified by teachers are lack of adequate funds, class sizes that are too large, and salaries that are too low (MetLife, 2005). In another survey in which the public was asked to identify problems in an open-ended question rather than from a preset list of problems, the lack of financial support topped the list, followed by overcrowding, lack of discipline, and use of drugs (Rose and Gallup, 2005).

Revisiting Charles Beckum's Perceptions of Students

Charles Beckum, the teacher at the beginning of this section, holds opinions about the students' behavior that may not always agree with those held by members of the community or even by the parents of the students. Charles believes that if members of the community knew more about the actions of the students in school, they would change some of their negative opinions. Therefore, Charles and other teachers at the school created **service learning** projects that will require the students to work with members of the community. Charles believes that collaborative service learning projects will help improve the public image of the school and its students.

Service learning. Learning that requires students to work with members of the community.

In What Types of Families Do Students Live?

*Seven-year-old **Marcus McLaurin** was standing in the recess line at Ernest Gallet Elementary School when a classmate asked a question about his mother and father. Marcus replied that actually he didn't have a mother and father, that he had two mothers instead. The curious classmate wanted to know why, and Marcus responded it was because his mother was gay. "What does that mean?" the classmate asked, and Marcus explained, "Gay is when a girl likes another girl."*

The teacher's response was swift and unequivocal. Marcus was chastised in front of his classmates and told that gay is a "bad word" that should never be spoken at school. He was denied recess and sent to the principal's office. The following week, he had to attend a special "behavioral clinic," where he was forced to write time after time, "I will never use the word 'gay' in school again." (Roffman, 2004, p. 34)

Diversity of Today's Families

Less than one in five persons in the United States is under the age of 18 and less than half of U.S. families have children under the age of 18 (U.S. Census Bureau,

Ed Lines

The stakes are especially high for children who are English language learners, who must master academic content and a new language at the same time. *(National Association for Bilingual Education, 2005)*

2006). Fifty-three percent of the families do not have school-age children (U.S. Census Bureau, 2006) and are not always advocates for education, especially when it comes to providing additional financial support. Families today are different than those in which our grandparents and great-grandparents were raised. Fifty years ago, couples married within a few years after they finished high school. The typical family included both mother and father and two or more children with the father usually working while the mother stayed at home to raise the children. Children were more likely to be born to married women, and divorce was rarer than today.

Types of Families   Families in the United States today are very diverse. They include mothers working while fathers stay at home with the children, stay-at-home mothers, single-parent families, two working parents, remarried parents, married couples without children, families with adopted children, gay and lesbian parents, extended families, grandparents raising grandchildren, and unmarried couples with children. Most children live with two parents, even though one of them may not be their natural parent (U.S. Census Bureau, 2006). As shown in Figure 3.2, however, single mothers, single fathers, grandparents, and other guardians raise approximately one of three children in the United States. Fewer African American students live with two parents than white and Latino students; half of the African American students are living in families with a single mother (U.S. Census Bureau, 2006). Five percent of households are partners of the same sex (U.S. Census Bureau, 2006) and some of these families are raising children.

Today there are more unmarried women than ever before, and they are having more children than in the past. In fact, one of three children is born to an un-

Figure 3.2 Types of families in which children live

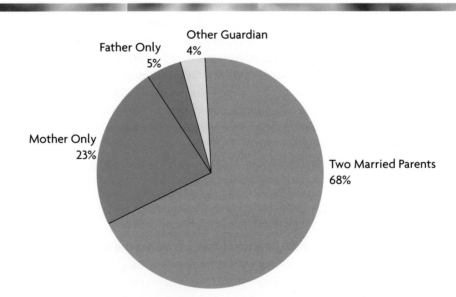

Source: U.S. Census Bureau. (2006). *Statistical abstract of the United States: 2006* (125th ed.). Washington, DC: U.S. Government Printing Office.

married mother (Federal Interagency Forum on Child and Family Statistics, 2004). Although children are advantaged when they they live with two caring and loving parents, living with two parents is not essential for success in school and life as shown by the number of successful professionals who were raised by a single parent. Problem behavior and lack of academic success are more directly related to poverty, conflict, and instability in families than family structure (Furstenberg, 1999). Unfortunately, poverty is a prevalent factor in families headed by single mothers. Their income is only 43 percent that of a married couple, making single mothers five times more likely to be below the official poverty line (U.S. Census Bureau, 2006). Poverty leads to children suffering from inadequate health care, hunger, and poor housing conditions that result from not enough money to support basic needs. In addition, one of three children now lives in communities with poor environmental conditions such as air quality (Federal Interagency Forum on Child and Family Statistics, 2004).

Children in single-parent families are more likely to be in poverty than those in two-parent families. A good education is critical for an economically independent future.

Size of Families   Although some families have many children, most married couples with children under 18 years old in the United States have one or two children (U.S. Census Bureau, 2006). The birth rate now is lower than it has been since the government began keeping records; the greatest drop is among African American teenagers (National Center for Health Statistics, 2003; Federal Interagency Forum on Child and Family Statistics, 2004). However, birth rates are higher for women of color, in part because the median age of persons of color is younger than for whites (U.S. Census Bureau, 2006). Therefore, a larger percentage of women of color are of childbearing age, leading to higher birth rates.

Revisiting Marcus McLaurin and His Dilemma

The teacher and administrators at Ernest Gallet Elementary School are unable to accept the fact that Marcus's parents are two women. As a result, they have punished Marcus for telling the truth—that his parents are lesbians. Even if an educator believes that homosexuality is wrong, should the child of gay or lesbian parents be treated differently than students living with heterosexual parents? Educators must be careful about stereotyping students because of the structure of their families. No matter who the parents are, teachers should be helping students to reach their fullest potential. They should not suffer indignities by educators because one or both of their parents are drug addicts, prisoners, homeless, unemployed, unmarried, gay, or lesbian.

How Does Culture Influence Students?

*Mr. and Mrs. Johnson believe that there is racial discrimination in many aspects of their daughter's school. They complain that the school pays little or no attention to black history and heroes. They point out that the school has lavish Halloween parties, but ignores the Martin Luther King, Jr., holiday. They are concerned that Susan is not progressing in her below-grade reading group. Her parents know that she likes reading and believe she is capable of achieving at a higher level. Susan's 4th grade teacher, **Mrs. White**, was surprised and concerned when Mrs. Johnson suggested that she was not helping Susan because of her race. After her encounter with Susan's mother, Mrs. White decided to spend more time encouraging Susan in her academic work. Mrs. White also decided it was time for her to examine her attitudes and beliefs about students from racial groups other than her own.*

Culture

Our culture defines us. Early in life, it guides our way of thinking, feeling, and behaving in our family and community. Members of a group develop behavior patterns that help them understand each other and be able to live together in relative harmony. Our cultural identity is not innately based on the culture in which we are born. For example, a Chinese infant adopted by Polish American, Catholic, middle-class parents will share a cultural heritage with middle-class Polish American Catholics, rather than with the Chinese.

We are comfortable with the members of our cultural group because we know the meaning of their words and actions. However, we may misunderstand the cultural cues of members of a different cultural group. We grow up thinking that everyone thinks and acts like us, not realizing that the experiences and conditions of other groups could lead to different **values**, behaviors, and knowledge. As a result, we may respond to differences as personal affronts, rather than as cultural differences. These misunderstandings may seem insignificant, but they can carry important cultural meanings to some groups. Examples include how loud is too loud, how late to arrive at a social event is acceptable, how close to stand to someone without being rude or disrespectful, and how to greet one another. Whether the palm faces the other person in a greeting, how the eyebrow is raised, and whether to bow when greeting someone are all culturally determined behaviors that gain respect or offend another person.

▶ **Values.** The ideals or morals that we believe are important.

Characteristics of Culture
Culture is learned, shared with others in our group, adapted to the circumstances, and dynamic. We learn our culture from our parents

Ed Lines

"A young child asks his mother why the man in the grocery store is so dark. Instead of answering, his mother tells him to be quiet, which tells the child it's not okay to discuss differences." *Beverly Daniel Tatum*

and caretakers. It is reinforced at places of worship, community events, and ethnic celebrations. We acquire our culture and become competent in its language and ways of behaving and knowing through a process called **enculturation**. We learn the social norms and expectations of society through the process of socialization. Thus, we learn what it means to be a mother, husband, student, or friend as well as the meaning of occupational roles such as teacher, business person, custodian, or politician. Nurses, physicians, teachers, neighbors, and religious leaders assist parents in enculturating and socializing children by modeling appropriate behavior and rewarding children and youth for acceptable behaviors. Shared cultural patterns and customs bind people together as an identifiable group that can be recognized by others. Members of the same cultural group may disagree about some aspects of the culture. Members of one culture may not always be aware of the points of agreement that include the way they communicate with each other, the foods they eat, and childrearing patterns.

> **Enculturation.** The process of learning your culture's expectations for behavior, communications, and ways of knowing.

To survive, cultures have had to adapt to environmental conditions, available natural and technological resources, and the relationship to the larger society. Thus, the Eskimo who lives with extreme cold, snow, and ice develops a culture different from that of the Pacific Islander, who has limited land, unlimited seas, and few mineral resources. The culture of urban residents differs from that of rural residents, in part, because of the natural resources available in the different settings. Cultures adapt as technology forces changes in available jobs and communication. The cultures of groups that suffer discrimination in society respond to the power relationships within society differently than the dominant group.

Expressions of Culture   Culture is expressed in an infinite number of ways as we meet our psychological and basic needs. For example, our culture is reflected in our values, which are the ideals and morals that we believe are important. They influence the importance of prestige, status, pride, family loyalty, love of country, religious belief, and honor. Values determine what is important in life. For some, it is the accumulation of material possessions such as a house, boat, luxury car, and exotic vacations. For others, it is the importance of education for the purpose of knowing. Others see education as a credential to a profession and financial success. For some, responsibility for civic and community service is the path of self-satisfaction and rewards.

Nonverbal communication patterns also are learned from culture. Our manner of walking, sitting, standing, reclining, gesturing, and dancing comes from our observations of others in our culture. Interpreting acts and expressions of people from other cultural groups as wrong or inappropriate can lead to unnecessary confrontations. A positive approach to overcoming miscommunications requires learning the meaning of communication patterns across the groups with which you will be working as a teacher.

Language is more than a means of communication. It also provides a way of looking at the world that cannot always be captured in the translation of one language to another. In the larger society, some dialects (e.g., standard English) are

Ed Lines

"It takes the whole village to raise the child." *African saying*

more acceptable than others such as black English or the dialects used by low-income families. Language patterns in the same language can have different meanings based on the speaker's culture. The speaker may intend a joke, but the listener may hear it as a criticism or abuse of power. Miscommunications are most likely to occur when the speaker and the listener are from different cultural groups.

▶ **Cultural relativism.** Judging other cultural groups through the lens of members of that culture rather applying the standards of one's own culture.

▶ **Cultural borders.** A social construct based on cultural membership that is political and involves differences in power.

Cultural Relativism   **Cultural relativism** requires that we not judge other cultural groups by our own cultural standards, but see the second culture as one of its members sees it. We might come to understand that the way of doing things in that culture has validity. As countries and cultures around the world become more interdependent, people will need to learn to respect other cultures and avoid relegating them to an inferior status. This stance is particularly important in schools as a growing number of students with foreign-born parents enter the classroom.

The principle of cultural relativism is not limited to cultures outside the United States. The cultures of many groups in the United States have been judged as inferior to the dominant and privileged Western European culture. We are likely to find children of immigrant parents, students of color, and students from low-income families in our classrooms. What do we really know about their cultures and their experiences in the community? When we expect students from cultural groups other than our own to act, think, and know as we learned in our own culture, we are placing a burden on the students to learn our culture. Your respect in the community will improve as you learn the cultures of the students and their families and begin to understand why they behave and think differently than you.

Biculturalism and Multiculturalism   We are all multicultural because we are members of more than one identity group within our culture. We behave and think differently about ourselves and the world based on our gender, ethnicity, race, language, religion, socioeconomic status, and abilities. We may act and speak differently in a professional setting than when we are interacting in the community in which we grew up. Males and females often exhibit different behaviors in social settings. As we grew up, we learned the competencies appropriate in our multiple identity groups. We can also learn the history, experiences, and cultures of other groups. As we learn to function effectively in two or more cultures, we become border crossers. We become bicultural or multicultural and often bilingual or multilingual as well.

Because most schools reflect the dominant society, students of color sometimes feel forced to adjust (or act white) if they are going to be academically successful. In contrast, most middle-class whites find almost total congruence between the culture of their family, schooling, and work. Persons of color, immigrants, and persons with low incomes must commonly be bicultural to fit in at work or school, maintaining their own cultural patterns at home and the cultural patterns of the dominant group at work and in school.

As discussed earlier, we belong to multiple cultural groups (for example, ethnic, religious, and socioeconomic groups) that define and identify us. When cultural differences result in one group being treated differently from another, **cultural borders** are erected between groups. Crossing these borders can be difficult, especially when behavior valued on one side of the border is denigrated or not tolerated on the other side. Borders are sometimes drawn in schools around speaking one's native language or dialect in school or wearing a head scarf as expected for one's faith.

Cultural borders are established in classrooms when teachers ground all activity and communications in one culture alone. Being able to function comfortably in different cultures allows educators to cross cultural borders, incorporating the students' cultures and experiences into the curriculum and classroom activities. It also allows teachers to model respect for cultural differences and the cultural borders some students must cross on a daily basis.

Most schools participate in competitive sports events. These events are used to develop school spirit that brings students and the community together.

School Culture

Schools have their own culture, which may differ from that of the family and broader community. The school rules regulate classroom behavior as well as determine acceptable dress and speech. Although they differ across schools and communities, students and educators practice many common rituals in athletics, extracurricular clubs, graduation exercises, and school social events. The signs and emblems of the school culture are displayed in school songs, colors, and cheers. Traditions in the school culture are associated with regional influences, the social structure of a community, and location in a rural, urban, or suburban area. Some schools are influenced greatly by the religion of the children's families; others by the presence of a large military base.

Schools develop histories that are transferred from generation to generation. Extracurricular activities, proms, awards and graduation ceremonies, fund raisers, school plays, bands, clubs, football games, and school trips take on different degrees of importance from one community to another and from one student to another. Some graduates retain lifelong feelings of pride about their schools. Others have less positive memories.

Hidden Curriculum In addition to the formal curriculum of academic and vocational courses, schools include a **hidden curriculum** that maintains the power relations between teachers and students and reinforces existing differences between socioeconomic levels through practices such as tracking and self-fulfilling prophecies. The problem with the hidden curriculum is that it privileges the cultural values and patterns of the dominant group and does not positively acknowledge the cultural differences that exist in many schools. As a

Hidden curriculum. The norms and values that define expectations for student behavior and attitudes and that undergrid the curriculum and operations of schools.

result, white middle-class students adapt easily to the school culture because it reinforces the behaviors they have learned from their families. Students from other cultures may find school practices different and sometimes contradictory to what they have learned at home. One example is a school's emphasis on competition over collaboration in academic work. In a collaborative mode, students work together on assignments and assist each other as needed. Educators should confront the discriminatory practices that are often inherent in the hidden curriculum in the classroom and ensure that the cultural patterns of all groups are respected and drawn upon to help all students learn.

The hidden curriculum also includes moral lessons as students study real and fictional characters, especially in English and social studies. Lessons sometimes deal with issues of social injustice such as slavery, homelessness, colonization, and genocide. The rituals and ceremonies of schools also provide nationalistic lessons as the pledge of allegiance is recited and patriotic songs are sang.

The hidden curriculum is supported by a set of classroom rules and regulations for appropriate behavior. Often these rules are posted and discussed at the beginning of the school year. They range from "be kind to each other" to "raise your hand for recognition before talking." Students who follow the teacher's rules become the "good students" who accept the teacher's authority and cause no classroom problems. The good students are not necessarily more intelligent than other students, but they are likely to receive more positive attention to their academic performance than the "bad students" whose attention from the teacher is more likely to be related to discipline than to learning.

Revisiting Mrs. White's Recognition of Differences

After a difficult encounter with a parent, the teacher at the beginning of this session began to take a closer look at the ways she interacted with students from cultures different from her own. She began to examine the teaching strategies she used and the materials she used to extend student learning. In the past, Mrs. White often referred to herself as **color-blind** meaning that she saw all students as the same and did not identify them by race or ethnic background. Now Mrs. White realizes that she must recognize the differences in culture each one of her students brings to school and learn to understand and respect these differences.

▶ **Color-blind.** A teacher's belief that race makes no difference in the lives of students and that the teacher treats all students alike regardless of their race.

What Happens when Students' Cultures Come to School?

In April, at a meeting of the school board in Muhlenberg, Pennsylvania, Brittany Hunsicker, a 16-year-old student at the local high school, stood up and addressed the assembled board members.

"How would you like it if your son and daughter had to read this?" Miss Hunsicker asked the board members. Then she began to recite from The Buffalo

Tree, a novel set in a juvenile detention center and narrated by a tough, 12-year-old boy incarcerated there. What she read was a scene set in a communal shower, where another adolescent boy is sexually aroused.

"I am in the 11th grade," Miss Hunsicker said. "I had to read this junk."

Less than an hour later, by a unanimous vote, The Buffalo Tree *was banned, officially excised from the* **Muhlenberg High School** *curriculum. By 8:30 the next morning, all classroom copies of the book had been collected and stored in a vault in the principal's office. Thus began a still unresolved battle over the fate of* The Buffalo Tree, *a young adult novel by Adam Rapp that was published 8 years ago by HarperCollins and had been on the 11th grade reading list at Muhlenberg High since 2000.* (Weber, 2005)

Religious and Moral Sensitivities

Some families are concerned that the books their children are assigned to read in school are immoral or inappropriate as defined by their religious beliefs. For example, some religious groups do not want their children to read the Harry Potter books because they are perceived as promoting witchcraft and wizardry. The American Library Association reports that "more than one book a day faces expulsion from free and public access in U.S. schools and libraries every year" (American Library Association, 2006, 1). Some groups pressure school libraries, video stores, or art galleries to remove books, music, videos, or artwork from their shelves or walls. In 2004, 547 books were challenged as compared to 458 in 2003 (Weber, 2005). The U.S. Supreme Court said in *Board of Education v. Pico* (1982) that books could not be removed from school libraries simply because someone does not like the ideas in the books. Some groups of parents calling for censorship

Teachers' Lounge

My Cultural Epiphany
I could write a book about all the funny things that have taken place in my 43 years of teaching, especially from my earlier years when we were just beginning to have a number of Latino students in our classes and their names were new to us. I will always remember a student named Salijo. I was very sure of myself the first time I called out her name in class, carefully pronouncing it "SAH-LEE'-HOE." She raised her hand and said, "Um, that's SALLY JO."

We had another student named Jesus, who was on the basketball team. I coached the cheerleaders, and one day we were at an away game. Each player's name was announced on the loudspeaker and the band was playing *Sweet Georgia Brown*, when they got to this student's name and pronounced it "JEE-ZUZZ" (instead of "HAY-SUCE"). We watched in amazement as the hometown crowd dropped to their knees and started crossing themselves.

● Nancy Estes
Broward Career Center Central

lobby a state or school district to adopt specific textbooks that reflect their religious values.

Calls for censoring books often split communities. Not all families agree with the censorship, leading to caustic relationships in communities. Both sides are sincere about their cause. One side believes the censorship is just and moral. They believe that the objectionable materials will "contaminate" the minds of their children and contribute to the moral decay of society. On the other side, opponents want their children exposed to the world and multiple perspectives. They do not find the materials objectionable to their religious beliefs. Instead, they find that they help their children explore reality and think critically about important issues in society. Educators should share with families the objectives of new curricula and materials. Communications with families is critical in reducing possible alienation between educators and parents over the inclusion of what might be viewed as controversial content in curriculum.

Cultural Clashes Related to Religious Beliefs Many Americans believe that religion is losing its influence. Religious leaders find this very worrisome. They and their adherents blame many of the problems in families and schools on the lack of the morals that are taught. Their frustration with student drug use, premarital sex, gang violence, and undisciplined students has led some religious groups to pressure schools to incorporate character education. They have campaigned to elect school board members who will push schools to return to what they perceive as the Christian values of the past. They may reject the introduction of multiple perspectives that give equal weight to the knowledge and experiences of religions other than Christianity.

The First Amendment and Teaching Religion in Schools The First Amendment of the U.S. Constitution requires the separation of church and state. The meaning of the First Amendment in schools is complex. Although the First Amendment requires the separation of state and church, public schools and religion do not have to be completely separated. Religion is a legitimate discipline that can be taught in public schools. A comparative religion course is taught in many high schools so that students can learn that the United States and the world are rich in religious diversity. The fine line in teaching religion is to ensure that students are not forced to practice a specific religion as part of the class. Courses that indoctrinate or try to convert students to a specific religion are illegal. Public schools can neither promote nor inhibit a religion. They must be religiously neutral, but protect the religious liberty of students. Teachers have a right to their own religious convictions. However, they cannot **proselytize** or promote their religion in the classroom.

One's religious orientation may strongly influence one's perception of objectivity, fairness, and legality in schools. While some families believe that schools should reflect their religious values, others believe that public schools already reflect Christian perspectives, denigrating their own religious beliefs when they are

▶ Proselytize. Recruiting
new members to one's
own faith.

Ed Lines

"In automobile terms, the child supplies the power but the parents have to do the steering." *Benjamin Spock*

not Christian. Some families have removed their children from public schools because they don't feel that the school reflects their values of appropriate student dress, language, and behaviors. Some families support prayer and religious clubs in schools—practices that are prohibited in public schools. Some complain that the curriculum and assigned readings are too **secular**, not acknowledging their beliefs. Non-Christians accuse schools of not respecting religious diversity, scheduling important assignments and celebrations on their religious holidays, singing Christian hymns during convocations and concerts, and expecting their daughters to attend coed physical education classes.

Understanding the importance of religion to students and their families provides an advantage to educators in developing effective teaching strategies for individual students. Educators should avoid stereotyping all students from one denomination or religion. Within each religious group are differences in attitudes and beliefs. Members of the same religion may be a part of a liberal or moderate group, whereas others would be identified as very conservative or fundamentalist. Educators must periodically reexamine their own interactions with students to ensure that they are not discriminating against students because of their religion.

Prayer in Schools   In 1963 the U.S. Supreme Court ruled that prayer could not be said in school. However, the law allows voluntary prayer by teachers and students. A private prayer can be said before a meal, between classes, and before and after school. Generally, students can initiate prayer at school events as long as school officials have not endorsed or encouraged it. Schools cannot support a moment of silence because the motivation for the moment of silence has been to encourage prayer. Public group prayer is unlawful in school or at school events such as a convocation or football game.

Evolution and Creationism   In the first half of the twentieth century, some states did not allow evolution to be taught in public schools. In the famous Scopes "Monkey Trial" in 1927 the Tennessee Supreme Court upheld the state's law requiring the teaching of the biblical version of creation. Not until 1968 did the U.S. Supreme Court declare a similar Arkansas law unconstitutional because evolution is a science and students should have access to such information. Trying to circumvent the court's decision, some states required that equal time be given to creationism when evolution was taught. In 1987, the U.S. Supreme Court also found this practice unconstitutional because creationism is not science and teaching it was advancing a religious belief. Proponents of creationism are changing the lingo from creationism to **intelligent design**, which is "the general belief that an intelligent cause has influenced the development of living things" (Cavanagh, 2005b, 18). They argue that scientific evidence supports intelligent design. However, a Pennsylvania court in 2005 told the Dover school board that it could not require the teaching of intelligent design because it was not based on science (Cavanagh, 2005a).

Secular. Not religious in nature: sometimes identified as based on science rather than religion.

Intelligent design. The belief that an intelligent being (for example, God) influenced the development of living things.

Ed Lines

"Children are likely to live up to what you believe of them." *Lady Bird Johnson*

Even though the courts have said that the teaching of creationism is unconstitutional, some states and school districts are still discussing this issue. For example, the Kansas State Board of Education adopted in 1999, science standards that did not require the teaching of evolution or the testing of students on evolution. A few years later when the majority of the board members were moderates, the standards were changed to require evolution. In 2005 with a majority of board members holding fundamentalist religious beliefs, the board held a number of hearings across the state about revisions to the science standards to include intelligent design. A school district in Georgia placed disclaimers on textbooks; the stickers said that evolution was "a theory, not a fact (Purrington, 2006)." A federal judge ordered the removal of the stickers in 2005.

Not all teachers are following the law. Surveys in the states of Oklahoma, Louisiana, Minnesota, Illinois, Pennsylvania, and South Dakota found that one of four teachers include creationism or intelligent design along with their teaching of evolution. In a CBS poll in November 2004, 65 percent of the responding adults favored the teaching of both evolution and creationism and 37 percent wanted creationism alone to be taught (Cavanagh, 2005b). The national professional associations of science teachers—the National Science Teachers Association and National Association of Biology Teachers—are outspoken in their support of teaching evolution and not including creationism or intelligent design in the school curriculum.

You will need to be aware of the religious orientation within the community before introducing materials, teaching strategies, and books that may be perceived as not reflective of community values. School administrators and experienced

Figure 3.3 Limited English proficient students enrolled in K–12 schools

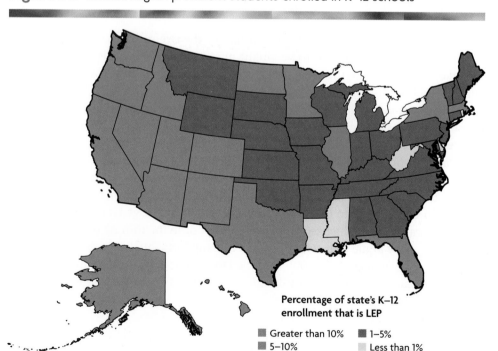

Percentage of state's K–12
enrollment that is LEP

■ Greater than 10%   ■ 1–5%
■ 5–10%   ■ Less than 1%

Source: Zehr, M. A. (2005, May 4). Newcomers bring change, challenge to region. *Education Week, 24*(34), 1, 19.

Figure 3.4 Students who speak a language other than English at home and have difficulty speaking English

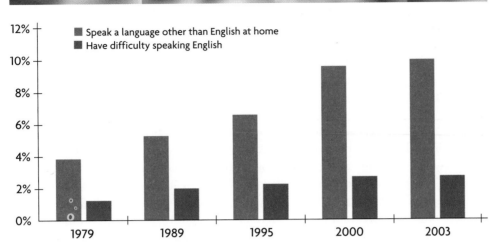

Source: U.S. Census Bureau. (2006). *Statistical abstract of the United States: 2006* (125th ed.). Washington, DC: U.S. Government Printing Office.

teachers can serve as barometers as to how students, parents, and the community will react to new materials. However, as indicted in the anecdote that opened this section, attacks on teaching a particular book can come as a surprise because the same book may have been taught for many years without controversy. As a new teacher, you should be able to recognize possible problem materials and content and be able to respond professionally to confrontations from students and parents. Schools often will allow a student to read a different book and be exempt from attending class during discussions of objectionable topics. Again, good communications with parents may be helpful in avoiding these situations.

Language

Over the past 10 years, the percentage of English language learners has increased by over 50 percent in the United States, but by 185 percent in Iowa, 212 percent in Missouri, 269 percent in Kansas, 320 percent in Nebraska, and 389 percent in Arkansas (Zehr, 2005). As shown in Figure 3.3, over 10 percent of the students in the southwestern states, Florida, and Alaska are English language learners.

As shown in Figure 3.4, ten percent of the students in K–12 schools speak a language other than English at home, but most of them speak English without difficulty. Speaking English, however, does not necessarily mean that they can function effectively with academic work that is written and discussed in English. Most students can become conversationally fluent within 2 or 3 years, but may require 5 to 7 years to reach the proficiency necessary for success in academic subjects such as social studies and English (Thomas & Collier, 1997). Students who are conversationally fluent may be assigned to English-only classrooms without appropriate support to ensure they can function effectively in academic work. In this case, these students may fall farther behind their classmates in conceptually understanding the subjects being taught.

The Supreme Court ruling, *Lau v. Nichols* (1974), requires school districts to offer language programs to help English language learners (ELLs) learn English. This case was brought on behalf of Chinese American students in San Francisco who argued they were being deprived of equal education because they could not understand the English that was being used for instruction. To help English language learners learn English and progress through school, schools most often offer either bilingual education or English as a second language (ESL). Teachers are expected to use the approach to teach ELLs that has been adopted by the school or school district.

Learning English When children speak little or no English upon entry into a classroom and neither the teacher or teacher assistant speak their native language, they may feel alienated and can become quite frustrated. Usually other children become their first allies as they try to communicate with ELLs with signs. When you enter your classroom as a teacher, you may have a number of students who speak languages other than English. School administrators and other resource people in the school district should help you know the approaches you should use to help these students learn both English and the academic content.

Bilingual education uses both English and the students' native language as the mode of instruction. It requires either the teacher or an assistant teacher to be bilingual. In bilingual education, the academic subjects are taught in the native language, giving English language learners the opportunity to learn at the same pace as their English-only classmates. Most schools offer transitional bilingual programs that move students from their native languages to English as soon as possible, usually between one and four years. Gradually, more and more of the instruction is conducted in English.

English as a second language (ESL) promotes English proficiency and is used extensively in the United States to move ELLs into English-only classrooms. Unlike bilingual education, ESL is conducted totally in English; the native language is not used at all for instruction. ESL is used in newcomer and sheltered programs for new immigrants who have limited or no experience with English and sometimes have limited literacy skills in their native language. Immigrant students are most successful when they are able to stay in these programs for at least 4 years (Genesee, 1999).

Families should be involved as a school decides the appropriate approach. Educators and parents together should decide whether they want to promote bilingualism so that ELLs become competent in both English and their native language. Families may want their children to move into English-only instruction as soon as possible, requiring a different teaching strategy. Some English-only families may advocate for an immersion program in which their children become fluent in a second language and culture. The effectiveness of different approaches to teaching ELLs are discussed in the Challenging Assumptions on page 111.

Maintaining the Native Language Although the majority of programs for ELLs are transitional, some bilingual programs are designed to help students maintain their native language. These maintenance programs promote the use of both languages and cultures as students become bilingual and bicultural with neither lan-

Challenging Assumptions
FINDINGS FROM RESEARCH

Do English language learners (ELLs) achieve at academically higher levels when they are in bilingual or English-only classrooms?

The Assumption: Proponents of English-only policies argue that ELLs learn English more quickly if they are immersed into classrooms in which only English is used for instruction. This argument has led to policies in some states and school districts that prevent instruction from being offered in the native language and English.

Study Design and Method: Two researchers followed every ELL in grades K–12 in five urban and rural school districts for 5 years. The school districts were located in the northeast, northwest, south-central, and southeast United States. The students represented 80 different languages, but the data analysis in three of the sites focused on Spanish speakers. Findings were tracked by the type of program the ELL was in or had participated in earlier in their schooling. The programs available to students in these five school districts included approaches that ranged from English-only without bilingual or ESL services to two-way bilingual immersion in which ELLs and students whose native language is English receive instruction in the two languages.

Study Findings: The researchers found that the reading and mathematics achievement of ELLs in English-only classrooms without bilingual or ESL services decreased by the 5th grade. The largest number of dropouts had been enrolled in these English-only classrooms.

The ELLs in the one-way developmental bilingual education program with 4 years of instruction in English and their native language in two high-achieving school districts outperformed the ELLs in all other programs and remained above grade level at the 7th grade. The one-way and two-way developmental bilingual education programs were the only programs that assisted ELLs in reaching grade level and maintaining it through the end of their schooling. These programs also had fewer dropouts.

When ELLs enter English-only elementary classrooms after ESL or bilingual education, they do not perform as well on tests given in English as their counterparts who were in English-only classrooms. However, the bilingually educated students reach the same level of achievement by middle school and outperform the monolingually schooled students during high school. Native English-speaking students in two-way immersion programs equaled or outperformed on all measures their comparison group who were in English-only classrooms. The highest quality ESL programs closed only about half of the achievement gap.

Implications: The findings of this and similar studies are important to policymakers and educators as they try to determine the best strategies for increasing the academic achievement of English language learners in pre K–12 schools. The results of this research suggest that ELLs should be placed in bilingual education programs to improve long-term academic achievement and reduce dropout rates. The researchers also found that students who do not speak English need to be placed in bilingual programs for 4 years or more. For best results, bilingual and ESL programs must meet students' linguistic, academic, cognitive, emotional, social, and physical needs.

Source: Thomas, W. P., & Collier, V. P. (2001). *A national study of school effectiveness for language minority students' long-term academic achievement.* Santa Cruz, CA: Center for Research on Education, Diversity & Excellence.

guage being the dominant one. This approach values the language and cultures of the students' families and promotes the development of a positive self-image as a bicultural individual. These programs support bilingualism and literacy in both English and the native language. In these programs, both English and the native language have equal status, and both are used interchangeably for instructional purposes. One approach is an immersion program in which English-only students are in classes in which the second language is used for instruction. Two-way immersion helps both English-only and ELLs develop bilingualism as language training is integrated with academic instruction. These classes usually have an equal number of English speakers and speakers of another language.

Revisiting Muhlenberg High School's Reading List

The conflict over curriculum and the personal beliefs of a student that arose in Muhlenberg at that beginning of this section might have been avoided had there been some discussion between school administrators and parents regarding the purpose of using a particular piece of writing in the high school English curriculum. Even though such conflicts may be fueled by impulses seen as counterproductive to the learning process, they do have a major impact on the climate for teaching and learning in today's schools.

How Should Teachers Work with Parents and Communities?

Janice Greer *is a German American first-year teacher of 4-year-olds in a Title I school that serves a very impoverished, primarily African American community. Many of her colleagues warned her that it would be difficult to involve parents in their child's education. Rather than being discouraged, Janice began the year by personally calling all of the parents of the children enrolled in her class to invite them to an orientation meeting at the beginning of the school year. Out of the 15 students enrolled in her class at the time, 13 parents came to the orientation.*

At the orientation, Mrs. Greer gave all of the parents a welcome letter that included both her home and cell phone numbers so parents could contact her with any questions or concerns. She explained the curriculum, the program, and her expectation that all of their children make good academic progress as long as the parents and teacher worked as a team to promote learning. She stressed the importance of the parents' role in their children's education and invited them to visit the classroom at any time to observe the class and the classroom routine. Finally, she invited them to accompany their child to school during the first week so he or she could adjust to going to school. As the year progressed, parents contacted her when they felt the need to discuss their child's progress or to ask for assistance with behavior problems or issues at home. She continued to encourage parents to contact her at any time in letters that were sent home throughout the school year. Several parents also attended a number of classroom parties, and there was a very large turnout at their end-of-year promotion ceremony and picnic. As a result of Mrs. Greer having opened the door to communications, parents responded by staying closely involved in classroom and school activities.

Working with Families as Partners for Student Learning

Teachers are encouraged to work as partners with families in helping students learn. In some schools, a high percentage of families are involved with their teachers and their children's learning. In other schools, contacting families can be quite a challenge. A growing number of families have limited proficiency in English, requiring translators at meetings. As you observe and work in schools over the next few months or years, ask to observe meetings with families, noting successful practices that support the involvement of families in their children's education.

Educators and families do not always see their relationships and expectations in the same way. For example, 9 of 10 principals report that their school is welcoming to parents, but only 6 of 10 parents see their school in the same way. Teachers and parents are a little closer in their evaluations. Approximately three of four are satisfied with their relationship with each other (MetLife, 2003). As a result of a poll of teachers and parents, Public Agenda (Farkas, Johnson, & Duffett, 1999) found that "parents say their child's teachers are accessible and caring, and teachers are more likely to be complimented, rather than criticized, by parents. At the same time, most teachers say that parental involvement at their school overall is either fair or poor. Parents agree that most parents need to be more involved in the child's education" (p. 9).

Families report that they are more involved in their child's education than their parents were, but they would like to do more. Urban teachers find that families are overwhelmed by personal problems. Suburban teachers say that the most common problem with families is the pressuring of children for good grades. The major conflict between families and teachers is around homework. Most teachers want parents to check their children's work, but most teachers don't think parents do it. Families, on the other hand, indicate that they monitor their children's homework, sometimes pushing the issue to the point of screaming. Some parents question whether all of the homework is actually necessary (Farkas et al., 1999). The differences in how parents and teachers view homework are explored in the Understanding & Using Evidence on page 114.

As you work with families, remember that the parents or guardians were the children's first teachers. They have the welfare of their children in mind when they push for services and attention to their children. In most cases, they are anxious to help their children do well in school and will support educators in that goal. Family involvement in schools and with teachers has proven to be an important variable in supporting student learning and successful school experiences. For students, it means "higher grades, test scores, and graduation rates; better school attendance; increased motivation, better self-esteem; lower rates of suspension; decreased use of drugs and alcohol; fewer instances of violent behavior; and greater enrollment in postsecondary education" (National PTA, 1998, p. 2). Family involvement contributes to better teacher morale, an increase in teacher effectiveness, improved job satisfaction, improved communications with families and students, and increased community support (National PTA, 1998). It also improves parents' relations with their children and teachers and improves their attitudes toward school and teachers (National PTA, 1998).

Understanding
& USING EVIDENCE

PARENTAL INVOLVEMENT IN HOMEWORK

Survey data can help educators think about their own practices and perspectives and test them against the perspectives of others. In a survey of parental involvement in schools, Public Agenda asked teachers to consider parental involvement in their children's homework. Parents were asked how they actually handled their children's homework. The following two tables show how the two groups responded.

	Teachers	
	What parents *should* do: (%)	What parents do: (%)
Check the work to make sure it was done and done correctly	57	10
Get involved in helping the student do the work	30	6
Ask the student if the work has been done and leave it at that	9	34
Leave it up to the student	2	44

Parents saying they have done the following:	%
Have had serious arguments with child where there was yelling or crying over schoolwork	50
Have walked away and let child deal with the consequences of not doing their schoolwork rather than dealing with child's constant stalling	49
Have done part of child's homework because it was too difficult for them or because they were too tired	22

Your Task: Surveys can help us understand how the perceptions of groups of people differ. As you examine the responses about homework from teachers and parents, what do you learn?

1. What do the tables tell you about the perceptions of teachers and parents regarding parental involvement in students' homework?

2. What other information do you wish you had about parental involvement?

3. Why do teachers think that parents are not assisting their children appropriately with their homework?

4. What do the data suggest about parent and teacher relationships and communication?

5. How might teachers be involved in improving parental support on homework assignments?

Refer to the **Understanding & Using Evidence Appendix** *at the end of the text for answers and information related to these activities.*

Source: Farkas, S., Johnson, J., & Duffett, A. (1999). *Playing their parts: Parents and teachers talk about parental involvement in public schools.* New York: Public Agenda.

Two sets of standards provide guidance as you think about working with families. The standards for new teachers by the Interstate New Teacher Assessment and Support Consortium (INTASC) expect teachers to work with families, communities, and other professionals for the purpose of helping students learn. The

Figure 3.5 INTASC Principle 10

The teacher fosters relationships with school colleagues, parents, and agencies in the larger community to support students' learning and well-being.

I. KNOWLEDGE

- The teacher understands how factors in the students' environment outside of school (e.g., family circumstances, community environments, health and economic conditions) may influence the students' life and learning.

II. DISPOSITIONS

- The teacher is willing to consult with other adults regarding the education and well-being of his or her students.

- The teacher is willing to work with other professionals to improve the overall learning environment for students.

III. PERFORMANCES

- The teacher makes links with the learners' other environments on behalf of students by consulting with parents, counselors, teachers of other classes and activities with the schools, and professionals in other community agencies.

- The teacher can identify and use community resources to foster student learning.

- The teacher establishes respectful and productive relationships with parents and guardians from diverse home and community situations, and seeks to develop cooperative partnerships in support of student learning and well being.

- The teacher talks with and listens to the student, is sensitive and responsive to clues of distress, investigates situations, and seeks outside help as needed and appropriate to remedy problems. The teacher acts as an advocate for students.

Source: Interstate New Teacher Assessment and Support Consortium. (1992). *Model standards for beginning teacher licensing, assessment, and development: A resource for state dialogue.* Washington, DC: Council of Chief States School Officers.

knowledge, dispositions, and skills expected of new teachers are outlined in Figure 3.5. The following National PTA Standards (1998) are written for families, but outline the key components of successful school-family relationships (p. 5):

1. Communicating—Communication between home and school is regular, two way, and meaningful.

2. Parenting—Parenting skills are promoted and supported.

3. Student learning—Parents play an integral role in assisting student learning.

4. Volunteering—Parents are welcome in the school and their support and assistance are sought.

5. School decision making and advocacy—Parents are full partners in the decisions that affect children and families.

6. Collaborating with community—Community resources are used to strengthen schools, families, and student learning.*

◄ *Excerpted with permission from National PTA, *National Standards for Parent/Family Involvement Programs: An Implementation Guide for School Communities* (Bloomington, IN: National Educational Service, 2004).

racism affecting the school's treatment of their children. They are able to focus solely on their children's experience in classrooms when they interact with teachers and other school officials (Lareau & Horvat, 2004).

Family involvement is related to better grades, higher test scores, better attendance, and fewer behavioral problems (Wallheiser, 2005, p. 30). Therefore, it is critical that you monitor your relationships with families to ensure that you are not privileging families from the same cultural groups as you. All families should have the same access to and support from teachers.

African American, Latino, and immigrant families have a history of discrimination in society and schools that makes them cautious of the treatment that their children receive. Many are distrustful of educators who do not seem to recognize that racism pervades their experiences. When they approach school officials, including teachers, they may be either extremely confronting or guarded. They may directly criticize educators, insinuating that their children are being discriminated against because they are African American or Latino or English language learners. They may even raise their voices as they make these accusations. Such behavior may not meet the school's standards of positive and supportive parents and are often rebuked or ignored by teachers and school administrators.

Family and Teacher Organizations   The relationship between families and schools is not always positive and supportive, especially when trust is lacking and families do not agree with the decisions being made about their children, the curriculum, or other school policies. Over time, families have allowed most of these decisions to be made by professional educators rather than parents. At the same time, most parents want to be involved in their children's education. They know that their children's education is not just the responsibility of schools. Most parents believe that what happens at home also affects student achievement. The problem is that many parents do not get involved in schools on their own, requiring educators to figure out how to involve them (Cutler, 2000).

One structured way of involving some parents is a parent-teacher organization. These groups began in the nineteenth century as local groups of mothers organized to support their children. The one that is most well-known today is the National PTA, which was founded in 1897 by Alice McLellan Birney and Phoebe Apperson Hearst as the National Congress of Mothers. The organization mounted efforts to create kindergarten classes, child labor laws, hot lunch programs, a juvenile justice system, and mandatory immunization (National PTA, 2005a). Anyone who is an advocate for students may join the National PTA. Local chapters can be found in many of the nation's schools with the goal of promoting partnerships between educators and families to advocate on behalf of children.

Relationship of Schools to the Community

The saying, "It takes a whole village to raise a child," applies to the communities in which schools are located. When the community cares about and is actively

Ed Lines

Family involvement in schools leads to higher grades, test scores, and graduation rates.
(National PTA, 2005)

involved in schools, they serve the community, families, and students well. According to the National PTA (1998), "when schools and communities work together, both are strengthened" (p. 20) in synergistic ways and make gains that outpace what either entity could accomplish on its own:

- Families access community resources more easily.
- Businesses connect education programs with the realities of the workplace.
- Seniors contribute wisdom and gain a greater sense of purpose.
- Students serve and learn beyond their school involvement.

Partnerships   The goal of school and community partnerships should be to improve the academic achievement and positive development of young people in the community. Partners should make an investment of time, money, people, and expertise as appropriate (Smith, 2005). Potential partners include businesses, the chamber of commerce, charitable organizations, churches, civic groups, foundations, local government, local media, museums, military groups, nonprofit associations, senior citizens, and youth groups. The partner provides support to schools in a number of ways, including assigning some employees or volunteers to work with the school, encouraging employees to assist teachers and administrators, and contributing equipment and other resources.

School and community partnerships should be two way: While the community contributes resources and expertise to schools, the school should help families know more about available resources in the community. Schools could distribute to families information about activities and agencies in the community. They could encourage community members besides parents and guardians to volunteer in schools. Finally, they could encourage both students and their families to be more involved in community service (National PTA, 1998).

Bringing the Community into the School   As a teacher, you could bring the community into your classroom in a number of ways. The parents and grandparents of your students can be excellent teachers of their own traditions and histories. You might consider asking a Muslim parent to explain to the class the meaning of Ramadhan or a Jewish parent to talk about Rosh Hashanah and Yom Kippur. Immigrant parents could talk about their country of origin and why they immigrated to the United States. Parents can be invited to talk about their jobs or a community project. Parents, of course, are not the only community resources. Grandparents, employees at local businesses, museum staff, and staff at community agencies have valuable information to share in classrooms. Public officials such as firefighters and police officers might be invited to talk about their roles, safety issues, or community involvement.

Field trips provide another opportunity to know the community. Many students don't have the opportunity to attend concerts or visit museums, fire stations, the zoo, or historical sites except through field trips. A school district should

Ed Lines

"Parents have become so convinced that educators know what is best for children that they forget that they themselves are really the experts." *Marian Wright Edelman*

have guidelines for selecting and conducting field trips. Families must be made aware of field trips and give permission for their children to participate.

Through school projects, students can learn to be involved in community projects that range from planting trees to cleaning up a park to assisting elderly people and young children. Students, especially older ones, might conduct research on a community need that could lead to action by a city council or state legislature. Some schools require students to provide community service by volunteering in a nursing home, child care center, nonprofit association, health clinic, or governmental agency. These projects help students understand their responsibility to the larger community.

Revisiting Janice Greer's Relationship with Parents

Janice Greer, the teacher at the beginning of this section, is well aware of the many ways to build a trusting relationship with the parents of her students and to create an open line of communication between the students' families and the classroom. She knows that family involvement is a strong indicator of a student's academic success. She encouraged parents to become involved by making them aware of her expectations for student academic progress, inviting them to participate in the class activities, and by making herself readily available to respond to parents' questions and concerns. Ms. Greer's dedication to her profession is evident in the effort she expended to help the parents become involved in their children's schooling.

Connecting
TO THE CLASSROOM

This chapter introduced you to public perceptions of schools and the importance of understanding the influence of culture on teaching and learning. Understanding communities and working with your students' families will be important in supporting learning. The following are some key principles for applying the information in this chapter to the classroom.

1. English proficiency is an attainable goal for all students.
2. Bilingual proficiency is desirable for all students.
3. Language and cultural diversity are assets in the teaching and learning process.
4. All students can achieve at high levels regardless of the structure of their families.
5. Teachers who are multicultural, bilingual, and bidialectal function effectively in a number of cultural groups.
6. Teachers cannot promote a religion in their classroom or any school activity.
7. Partnerships between teachers and families can improve the learning of students.

2. Observe a teacher-parent meeting and take notes about how the teacher prepared for the conference. Also record the questions that parents asked and your impressions of how effective the conference was. Analyze the conference and indicate the strengths and weaknesses of the interactions between the teacher and parent. Indicate any suggestions that you have for making the conference more effective.

Self-Assessment *What Am I Learning?*

How ready are you to teach in a classroom with English language learners? Using the following rubrics selected from the five standards domains of the Teachers of English to Speakers of Other Languages (TESOL), highlight the knowledge and skills that you currently possess in the three middle columns and give yourself a readiness score in the far right column. After completing the rubric, list the steps you need to take to be better prepared when you begin your first teaching job.

Performance Indicator	Approaches Standard (Rating = 1)	Meets Standard (Rating = 2)	Exceeds Standard (Rating = 3)	Score
3. Planning, Implementing and Managing Instruction Incorporates activities, tasks, and assignments that develop authentic uses of language, as students learn about content area material	Am aware of the need for authentic uses of language in ESL, and content-area learning and the need to design activities and assessments that incorporate both	Incorporates activities, tasks, and assignments that develop authentic uses of language, as students access content-area learning objectives	Designs authentic language tasks, as students access content-area learning objectives Collaborates with non-ESL classroom teachers to develop authentic uses of language and activities in content areas	
4. Assessment Demonstrates an understanding of the limitations of assessment situations and makes accommodations for ESOL students	Am aware of some of the limitations of assessment instruments for ESOL students	Accommodates for psychological situations (e.g., anxiety over timed tests with high-stakes consequences, limited experience with tests) Accommodates for cultural bias (e.g., unfamiliar images and references) Accommodates for linguistic bias (e.g., test translations, specific test formats) Uses L1* assessment results to determine language dominance	Evaluates formal and informal technology-based and nontechnology-based assessment measures for psychological, cultural, and linguistic limitations	

*L1 refers to a student's first language.
Source: Teachers of English to Speakers of Other Languages. (2003). *Standards for the accreditation of initial programs in P–12 ESL teacher education.* Washington, DC: Author.

Using the Web

1. To see the full report of the Phi Delta Kappan/ Gallup Poll, go to **www.pdkintl.org/kappan/ kpollpdf.htm**.

2. For a Spanish and English website for families and educators with resources for teaching English language learners, visit **www .colorincolorado.org/**.

3. Online professional development courses and resources for teachers in multilingual class-rooms can be found at **www.ncte.org/ profdev/online/colearntesol/108671.htm**.

4. For a discussion of regional, ethnic, and social dialects of education and curriculum materials from PBS's *Do You Speak American?*, visit **www .pbs.org/speak/education/**.

5. To see guidelines and resources for teachers on First Amendment freedoms, including the freedom of religion, go to **www .firstamendmentcenter.org/**.

Your Professional Library

Chang, J. (2004). *Family literacy nights: Building the circle of supporters within and beyond school for middle school English language learners*. Santa Cruz, CA: Center for Research on Education, Diversity & Excellence.

This report is based on a project with the families of low-performing Asian American English language learners. It includes practical strategies for school and family partnerships.

Dalle, T. S., & Young, L. L. (2003). *PACE yourself: A handbook for ESL Tutors*. Washington, DC: Teachers of English to Speakers of Other Languages.

This easy-to-follow guide for inexperienced tutors provides a structure and recommendations for teaching English language learners through English as a second language (ESL).

Haynes, C. C., & Thomas, O. (2001). *Finding common ground: A guide to religious liberty in public schools*. Nashville, TN: First Amendment Center.

This practical resource for teachers addresses contentious First Amendment issues in schools and related legalities. It includes guidance for teachers, sample policies, and other resources for the classroom.

Henderson, S. (2003). *Teaching about religion in public schools: Where do we go from here?* Nashville, TN: First Amendment Center and The Pew Forum on Religion and Education.

Leaders from diverse faiths discuss the teaching of religion in public schools. The discussion provides insights into interfaith respect for others.

National PTA. (2000). *Building successful partnerships: A guide to parent and family involvement*. Chicago: Author.

This guide for quality parent involvement in schools includes project ideas, survey forms, worksheets, and resources for involving parents.

National PTA. (1998). *National standards for parent/ family involvement programs*. Chicago: Author.

The six standards for family involvement in schools are described in detail in this booklet, which also includes suggestions for implementing the standards.

Shaikh, M. A. (Ed.). (1995). *Teaching about Islam and Muslims* (3rd ed.). Fountain Valley, CA: Council on Islamic Education.

This handbook for teachers introduces educators to Islam. It includes a useful guide to making appropriate and legal accommodations for the religious needs of Muslim students.

Short, D., & Boyson, B. A. (2004). *Creating access: Language and academic programs for secondary school newcomers*. Santa Cruz, CA: Center for Research on Education, Diversity & Excellence.

Practical strategies for working with new immigrant students in middle schools and high schools are the focus of this book.

ful, beautiful bulletin boards. They are nice—but I want to see children's work so that other children can see what good work looks like. I expect to see teachers engaged in learning with their children. I don't expect to see teachers sitting at their desks. I want them either working with small groups, or in front of the class if it is to model and present, and then get those questions going with children and conversations.

❖ *How do you know that a teacher has made a difference in student learning?*

We do a lot of testing. A lot of it, also, is seeing where the child started from. We do beginning-of-the-year assessments and we do running records for reading. I also look at attendance. If they are coming more than last year, then we are being successful with their parents or they are being more successful in their learning. If we see growth and we see their scores going up, then we know that we are making a difference. We look at the library. Are kids checking out a lot of books? Are they really engaged in reading? Then we know there is a difference in student learning and in that classroom. When kids bring their books to the cafeteria, you know learning is going on.

When I need a break and I want to see kids excited, I'll go into this one classroom. The kids are excited about what they are doing; they are telling me about what they are doing. I don't have to ask them. If I do ask, they are telling me this is what I have done, this is what I am doing, this is why I am doing it. These are 2nd graders. I know that teacher is making a difference in student learning. And they are improving!

It is one thing to love the kids, be sympathetic, and have the pobrecito syndrome ("my poor little thing")—but there is no learning going on and it has not made a difference in the kids. However, if I see reading improvement and math improvement, then I know the teacher is making a difference.

❖ What brings you joy in teaching?

I get excited when I see the kids get excited about their learning; seeing my teachers put into practice what they have been learning in training and making a difference in the classroom. Every day is new. Seeing the kids smiling and happy to be here. Seeing the teachers really work with their kids. When I see that 98 percent of my kids pass in reading, then I am really excited. When I sit with a team and I hear their conversations about student learning, I am excited. They are such a good team and working together.

❖ What do you expect a first-year teacher to know and be able to do?

Do they have a sense of teaching and can they reflect on that experience. Let me give an example: We were hiring a 4th grade teacher and were interviewing the three finalists. We asked each of them to teach a short model lesson to a small group of students. I was nervous about asking them to do this. When I put myself in the position of the new teacher, I would be concerned. I planned to put the person at ease. We provided the book, if they would come by and pick it up. We selected five kids who were not going to be challenges. It was not student behavior I was looking for, it was how the candidate interacted with the kids. After they had done their model teaching, I asked them, "What do you want to tell us about your teaching?"

One of them told us what her goal was and went through the whole thing. But then this teacher said, "After I have thought about it, I think I would change this in my presentation to the children. You know, I didn't have enough time to do this, but as I think about it . . . ." So even as she was teaching the small group, she was reflecting on what was working and what was not working. This is a teacher who was going to look at what was happening and instead of saying it is the kids, she is looking inside. What could I do differently? Those reflective teachers are the ones who are going to grow and make a difference.

Being able to ask for help is another big thing I look for. Not drowning, but knowing that it is OK to come and ask for help. Schools are big, and if you are drowning, and don't come and ask for help, then sometimes even with a mentor you will sink. Knowing that it is OK to say "I don't know enough about classroom management" is important.

❖ What are important themes in the organizational culture of your school?

A really big theme in our school is collaboration. When I talk about collaboration, it is the ability to be honest with each other and to help each other work together—instead of planning together and thinking we have to be best friends. That would be nice, but that is not what we are about. I want the teachers to know that this 1st grade child belongs to all of us, not just that 1st grade teacher. We all take responsibility for all children. It is everyone helping to move the campus forward. If one teacher doesn't show up, we split the kids among all the teachers. No extra pay, it is what we do. Student achievement and kids come first.

❖ How does teacher leadership come about in your school? Is there a leadership team?

Yes, we have a campus advisory council, which is mandated by the state. It is composed of six elected teachers, six parents, and community representatives. They work on the campus improvement plan and are the advisory council for the school. Then we have academic team managers. They lead weekly planning meetings with their teams. They volunteer and have to make a 2-year commitment. They must be really interested in working on aspects of the curriculum. Another leadership team is called the Nuts and Bolts. They do all the management, coordinating field trips, facilitating fund-raisers, and coordinating ordering of curriculum materials.

We also have instructional coaches. They represent different subject areas and are responsible for looking across grade levels. Currently, they are leading the development of team tests, which are being administered at each grade level. The results are shared across the school so that there is a vertical view of the curriculum and there is alignment and rigor in the expectations for student learning.

Questions to Consider

1. What do you know about the working relationship between teachers and their principal?
2. What was your reaction to Principal Diaz selecting round tables for students in her school, rather than individual desks?
3. In what ways do you see joy in teaching in Principal Diaz's school?
4. What would you expect to be the influences of the school district and state and federal governments on how Principal Diaz and her teachers do their jobs?

Becoming a successful teacher entails understanding teaching, standards, students, and parents. Becoming successful also requires beginning teachers to understand how schools are staffed, organized, financed, and the different ways that funds are spent. As is true for other types of businesses, schools are organizations comprised of employees who produce a product or service. To be successful, all organizations must organize the work and attend to the well-being of the workers. A unique characteristic of schools as organizations is that all of the workers are not paid a salary. Teachers, principals, custodians, cafeteria workers, and other adults receive paychecks. Students are workers too, but their "pay" is in a different form. Rather than receiving money, students are rewarded in other ways, including the joy of learning, the satisfaction of participation, feedback on assignments, grades, and ultimately earning a diploma.

Another special characteristic of schools as organizations is that the largest component of the labor force is composed of professionals: teachers. Professionals have higher levels of education and expect to have more autonomy in organizing and doing their work than would be acceptable for other types of workers. Professionals also expect to have strong input into how the whole school is organized and which tasks they will do. Because they are staffed by professionals, schools are unique organizations in many ways. The organizational structures, the degree of employee involvement in decision making, and the way schools are financed, as well as how the money is spent, are designed differently than would be true of a manufacturing business or a bank.

In this chapter, learning about schools as organizations is the topic. One way of understanding schools as organizations is learning about their structure. The role of teachers, principals, teacher leaders, and other personnel is described and charted. Schools should not be thought of as isolated and autonomous. Instead, schools are clustered into school districts. In addition, schools are accountable to their state and the federal government. Two other ways to understand schools as organizations are related to how schools are financed and how the money is spent. Each of these ways of understanding schools as workplaces is presented in this chapter. The final major section of this chapter will introduce a number of issues and implications of these different ways of understanding schools as the workplace for students and teachers.

Focus QUESTIONS

After reading this chapter, you should be able to answer the following questions:

1. Who has the final say about what happens in schools?

2. What are the most important functions of school districts and state government as they affect teachers?

3. In what ways is the federal government increasing its role and influence over schools?

4. Where does the money come from to pay for schools?

How Are Schools Staffed and Organized?

Tony Rodriguez is really enjoying his first year as a science teacher. He has been able to teach both freshman and advanced biology classes. One day in January when picking up his mail in the high school staff lounge, he discovers a note from Mr. Robinson, the principal: "Please see me at the end of school today." Tony briefly wonders what this is about, but immediately becomes consumed in preparing for the day's labs.

When Tony reports to Mr. Robinson at the end of the day, the principal states, "I hear that you have been talking with Dr. Johnson [assistant superintendent for curriculum] and requesting funds to buy more lab supplies."

Tony, "Yes, we need a number of items for . . . ."

Mr. Robinson, interrupting, says, "Young man, if you want to survive here, then from now on, you darn well better follow the chain of command. That is all."

Principals, assistant superintendents, and chains of command are examples of the concepts that are used to describe the organizational structure of schools. In the structural view, schools as organizations are defined in terms of roles, tasks, work responsibilities, and role relationships. In its purest form, the structural view of schools does not deal with workers' feelings and perceptions. Instead, the focus is entirely on the work at hand, who does what, and who is responsible.

Roles of Adult School Workers

Role differentiation is a key to understanding the organizational structure of schools. All of the adults do not do the same things. Instead, roles are defined in relation to the accomplishment of organizational tasks. The two key worker roles for the adults in schools are administrators and teachers. A number of other roles are important to know about, including resource teacher, counselor, secretary, and custodian. There are a number of additional roles that are officed outside of the school but that directly impact what teachers do; for example, school psychologists, coordinators of special programs such as those for English language learners (ELL), and school bus drivers.

Principal   The administrator with final authority over everything that goes on in a school is the principal. The principal is responsible for hiring and supervising all teachers and other school personnel. The principal is the person who is charged with the responsibility for evaluating all teachers, especially beginning teachers. Earlier in their careers, nearly all principals were teachers. Therefore, it is assumed that principals are experts in curriculum and instruction, as well as knowing about all of the other aspects of running a school organization. In addition, principals are in charge of discipline, enforcing rules of student behavior, and making sure that all of the employees and students obey all laws, statutes, policies, rules, and regulations. Principals also work with parents, community groups, and the various committees that are established for involving teachers, students, parents, and others in doing the work of the school.

Assistant and Vice Principals and Deans   As the brief summary of the principal's role suggests, the job expectations cover more areas and tasks than one person can do. The organizational structure solution to this problem has been to create another administrator role, that of assistant or vice principal. Depending on the size of the school, there may be one, two, or no assistant/vice principals. For example, elementary schools typically will need to have over six hundred students before they will have an assistant principal. As high schools increase in size from under one thousand to two or three thousand students, the number of vice principals will increase from one to three or more. Typically, the individuals in this role share in accomplishing the tasks that are formally the responsibility of the principal. Assistant/vice principals may evaluate teachers, although normally not probationary teachers. Assistant/vice principals may have full responsibility for certain tasks, such as discipline or managing the school's budgets. They also will assume authority for the school during times when the principal is out of the building. High schools will often have deans with specialized responsibility, such as student discipline.

Teachers   The other obvious role in the organizational structure of schools is that of teachers. Here, too, there is differentiation within the role. One form of differentiation is by the level of schooling where the teacher works. Elementary, junior high, and high school teachers are viewed as specialist within that level of schooling. There are other ways that the teacher role is differentiated. For example, elementary teachers are classified as primary (grades K/1–3) or intermediate (grades 4–5/6), while secondary teachers are either junior high (grades 6–8), middle school (grades 6–8/9), or senior high school (grades 9–12). Teachers also may specialize in other ways including:

- Subject(s) taught: Specializing in terms of subject(s) taught is the regular pattern in junior and senior high schools. For example, teachers are specialists in teaching mathematics, English, social studies, science, physical education, music, or technical areas.

- Types of students taught: Teacher roles may be specialized according to the needs of particular students such as resource teachers (for students with special needs), bilingual or ELL teachers for students whose first language is not English, and Title I teachers who teach students who are from low-income families and may be at risk of falling behind.

Department Chairs and Teacher Leaders   As schools have grown in size, another important role has developed: department chair and team/grade-level leader. The widespread staffing pattern in secondary schools is to have teachers organized into departments by subject matter. One of the teachers will serve as chair. At a minimum, this way of structuring work facilitates communication between teachers within the subject area. Typically, the department chairs will meet regularly with the principal and serve as a communication channel by passing on to teachers information that is received from the principal. In most schools, department chairs do not evaluate teachers; instead, their primary task is to facilitate communication and coordination of teacher work within the particular subject area. Department chairs also are important resources of ideas and assistance for new teachers. A similar coordination and communication role is assumed by grade-level teacher leaders in elementary schools.

Organization Charts

▶ **Organization chart.** A graphic depiction of the formal relationships between different roles and positions in an organization.

▶ **Line relationship.** Where one position in an organization has direct supervisory authority over another.

▶ **Staff relationships.** When one position does not have direct supervisory authority over another but there is an expectation that the two will communicate, coordinate, and work together.

An **organization chart** is a graphic that depicts the formal relationships between different roles and positions in a particular organization. The organizational structure of schools in terms of the defined roles, areas of responsibility, and authority is presented in Figure 4.1. A number of the important characteristics of organizational structure are represented in this type of chart. One that is very important for beginning teachers to understand is the difference between line and staff relationships. **Line relationships** are those in which one position has direct supervisory authority over another. In the organizational structure of schools, the principal is in a line relationship with all teachers, the assistant/vice principals, and all other school-based personnel. **Staff relationships** are those in which one position does not have direct authority over another but there is an expectation that the two positions will communicate, coordinate, and work together. For example, in secondary schools, there is a staff relationship between the various de-

Figure 4.1 School organization chart

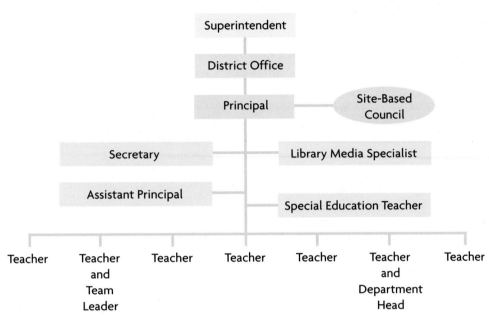

Adapted with permission from Johnson, J. A., Musial, D., Hall, G. E., Gollnick, D. M., & Dupuis, V. (2005). *Introduction to the foundations of American education* (13th ed.). Boston: Allyn and Bacon.

partment chairs, and in all schools, assistant/vice principals are in a staff relationship with teachers. Teachers are in staff relationships with other teachers.

Communication Is Important   One of the reasons schools are structured as they are is to facilitate communication. There is a continual risk that teachers will become isolated within their classroom, grade level, or department and not be aware of schoolwide needs and initiatives. The reverse risk also is very real; one teacher, a team, or a department may be doing something very wonderful but without communication, the rest of the organization does not learn about it. Two types of communication are built into the structure of the school organization chart: vertical and horizontal. **Vertical communication** is that which moves down, and up, the organization chart. This is where the phrase, "the lines of communication," comes from. An important responsibility of people in each role is to initiate and facilitate communication up and down the lines of authority. However, vertical communication is not sufficient; there also needs to be communication across the various levels in the organization chart—in other words, **horizontal communication**. One example of horizontal communication is when a veteran 4th grade teacher tells a first-year 4th grade teacher about an upcoming professional development workshop. Another example would be when a department chair tells another about an interesting idea that the principal proposed in an informal conversation. In schools that are more successful, there will be a greater amount of vertical and horizontal communication.

Vertical communication. The passing of information up and down the organization chart.

Horizontal communication. Passing information to others at the same level in the organization chart.

Teachers' Lounge

Lauren's Lip Gloss

As my 7th grade students entered for their sixth period math class, they began working on their warm-up problems. One of my students, Lauren, had a desk right next to mine.

"Lauren, I've got good news for you!" I exclaimed.

She looked at me a little puzzled and asked, "About lip gloss?"

Now she had me confused. "Lip gloss? What about lip gloss?" I asked. "Lauren, I have good news about your geometry test." I explained.

Still puzzled, she continued to question me, "Geometry test? Did we take a geometry test?"

"Yes, Lauren, you took a geometry test," I replied.

"Are you sure?" she asked again.

"Yes, I'm sure; I graded 160 tests," I replied.

Still confused, Lauren probed even further, "We really took a test? Was I here that day? What day did we take it?"

I finally gave up and handed her test to her. "Yes, you really took a test on Wednesday and you were here."

Go figure: She had gotten 100 percent on the test.

● Tracy Schroeder
8th grade mathematics teacher
Canarelli Middle School, Las Vegas, Nevada

Chain of Command   Tony's story at the beginning of this section illustrates a mistake that many new members of organizations make. Using the ideas about organization structure that have been introduced, we can now analyze the mistake made by first-year teacher Tony Rodriguez. When Principal Robinson referred to the chain of command, he was talking about line authority and vertical communication. **Chain of command** refers to the process of having information passing up and down the line of authority without skipping a level. Look once again at Figure 4.1. Note that there is a line of authority connecting the principal to the superintendent. This means that the principal reports to and is evaluated by the superintendent. When beginning teacher Rodriguez did not tell the principal that he had talked with the assistant superintendent, he failed to understand at least two significant consequences of line relationships and organization structure. Failure 1: Whenever an assistant superintendent hears about something going on in a school, there is a high likelihood that he or she will talk with the principal about it. Failure 2: Principals like to know when one of their teachers is going to or has talked with their supervisor. When the principal finds out after the fact, they may develop concerns about the possibility that their supervisor might conclude that they are not "on top" of what is going on in the school. At the very least, it leaves

▶ **Chain of command.** The uninterrupted linkage of line positions from top to bottom in an organization chart.

Although the principal has final authority, teachers assume major responsibility for tasks, including school improvement planning. Will you be ready to help accomplish some of these tasks?

the principal in the position of not being able to support the request for more funds for lab supplies because he or she knew nothing about it.

Variations in School Staffing Patterns

To this point, the description of the organizational structure of schools has been based in how most schools are organized. There are many interesting variations to consider, some of which are presented next.

Variations in Teacher Roles   There are many variations in the assignments of teachers. For example, the intermediate grades in elementary schools can be "departmentalized." Instead of each teacher being responsible for one group of 25 to 35 students for all subjects, teachers will specialize by teaching one subject to all the students at a particular grade level. For example, one 6th grade teacher teaches mathematics, while another teaches social studies and another specializes in literacy. A variation on this staffing model is to have one teacher lead in the preparation of the instruction, and each teacher then uses the same lesson plan and materials to teach his or her class.

Looping   An interesting staffing variation used in some elementary, junior high, and middle schools is looping. In **looping**, teachers follow their students to the next grade. For example, the teacher of a 1st grade class one year moves to teaching 2nd grade the next year and keeps the same students. An obvious advantage is that the teacher knows the students and the students know the teacher which means less time loss to diagnostic assessments at the beginning of the year. Of course, looping also requires teachers to develop new preparations for use in the second year.

Looping. A staffing arrangement that has teacher assignment move with their class to the next grade level.

Team Teaching   **Team teaching** is a staffing plan that has two or more teachers working together to plan and teach a common group of students. Team teaching is used in many configurations in both elementary and secondary schools. In some schools, two to four teachers are assigned a large block of students and they are responsible for all of the instruction all day. This configuration is frequently applied in elementary schools. It also is used in middle schools that are using interdisciplinary curriculum. A frequent variation on this approach is to have teachers team for part of the day and for the remainder of the day each teacher teaches their "own" students. The organizational support of teachers to team will vary, too. In some schools, teams have to do their planning before and after school. In other schools, there will be a scheduled team planning period. In others, there will be an "early release," which means that on certain days students leave school early in order to provide time for teacher teams to plan.

Organizing Student Workers

Organizing the adults in the school seems relatively easy in comparison to organizing the students. A variety of organizational structures, methods, and groupings have been tried. (For many of these structures, there are continuing debates about their effectiveness.) Curiously, some of the structures seem to have become fixed in concrete. Think about it: What is the first step in organizing school students for doing their work? What characteristic of students is determined first in deciding their placement? This characteristic of students is not used in any other type of organization as the basis for organizing the workers. It is their age! Students cannot begin schooling until they have passed a certain birthday. Students cannot leave school until they have reached a particular birthday. At its simplest, grade levels are groupings of students by their age. There are a number of additional considerations and variations in the ways that students are organized to do their work.

Team teaching. A staffing pattern in which two or more teachers jointly plan and teach a group of students.

Self-contained classroom. An assignment where a teacher is responsible for a class of students for the whole day.

Self-Contained Classrooms   In most settings, **self-contained classroom** means that one teacher stays in a classroom and is assigned responsibility for teaching all subjects to one set of students. The self-contained classroom continues to be the dominant structure for U.S. elementary schools. However, an interesting variation on the meaning of self-contained classroom is being tested in some high schools in New York City. In this variation, the students stay in one classroom and the teachers change rooms. This variation seems to be reducing the isolation that so many students experience in high schools, especially those with thousands of students.

Organizing Students for Work   Continuing the use of the metaphor of students as workers leads to an examination of how they can be organized for learning. Table 4.1 presents a brief summary of the range of ways that students can be grouped. At different times in your career as a student in schools, you will have experienced each one of these and probably prefer some ways over others. Each of these ways carries important consequences for the teacher, as well as for student learning. For example, presenting a lecture to the whole class provides the teacher with a way to "cover" the content, but brings with it very limited opportunities to check for individual student understanding. As another example, consider the different ways of

Table 4.1 Ways of Organizing Students to Do Their Work

Structure	Description	Advantages	Teacher Challenge
Whole Class	Students taught as a single intact group	Lesson presented at the same time to all students	Difficult to address individual differences in understanding
Small Groups	Typically three to five students per group	More opportunity for each student to participate	Some students may do most of the work, difficult to determine each student's effort
Dyads/Pairs	Two students work together	Each student has opportunity to participate	Managing and monitoring all dyads at the same time
Individuals	Each students does own work without dialogue with others	Each student learns at own rate	Managing and monitoring all students at the same time
Homogeneous	Grouping like students together	Students progress at same rate	Risk of labeling and neglecting "fast" and "slow" groups
Heterogeneous	Groups composed of mixed levels	Helps all students learn	"Slow" or "fast" students may be neglected
Stable	Keeping the same students together over extended time	Students and teachers know what to expect	Some students may dominate; others may not do their share
Flexible	Routinely changing group membership	Provides fresh opportunities	Monitoring to be sure that certain students do not stay together
Cooperative	Organized process in which each group member has a prescribed role (e.g., facilitator and note taker)	Students learn roles for facilitating group work; some research suggests students learn more	Students have to be trained in doing roles

organizing small groups. The teacher role is changed dramatically from being a dispenser of information, or directions, to a monitor and facilitator of group work. Each time a lesson is planned, the teacher has to decide how the student workers will be organized. Table 4.1 will be of help in thinking about this important element of teaching. Also see the Challenging Assumptions on page 140.

Revisiting the Tony Rodriguez Dilemma

Tony's reaction was:

Geez! I had no idea that telling the principal that I met with Dr. Johnson [assistant superintendent] was so important. Now, I can see that from his point of view Mr. Robinson felt that he was being blindsided. I didn't mean anything; I was just advocating for my students. But, next time I will be sure to let my principal know beforehand if I am going to be seeing a central office administrator, and I sure will tell them later if it happens by chance.

Challenging Assumptions
FINDINGS FROM RESEARCH

Student grouping: Which is best—tracking or mixed ability?

The Assumption: Teachers, parents, school leaders, and policy makers have long debated which is best—homogenous or heterogeneous grouping of students? The debate can focus on what a teacher should do in grouping students for a day's lessons or how students should be grouped for an entire school year. When students are grouped according to ability for a semester or longer, it is called tracking.

What is your current position about this important question? Do you believe that students will make greater progress if they are placed with like students so that all can move at the same pace? Or, do you believe that students can learn from each other and that it is not fair to label some as being in the "slow" group?

Study Findings: Although there have been literally hundreds of studies, there still are no definitive answers, but a set of subquestions have become clear:

1. In which grouping pattern do students learn more?

2. What difference does grouping patterns make in students' attitudes about learning and self-perceptions?

3. What difference do teachers make in determining the effects of grouping arrangements?

Two decades ago, Oakes (1985) and Slavin (1987) argued for all students being placed in heterogeneous classes. A main theme in their position is that a democratic ideal is not to create different categories of people and there needs to be equal opportunity for all students. They also reported that there was no clear pattern of gains in student learning with homogeneous grouping.

The grouping question is so important that it is a continuing topic of inquiry in other countries

and is a component of the Trends in International Mathematics and Science Study (TIMSS) research as well. For example, in a recent study of grouping of 5th and 8th grade students in Canada, Shields (2002) reported that the academically talented self-contained classes had higher student achievement. However, there was "considerable overlap (from 46%–88%) in the scores of the two groups." In other words, students in both the gifted and heterogeneous classes were achieving. (An important contextual factor to keep in mind is that Canada has offered self-contained programs for elementary school academically able students since 1934.)

Although the findings about perceptions and attitudes were more complicated, Shields concluded:

> These data do not suggest that the needs of all students would be better served if they had all been grouped in a single heterogeneous class; rather, in this study, homogeneous grouping for academically talented and gifted students was associated with positive student perceptions of themselves as learners and of their total school experience. Likewise, students placed in a heterogeneous classroom demonstrated similarly positive attitudes and perceptions.

Implications: Across the many studies of student grouping, a key factor that is emerging as probably the most significant is that of the teacher's attitudes and teaching approach. When the teacher sets high expectations for learning and presents all students with the same curriculum, students learn in either grouping arrangement. Student attitudes and perceptions can be positive in either grouping arrangement; again, dependent on the teacher's attitudes and expectations. Still, much of the research indicates that placing more able students in a homogeneous group advances their level of achievement while not diminishing other students having success in heterogeneous groups.

Sources: Oakes, J. (1985). *Keeping track: How schools structure inequality*. New Haven, CT: Yale University Press; Shields, C. M. (2002, Spring). A comparison study of student attitudes and perceptions in homogeneous and heterogeneous classrooms. *Roeper Review, 24*(3), 115; Slavin, R. E. (1987). Ability grouping and student achievement in elementary schools: A best-evidence synthesis. *Review of Educational Research, 57*, 347–370.

141

What Is the
Relationship of Schools
to School Districts
and the State?

In most schools there is a sense of collegiality, shared effort, and mutual support. What indicators can you use to get a read on a school's organizational cimate?

What Is the Relationship of Schools to School Districts and the State?

*Even though he was only a first-year teacher, word quickly spread about how ef-fective **Jeff Shih** was in teaching mathematics. The joy of learning was alive with all of the students in his classes and they were doing well on the various assess-ments that Jeff used and in the district and state testing. By the middle of the year, many of his teacher colleagues were seeking him out for ideas about inter-esting ways to assess student learning.*

In late January, he received a phone call from the district mathematics co-ordinator! Jeff did not know this person or what her role was, but when asked, he agreed to serve on a district curriculum committee and to offer a district-wide workshop the following August. As he attended the curriculum committee meetings that took place at the district office, he discovered that there were a surprisingly large number of people doing a wide variety of tasks in the "head shed." At first the unfamiliar position titles did not make sense, but gradually he discovered that most of these people were bright and very hard working, and that each had an important role that in some way was designed to support him as a teacher, his students, and his school. However, it did take him quite some time to figure out who was responsible for what and why. Just as he had the district figured out, Maria Jones from the state education department called and asked him to make a presentation to the state board of education, which Jeff had never heard of.

Teachers and the Law

Two areas of law relating to school organization and finance that are particularly important for future teachers to understand are those that address discrimination in employment and the judgments from the many recent court cases relating to taxation and budgeting of public schools. That discrimination in the workplace is not to be tolerated has been addressed in the U.S. Constitution and through federal statutes. The U.S. Supreme Court has accepted using local property taxes as a source of funds for schools. In recent years, more than 40 states have had lawsuits related to questions of equity and adequacy in the distribution of funding to local school districts.

DISCRIMINATION

Do teachers and students have protection against discrimination?

Yes. The first source in addressing this question, as for any legal question, is the U.S. Constitution. As has been described in this chapter, the Equal Protection and Due Process Clauses in the Fourteenth Amendment are fundamental for answering any question of discrimination. There also are a number of federal statutes, with the Civil Rights of Act of 1964 being the most fundamental effort to prohibit discrimination. Title VII is the section of the Civil Rights Act that addresses discrimination in the work-

place. The following excerpts make it clear that discrimination in the workplace is not allowed:

Section 703

(a) It shall be an unlawful employment practice for an employer

(1) to . . . discriminate against any individual with respect to his compensation, terms, conditions, or privileges of employment, because of such individual's race, color, religion, sex, or national origin; or

(2) to limit, segregate, or classify his employees or applicants for employment in any way which would deprive or tend to deprive any individual of employment opportunities or otherwise adversely affect his status as an employee, because of such individual's race, color, religion, sex, or national origin.

. . .

Section 706

(g) If the court finds that the [employer] has intentionally engaged in . . . an unlawful employment practice . . . the court . . . may order such affirmative action as may be appropriate.

What about sex discrimination in selection of principals and specialty positions where there is greater responsibility and extra pay?

No. In *Marshall v. Kirkland* (U.S. Court of Appeals, Eighth Circuit, 1979 602 F.2d 1282), the school district was not supported in its argument that men were better qualified for all of the administrative and specialty positions that included an increment

---

▶ **Local education agency (LEA).** A school district or regional clustering of public schools.

▶ **State education agency (SEA).** Each state's department of education.

Schools are not isolated and autonomous organizations. Instead, schools are clustered to form school districts, also called **local education agencies (LEAs).** The primary factor for determining an LEA is geography. School districts typically encompass all of the public schools within a certain area such as a town or city. In a few states, such as Nevada and Florida, the geographic area of the school districts is the same as for the counties. All of the schools and school districts within each state are accountable to the state. Each state has a state department of education, also called the **state education agency (SEA).** The SEA is the oversight authority for all K–12 education, public and private, within the state. Also see the Teachers and the Law above.

Organization of School Districts

Mapping the geographic area covered by a school district is one way of understanding its size. Another is the levels of schooling that are covered. For example,

of pay, except for home economics and girls' physical education.

Is it legal for school districts to have policies mandating leave at a particular time in a pregnancy and rules related to reemployment after delivery?

No. In *Cleveland Board of Education v. La Fleur*, 414 U.S. 632 (1974), the Court ruled that specifying the number of months in anticipation of childbirth violated the Due Process Clause of the 14th Amendment.

Is it legal to wear religious garb or dress as a public school teacher?

No. A number of states have statutes that expressly prohibit the wearing of religious garb. "Garb" includes dress, markings, emblems, and insignia indicating a teacher's membership in a religious order or sect. For example, see *United States v. Board of Education for the School District of Philadelphia*, 911 F.2d 882 (3rd Cir. 1990).

Is it legal for schools to distribute condoms in an effort to reduce student pregnancy and the spread of AIDS?

Yes. The spread of sexually transmitted disease and AIDS/HIV are of increasing concern, especially with students in grades 7 through 12. In response, some schools have made condoms available to students who request them. The courts have ruled that these programs do not violate parental privacy rights and that parents do not have the right to expect schools to tailor programs to meet their individual religious or moral preferences. See *Curtis v. School Committee of Falmouth*, 652 N.E. 2d 580 (Mass. 1995); *Parents United for Better Schools, Inc. v. School District of Philadelphia*, 148 F.3d 260 (3rd Cir. 1998).

FINANCE

What about using local property taxes to fund schools? Some communities are richer than others. Is this legal?

Yes. In a five-to-four decision, the U.S. Supreme Court ruled that although not perfect, it is permissible to fund public education with local property taxes. See *San Antonio Independent School District v. Rodriguez*, 1973 411 U.S. 1.

But what about issues of equity and adequacy?

A short drive around any city will quickly reveal that the "rich" suburbs have better and newer schools than the urban areas. When property taxes are used locally to fund schools, there can be very obvious differences in equity and adequacy, which is what the 40-plus states with school finance lawsuits have been addressing. For example, in California, the state supreme court ruled that the quality of a child's education should not be based on the wealth of the local community; instead, it should be based in the wealth of the state. Further, the state has the responsibility to demonstrate that the plan for financing all local schools meets the Court's standard of "fiscal neutrality." See *Serrano v. Priest*, 487 P.2d 1241 (Cal. 1971) (Serrano I).

Source: LaMorte, M. W. (2002). *School law cases and concepts* (7th ed.). Boston: Allyn and Bacon.

most school districts encompass all elementary and secondary schools within a certain geographic area. However, in some states, such as Arizona, some school districts are responsible for elementary schools only. A separate school district will be responsible for the secondary schools. Another way to understand the size of a school district is to discover the number of schools within the school district. Extremely small districts may have as few as one or two schools. The largest school districts will have two hundred or more schools.

An organization chart for a typical school district is presented in Figure 4.2. One of the first impressions from studying this chart should be the fact that there are many roles and functions that are not directly related to teaching and learning. As is true for organizations in business and industry, a number of support functions must be addressed and staffed. Personnel are needed to hire employees, see that they are paid, and see that they have health and retirement programs (benefits). Organizations need specialists to manage and audit the budgets. (School

Figure 4.2 School district organization chart

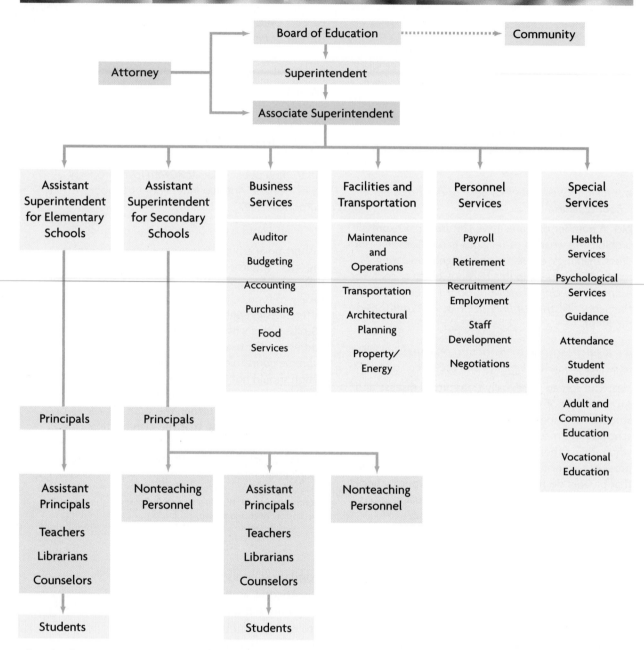

Adapted with permission from Parkay, F. W., & Stanford, B. H. (2004). *Becoming a teacher* (6th ed.). Boston: Allyn and Bacon.

districts will have annual budgets in the millions of dollars.) There also will be a maintenance department for buildings, grounds, and transportation.

A number of functions are unique to schooling including the various special services for students and their families. Of course, the instructional support func-

145

What Is the
Relationship of Schools
to School Districts
and the State?

tion must be staffed as well. A function that has grown significantly in importance is the research and evaluation office. With the current heavy focus on testing, experts are needed to organize and analyze test data. As never before, teachers, administrators, parents, policy makers, and the public are demanding quick turnaround and understandable reporting of data about student achievement.

School District Superintendent   The chief executive officer (CEO) of the school district is the **superintendent**. This person has the overwhelming responsibility of leading the entire school district. As is reflected in the organization chart (Figure 4.2), all of the district office and school personnel are in a line relationship with the superintendent. As President Harry Truman was known to say, "The buck stops here." In the end, the superintendent is accountable for everything that happens, should happen, and should not happen within the school district. In a large school district with many layers to the organization chart, holding the superintendent responsible for everything is very unrealistic; however, in the structural view of organizations that is the reality.

Superintendent. The top executive who has overall line authority and responsibility for a school district.

Most superintendents are appointed and will have a contract for 1 to 3 years. There are some exceptions, such as occurs in Florida, Indiana, and a few other states where some superintendents are elected through a communitywide vote. One of the consequences of their being elected is that the individual may not have any background in education either as a teacher or administrator. In some cities, the superintendent is appointed by the mayor.

Superintendents do not have tenure in the position and may be removed at any time. One unfortunate consequence of this fact is that there is a large turnover in the superintendency each year. Some years, a state will have one-third or more of the school district superintendents change. In urban school districts, the

Parents and other citizens can be very active in making their views known to their school board. How would you react if a parent or community member threatened to take a complaint to the school board?

average longevity of superintendents is under 3 years. One important consequence of this rapid turnover is that with the arrival of each new superintendent, the strategic directions and priorities within the school district change. One direct consequence is that district and school administrators, as well as teachers and families, are unable to develop and sustain initiatives and directions across the 3 to 5 to 8 years it takes to make meaningful changes. This places significantly heavier responsibility on principals and teachers to maintain a focus on the most essential long-term efforts that will benefit students the most.

► **School board.** The local committee, normally elected, that has been granted authority by the state for oversight of policy and operation of a school district.

► **Policy.** Formal statements that specify for an organization what can and cannot be done.

► **Prescriptive policy.** Formal statements that identify a target and that specify how personnel are to achieve that end.

► **Empowering policy.** Formal statements that set targets for action but leave open who personnel are to approach achieving the end.

School Boards   The school district governing body is the **school board**. School boards typically consist of 5 to 11 members. (The reasoning behind having an odd number of members is to reduce the chance of having tie votes by the board.) In most communities, school board members are elected by voters in a designated geographic part of the community or by the community at large. In some cities, such as Chicago and Hartford, Connecticut, the mayor or the city council will appoint some or all of the school board.

Downey (1988) identified two major obligations of school boards:

1. To process the values, needs, and demands of society and, in so doing, to determine which of these are to be accepted as the official guidelines for the educational system

2. To set the guidelines for action which are, in effect, the directions or general rules for the operation of the school system (p. 18)

The primary role of school boards and other governing bodies is to establish policy.

Policy   **Policy** is a guideline for action. Policies can be **prescriptive** by setting limits and specifying the procedures that are to be used, or they can be **empowering** by identifying the target or vision and leaving open the means for achieving the desired end. For example, a school board could set in policy that the school district should achieve a 10-point increase in the percentage of high school graduates that go on to some type of postsecondary education. This would be an empowering policy; district administrators and teachers would be expected to devise the steps to be taken to achieve the goal. If the school board established a prescriptive policy, they would specify the approach to be used, such as "no-pass/no-play policy for athletics" or that all students would be required to take algebra I. With prescriptive policies, administrators and teachers have little or no say in the strategies to be used and instead are charged with implementing the policy mandate.

Many consequences are derived directly from policies whether they are empowering or prescriptive. For example, administrators and teachers as education professionals believe they know which approaches are best. Therefore, they do not like prescriptive polices. On the other side, school board members are uncomfort-

Ed Lines

Connecticut's Beginning Educator Support and Training (BEST) Program provides useful standards and rubrics for assessing beginning teachers.

147

What Is the
Relationship of Schools
to School Districts
and the State?

able with leaving the selection of the approach open ended. They see themselves as accountable for making clear which steps should be taken.

School Board Responsibilities   One of the most important school board responsibilities is hiring the superintendent. Another is approving the employment of all district personnel, including teachers. Beginning teachers will turn in their signed employment contract to the district office of human resources, but the contract is not official until it has been approved by the school board. School boards are responsible for the oversight of all administrative and educational matters, including review and approval of the district budget, large purchase orders, trip travel support for student groups such as choir or band, and review of test scores. Boards also evaluate the performance of the superintendent. In the ideal setting, the board will turn to the superintendent, as the CEO, to lead the day-to-day operations of the district. Unfortunately, in too many districts, school board members are not satisfied with limiting their role to establishing policy and oversight of district operations. Many board members seem to be most interested in pushing a pet agenda, such as a particular curriculum approach or trying to "get" a particular district employee. Many boards also have a tendency to become overly involved in the day-to-day operations of the district (**micromanaging**). This is a significant contributing factor to the high rate of superintendent turnover.

Micromanaging. To closely supervise, control, and/or direct the work of others.

Organization of Education at the State Level

In the distant past, the governance of schools was primarily a matter of local interest. School boards set most policies and obtained financial support locally. In the last 50 years, much of the control has shifted to the states. This shift has come about, in part, because the funding of public schools is a very large part of state budgets. Also, state policy makers have a right to take an active interest in education. In fact, all states have laws related to the responsibility of the state to assure that all citizens have access to education. For example:

Arkansas
Intelligence and virtue being the safeguards of liberty and the bulwark of a free and good government, the State shall ever maintain a general, suitable and efficient system of free public schools and shall adopt all suitable means to secure to the people the advantages and opportunities of education. . . . Arkansas, State Constitution, Article 14, Education, Section 1, Free school system.

California
The Legislature shall provide for a system of common schools by which a free school shall be kept up and supported in each district at least six months in every year, after the first year in which a school has been established. California Constitution, Article 9, Education, Section 5.

Ed Lines

There were more than 3.5 million teachers in the 2005–06 school year. *(National Center for Education Statistics)*

Vermont

The right to public education is integral to Vermont's constitutional form of government and its guarantees of political and civil rights. Further, the right to education is fundamental for the success of Vermont's children in a rapidly changing society and global marketplace as well as for the state's own economic and social prosperity. To keep Vermont's democracy competitive and thriving, Vermont students must be afforded substantially equal access to a quality basic education. However, one of the strengths of Vermont's education system lies in its rich diversity and the ability for each local school district to adapt its educational program to local needs and desires. Therefore, it is the policy of the state that all Vermont children will be afforded educational opportunities which are substantially equal although educational program may vary form district to district. (Vermont: Added 1997, No. 60, §2, eff. June 26, 1997)

Today, all three branches of state government—legislative, administrative, and judicial—are extremely active when it comes to public education. Figure 4.3 is an organization chart for state government.

Figure 4.3 Organization chart for state government

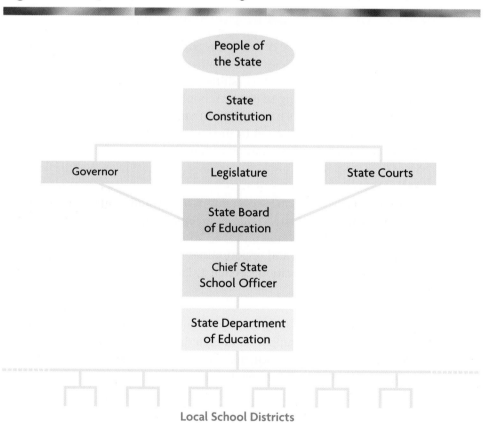

Adapted with permission from Johnson, J. A., Musial, D., Hall, G. E., Gollnick, D. M., & Dupuis, V. (2005). *Introduction to the foundations of American education* (13th ed.). Boston: Allyn and Bacon.

State Governors Because citizens are concerned about the quality of schools and the costs of education, it is logical that political leaders would be attending to education problems and needs. The phrase "education governor" is being applied so frequently that is becoming a cliché. However, being an education governor is good politics. For example, the last two presidents of the United States, Bill Clinton and George W. Bush, previously were governors who launched major education initiatives in their states.

State legislatures have the primary responsibility for financing public education and setting its priorities. What are the education priorities for the legislature in your state?

Governors are able to establish aspirations and vision for a state's education system. In some states, they have a major say over the state budget and in all states can propose changes in state policies that they believe will improve schools. In some states, the governor appoints members of the state board of education and/or the state superintendent. In other states, the legislature may appoint or will need to approve appointment of the state superintendent and state board members.

State Legislatures The primary policy-making body for education is the state legislature. State legislatures can create new education policies in any area from student discipline to curriculum to standards for hiring teachers and administrators. A significant responsibility of state legislatures is to establish the state budget for education, which necessarily is linked to state sources of funds such as income and sales taxes. Within whatever limits have been set by a state's constitution, the legislature can prescribe what the state board of education and other education agencies can and should do.

State Board of Education State boards of education have become very important bodies. As the legislators and governors have become more engaged with education issues, the state boards of education have been given more authority and charged with greater responsibilities. The state board and the staff of the state education department must ensure that all school districts and schools are performing in compliance with state policies and statutes. Other responsibilities include setting standards for teacher licensure, establishing processes for developing and approving curriculum standards, and organizing test data and other data from schools in order to prepare reports about school and student performance for the legislature, the public, and the federal government. State boards also are the body to review cases of teacher malpractice and the revocation of teacher licenses. Most state board members are either elected or appointed by the governor.

Chief State School Officer   The chief state school officer, state superintendent of public instruction, or commissioner of education is the CEO for the state board of education. This person is responsible for supervision of the staff and work of the state education department. They also play a key leadership and advocacy role for education with the legislature, the governor, school districts, and the state. In some states, these "chiefs" are elected at-large; in others, they are appointed by the state board of education or the governor.

State Courts   As the cost of public education has increased and as concerns about the adequacy of school have increased, the courts have become more instrumental in shaping the directions of education. In the past, the courts mainly addressed contractual issues and made determinations about the rights of students. In the last 15 years, state courts have been asked to address issues of funding adequacy and equity. In fact, some 38 states have had, or have, lawsuits related to the funding of the schools working their way through state judicial systems.

The precedent-setting case was filed in the 1980s in Kentucky. Using the wording in the Kentucky Constitution, the state supreme court ruled in *Rose v. Council for Better Education* 1989 that the entire system of public education in Kentucky was "inadequate." Going even further, the court ruled that the entire system and organization of the State Education Agency (SEA) and the Local Education Agencies (LEA) was "unconstitutional." The court then directed the governor and the legislature to develop a new system of education. The result was the Kentucky Education Reform Act (KERA), which was passed in 1990. KERA mandated a number of important reforms including integrated primary, school-based management councils, major changes in high schools, and a system of annual standardized testing of students. Since then, a number of other states including Arkansas, Kansas, Ohio, and New York have had state courts review and rule on the quality and adequacy of the state's education system. However, to date no other state has been as ambitious in its attempts to redress past inadequacies and to implement dramatic changes in practice.

Revisiting Jeff Shih, the Mathematics Teacher

In the anecdote presented at the beginning of this section, a successful first-year mathematics teacher, Jeff Shih, was asked by the district math coordinator to participate on a district committee and to present at a teacher workshop the following summer. He also was contacted by the state education department mathematics coordinator. Although Jeff was not fully understanding of the different organizational levels and roles both at the district and state level, they had heard about him. This is an example of the importance of horizontal and vertical communication. Through some sort of communication path(s) beginning with his principal or fellow teachers, word was spreading about his successes. The first moral of this story is that communication is important. The second moral has to do with line and staff

Ed Lines

151

What Is the Role of
the Federal
Government in
Public Schools?

relationships. Neither of the mathematics coordinators were in a line relationship with Jeff; theirs are staff relationships. In an organization of professionals, all communication does not need to follow the chain of command. Of course, Jeff should remember to tell his principal about the calls and opportunities. The upcoming experiences will allow this beginning teacher to learn very early in his teaching career about the important roles of LEA and SEA curriculum staff. They play key roles in supporting curriculum selections and teacher professional development at the district and state levels. These opportunities will also bring additional joy to Jeff's teaching through sharing with and learning from colleagues.

What Is the Role of the Federal Government in Public Schools?

Sara Sandefur is a dedicated and excited first-year teacher. As is typical in most school districts, Sara's first teaching assignment was in an at-risk school. Most of the children were eligible for free or reduced lunch, and many were just beginning to learn English. Sara was prepared and ready to teach all of these students. What came as a surprise was that the school had been labeled a "school in need of improvement." The newspaper headlined her school as low performing and in the article described how much lower the test scores were in comparison to other schools within the district and from around the state. As if this was not bad enough, a number of experts, consultants, and "turnaround specialist" were in the school constantly. All of the teachers had to attend workshops, and student test scores were watched very closely. The principal always seemed worried and preoccupied.

As Sara asked what all of this meant, she was told that it was one of the mandates from the No Child Left Behind (NCLB) act and the state had no choice but to intervene.

For any level of government, the role and authority of all bodies—executive, legislative, and judicial—is derived from what is stated in the related constitution. As was just described, each state's constitution sets the beginning expectations for education. Curiously, the U.S. Constitution includes no statements about expectations or responsibility for education. Through interpretation of what is said, the states have been assigned responsibility for education. However, over the last 50 years, the federal government has increasingly become engaged with and increasingly directive about what states, school districts, and schools should be doing.

The U.S. Constitution and the Responsibility for Education

The U.S. Constitution is composed of six articles. Shortly after it was approved, the Bill of Rights was added. The Constitution itself has been stable over time. However, over the last two centuries, 26 amendments have been added. As is

Ed Lines

There were 95,726 public elementary and secondary schools in the United States in the 2003–04 school year. *(National Center for Education Statistics)*

frequently stated, the U.S. Constitution is "the law of the land." All other laws, statutes, each state's constitution, and the actions of governments at all levels must be consonant with the U.S. Constitution. Because the Constitution does not directly address education or schooling, several of its amendments have been interpreted by the U.S. Supreme Court and various governing bodies in ways that assign responsibility to the states. The Tenth Amendment is the key.

The Tenth Amendment: Grants Responsibility to the States   The Tenth Amendment was adopted in 1791 in order to make clear that the civil rights of citizens would be protected against state actions. The Bill of Rights protected citizens against actions of the federal government, but not necessarily a state's. The Tenth Amendment is:

> The powers not delegated to the United States by the Constitution, nor prohibited by it to the States, are reserved to the States respectively, or to the people.

Because education is not mentioned in the U.S. Constitution it is reserved to the states. As was illustrated in the earlier section of this chapter, each state's constitution in some way assumes responsibility and assigns authority for education.

The First and Fourteenth Amendments of the Constitution also continue to be of major importance to schools, teachers, and students.

The First Amendment: Freedom of Speech and Religion   Passed in 1791, the First Amendment states:

> Congress shall make no law respecting an establishment of religion, or prohibiting the free exercise thereof; or abridging the freedom of speech, or of the press; or the right of the people peaceably to assemble, and to petition the Government for a redress of grievances.

Two clauses in the First Amendment have become central to the role of schools and the rights of teachers and students:

- The "establishment" clause is "Congress shall make no law respecting an establishment of religion." Today, interpretation of this clause has taken center stage as various individuals and groups advocate for prayer in schools and use of public dollars to fund educational activities in buildings and programs sponsored by religious groups. The founders of this country had serious concerns about the possibility of government supporting a religion or punishing citizen participation in a religion. There is a continuing debate about how to balance between what government can do and the need to provide educational opportunities for all students without it being seen as government support of a particular religion.

- The "free speech" clause has been used to challenge a variety of topics such as the extent of teacher academic freedom, the amount of freedom of school-sponsored student newspapers, and dress codes. Because there have been a number of past court decisions, there are fewer questions in this area at this time.

153

What Is the Role of
the Federal
Government in
Public Schools?

The Fourteenth Amendment: Due Process   Passed in 1868, the Fourteenth Amend-ment states in part:

> No State shall make or enforce any law which shall abridge the privileges or im-munities of citizens of the United States; nor shall any State deprive any person of life, liberty, or property, without due process of law; nor deny to any person within its jurisdiction the equal protection of the laws.

Due process is an important right granted to all citizens, including students in public schools. There are two components: substantive due process and procedural due process. **Substantive due process** has to do with protection against the loss of the rights granted in the Constitution, such as freedom of expression. The government cannot be arbitrary, capricious, or unreasonable in their actions relative to the rights of all citizens, including educators and students. Administrators can enforce rules of behavior, but all students must be treated similarly. **Procedural due process** deals with whether a person has been treated fairly and that proper procedures have been followed. Procedural due process has been at the center of many student suspension cases.

Substantive due process. Constitutional protection against the loss of rights guaranteed in the U.S. Constitution.

Procedural due process. The steps to be taken to be sure that a person is treated fairly as stated in the U.S. Constitution.

Three Parts of the Federal Government: Three Sources of Education Policy

As you learned in social studies, the U.S. Constitution specifies that the federal government is comprised of the executive, legislative, and judicial branches. The architects of the Constitution wished for balance and equality in power between the three. Although at times in history there have been imbalances, in general, the three-way approach has been maintained. Today, all three branches play activist roles in regard to what should, and should not, occur in public schools.

President of the United States   In the last 50 years, each president has had a strong interest in public education. For example, in 1965, as one of the major pieces of legislation within his Great Society program, President Lyndon Johnson led the passage of the first Elementary Secondary Education Act (ESEA). This act established a number of national priorities for improving schools and education. Federal funds were targeted to improving libraries, teacher professional development, improving teacher education, support for bilingual and special education, the development of national statistics about education, and through the National Assessment of Educational Progress (NAEP) regular study of student learning within each state. ESEA has been reauthorized every 4 to 5 years since that time. In 2001, President George W. Bush took the lead and that reauthorization of ESEA is called No Child Left Behind (NCLB).

U.S. Congress   Many members of the House of Representatives and the Senate have a very strong interest in schools and education issues. As a result, each year there are a number of education bills and statutes initiated and approved by both houses. Of course, each does not become law until signed by the president. An important understanding related to legislative bodies, such as the Congress, is that two pieces of legislation are needed to accomplish a change. First, a bill must be passed to **authorize** the program or activity. This bill does just what its name implies; it places into law authorization for schools (or any other body) to engage in a specified activity. No dollars are provided with authorization, although frequently the bill will set a limit on how much can be spent. Funding for an authorized activity or project comes through separate **budget legislation**. Although the major budget bills for the federal government are supposed to be approved by Congress early in the year, it seems to be typical to have them not approved until well into fall. A regular occurrence in the budget process is that an education activity that was authorized earlier will not be funded, or the budget bill will include funding far below what was authorized and desired.

U.S. Supreme Court   At the top of the judicial branch is the U.S. Supreme Court. This court is the highest court in the nation and has the final word on any legal issue in the United States; it is really the court of last resort. The justices are appointed for life. Over the years, the Court has reviewed many cases and made a number of significant decisions that have had direct and long-lasting impact on schools, students, teachers, and communities. Several of these are summarized in Figure 4.4.

Authorizing legislation. Legislative acts that grant authority for a certain activity.

Budget legislation. Statutes that provide for an authorized activity.

Administrative law. Rules and procedures developed by the executive branch of government that have the authority of law.

U.S. Department of Education   Another important component of the federal government is the various departments and offices that, in theory, are part of the executive branch. They are "in theory," because, in many ways, these departments can facilitate, limit, and direct through the establishment of rules and procedures, which are called **administrative law**. When Congress and the president pass a bill, it becomes federal law. Implementation of the law becomes the responsibility of the various federal agencies and departments. The same is true when the Supreme Court makes a decision. One or more offices of the federal government will be responsible for seeing that steps are taken to implement the decision.

A number of federal agencies have authorities and responsibilities related to schools, but the largest and most visible is the U.S. Department of Education (ED). The major program offices of ED include the Institute of Education Sciences (IES), the Office of Civil Rights (OCR), the Office of Elementary and Secondary Education, and the Office of Special Education and Rehabilitative Sevices (OSDFS). There also are a number of management and staff offices, as well as an office for White House initiatives. During President George W. Bush's administration, these initiatives have included:

- Center for Faith-Based and Community Initiatives
- Historically Black Colleges and Universities
- Tribal Colleges and Universities
- Educational Excellence for Hispanic Americans

ED also houses a number of organizations that provide research, evaluation, and statistics about schools and higher education. Significant among these for teacher-education candidates are:

Figure 4.4 A sample of U.S. Supreme Court decisions that have had major impact on schools, students, teachers, and communities

Religion and Public Schools

- A state cannot require that schools teach the biblical version of creation. *Edwards v. Aguillard* (1987)

- If one noncurriculum-related student group is permitted to meet at a public school, then the school may not deny other clubs. *Board of Education of the Westside Community Schools v. Mergens* (1990)

- School districts cannot have a policy supporting student-led prayer before football games. *Santa Fe Independent School District v. Jane Doe* (2000)

School Finance

- Local property taxes can be used as a basis for financing schools. *San Antonio (Texas) Independent School District v. Rodriquez* (1979)

Desegregation

- Separate-but-equal systems are unconstitutional. *Brown v. Board of Education of Topeka* (1954)

Teacher Rights

- School districts cannot have a policy forcing pregnant teachers to take mandatory maternity leave. *Cleveland Board of Education v. La Fleur* (1974)

- Nontenured teachers with a 1-year contract do not have a property interest that would entitle them to procedural rights under the Fourteenth Amendment. *Board of Regents of State Colleges v. Roth* (1972)

- Teachers have First and Fourteenth Amendment rights and may criticize a school board and superintendent in a letter published by a local newspaper. *Pickering v. Board of Education* (1968)

Student Rights

- Only in an emergency can a student be suspended without a hearing. *Goss v. Lopez* (1975)

- States may constitutionally authorize corporal punishment. *Ingraham v. Wright* (1977)

- School officials must have a reasonable cause when engaging in student searches. *New Jersey v. T.L.O.* (1985)

- National Center for Education Statistics
- National Assessment of Educational Progress
- National Institute on Disability and Rehabilitation Research

Each of these offices, initiatives, and institutes has its own home page and all can be found within the ED home page at www.ed.gov.

No Child Left Behind Act

Currently, the most significant education-related law to come out of the federal government is the **No Child Left Behind Act of 2001 (NCLB)**. Within its 2,100 pages, the statue sets expectations for levels of student performance and backs these expectations with an array of mandates to states, school districts, schools, and teachers. The overall aspiration is admirable. No American wants to see any child left behind educationally and not equipped to participate and contribute in society. At the same time, NCLB represents a new high in terms of federal

No Child Left Behind Act of 2001 (NCLB). The 2001 reauthorization of the Elementary and Secondary Education Act (ESEA).

involvement in public education, which in the past was seen as solely the responsibility of the states.

NCLB was the education legislative initiative of President George W. Bush. Many of the ideas were derived from his earlier initiative when he was the governor of Texas. The expressed intent was to raise student achievement, increase teacher quality, and to make schools safer. The bill was passed by both houses of Congress in 2001 and signed into law in January 2002 by President Bush.

Three important areas of NCLB mandates that have direct consequences for teacher education candidates are highly qualified teachers, adequate yearly progress, and school in need of improvement. Within each of these components are many expectations and explicit directives that have all of the nation's schools, teachers, and administrators struggling to comply. An added observation about NCLB, that is true of many other pieces of federal and state legislation, is that the act has not been funded at anywhere near the level that would be necessary to make total compliance a reality.

Highly Qualified Teachers   NCLB sets specifications for highly qualified teachers (HQT). Note that the term is "highly qualified," not "high quality." The intent is to assure that all classrooms are staffed by teachers who have met a set of minimum criteria. By 2006, all teachers in public elementary and secondary schools must:

- Be fully licensed by the state and must not have any certification requirements waived on an emergency or temporary basis
- Have at least a bachelors degree and demonstrate competency equivalent to a major, a graduate degree, or advanced certification

In addition, new teachers must:

- Pass a state test of subject matter knowledge and teaching skill

Another HQT requirement is that the LEA must notify parents of the availability of information on the professional qualifications of the student's classroom teachers and whether the teacher meets state qualification and licensing criteria. In other words, when you become a teacher, NCLB mandates that your district has to inform parents of your professional qualifications, if they ask.

As with many other parts of NCLB, the states are mandated to determine the details of what HQT means. In most states, this has meant that before receiving a license to teach, candidates must pass a standardized test, such as PRAXIS II. However, the test score that a candidate needs to make can vary by state, because each state can set its own **cut-off** or **cut score**. At least one state, Connecticut, is not relying on a single high-stakes test and instead is continuing to use beginning teacher portfolios, which have been an established part of its Beginning Educator Support and Training (BEST) program. Early in your education process, you should seek out the HQT criteria that have been established for the state in which you plan to teach.

▶ Cut-off scores/cut scores. The raw score on a test or performance measure that is set as the minimum necessary to be judged as a pass.

Adequate Yearly Progress   Another significant NCLB component has to do with student achievement as measured on standardized tests. The adequate yearly progress (AYP) mandate includes:

- All grade 3 to 8 students must be tested annually in math and reading/language arts and at least once in grades 10 to 12.
- For each school and school district, student test performance must be disaggregated, using a number of demographic factors such as boys and girls, ethnicity, special education, and ELL.
- Students in each of the subgroups must make progress each year.
- By the end of school year 2013 to 2014, all subgroups of students must score at the proficient level on the state's assessments.
- Annually, 95 percent of all students in a school must be tested.

"They meet in there. Some kind of support group."

In addition to implementing statewide annual testing programs, responding to the AYP mandate sets the expectation that each year between the 2002 and 2014 test scores all students who have scored below the proficient level will make progress toward scoring at the AYP proficient level.

Schools in Need of Improvement   Failure of a school to make AYP brings with it an escalating set of consequences for the school and the school district.

- Students in all schools must make AYP in each of the subgroups that have been identified.
- Failure to make AYP in any one category means that the school will be placed on the list of schools in need of improvement (SINOI).
- SINOI parents can request and the school must pay for approved supplemental education services, such as after-school tutoring.
- The district needs to offer transfer options to other public schools.
- A report card must be prepared and disseminated to parents and the public that
  Names each SINOI
  Provides the number and percentage of SINOIs and how many years they have been on the list
  Comparison of student achievement of the LEA to the state
  Comparison of the SINOI student achievement to the LEA and the state

There is much more prescribed in NCLB. Although the aspiration is admirable, the act is requiring a great deal of additional work on the part of teachers, administrators, states, and students. Only with time will the country know the extent to which the admirable goals are approached, and the degree to which the added burdens, with limited funding, have contributed to their increased—or diminished—progress.

Revisiting Sara Sandefur's Dilemma

Based on the description of the structure and role of the federal government, as well as some of the pieces of NCLB, the experience of Sara Sandefur, as described in the introduction to this section, should now be making sense. National policy makers are very concerned about the quality of schooling and the level of student performance on tests. Their solution approach is to mandate certain steps. If students fail to achieve at the proficient level or to show sufficient progress, then a series of remedial steps and sanctions are required of the school and school district. Thus Sara's school had its name reported in the newspaper, along with the low level of student performance. Her school has been labeled a "SINOI," and an array of remedial steps, including consultants and teacher training, are taking place. What Sara may not yet understand is that if her school fails to make improvement in AYP, in 1 or 2 years, her school will be identified as in need of "corrective action or restructuring." At that time, one alternative under NCLB would be to replace all of the staff in the school.

How Are Schools Paid for?

Principal Pankratz was in conference with Mrs. Buckley, who was this year's chair of the Chaparral Parent Boosters Club (CPBC). Mrs. Buckley was extremely upset over the district's decision to cut the funding for junior varsity sports, including football. "I don't understand this! My husband and I pay a lot of taxes. We pay a state income tax, federal income tax, sales tax, and property taxes. All of them keep going up! And at the same time, the school district is cutting its support for athletics. We even voted for the state lottery, although we don't play that. This is ridiculous. If there is a need to cut spending, then get rid of some of those high-priced administrators in the district office."

Principal Pankratz appreciates her frustration; he is a taxpayer, too. He also understands the different sources of revenue that finance schools, as well as how the funds are spent. His dilemma: "How do I explain to Mrs. Buckley where the funds for schools come from and that most of the money is spent on instruction?"

Paying for all of the schools and school districts requires that a large amount of money be found each year. In the last year for which the statistical analysis has been done (2000–2001) nearly $373 billion of revenue were raised. These funds were for elementary and secondary education only. Of course, the amount of revenue raised within each state varied depending on a number of factors including the numbers of students. For example, the highest was California, which had revenues of around $45 billion, while the lowest was North Dakota with revenues of

Understanding & USING EVIDENCE

SCHOOL FINANCING

Parents are not the only ones who need to understand the basic financing of schools. Teachers also need to understand where the money goes. The table presented here summarizes the budget for one school.

Gold Flake School	Amount
Enrollment: 1,657	
Instruction	$5,876,265
Instructional Support	$1,923,388
Operations	$2,524,402
Other Commitments	$0
Leadership	$772,706
Total School Expenditures	$11,096,761

*Refer to the **Understanding & Using Evidence Appendix** at the end of the text for answers and information related to these activities.*

Your Task: Many people find it difficult to make sense out of a table of numbers. Using the budget numbers for this school, develop two other ways of describing how the budget is being spent. Hint: Look for ideas in Figures 4.5, 4.6, and 4.7.

$750 million. Revenues increased an average of 7.4 percent over the previous year. Once the funds are raised, states, school districts, and schools spend the money, with most of it being spent on instruction.

Sources of Revenue: Where the Money Comes from

The money for the funding of schools comes from a number of different sources. The obvious sources are income, sales, and property taxes. There are several other sources including estate taxes and lotteries. In addition, as the schools' need for funds has increased, a number of additional sources are being created. Refer to the Understanding & Using Evidence above.

Income Tax   The first tax considered by most when we hear the word "taxes" is income tax. Implicitly, we are thinking about a **personal income tax**, which are the taxes individuals pay to the federal and state governments based on their level of income. What is not thought about is that businesses also pay a **corporate income tax**. Governments rely heavily on these two forms of income tax. One of the important features of income taxes is that those with higher levels of income pay more. The term for this is **progressive**. In other words, the income tax is graduated with those having a higher level of income paying a larger amount. The assumption is that a progressive tax is correlated with the ability to pay, and that there will be less impact on those with less income.

Property Tax   Property taxes are those paid on tangible and intangible property. Tangible property includes real estate, vehicles, boats, computers, livestock, and

Personal income tax. A proportion of an individual's income that is paid as a tax.

Corporate income tax. Taxes paid by businesses based on their income.

Progressive tax. A tax that increases as one's ability to pay increases.

equipment, while intangible property are those forms of wealth that do not have a physical existence such as stocks, bonds, and savings. Property taxes, especially real estate, have been a primary source of funds for public schools. Advantages of this form of taxation are that the property can be objectively evaluated and a tax rate determined. It also doesn't move away or have its value change very rapidly. Therefore, over time, there is a predictable evenness to the revenue. A disadvantage is that only those who own property pay the taxes. For example, apartment renters do not directly pay property taxes.

Another significant disadvantage of the property tax is that the value of real estate is not the same for every community, which limits the ability of each school district to raise the money that it needs. For example, a school district that has a popular shopping mall in its tax district will have a significant source of revenue in addition to the property tax on homes. However, a school district that has a high proportion of older homes and the only local "industry" is a closed manufacturing plant will not have the same ability to raise revenue through a local property tax. As will be discussed at the end of this chapter, these local differences in ability to pay for schools has led to school finance lawsuits in most states.

Sales Tax   Sales taxes are based on consumption. When various products and some services are purchased, a certain percentage may be added to the price as a sales tax. The dollars from sales tax typically go to the state, however, in some localities a proportion will be a source of local or regional revenue. For example, the total of the sales tax may be 7 percent with 5 percent serving as the state sales tax and 2 percent going as a local city tax. This form of taxation is **regressive**, which means that it proportionately costs more for those with lesser ability to pay.

▶ **Regressive.** A tax that is proportionately higher for those with less ability to pay.

Lotteries and Gambling   Income, sales, and property taxes are direct forms of taxation. These taxes are mandatory, too; everyone has to pay them. Taxes also are politically unpopular, which has led policy makers to seek other forms of taxation, especially ones that would be less direct and more open to citizen discretion. In other words, policy makers have turned to sources of revenue that are "voluntary." For example, lotteries and increasingly gambling are being made legal and taxable. It is up to the individual to decide whether to play.

Beginning in the mid-1960s, New Hampshire and New York established lotteries. Over the last 50 years, nearly all of the states have their own or participate in a multistate lottery. In lotteries, a portion of the funds received through the sale of tickets is used to pay for the prizes. There also are administration costs. The remainder becomes revenue. Initially, in each state, the proponents of lotteries promise new funds for schools and other well-thought-out needs. For example, the original intent in Florida was that the lottery profits would be used for add-on and special projects in schools. However, in a tight budget year, the legislature very quickly rolled lottery revenues into the base funding for schools. No more funding for special projects. This has been the trend across the United States. Very quickly, the extra revenues from lotteries and gambling become absorbed into the

Ed Lines

In the 2003–04 school year there were 14,383 school districts across the United States.
(National Center for Education Statistics)

regular budgets and are used to offset, or even reduce, past levels of spending. In addition, although the revenues from lotteries sound large, in terms of the overall budget for schools, the revenue is at best 1 or 2 percent of the total budget.

In the last decade, many states have turned to gambling as another source of revenue. Some states have permitted the opening of casinos and others have approved riverboat gambling. This is another form of revenue gain that is voluntary. People do not have to buy lottery tickets, and they do not have to gamble in casinos or play video poker. For those who do, there is a tax on the casino's "take" and a licensing fee for each machine. In addition, in states with an income tax, winners must pay state and federal income taxes.

Critics argue that lotteries and gaming are played most by those who can least afford to spend their money that way. Low-income adults play more than the well-to-do. Other critics are concerned about the many who become problem gamblers. Also, the odds of wining are infinitesimally small. People have a much higher probability of being hit by lightning than winning a lottery. Still, the states have become addicted to these indirect sources of revenue and other forms of taxation have not had to be raised as much to cover the level of services provided.

Citizens Fight Back   Given all of the forms of taxation, including a number not mentioned here (such as the federal excise tax on car tires and phone calls), it is not surprising that many citizens are unhappy with the current tax system. As a result, various forms of tax rebellion such as citizen referendums and the **underground economy** have been growing. The now-infamous Proposition 13, which was passed by the voters in California in 1978, has since been replicated in a number of other states such as the Tax Payer Bill of Rights (TABOR) in Colorado. Citizen initiatives begin by seeking signatures and placing on the ballot a constitutional referendum that, if approved by the voters, sets a cap on tax rates and/or government spending. Typically, these initiatives sound extremely good to frustrated taxpayers and in the short term appear to work well. Depending on the size and rate of growth of a state's economy, as well as the restrictions in the referendum, a state may be able to continue for quite some time before the unintended consequences become visible. For example, it has taken some 25 years for the long-term consequences of California's Proposition 13 to become visible. A key reason for California's current serious financial problems and the sad decline in the quality of its schools can be traced back to the loss of revenue from property taxes that resulted from passage of this bill. The consequences were observed sooner in Colorado, where recently there have been local and statewide votes to override the TABOR caps.

Creative Sources of Funds for Schools   Given how tight school district budgets have become, educators too have become creative about fund-raising. Unfortunately, bake sales are no longer sufficient. Now there are fees for participating in athletics and product advertising painted on the sides of school buses. Even the cola war is being played out in school districts with school

Underground economy. The practice of barter, work exchange, and sale of products and services between individuals that is not reported to any of the taxing agencies.

Ed Lines

boards making the decision to only allow one or the other brand to be available—of course, each of these decisions has a price.

Distribution of Revenue: By Different Levels of Government

The money that funds education comes from a variety of local, state, and federal sources. The national average for each of these sources is pictured in Figure 4.5. Note that, according to the National Center for Education Statistics (2003), 92.7 percent of the revenue for schools comes from the state and local level. In other words, the amount of federal financial support of schools is relatively small. Also, these ratios have not changed significantly over the last 30 years.

However, across the states, there are large differences in the proportion of revenue that comes from local sources. The lowest is 14.4 percent (New Mexico) and the highest is 65.8 percent (Nevada). There also is a wide range in the proportion of revenue from state sources. Nevada schools receive less than 30 percent (29.1%) from the state while the highest proportions are for Vermont (73.6%) and New Mexico (71.5%).

Expenditures: How Schools Spend the Money

Once the funds have been collected and allocated to school districts and schools, budgets are constructed and the funds are spent. There are several ways to analyze

Figure 4.5 Sources of revenue for public schools: school year 2002–2003

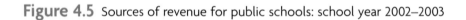

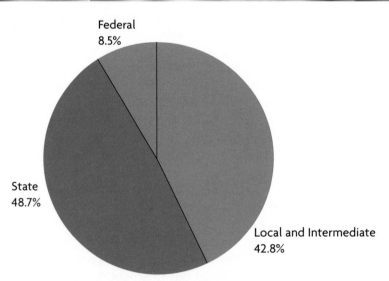

NOTE: Percentages may not sum to 100 due to rounding. Intermediate revenues were combined with local revenues.
Source: U.S. Department of Education, National Center for Education Statistics, Common Core Data, National public education financial survey school year 2002–2003. Washington, DC: Author.

and summarize the way that the money is spent. One, which was alluded to in the anecdote at the beginning of this section, is to compare how much is spent on instruction versus for administration. Another commonly employed statistic is to compare the amount of money spent per pupil.

Balancing Instruction with Other Costs   Clearly the most important component of spending should be directly related to instruction. Teacher salaries, curriculum materials, technology for instruction, and school library resources are some of the direct costs for instruction. Figure 4.6 presents the national averages for **current expenditures** by function, which are the funds spent during the 2002 to 2003 school year. Note that there are other expenditures, such as payment on school construction bonds, that are in addition to those identified in Figure 4.6. In this figure, the category of instruction represents more than three-fifths of the budget. This is a conservative statistic because the definition of what is included in this category is very restrictive. It only relates to teachers and resources for classrooms. For example, the principal's salary and that of the school secretary, as well as the cost of the library are included under support services. Other support services include items such as student counseling and transportation, which most school and community members see as having a direct influence on instruction and student learning. Thus, this is a conservative statistic, and still it is clear that at least two-thirds of a school district budget is directly related to teachers and what they do in the classroom. From this perspective, another way to summarize the information in Figure 4.6 is to say that only 4 cents of every education dollar went to activities that were clearly noninstruction related.

Current expenditures. Funds spent in the current budget year.

Figure 4.6 Distribution of expenditures for public schools: school year 2002–2003

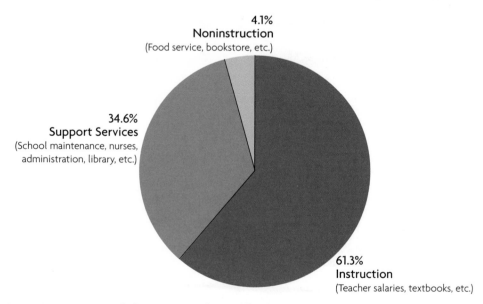

4.1%
Noninstruction
(Food service, bookstore, etc.)

34.6%
Support Services
(School maintenance, nurses, administration, library, etc.)

61.3%
Instruction
(Teacher salaries, textbooks, etc.)

Source: U.S. Department of Education, National Center for Education Statistics, Common Core Data, National public education financial survey school year 2002–2003. Washington, DC: Author.

Per-Pupil Expenditure One useful statistic for comparing school funding is to compare how much one district, or state, spends for each student. Basically, this statistic is derived by dividing the total number of dollars spent by the number of students. Per-pupil expenditure is used regularly as an indicator of a community's commitment to, and support of, public education. As can be seen in Figure 4.7, per-pupil expenditure also is useful in comparing each state's investment in its schools.

Figure 4.7 Per-pupil expenditures for elementary and secondary schools: school year 2002–2003

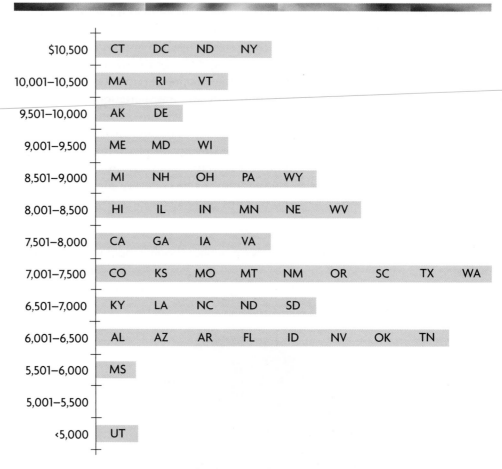

$10,500	CT	DC	ND	NY				
10,001–10,500	MA	RI	VT					
9,501–10,000	AK	DE						
9,001–9,500	ME	MD	WI					
8,501–9,000	MI	NH	OH	PA	WY			
8,001–8,500	HI	IL	IN	MN	NE	WV		
7,501–8,000	CA	GA	IA	VA				
7,001–7,500	CO	KS	MO	MT	NM	OR	SC	TX	WA
6,501–7,000	KY	LA	NC	ND	SD			
6,001–6,500	AL	AZ	AR	FL	ID	NV	OK	TN
5,501–6,000	MS							
5,001–5,500								
‹5,000	UT							

NOTE: Current expenditures include salaries, employee benefits, purchased services, and supplies, but exclude capital outlay, debt service, facilities acquisition and construction, and equipment. Dollar amounts for states and the District of Columbia were grouped in $500 ranges (e.g., $8,501–$9,000).
National average: $8,401   Median: $7,574
Source: U.S. Department of Education, National Center for Education Statistics, Common Core Data, National public education financial survey school year 2002–2003.

Ed Lines

"**The Constitution only gives people the right to pursue happiness. You have to catch it yourself.**" *Benjamin Franklin*

Funding Formulas   Once the funds are collected, each state has to determine how the funds will be distributed to each school district. The basis for doing this is a **funding formula**, which lays out those factors and characteristics of schools and school districts that in combination will determine the relative amount of state funding each district will receive. Typically, each school district will have a funding formula to determine how much money each school will be given. Typical factors that will be included are the number of elementary and secondary students, the number of students with special needs, the number of schools, an accommodation for a district being extremely large or small, how rural or urban the district is, and increasingly the extent of wealth of the local community. For example, if the local community has a higher tax base such as through more expensive housing or having a shopping mall, then, on that factor, the district would receive less funding from the state. The exact specification of the state funding formula will be determined by the legislature.

Schools continue to search for new sources of revenue. What do you see as possible issues with turning to advertising and limiting purchases to certain commercial brands and products?

Balancing the Budget in Tight Times   School districts and states are required to balance their budgets each year. In times of tight budgets and tax limitations, difficult choices have to be made. Districts may increase the number of students in each class. Increasing the average class size by one student across all schools will save significant dollars by reducing the number of teachers who need to be employed. Building maintenance may be deferred and computers kept for another year. In extremely difficult financial times, districts will turn to a number of other money-saving strategies.

Outsourcing/Privatizing   This is one such strategy. Instead of having district employees do a particular function such as cleaning buildings or driving school buses, contracts are made with outside companies to provide these services. The district then can reduce the size of its payroll and hold the outside contractor accountable for the quality of service. Unfortunately, this strategy, as well as across-the-board budget cuts, likely means that a number of district employees will lose their jobs. Another consequence is that the quality of service is not at the same level as before. For example, the district-employed high school custodian will note

Funding formula. The use of selected factors and characteristics of schools and school districts to determine the relative amount of state funding.

Outsourcing. Contracting to an outside organization for a service or product that historically had been done internally.

Ed Lines

In Spring 2003, about 1.1 million, or 2.2 percent, of all students were home schooled.
(National Center for Education Statistics)

Connecting
TO THE CLASSROOM

The organization of schools, school districts, and state education systems have been described in this chapter. School finance, taxation, and how the money is spent were the other main topics in this chapter. These topics may seem remote for candidates who are at the beginning of their teacher preparation program. However, each of these topics will become increasingly important to understand as you begin having clinical and field experiences, and as you have conversations with parents and community members.

1. In many ways schools are professional organizations. One consequence is that teachers have more autonomy and greater responsibility than would be possible for workers in other organizations. Teachers must be very careful to demonstrate that they are ready and able to accept these high-level expectations.

2. Teachers have a responsibility to communicate with colleagues and administrators when there is a problem, when they have successes, and when they have questions.

3. Keep in mind that teachers and schools are not autonomous; they are subparts of school districts and each state's education system.

4. The federal government is playing an increasing role in public schools as is demonstrated in the NCLB legislation. Teachers are not free to do whatever they may desire.

5. Be respectful of the fact that a large proportion of the taxes you and others pay are used to fund schools.

6. Local control can be talked about in the abstract but is quite limited at this time.

when a door is left open at the end of the day and know that it needs to be closed. The outsourced employee understands that his or her job description is to sweep the floor. Nothing is in the contract about keeping doors closed.

Revisiting Mr. Pankratz's Dilemma

Parents, business leaders, and elected officials are continually reminded of the fact that schools require money. Nearly everyone understands the need for having good schools. The debate centers on how good is good enough and how much money is enough. Mr. Pankratz, as a principal, should know most of the statistics presented in this section. In addition, he would need to have detailed knowledge about spending by his school district and how that affects the funds spent on his school. Some of these statistics could be used to illustrate how well, or how poorly, his community is doing in funding schools. He also could point out one or more interesting activities that have been initiated in the school that are a direct result of how the school is funded. Sometimes parents as taxpayers just need to be reassured that the hard-earned money they pay in taxes is being used well.

Chapter Summary

In this chapter, schools have been described as the workplace for adults and students. We also have examined governance, where the money comes from, and how it is spent. One impression that you should understand is that public education is a very big business. As is true in any industry, a large business needs to be organized, employees have to do their jobs, and there has to be accountability for the quality of the product or service that is produced. One of the unique elements in education is that, in large part, teachers see themselves as professionals and their work is structured accordingly. One complicating factor is that all students do not arrive at school as skilled workers. Another is that student learning takes time. In fact, it takes 13 years for one student to begin learning in kindergarten and advance to the level of skill and learning that is expected of a high school graduate. This is a long time in the minds of students, teachers, administrators, and policy makers; which is why the various ways of describing schools that have been introduced in this chapter are so important for future teachers to understand.

Why are schools organized the way they are?
In many ways the organization of schools at this time is a direct result of the Industrial Revolution. Just think about the photos you have seen of factory workers standing at their station as the assembly line produces the Model T Ford, textiles, or soft drinks. For the assembly line to work well, each worker has a prescribed job. There are supervisors and managers, too. Even the timing of tasks and the work day are specified. Many of these ideas about how to structure an organization are now institutionalized in schools. Line and staff relationships, organization charts, position descriptions, and 50-minute class periods with bell ringing, are well-

defined components of schools. Think about the typical junior high school and high school. Each teacher is a specialist in a subject, the bells ring at specified times, and the students move to their next "work station." The principal and assistant principals monitor the movements and press to make sure everyone is "at their station" for the next 50-minute period. The structural view of schools continues on.

How do schools, school districts, and the state work together to improve student learning?
Beginning teachers need to learn quickly that in today's schools, no one can simply close their classroom door and teach. Each teacher and classroom is a key element of the school. All of the schools within a district play key roles in serving all of the students within their shared attendance area. From a structural perspective, there is a straight-line chain of command from the state, to the school district, and on to each school. Each state has constitutional authority and responsibility for educating its citizens. Education is most successful when all of these agencies and personnel work together with a shared vision for how best to help all students learn.

Where does the federal government fit into the overall scheme for education? This is an increasingly important question. Although the federal government provides a small proportion of the funds (around 7%), its influence over schools has been steadily increasing. The federal government has two important levers for influencing schools: the U.S. Supreme Court and legislation. When the Supreme Court rules, as it did in *Brown v. Board of Education of Topeka*, there can be major implications for schools. Legislation, such as NCLB, when passed by both houses of Congress and signed by the president also can have major implications for schools.

Where does the money come from to pay for schools? The primary source of funds for schools is taxes. Most people think first of income taxes; however, in most states, property taxes are a much more important source of funding for schools. In most states, half of the funding for local schools comes from the state. School district budgets direct nearly all of the funds in ways that directly support student learning. In fact, some 95 percent of the school district's budget is spent on instruction and student support services.

This chapter has presented different ways that schools are viewed as organizations. Of course, the work of teachers is teaching—but teachers do their work in an organizational setting. This setting can be thought about in terms of how work is structured and governed. The work has to be paid for, too—and there are issues. However, don't lose sight of one final important idea: in the United States, the ideal of all children going to school is a reality. It is stated in some way in each state's constitution. This core principle is reflected in the high expectations for teacher quality and student learning. A shared theme is that teachers, and schools, really do (and must) make a difference in student learning.

Class Discussion Questions

1. Accountability for schools, teachers, students, and school districts is not going away. The form(s) that accountability will take is where the debate will take place. Which forms do you think should be used to hold teachers, students, and schools accountable? Are test scores sufficient? Should test scores for students and teachers be high stakes?

2. The role of school boards has been reduced in many ways. Some argue that local school boards are no longer needed. Others argue that school boards are an important component of democracy and having local citizen representation is very important to the process. What do you say?

3. What is the "price" of allowing advertising in schools? Is the money worth it? What is the downside?

Field Guide for School Observations

An important key to success as a teacher is to develop an understanding of the organizational culture of the school. A large proportion of this understanding comes about during the very first contacts with the school. The design of the campus, the parking lot and playground, and the appearance of the entryway all contribute to one's initial impression. All of these first impressions are just that; hunches about what is important in this school.

For this assignment, prepare yourself for your next visit to a school. This could be a school where you have been before or one that is new to you. Either way, be a careful observer of the facts. Fold your note paper from top to bottom so that you can write in two columns. Begin with observations of the neighborhood and observations of the grounds and entryway. Be very careful to stick to observations. What are the facts? List your observations in the left column.

Once you have your field notes listed, turn the paper over to make inferences about what they mean. In the right column, make notes about your inferences—but the key is to find out what they mean to the workers in the school. Don't be pushy or impolite. As part of conversations, you will hear explanations. Some will be provided in school documents; it is OK to ask about some that have piqued your curiosity.

Ask a Teacher or Principal

Ask a veteran teacher about the relationship with his or her principal. When is the principal clear about there being a line relationship? How much autonomy as a professional does the teacher have?

Ask a school administrator about his views in regard to whether local control is important. What are the important trade-offs with increased federalism?

Journaling Becoming a Thoughtful Teacher

In the past, local control was an important argument against state and federal governments intruding on what were local issues, such as local communities and school districts selecting curriculum and determining the qualifications of teachers and principals. Now, the state and federal governments are making most of the decisions about schools. What is your position? What do you see as being gained? What is lost with the current trend toward increasing centralization?

Portfolio Task

Go to the website for the state department of education in a state where you attended school. In the state's website will be an area that reports on how well each school is doing with the annual testing mandated by No Child Left Behind. Look up the test results for one school that you attended. Print the results and examine them closely. In which categories of student performance is the school doing well? Which categories are in need of improvement? What would you want to see addressed if you now were a teacher in that school?

Self-Assessments What Am I Learning?

Complexity of Thinking Rubric

One of the indicators of understanding is to examine how complex your thinking is when asked questions that require you to use the concepts and facts introduced in this chapter. Answer the following questions as fully as you can. Then use the Complexity of Thinking rubric to self-assess the degree to which you understand and can use the organization and finance ideas presented in this chapter.

1. How would you explain the authority of the school principal to a friend?
2. What are the roles and responsibilities of the school district?
3. How is the federal government able to influence schools so much, especially when there is no mention of education in the U.S. Constitution?
4. What's wrong—and right—about relying on property taxes to pay for public schools?

Complexity of Thinking Rubric

	Parts and Pieces	Unidimensional	Organized	Integrated	Extensions
Indicators	Elements/concepts are talked about as isolated and independent entities.	One or a few concepts are addressed, while others are under-developed.	Deliberate and structured consideration of all key concepts/elements	All key concepts/elements are included in a view that addresses interconnections.	Integration of all elements and dimensions with extrapolation to new situations
Organization Structure	Names some roles and organization concepts.	Describes school-based roles and line relationships, but not LEA or SEA.	Describes school-based, LEA, and SEA roles and relationships.	Describes role, line, and staff relationships at all levels and issues related to communication.	Uses concepts to analyze an organization problem.
School Finance	Selected facts only are described.	Taxation or spending is described in part.	Both taxation and spending are described separately.	Taxation and spending are described along with interconnections.	Implications for public education are drawn out of the descriptions of taxation and spending.

Using the Web

Go to the website of your state and look up the education budget. How is the level of funding for each district determined?

Your Professional Library

Hord, S. M., Editor. (2004). *Learning together, leading together, changing schools through professional learning communities*. New York: Teachers College Press.

A very informative reading for learning about schools as professional learning communities.

To access chapter objectives, practice tests, weblinks, and flashcards, visit the Companion Website at **www.ablongman.com/hall1e**

(mylabschool
Where the classroom comes to life!

Log on to Allyn & Bacon's MyLabSchool (**www.mylabschool.com**). Enter Assignment ID **ELV1** in the **Assignment Finder** and view the video clip, *The Principal as a Leader*. Consider what you have read in this chapter along with Dr. Loraine Monroe's comments about the responsibilities of school principals. For each of the following terms or concepts, offer one way that a principal can lend support to students and schools.

1. Staff Development
2. Inspiring People
3. Modeling
4. Diversity
5. Being a Resource
6. Classroom Observation
7. Delegating Authority

Describe one other way that you have observed principals helping students and teachers in schools.

The History of Schools in the United States

Educators in Real Schools

MEET

Verna Jessen

Teacher in a one-room schoolhouse, Eastern Montana

Verna Jessen teaches at Sand Springs Elementary School, a one-room schoolhouse located in eastern Montana. It is more than 120 miles to a town of any size. Mrs. Jessen has been teaching at Sand Springs for 6 years. She drives 32 miles one way and picks up one of her students on the way.

Mrs. Jessen is the only teacher for all students from kindergarten to 8th grade. Following 8th grade graduation, students transfer to a district high school that is located in a distant community. Some students will stay in town, because the driving time from their family homes could be more than 50 miles one way.

This year, Mrs. Jessen has one student in kindergarten, 1st, 4th, 5th, and 6th grades. There are five boys and one girl. In her first year of teaching, she had 12 students; one in each grade except 3rd. One family drives their child to school 18 miles one way on dirt roads. When the weather is bad, she has her students take their books and assignments home. She then works with them via telephone. The school is equipped with technology, including a computer for each student. They have access to the Internet via satellite.

Here's how Mrs. Jessen responded when asked to explore her thoughts and experiences about teaching:

❖ *What do you expect when you are looking for excellence in teaching?*

Teachers need to have lots of tolerance for the different personalities and the different family situations they will deal with. They need to have respect for the differences in family

Chapter 5

beliefs. They should have compassion for what the students need—and, of course, they need to have knowledge of the subjects they will teach.

❖ *How do you know when you have made a difference in student learning?*

There is a light that comes on in their eyes when they finally get it. You have been working so hard to teach them something; you finally did something right and they got it. When a student comes up and gives you a hug for no reason. When they talk to you in public away from the school. Let me describe it another way. In my second year of teaching, I had a student come in the middle of the year. When she went to high school, the English teacher had them write a letter to someone who had made a difference in their life. She wrote me a letter about how I had helped her. She struggled and I helped her. I changed the curriculum, and that is one of the best things about a one-room school. Because you will only have one or two students in a grade, you can slow the curriculum down if they are not understanding, and you won't be slowing anyone else down. You can really adjust the curriculum to fit the student.

Each grade has its own standards, with the exception of science, Spanish, computer, art, music, and PE (physical education). Anything I can combine I try to, but as it is, I teach 10 different subjects in a day. When I can combine, I teach everyone the information, but when I make up the test, it is done for each grade. Obviously, I would expect more from my 6th grader than from my 3rd grader. The state standards require that 8th graders learn a foreign language. I talked with the school board about starting early, so, we are learning Spanish together.

❖ *What brings you joy in teaching?*

When the students finally understand a concept that you have spent so long trying to get them to

understand. I enjoy learning the new things along with them. I enjoy when the kids are interested.

After being here 5 years, I have really bonded with the kids. They told me that I can't leave because another teacher would not understand their sense of humor. I can joke with them in ways that I couldn't with students whom I did not know. I might hurt their feelings and they wouldn't know that I was just joking. After 5 years, they know when I am kidding, and they know when I am serious. When I am having a bad hair day, they tell me about it.

❖ *How is teaching in a one-room schoolhouse today different than in the past?*

We have more of the modern conveniences. We have indoor plumbing and propane heat. One of the parents went to school here. He said they would put potatoes on top of the wood stove and by lunch they would be done. We don't do that anymore; we have a microwave. There are some country schools that lack technology, but we are fortunate with what we have.

❖ *What advice would you have for a teacher education candidate who is interested in teaching in a one-room schoolhouse?*

I think it is a really fun experience and you get a lot of experience fast. In the 7 years I have been teaching, I have taught every subject and every grade. For the first several years, they need to buckle down and be willing to learn the information so that they can get it across to kids. Be open to new ideas about teaching because all kids do not learn in the same way. Help the kids learn academically, but don't make references about how their parents should be raising them.

You need to learn to switch gears really fast. You could be helping an 8th grader with algebra and then turn to your right and help a 1st grader with language. At first it is hard. Usually a teacher can set their mind on one thing. In a country school, you have to be thinking about math, language, and social studies. You might be doing it all at the same time. When I first started, it could be overwhelming.

Beginning teachers should not be reinventing the wheel. They must be willing to share their ideas about how to run a classroom and on how to teach subjects. Ask a lot of questions. Listen to what other people are doing, and listen to your kids on what it takes for them to learn.

Questions to Consider

1. Did you know that one-room schoolhouses still exist in the United States? What do you see as the advantages and disadvantages of teaching in one?

2. What knowledge and skills would be particularly important for teachers who teach in a one-room schoolhouse?

3. How do you think today's one-room schoolhouses are the same and different from schools in colonial times?

Knowing the past helps us plan the future. Since the Boston Latin School was established in 1635, the nation has adopted universal schooling for all children, established a public education system, desegregated schools, and opened postsecondary education to almost any student who desires it. In studying the history of education, we find that some educational practices appear cyclical, reappearing in a different form every few generations. Movements such as progressivism have a lasting effect in some aspects of schooling, even though it fell out of favor as a movement before the mid-1900s. Reforms of schools come and go as school administrators and policy makers strive to find the magic curriculum, teaching strategies, and system that will ensure that students learn at high levels.

Focus QUESTIONS

After reading this chapter, you should be able to answer the following questions:

1 For what reasons did the states gradually decide to establish free and universal education?

2 What were the practical and pedagogical reasons for establishing high schools, middle schools, and preschools?

3 Who has been influential in determining school curriculum over the past two centuries?

4 How has the education of American Indians, African Americans, Latinos, Asian Americans, and whites differed over the past century?

5 How have the lives of teachers changed between the nineteenth century and now?

How Did Education Become Free and Universal?

"A bill for the more general diffusion of learning . . . proposed to divide every county into wards of five or six miles square; . . . to establish in each ward a free school for reading, writing and common arithmetic; to provide for the annual selection of the best subjects from these schools, who might receive at the public expense a higher degree of education at a district school; and from these district schools to select a certain number of the most promising subjects, to be completed at an University where all the useful sciences should be taught. Worth and genius would thus have been sought out from every condition of life, and completely prepared by education for defeating the competition of wealth and birth for public trusts." (Thomas Jefferson to John Adams, 1813)

CHAPTER 5
The History of Schools
in the United States

▶ Free and universal education. Public education for all children and youth.

Today, teachers, parents, policy makers, and society in general, expect that all children in the United States are entitled to a public school education. The expectation is that it should be free, it should be available in every community, and it should be open to all children regardless of age, race, ethnicity, religion, or social economic status (SES). We may debate the amount of money that should be spent, or where attendance boundaries should be drawn, or whether a teacher or principal is doing a good job. However, we now believe that a **free and universal education** is the right of all children. It may come as a surprise to learn that this has not always been the case. In fact, in colonial times, the exact opposite assumption was true. Only the elite had schooling in basic literacy and numeracy. Many hard-fought political and legal battles occurred over the past four centuries to realize this right. A critical theme in these debates was the rights of individuals to decide for themselves whether to attend school and the basic requirements necessary for all citizens in a democracy. Other themes included how much education citizens must have to sustain a democratic form of government, and what the state's role should be in determining what children will learn.

The Puritan Influence   As with many other aspects of early society in the colonies, the Puritans transferred their views and expectations for education from England to the United States. Higher education was most important for well-to-do individuals who were preparing for the Protestant ministry and public leadership. The main reason other children were taught to read and write was to learn to obey the laws of God. The poor and lower classes did not attend school. If they received formal education, it was in the form of training for a trade, often as an apprentice. However, advocates for universal education were also present. Some colonies moved more quickly toward that goal than others. The Massachusetts Bay Colony is credited with being the first in which all children were required to receive formal education. The Massachusetts Law of 1642 called for children to learn to read for the purpose of understanding their religion and the country's laws. A 1647 statute, the Old Deluder Satan Law, moved even further by requiring towns to appoint a teacher and collect taxes to support schools. In 1650, Connecticut established its own school statutes. Other colonies

© Bob Schoechet.

"I THINK WE'VE DISCOVERED THE CAUSE OF THEIR DOWNFALL."

were slower to engage with these core issues, and the South resisted the estab-lishment of schools for anyone other than aristocrats.

One of the beliefs of Puritans and other Protestant groups was that children were born evil. Education at home and school focused on religion and **morals** to rid them of that evil. Teachers were **authoritarian**, controlling and punishing students. Instruction focused on memorization and recitation of lessons.

Expanding the System of Public Education

As the eighteenth century began, it was broadly understood that the states were supposed to assume responsibility for education. Most citizens were coming to understand that their own well-being was dependent on everyone having a basic education. As the 1800s unfolded, the debates changed to determining how much education a state should provide and whether attendance should be **compulsory**. There were challenges to the states' role in education and statutes had to be set with regard to who should attend school and for how long. Throughout the twentieth century, the system of education continued to expand as did society's expectations for what public schooling could accomplish.

The U.S. Constitution makes no reference to education. Some of the founders wanted education to be a federal responsibility, but their view did not win out over those who believed it should be a responsibility of the states. The Tenth Amendment states that "(t)he powers not delegated to the United States by the Constitution, nor prohibited by it to the States, are reserved to the States respectively or to the people." Thus the states were seen as responsible for education to the extent to which each state's constitution prescribed. State legislatures were responsible for establishing education policies and financing a free and uniform public education system.

That the states should be responsible for education was seen as important even before the Constitution was written. In the 1780s, the Continental Congress passed several ordinances related to the opening up of lands in the west. For example, the Land Ordinance of 1785 specified that each new township designate one section (1 square mile) of its 36 allocated sections of a township for public schools. This ordinance required each new state to form a central government and to address education as a component of its founding laws. In addition, the legislatures were required to oversee the use, or sale, of the lands set aside in each township for education. The Northwest Ordinance of 1787 encouraged the establishment of schools because religion, morality, and knowledge were critical for a good government (Tyack, 2003).

Revisiting Thomas Jefferson's Vision

Thomas Jefferson's vision for public education came to fruition during the nineteenth and twentieth centuries. All children now have access to a public school in their communities and are required to attend school until they are at least 16 years old. Higher education has become available to far more people than the select "promising subjects" that Jefferson recommended in 1813.

Morals. Generally ac-cepted notions of right and wrong or good and bad behavior.

Authoritarian. Leader-ship that requires blind submission to the rule of a teacher or another person.

Compulsory attendance. Required attendance at school until an age (now 16) set by state legislatures.

Why Do We Have Schools for Students of Different Ages?

"It [the common school] is a free school system, it knows no distinction of rich and poor. . . . it throws open its doors and spreads the table of its bounty for all the children of the state. . . . Education then, beyond all other devices of human origin, is the equalizer of the conditions of men, the great balance wheel of the social machinery." (Horace Mann, 1868)

Schools were initially organized to teach children how to read, write, and be a good citizen. However, children and young people were also expected to contribute to the family by working. In rural areas, they had to help with farming, which required planting in the spring and harvesting in the fall. Students could not be in school at certain times of the year or had to be excused when they were needed at home. A 9-month school "year" from mid-August to mid-May was informally established and continues to operate in most communities today.

Higher education has been important for selected students beginning in the seventeenth century when a number of religious groups established colleges. Those students were prepared in the Latin grammar schools of the time. It was not long before families who were not as well off saw the value of education for their own children. Beginning with common schools for elementary-age children, schooling expanded to high schools by the end of the nineteenth century. As more and more children attended school and psychologists identified developmental stages based on age, education became further divided into early childhood education and middle-level education to better meet the needs of children.

The Common School

As early as the eighteenth century, educators and policy makers were concerned about the lawlessness of young people from low-income families. They envisioned schools as a way to overcome poverty and crime by inculcating a good moral character into students whom the reformers believed lacked good parental guidance. Charity schools and juvenile reformatories were developed for this purpose. Although some students from low-income families attended the private and public schools that existed during this period, many, including African American students in the North, attended charity schools while more well-to-do children attended private or other public schools (Spring, 2001).

The charity schools were the forerunner of the common school. In the 1830s and 1840s, the father of common schools, Horace Mann, was concerned with divisions between social classes and saw mixing the social classes in the common school as one way to reduce the tensions between groups. His recommendations were supported by the working men's parties who viewed education as a way to help workers protect themselves from exploitation by capitalists (Spring, 2001, 87). In 1837, Mann applied his ideas to schools when he became the first secretary of the Massachusetts Board of Education.

Understanding & USING EVIDENCE

PUBLIC SCHOOL STATISTICS IN 1880

The federal government has collected data on the population and institutions for over 100 years. These data provide demographic information, but also assist policy makers and other leaders in planning for the future.

The following statistics on the school populations by selected state were reported by the federal government in 1879.

STATES AND TERRITORIES	School age	School population	Number between 6 and 16 years of age	Number enrolled in public schools	Average daily attendance	Average duration of school in days
Alabama	7–21	376,649	—	174,585	112,374	84
California	5–17	216,404	—	156,769	98,468	149
Colorado	6–21	29,738	—	14,111	10,899	89
Florida	4–21[b]	72,985[c]	—	36,964[b]	23,933[b]	105.8[b]
Illinois	6–21	1,000,694	—	693,334	404,479	150
Kentucky	6–20[d]	539,843	—	227,607[e]	160,000[e]	110[e]
New York	5–21	1,628,727	—	1,030,041	570,382	179
Pennsylvania	6–21	1,200,000[h]	—	935,740	587,672	149
Texas	8–14	208,324	—	192,616		80
West Virginia	6–21	206,123	—	135,526	90,268	100.76

[b] In 1878. [c] In 1876. [d] For colored population the school age is from 6 to 16. [e] In 1877. [h] In 1873.

Source: U.S. Census Bureau. (2006). *Statistical abstract of the United States: 2006*. Washington, DC: U.S. Government Printing Office.

Your Task. Using these statistics, answer the questions to compare attendance and length of school years in 1879 to today.

1. How do the ages of students in 1879 compare to the ages of students in schools today?

2. What percent of the school-age population was enrolled in schools in 1879?

3. How many months did students in schools in 1879 attend school? How does the length of the school year compare to the time spent in schools today?

4. What percent of the enrolled students in 1879 attended school daily?

For statistics on students and schools today, visit the *Statistical Abstract* of the U.S. Census Bureau at www.census.gov/compendia/statab/2006edition.html.

*Refer to the **Understanding & Using Evidence Appendix** at the end of the text for answers and information related to these activities.*

Mann's concept of the common school became the dominant educational model for the industrial era in the United States. The **common schools** became tax-supported, locally controlled elementary schools. The curriculum included the skills needed for everyday life, ethical behavior, and responsible citizenship with standardized subject matter in reading, writing, arithmetic, spelling, history, and geography (Cremin, 1951). To encourage a common experience for all learners, standardized teaching methods were taught in teacher institutes and normal schools.

Mann believed all students should be taught the rudiments of government and the Constitution in order to better serve the nation. Common schools were also expected to create conformity in American life by imposing the language and ideological outlook of the dominant Anglo American Protestant group that governed the country. Education in common schools was seen as a venue for upward social and economic mobility for "native" whites and European immigrants in the United States. Both girls and boys attended the common schools, usually together. In the first U.S. Census of 1879, statistics on school attendance were collected as shown in the Understanding & Using Evidence on page 179.

▶ **Common schools.** Eighteenth-century schools that mixed students from different socioeconomic levels in the same classes and taught the same curriculum to all students.

Elementary Schools

Before communities built schools, children were often taught by women in their neighborhoods who established "dame schools" in their homes. The first schools built in many communities were one-room schools with a teacher who taught all subjects to students who sometimes ranged in age from 5 to 20. In rural areas, these schools were built of wood, brick, or sod by members of the community who had decided they needed a school. Sometimes the schools had desks, but often students sat together on long benches.

School Design   Many urban schools in the 1800s had classrooms for over a hundred students. One teacher managed the classroom with the assistance of student mentors who were selected from the better students. In this Lancasterian method, developed by Englishman Joseph Lancaster, students sat in long rows and the teacher sat at a desk on a raised platform at the front of the room. When it was time for instruction by the teacher, students marched to the front of the room. Afterwards, they were replaced at the front of the room by another group. The first group of students moved to another section of the classroom for recitation and drill with one of the mentors. Throughout the day, students moved from one part of the room to another to work with different mentors with several recitations occurring simultaneously in the room. Many educators and politicians of this era saw this very structured and orderly learning environment as the panacea for efficient schooling of the masses.

In 1848 Boston established Quincy School, the first school based on grades. Teachers had their own separate classroom and each student had a desk in classrooms designed for 56 students. By 1855, all Boston schools were graded. Other

Ed Lines

"**Truth is proper and beautiful in all times and in all places.**" *Frederick Douglass* cities and communities soon adopted the Quincy model, setting the stage for the graded schools of today.

By the beginning of the twentieth century, the standard classroom had rows of desks bolted to the floor. A classroom had 48 permanent desks for grades one to four; 45 desks for grades five to six; and 40 for grades seven to eight. As the century progressed, many educators moved from lecture and recitation to student-centered activities, which called for smaller classes that allowed experimentation and flexibility. New York City classrooms, for example, averaged 50 students around World War I; by 1930, the average was 38 students (Spring, 2001). Elementary classrooms averaged around 30 students for the rest of the twentieth century with rural schools generally having fewer students than urban schools.

The Lancastarian classroom was designed for one teacher to manage the education of as many as 100 students at one time in the same room.

The Textbooks   The *New England Primer* was the first widely used textbook in colonial days. The primer included the Lord's Prayer, the Ten Commandments, and a list of the books of the Bible. Students were asked to memorize the primer's **catechism**, which was a series of questions and correct answers that taught the Protestant faith. For example, one of the questions asked "What rule hath God given to direct us how we may glorify and enjoy him?" The answer recited by students was "The word of God which is contained in the scriptures of the Old and New Testaments is the only rule to direct us how we may glorify and enjoy him" (see Spring, 2001, 16).

Catechism. Series of questions and answers, usually on religious doctrine.

The elementary school curriculum in the first half of the nineteenth century was influenced greatly by the spellers and textbooks written by Noah Webster. His influence was not only on schools; he wrote an American dictionary with which many may be familiar because current versions are online. Webster was a schoolmaster who, in 1779, had an idea for a new way of teaching that included a spelling book, a grammar book, and a reader. When he finished writing the books 5 years later, he became an itinerant lecturer, riding through the country selling his books. He was a good salesman, selling one and a half million copies by 1801; by 1875, 75 million of the spellers had been sold. In addition to helping students learn to read and write, Webster believed his books "should produce good and patriotic Americans, develop a unique American language, and create a unified national spirit" (Spring, 2001, 48). Like The *New England Primer*, Webster's books contained catechisms, but did not limit the recitation to religion. He included a moral catechism and a federal one that stressed nationalism and patriotism.

Ed Lines

"Invest in yourself, in your education. There's nothing better." *Sylvia Porter*

The Webster spellers were replaced in the last half of the nineteenth century by the *McGuffey Readers*, which were written by William Holmes McGuffey, a former teacher and faculty member at Miami University, located in Oxford outside of Cincinnati, Ohio. The readers, which were written specifically for the common school, provided moral lessons for an industrialized society. The leading characters in the readers were stereotypically male; girls were missing from most stories. Although the stories were more secular than earlier textbooks, religious selections were included along with stories focusing on moral character and the importance of charity. The *McGuffey Readers* were in use for over 80 years between 1836 and 1920, selling over 120 million copies. They are credited with influencing the public's attitudes about moral, political, and economic institutions through conservative messages that were distrustful of popular participation in government (Mosier, 1965).

Textbooks in the twentieth century became much more secular to the chagrin of some fundamentalist church leaders, who sometimes suggested that the nation would be better off if textbooks and schools returned to their Puritan roots. The content of textbooks continues to be debated with some groups calling for the censorship of books that they find offensive to their values and beliefs. Groups that have historically been left out of textbooks want to see their cultures and histories represented. By the end of the twentieth century, textbooks included many more females than were found in the *McGuffey Readers*, and they appeared in both traditional and nontraditional roles. In a number of states, the content is still controlled by the government through statewide adoptions of textbooks. Large states like Texas and California can force authors and publishing companies to include or exclude information in order for the book to be placed on the state list.

High Schools

In the early 1800s, universal education in most states was only for children of elementary ages. The early common schools did not include kindergarten or secondary schools. Massachusetts was again in the lead with the first high school established in Boston in 1821. As with other innovations in education, the establishment of high schools entailed an extended debate. Throughout the 1800s, the debate continued around the use of public funds, competition with existing academies, and the real need for them. As seen today, the objections were overcome and with time high schools became an essential part of the education system.

Academies   During the colonial period, a struggle for intellectual freedom was underway in England to expand education beyond the classical study of Latin and Greek. Dissenters believed that schools were limiting the freedom of ideas by teaching students to be obedient to a church or the government. The scientific revolution fueled the debate, and intellectuals such as Francis Bacon argued that education should provide the intellectual tools and scientific knowledge required to create a better society. This movement led to the development of what were called *dissenting academies*.

When they crossed the Atlantic Ocean, academies became a popular alternative to the Latin grammar schools of the seventeenth and eighteenth centuries. An early model of a high school, the academies taught ideas and skills related to the practical world, including the sciences and business. They provided useful education and transmitted the culture that helped move graduates into the middle class. Sometimes the academies were considered small colleges; at other times, high schools.

To address the need for preparing students for college, some states, including Massachusetts and New York, established systems of county academies. Most were residential and charged fees. Some had limited financial support from the town or the state. Still, through the nineteenth and early twentieth centuries, most college preparation was done in private academies. By the end of the nineteenth century, the demand for secondary education outgrew the availability of academies. Not all families could afford to pay the tuition, and many lived too far away for students to live at home and attend them. Thus, they became identified with preparing the elite class in boarding schools.

Birth of the High School   Boston founded the English Classical School in 1821 as an alternative to boarding schools and the Boston Latin School, which provided a classical education. The curriculum included English, geography, arithmetic, algebra, geometry, trigonometry, history, navigation, and surveying. A few years later, it was renamed the English High School, becoming the first high school in the United States.

In 1838, Connecticut's secretary of the board of commissioners of the common school, Henry Barnard, defined the high school as "a public or common school for the older and more advanced scholars of the community . . . [with] a course of instruction adapted to their age, and intellectual and moral wants and, to some extent, to their future pursuits in life" (Reese, 1995, 35). Barnard, who was trained as an attorney, became an educational leader who promoted the common school and public funding of education. When he became Connecticut's state superintendent of schools in 1850, he was also the principal of the New Britain Normal School, which later became Central Connecticut State University. Barnard became the United States' first commissioner of education in 1867.

Advocates for high schools in the mid-1800s argued that they were needed for a number of reasons. They believed that well-educated people would learn that equal educational opportunity through schooling justifies social differences based on income and wealth. These schools could promote the idea that achievement is an individual responsibility and undercut the potential for political revolution. As with the earlier charity schools, they were also expected to teach obedience to the law and reduce crime by instilling basic moral values.

Debates about the purpose of high schools were similar to those that led to the development of academies during the colonial days. Not everyone believed that a community should have a high school as shown in the Teachers and the Law on page 203. Some people argued that they should develop a well-disciplined mind in the tradition of the old grammar schools. Others believed that the curriculum should prepare students for the practical world and occupations. Most of the early high schools ended up focusing on advanced science, math, English, history, and the political economy, but the curriculum was generally determined by the textbooks of the period.

The high school curriculum was not set in stone. The purposes of high schools continued to be debated by teachers and college professors as well as the public. The National Education Association (NEA) provided the early leadership for setting public educational policy. NEA formed the Committee of Ten on

Secondary School Studies in 1892. Chaired by Harvard's president Charles Eliot, the committee was initially charged with developing uniform requirements for college admission. However, its final report identified goals for secondary education. The committee recommended that the children of wealthy and low-income families take the same course of study, regardless of whether they would attend college. The committee wanted to avoid class-based education. The report called for at least 4 years of English, 4 years of a foreign language, and 3 years each of mathematics, science, and history. All graduates would be eligible for college. Critics of the report charged that it was elitist because it did not propose a special course of study for students not planning to attend college.

The number of high schools grew dramatically at the end of the nineteenth century and the beginning of the twentieth century. They were also establishing their role in college preparation. Seventy percent of the students entering college in 1872 were graduates of academies; by 1920, 90 percent were high school graduates (Alexander & Alexander, 2001). The Great Depression pushed children out of the workforce and into high schools in the 1930s. During this period, many states raised their compulsory school attendance to ages 14 to 16 (Olson, 2000a), contributing to high schools becoming an important institution in society.

It was not until after World War II that the need for a high school education became widespread. By the 1950s, a majority of teenagers were earning high school diplomas. Although more students were attending high school, not all of them were happy with the curriculum and the way they were treated. By the end of the 1960s and into the 1970s, African American students were rioting or causing disruption in many high schools as they confronted discrimination and demanded that their cultures be included in the curriculum. High schools entered the 1980s more peacefully, but with more rights for students due, in part, to a number of court cases. The curriculum and textbooks began to incorporate content on the experiences and history beyond those of white, Anglo Saxon, Protestant males.

Middle-Level Education

NEA's Committee of Ten on secondary education and Committee of Fifteen on elementary education concluded in the 1890s that college preparatory courses should begin before high school. At the same time, psychologist G. Stanley Hall was arguing that early adolescents were neither children nor adults. He believed that separate education would better serve the students between elementary school and high school rather than pushing them into high school to be influenced by older students or leaving them in elementary school too long (Beane, 2001). Before long, junior high schools were opened for this purpose.

Junior High Schools Although some educators and psychologists were beginning to call for schools between elementary school and high school, the first junior high schools were established in response to a set of social conditions. They were established around 1910 because elementary schools were becoming overcrowded with the large influx of immigrant children and the increasing number of students not passing to the next grade (Beane, 2001). Junior high schools were often attached to high schools.

By 1960, four of every five high school students had attended junior high school, but the number of junior high schools peaked at 6,000 in that decade; by 2001, the number had dropped to 632 (McEwin, Dickinson, & Jenkins, 2003). For the most part, they had become miniature high schools that many believed were not effectively serving young adolescents. In his popular 1970 book, *Crisis in the Classroom*, journalist Charles Silberman said "the junior high school, by almost unanimous agreement, is the wasteland—one is tempted to say 'cesspool' of American education" (Silberman, 1970, 324).

Middle Schools   Still believing that early adolescents deserved an education that was different from that provided in elementary and secondary schools, middle-level educators proposed a new structure. Like junior high schools, middle schools evolved, in part, because of the practicalities of the times. By the late 1950s, the baby boom generation was overcrowding elementary schools, which suggested building more elementary schools. Another option was to add a wing to the high school and move the 9th grade from the high school and the 6th grade from the elementary school to it. Some communities built a new high school and remodeled the old one for grades six through eight. Sometimes the 5th grade was also moved into the new intermediate schools.

Another reason for the establishment of middle schools was the release of research from England in the 1950s that reported that the average age for puberty had declined from 12–15 to 10–14. The research suggested that grades five or six through eight were most appropriate for young adolescents (Beane, 2001).

Middle-school advocates argued that schooling for young adolescents should focus on their developmental and academic needs. Rather than a large, departmentalized school like high school, their vision was smaller clusters of teachers and students. Teachers and other school professionals in these schools would provide guidance to help students maneuver though their changing social and physical development. Educators were to be more affectionate and sensitive to young people. Leaders of the movement publicized their ideas through committees in national professional associations, educational publications, and weekend conferences sponsored by the Educational Leadership Institute. In the mid-1970s, the National Middle School Association (NMSA) was established for professionals in the field and the parents of middle-school children.

In its 1968 study, NMSA defined the middle school as "a school having at least three grades and not more than five grades, and including at least grades six and seven" (Alexander, 1968, 1). As the popularity of junior high schools declined, the number of middle schools grew quickly to over 13,000 by 2001. With the emphasis on academics in the 1990s, middle-level educators pushed for a curriculum that would provide access to more knowledge in a positive and nurturing climate. Teachers are encouraged to use collaborative and cooperative learning. One current goal is to eliminate the tracking of students by creating heterogeneous groups in which cultural diversity is celebrated and diverse learning styles are recognized. Another goal is to more effectively connect schools to community life. Team teaching and block scheduling are used in many middle schools.

Early Childhood Education

The work of G. Stanley Hall also had a major influence on early childhood education programs. As a professor at Johns Hopkins University at the end of the nineteenth century, he established child development and child psychology as fields of study. He defined childhood as the years between 4 and 8, which remains the range for primary education. Early childhood programs between 1930 and the 1950s had a behaviorist orientation, in which good habits were developed through exercise and drill. After the 1950s, the field shifted to a developmental emphasis with renewed interest in Piaget and others who described the developmental stages of childhood. By the beginning of the twenty-first century, the field was forced to address academic achievement and standards-based assessments, sometimes with high stakes for teachers, schools, and children.

Daycare and Preschools   Throughout history, some mothers have had to work to support their families. Almost always, they have had to leave their children with someone, often a relative or a neighbor. Some women in the neighborhood watch several children. However, organized schools with child care providers were not available until the nineteenth century. Robert Owens opened the first known child care center at a mill in New Harmony, Indiana, around 1825. More than one hundred children were enrolled (Ranck & NAEYC's History & Archives Panel, 2001). During the Civil War, daycare for working mothers became institutionalized (Hewes, 2001).

Around 1925, a distinction was made between nursery schools, which were based on child development and psychology, and the day nurseries that served low-income and immigrant families. The nursery schools served a more well-to-do population. To try to control the conditions and quality of the day nurseries, some cities and states developed a licensing system in the 1930s. However, the systems lacked consistency and the requirements were not enforced. The federal government established a national preschool program in the 1930s to serve poor children affected by the economic downfall of the Great Depression. Teachers, nurses, and social workers were hired to staff these nursery schools. When mothers returned to work to support the war efforts from 1941 to 1945, the federal government supported child care, but declared that its involvement in child care would be limited to the time of the war. Following World War II, federal funds for child care were gradually withdrawn. It

Early nursery schools were developed in the 1920s and 1930s on what was known from the emerging fields of child development and psychology.

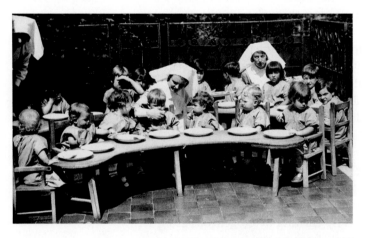

Ed Lines

"I have never let my schooling interfere with my education." *Mark Twain*

was not until 1962 that Congress again supported child care by providing assistance to mothers on welfare who were working or in job training. The breakthrough for federal support occurred with the passage of the Economic Opportunity Act of 1964 that established Head Start to provide comprehensive services to preschool children of families with low incomes with the goal of preparing them to start school on an even par with their middle-class peers.

In 1985, the National Association for the Education of Young Children (NAEYC) developed a voluntary accreditation system with standards for preschools, kindergartens, and child care centers, which now accredits over 10,000 programs. Over time, the qualifications for preschool teachers have also increased. A growing number of states requires teachers to complete a bachelor's degree and be fully certified. Many community colleges have developed associate degree programs for day care workers. However, unlike many other industrialized nations, the United States continues not to support universal child care, viewing it as a family responsibility.

Kindergarten Friedrich Froebel opened the first kindergarten in the 1840s in Germany. He saw kindergarten as a way to move children "from a world concentrated on self to a society of children" (Spring, 2001, 209). He believed that the kindergarten teacher should not be an authoritarian as was the standard in the common schools. Froebel saw the teacher as passive and protective, supporting creative play and self-expression.

The first public kindergarten in the United States opened in St. Louis in 1873 to save children in poverty from the corruption of their neighborhoods. Children were to learn the virtues and manners, moral habits, cleanliness, politeness, obedience, promptness, and self-control that they may not be exposed to at home. By attending kindergarten, children were also expected to be ready for elementary school.

Beginning in the 1880s, Froebelian kindergartens were popular in the United States, but by the beginning of the twentieth century, the focus of a kindergarten class was on creating order and discipline in the child's life. As child care professionals participated in state and national organizations in the early 1900s, the curriculum and structure of kindergartens became grounded in the research about child development and age-appropriate instruction. Children were encouraged to play and be creative. By the beginning of the twenty-first century, teachers were expected to instill kindergartens with the basic rudiments for literacy and numeracy. Free play had become something of the past.

Revisiting Horace Mann's Common School

Horace Mann's vision of education in the 1830s was the common school with the same curriculum for all students no matter their economic condition. Text-books and national reports recommending curriculum content contributed to a common

Ed Lines

"An honest heart being the first blessing, a knowing head is the second." *Thomas Jefferson to Peter Carr, August 19, 1785*

curriculum in schools across the country. However, curriculum has been influenced by local cultures and beliefs. Although states and school districts have responsibility for the control of their schools, the curriculum has become more common across the country since 1990 when national standards for P–12 students and teachers emerged.

What Is Included in the School Curriculum?

"The Congress hereby finds and declares that the security of the Nation requires the fullest development of the mental resources and technical skills of its young men and women. The present emergency demands that additional and more adequate educational opportunities be made available. The defense of this Nation depends upon the mastery of modern techniques developed from complex scientific principles." (National Defense Education Act of 1958)

*E*ven though schools look pretty much the same today as they did at the turn of the nineteenth century, the present never exactly mirrors the past. Curriculum has gone through some major changes since the first schools were established in the Plymouth colony. From schooling in colonial America to the present-day concerns with teaching reading and equal access for all students to learn, the intensity of debates among educators, politicians, and the population in general about what should be taught and how it should be taught has never faltered.

Preparation for Industry

As industrialization took hold in the cities of the northeastern United States at the end of the nineteenth century, schooling was greatly influenced by the need to help new immigrant populations become literate and disciplined workers. Education was becoming more standardized, compartmentalized, and centralized. The New York Free Society introduced the Lancasterian system to the United States, first in charity schools and later in common schools as an inexpensive solution to mass education. Proponents also claimed that the system could guarantee that students would learn the basic skills in the few years they had available for education.

The move toward preparing young people to contribute effectively to the industrial revolution was assisted by the work of psychologists at the turn of the century. Harvard philosopher and psychologist, William James, found evidence that the stimulus-response, or behavioral, concepts of learning could be used to help children develop desirable habits. His ideas were expanded by one of his most famous students, Edward Thorndike, who published in 1913, *Educational Psychology*, which guided education for the next few decades. He "viewed teaching as a science concerned with the control of human behavior" (Spring, 2001, 278), which included rewards and punishment. He also promoted testing as a way of determining which people were suited for which social roles. Thorndike's principles were applied to schools in the popular textbook, *Classroom Management*, by

curriculum until immigrants from other countries sent their children to school in the mid-1880s. The cultural wars about curriculum have been an undercurrent in education since Irish immigrants and Catholic leaders questioned the use of the Protestant Bible in schools. Periodically, the cultural wars become highly publicized when parents protest curricula and books at school board meetings and in other forums.

In the 1830s and 1840s, Catholics did not feel welcome in the nation's common schools. Most Protestants were very hostile to Catholics and refused to stop using the Protestant Bible for readings in the public schools. Not wanting their children exposed to the religious instruction of Protestants and the anti-Catholic hostility in schools, Catholics in New York City demanded that public funds be shared with them to establish their own schools. Emotions about this issue erupted into a riot between anti-Catholic and Irish Catholics in New York City in 1842. Riots erupted again in Philadelphia a year later after the school board declared that Catholic children could read their own Bible and be excused from Protestant religious instruction. People were killed and a Catholic church burned during the riot. Less intense riots occurred around the country. As a result, Catholics ended up establishing their own school system without public funds.

During the Protestant and Catholic conflicts, New York City schools began to remove anti-Catholic rhetoric from their textbooks. However, it would take more than 100 years to make the school curriculum secular by removing religious instruction, Bible readings, and prayer. Other religious groups took their complaints to the courts for resolution. For example, in the 1943 *West Virginia State Board of Education v. Barnette*, the U.S. Supreme Court affirmed the right of Jehovah's Witnesses to refuse to salute the American flag. The Supreme Court exempted Amish children from compulsory school attendance after the 8th grade in *Wisconsin v. Yoder* in 1972.

Some fundamentalist Christians do not limit their concern about the curriculum to religious instruction. They believe that the curriculum should be based on the absolute truths that are fundamental to their religion. Therefore, they attack the teaching of evolution as a contradiction to creationism or intelligent design. They fight sex education because it teaches about contraception, which is viewed as being against abstinence before marriage. These groups also call for the censuring of books and curricula that present perspectives or interpretations contrary to their religious beliefs. They also attacked a number of the innovative curriculum packages developed by leading scientists as part of the NSF projects after *Sputnik I*, leading to them being withdrawn by school districts.

Religion is not the only contentious curriculum issue in the nation's schools. Patriotism and nationalism have also led to many accusations and attacks on schools from both sides of the issue. The country has a long history of promoting the Anglo American culture as the one that must be adopted to become a citizen. The Americanization programs for southern and eastern Europeans at the end of the nineteenth and beginning of twentieth centuries were designed to teach the immigrants English and American ways, including patriotism and national heroes. Cultural pluralism was not to be tolerated,

Ed Lines

"Let us think of education as the means of developing our greatest abilities, because in each of us there is a private hope and dream which, fulfilled, can be translated into benefit for everyone and greater strength for our nation."
John F. Kennedy

requiring immigrants to abandon their own native cultures. Textbooks did not reflect the cultures or contributions of the new immigrants nor those of the non-Anglos who had been in the country for centuries. By the 1960s, inclusion of the missing groups in the curriculum was one of the demands of the civil rights movement. In the 1970s and 1980s, colleges established African American, Chicano, Asian American, American Indian, and women's studies programs. Textbook publishers were incorporating the history and narratives of these groups in elementary and secondary books often as a separately set off section rather than integrating them into the master narrative that still highlighted the Anglo Saxon culture as it had been adapted by the dominant society. Although groups of color and women are now included in the curriculum, the themes of freedom, equality, and opportunity are not often analyzed as part of the presentation or discussion. Students are not usually encouraged to question the master narrative and may be labeled as unpatriotic for doing so.

Whose stories should be included in the curriculum came to a head when the federal government supported the development of national standards in the late 1980s. The history standards, which were developed by a group of historians, were attacked at the highest levels for including the stories of the diverse ethnic and racial groups in the country at the expense of leaving out the study of some historical heroes. These traditionalists believed that this change would undermine patriotism. Religious conservatives found a curriculum dangerous that encouraged students to inquire into human behavior and values; they believed that the social studies curriculum should be built on absolute truths. Critics of the standards took

Teachers' Lounge

He Proved It...

Trust students to milk every situation for its fun quotient. Years ago in my senior-level high school biology class, we were investigating pulse and breathing. I had connected one of my male students to a kymograph—a fairly antiquated device for measuring blood pressure changes. I had calibrated the paper drum and needles and all was progressing well. I asked one of the girls in the class to come up and hold the young man's hand so that we could look for observable changes in his pulse and breathing. Unbeknownst to me, she was actually his current girlfriend, and thus began the fun. She saw the needles going and apparently decided that she would prove forever that she had power over him. She leaned over and kissed him. It was a very demure kiss on the cheek, but enough to turn him bright red and cause the needle to go crazy. The class cracked up! He was a good sport, took the ribbing he got from his classmates, and eventually all returned to calm—and normal needle fluctuations! The students in the class wrote a report about their "findings," presented it first to me for grading, and then to him as a medical diagnostic report. He and the girl remained friends, though she forever claimed that she had an irresistible effect on men backed up by full scientific proof.

● Barry Mitchell, Ph.D.
School of Education,
Brigham Young
University—Hawaii

American Indians. They were not the native inhabitants of the United States. For the most part, they had not chosen to immigrate to the United States, but entered involuntarily by force. They did not own land that the settlers wanted, but they were a critical source of labor necessary for the Southern economy. They were owned and sold and had no control over their own lives.

Until the early part of the twentieth century, most African Americans lived in the South where it was illegal to attend school before the Civil War. Although literacy was a punishable crime for African slaves in the South, at least 5 percent of them were literate by the outbreak of the Civil War. If they lived in the North, they most often attended segregated and inferior schools. Charity schools for freed slaves opened in Philadelphia in 1770, in New York City in 1787, and in Baltimore in 1792 (Kaestle, 1983). African American children could attend Boston schools at that time, but most did not because of their poor economic situations and the hostile reception of them in schools. In 1798, a group of black parents petitioned the Boston school committee for a separate school to protect their children from the hostile environment. The school committee did not accept the parents' proposal at first, but changed its position in 1806 and opened a segregated school with public funds and money from white philanthropists.

By the 1820s, black parents decided that the segregated school was providing an inferior education for their children and began to demand better conditions and teachers. In 1846, African Americans petitioned the Boston School Committee to desegregate schools. Even though the school committee found the segregated schools unacceptable, it took no action to change those conditions or to require its public schools to be open to African American children. In response, Benjamin Roberts sued the city for excluding his daughter from all-white schools near their home. He lost his case before the Massachusetts Supreme Court when it ruled that the city had provided a "separate, but equal" school for his daughter. Not long afterwards, in 1855, however, the state legislature passed a law that prevented the segregation of schools based on race or religion, becoming the first state to outlaw school segregation. The Boston schools were integrated that year. African Americans in other parts of the country were also challenging segregation and racial discrimination in their schools.

Before the end of the Civil War, former slaves in the South were fighting for universal education, which would have expanded schooling beyond the private academies for the children of land owners. They craved literacy, but were unwilling to wait for the government to provide schools. They established and staffed their own schools with African American teachers throughout the South. The black teachers, school officials, and other leaders adopted the common school ideal with the New England classical liberal curriculum. The curriculum in elementary schools included reading, spelling, writing, grammar, diction, history, geography, arithmetic, and music. In the black colleges, students studied Latin, Greek, mathematics, science, and philosophy.

To pursue the goal of universal education, the former slaves sought the help of Republican politicians, northern missionary societies, the Union army, and the Freedmen's Bureau that had been created by Congress in 1865. However, it was very important to them that they control their own education, which was sometimes difficult as northern missionaries moved into the South to establish schools.

When John W. Alvord was appointed the national superintendent of schools for the Freedmen's Bureau in 1865, he discovered a system of at least 500 "native schools" as he traveled across the South (Anderson, 1988). These schools had been established and were being managed by ex-slaves who were committed to ensuring that African American children and adults would learn to read and write as soon as possible. In some communities, black churches developed Sabbath schools that offered literacy instruction in the evenings and on the weekends. In these schools, the speller was as prevalent as the Bible.

Although a few planters were supportive of black education, most resisted universal education for former slaves and impoverished whites. Their opposition was, in part, due to economics. The planters needed a workforce that would work for low wages. They also depended heavily on child labor, which led to schools being opened as late as December. By the 1870s, the planter class had regained control of state governments. Those in power supported low taxes, opposed compulsory school attendance, and discouraged universal public education. They began to provide schools for low-income white students, but failed to provide schools for black children in most communities. The gains made by African Americans in the 1860s were quickly stymied and the proportion attending school began to drop. Nevertheless, African Americans persisted in their goal of becoming literate. "The 95 percent illiteracy rate in 1860 had dropped to 70 percent in 1880 and would drop to 30 percent by 1910" (Anderson, 1988, 31).

As the nineteenth century was ending, educators and political leaders disagreed on the curriculum for African American children. Although ex-slaves founded their schools with a classical curriculum, some leaders questioned the need for such advanced study. They argued that black children would be better served with training for the trades and learning their appropriate role in the southern culture. With this goal in mind, northerner Samuel Chapman Armstrong founded Hampton Institute in Virginia to prepare teachers who would teach students to be good workers. Most of Hampton's early students had completed only the 8th grade. They were required to work long hours in a sawmill, on the school's farm, or in the school's kitchen or dining room to develop the ethic of hard work that southern land owners expected of their laborers. One of Armstrong's top students, Booker T. Washington, founded Tuskegee Normal and Industrial Institute in 1881 to extend further Armstrong's pedagogy and ideology about preparing African Americans for their subordinate role in the southern economy. Many white philanthropists and politicians supported the Armstrong and Washington vision of industrial education in segregated schools.

Most African Americans had a different vision for their education. They saw Washington as giving in to the white demands of industrialists who wanted a steady, complacent workforce at low wages. The primary spokesperson for a different vision was W. E. B. Du Bois who wanted no compromises with the powerful white elites. He argued that black education should be about preparing the African American leaders of the future. He supported the classical education that was available in black colleges like Atlanta and Wilburforce,

Ed Lines

"Success isn't measured by the position you reach in life; it's measured by the obstacles you overcome."
Booker T. Washington

both at which he taught during his career. People on the Du Bois side of the argument believed that blacks should not learn to accommodate the oppressive Southern economy, but instead challenge it. While Washington supported segregated schooling, Du Bois became one of the founders of the National Association for the Advancement of Colored People (NAACP)—the organization that spearheaded the effort to desegregate schools later in the century. By 1915, Du Bois supporters had prevailed; the Hampton-Tuskegee model began to lose favor among its previous supporters.

At the beginning of the twentieth century, most black children did not attend elementary school because no schools existed for them, and they were not allowed to attend the schools that white children attended. If they wanted a school, African American families in the South often had to build their own schools even though they paid local and state taxes to support white segregated schools. When African American children could attend school, their schools were usually inferior to those attended by white students. The schools lacked equipment and supplies. They were allocated textbooks after they had worn out their usefulness in the white schools. Black students were not receiving an equal share of the tax dollar that a city or rural area was spending on public education. Families and leaders in the black community turned to the courts for support in being granted equal resources.

The equal protection clause of the Fourteenth Amendment has played an important role in the struggle for education equality for blacks and other groups of color. It reads:

> . . . No State shall make or enforce any law which shall abridge the privileges or immunities of citizens of the United States; nor shall any State deprive any person of life, liberty, or property, without due process of law; nor deny to any person within its jurisdiction the equal protection of the laws. (Legal Information Institute, 2006)

Nearly 100 court cases from 20 states and the District of Columbia were filed in the nineteenth century. African Americans in the North won a majority of their cases, prohibiting segregation in their public schools (Hendrie, 2000).

Nevertheless, segregation continued in the South. After Homer Plessy, who was one-eighth black and seven-eighths white, was arrested for refusing to ride in the "colored" section of a train in Louisiana, he protested that his Fourteenth Amendment rights had been denied. The U.S. Supreme Court disagreed, ruling in its 1896 *Plessy v. Ferguson* decision that "separate but equal" facilities were legal. This decision supported the segregation of schools for the next six decades. In addition, state laws in the South curtailed the right of African Americans to vote and created other segregated public institutions. These patterns of **institutional discrimination** were not reversed until the 1950s and 1960s.

Institutional discrimination. Policies and practices that give advantages to one group over another.

The NAACP decided to pursue a legal path toward desegregating public schools. Five cases were percolating in the lower courts at mid-century: *Briggs v. Elliott* in South Carolina, *Davis v. County School Board of Prince Edward County* in

Ed Lines

Virginia, *Gebhart v. Belton* in Delaware, *Brown v. Board of Education of Topeka* in Kansas, and *Bolling v. Sharpe* in the District of Columbia. The first four cases were argued before the U.S. Supreme Court in 1952 and 1953 by Thurgood Marshall, who later became the first African American appointed to the Supreme Court. In 1954, the Court declared that "In the field of public education the doctrine of 'separate but equal' has no place. Separate educational facilities are inherently unequal" (National Center for Public Policy Research, 2006). The fifth case, *Bolling v. Sharpe*, settled a year later, declared that the federal government could not segregate schools in the District of Columbia.

In 1955, the Supreme Court sent all school integration cases back to the lower courts, asking states to desegregate "with all deliberate speed." A few years later, the courts also called for the desegregation of metropolitan areas in the North, often requiring the bussing of students across city lines to ensure integration. Most school districts did not respond to this mandate for years. Many white families fiercely resisted the desegregation of their schools. In cities like Little Rock, Arkansas, the National Guard had to protect African American students entering white schools for the first time. Many white families established private Christian schools or moved to the suburbs where the population was primarily white to avoid integration. Many African American teachers and principals who had worked in segregated schools lost their jobs and were not invited to teach in the integrated schools. In the three decades following the *Brown* decision, the race of the students in schools did change. In the mid-1960s only 2 percent of black students attended integrated schools; by the late 1980s, 45 percent of them were in integrated schools.

▶ *De facto* segregation. The voluntary separation or isolation of racial, ethnic, or socioeconomic groups in a community, leading to neighborhood schools attended by students from one group.

By the mid-1980s, federal court sanctions for integration began to be lifted. School districts were allowed to return to neighborhood schools. Because of ***de facto* segregation** in many communities, neighborhood schools were often comprised of students of the same race. Segregation in many schools had returned to pre-1970 levels. Leading researchers of desegregated schools reported that at the beginning of the twenty-first century black students are the most likely racial group to attend "apartheid schools," in which 99–100 percent of the population is students of color. These schools are characterized by poverty, limited resources, social strife, and health problems. One of six black children attends these schools (Frankenberg, Lee, & Orfield, 2003).

Latinos

When the Mexican-American War ended on May 30, 1848, Mexican citizens in the newly acquired territory in the Southwest were promised

African American students at Little Rock's Central High School had to be protected by the National Guard as they desegregated the school in 1957.

U.S. citizenship as part of the Treaty of Guadalupe Hidalgo. However, their citizenship was delayed until Congress felt assured the Mexicans were ready for citizenship. Like African Americans and American Indians, the Mexicans who lived in the territory conquered by the United States were not allowed to be full citizens until after the Civil War.

Mexican American families fought for the education of their children, many of whom were attending inferior segregated schools. Whether they could attend the same schools as whites depended on whether they were classified as white. There was no common agreement on the race of Mexican Americans. In 1897, Texas courts ruled that Mexican Americans were not white. However, California classified them as Caucasian until 1930 when the attorney general categorized them as American Indians. He argued that "the greater portion of the population of Mexico are Indians"; therefore, individuals were as well (Spring, 2001, 171). As a result of not being white, most Mexican American children attended segregated schools through the first half of the twentieth century. The same separate but equal laws applied to them as to African Americans.

In addition to being in segregated schools, students often were not allowed to speak Spanish in school. To ensure that teachers would deliver instruction in English, states passed laws: California in 1855 and Texas in 1870. In 1918, Texas made it a criminal offense to use any language other than English for instruction. Often, students were forbidden the use of Spanish at any time while they were in school. In the last half of nineteenth century, Mexican Americans sent their children to Catholic schools or nonsectarian private schools to escape the anti-Mexican attitudes of public schools. Catholic schools were more likely to provide bilingual instruction. Many Mexican American children were not attending school at all at the beginning of the twentieth century. Many farmers used Mexican Americans, including children, as laborers and were not supportive of releasing them to attend school. On the other hand, many school officials wanted them in schools to Americanize them and rid them of their cultures and language.

Concerned about discrimination against Mexican American students in public schools, the League of United Latin American Citizens (LULAC) called for bilingual instruction and the maintenance of Mexican cultural traditions in schools as early as 1929. However, these English-only laws were not repealed until the 1970s when the federal government supported bilingual education as an option for teaching English language learners. As the federal policy moved away from support of bilingual education, some states have now returned to laws prohibiting bilingual education and the use of any language other than English for classroom instruction.

Mexican American families were fighting for the right to attend white schools at the same time that African Americans turned to the courts for assistance. In the 1930s, the Texas courts upheld the right of school boards to provide segregated education for Mexican Americans. The first breakthrough for integration occurred with the 1940 *Mendez v. Westminster* decision that required a California school district to allow a Mexican American girl to attend the white school. The Mexican American Legal Defense and Education Fund (MALDEF) was established in 1967 to continue suing for the civil rights and equality for Mexican American students.

Court cases since then have focused on discriminatory practices in the funding of schools, the sole use of English in classrooms, and the disproportionate placement of Spanish-speaking children in special education classes as a result of biased tests or tests being given in English. The court's ruling on inequitable funding in the 1971 case brought by MALDEF is discussed in the Teachers and the Law on page 203.

Education for students in Puerto Rico has been interrelated with a history of occupation by the United States. Puerto Rico had just received its autonomy from Spain before it came under the control of the United States as part of the spoils (along with the Philippines and Guam) from the Spanish-American War at the end of the nineteenth century. With the 1900 Foraker Act, Congress established a colonial government to replace the military rule in Puerto Rico and appointed the first U.S. commissioner of education for Puerto Rico. Just as with the Native Americans, the federal policy was to Americanize the Puerto Ricans through education. Before long, the language of instruction was to be in English. Because many Puerto Rican teachers spoke only Spanish, teachers were brought in from the United States. Not only were students expected to learn English, they were also supposed to learn American ways. Educational policies required celebration of the U.S. patriotic holidays, such as the Fourth of July. Students were required to pledge allegiance to the U.S. flag and study U.S. historical heroes. Local textbooks were replaced with U.S. textbooks. When new teachers applied for a teaching certificate, their test included an English examination.

Puerto Ricans were not interested in becoming Americans and losing their own native language and culture. In 1912, the Puerto Rican Teachers Association began to defend Spanish as the language of instruction. When a student at San Juan's Central High School was expelled in 1915 for collecting signatures in support of instruction in Spanish, a student strike was sparked. Calls for nationalism and independence were common. Without asking Puerto Ricans whether they wanted to be citizens of the United States, Congress granted them citizenship in 1917. As a result, they were obligated to serve in the military. However, they were not granted the right to vote in elections and still do not have the right to vote or elect a representative to Congress.

Tensions increased in the 1920s when a Puerto Rican who supported the U.S. assimilation policies became the commissioner of education. He pressed his predecessor's policies even further. He required seniors to pass an English examination before they could graduate. He banned school newspapers in Spanish. Teachers were required to use English in teacher meetings and in informal discussions with students. Protests by teachers, professors, and college students expanded. College students were expelled for participating in anti-American marches. Professors were warned to stop supporting student protests.

Their efforts to change U.S. educational policies in Puerto Rico resulted in the Padin Reform of 1934 that restricted English instruction to high schools. Spanish could be used at other levels. However, textbooks continued to be printed in English. After the teachers association successfully lobbied the Puerto Rican legislature to pass a bill requiring the use of Spanish, President Harry Truman vetoed it. After Puerto Rico was granted commonwealth status in 1951, Puerto Ricans gained greater control of their school systems, restoring Spanish as the language of instruction (Spring, 2001).

Teachers and the Law

EQUAL PAY BASED ON GENDER

Is there any time that men can be paid more than women for the same job?

Yes. The plaintiff must show that the jobs are comparable in responsibility, skills, effort, and working conditions. In 1994 the head coach of women's basketball sued her university because the head coach of the men's team was paid more. The university provided evidence that the male coach had greater responsibilities, including the pressure to raise significant revenues. The court ruled that the jobs were not equal, and salaries could be different. Salary differences based on gender are less likely to occur at the P-12 level where salaries are based on degree level and experience.

PUBLIC HIGH SCHOOLS

Do states have the authority to establish public high schools?

Yes. The answer to this question came in *Stuart v. School District No. 1 of Village of Kalamazoo* (1874). Kalamazoo College, a private academy, had been es-tablished in 1855. As demand for high school education increased in 1858, the district superintendent created a union high school, which was successful. The college was concerned because the high school pulled some students away and some taxpayers objected to paying for the high school. In 1873, the college and a group of prominent citizens filed suit. The case was decided in support of public high schools by the Supreme Court of Michigan.

INEQUITABLE FUNDING OF SCHOOLS

Is the funding of schools a constitutional issue?

No. The Mexican American Legal Defense and Education Fund filed a class action suit on the behalf of a group of Mexican American parents against the inequitable funding of Texas schools. In 1971, the federal district court ruled in *Rodriguez v. San Antonio Independent School* that the Texas school finance system was unconstitutional based on the equal protection clause of the 14th Amendment. In 1973, the U.S. Supreme Court ruled that school finance was not a constitutional issue, pushing the cases back to state courts for resolution.

Source: Cambron-McCabe, N. H., McCarthy, M. M., & Thomas, S. B. (2004). *Public school law: Teachers' and students' rights* (5th ed.). Boston: Allyn and Bacon.

Asian Americans

Asian Americans have a shorter history in the United States than the other ethnic group discussed so far. The first Chinese migrants arrived in California in the 1850s to join the gold rush as free laborers; by 1852, 20,000 had immigrated to California. After mining profits fell, they helped build the transcontinental railroad at much lower wages than whites would accept. They also faced a great deal of hostility and discrimination from the dominant white group. The courts considered Chinese immigrants as having the same status as Native Americans. In 1853, the California Supreme Court denied their right to testify in a court case based on a ban against the testimony of Native Americans. In 1855, the U.S. Supreme Court ruled in the *Chan Yong* case that Chinese are not white and not eligible for citizenship. By 1882, anti-Chinese sentiment was so great that Congress banned Chinese workers from the United States. When the court ruled in 1885 that native-born Mamie Tape had equal access to public schooling, the California legislature responded by allowing school districts to establish segregated schools for Asian Americans. By 1905, the segregated system in San Francisco was being broken as Chinese youths were admitted to the regular city high schools.

Japan law forbade Japanese students from traveling to foreign countries until 1868 when some Japanese laborers were contracted to work on Hawaiian plantations and in the silk industries of California. Koreans began to immigrate to Hawaii in the first decade of the twentieth century. In 1907, Asian Indians began to immigrate to the United States mainland, and Filipinos were recruited to work in Hawaii and on the mainland.

Asian American families in the South wanted their children to attend white schools, but school boards forced them into the black segregated schools. The family of a Chinese American girl argued that she was not black and therefore should be able to attend the white school. However, the court ruled that she was not white and gave schools the authority to determine the race of their students.

Policies related to citizenship continued to discriminate against Asians. For example, Takao Ozawa was born in Japan, but was educated in the United States and was a Christian. The U.S. Supreme Court ruled in 1922 that Ozawa was not white and thus not eligible for citizenship. The next year the Court ruled that Asian Indians were also ineligible for naturalized citizenship. The court argued that "the intention of the Founding Fathers was to 'confer the privilege of citizenship upon the class of persons they knew' " (Spring, 2001, p. 177). It was not until 1943 that the Chinese Exclusion Law was rescinded, allowing Chinese immigrants the right to become naturalized citizens. With the passage of the 1965 Immigration Act, citizenship discrimination against Asians was ended, and the number of Asian immigrants began to grow.

As the number of Asian immigrants increased, schools in cities such as San Francisco were faced with a growing number of students who spoke languages other than English. Because the language of instruction was English, parents worried that their children were not able to achieve at the high academic levels that they expected. They sued the San Francisco school system and in 1974, in *Lau v. Nichols*, won the right to have their first language used in instruction. The court said "under state imposed standards, there was no equality of treatment merely by providing students with the same facilities, textbooks, teachers, and curriculum; for students who do not understand English are effectively foreclosed from any meaningful education" (*Lau v. Nichols*, 1974).

Revisiting W. E. B. Du Bois and Equal Educational Opportunities

The school in which W. E. B. Du Bois taught in the 1880s provided education for African American children when they could be released from their farming and babysitting responsibilities. It was a period in which it was illegal for students of color to attend a white school in many parts of the country. Families of these students fought in the courts to overturn the separate but equal policies that allowed segregated schools in which resources were much more abundant for the schools of white students. Although *de jure* segregation has not been legal for over 50 years, schools are no longer required to be integrated as the courts have allowed school districts to return to neighborhood schools that are often *de facto* segregated.

▶ *De jure* segregation. State policies or laws that separate or isolate racial, ethnic, or socioeconomic groups in a community, requiring students of one group to attend the same school.

How Have Teachers Evolved?

Two-thirds of the teachers attending the 1853 national convention of the National Education Association were women. However, women teachers were not allowed to speak publicly. When the discussion turned to why the profession of teaching was not as respected as that of lawyer, doctor, or minister, women's rights leader, Susan B. Anthony, determined it was time for her to speak. Her biographer, Ida Husted Harper, recounts what happened next:

> *"A bombshell would not have created greater commotion. For the first time in all history a woman's voice was heard in a teachers' convention. Every neck was craned and a profound hush fell upon the assembly. Charles Davies LL.D., author of Davies' textbooks and professor of mathematics at West Point, presided. In full-dress costume with buff vest, blue coat and brass buttons, he was the Great Mogul. At length recovering from the shock of being thus addressed by a woman, he leaned forward and asked with satirical politeness, "What will the lady have?" "I wish to speak to the question under discussion," said Miss Anthony calmly, although her heart was beating a tattoo. Turning to the few rows of men in front of him, for the women occupied the back seats, he inquired, "What is the pleasure of the convention?" "I move she shall be heard," said one man; this was seconded by another, and thus was precipitated a debate which lasted half an hour. . . . At last a vote was taken, men only voting, and it was carried in the affirmative by a small majority. Miss Anthony then said: "It seems to me you fail to comprehend the cause of the disrespect of which you complain. Do you not see that so long as society says woman has not brains enough to be a doctor, lawyer or minister, but has plenty to be a teacher, every man of you who condescend to teach, tacitly admits before all Israel and the sun that he has no more brains than a woman?" and sat down. She had intended to draw the conclusion that the only way to place teaching upon a level with other professions was either to admit woman to them, or exclude her from teaching, but her trembling limbs would sustain her no longer. The convention soon adjourned for the day and, as Miss Anthony went out of the hall, many of the women drew away from her and said audibly: "Did you ever see such a disgraceful performance?" "I never was so ashamed of my sex." But a few of them gathered about her and said: "You have taught us our lesson and hereafter we propose to make ourselves heard." "* (see Grant & Murray, 1999, 83–84)

It would be over 50 years before women were allowed to vote at NEA conventions, and over 100 years before teachers actually controlled the NEA, which had been controlled by administrators. The role of women in teaching defines the profession. Historically, they have provided a stable, inexpensive, and moral teaching force for the country. As the educational system became standardized, teachers were supervised by county or city superintendents. The emerging pattern in the nineteenth century was men administrators managing women teachers.

Women were not always the majority of teachers. During the colonial period, teachers were men except in the dame schools. After the Revolutionary War, females began to be recruited as teachers. New teachers whose families did not live in the communities in which they taught often boarded in their students' homes, moving from home to home every week or so.

During the nineteenth century, many teachers went west with settlers. Some were sent to Indian tribes by their churches to convert American Indians to Christianity while teaching them to read and write in English. Isolation and danger sometimes took their toll on these teachers. Wives and daughters of settlers in the West staffed many of the schools in the prairies and mountains.

Teacher Preparation

To ensure that teachers were teaching the curriculum that educational leaders desired, teacher education programs were developed. Reverend Samuel Hall is credited with establishing one of the first institutions for preparing teachers in 1823 in Concord, Vermont. However, Emma Willard had opened the Troy Female Seminary in 1821. Completion of these programs eventually led to certification, which many school boards required. However, certified teachers were not readily available in many rural areas for another century.

Teacher Institutes The first teacher institute was established in 1839 in Connecticut by Emma Willard and Henry Barnard. New and experienced teachers attended the institutes during breaks to learn new teaching strategies and improve their knowledge about the subjects being taught. Institutes were usually held one to two times annually for 2 to 4 weeks. Teachers usually had to travel to another town for the institutes, providing the opportunity to interact with other teachers in the area on a personal as well as professional level.

The focus of the teacher institutes was on the development of moral character in students. They learned their role in teaching religion and patriotism. They were expected to prevent social problems in schools, but not to be actively engaged in solving existing social problems.

Normal Schools Normal schools were established in 1839 in Lexington, Massachusetts, to prepare teachers for the elementary school. In most of the nineteenth century, most students were women who had completed elementary or common schools, but had not completed high school. Secondary teachers had completed college or university, were more likely to be male, and were paid more than their women counterparts (Cordier, 1992).

Curriculum in the normal schools required 1 to 2 years of study in which the elementary school curriculum was reviewed, classroom management studied, and teaching methods taught. Students

Teachers in the one-room schools of the past and today serve not only as the teachers, but also as the custodian, nurse, secretary, and principal.

also learned about lesson plans, which were developed by German psychologist Johann Herbart (1776–1841). The lesson plan was to be developed around the interest of students. Herbartian lesson plan included preparation, presentation, comparison and abstraction, generalization or definition, and application.

By 1900, most teachers in the United States still had not attended normal schools. Many of today's state colleges and universities began as normal schools. They changed their names and expanded their missions beyond the preparation of teachers in the mid-1900s. Today, they continue to prepare the majority of teachers in the country. At one time many females and students of color selected teaching as their career goal, in part, because they were not welcome in many other professions. As they moved into other fields of study after the 1960s, some people began to question the academic qualifications of new teachers, which is discussed in the Challenging Assumptions on page 208.

Teacher Autonomy

Teachers have long been under the control of school boards and administrators. Even their organization, the NEA, included school administrators and professors who served as the elected leaders for its first 100 years. Not only did administrators oversee the work of teachers and select their textbooks, they also monitored their personal behavior.

Moral Behavior   Teachers were expected to live exemplary moral lives. Their social activities were controlled by school officials throughout the nineteenth century and well into the twentieth. Of course, teachers were expected to be more than models of good moral behavior. Horace Mann in 1840 identified the qualifications for a teacher as having

1. "perfect" knowledge of the subject being taught
2. an aptitude for teaching, which he believed could be learned
3. the ability to manage and govern a classroom and mold moral behavior
4. good behavior as a model for students
5. good morals

Even though morals were only one of Mann's five qualifications (Spring, 2001), it appeared to be one of the most important to school superintendents and school board members. Contracts for women teachers sometimes did not allow them to socialize with men or be married. The emphasis on high moral character continued into the early twentieth century. In her diary, Rosa Schreurs Jennings wrote:

> Teachers were surrounded with prohibitions, some by contract, others by custom—no drinking, no dancing or card-playing where the community attitude was against it, no "gallivantin' around," no slang. . . . We wore ruffled thing-a-mabobs to conceal our maidenly forms. Neither did we show our legs—high-button shoes and three petticoats, one short and two floor-length, under a dress five yards around the bottom, took care of that. (Cordier, 1992, 34)

Challenging Assumptions

FINDINGS FROM RESEARCH

Are college students preparing to be teachers as smart as students preparing for other jobs?

The Assumption: Teachers of children in the 1700s had not always finished elementary school although teachers of adolescents may have attended college. The amount of education increased in each century that followed. In the 1800s, a growing number of elementary school teachers completed high school and began to attend teacher institutes and normal schools to further develop their knowledge of the subjects they were teaching as well as their teaching skills. It was not until the mid-1900s that most teachers completed a 4-year college, which is now required for a teaching license in all U.S. states. Into the mid-1900s, teachers had more education than most members of their community. However, by the beginning of the twenty-first century, a larger proportion of the population had a bachelor's degree than in previous centuries. Some critics of teachers and education have charged that college students who choose a teaching career are not as academically talented as other college students.

Study Design and Method: Researchers at the Educational Testing Service (ETS) examined college students' performance on the SAT and ACT to determine whether this assertion was true. ETS began its study by determining which students who had indicated on their college entrance examination that they planned to teach actually entered a teacher education program as determined by their later taking Praxis II, the test for content knowledge.

Study Findings: Researchers found no differences between the performance of teacher candidates in secondary programs and other college students majoring in the field. Scores on college admissions tests and the licensure test on content knowledge does indicate that as a group, teacher candidates in early childhood education, elementary education, special education, and physical education do not perform as highly as other college students.

Implications: Many people argue that a single standardized test is not a good measure of intelligence. Multiple assessments that include actual performance in classrooms would provide a more accurate picture of what teachers know and are able to do. College students who decide to pursue a teaching license are required to show evidence before they finish their programs that they know the subjects they will teach, understand the developmental stages of the children in the grades they plan to teach, and can help students learn. Although some college students may enter a teacher education program with lower test scores, they must be able to show evidence that they meet state and professional standards by the end of the program as shown through multiple assessments.

Source: Gitomer, D. H., & Latham, A. S. (1999). *The academic quality of prospective teachers*. Princeton, NJ: Educational Testing Service.

Although moral character is not included in today's teacher contracts, teachers are still expected by the public to be models of high moral character.

Under Attack At the beginning of the twentieth century, the NEA partnered with a number of groups to support patriotism and nationalism in the nation's schools. For example, after World War I, the American Legion partnered with the NEA to rid schools of radical ideas in the curriculum and what they called subversive teachers. "In the 1930s, the National Association of Manufacturers launched the 'American Way' campaign through schools and other organizations to try to create an automatic association in the public mind between democracy and capitalism" (Spring, 2001, 317).

These partnerships with businesses and patriotic organizations did not last. In 1932, the U.S. Chamber of Commerce was considering recommendations to their communities to cut evening classes and kindergartens, shorten the school day, increase class sizes, and charge tuition for high school attendance. At the same time, many educators were attacking the country's economic policies. In response the NEA established the Joint Commission on the Emergency in Education (JCEE) in 1933 to counteract the chamber of commerce's proposals. This commission joined the honorary education fraternity, Phi Delta Kappa, to analyze public criticisms of schools. The top five criticisms were "soft pedagogy, lack of contact with life, overemphasis on vocations, severe discipline and overwork, and neglect of character" (see Tyack, Lowe, & Hansot, 1984, 75).

Some educators (for example, George Counts at the 1932 annual meeting of the Progressive Education Association) issued radical critiques of the economic system and proposed using the schools for social reconstruction. The business community worried about radical educators taking over the schools. The social reconstructionist movement contributed to the image that educators were among the most liberal group in society.

Following World War II, the radical right charged that the teaching profession had been infiltrated by Communists. They demanded the removal of what they perceived to be anti-American literature and left-leaning teachers. "By the 1950s, business had joined with politicians to declare that professional educators had made the schools the weakest link in America's defense against communism" (Spring, 2001, 318). Historian Arthur Bestor decried the anti-intellectualism in schools at the 1952 annual meeting of the American Historical Association. He called for a closer working relationship with professional educators. Bestor wanted schools to reject their emphasis on socialization and sorting, calling for a curriculum organized around subject-matter disciplines. In 1956, he helped organize the Council for Basic Education, which influenced curriculum and policy for nearly 50 years before its demise. Vice Admiral Hyman G. Rickover, the "Father of America's Nuclear Navy," also attacked professional educators for anti-intellectualism and being a weak link in the country's defense strategy.

In the 1960s, the radical right blamed the decline of academic standards on the Communist infiltration of education. The academic community accused professional educators of being anti-intellectual and argued that scholars should determine the public school curriculum. Educators continue to be blamed when students are not scoring higher than students in other nations of the world, when employers are unhappy with their preparation, when not enough students are enrolled in mathematics and science, and when students misbehave in the community. Schools are blamed when business and political leaders declare that the United States is no longer being competitive and the economy is in recession. However, they are not given the credit when the economy is performing well and scientists are making new discoveries.

Remember that if it were not for good teachers, the country would not have the scientists, mathematicians, medical professionals, and business persons that it does. Teachers in public schools have taught most of the United States' Nobel Prize winners and the country's leaders. Most of these leaders, sports stars, and the parents of your students can identify teachers who have made a difference in their lives. Hopefully, one of your goals is to make a difference in the lives of the students that you teach.

Revisiting Susan B. Anthony's Response about Teaching as a Profession

The question that Susan B. Anthony chose to respond to at the 1853 convention of the National Education Association was one that continues to be asked today: Why is the profession of teaching not as respected as that of doctors and scientists? Teachers today are even more likely to be women than when Susan Anthony spoke, which may contribute to the lower status attributed to teaching. Much has occurred since 1853 to make teaching a profession. Teachers must hold a baccalaureate degree and sometimes a master's degree. They study learning and child or adolescent development along with the subjects they will be teaching. They pass licensure tests that indicate they know the subjects they teach. They practice their craft under the tutelage of experienced educators. They continue today to fight for recognition as professionals.

Connecting
TO THE CLASSROOM

This chapter has provided you with some basic information about how schools and the education of different students have evolved to the schools we know today. The following are some key principles for applying the information in this chapter to the classroom.

1. The history of education helps us understand teaching practices that have been tried previously by educators, the reasons for their falling out of favor, and the possibility of their recycling again as desirable practice.

2. Teachers should be diligent in checking their classroom practices and interactions with students to ensure they are not sorting students by the income of their parents under the guise of their being more or less intelligent.

3. Teachers in primary and middle schools are expected to provide age-appropriate education for students based on what is known from child and adolescent development.

4. Good teachers are able to analyze and evaluate the different curriculum packages their school districts are likely to impose on them during their careers, and make wise, pedagogically sound decisions about their use in their classrooms.

5. The civil rights movement of the 1960s and 1970s was the foundation for ensuring that an equal education could finally be accessible to all children regardless of their race, ethnicity, socioeconomic status, language, gender, and abilities.

Chapter Summary

The history of education helps us understand how we arrived at the schools in which you will soon be teaching. We should learn from past mistakes and successes in carving out the schools of the future—and, most important as teachers, we should become an active participant in determining the curriculum and practices of our profession.

How did education become free and universal? Schooling in colonial days was based on the influence of the Puritans and other Protestant groups, who viewed it as a way to teach religion, instill moral values in children, support the Anglo Saxon culture, and develop allegiance to their new country. Following the signing of the Declaration of Independence, the country's leaders debated the purposes of education as a benefit to individuals or preparation for participating in a democratic society. The Constitution indicated that states would be responsible for education, and new territories were expected to set aside land for the establishment of a school.

Why do we have schools for students of different ages? The first schools in the colonies were Latin grammar schools, which were attended primarily by the children of the elite. In the 1800s, Horace Mann led the movement for common schools that would mix students from both low-income and well-to-do families. The first common schools focused on elementary education and were guided first by Noah Webster's spellers and readers, followed by the *McGuffey Readers*, both emphasizing moral behavior and patriotism. By the end of the nineteenth century, high schools had evolved out of academies to serve adolescents. Around 1910, the first junior high schools emerged as a bridge between elementary and high schools. Beginning in the 1970s, they became middle schools, often with the 6th and 9th grades. Organized preschools for the children of working mothers began at a mill in Indiana in 1825, but really came into their own with the nursery schools of the 1920s and 1930s.

What is taught in the curriculum? The curriculum in colonial schools focused on reading, writing, and arithmetic with strong religious and nationalistic themes. As the industrial revolution developed in the 1800s, schools themselves became more efficient, sometimes trying to educate 100 students in a classroom. Following World War I, IQ tests were used to sort students into curriculum tracks to prepare them for the jobs that they were best suited. The progressive movement that evolved at the beginning of the twentieth century was more student centered and viewed education as a means to reform society. After the Soviet Union beat the United States at launching a satellite in 1958, Congress passed the National Defense Education Act to prepare more students in mathematics and science. The content of curriculum continues to be debated by religious groups and groups that have historically not been well served in society.

How have different groups fared in the education system? For the most part, colonial schools and schools into the late 1900s were for white children. The federal goal for educating American Indians was to convert them to the Anglo Saxon culture and religion. African Americans, Latinos, and Asian Americans were taught in segregated schools that were underfunded and inferior to the schools of white children. Desegregation of schools did not occur until the mid-1900s when barriers to equal education were broken through a number of court cases, including the 1954 *Brown v. Board of Education of Topeka*.

How have teachers changed? In colonial days, completion of elementary school was usually enough to land a teaching job for younger children. The male teachers of older children usually had completed high school or college. Beginning in the 1800s, teachers could attend teacher institutes during school breaks to learn more about the subjects they taught and pedagogy. Normal schools were established to provide 1 to 2 years of preparation for teaching. These continued to operate into the mid-1990s when most of them became 4-year colleges and universities. Teachers have had little autonomy in their work with curriculum being determined by others and managed by school boards and administrators. For most of U.S. education history, their moral behavior has also been monitored through contracts.

Class Discussion Questions

1. Today Americans assume that a free and universal education is a "right." They probably give no thought to whether this has always been the way. What are your thoughts now? If you had been a participant in the various debates of the past three centuries, what would have been your position? Would you have argued for, or against, the state establishing common schools? How about expanding to include high schools? Having citizens taxed to pay for public schools for all children?

2. Historically, not all children have had access to the same quality of education, sometimes legally being barred from learning. What groups have had to fight to receive an education at public expense? What were the factors that prevented them from participating equally in the education system? What factors led to the changes that occurred in the 1960s and 1970s?

Field Guide for School Observations

When you begin teaching, you will probably work in a preschool, kindergarten, or primary, elementary, middle, or high school. Your teaching license may allow you to teach at two or more levels. The levels are different not only in the curriculum taught, but also the organization of a school day and the interactions of students and teachers. As you observe teachers in schools at two different levels (for example, middle and high school), make notes of the similarities and differences between the levels. You could organize your notes into a table or narrative. Write a brief paper on what level you would prefer to teach and why.

Ask a Teacher

Identify a teacher who has been teaching for over 20 years and ask him or her to describe some of the curriculum packages or programs the school system has asked them to use over the years. How long did most of them survive? Why were they successful or not successful? What does the teacher think are keys to a curriculum package being successful?

Journaling   Becoming a Thoughtful Teacher

Expectations for education have come a long way since colonial times. Take a few minutes to write a brief summary of how the curriculum has developed over the last 300 years. Describe some of the debates that have occurred over time. In what ways were the debates in the past similar to those heard today about what should be taught in schools?

Portfolio Tasks

1. Take a look at the constitution for your state. What does it say about the state's responsibility to offer a free and universal education? Then dig into state statutes

and regulations to see what is said about compulsory attendance. When were the compulsory attendance laws passed? How does that timing relate to the establishment of child labor laws in the early parts of the twentieth century?

2. A curriculum document may not provide the most stimulating reading material. However, understanding the ways in which curriculum documents can be transformed into learning activities helps a new teacher develop a sense of respect for the process of curriculum development. Prior to observing in an elementary or secondary classroom during your teacher education coursework, ask the cooperating teacher to share with you the curriculum elements they plan to include in the lesson. Compare those elements to the instruction and activities that the students are engaged in during the lesson. Describe, using this observation as an example, how curriculum is translated into instruction.

Self-Assessment *What Am I Learning?*

The Constitution of the United States and its amendments have guided the development of education since 1787. How have the following influenced the way education looks today? For assistance, check www.law.cornell.edu/constitution/constitution.table.html#amendments.

1. First Amendment
2. Tenth Amendment
3. Fourteenth Amendment

Using the Web

To learn more about some of the issues discussed in this chapter or to check your knowledge in this area, check out the following websites:

1. To learn more about Jefferson's Bill for the More General Diffusion of Knowledge, go to **http://etext.virginia.edu/jefferson/biog/lj13.htm**.

2. For a more thorough look at Rush's ideas on the education of women, visit the John and Mary's Journal on the Dickenson College website at **http://chronicles.dickinson.edu/johnandmary/JMJVolume13/campbell.htm**.

3. To find out more about Noah Webster, visit **www.lexrex.com/bios/nwebster.htm**.

4. For a description of the Lancaster Monitorial System of Education, visit **www.constitution.org/lanc/monitorial.htm**.

5. To hear National Public Radio's discussion and background on the historical *Brown v. Board of Education of Topeka* by historians, political leaders, and educators, visit **www.npr.org/news/specials/brown50/**.

6. To test your knowledge of the civil rights movement, go to **www.civilrightsteaching.org/**.

Your Professional Library

Education Week. (2000). *Lessons of a century: A nation's schools come of age*. Bethesda, MD: Editorial Projects in Education.

Articles by *Education Week* staff that address the issues, trends, and personalities that have shaped education in the United States since 1900 are compiled in this book. The chapters address everything from curriculum and teaching to governance and student life.

50 Years Later: Brown v. Board of Education. (Spring 2004). *Teaching Tolerance*, 25.

This issue provides a detailed outline and discussion of the court cases that led to *Brown v. Board of Education of Topeka* and the ones that stopped desegregation later in the 1900s. Prominent education, political, and media leaders also reflect on the importance of the *Brown* decision.

Menkart, D., Murray, A. D., & View, J. L. (2004). *Putting the movement back into civil rights teaching*. Washington, DC: Teaching for Change and the Poverty & Race Research Action Council.

The resource guide for educators moves the civil rights movement from heroes and holidays to the human story of the ordinary people who changed the history of the United States. It includes the stories of these heroes and lesson plans for teaching them.

Mondale, S., & Patton, S. B., Eds. (2001). *School: The story of American Public Education*. Boston: Beacon Press.

Prominent educational historians summarize the movement to common schools, the expansion of the public schools in the first half of the twentieth century, the desegregation of schools, and the increasing connections between schooling, national security and global competitiveness. The book includes many photos and interesting quotes.

Tyack, D. (2003). *Seeking common ground: Public schools in a diverse society*. Cambridge, MA: Harvard University Press.

In this wise and enlightening book, the difficult task of creating political unity and social diversity is examined. Tyack helps us see that debates about the civic purposes of schools are critical to a democratic society.

To access chapter objectives, practice tests, weblinks, and flashcards, visit the Companion Website at **www.ablongman.com/hall1e**

Log on to Allyn & Bacon's MyLabSchool (**www.mylabschool.com**). Enter Assignment ID **FDV3** in the **Assignment Finder**. View the clip *Brown v. Board of Education*. Answer question 1 at the end of the clip.

Enter Assignment ID **FDRN** in the **Assignment Finder** and launch Research Navigator. Go to the Link Library and search by the subject *Education*.

Under *Education in the U.S.* scroll down to the Modern Period of American Education (ca. 1920–present). Read the *Pierce v. Society of Sisters* account. Both the video clip and the written account offer evidence of the ways society, culture, and government have intersected during the history of education in the United States.

1. Use the MLS resources to identify another example of a pivotal occurrence in the history of education.

The Social Context of Schools

Educators in Real Schools

M E E T
Les Nakasaki

1st grade teacher, Rosemead, California

Les Nakasaki is beginning his 32nd year as a 1st grade teacher in Rosemead, California, east of Los Angeles. He is currently teaching at Arlene Bitely Elementary School, which has 520 students in kindergarten through 6th grade. His class usually has 20 students from ethnically diverse families. The school population is 55 percent Asian American, 40 percent Hispanic, and 5 percent from other ethnic groups. Many families speak languages other than English, including Spanish, Vietnamese, Cantonese, Mandarin, and other Chinese languages. Over 90 percent of the students receive free or reduced lunches, making the school eligible for Title I funds. Unlike many other low-income communities, the transient rate is low; families stay in this school district. Although children in many communities with large numbers of low-income families achieve at low levels on national achievement tests, Arlene Bitely Elementary School is an exception. It not only meets AYP (adequate yearly progress), but is an academic improvement school that has been designated as a California distinguished school.

Here's how Mr. Nakasaki responded when asked to describe his teaching experiences and thoughts about teaching.

❖ *What is excellence in teaching?*

Excellence in teaching is getting the most from your students to the best of their abilities. A teacher needs to look at the whole child. To help all students learn, a teacher must have the knowledge, skills, and dispositions for teaching effectively. Students who are learn-

ing are actively engaged in their work and are capable of telling the teacher what they are doing. They are able to demonstrate their knowledge by applying it to a new situation. Among my favorite sayings are "to teach is to touch a life forever" and "children come first."

❖ *How do you know when you have made a difference in student learning?*

When students are actively engaged in their learning and can talk about their work, I know they are learning. I am able to follow my 1st graders as they progress through 6th grade at my school. I observe a give-and-take attitude between teachers and students that contributes to their learning. The learning and educational needs of the child are communicated jointly between me as the teacher and my students.

I invite parents to visit my classroom at any time. I provide positive reinforcement to them on how well their children are doing. If children need help, I try to work with their parents as partners. I also encourage parents to become involved in different school committees, the PTA, school site councils, and school advisory committee meetings. I also encourage them to attend school and district functions. Being connected to parents is very important in supporting student learning.

❖ *What brings you joy in working in a classroom?*

Seeing students' eyes light up. Also when kids come up and say they got it, and you know they did because they demonstrate it. For a 1st grader, it is the smile. Students show confidence in what they are doing and begin to find the work easy. After Christmas, I always see the second semester blossom. The kids have moved into the routines of being in school; they know how school works. What they once struggled with is now comfortable. They begin to like math and reading. They want to learn and learn more. As they grow up, some come back to say thank you. After they leave 1st grade, they return to just talk, show me their work, and talk about what is happening in their lives. I love teaching.

❖ *What are some of the social issues that challenge your students and their families?*

Overall, the economic conditions affect their access to reading materials at home. Students don't have computers in their homes. Although my classroom has four computers and the library has computers that students enjoy, they don't have access after school and in the summers.

The mothers of a number of my students are teenagers who are not married and suffer economic hardships. It is more difficult to communicate with single parents because they lack the time and resources. Many of them are working long days that make it harder for them to be involved in the school. They have to rely on family members to provide child support.

❖ *What advice would you have for a new teacher?*

First, find the grade level with which you feel comfortable and are good at. If you feel successful, you will be successful. Communicate with colleagues about the realities of being a first-year teacher. Listen and learn from them about working in the classroom. Don't be afraid to ask questions. There is no such thing as a dumb question. Experienced teachers have probably asked the same question at some time.

Questions to Consider

1. What stereotypes about 1st grade teachers does Les Nakasaki break?

2. Why are communications with parents so important, especially in primary grades?

3. What are challenges that students may face in school and their lives as a result of their race, economic conditions, and pressures of growing up?

▶ **Sociology.** The study of society, its members, and their interactions.

Sociology is the study of society, its members, and their interactions. It examines the historical, economic, political, and psychological influences on how people interact with each other and society. It helps us examine social and cultural groups, individualism, and identity and explore issues such as the interaction of race, class, and gender in determining one's identity and society's response to groups that are not privileged. Sociology provides the tools for studying conflict among individuals and groups and the reasons for the conflict. It includes an examination of society's institutions such as schools, government, welfare, prisons, faith-based groups, families, health, and the like. The findings from sociological

221

How Does Sociology
Help Us Understand
Schools and the Work
of Teachers?

When conflict theory is applied to education, schools are found to be structured for the purpose of maintaining the power and control of the dominant group—those people with the greatest wealth and power. Schools legitimize inequities as children of the upper class and upper middle class attend schools that are attractive, clean, and well-equipped with technology, a swimming pool, a football field, gyms, and other amenities while schools for children from low-income families often are unattractive buildings that lack appropriate equipment for science and computer labs and sports such as swimming or football. In the 1976 publication of *Schooling in Capitalist America*, Bowles and Gintis (1976) charged that schools prepare students for their future class positions by providing a different education to the children of capitalists, who will be managers, and of the working class, who will work for them.

Resistance Theory   Some sociologists have found that neither of these theories fully describe society and schools. Students do not always accept their inferiority status. Some students resist following the school rules and participating in class activities. This theory suggests much more interaction between students and teachers than is explained by the previous two theories. It also allows for the possibility that social systems can be changed, especially when schools are not based on domination and submission, but model democracy in which students' voices are valued. If schools allow it, students can become active participants in defining and redefining schools.

Purposes of Schools

Schools are one of society's institutions that, along with parents, prepare children and youth for their adult roles. How schools go about that task depends, in part, on the philosophical, religious, and political perspectives of educators and the communities in which they are working. Some people view education as a public good in which all students should receive a liberal arts education and learn to be productive citizens in a democracy. Others believe that the primary role of schools is to prepare students for future jobs. Still others see schooling as a means for social mobility in which education is an asset to be accumulated and used to gain a competitive advantage over others to secure a desirable position in society.

Traditionally, schools have been expected to reproduce the cultural, political, social, and economic order of society. A problem with this approach is that it not only reproduces the positive characteristics of society, but also the negative characteristics such as discrimination against the least powerful. It generally supports the current power structure that favors the children of families with higher incomes through placements with the best teachers in gifted programs and advanced placement courses. The sociological theories outlined earlier provide contradictory descriptions of how schools carry out their reproductive role for society.

Ed Lines

"We cannot change anything unless we accept it." *Carl Jung*

Some educators believe that schools can do more than just reproduce society. They believe that schools can transform society to be more equitable across groups of students. These reconstructionists believe that all students can learn at a high level regardless of their race, ethnicity, gender, or socioeconomic status. These educators manage democratic classrooms in which both students and teachers are active learners and participants. The curriculum is experiential, encouraging students to learn by studying the positive and negative realities of society and confronting inequitable practices. Together, students and teachers work for the good of the community. Reconstructionism is built on the core values of social justice, human rights, human dignity, and **equity**. In the process, the school leads, rather than follows, societal practices for a democratic equitable society.

▶ Equity. The state of fairness and justice across individuals and groups; it does not mean the same educational strategies across groups, but does expect equal results.

School boards, educators, parents, and politicians have their own opinions about the primary purpose of schools. These opinions may be based on their own experiences in schools, their politics, or their religion. They may be influenced by local, state, and national reports, and debates on education. However, most of us refine and redefine our ideas about the purposes of schools over time. Our views may be dependent on our changing relationship with schools as students, parents, grandparents, or taxpayers. The four purposes of schools described here are those most often supported by educators and the public. Most schools address all of them, but one purpose may receive more prominence than others at a given time in a given school.

Citizenship

Almost everyone agrees that schools should help students become good citizens, but they may disagree on how students become good citizens. Some people believe that schools should ensure that students follow the rules of society, are patriotic, and know how government works. Others believe that students should be active participants in their learning and community. Students should be encouraged to question the inequities that exist in society and to fight for the civil rights and human dignity of all citizens.

In some schools, especially elementary schools, students may be graded on their citizenship within the classroom; this grade is often based on "good" behavior. Students usually take a civics or government course or study them in social studies. The focus in these courses is usually on the U.S. political system and documents that provide its foundation such as the Constitution and Bill of Rights. Patriotism and loyalty are implicit citizenship values taught in schools through reciting the Pledge of Allegiance, singing the national anthem, and celebrating national holidays in school assemblies and class activities.

Citizenship is not a proficiency that is taught in a single course. It is learned through observations of teachers, parents, and leaders who respect each other; believe in human dignity; are concerned about and care for others; and fight for justice, fairness, and tolerance. Students who are encouraged to participate in their community through service learning or volunteer work learn to be active, involved citizens. As educators, we can model democratic and equitable practices for our students.

Basic Skills for Work

Most parents would like their children to leave school with the basic skills needed to find and keep a job or begin college. Many communities have vocational high schools to teach specific occupational skills. Some school districts have also established magnet schools with single purposes, includ-

223

How Does Sociology
Help Us Understand
Schools and the Work
of Teachers?

Students learn early in
their school careers
the symbols of citi-
zenship such as
pledging allegiance to
the flag and singing
the national anthem.

ing career preparation in the arts, health fields, computing, and service areas such as restaurants, hotels, and tourism. Nevertheless, some employers complain that many young people cannot read, write, or compute at the level needed for the available jobs.

Educators, policy makers, and employers debate what students should be taught. All agree that students should know how to read, write, and compute at a level necessary for a job and managing their own affairs. State and national standards push for greater proficiency in reading, mathematics, and science. Education critics worry that schools are offering frivolous electives that may be interesting, but are not helping students learn the basics. Periodically, they call for a return to the basics of writing, reading, and computing, which can be measured by standardized tests. In addition, students need to learn to think, adjust to change, and be lifelong learners, in part, because certain jobs may become obsolete after a few years.

High Academic Achievement   Some school districts base their reputations on how well their students perform on standardized tests and how many are admitted to elite universities. Some parents try to ensure high academic achievement for their children by enrolling them in the best preschool in the community, hiring tutors for them, and lobbying for their acceptance in gifted programs.

State and national standards in academic areas, the arts, health, and physical education outline the proficiencies that students are expected to accomplish at different grade levels. Low-income students and students of color are expected to learn at the high levels historically expected of white upper-middle-class students. School systems' reputations and their state funding are dependent on how well students perform on these tests. Comparisons of test performance across schools, states, and nations is common. When other countries outperform U.S. students, politicians and policy makers call for reform of the curriculum, which has led to longer school days, reduction of social promotion from one grade to another, more rigorous standards, and more and more tests.

Social Development   Schools also provide opportunities for students to develop the social skills needed to work with others. In this process, students learn the rules for working appropriately with peers and adults. Appropriate behavior is constantly reinforced by teachers and other school personnel in the classroom and on the playground. Cooperative learning activities can be used to help students learn to work together. As teachers, we can assign students from different cultural backgrounds to a heterogeneous group. Internet and two-way video connections also allow students to talk directly with students in another part of the city or country, and even outside the United States.

Revisiting Johnny Wyche's Approach to Citizenship

The teacher whose story opened this section, Johnny Wyche, strongly believed that one of the purposes of schooling should be to learn to be a democratic citizen by practicing democracy in his social studies classroom. He, like Thomas Jefferson, believed that citizens would contribute to society most effectively if they were literate and learned how to participate. Some magnet schools are designed with the purpose of preparing students to be active participants in government. Other schools have other more general or specific purposes. Teachers themselves reinforce a school's purpose in different ways, focusing on one over others.

How Is Knowledge Socially Constructed?

Marilyn Johnson is selecting the literature that middle school students will read in her English class during the year. She knows that she should assign stories by African American writers in February to celebrate Black History Month and women writers in March to celebrate Women's History Month. She is sure there must be a month to celebrate American Indian and Latino heritage as well, but she can't remember when those are. Besides, she doesn't see any Latino or American Indian authors on the list of books and readings supplied by the school district. She wonders how she can begin to cover all of these ethnic groups and still read the classics that she read when she was in junior high.

What is knowledge? According to the 11th edition of the *Merriam-Webster's Collegiate Dictionary* (2005), it "applies to facts or ideas acquired by study, investigation, observation, or experience"; a related concept is learning, which "applies to knowledge acquired especially through formal, often advanced, schooling." Although the development of knowledge is the work of schools, it is also imparted

Ed Lines

"The chief cause of stress is reality." *Lily Tomlin*

by parents, friends, religions, mass media, places of business, and everyday experiences in society. Many of us have learned that the knowledge taught in schools
is objective and true; that it has been codified through a rationale process with
which almost everyone agrees. What a surprise to learn that knowledge is actually
socially constructed. It is influenced by the ideas, values, and interpretations of
the authors who have placed the facts in textbooks and scholarly documents. It is
also influenced by the author's identity, which is based, in part, on their group
memberships and experiences in society.

Because most recognized scholars in the United States who codified what is
known about an academic discipline over the centuries were white, upper-middle-
class, Protestant males, the perspectives of the powerful in dominant society are
reflected in their work. Many of these scholars and the consumers of their work
have come to identify their knowledge as accurate and true, the norm against
which other scholarship should be judged. Scholars with different racial, class, and
religious identities or from other countries question traditionally accepted knowledge and reconceptualize it from their own perspectives and world views. Thus,
the Western canon, which had been instilled into schools as the official curriculum for most of U.S. history, is labeled by these nontraditionalists as limiting and
exclusive with its focus on the history, literature, and arts of northern and western
Europe and the dominant group in the United States.

Early in the twentieth century, sociologists began to study knowledge with a
focus on the formal systems of ideas, particularly the worldviews and politics of
intellectuals. More recently, knowledge has been linked to broader cultural patterns and social consciousness. Sociologists now examine political and religious
ideologies as they are reflected in formal and informal types of knowledge. In this
section, we will explore the expansion of what is being taught in schools beyond
the traditional Western canon.

Whose Knowledge?

Knowledge valued by one group may be unimportant or known to be inaccurate
by another group. Whose knowledge should be taught in the curriculum? Western
traditionalists argue for the dominance of western civilization in the curriculum.
At the other end of the continuum, multiculturalists argue that the curriculum
must also include the marginalized experiences of people of color, the labor class,
women, and non-Christian believers. They believe that the curriculum should
more accurately reflect the histories and cultures of many groups and be presented
from multiple perspectives.

The curriculum of most schools remains centered in the cultural heritage of
northern and western Europe. It does not always incorporate the histories and experiences of groups whose families or ancestors were indigenous to the United States
or came from Asia, Africa, and South and Central America. The curriculum often
supports the superiority of Western thought over all others and is silent about issues
such as racism and oppression that affect the lives of many students. Study of

Ed Lines

"You lose a lot of time hating people." *Marian Anderson* non-European groups may be included as a unit during a school year or during the month set aside to address a group (for example, black history month). The goal, however, should be to integrate the major U.S. ethnic and racial groups plus the groups in the community throughout the curriculum and school activities.

Some parents are concerned that the public school curriculum does not reflect the values of their religion. They may even think their religion is purposefully denigrated in the curriculum. These differing perspectives on knowledge lead to controversies about the teaching of evolution, sex education, and other areas discussed in Chapter 3. These families may protest readings and books assigned to their children. Teachers should understand the values of the community in which they are teaching before making assignments that could be controversial.

The communities from which students come should provide the real-life examples that teachers draw on as they teach. One of the goals of teaching is to help students learn the academic skills for competing effectively in the workplace. Another goal is to acknowledge and respect the race and ethnicity of students to prevent them from becoming alienated from their families and communities. We are helped in accomplishing this goal by accurately reflecting the cultures and histories of our students in the curriculum.

Teaching the Cultures of Students   One approach to studying different racial and ethnic groups is **ethnic studies**, which provides in-depth examination of the social, economic, and political history and contemporary conditions of a group. Colleges and some high schools have ethnic studies courses, such as African American, Asian American, Native American, and Latino studies. These courses help fill in the gaps in knowledge about a specific group. If you have little exposure to the examination of an ethnic group different from your own, you should consider taking some college courses or undertaking your own individual study.

Another approach to incorporating students' cultures into classrooms is an **ethnocentric curriculum**. Some immigrant groups historically have established their own schools, with evening and weekend classes to teach their children the values, traditions, and language of their native homelands. Today some ethnic groups are establishing their own charter or private schools with curriculum centered on the history and values of their own ethnic group rather than the dominant western European orientation of most schools. Some Native American tribes have established tribally controlled schools in which the traditional culture provides the social and intellectual starting point.

Some African Americans have pushed for an **Afrocentric curriculum** to challenge Eurocentrism and tell the truth about black history. Proponents argue that centering the curriculum in the roots of Africa will improve their children's self-esteem, academic skills, and values and encourage them to develop a positive African American identity. The African perspective of the world and historical events is at the core of this approach. These schools are now located in a number of urban areas with large African American student populations.

Multiethnic Curriculum   The most common approach to integrating race and ethnicity into instruction is a **multiethnic curriculum**, which calls for all courses to reflect accurate and positive references to racial and ethnic diversity. The spe-

▶ **Ethnic studies.** A curriculum or courses that focus on the history, contributions, and conditions of a specific ethnic group (for example, Asian American studies or American Indian studies).

▶ **Ethnocentric curriculum.** A curriculum that is centered in the ethnic roots of an ethnic group.

▶ **Afrocentric curriculum.** A curriculum that is centered in African history, culture, and experiences.

▶ **Multiethnic curriculum.** A curriculum that integrates the history, culture, contributions, and experiences of multiple ethnic groups. The ethnic groups included in a multiethnic curriculum usually include the major ethnic groups in the United States and specific groups in the community served by a school.

cific content about groups differs based on the course being taught. In this approach, the diversity of students in the classroom does not determine the curriculum. All students study the racial and ethnic diversity of the United States and world. Multiple perspectives from different groups are used to explore critical issues in the curriculum.

Bulletin boards, resource books, and films should reflect ethnic diversity and the realities faced by different groups. Persons of color and new immigrant groups are studied in social studies. Students in language arts read stories about groups other than their own and by authors from different ethnic and racial groups. Students in the sciences, mathematics, the arts, and physical education learn that persons from many different cultures have contributed to these fields. The examples used to teach lessons should be drawn from the experiences of diverse groups, not just the group to which the teacher belongs.

As educators, we should ensure that ethnic and racial groups become an integral part of the curriculum. Although time will not allow us to discuss every ethnic group, we should ensure at a minimum that we include the groups represented in our community or state. If our textbooks do not include information about these groups, we need to find supplementary materials. Invite experts from the community to make a presentation or assist with lessons. Become acutely aware that teachers need to intervene when the curriculum is focusing solely on the dominant group.

Multiethnic education also helps students examine their own stereotypes about, and prejudices against, other racial and ethnic groups. Although these topics are not always easy to address, they should be a part of the curriculum beginning in preschool. Middle and high school students sometimes resist discussions that suggest they may be prejudiced or racist, often becoming very defensive. A safe classroom climate can be created by establishing clear guidelines for such discussions. Racial incidents in the hallways, on school grounds, in classrooms, and in the community can provide teachable moments to help students address their stereotypes and biases.

Multicultural Education

Multicultural education embraces the diversity of students, strives to help all students learn regardless of their group memberships, and promotes social justice. It is concerned with equity in the curriculum, relationships between teachers and students, the school climate, staffing patterns, and the school's relationships with parents and communities. Multicultural educators are able to view all aspects of the educational process through a critical lens that has the needs and learning of students at the center. Multicultural education usually refers to the content of the curriculum, which could include human relations; the study of ethnic and other cultural groups; the development of critical-thinking skills; and the examination of issues such as racism, power, and discrimination. The provision of education that is multicultural requires educators to

1. Place the student at the center of the teaching and learning process
2. Promote human rights and respect for cultural differences

3. Believe that all students can learn

4. Acknowledge and build on the life histories and experiences of students' cultural group memberships

5. Critically analyze oppression and power relationships to understand racism, sexism, classism, and discrimination against persons with disabilities, gays, lesbians, the young, and the aged

6. Critique society in the interest of social justice and equality

7. Participate in collective social action to ensure a democratic society (Gollnick & Chinn, 2006, 357)

Multicultural education is meant for all students regardless of their group memberships. Unfortunately, many educators have thought that it is only for students of color, believing that white students did not need to explore the issues that are so disruptive to society (for example, racism and discrimination) or to know about other groups and perspectives that help explain the different conclusions reached by groups about history, events, and subjects. Most textbooks today refer to diverse ethnic and racial groups, and most teachers include information about groups other than their own in a lesson, particularly during the months that have been highlighted for African American, Latino, or women's history. However, in some schools, attention to multiculturalism begins and ends with tasting ethnic foods and participating in ethnic festivals organized by parents, which provide only a superficial understanding of differences. Multicultural education, on the other hand, goes much further by integrating diversity and equity throughout the curriculum and school environment.

Teachers' Lounge

Bewitched

As a new art teacher in a rural Kansas junior high, I approached human figure drawing with care.

A few days before Halloween, I was working with my students on the correct proportions for human figures using a department store mannequin. In light of the way they feel with their bodies, figure drawing for students at this age can be awkward. As I walked around the room observing the drawings, however, I noticed that one of my more precocious students had drawn me naked on a broomstick wearing a witch's hat. I quietly slipped his drawing off his desk, replaced it with a blank sheet of paper, and told him he could begin again. His plan was foiled. A few minutes later, the class bell rang and I headed to the teachers' lounge for a mid-morning break. When I shared this story with those in the room, my colleagues roared with laugher. That incident occurred over 25 years ago and it still brings a smile to my face.

● Dawn Yonally, Ph.D.
Northeastern State
University

Culturally Responsive Teaching   **Culturally responsive teaching** is based on the premise that culture influences the way students learn (Gay, 2000; Darling-Hammond, French, & Garcia-Lopez, 2002). Culturally responsible teachers affirm the cultures of students, view the cultures and experiences of students as strengths, and reflect the students' cultures in the curriculum. Students learn to be proud of their ethnic and cultural identities. Teachers build on the students' diverse ways of knowing as they teach. The curriculum expands beyond the traditional canon grounded only in the knowledge and experiences of western and northern Europeans. It helps students learn about cultures other than their own with a goal of respect for and acceptance of differences as the natural state of a diverse society.

The real-life experiences that students bring to the classroom are often given no credibility in the classroom. School behavior and prior knowledge are related to what is learned to survive and thrive in their community environments. Most students who live in poverty have learned how to live in a world that is not imaginable to most middle-class students or teachers. However, their knowledge and skills do not always fit into the middle-class orientation of schools. Classrooms serving students from low-income families should see ordinary working people as valued members of society. They should see themselves and their families as valued, contributing members of the school community, rather than as second-class citizens who are not expected to compete at a high level with their more economically advantaged peers.

Students should be encouraged to expand their knowledge about others as they read novels and short stories about people from different socioeconomic levels. They should examine current and historical events from the perspective of the working class and those in poverty, as well as from the perspective of the middle-class and political elite. Learning is enhanced when teachers use representations from the experiences of students. Schooling should help expand students' knowledge of the world, not hide them from the unpleasant realities that exist. Students of all socioeconomic classes should develop critical-thinking skills that push them to question and investigate what they read, see, and hear in textbooks, the mass media, and discussions with friends. A curriculum for equality encourages them to identify inequities across groups and ask why.

Culturally responsive teaching. An educational strategy that affirms the cultures of students, views the cultures and experiences of students as strengths, and reflects the students' cultures in the curriculum.

Social Justice Education   The principle of social justice expects us to provide for those persons in society who are not as advantaged as we are. It is a value in most religions, suggesting that all people be treated equitably and with dignity. The philosopher and educator John Dewey (1997) called for social justice in education when he said, "What the best and wisest parent wants for his [or her] own child, that must the community want for all of its children" (p. 3).

Providing a socially just education requires taking steps to eliminate inequities within the classroom and school. Teaching for social justice requires what the president of the American Educational Research Association, Marilyn Cochran-Smith (2004) calls "teaching against the grain." It is more than teaching the literature and history of one's own group along with that of the dominant society. It also means confronting the inequities of society and working toward eliminating them.

Students who are involved in social justice programs may volunteer to work in the community on projects such as assisting the elderly.

Socially just teaching examines and critiques equity across groups. It confronts the social and economic inequities that prevent students from learning and participating effectively in schools (Apple, 2004).

Teachers for social justice feel a social responsibility for persons who are not advantaged. They believe that the great disparities between the rich and poor are too great and should be reduced. They also believe that everyone has a right to decent housing, health insurance, education, and adequate food and nutrition, regardless of their ethnicity, race, socioeconomic status, sexual orientation, or disability.

Revisiting Marilyn Johnson's Reading Selections

▶ **Multicultural curriculum.** A curriculum that incorporates the history, culture, contributions, and experiences of multiple ethnic, socioeconomic, language, and religious groups as well as females, males, and students with exceptionalities. A multicultural curriculum also addresses issues of power, discrimination, and inequality.

When Marilyn Johnson was making the literature selections for her class at the beginning of this section, she was aware that she should include writers of color and women. However, she viewed them as additions to the regular curriculum rather than an integral part of the curriculum. In a **multicultural curriculum**, students read a diverse group of authors throughout the year. They are aware of the ethnic identity of the authors and can discuss how their ethnicity or gender may have influenced their perspective on a story. The literature studied provides a look into the world from diverse and multiple perspectives, making it interesting and real to all students as they see themselves in the stories or can see a link between themselves and the characters in the stories.

How Important Are Class and Race in Providing an Education?

Finland provides families a number of educational options at public expense. For example, they can choose to place their preschooler in the town nursery school with about 40 other children. This school has an experienced principal, four teachers with master's degrees, two teacher's aides, and a cook. The child "would hear books read aloud every day, play games with numbers and the alphabet, learn some English, dig in the indoor sandbox or run around outside, sing and perform music, dress up for theatrical games, paint pictures, eat a hot lunch, take a nap if she wanted one, learn to play and work with others" (Kaiser, 2005, B1).

However, most parents in this small town choose to place their 4-year-olds in home care with three or four other children. The caretaker "doesn't have a master's, but she has received extensive training, has provided day care for two decades and has two grown children of her own. The kids in her charge do most of the things those at the center do, but with less order and organization. They also bake bread and make cakes" (Kaiser, 2005, B1).

Finland allows families to choose the form of day care they desire. The schooling that follows preschool will be essentially identical for all children regardless of their family's economic condition. "There is no 'elite' choice, no working-class choice; everyone is treated equally" (Kaiser, 2005, B1). And yet, Finnish children are scoring at the top levels on international academic achievement tests.

In his 1970 critique of sociology of education, *Reproduction in Education, Society and Culture* (1990), Pierre Bourdieu introduced the term *cultural capital* as the endowments we gain from our families such as cultural and linguistic competence. He claimed that schools are not as neutral and objective as many think because they value and reinforce the cultural capital of middle- and upper-class families, placing the children of working-class families at a disadvantage. The language, ideas, and knowledge of the arts that is learned in many upper- and middle-class homes provide children an "important exchange value in the educational and cultural marketplace" (Sadovnik, 2004, 17). Thus, families who do not adopt the language, ideas, and arts of the dominant group are at a disadvantage in schools. Their own cultures are not valued or rewarded in schools. In most instances, their children must adopt the dominant culture or become bicultural to be successful in schools. In this section, we will examine the cultural capital of class and race and the roles they play in schools.

Class

Class is used by sociologists to identify economic and social factors that determine differences among individuals and families. As indicated earlier, Marx established the class analysis in the nineteenth century by focusing on economic determinants such as owning property or capital, skill, and education. The study of class is a Western tradition led by British and U.S. sociologists who have divided the population into different classes based on the type of work in which they are engaged. Some sociologists argue that class is a weak determinant of life chances because social mobility allows many people to move from one class to another during their lifetimes. They believe that race and gender may be more important determinants of how people think and act. Other sociologists argue that class or SES has the greatest impact on families and students; see the Challenging Assumptions on page 232 for this perspective.

Class. Group of people, such as working class, who share the same social status based on socioeconomic status (SES).

Challenging Assumptions
FINDINGS FROM RESEARCH

Is the academic achievement gap between African Americans and whites primarily due to racial differences?

The Assumption: The disaggregation of scores on state and national achievement tests of academic knowledge shows that African American, Latino, and low-income students along with English language learners and students with disabilities perform at lower levels. Some researchers and policy makers have concluded that the differences in test scores are due to the race of students.

Study Design and Method: Richard Rothstein, a research associate with the Economic Policy Institute, argues that the achievement gap is primarily based on social class. He reviewed the data on test scores by different ethnic and racial groups and other factors such as family income to determine characteristics that correlated with lower test scores.

Study Findings: Rothstein's review of the impact of social class on learning identifies a number of critical characteristics. First, distinctively different child-rearing patterns exist across socioeconomic groups although not all families at a certain socioeconomic level exhibit the same patterns. These include the way families discipline their children, the way adults and children communicate, and the way adults read to their children. These differences are grounded, in part, in the types of jobs that adults in the family have. "If upper-middle-class parents have jobs in which they are expected to collaborate with fellow employees, create new solutions to problems, or wonder how to improve their contributions, they are more likely to talk to their children in ways that differ from those of lower-class parents whose own jobs simply require them to follow instructions without question" (Rothstein, 2004, p. 106).

Health differences among socioeconomic groups also have important implications for learning. Children from low-income families are more likely to have poor vision, poor oral hygiene, lead poisoning, asthma, poor nutrition, inadequate pediatric care, exposure to smoke, and other health problems. The lack of affordable housing for low-income families often means they are forced to move much more often than middle-class families. As a result, their children may attend one or more schools in a year. Some schools in low-income neighborhoods have almost a complete turnover of students during a school year as families move from one district to another.

Differences in the wealth of families are often overlooked by researchers who compare students based on their family incomes. White families with incomes similar to black families are more likely to have assets such as a house, allowing them to be ranked differently in the socioeconomic structure.

Little is known at this time about socioeconomic differences in noncognitive skills such as "perseverance, self-confidence, self-discipline, punctuality, the ability to communicate social responsibility, and the ability to work with others and resolve conflicts" (Rothstein, 2004, p. 108). Some students from low-income families score at the same or higher level as upper-middle-class whites on standardized achievement tests. They show great resiliency in overcoming the characteristics of an economically disadvantaged environment that contributes to students performing at lower levels in school.

Implications: The achievement gap appears to be between white students and students of color. However, students of color are more likely to live in a low-income family than white students. Rothstein concludes that more needs to be done to "narrow the social and economic gaps between lower- and middle-class children. These policies can probably have a more powerful impact on student achievement (and in some cases, at less cost) than an exclusive focus on school reform" (Rothstein, 2004, p. 109).

Source: Rothstein, R. (2004, October). A wider lens on the black-white achievement gap, *Phi Delta Kappan, 86*(2), 105–110.

Social Stratification   **Social stratification** categorizes individuals and families based on the interrelated factors of income, education, occupation, wealth, and power in society. These five factors are interrelated. For example, the higher your income, the more likely you will have an advanced college degree, a professional or managerial job, own stocks and property, and have influence in your community. Differential rankings in this social stratification system lead to inequality as some jobs are viewed as more worthy, more important, more prestigious, and more preferable than others. People who hold high-ranking positions try to maintain their positions and the accompanying power. They establish policies and practices such as required educational credentials that limit the access of others.

Rankings are not always based on merit or ability. A socially stratified society assigns low-prestige rankings to women, people with disabilities, the elderly, children, people of color, and persons with low incomes. At the same time, not all white, able-bodied men achieve a high-ranking position. Some are homeless and others are billionaires, but they and their families are overrepresented at the highest socioeconomic levels. Conversely, members of most oppressed groups can be found at all levels of the continuum, with a few at the top of the socioeconomic scale.

Meritocracy   **Meritocracy** is a system in which individuals who are the most talented and ambitious are expected to achieve at the highest social and economic levels. Proponents of meritocracy believe that everyone has the opportunity to be successful if they are smart enough and work hard enough. They accept **sociobiology** or the belief that intelligence and achievement are based almost solely on genetics. Socioeconomic status, race, or gender is not seen as contributing factors in academic achievement and financial success. They believe that individuals are totally responsible for their own achievements and do not accept the premise that being born into a wealthy family gives one an advantage. They do not accept discrimination and societal constraints on groups as reasons for their members to be less successful. They argue that members of such oppressed groups do not possess the intelligence, drive, or personal characteristics necessary to be successful. Inequalities are seen as natural, fair, and just.

Meritocracy is supported by at least three factors that drive the dominant view of U.S. society. First, the individual is valued over the group. Many people argue that policies such as affirmative action and sex equity inappropriately grant advantages to members of a group rather than allowing persons of color and women to compete equitably with others. They believe that these programs promote reverse discrimination against members of the dominant group.

The second factor promotes competition that stresses differences based on intelligence and talent. We compete with each other through IQ and achievement tests, which have become an integral part of education today. We are rewarded for the best grades, winning sports events, and receiving awards for our artistic accomplishments.

The importance of internal characteristics such as motivation, intuition, and character comprise the third factor. When people cannot be economically or socially successful as defined by the dominant society, they are blamed for not trying hard enough. External conditions such as racism and poverty are not recognized as

Social stratification. Levels of social class ranking based on income, education, occupation, wealth, and power in society.

Meritocracy. A system in which individuals who are the most talented and ambitious are expected to achieve at the highest social and economic levels.

Sociobiology. The belief that intelligence and achievement are based almost solely on genetics or heredity.

the roots that make it very difficult for most people with low-incomes and persons of color to compete at the same level as others.

The theory of meritocracy is applied to education through the provision of equal educational opportunity. This approach is supposed to level the playing field by ensuring that all students, regardless of their group membership, have similar chances for success or failure in school. These include programs such as Head Start and Title I, which are designed to provide compensatory education for children in low-income families to make up the education deficiencies they may have because they were born into a family with few economic resources.

Critics of meritocracy argue that equal educational opportunity programs are not able to overcome the disparities that exist between affluent families and families in poverty. They contend that children born with advantages are almost always able to hold onto and extend those advantages throughout their lives. Their families want to pass on their advantages and are often resistant to the equitable participation of less-advantaged students in gifted and talented programs, advanced placement courses, and the educational enrichment programs that accompany these programs.

Educational Practices   As shown in Figure 6.1, educators in the largest school districts face many students from low-income families who are eligible for free or reduced lunch. Poverty also exists in many rural and some suburban schools. These students live in environments outside school that are very different from those where most teachers live. Students who live in poverty have strengths that often are not recognized or supported by educators. Many are very resilient under conditions that provide obstacles to their well-being and academic achievement. Schools with large numbers of low-income students require competent educators with "commitment, enthusiasm, compassion, solidarity, and love" (Noguera, 2003, 21).

Teacher Expectations   Sociologists have documented the classification and segregation of students based on their class and race beginning in their first days in school. Most teachers can quickly identify the cultural capital that students bring to school. At the same time, many teachers develop expectations for their students' behavior and academic achievement based on these factors. Often unknowingly, they then develop instruction and interactions with their students that ensure they will behave as the teachers expect—a phenomenon called the **self-fulfilling prophecy**. Some teachers divide a class into learning groups based on nonacademic factors such as their clothing, cleanliness, or dialect. Students in the group expected to make the most academic progress may have been chosen because they are well-groomed, arrive in relatively new and well-pressed clothes, and use standard English. Students expected to have trouble learning may be wearing less-attractive clothing and live with single mothers. They use a lower-class dialect, and their parents or guardians do not have stable jobs. If the teacher's goal is to spend extra time with students in the second group with the goal of ensuring that they develop the academic skills necessary to move to the next grade, this grouping strategy might be successful. The problem is that too often students identified as having lower academic ability at the beginning of the year end the school year

▶ Self-fulfilling prophecy. Teacher's expectations for student achievement at the beginning of the year being realized by the end of the year.

Figure 6.1 Diversity of students in the six largest U.S. school districts in the 2001–2002 school year

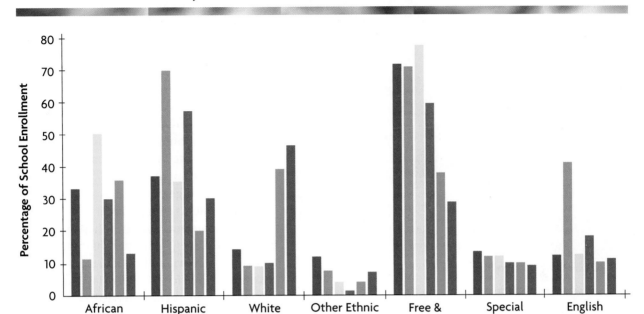

Source: Council of Great City Schools. City-by-city statistics: 2001–2002. Retrieved on January 1, 2005, from www.cgcs.org/pdfs/citybycity03.pdf.

with little improvement in their skills just as the teacher projected early in the year. Unfortunately, their lack of academic growth during that year usually follows them throughout their school career.

When teachers make such judgments about students based primarily on their class status, they are preventing them from having an equal opportunity for academic achievement. In these cases, a teacher's expectations for student achievement lead to the confirmation of the self-fulfilling prophecy. The practice is not congruent with the democratic belief that all students deserve an equal education. One of the joys of teaching is to overcome the odds against students whose families are low income by caring about them and guiding them to academic performance at the same level as their more affluent peers.

Tracking **Tracking** is an educational strategy that separates students for instruction based on their academic abilities. Students may be placed in a specific education track based primarily on their native language or disability. Students may choose or be assigned to a college, vocational, or general track that determines the courses they take. These assignments are sometimes based on judgments by

Tracking. The practice of separating students based on their academic abilities to receive instruction that is supposed to be most appropriate for their abilities.

In some schools, students are placed in academic tracks as early as preschool. Unfortunately, they are likely to stay in those same tracks for the remainder of their school careers.

teachers or counselors of a student's future potential. Some students are placed in gifted programs and others in programs that are clearly designed for low-ability students.

Socioeconomic status (SES) matters in tracking practices. Test scores, which may be used to track students, are correlated to the education level, or social class, of students' parents (Gamoran, 2004). Placement in high-ability classes is more closely correlated to family background and SES than intellectual potential (Ball, 2003; Brantlinger, 2003; and Welner, 2001). Students in high-ability courses and programs are academically challenged with enrichment activities that improve their intellectual and critical-thinking skills. Courses for students classified as low ability are often characterized as uninviting and boring. They include oral recitation and structured written work that are related to low-status knowledge. In addition, too many teachers in these classrooms spend more time on administration and discipline than actually teaching the subject matter, keeping students at the lowest level of academic achievement. These students are most likely to be taught by the least qualified and least experienced teachers who have a negative view of low-track students. Students from low-income families are also disproportionately assigned to low-ability groups. They are more likely to be classified as mentally challenged than their middle-class classmates.

Tracking has led to the resegregation of students based on race, class, and language into separate programs within the school. White, middle-class students are disproportionately represented in gifted and talented programs while African Americans, Latinos, students from low-income families, and English language learners are the majority of the students in low-ability classrooms. Schools could be accused of discriminatory practice in placing these students in low-ability courses and programs because they are limiting students' educational opportunities and potential for later occupational and economic success. A school district must notify parents of the requirements for advanced courses to provide all possible options for their children. With the emphasis on testing today, some parents are suing school districts because they have not hired qualified teachers to prepare their children to pass standardized tests. The Teachers and the Law on the facing page explores the legal ramifications of this issue.

Race

Sociologists do not regard "race" as a valid scientific category for explaining human behavior (Abercrombie, Hill, & Turner, 2000). It is a socially constructed

Teachers and the Law

TRACKING STUDENTS

Can students be grouped by ability or achievement?

Yes, unless the practice results in discrimination against a group of students. In the most publicized case, *Hobson v. Hansen*, parents in Washington, D.C., in 1967, argued that their children were assigned to lower tracks with limited curriculum and little chance for moving to higher levels. The court found that the testing methods used by the school district discriminated against students of color. Testing instruments used to make decisions about placement must be reliable, valid, and unbiased. They cannot be racially biased or administered in discriminatory ways. They must be administered in the student's native language and with appropriate accommodations for students with disabilities.

STUDENTS' FREEDOM OF EXPRESSION

Can students criticize governmental policies or practices in school?

Yes, as long as the action is not disruptive. The 1965 *Tinker* decision is the basis of most decisions related to students' freedom of expression. In this case, three students were sent home for wearing black armbands to protest the United States' involvement in Vietnam. The Supreme Court ruled that students are allowed to express their views in an orderly way.

The First Amendment allows both students and adults the right to express themselves and the right to be silent. For example, students cannot be forced to salute the American flag or to say the Pledge of Allegiance. However, some student expression is not covered by the First Amendment. School officials can take action against a student whose written or oral language is defamatory, shaming, or ridiculing others. The Supreme Count in 1986 ruled in *Bethel School District v. Fraser* that school officials could censor lewd, vulgar, and indecent student behavior. Courts have also upheld schools' rights to discipline students for inflammatory expression such as threatening other students or teachers.

REPORTING CHILD ABUSE

Can teachers be held liable for not reporting suspected child abuse?

Yes. Teachers are among the professionals who are required to report signs of child abuse. Penalties for not reporting include fines and/or prison terms. School districts may also impose disciplinary action. For example, the Seventh Circuit upheld the suspension and demotion of a teacher-psychologist who did not promptly report suspected abuse in *Pesce v. J. Sterling Morton High School District 201, Cook County, Illinois*, in 1987. School districts usually have procedures for reporting suspected abuse, including to whom the abuse should be reported. In 1998, the Kentucky Supreme Court ruled that once the abuse is reported to a supervisor, the supervisor has the responsibility for reporting it to the appropriate authority. However, teachers should check to ensure that the appropriate agency has been notified.

Sources: Cambron-McCabe, N. H., McCarthy, M. M., & Thomas, S. B. (2004). *Public school law: Teachers' and students' rights* (5th ed.). Boston: Allyn and Bacon; Essex, N. L. (2005). *School law and the public schools: A practical guide for educational leaders*. Boston: Allyn and Bacon.

concept based on society's perception that racial differences exist. In the United States, race has become equivalent to caste in other societies because persons with darker skin have been treated as inferior to whites. This practice has resulted in overt discrimination and inequality against persons of color. For example, immigrants had to be white to be eligible for naturalized citizenship until 1952. Race continues to be codified in this country. We are often asked to identify our race when we complete government forms. It is also used to track the participation of groups in schools, colleges, and professional fields to determine discriminatory practices.

Many adults are not aware of the number of children who live in poverty. They do not understand the pressures that youth experience in their homes, schools, and communities. The contributions young people make to their schools and communities are often not acknowledged by adults or publicized in the media. As a result, many adults see children and young people as a drain on society's resources through taxes for schools and youth services. Their fear of the violence of youth has led to policies of zero tolerance, tougher sentencing requirements for young people, and abusive corrective camps to straighten them out. The inattention and lack of support by adults has made many children and youth feel devalued by a society that often resents or fights governmental support for their well-being and safety. Schools often are a haven for children and youth. They are usually seen as a place with supportive adults who care about their growth and potential. As a teacher, you can be one of those adults who make a difference in the life of students.

Children are becoming a diminishing proportion of the U.S. population. They were 36 percent of the population in 1960. By 2025, they will be less than 24 percent of the population; Americans over 65 years old will outnumber persons between the ages of 5 and 17 years old (Nichols & Good, 2004). As adults, these young people will be expected to provide the resources for this large aging population.

Unlike the period in which their grandparents grew up, many youth today are expected to work part-time and attend school as well as participate in sports and/or extracurricular activities and religious or community activities. In fact, nearly one-third of 16- to 19-year-olds are working while they attend school (U.S. Census Bureau, 2006). They are expected to enroll in postsecondary education after high school and not have a full-time job until they are in their twenties. They marry later than their elders and will have fewer children or no children at all. Activities that they share with adults are more limited, leaving them to socialize themselves and seek assistance and approval from their peers. They have great access to media and their stereotypical images of youthfulness. They also have access to instant communications with peers from all over the world through the Internet (Nichols & Good, 2004).

Health and Fitness

The nation is at risk of raising unhealthy children and youth. Their education is not providing them information about good nutrition and it is no longer requiring them to participate in regular physical activity that is critical for a healthy life. Many schools have eliminated physical education and health as part of budget-cutting measures. When teachers are asked to concentrate almost solely on the subjects on which students' academic achievement will be tested, little time is left in the school day for what some policy makers call frivolous activities such as physical education—and, yet, healthy children perform better in school.

The Way They Look   Beginning as early as elementary school, some students, especially girls, worry about their looks and weight. Some young people are just not

Ed Lines

"**We must change in order to survive.**" *Pearl Bailey*

Connecting

TO THE CLASSROOM

This chapter has provided you with some basic information about the role sociology plays in our understanding of schools and students. The following are some key principles for applying the information in this chapter to the classroom.

1. Positively incorporating the cultures of students in the curriculum shows that teachers value cultures other than their own.

2. Students in poverty and from low-income families need more, not less, attention from teachers.

3. When teachers hold high expectations for the academic achievement of students, students almost always meet those expectations.

4. Assessments used to group students must be unbiased, valid, and reliable to prevent discriminating against a group of students based on their ethnicity, race, socioeconomic status, language, gender, or disability.

5. Teachers and parents can influence the choices that students make about sex, drugs, and other potentially harmful choices.

Males are less likely to finish high school than females, and a larger percentage of females are entering college than males. High school graduates (94.5%) are more likely to be employed than dropouts (91.2%) and to have higher incomes. The median income for a male who went to high school but did not graduate was $29,100 in 2003. In that same year, it was $38,337 for a high school graduate and $81,007 for a college graduate. Women earned less than men, but education increased their earnings from $21,426 if they had not graduated from high school to $53,215 if they completed college (U.S. Census Bureau, 2006).

Revisiting Carmen Vasquez's Classroom

The teacher who opened this section, Carmen Vasquez, has recognized that learning is affected by many factors other than intelligence. The behavior of students may be influenced by the conditions they face in their families and communities that can have positive or negative impacts in the classroom. Their self-esteem may be high or low based on factors such as their weight, sexuality, or use of illegal substances. Carmen has been effective in helping them understand the conditions that affect their lives and in helping them express themselves as they write.

Chapter Summary

Schools are one of society's most important institutions because they help prepare children for their adult lives. The content of the curriculum in schools is studied by sociologists. Sociology also includes the examination of the academic and social performance of students, student and teacher interactions, educational equality across groups, and the social well-being of students.

How does sociology help us understand schools and the work of teachers? Sociological theories provide different ways of interpreting the roles of schools in society. Functionalism is concerned with developing a cohesive society through assimilation into a common culture. Conflict theorists see schools as serving the needs of a capitalist society by preparing students for the different jobs needed to sustain capitalism. Resistance theorists see students and teachers as playing more important roles in the education of students as they interact in the classroom. Educators and the public help determine the purposes of schools in their communities, giving priority to different purposes at different times in history.

What does social context have to do with what teachers teach? Knowledge is socially constructed and thus controlled by those who write textbooks and curriculum. Some states manage a statewide textbook adoption process in which they can demand that certain subjects be included or excluded from textbooks. Teachers who believe there are no absolute truths to be taught incorporate multiple perspectives on a topic into their teaching. They bring the cultures and experiences of their students into the curriculum. They systematically incorporate information and examples from diverse ethnic groups as they deliver multiethnic education. Multicultural education opens the curriculum beyond ethnicity to address the history and experiences of other groups such as women, people with disabilities, economically disadvantaged groups, English language learners, and religious groups.

How important are race and class in providing an education? Our educational system does not appear to serve students of color or of low-income equitably. Their schools too often have inadequate resources, unprepared teachers, and unsafe environments. They have not been expected to achieve academically at the same high levels as their white, middle-class counterparts. The inequity in educating these students is complicated by the racism and classism in society that prevents educators and others from respecting them and holding high expectations for their academic and social behavior. As schools are forced to focus on achievement results across racial and economic groups, it is becoming clear that these students are still not being well-served in our schools.

What other societal challenges affect students? Children and young people face a number of societal challenges as they make decisions about themselves. They are influenced by their peers, their parents, other adults, and the media about appropriate behavior. These sources of information sometimes provide conflicting messages, particularly about issues related to appearance (that is, being thin or muscular) and sexuality. Some students experience violence in schools as they are bullied or harassed; others are abused at home. Many teenagers experiment with drugs and alcohol, but the numbers who do have been dropping over the past 10 years. The most recent data on school dropouts show that as many as 50 percent of the students in urban areas are dropping out of school, a much higher rate than school districts had reported in the past.

Class Discussion Questions

1. Sociology helps us understand society and its institutions, including schools and how students are treated in them. How do you think sociology can contribute to our knowledge about teachers and schools? What data about the culture of schools and their students could be helpful to you as a teacher?

2. Sociology suggests that schools often perpetuate inequities based on the race and class of their students. How could you check for your own biases and begin to ensure that you do not discriminate against students of color and/or students from low-income families?

Field Guide for School Observations

In culturally responsive teaching, one of the goals is to connect the concepts being taught to the students' real lives. The teachers whom you are observing during this school period may use a number of different strategies to make the curriculum authentic and meaningful to their students. As you visit classrooms, look for evidence of how the teachers you observe are connecting the curriculum to students' lives by using the following rubric from the *Standards for Effective Pedagogy* of the Center for Research on Education, Diversity, and Excellence. Begin the process by identifying the school and the group memberships of the teacher and students being observed.

School:

Location of the School:

Race and Gender of the Teacher:

Race, Gender, Native Languages, and Class of Students:

Standard	Not Observed	Emerging	Developing	Enacting	Integrating
Making Meaning— Connecting School to Students' Lives	Contextualization is not observed.	(a) The teacher inquires about students' knowledge and experiences from outside school, or (b) parents or community members participate in activities or instruction, or (c) classroom activities are connected only by topic.	The teacher makes incidental connections between students' prior experience/ knowledge from home, school, or community and the new activity/ information, or some aspect of students' everyday experience or prior knowledge is included in instruction.	The teacher integrates the new activity/ information with what students already know from home, school, or community.	The teacher designs, enacts, and collaboratively contextualizes activities, demonstrates skillful integration of multiple standards simultaneously.

Comments:

Ask a Teacher

One of the purposes of schools is to help children become literate. However, schools serve other purposes as outlined in this chapter. Magnet schools are designed to prepare students in a particular field such as government, the arts, or mathematics and science. Ask several teachers in the same or different schools what they believe to be the purposes of the school in which they are working. Ask them how their teaching contributes to those purposes. What purposes do they wish their schools had? Why?

Journaling *Becoming a Thoughtful Teacher*

Think about the last three fiction or nonfiction books that you have read. Whose knowledge did it reflect? Were the stories grounded in U.S. dominant society or did they introduce you to other cultures? Why do you think you are choosing these books?

Portfolio Tasks

1. When you begin teaching, you may have a class with students from ethnic or racial groups with which you are not familiar. You should be able to incorporate information about your students' culture into the curriculum and draw on their cultures to provide examples to help them learn. To provide you a beginning, identify instructional resources on African Americans, Asian Americans, Latinos, or American Indians that can be incorporated into lesson plans for the future.

2. The sexual harassment of students by teachers or other students is illegal. Gay and lesbian students report fairly regular harassment from other students, particularly verbal abuse. How will you respond if students in your class or within your hearing are verbally taunting gay or lesbian students? How will you help the gay and lesbian students in your classroom to handle the harassment? Develop a plan for confronting harassment in your classroom. See Using the Web for websites that may provide information for developing the plan.

Self-Assessment *What Am I Learning?*

Using the rubric in the Field Guide for School Observations, assess your preparedness for this important task. Where do you rate yourself?

Using the Web

1. For guidance on preventing sexual harassment, visit **www.aauw.org/ef/harass/pdf/ completeguide.pdf**.

2. For information on supporting a no name-calling promotion in schools, go to **www .glsen.org/cgi-bin/iowa/educator/library/ record/1903.html**.

3. To find assistance on identifying and reporting child abuse, check **www.calib.com/nccanch/**.

4. For suggestions on working against hate and prejudice in schools, get a free subscription to *Teaching Tolerance* at **www.splcenter.org/ center/tt/teach.jsp**.

Your Professional Library

Hersch, Patricia (1999) *A tribe apart: A journey into the heart of American adolescence*. New York: Ballantine.

A journalist describes the experiences of eight teenagers in Reston, Virginia, a suburb of Washington, D.C. She pleads with adults to set aside their stereotypes and fears about teenagers to see their world as they see it.

Moran, J. P. (2000). *Teaching sex: The shaping of adolescence in the 20th century*. Cambridge, MA: Harvard University Press.

This history of sex education in the twentieth century provides insights into the current struggle between comprehensive and abstinence-only programs.

Nichols, S. L., & Good, T. L. (2004). *America's teenagers—Myths and realities: Media images, schooling, and the social costs of careless indifference*. Mahwah, NJ: Lawrence Erlbaum.

The myths about today's teenagers are explored and corrected with data in this book. The authors' recommendations can help teachers, parents, policy makers, and citizens in responding to teenagers in meaningful and proactive ways that will improve their quality of life.

To access chapter objectives, practice tests, weblinks, and flashcards, visit the Companion Website at **www.ablongman.com/hall1e**

mylabschool

Log on to Allyn & Bacon's MyLabSchool (**www. mylabschool.com**). Enter Assignment ID **CS17** in the **Assignment Finder** and read the case study, *Multicultural Education: Parents as (subversive) Partners*, and read about Susan's attempt to introduce a multicultural curriculum.

Teachers are expected to deliver curriculum that meets national, state, and local school district standards. Additionally, teachers must be mindful of the social context of the school in which they teach and the prevalent attitudes and beliefs of the parents of their students. The teacher in this case, Susan, has worked creatively to develop a multicultural curriculum to provide her students with knowledge of the contributions to American society of diverse cultures and ethnic groups. Her efforts have met with discouraging reactions from a couple of parents. Consider what you have read in this case along with the information in this chapter to answer questions 5, 6, and 7 at the end of the case about Susan's attempt to introduce a multicultural curriculum.

5. Should Susan talk to Mrs. Woods and Mrs. Myers? If so, how should she approach the conversation? Should Susan talk again with her principal? Explain your answer.
6. What could Susan have done to avoid this problem?
7. What should she do now?

Thinking about Teaching and Learning

Educators in Real Schools

MEET
Lisa A. Mason-Sykes
George H. Corliss High School

George H. Corliss High School, located in the historic Pullman community on Chicago's far South Side, serves approximately 1,100 students, most of whom are African American. About 75 percent of Corliss students participate in Education-to-Career (ETC) programs that include accounting, carpentry, chorus, computer programming, commercial art, culinary arts, information processing, band, and naval JROTC. Of the 82 teachers at Corliss, 42 hold a master's degree and one of the teachers holds a doctorate.

Eldorado High School located in Henderson, Nevada, "provides relevant experiences that develop skills necessary to succeed in an ever-changing world." Of the nearly 3,000 students at Eldorado, more than 60 percent are from minority groups, and nearly 20 percent are students with limited English proficiency. English classes at Eldorado average 31 students per class.

Lisa A. Mason-Sykes is a teacher on the move. She teaches high school English to sophomores and seniors. She began her teacher career at Corliss high school before moving across the country to be closer to her grandmother. She now teaches at Eldorado high school, where she serves as the English department chair, coaches girls' basketball and softball, and is a mentor for three new teachers. Lisa says that it was inevitable that she would become a teacher even though she left Southern University and A&M College in Baton Rouge, Louisiana, before completing her degree to enter the world of business.

Chapter 7

❖ Why did you become a teacher?

Teaching is in my blood. Everyone in my stepfather's family is in education. When I left college to begin working in the business field, I thought I had made the right choice. In time, though, I saw that I needed to finish my college degree in order to reach the goals that I had set for myself. My stepdad, a teacher and administrator, had a great influence on my decision. He often said he didn't care what I could do without an education, he wanted to know what I could do with one. So I left my job as a sales and special projects manager and went back to college in Chicago to finish what I had started in Louisiana. When I received my degree from Chicago State University and obtained a teaching license in Illinois, I knew that I was carrying on the legacy of the family.

❖ What do you see when you see excellence in teaching?

I see a teacher who doesn't waste a second. The time students spend in high school can seem like an eternity to some, but in reality it is such a short time to learn so much. Not a minute can be wasted. An excellent teacher teaches from bell to bell. The moment kids come into the classroom they should have something to do that engages them in learning. My students are required to journal every morning. I give them random topics related to real life and they must write a minimum of 11 sentences about the topic. They write, and, while they're writing, they're reading. Sometimes excellence in teaching is tricking students into doing the work. Kids don't always want to learn what they need to and it is up to teachers to surprise them into learning. Excellent teachers are creative and enthusiastic and often entertaining. They make learning fun by sharing the fun of teaching with the students. I tell my

students to not ever let a teacher steal a paycheck. Teachers who don't demand learning from their students aren't doing their jobs.

❧ How do you know that you have made a difference in student learning?

I know I've made a difference in student learning when they ask questions about the content. You can see the difference you've made on their faces. Sometimes it's possible to see the spark of understanding in students' eyes. When teachers take the time to look closely at their students' faces they often notice a cloud of confusion or misunderstanding lift to be replaced by a glow of learning. If I help only one kid out of a hundred, I have made a difference.

❧ What brings you joy in teaching?

If just one kid says, "Thank you, Mrs. Sykes" my day is made. There is nothing more rewarding than knowing my time and energy have been appreciated. Life today is fast paced. At times it is exhausting; at times it is exhilarating. Seeing the effort you have expended acknowledged by your students is a great rush in teaching. Of course the joy in teaching works both ways. When teachers are joyous about the accomplishments of their students, the students may reciprocate in kind by showing their joy in learning. Expressions of appreciation may be so subtle that a teacher might miss them, but when you do notice them, it's great.

❧ How did you go about developing a personal philosophy of teaching?

There is no direct methodology as to how I came up with my philosophy of teaching. I have always been the type of person who learns by living. Why should teaching be any different? I learn by teaching and I gain my philosophy along the way. I have always believed that our youth have been given a bum rap and that they are often looked at as a generation lost. This method of thinking is derived from people who don't deal with our youth on a regular basis. It comes from the people who let what they "think they know" interfere with what is reality. I look at each student and I make my own decisions based on my conversation with that student. I don't lump students together. My philosophy began to develop the first day I stepped foot into a classroom and it continues to evolve as I encounter more students. I pay close attention to the habits and needs of my students which is why I can relate to them.

❧ What philosophical perspectives influenced the development of your philosophy of teaching?

I don't want to make it seem like I don't listen to the different philosophies because I do take in much of that information, though it is up to me to decide if aspects of one or another of the philosophies fits into my situation. I like what Sonia Nieto says about making sure that we view our students as individuals. I think that idea alone can make a great philosophy. If you look at each student as an individual, then you won't be so quick to make a judgment on the entire class of students. As I said before, I learn from my daily interaction with my students. What one says is a great concept of teaching might be good for that group but not for the next group. My experience in the Chicago Public School system really opened my eyes to that reality. My students were diverse in background and one concept did not always work for the entire class; that is when your creativity as a teacher must come into play. If a teacher is not motivated for the "cause," then it's the students that suffer.

❧ *If your personal philosophy of teaching ever came in conflict with the status quo, how did you negotiate/manage the conflict without surrendering your ideals?*

I feel that my philosophy is always in conflict because the people who are making the decisions for our children do not come in contact with our children. The people making the rules and program guidelines don't get input from the people who are in the trenches and so how can my philosophy not come into conflict with the status quo? What I see as best for my students, the "suits" do not. What I know about my students, the "suits" do not. I never surrender because we are at war for our students. I am the general in charge of leading my students to victory. Why would I ever give up? Never! I just make slight adjustments so that the students still come out as the winners. It is a rough war and it is hard fought but I am not ready to wave the white flag.

❧ *How is your personal philosophy of teaching translated into instructional practices?*

I know that students learn better when they have an active part in the process. If I see that my students do not understand a concept, I often come up with some sort of "authentic pedagogy" project that they can create. When students can see or feel a concept then it is easier to understand. I often use popular culture as a tool for learning as well. This means that I will make a parallel with the literature and something that exists in their world. The way that movies are being produced today, it is easy to use a popular movie to teach the students techniques that they use every day. Many techniques are used and the students don't realize it. When you use something that they are familiar with to show a particular skill, you see that look on their faces that lets you know that you have made a difference. That look that lets you know that you have given that student something that they will take with them for life.

Questions to Consider

1. Do you recall a time when one of your high school teachers was able to help you understand a difficult concept by relating it to something in your personal life? Why does this strategy seem to work?

2. How do teachers demonstrate joy in what the students are learning? In what ways can a teacher's demonstration of joy over student learning be contagious?

3. How might a teacher manage to avoid thinking of all students as cut from the same cloth? What are some strategies a teacher could use to recognize and appreciate the individual differences among students?

Professionals worthy of the title spend most of their waking moments, and even some moments deep in sleep, thinking (or dreaming) about their work. Contemplating teaching is what good teachers do. They play questions over and over in their minds seeking solutions to complex and often baffling problems. Socrates felt that the unexamined life wasn't worth living, and perhaps teachers who do not constantly think about and question the art and science of teaching may not be worthy of being called teachers.

As you train for and eventually enter the profession as a fully qualified, full-time teacher, you will enter a world of debate, dissonance, and delight. The people you work for and with will at times seem to be faithful comrades, compatriots in mind and action, and at other times opponents of all you hold true and dear. How each person thinks about teaching reflects not only their personal values but also the values of society. The socioeconomic status we enjoy, the experiences we have had, and what is happening in our local society and the world in general all influence the ways we think about teaching and learning. One individual's interpretation of events may conflict with another's and result in discord. Upheavals in our lives and in society have great power to alter the way we perceive the future and in some cases to change our thinking about what future citizens must know and be able to do.

Few modern educators would argue that there is but a single way to learn, or a single way to teach the skills, facts, and concepts deemed essential to a contemporary education. However, there are those who would argue that one particular way of teaching is inherently better or more efficient than another. Listen to teachers talk about how they teach their students to read or spell, and chances are that you will hear quite different philosophies regarding learning, methods, and materials. Such discussions often generate more heat than enlightenment and provide proof of the value we place on our own firmly held opinions.

In this chapter, you will begin to understand the ways that teachers must confront the assumptions that guide their behavior and practice in classrooms. For the most part, teachers must enact what policy makers propose. They have to work constantly to adjust their personal and professional ideals to meet others' expectations. They compromise their own emotions and intellectual abilities to accommodate such expectations. People outside of the daily act of teaching seldom think about this. Teachers contemplate it constantly. To be well informed, they must know and understand what policy makers and academics recommend. Alan Tom in his 1997 book, *Redesigning Teacher Education*, examines the role that teacher education must play in preparing teachers to incorporate and connect ideas and to prepare them for the purposeful act of teaching through integration of knowledge, skill, and a lifetime of opinions.

Focus QUESTIONS

After reading this chapter, you should be able to answer the following questions:

1 How do teachers learn to recognize the difference between good and not-so-good ideas about teaching and learning?

2 What factors influence the development of teachers' beliefs and assumptions about teaching and learning?

3 How might thinking about teaching foster new ideas?

4 How might a teacher develop a pedagogical vision?

5 Why is it important to have a personal philosophical perspective toward teaching and learning?

Where Do Good Ideas about Teaching and Learning Come from?

Natalie has had to give considerable thought to her actions and make many decisions during her teacher-education coursework and during her practicum and student-teaching assignments. She is well aware that as a full-time teacher she must carefully think through her actions as a teacher, and that she will be required to make even more decisions than she has had to make as a teacher education candidate. In one of her classes, she heard that the only job more demanding than teaching in the area of rapid decision making is that of an air-traffic controller. Sometimes teachers can make as many as a thousand decisions a day. Of course the decisions teachers make aren't likely to result in crashes or close calls. However, Dr. David Berliner, a professor at Arizona State University, did once suggest that if students fell out of their seats as the result of bad decisions on the part of the teacher, all teachers might give more thought to the decisions they make about teaching. It has occurred to Natalie that thinking about teaching and making decisions can be more exhausting than playing three set of tennis with Nancy on Saturday mornings. What Natalie is most concerned about, however, is that the thinking she does results in good ideas. She has seen enough examples of not-so-good ideas being demonstrated in classrooms that she wants to make certain that the ideas she comes up with are always a benefit to her future students. Because of this desire, Natalie has taken particular pains to read about different approaches to teaching and understand the tenets underlying a variety of teaching strategies. She also tries to identify particularly good ideas about teaching and to document how they are actually used in the classroom.

Someone once said that good ideas just blossom, arise up out of the minds of people close to the action, and are fertilized by knowledge, creativity, and enthusiasm. Ideas about teaching and learning are in abundance, and, because not all ideas are of equal value, it can be difficult to weed out the good from the bad. Some ideas are priceless—while some are not. Some are in direct conflict with one another. Ideas germinate in knowledge and are driven by opinions, beliefs, assumptions, and experiences, and the context in which the ideas blossom. Unfortunately, in education, as in all areas of life, some good ideas are stamped out before they have a time to bloom, while some bad ideas flourish in unguarded cultures.

Good ideas are often based in one or another of the established philosophies of life. There will be more about this later in the chapter. Good ideas can come out of educational research conducted by professors and research centers dedicated to the study of teaching and learning. Good ideas also emerge from teacher educators and teachers practicing their craft, collecting data, and making grassroots changes in practice. Some of the teacher educators and teachers who have generated great ideas for future generations of teachers and learners are famous. All have, through thinking about teaching and learning, contributed to the profession.

Good Ideas

Great minds in U.S. education wrestle with ideas of what should be taught in America's schools, how it should be taught, and when it should be taught. As U.S. education has evolved, a number of approaches from European to homegrown ideas and programs have been tried. Room arrangements from the utilitarian, efficiency approach of nailing rows of desks to the floor to facilitate organization and directing student attention forward, to classrooms with tables and multiple activity centers and all the interaction such an arrangement might offer, have been tried. Some experts have recommended managing student behavior from a laissez-faire approach. For example, A. S. Neill's Summerhill style of schooling does this by allowing students free rein to decide when to play and when to work. For more information on the Summerhill approach, visit www.summerhillschool.co.uk/. In B. F. Skinner's behavior modification approach, actions are controlled through reinforcement. Nearly everyone you talk to has some idea about what should be happening in school. The popular press has nearly as much to say about teaching and learning as educators. Even Oprah's favorite philosopher, Dr. Phil McGraw, offers his ideas about raising the perfect child (2004). The range of ideas teachers are confronted with is staggering.

Numerous ideas about structuring curriculum and methods for delivering the curriculum have been tried, revamped, and retried. The book of Ecclesiastes says that there is nothing new under the sun. Teachers who have been around for any length of time and have experienced the ebb and flow of programs and approaches to teaching will tell you that many of the new programs they are asked to implement are really only revamped versions of tried-and-true methods. The fact is that data collected on some of these tried-and-true methods are frequently used to improve them. Constant thinking about teaching can lead to new ideas that will improve education for teachers and learners alike.

While educators know an informed populace helps build a democratic society, they don't know exactly what skills a 5-year-old of today will need 30 years down the line in order to be successful and to contribute to the well-being of society. The constant generation of ideas about teaching and learning is one way educators attempt to imagine and prepare for the future.

Way of Thinking about Teaching   The Western world's first great philosophers came from Athens, Greece. The names of three of these philosophers are no doubt familiar to you: Socrates (470–399 BCE), Plato (427–347 BCE), and Aristotle (384–322 BCE). Socrates is famous for creating the **Socratic method** of teaching still used by many teachers today. These teachers ask a series of questions that leads the student to a certain conclusion. Plato believed that each person's abilities should be used to serve society and should be developed to the fullest capacity. Aristotle favored the scientific, the practical, and the objective in learning, and believed that the quality of a society was determined by the quality of the education that society promoted.

Socratic method. A method of teaching or discussion in which the teacher asks a series of questions that lead the answerer to a logical conclusion.

John Dewey (1859–1952)   It would be folly to try to adequately cover the contributions of Dewey's ideas to U.S. education in this chapter. Suffice it to say he was a giant among the thinkers of the twentieth century. John Dewey inspired several movements that shaped twentieth-century thought. For over 50 years, Dewey was the voice for a liberal progressivism that helped shaped the destiny of education in the United States. Dewey's thoughts on pedagogy, epistemology, and his pragmatic approaches to ethics and aesthetics remain influential in education today. You should become familiar with John Dewey's name and ideas as you progress through your teacher education coursework. His ideas can provide a basis for you to establish your own pedagogical vision. Visit http://dewey.pragmatism.org/ for a comprehensive coverage of Dewey and his accomplishments.

Dewey started his teaching career at the University of Michigan and later moved to the University of Chicago where he was chairman of the department of philosophy, psychology, and pedagogy. He established the Chicago Laboratory School for the purpose of testing the sociological implications of his educational theories and the effect his theories had on student learning. Dewey called his laboratory school a "miniature society," an "embryonic community" in which children learned collaboratively by working together to solve problems (Martin, 2002, 199–200). Dewey described "the fundamental factors in the educational process as (1) the learner, (2) society, and (3) organized subject matter" (Dewey, 1974).

The University of Chicago Laboratory School was John Dewey's vehicle for reforming classroom education.

John Dewey was way ahead of other theorists of his time. His ideas in *The School and Society* (1943) have remarkable significance to the field of education as we now know it. Dewey's ideas about the needs, the problems, and the possibilities of education are detailed in *Experience and Education* (1963), perhaps the best concise statement on education ever written. It is a must read for all students of education.

Dewey devised a five-step process-oriented method for students to approach problem solving. Simply put, his steps involved:

1. Encountering a problem that needed to be solved
2. Defining the problem, asking questions that would help clarify exactly what needs to be solved
3. Collecting information about the problem
4. Making tentative hypotheses and reflecting on possible actions and outcomes
5. Acting on a hypothesis that is likely to solve the problem

For Dewey, problem solving using the scientific method, action, and empirical testing is the most effective strategy for teaching and learning. He believed that schools should teach children not what to think but how to think through "continuous reconstruction of experience." It would be almost impossible not to have directly experienced Dewey's five-step method somewhere along your education journey.

Ralph W. Tyler (1902–) Ralph W. Tyler's innovative ideas made him one of the most influential men in U.S. education. He began a life career in education following a stint as a science teacher in South Dakota. He served the profession as teacher, scholar, administrator, creator of institutions, policy maker, and advisor to presidents and foreign educational institutions. Tyler believed that successful teaching and learning could be determined by scientific study, but stressed that evaluation should start with objectives and not rely entirely on a statistical process. His insights into educational evaluation affected the lives of generations of students whose performance and potential are frequently tested. As director of the *Eight-Year Study* (from 1933 to 1941) he helped convince the educational community that schools that offer programs that are interesting and useful to their students can help students become successful in college.

Tyler's 83-page book, *Basic Principles of Curriculum and Instruction*, published in 1949, made an indelible mark on the field of curriculum theorizing, as well as on teaching practices in U.S. public schools. This short text was originally the syllabus for one of Tyler's courses at the University of Chicago. In the text, Tyler espoused four ideas regarding the development of curricular projects. These four ideas remain as relevant today as they were 60 years ago for teachers and anyone else who develops curricula; they serve as a framework for selecting appropriate strategies to use to connect the learner and the content.

They are:

1. Define appropriate learning objectives.
2. Establish useful learning experiences.
3. Organize learning experiences to have a maximum cumulative effect.
4. Evaluate the curriculum and revise those aspects that do not prove to be effective.

These simple yet powerful ideas shifted the role of the teacher and curriculum specialist to that of scientist, establishing and testing hypotheses directly related to learning outcomes for students. Teachers became scientific observers of student behavior, checking for evidence of student learning and making modifications to plans when necessary to guarantee results. Tyler's ideas were so powerful, functional, and easy to apply that they are still widely implemented in the curriculum of public schools today.

Hilda Taba (1902–1967) This Estonian-born U.S. educator spent much of her professional career contemplating ideas concerned with the development of thinking skills in students. She was able to combine her own ideas with other

Ed Lines

"Survival is a race between education and catastrophe." *H. G. Wells*

great ideas to develop models for teaching and curriculum development. She believed that students make proper generalizations only after information is organized, and they could be led toward making generalizations through concept development and concept attainment strategies. She based her teaching model on three main assumptions:

1. Thinking can be taught.
2. Thinking is an active transaction between the individual and data.
3. Processes of thought evolve by a sequence that is "lawful." (Joyce & Weil, 2000, 131)

Believing that process translates content into learnable tasks, she developed a system of cognitive processes and a set of eliciting questions for use with each of the cognitive tasks of concept formation, development of generalizations, and application of principles to new situations. Each set of questions was organized to elicit certain learning behaviors by students necessary to the completion of the tasks (Taba, 1965).

According to Taba, "efforts to develop thinking take a different shape depending on whether the major function of education is seen as fostering creative thinking and problem solving or as following the rational forms of thinking established in our classical tradition. As such, differences in these concepts naturally determine what are considered the essentials and the dispensable frills in education" (1962).

Hilda Taba generated the idea that curriculum could be built through implementation in classrooms. Hers was a grassroots method in which teachers design experimental units, test them with their students, then collaborate with others who have also created experimental units to develop a scope and sequence. When a workable plan is established, those who have created the units provide in-service training for others. Refining Tyler's procedure of developing school curriculum, Taba included seven major steps in the design of any curriculum.

1. Diagnosis of needs
2. Formulation of objectives
3. Selection of content
4. Organization of content
5. Selection of learning experiences
6. Organization of learning experiences
7. Determination of what to evaluate and the means of doing so

Hilda Taba was famous for her work in concept development in social studies. For a look at how Hilda Taba's ideas on concept attainment can be applied in a classroom, visit the Global Connections for Elementary Students website at www.globaled.org/curriculum/tomcollins.html.

Ed Lines

"**We are what we think about all day long.**" *Ralph Waldo Emerson*

Good Ideas and Conflicting Perspectives: An Example

There is a back-and-forth nature in the struggle to educate. Perpetual controversy over one or another reigning educational philosophy and the give and take regarding ideas about classroom practices often create a cyclical effect. Ideas in education have been batted back and forth like ping-pong balls, falling out of favor only to be, at some later date, reembraced as brilliant. Education is neither here nor there, one way or another. It is what works and what actually works is not always most commonsensible.

During the 1960s, a period of unprecedented upheaval and change in the field of education in the United States, two men in particular, Jerome S. Bruner and David P. Ausubel, came to symbolize a dichotomy of viewpoints regarding the methods and means of teaching and learning, and, between them, defined the terms of a debate that continues unabated to this day.

For his part, Jerome Bruner theorized that by categorizing his or her environment, the learner is better able to comprehend it. His learning theory, which emphasized the structure of disciplines and the use of inquiry and came to be called the **discovery method**, contributed to a large number of the curricular reforms of the 1960s. Bruner stressed the importance of teaching the type of thinking skills necessary to the development of problem-solving abilities. His attainment theory was based on the technique of combining rules learned by discovery into a concept the learner desires to understand. This discovery or experience of the learner became the "moving force" Dewey describes as central to learning (p. 38).

It was David Ausubel's view, on the other hand, that the teacher's major task is to transmit large bodies of already organized knowledge to the learner through a **reception-receptive method**—the relationship between the way knowledge is organized and the manner in which the mind works to process such information. Ausubel, held to be the more traditional of the two thinkers, was opposed to most learning activities that could be described as discovery and felt "discovery" was not an indispensable condition for the occurrence of meaningful learning (Ausubel, 1967).

Jerome Bruner attempted to find new answers to basic questions of how boys and girls and men and women learn, and from there to lead learners to construct models of reality on their own terms (Bruner, 1969). David Ausubel's professional interest was more specifically in whatever meaningful symbolic learning takes place within the classroom. Ausubel considered it important to distinguish among the principle kinds of learning that can take place in the classroom. He was adamantly opposed to passive learning on the part of the student and unyielding in his insistence that receptive learning could be meaningful, arguing that just because learning by reception implies the material is "presented" rather than "discovered" does not make it inherently less meaningful (Ausubel, 1963).

Bruner's and Ausubel's contrasting theories came into prominence on the education scene as progressivism entered its final stage, and there was a desire for some sort of orderly guidance, some sort of basic adjustment to the entire education system, from top to bottom. As U.S. education flexed its newfound muscles during the early 1960s, Bruner and Ausubel found their models of learning increasingly at the center of debate over how to best help students become proces-

▶ **Discovery method.** A method of teaching that introduces a general concept through questioning and problem solving.

▶ **Reception-receptive method.** A method of teaching that makes large bodies of already organized knowledge available to learners.

269

How Does Philosophy
Help Teachers
Understand
Teaching and
Learning?

sors of information. Oddly enough, within their theories are many broad areas of agreement, although they have never been of much interest to the "warrior-pedagogues" of the continuing methods wars.

Their ideas were well founded, based on research and clear thinking. Both men supported the necessity of the teacher as director in the classroom, although from Ausubel's point of view, the most efficient arrangement for the acquisition of knowledge involved the teacher telling the student what needed to be known. Ausubel did not consider discovery a prerequisite for understanding, believing instead that it was possible to teach students to think deductively. Though Ausubel did not deny the usefulness and practicality of problem-solving skills, he regarded "knowing" as a substantive phenomenon, not a problem solving capability.

Revisiting Natalie's Concern for Good Ideas

Natalie, the teacher education candidate at the beginning of this section, is worried that her ideas might not be of the highest quality. While Natalie's desire to have only good ideas is admirable, it may not be entirely practical. Teachers sometimes have not-so-good ideas that flop in action. Smart, thoughtful teachers learn from their mistakes and this learning can result in more excellent ideas in the future. Natalie should also take comfort in the wealth of good ideas available to her from educators who learned their lessons long ago. From the thinking of the teacher across the hall, to the thinking of great names in American education history, to education bloggers on the Internet, Natalie can draw from the best ideas educators have to offer.

How Does Philosophy Help Teachers Understand Teaching and Learning?

*It's been a bad day for **Chad**. He had to ask for an extension on an assignment due today in the general teaching strategies class he is taking. The assignment was to write about an experience he had as a student when he simply didn't understand something the teacher was trying to help him learn. Initially, he thought the assignment would be easy because there were a lot of times in his schooling when he didn't understand directions, explanations, or even the outcome of lab experiments, but writing such an experience down in a meaningful way that would fully express the frustration and shame he felt was easier considered than done.*

One incident he thought about happened when he was in the 5th grade. He just didn't seem to be able to complete an essay and his teacher told him to think about it. He went home that night and sat on his bed and wanted to cry because he wasn't sure if he knew how to think. Thinking about that incident from his past made him think about thinking. How do teachers learn to think clearly about teaching and their students? How do teachers help students learn to think? He posed these questions to Ann, a fellow student. She gave him her famous cold, 20-yard stare and said, "What are you thinking?" He wasn't sure.

All human knowledge arises from thinking.

Later that day he read two signs in the halls of the education building. One asked, "Are we thinking here or is this just so much pointing and clicking?" The other sign was a quote by Seymour Papert, "You cannot think about thinking, without thinking about thinking about something." Maybe he should have paid closer attention in his freshman philosophy course. And as a fitting end to a rather confusing day, his car wouldn't start when he was leaving school to head for his part-time job and the only person who could give him a ride was his mother. Chad was grateful that she brought along a sandwich. That was certainly food for thought.

Thinking is what philosophy is all about. Philosophy underlies all disciplines. Philosophy investigates fundamental questions concerning the ultimate nature of values, knowledge, and reality. The practices of philosophy can help people interpret their experiences. You will no doubt take a philosophy or logic course as part of the core requirements for your degree. Understanding philosophical thought prepares teachers for critical thinking and reasoning and constructing logically sound arguments. The study of philosophy helps teachers sift through ideas and articulate thoughts in ways that others can follow. Understanding the practices of philosophy helps teachers learn how to look and listen and how to engage in meaningful discussions.

In 1958, Professor Curt J. Ducasse delivered a paper on the practical contribution that philosophy can make to the urgent task of bringing intelligent order, responsibility, and efficiency into what he termed "the chaotic educational situation." In his paper, he suggests that so far as philosophy has practical value, it "consists in making clear what, in given circumstances, and on the whole, is the best use to make of such powers as one happens to have, or what is the best means to employ, out of several at one's command, in order to achieve a chosen end."

Like Chad at the beginning of this section, we all seek answers to questions in order to make sense of our worlds. In translation, the word *philosophy* can be defined as "love of wisdom," though it's clear we don't all have the same questions or view wisdom in the same way. Philosophers have thought long and hard about their philosophies and about the implications their perspectives have for learning and teaching.

Three different branches of philosophy are concerned with seeking answers to different types of questions. **Metaphysics** is concerned with questions about the nature of reality and humans' attempts to find coherence in the realm of thought and experience. Typical questions examined from this perspective might explore the relationship between learners and teachers. **Epistemology** examines questions about how and what we know and how knowing takes place. Questions dealt within the study of epistemology may include "Where do ideas come from? How do we pose and solve problems?" The **axiology** branch of philosophy deals with questions concerning the nature of values. Questions examined from the axiology

Metaphysics. The branch of philosophy that seeks to explain the nature of being or reality.

Epistemology. The branch of philosophy that seeks to explain knowledge and knowing.

Axiology. The branch of philosophy that examines values and ethics.

271

How Does Philosophy
Help Teachers
Understand
Teaching and
Learning?

perspective deal with what should be or what values we hold: "What is good for students?" "How should students behave?" As you can see, the questions that are the focus of each branch of philosophy are related to different aspects of education. Such questions posed by the different branches of philosophy can be found in educational concerns over curriculum, methods, and teaching behaviors.

The Metaphysical Questions of Content or Child

In 340 BCE, Aristotle declared that metaphysics involves intuitive knowledge of unprovable starting points (truth) and demonstrative knowledge of what follows from them. Teachers want to know why some students are successful at particular tasks while other students struggle with them. Can a child choose whether to learn? Is the ability to learn determined by factors outside of a student's control? Is understanding of specific content necessary to a successful life or is the way in which the content is learned of utmost importance to the learner? The manner in which a teacher approaches the content and how the child interacts with the content depends somewhat on the teacher's attitudes about human nature (Johnson, 2005). Diann Musial (2005) from Northern Illinois University believes that a

Teachers' Lounge

Breakfast with Jeremy

Years ago during my first year teaching 5th grade, I had a young man named Jeremy. He was kind of a scraggly kid with a charming smile, messy clothes, dirty blond hair, and a long rattail. For the first month of school, he was late for school every day except one. I would admonish him for being late, give him a little lecture on responsibility, and remind him of the school rule requiring after-school detention for every three tardies. He would just shrug his scrawny shoulders and head to his desk in the back of the classroom.

The day he arrived on time, I asked him, "Why are you late all the time but were on time today?" Jeremy quietly explained, "My dad does not live with me and my mom, and she goes to work before I wake up in the morning; I am on my own to get up and off to school. My mom was

sick this morning so I got up early to take care of her."

Jeremy and I came up with a plan: I would call him every morning at 6:30, and he would get up and get himself to school. If he could get to school on time for 2 weeks, I would take him to breakfast. Jeremy came to school for 2 weeks on time and we went to breakfast. Then another 2! At the end of about a month, he told me he thought he could get to school on his own but that he really appreciated my help.

Just recently Jeremy came up to me at a local festival and reintroduced himself. He shook my hand and told me what a difference I had made in his life, how he prides himself on being on time, that he had a great job and a great family . . . and that he learned to be a responsible person in 5th grade! He still had the rattail . . . but he looked great!

● Rich Smith
5th grade

teacher's classroom approach is linked to the teacher's metaphysical beliefs. "If the teacher believes that very specific basic knowledge is crucial to the child's intellectual development, it is likely that this teacher will focus on the subject matter. If, on the other hand, the teacher holds that the child is more important than any specific subject matter, it is likely that this teacher will focus on the child and allow the child to provide clues as to how he or she should be instructed" (p. 308).

Ways of Knowing, Learning, and Teaching

In the concern over how students learn, what they should learn, and how they should learn it, educators connect epistemology and education. Epistemology is the study of the origin, nature, methods, and limits of knowledge. Epistemology is the science of how we learn and teach and encompasses the range of questions educators face in designing the very best schooling for children. Education is focused on how students best learn the knowledge they must have and how teachers learn the necessary behaviors to facilitate student learning.

When classroom teachers puzzle over which educational goals should be met and how these goals might be achieved through teaching practices, they are dealing with questions about knowing, learning, and teaching. In Plato's discussion of epistemology, he argued that in order to grasp reality or know, individuals use understanding, reason, perception, and imagination. Check out a straightforward discussion of *Plato's Epistemology in a Nutshell* on the Sophia Project Resource website at www.molloy.edu/academic/philosophy/sophia/plato/plato_epistemology.htm.

Teachers implement Plato's ideas of knowing when they plan and structure lessons and decide which methods are most appropriate to a specific learning task. As you progress in your teacher education coursework, you will no doubt become very familiar with the theory of constructivism or constructivist teaching. When you study this approach to teaching and learning, think of it as an epistemological view. Constructivist approaches to teaching take into account the ways that children learn and what conditions are necessary to promote such learning. The theory of constructivism ponders how knowing is achieved. You will also learn about Jean Piaget in your coursework and how his program of naturalistic research helped teachers understand child development. Piaget was primarily interested in how knowledge developed in human organisms and he termed his general theoretical framework genetic epistemology.

The Role of Values and Ethics in the Classroom

There are many reasons that parents care a great deal about who teaches their children. Certainly parents hope for a teacher who is knowledgeable. They hope for one who will be sympathetic to any idiosyncratic behaviors or learning styles their particular child might possess—but probably nothing concerns

Ed Lines

"There is nothing either good or bad, but thinking makes it so." *Shakespeare,* Hamlet, *Act II, scene ii*

273

How Does Philosophy
Help Teachers
Understand
Teaching and
Learning?

parents more than the moral values or ethics the teachers of their children demonstrate. Parental concern over the moral values of individual teachers as well as those expressed by schools has given rise to an increased interest in home schooling and school vouchers. As one example, the National Character Education Center relates core values to human anatomy and gets at the heart and mind of values in action. In this approach, the seven virtues attributed to respective body parts are respect (eyes and ears), integrity (mouth), compassion (heart), perseverance (stomach), cooperation (hands), initiative (feet), and positive mental attitudes (mind) (Bedley, 2001).

Another initiative to accomplish the teaching of core values is the Institute for Global Ethics (2006). It provides guidelines for ethical literacy through ethical fitness (2006). The character education website at www.ethics.org discusses the questions of whether schools should be teaching values and, if so, whose values should be taught. Ethics is a way of processing behavior. Teachers weigh various elements of their own behavior and the behavior of their students differently depending on their own set of ethics and values.

While aesthetics might provide food for thought, not everyone has the same beliefs that public institutions should dictate to individuals what should be considered an acceptable form of conduct. Teachers must negotiate the omnipresent conflict between societal values and individual values in the classroom. A well-informed teacher understands and respects the diversity of cultural and ethnic thought in any community and uses this knowledge to help all students learn. Teachers faced with questions about values are dealing with the axiology branch of philosophy. Differing beliefs and values can give rise to heated debate. See the Teachers and the Law on page 274.

Opinions, Values, and Beliefs Opinions about public school teaching and learning begin with the very first moment we enter schools as students. Every beginning teacher's knowledge of teaching is more memory than schema. Beliefs are the frameworks in which all subsequent knowledge is incorporated. It is necessary for teachers to categorize their thinking and understand the traditions of practice and the historical circumstances out of which certain kinds of thinking arise. Change is endemic to education. That's not a bad thing. What is difficult is letting go of no-longer-useful ideas. For example, the concept of open classrooms, classrooms without doors and walls, was brought to life in the late 1960s and early 1970s. It was an idea to promote communal learning and many schools were built across the nation to house the open classroom concept. It didn't take long for educators to realize the negative impact such school structure had on instruction and learning and open schools were quickly enclosed. However, today, there are still some open schools in operation. Why? Are some open schools still in operation in the country merely because of a tradition of practice or some long-held belief that open schools were and still are a good idea?

Ed Lines

"Accuracy of observation is the equivalent of accuracy of thinking." *Wallace Stevens*

Teachers and the Law

WHOSE VALUES REIGN?

Do teachers have the right to deliver any curriculum they choose?

Even though the Constitution of the United States of America specifies that "Congress shall make no law respecting an establishment of religion, or prohibiting the free exercise thereof; or abridging the freedom of speech . . . ," court cases challenging the details of this first amendment to the Bill of Rights are never in short supply. One of the most famous cases, *State v. Scopes* (known as the Scopes Monkey Trial) held in the summer of 1925, clearly demonstrates the emotions that discussions of "what will be taught in schools" can evoke. Douglas Linder (2002) has written a fascinating narrative of the trial. He begins his description with the historical perspectives that added fuel to the debate,

> The early 1920s found social patterns in chaos. Traditionalists, the older Victorians, worried that everything valuable was ending. Younger modernists no longer asked whether society would approve of their behavior. . . . Intellectual experimentation flourished. Americans danced to the sound of the Jazz Age, showed their contempt for . . . prohibition, debated abstract art and Freudian theories. In a response to the new social patterns set in motion by modernism, a wave of revivalism developed, becoming especially strong in the American South.
>
> Who would dominate American culture—the modernists or the traditionalists? Journalists were looking for a showdown, and they found one in a Dayton, Tennessee courtroom in the summer of 1925. There a jury was to decide the fate of John Scopes, a high school biology teacher charged with illegally teaching the theory of evolution. The guilt or innocence of John Scopes, and even the constitutionality of Tennessee's anti-evolution statute, mattered little. The meaning of the trial emerged through its interpretation as a conflict of social and intellectual values.

Read the entire narrative at www.law.umkc.edu/faculty/projects/ftrials/scopes/evolut.htm.

You might be surprised at what some parents would consider inappropriate content for teachers to teach. When I was teaching 3rd grade in Beaverton, Oregon, I read my students Baum's *The Wizard of Oz*. Parents of a child in my class took umbrage to the text because of the "communistic" overtones it contained. They asked the school district to remove the book from the school libraries and to forbid teachers to share it with their students. I was amazed. I thought the flying monkeys were the worst things in the book.

With your classmates, list certain content that teachers are duty-bound to cover that might result in a conflict of values with parents and the community. Consider this content from varying social, economic, ethnic, political, and religious perspectives.

Source: Linder, D. (2002). The Scopes Trial: A final word. Retrieved July 7, 2006 from www.law.umkc.edu/faculty/projects/ftrials/scopes/evolut.htm.

275

How Does Philosophy
Help Teachers
Understand
Teaching and
Learning?

Philosophical Perspectives that Influence Education

Various **schools of philosophy** seek to answer the broad philosophical questions posed through metaphysics, epistemology, and axiology from differing perspectives. The schools of philosophy most often mentioned in terms of the implications they have for education are idealism, realism, perennialism, pragmatism, progressivism, essentialism, and existentialism. These philosophies represent a broad spectrum of influence on educational practice and thought and ways of knowing. Some schools of philosophy give rise to compatible educational theories; others generate quite opposite and competing points of view. Some of the philosophical perspectives listed here may not be considered schools of philosophy in the truest sense. However, their impact on education has given them a relevant stature in the realm of thinking about education. Observance of one or another of these philosophical perspectives, or a combination of two or more, could produce differing school structures, curriculum, instructional methods, and classroom practices for teachers and students. What follows is a succinct description of some of the schools of philosophy teachers should be familiar with as they undertake construction of their own personal philosophy of teaching.

Schools of philosophy. Groups of philosophical thought that provide frameworks for categorizing an array of ideas.

Idealism. A school of philosophy that holds ideas as the only true reality.

Confucianism   Confucius (551–479 BCE) is in many cultures regarded as the world's foremost and greatest philosopher. Confucius' teachings, a source of perennial good sense, encourage people to lead good lives by doing what is right. At some time in your preservice teacher education coursework and during in-service professional development, you will no doubt see or hear one of Confucius' many axioms. One of the most frequently displayed is: "I hear, I know. I see, I remember. I do, I understand." Another is: "If you think in terms of a year, plant a seed; if in terms of 10 years, plant trees; if in terms of 100 years, teach the people." Confucius taught that there are three methods to gaining wisdom. The first is reflection, which is the highest; the second is imitation, which is the easiest; and the third is experience, which is the bitterest method. As a teacher education candidate, you will have the opportunity to use all three methods to gain wisdom.

Idealism and Realism   **Idealism**, the oldest of the western philosophies, originated with Plato. Idealism refers to a rational world of the mind where ideas or concepts are the essence of all that is worth knowing. The *American Heritage Dictionary* (2004) defines idealism as the philosophy that guides behavior or thought based on the theory that the objects of external perception consist of ideas. Universal and absolute truths offer examples of the ideal to which to strive. Because ideas are consistent in an ever-changing world, they should be

Our concerns and insights as educators are timeless as Confucius' "Words of Wisdom."

learned and understood. The ideal should be sought and emulated when found. Hegel's (1770–1831) absolute idealism posits that because ideas about reality are products of the mind, there must be a mind at work in the universe that establishes reality and gives it structure. Idealism is used to refer to any metaphysical theory positing the primacy of mind, spirit, or language over matter.

Realism: Aristotle built upon the ideas of his famous teacher, Plato, to describe a world in which material objects exist in themselves apart from the mind's awareness of them. That world is real and exists whether a mind is there to perceive them. Remember the questions of the tree falling in the forest that you discussed in your first philosophy class? If a tree falls in the forest and no one is there to hear it, does it make a sound? Imagine the answer from both an idealist and a realist perspective. In realism, laws of nature and the order of the physical world override the idealist notion that ideas are the ultimate reality. In a realist's world, we respond to what is seen and sensed. According to John Locke's (1632–1704) *tabula rasa* theory, we all begin as blank slates and our senses help us fill the void with knowledge. Plato's idealistic perspective has us full of ideas at birth and life's experiences help us eventually know these ideas.

> **Realism.** A school of philosophy that holds reality exists independent of the human mind.

> **Perennialism.** A school of philosophy that seeks enduring truths and ideas that are everlasting.

> **Essentialism.** A philosophical belief that for any specific entity it is theoretically possible to specify a finite list of characteristics.

> **Pragmatism.** An American school of philosophy that stresses purpose of thought in action.

Perennialism and Essentialism   The roots of **perennialism** lie in the philosophies of Plato and Aristotle and also of St. Thomas Aquinas. Perennialism offers a conservative and traditional view of human nature. In this school of thought, humans do not change much, but they are capable of analytical thinking, reason, and imagination, and should be encouraged along these lines. Through reason lies revelation. When certain perpetual truths are learned, individuals will develop rationality. While human nature is somewhat predictable, it is possible to improve the human condition through understanding of history, the great works of literature, and art.

Essentialism became a popular educational philosophy in the United States in the 1930s following what was considered an excess of progressive education. Essentialists believe there is a fundamental core of knowledge that any functioning member of society must possess. Such knowledge is absolutely essential for an individual to lead a productive life. Learning takes place through contact with the physical world as well as with specific core disciplines. Goodness lies in acquisition of certain essential knowledge. E. D. Hirsch clearly delineated the finer points of essential knowledge in his 1987 book, *Cultural Literacy*, making clear the exact information that every literate person should possess. Teaching the essentials has since colonial times been the dominant approach to U.S. education. The testing frenzy of the current No Child Left Behind movement would attest to the staying power of essentialism in U.S. education. "While essentialism reflects the traditional view that the 'real' world is the physical world we experience with our senses, perennialism is more open to the notion that universal spiritual forms are equally real" (Sadker & Sadker, 2000, 400–401).

Pragmatism and Progressivism   **Pragmatism** was first introduced in philosophy by Charles Peirce in 1878. The term *pragmatic* is derived from the Greek word

Ed Lines

"When the mind is thinking, it is talking to itself." *Plato*

pragma, meaning action, also the source for the words *practice* and *practical*. The universe of pragmatism is dynamic and evolving. Change happens and humans are constantly in the process of becoming, evolving to reach ever-greater understanding. "Truth" is what works in one place and time and even if it worked once, it might not work again given different variables. Concepts and outcomes should be tested by their practical results. Maybe your university professor who answers "depends" to your questions about what works best is taking a pragmatic point of view. Pragmatism shares some views with Aristotle's realism but is less rigid because in pragmatism, experience is of utmost importance. Because of the changing nature of truths, individuals must be flexible and be capable of dealing with change. The United States was founded on pragmatic ideals. Since the arrival of the first explorers and settlers, Americans have spent a large portion of their energy adapting to one another and to ever-changing environments.

WHAT WORKS ONCE, MIGHT NOT WORK THE NEXT TIME. WHAT DIDN'T WORK LAST TIME, MIGHT FULFILL THE NEEDS NEXT TIME.

Progressivism marked by progress, reform, or a continuing improvement became popular in the 1920s through the work of John Dewey. The tenets of progressivism demonstrate respect for individuality, a high regard for science, and receptivity to change. According to Dewey, humans are social animals who learn through interaction with one another. Learning increases when we are engaged in activities that have meaning for us (Dewey, 1963). The influence of progressivism helped U.S. educators take a closer look at the role of the learner in any acquisition of knowledge.

YOU'RE NOT ALWAYS CORRECT. DON'T BE AFRAID TO CHANGE YOUR GAMEPLAN MIDWAY THROUGH THE COURSE.

Existentialism   **Existentialism** rose out of the cult of **nihilism**, a philosophical position that argues the world, and especially human existence, is without objective meaning, purpose, comprehensible truth, or essential value, and **pessimism**, a general belief that things are bad and tend to become worse, following the destruction of European civilization in World War I and more particularly the apparent ineptitude of France during World War II. Existentialism presents a world in which individuals determine for themselves what is true or false. Only through free will can individuals oppose hostile environments. The first principle of existentialism, according to Jean-Paul Sartre, is man is nothing else but what he makes of himself (Kreeft, 1988). The caterpillar in Alice in Wonderland asks, "Who R U?" If Alice had been an existentialist, she might have answered, "Yes, who am I and what should I do?"

Existentialism. A school of philosophy that stresses the free will of individuals.

Nihilism. The denial of any basis for knowledge or truth.

Pessimism. Expecting the worst outcome in any circumstance.

Maxine Greene, a long-time professor at Columbia Teachers College, contends that living is philosophy and that freedom means overcoming obstacles that obstruct our attempt to find ourselves and fulfill our potential (Greene, 1988). The writings of Friedrich Nietzsche (1844–1900) offer a framework for cultivating a healthy love of self. He wanted to help liberate people from the oppression of feeling inferior. Carl Rogers (1902–1987), the founder of humanistic psychology, made outstanding contributions to the field of education. His writings focus on empowering individuals to achieve their full potential, in other words, becoming self-actualized. According to Rogers, existential living means living in the here and now, being in touch with reality, while learning from the past and dreaming of

Ed Lines

"**You can't change the past, but you can learn from it.**" *Rafiki in* The Lion King

the future. Though the ideas of existentialism seem radical to many people, Donald Kauchak and Paul Eggen (2005) point out that "Existentialism makes a contribution to education because it places primary emphasis on the individual, and in doing so, it reminds us that we don't teach math, science, reading, and writing; rather, we teach people, and the people we teach are at the core of learning" (p. 214).

There are far more philosophical perspectives than have been mentioned here. When you read of the naturalists or of scholasticism, humanism, or social reconstructivism, you will be increasing your knowledge of the ideas that have influenced how you may be expected to perform in the classroom. Most philosophical perspectives hold increased knowledge or understanding as good. For more details on schools of philosophy and their implications in education, visit the Berglund Center Summer Institute website at http://education.edu.pacificu .edu/bcis/workshop/philosophy.html or the website of the Sophia Project of the Molloy College Philosophy Department at www.molloy.edu/academic/ philosophy/sophia/TOPICS/education.htm. The Sophia website lists numerous links to the thinking and writing of educational theorists, while the Berglund Center website identifies seven modern philosophical orientations.

Knowledge of teaching and learning is always incomplete even though there are a wealth of theories to support many of the practices and policies that exist. Knowledge and attitudes about education grow and change as the physical and social world changes. Teachers construct a personal philosophy toward teaching and learning in order to make sense of the complexities of their craft. A teacher may not be able to name a specific school of philosophy that he or she adheres to in daily practice, but he or she will certainly be able to give you thoughts on how children learn, what they should learn, and how they should be learning it. Most teachers select ideas from a number of schools and apply what works best for them given the requirements of their teaching situation. In order to maintain a sense of humor and hope in teaching, most teachers are pragmatic and operate from a philosophical viewpoint of eclecticism; they select ideas from various systems in the same way they gather materials from various sources. Such is the practical world of teaching.

279

How Do Teachers
Develop Personal
Philosophies Toward
Teaching and Learning?

USING EVIDENCE

CHANGING VALUES

From 1950 to 1990, American values have experienced radical change. Consider the following, and then discuss with your classmates the consequences such changes may have had on U.S. education. How do current American values compare?

1950	1990
delayed gratification	instant gratification
middle class	underclass
"We"	"Me"
heroes	cover girls
value added	charge cards
Ozzie & Harriet	latchkey kids
unionization	bankruptcy
equity	renting/leasing
public troubles	private issues
"Do what you're told"	"Do what you want"
public virtue	personal well-being
achievement	fame
regulation	deregulation

Refer to the **Understanding & Using Evidence Appendix** *at the end of the text for answers and information related to these activities.*

What we teach is also highly influenced by current values. The Understanding & Using Evidence provides examples of change in values over time.

Revisiting Chad's Thinking about Teaching

Chad is no philosopher but he is thinking about the profession he has chosen from a pragmatic and realistic perspective and is trying to understand its many dimensions. The more he learns about teaching and the more experiences he has interacting with teachers and students, the more he will learn about education. The best tool that Chad can employ at the beginning of his career is to become fully aware of his assumptions and opinions about teaching and learning and to examine them through a variety of philosophical lenses.

How Do Teachers Develop Personal Philosophies Toward Teaching and Learning?

Candice is a teacher education candidate at a large university in a metropolitan area of the southwest. Last semester, she participated in a field-based teacher education program in which she spent her days substituting in classrooms in the local school district or working alongside a cooperating teacher and her evenings attending class on the university campus. It was a grueling schedule and a challenging semester but she believes the practical application of the knowledge and theories from her courses is helping her be better prepared for her own future classroom. She has been able to see firsthand what it is like to be completely in charge of a classroom. She is now aware that students learn all of the time, not just in class, and that they are more willing to take risks when their teachers take risks.

The students she has encountered in the "real" world of teaching have lived up to and often exceeded her expectations. She has begun to believe that quality is more important than quantity because her students seemed to learn more when she taught a small amount of content in great depth. She has discovered that process and product work better together than apart and through experience has seen a good process produce a desired product; she now understands that a good product cannot be consistently achieved without a quality process.

Candice's previous attitudes about teaching and learning are being reshaped. The information she is constantly adding to her knowledge of teaching and learning is helping her form new opinions and integrate these with the ones she developed over the course of her time in classrooms as a student. Candice may think that she is finally establishing a well-developed, permanent personal philosophy toward teaching, but in reality, her attitudes toward her craft will continue to evolve throughout a lifetime of teaching.

*E*veryone operates from a personal philosophy. Personally, we know what makes sense to us; what is important and what is good. When you become a teacher, you take your personal vision of the world into the classroom with you. This personal vision affects everything you do in your classroom and with your students. It is necessary to understand your personal philosophy so that you can understand and reflect on what you are doing and why you are doing it. You develop your philosophy of teaching out of your personal belief system. The two are completely intertwined and either grow with vitality or wither together on the vine. Teachers who do not know or understand themselves can be of little service to the students in their classrooms—or as Confucius put it, "What has one who is not able to govern himself to do with governing others?"

Drafting a Personal Philosophy of Teaching Statement

An educational philosophy consists of the beliefs and principles that guide teaching and learning practices. Teacher education candidates are usually asked to draft a statement that organizes their thinking about how students learn and how teachers should teach. Revisiting this original philosophy statement throughout your program is one way you can keep track of your growth as a professional. As you acquire more wisdom and encounter new ideas, you will develop new atti-

Ed Lines

"A great many people think they are thinking when they are merely rearranging their prejudices." *William James*

281

How Do Teachers
Develop Personal
Philosophies Toward
Teaching and Learning?

tudes and opinions that will cause changes to your personal philosophy. For instance, consider the English composition teacher who requires students to attach all previous drafts of a composition to the final copy that is being submitted. This allows the teacher to evaluate the students' growth in their writing ability and also to see whether students have incorporated or learned from the teacher's editorial comments. The final packets can be rather substantial, but they do represent effort and the process of coming to a final, publishable paper. Keeping copies of your original and subsequent philosophy statements will provide you with a graphic representation of the changes in your thinking as you become more knowledgeable about teaching.

The Fast Track to a Personal Philosophy of Teaching

Whether it's fair or not, you will be expected to do the same job on your first day of work as a veteran of 5 or 10 years. Logically, this doesn't seem possible, but who can argue with the fact that the children in your classroom deserve no less than the children in Mrs. Bulow's room who has been teaching for 20 years. Beginning teachers may react to this dilemma by performing certain actions that make them appear capable of keeping up with the more experienced teachers, even when those actions don't exactly mesh with their own personal philosophy of teaching. Nothing can be more exhausting than maintaining a false front or upholding the assumptions of others. Ideas need time to percolate in the reality of full-time teaching. One of the major causes of teacher burnout is the burden of operating under expectations counter to what we believe. For many first-year teachers, discouragement raises its ugly head about mid-December when they begin to realize that the theories they have put into practice are not working. Formulating who you are going to be as a teacher will prepare you to act on your own beliefs and assumptions rather than someone else's. When you do this, you increase your chances of success and happiness as a teacher.

Using tenets of known philosophies as keystones for developing your own philosophy about teaching and answering some of the questions these philosophies pose can help you decide who you are going to be as a teacher. Do you think that the world is an orderly, logical place—or do you see it as chaotic and random? Obviously these two views would have a strong influence on how, for example, you arrange your classroom and lessons. Do you learn by repetition or by connecting what you know to the new learning? What senses do you find most important? In other words, how do you learn about the world around you? If you do feel that you learn best in one specific way, you must become familiar with all the other ways that people learn so that you offer a variety of learning opportunities in your classroom. Do you believe there are clear right and wrongs in life (black and white) or is life a series of slightly differing gray areas? Do you feel it is possible to understand everything if enough intelligence and logic is applied or do you believe some things must simply be taken on faith?

Ed Lines

"I like thinking big. If you're going to be thinking anything, you might as well think big."
Donald Trump

The Effect of Stories in Building a Personal Philosophy of Teaching

There are defining moments in everyone's life; we tell stories about them. Stories are powerful. We all remember a good story whether true or not. Stories can alter our perception of things. That's one reason the news media and television are so powerful. The stories we hear and tell can frighten us or evoke courage. Sooner or later, the stories we tell about our lives become our lives. We can make the stories we tell about our lives healthy or destructive. The choice is ours. Stories provide us with ideas, actions, and tools for working toward goals. Stories are what Robert Coles (1989) refers to as "reservoirs of wisdom" (p. xii).

Marty Learns from Teachers' Stories

Marty is a student teacher in an 8th grade English language classroom in a middle school in a small town of 6,000 people. The teachers in the school live among the students and their families and appear to know one another quite well. Marty is completing his student teaching through an out-of-state student-teaching program run by his home state college and is new to the area and town. He was warned by his instructors in his teacher education courses to be wary of the teachers' lounge and the often negative stories that can be heard there. Still, Marty feels it is in his best interests to get to know other faculty and staff, and since his cooperating teacher has encouraged him to spend his lunch break in the teachers' lounge with her, he makes it a point to spend at least 20 minutes each day in the teachers' lounge smiling and listening to conversations.

What Marty soon discovers is that the stories teachers at this school tell about their classes, individual students, and the lessons they teach provide him with a wealth of knowledge about the students, the school, and the teachers that he could gain no other way. As he listens to teachers talk about how a particular lesson on grammar went or what caused a class discussion to get entirely out of hand, he realizes that the strategies teachers use, the ways they interact with their students, and the lessons they plan are as different as the personalities involved. As he begins to feel more comfortable with the other teachers, he begins to ask questions about how to help specific students, or if other teachers get the same number of complaints from students about homework assignments, or how to cover the curriculum required in 8th grade English. The teachers laugh and nod their heads knowingly and sometimes offer suggestions in ways that don't make them seem like criticisms. Marty is encouraged by their camaraderie and on occasion offers a story of his own—and through the telling of his own stories, he is able to reflect on his growth as a teacher and the achievement of his students.

Marty continues to visit the teachers' lounge and learn about teaching through the stories that are told there. Sometimes he brings snacks to share because this seems to be a norm with the teachers at his school. Marty discovers that at the end of a hectic day, it is nice to have something sweet in his stomach while reflecting on a busy day of teaching and making shifts in his personal philosophy of teaching.

283

How Do Teachers
Develop Personal
Philosophies Toward
Teaching and Learning?

The example of Marty's story is one way that teachers construct personal philosophies of teaching and learning. As a novice to the profession, Marty has brought preconceived notions of teaching from his experiences as a student and from the theories he studied as a teacher education candidate. The real world of teaching will provide him with additional information that he will incorporate into his emerging personal philosophy of teaching.

Defining Events in Building a Personal Philosophy of Teaching

Certainly, high-profile events on the education scene affect the type of teaching and the content you are required to study. Knowing the effect certain events have had on teaching and learning when you were a student will help you better understand your own philosophical perspectives toward schooling. There have been defining moments in society as in our own lives. We learn about defining moments in the world of education in history and foundations of education courses. Defining moments change the way we go about our business. In many ways, the launch of *Sputnik* in 1957 was a 9/11 of the mind. It changed the ways Americans thought about the future. It initiated a reexamination of the purpose of schooling and school curriculum. The National Science Foundation (NSF) made millions of federal dollars available for the development of modern science and mathematics programs and materials. Another defining moment was the publication of *A Nation At Risk* (1983) that prompted a renewed focus on student achievement and the condition of schooling in America.

Keeping a record of your own stories of teaching and events in a journal or diary can also help you build a data reference system for comparing new ideas you encounter with the old ones you have used. The act of looking back to remember which way you've come is a device that has been used by travelers and learners for centuries. From time to time, you need to revisit your journey as a teacher with a critical eye. By checking where you've come from, you will have a better idea of where you are headed. Looking back can help you to assess the defining moments in your professional development and to prepare for the future.

Candice Revisits her Assumptions

Defining moments in Candice's development as a teacher (the teacher education candidate at the beginning of this section) have occurred most recently during her experiences as a substitute teacher. Even though her coursework provided her with information on conducting lessons and interacting with children in classrooms, nothing could prepare her for the physicality of being responsible for the learning of a large number of students over an extended period of time. She has had to revisit previously held assumptions and beliefs about learning and teaching. She is actively integrating new ideas with the old to further understand the connection between the theories she has learned and their practical application in teaching and learning.

How Do Philosophies of Teaching Translate into Practice?

Kenneth is a high school history teacher. He is fascinated by reasons and events that determine the rise and fall of governments and civilizations. He recognizes how the outcomes of conflicts shape the destinies of people and that there is much to be learned from lessons of miraculous accomplishments as well as the past mistakes of cultures and their leaders. He believes that in order for his students to understand the importance of historical events and the lasting influence such events can have on the ways we think and live in today's world, the students must know dates and outcomes of pivotal events as well as the names of the major players in these events.

His favorite course in college was history of western civilization and he remembers fondly the heft of the textbook he had to read for the class. He is also a fan of Shakespeare and whenever he can, he attends the summer Shakespearian festival in Ashland, Oregon. The combination of his love of history and the plays of Shakespeare make him an entertaining teacher, always ready to quote lines relevant to a topic or don a period piece costume to heighten students' anticipation of a lecture.

Though his students are nearly always captivated, some of them have difficulty grasping the content of the course and wonder how it relates to their personal lives. When one student asked "Why do I have to know this stuff?" during a lecture on the crowning of Charlemagne by the pope as the Holy Roman Emperor, Kenneth was nearly at a loss of words. He knew his quick response "Because every educated person should know of the importance of this defining moment in the history of the world" didn't even come close to satisfying the student's question. However, it did clearly express what Kenneth believed.

*E*very teacher has moments in the classroom when they are captivated by the topic they are teaching only to be caught short by blank stares or questions from left field. It is at such moments that teachers begin to realize that their perspectives on what is important to know may not be universally shared. The knowledge one person believes fundamental from say a perennialist's point of view may seem like so much intellectual domination to another. Any personal philosophy of teaching sets the stage for plans and actions. Teachers, by nature of the profession, must make decisions that incorporate a range of philosophical perspectives that are doable and that "work" given a variety of contexts.

Teacher-Focused Classrooms

Room arrangement may not be the best clue as to a teacher's views on what and how children should learn, but it is an indicator. Picture students seated in individual islands separate from other students with eyes directed toward a teacher at the front of the room explaining or demonstrating something the students are expected to remember. The students are quiet. The teacher is talking. We've seen examples of this style of teaching in movies and on television. Unfortunately,

Challenging Assumptions
FINDINGS FROM RESEARCH

Is one method of teaching reading skills universally better than another?

The Assumption: Teacher-focused direct instruction is not as effective as the child-centered, constructivist method in helping children learn, retain, and apply reading skills.

Teacher educators, teachers, and school administrators have long debated the effectiveness of a whole-language approach versus the direct-instruction approach to teaching early reading skills. Critics of the whole-language approach blame colleges of education for continuing to advocate a teaching method that does not seem to be working for all students, while proponents of the whole-language approach argue that the direct-instruction method constrains a child's learning style. According to educators who advocate the whole-language approach, the child-centered focus of this method introduces students to reading in a way that makes them enjoy reading and become lifelong readers.

Study Design and Method: Schug, Tarver, and Western (2001) of the University of Wisconsin–Madison examined the issue of direct instruction in their study titled Direct Instruction and the Teaching of Early Reading. Their goal was to conduct research on direct instruction in authentic settings using methods that would capture the rich complexity of classroom experience. Six schools in Wisconsin participated in the study. The researchers observed and conducted interviews related to the use of direct-instruction programs in these schools. In this qualitative study, teachers and principals reported positive effects from use of direct instruction for both regular-education and special-education students in reading, decoding, reading comprehension, and attitudes toward reading. Teachers also reported other positive effects that included improved writing skills, improved capacity to focus and sustain effort, and, generally, improved student behavior. Teachers also reported no evidence of the various negative effects critics have attributed to direct instruction methods.

Implications: Since not all individuals learn, retain, and apply information in the same way, it is important for teachers to use a variety of instructional methods to meet the needs of all students. One approach to teaching reading may gain popularity to the detriment of other equally effective methods. It is important for teachers to be aware of the role of academic fashion in instructional programs, and to examine research results.

Source: Schug, M. C., Tarver, S. G., & Western, R. D. (2001). Direct instruction and the teaching of early reading: Wisconsin's teacher-led insurgency. Wisconsin Policy Research Institute Report, (14) 2. www.wpri.org/Reports/Volume 14/Vol14no2.pdf

in most of these examples, the teacher is oblivious to what the students are doing or thinking.

Teacher-focused approaches to teaching, in which the teacher is master of the knowledge to be learned and is dispensing it to all students at a specified rate over a specified period of time, adhere to the essentialism school of philosophy in which learning the content is of major concern. The teacher-focused approach also follows a perennialist perspective, believing that education serves to inform students of knowledge that will remain constant through life (Oliva, 2005). In education, essentialism and perennialism perspectives dictate basic and prescribed subject matter. Learning is transferred in a programmatic fashion from teacher to students. The benefits of one method of teaching over another are often tested through research. See the Challenging Assumptions.

Connecting
TO THE CLASSROOM

This chapter has provided information on some of the widely held philosophical perspectives that influence attitudes about what and how children are to learn and how teachers are to teach. It is likely that during your teaching career, you will have firsthand experience with more than one philosophical perspective. The following are some ways to recognize and become familiar with different philosophical perspectives in instruction and in interactions with students, their families, and teacher colleagues.

1. Keep a list of the questions teachers ask during instruction. Do the questions seem to ask for recall of facts or are the opinions of students considered? Are students often asked to make inferences or does that teacher provide conclusive statements for the students to record and remember? At what point do the students seem to be most engaged in answering the teacher's questions?

2. In a previous chapter, it has been suggested that you take part in a parent-teacher conference. You can learn much about the philosophical perspective of teachers and parents when observing a parent-teacher conference. Pay close attention to how the teacher conducts the conference. In what ways does the teacher express his or her personal philosophy of teaching? Are the parents given equal opportunity to express their attitudes about what their children are learning in school?

3. When teachers agree with one another and with their administrators, the school climate is pleasant and productive. On the other hand, when there are glaring differences among colleagues regarding content, conduct, and teaching strategies, discord may permeate the school. What actions have you seen teachers and administrators take to alleviate the disagreement among colleagues that stems from belief in the tenets of different schools of philosophy?

Student-Focused Classrooms

Student-focused approaches to teaching correspond to the pragmatism and progressivism schools of philosophy. In education, these philosophical perspectives view the major role of schools and teachers as being to create learning opportunities that will allow students to construct knowledge relevant to a specific task or situation through self-interest and dialogue with others. The tenets of a constructivist teaching style are closely associated with progressivism, emphasizing hands-on, activity-based learning. The room arrangement in a student-focused classroom is open and flexible. Students can easily interact with one another. Motivation is encouraged through intrinsic rewards. Teacher and learners share control of behavior and the learning environment. Inquiry is promoted and divergent points of view are respected. The teacher models participatory evaluation through questioning and student-led discussions of results. The students value themselves as learners and welcome the active role they have in directing their education along the lines of their own interests. In a student-focused classroom, the curriculum should take into account students' interests. Students construct knowledge through interaction with others.

The Changing Focus   In any given day in a classroom, the focus shifts from teacher to students and back again. This is not a wishy-washy approach; it is merely a fact of the profession. In much the same way as a world-class photographer will shift the focus on a scene to emphasize or pick up an unusual feature, an effective teacher is able to view the classroom as a vibrant life form, taking note of all movement and features. In doing so, the teacher may find it necessary to redirect student attention or perhaps momentarily call a halt to all activity. Learning how to combine parts of different educational philosophies for the benefit of all of the students may be one of the hardest tasks a new teacher must learn.

Revisiting Kenneth's Dilemma

Kenneth, the teacher at the beginning of this section, doesn't necessarily need to discard his firmly held beliefs, but he does need to go back to the drawing board to think about different ways he can present the content required for the course. We all don't think alike and we all don't learn alike. Even perennial truths can be taught through student-focused approaches to teaching.

Follow the directions in Connecting to the Classroom on page 286 to learn more about the effect of differing philosophical perspectives.

Chapter Summary

There are many ways to think about teaching and learning and, because of this, identifying a particular philosophical point of view for your approach to teaching can be like looking for a needle in a haystack. Don't worry. Be happy that there are so many possibilities and ideas. It is important for you to become familiar with a variety of philosophical perspectives in order to organize your own thinking and develop a personal wellspring of original and useful ideas to help your students learn. The more you think about teaching and the more you hear how others think about it, the easier it will be for you to construct a personal philosophy of teaching.

Where do good ideas come from? Great ideas and grand plans for educating the children and young adults of this country can come from almost anywhere. Such thoughts may spring forth from the minds of the country leaders as they did from Thomas Jefferson, from the minds of business executives such as Andrew Carnegie, or, as is often the case, from the minds of leaders in the field of education such as John Dewey. While tried-and-true ideas are being implemented, newer and seemingly more radical ideas are being proposed. The continuous flow of refreshing ideas is part of the reason many have been drawn to the profession. Teachers constantly work with ideas. Teachers also represent a rich pool of creative thinking that has the power to stimulate major changes in education as well as in student learning. Everyone has an opinion though sometimes the ideas that reach popularity are not of the highest caliber. Regardless of where the ideas about education come from, they are put into play by a classroom teacher. Translating ideas into practice is a heavy responsibility and takes a courageous heart. In order to fulfill this responsibility, teachers must be knowledgeable of the ideas of numerous others who have encountered the same concerns and have established theories that have practical application in teaching and learning.

How does philosophy help teachers understand teaching and learning? Thinking and trying to find answers to questions is much of what teaching is about. A teacher who is perplexed by certain student behaviors or by the content of the textbooks mandated by the school district administrators can find comfort in the teachings of philosophers. With a little effort, teachers can use the great ideas from different philosophical perspectives to help them understand human learning, behavior, and value systems. As your knowledge of teaching practices increases, so must your understanding of the basis for such practices. Do not take anything on hearsay. Seek the answers to your questions and build a cognitive framework of theory and practice to rival the architecture of the Taj Mahal. The mind should be a beautiful thing.

How do teachers develop personal philosophies toward teaching and learning? Many of the professors where you are preparing to be a teacher have been classroom teachers—or still are. They may work in classrooms, serve as mentors for new teachers, or work with teachers in professional development seminars. They have had the benefit of experience to help them mold their philosophies of teaching. They have no doubt kept track of their professorial careers through portfolios and tenure and promotion files. Talk to them about the defining teaching moments in their lives that helped them construct a specific approach to teaching. Teaching is a people profession. People like to talk and tell stories about their lives.

Researchers and writers have looked at teachers and listened to their stories of teaching to unravel the mysteries of the profession (Lorti, 1977; Liberman & Miller, 1984). Clark & Peterson (1986) listened to teachers talk about planning. They then mapped their stories into flowcharts for new generations of teachers to follow and learn from. Marianne O'Grady, featured teacher in *Why I Teach* (1999), says "There is a moment when the struggle to master an activity or subject ceases and the action becomes familiar and regimented. Teaching is hundreds of such moments, strung together to create a career" (p. 11). As you try out your ideas, you will become more familiar, and therefore comfortable, with what works in a variety of contexts. You are fortunate to be learning to teach in this period of time. Life is full of choices and many of those choices add depth and breadth to your ultimate practice in the classroom. What happens in classrooms will continue to accommodate evolving ideas and trends about which learning is of most worth.

How do philosophies of teaching translate into practice? Joel Walton and Eve Adamson's (2000) management, relationship education (MRE) system for training dogs is a simple theory and probably works pretty well when training any dog (2000). However, humans have to learn so much more than animals that any single theory or simple approach just won't do. The combined teacher-focused and student-focused approaches to teaching and learning can encompass the spectrum of philosophical perspectives that underpin decision making and curriculum in education. It is the teacher's responsibility to continuously question what to teach and how to teach it and to learn about and develop skill in using methods that have their roots in differing philosophical approaches to teaching.

Class Discussion Questions

1. Experiences you have had as a student quite likely will shape your attitudes and beliefs as a teacher. Discuss one experience that stands out from the rest. Refer to particular schools of philosophy to explain why the experience was so important to you.

2. In schools where teachers follow the same philosophical perspective as their colleagues or students' families, there is probably a great deal of agreement and comfort in the curriculum that is being taught and the instructional methods that are used to teach it. What issues might arise, however, if many of the teachers follow the tenets of the progressive school of philosophy, while many of the families of the students follow the tenets of essentialism, and the administration mainly expresses a perennialist's point of view?

3. Describe stories from your experiences that have shaped your philosophy of teaching. What critical events have given rise to strongly held opinions?

4. Pick a philosophical perspective. What role might reflection on student achievement play for a teacher from that perspective?

Field Guide for School Observations

Classrooms are different. They come in different sizes and shapes and they are populated by people who also come in different sizes and shapes. It is interesting to compare classrooms, but it is also interesting to compare the public impression of classrooms with the reality of what really happens in classrooms during the school day.

Before your next observation visit or day of practice teaching, browse at least three popular magazines similar in content to *Good Housekeeping, Woman's Day, Prevention, Family Circle*, and the like. Write down the titles of at least three articles that deal with child development, learning, teaching, schooling, or health issues related to children. Under each title, list one or two of the ideas expressed in each article. Leave space between each title and list of ideas for your field notes.

While observing, refer to your list and take notes on what is happening in the classroom that might relate to the information in the articles you listed. Does there seem to be a link between what the public is reading about children, learning, and schooling and what you are observing? If there does not seem to be a link, what do you think might be the reason for the gap between the public view of classrooms and learning and what actually occurs? How important is it for members of society to share a common knowledge of what is happening in classrooms?

Ask a Teacher or Principal

Ask two separate teachers to share with you their opinions of how students learn. Ask how they know when their students have actually learned the information being taught. Do they believe that learning one piece of information automatically leads to learning a subsequent piece of information? In their opinion, is all learning of equal value? Will "knowing" help students lead a better life?

Journaling Becoming a Thoughtful Teacher

Think about the teachers you have encountered over your years as a student in classrooms. Explain why you believe that a certain teacher had a specific philosophy of teaching and learning. What do you remember of their actions in the classroom that would lead you to this conclusion? Did you find their teaching methods compatible with your own style of learning? Is it easy to determine someone's personal philosophy of teaching just through observation? How might someone who watched you teach identify your personal philosophy of teaching?

Portfolio Tasks

In order to recognize the influence of life events on the adoption of a personal philosophy of teaching, create an educational autobiography by documenting at least three critical events that had an impact on your schooling. Some questions you might consider are: What were the major events taking place in the world during your childhood years? What were some of the learning experiences you had in school that are still vivid memories? Which of your teachers did you like or dislike the most? Why? Who were your heroes? What was of major importance when you graduated from high school? What did your family expect you to do with your life?

At the end of your autobiography, reflect on how your experiences might be alike or different from your students' experiences.

Self-Assessments *What Am I Learning?*

Dr. Mark Bailey of Pacific University School of Education offers eight critical dimensions of an educational philosophy. In order to build an educational philosophy, Bailey (2006) poses the following questions for teacher education candidates to consider.

1. What is knowledge and understanding?
2. What is worth knowing?
3. What does it mean to learn?
4. How do you know that learning has taken place?
5. What should be the role of a teacher?
6. What should be the role of the student?
7. What is the ultimate purpose of education?
8. What are your core educational values?

Respond to these questions when creating your personal philosophy of teaching statement. Over the course of a year, while you are enrolled in teacher education coursework, reread your personal philosophy and revise it according to any changes in your philosophical perspective. If you are in a practice teaching situation, examine how your philosophy of teaching is enacted through your teaching behaviors. Do you walk your talk or do your actions contradict your espoused philosophy?

Using the Web

There are over 12,000 sites to visit on the Internet for teacher-focused lesson plans, and there are over 31,000 sites to visit when you search the Internet for constructivist lesson plans. Does this mean that student-focused approaches to teaching are more popular than teacher-focused ones in the nation's schools? Or is this an idea that sounds excellent in theory but is difficult to put into practice? Visit **www.interventioncentral.org** for suggestions using teacher-focused strategies to increase student learning. Then go to **www.thrteen.org/edonline/concept2class/constructivism** to learn about teaching strategies in student-focused classrooms.

Your Professional Library

Bruner, J. S. (1962). *On knowing: Essays for the left hand.* Cambridge, MA: Harvard University Press.

> This book takes a fascinating look at the influence of intuition, feeling, and spontaneity in determining how we know what we do know; how we can teach others what we know.

Palmer, P. J. (1998). *The courage to teach: Exploring the inner landscape of a teacher's life.* San Francisco: Jossey-Bass.

> In the book, Parker Palmer discusses emotional and social aspects of the profession that have a tremendous effect on the way a teacher might understand and approach the art and science of teaching and learning.

To access chapter objectives, practice tests, weblinks, and flashcards, visit the Companion Website at **www.ablongman.com/hall1e**

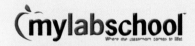

Go to Allyn & Bacon's MyLabSchool (**www.mylabschool.com**). Enter Assignment ID **FDV4** in the **Assignment Finder**. View video clip, *Developing a Philosophy of Education.* Then consider what you have seen along with what you have read in Chapter 7 to respond to the following questions:

1. As you listened to the teachers in the video clip express their personal philosophies of teaching, what was one similarity among all of the teachers' philosophies?

2. Why is it important for new and experienced teachers to develop and revisit a personal philosophy of teaching?

3. What would be one philosophical perspective that you read about in Chapter 7 that might have the strongest influence on your personal philosophy of teaching?

Focusing on Learning and Results

Educators in Real Schools

M E E T
Merrie Schroeder

Malcolm Price Laboratory School

Merrie Schroeder's career as a teacher has spanned 35 years. She began teaching middle grade mathematics in Iowa, then taught K–12 mathematics students as a consultant, and taught K–12 teachers of mathematics as a professional development coordinator. She also taught undergraduate and graduate students in elementary and secondary methods of teaching and classroom management. Merrie's lengthy career as a teacher began when a teacher she admired in middle school said she thought Merrie should go to college. As Merrie explains,

I was amazed that she would consider me, the last of three sisters she had in class, as college material. We were a very blue-collar poor family, and all the way home from school—1.6 miles of hoofing—I played the teacher's words over in my head. I was so thrilled, but I knew my mom would huff and say, "Where are we supposed to get the money?"

Mom was curling her hair in front of the big double mirrors used for fitting clients for whom she was a seamstress, curling her hair. Without hesitation and without even looking at me, she asked, "What are you supposed to be?" I was shocked at the question. "I don't know. She didn't say." "Well," my mother replied, "Go back and ask her." So, the next day, I waited for just the right moment to ask the big question. My teacher's reply was an emphatic, "Well, a TEACHER, of course! The world needs more good teachers!" And that is what I set as my life's goal—to be a good teacher.

Chapter 8

Malcolm Price Laboratory School, located on the campus of the University of Northern Iowa (UNI), serves approximately 350 children who live within the Cedar Falls/Waterloo metro area of Iowa. The students who attend the lab school range from 6 weeks old through grade 12. Twenty-four percent of the students come from diverse cultural and ethnic backgrounds. There is a nearly even split between male and female students. Slightly more than 7 percent of the students participate in the free and reduced lunch program, and 12 percent of the student population receives direct and indirect special education services. Because of the commitment to diversity at the lab school, the instructional programs reflect an array of multicultural opportunities and activities that include family and consumer sciences, band, choir, orchestra, technology education, and world languages (French, Spanish, and Russian). Cocurricular activities include, but are not limited to, speech, band, and choral contests, an array of sports activities, National Honor Society, Math Counts, Model State Legislature, and the Iowa History Day Competition.

❖ What does excellence in teaching look like?

To me, excellence in teaching looks more like excellence in listening. When I hear teachers listening to their students, then I know that something powerful is happening in that room. Teachers who listen ask the kinds of questions that allow students to talk—to reveal what they know and are curious about. Excellence in teaching is seeing a web of conversation in the room, with the teacher as one of the nodes, not always the center. Excellence in teaching—yes, even in mathematics—is also about being a learner with the students, trusting students to think of new ways of understanding the same concept or discovering a different solution to a very unusual problem. Excellence is when students and teachers have "eurekas" together about some-

thing they all thought they already knew. Excellence is artfully helping students keep the tools of learning sharp and clean for use at any moment . . . and that can include old-fashioned games that inspire and motivate speed and accuracy in knowledge.

❖ What are the characteristics of an excellent teacher?

Excellent teachers are able to identify solutions to problems through their experience, rather than through a formula or recipe. Excellent teachers take time to go deep into problems, not just attack them from the obvious, surface level of understanding or from passed-on knowledge. Delving into problems, whether behavioral or pedagogical, reveals unanticipated symptoms and leads to unique, personalized responses by the seasoned expert teacher.

Excellent teachers know that every student has a great deal of knowledge that needs to be shared and connected to the topic at hand. Excellent teachers know that opening up students to learning requires patience in bringing out the learner and the learning, and that requires revisiting the same topic or concept multiple times throughout the year, in multiple contexts. I am always amazed at how much there is in the most silent student. It's the silent ones who really do run deep, and a critical quality of an excellent teacher is to "fish" for that silent voice, to validate their offerings, and to connect those offerings to the topic.

Excellent teachers don't choose between the student and the curriculum. Young adults, preparing to teach, often express the desire to become teachers so that they can deliver what their students need, and "the district's curriculum be hanged!" Expert teachers know that students need the curriculum, and they know how to deliver, and this does include the affective as well as the cognitive.

❖ How do you know when students are learning?

When students become more confident in the kinds of questions they ask, and when they refer to something we have done before, bringing it into a new context—that is a powerful indicator that learning is happening. The learning I look for is in making connections in knowledge and concepts. The way students express themselves early in the year and the way they open up throughout the year can likely come from my goal for them—the classroom as a place to stretch their capacity for knowing, connecting, and expressing ideas—to solve problems in original ways.

A great indicator that students are learning is vocabulary. I work hard at all levels of teaching to insist on the "vocabulary of the profession," and that means 7th graders talking like mathematicians, not "valley adders"! It's not just the vocabulary, but how the students use the language to communicate their concepts. When students can teach each other and listen to each other as colleagues, they are learning what I want them to learn.

Another measure of learning is a strategy I have used that engages students in writing their own exams and determining how the exam shall be scored. Sometimes I write the beginning draft of the test and then consult them for refinement. Both the writing and the refining processes give excellent information about how well the class as a whole has understood the material. How they choose to score the exam also indicates their level of confidence in what they know. Of course, we often rehearse for the exam, including scoring strategies. This is a great opportunity for students to use their mathematical language and provide clues about their knowledge/concept attainment.

❖ What brings you joy in teaching?

The joy in teaching is the unexpected interplay of thoughts that come from students who feel uninhibited. I've had older people in my professional development courses, college kids, and 1st graders surprise me to pieces with their ideas. With laughter comes joy. Every teacher and student has a chance to be Burns and Allen. We just need to set up the environment to make it happen. Coming to school means putting aside my own trials at home and getting lost in my students' ideas. For me the joy of teaching is trying to find that space between the stars—the invisible student—and turn her into a star!

❖ *What is your perception of the increased focus on standards/accountability and testing to ensure student learning?*

If we are to be a profession, standards and accountability are critical, especially to assure families that their children are gaining what can't be taught at home. Knowledge is what we can see, like the stars in the sky, and so we can measure it. Our assessments allow us to say that our students are X bright, based on those measures. But today's schools are, or must be, more about what lies between those stars of knowledge—the students and what happens in transforming knowledge to concepts in the dynamic minds of students. Benchmarks and standards must reliably and validly assess what they can, which is more often knowledge bases rather than the interplay of achieving knowledge as a community of learners. Harder yet is identifying how to measure that which we cannot see. So we measure what we *can* see, and our real goals are just going to have to bend toward that which we can measure. The result is that a knowledge-based curriculum becomes the focus, not the dynamic creators of knowledge. That's too bad for children, for schools, and for society. It can make teaching less rewarding, but certainly more challenging.

Questions to Consider

1. How strongly did teachers you had in elementary, middle, or high school influence your desire to become a teacher? Did any of your teachers directly encourage you to consider teaching as a career?

2. How can listening to students and encouraging students to express themselves help students learn?

3. Merrie talks about revisiting the same topic or concept multiple times throughout the year. Why might students not learn something the first time it is presented?

You are starting down the road to becoming a teacher at a time in the history of U.S. education when all eyes—public, political, parental, and even those of your peers—are focused on student learning as something that can be viewed as a direct result of teacher performance. You are going to be in the spotlight. The long, hard look directed at what students and teachers know and know how to do has given rise to all manner of standards, benchmarks, and criteria for determining whether education is on target or floundering around somewhere in the abyss between orderly know-how and utter chaos. Some find the national focus on teacher and student performance cumbersome and doomed to failure.

"The national movement to create standards is dead of multiple wounds, some self-inflicted, others from our culture wars, still others from congressional antipathy to any federal initiative, and most from American educators who have long resisted establishing a common core of academic learning" (Gagnon, 1995, 1). Others consider the attention on standards crucial to setting education on a straight course. "Organizing schooling around standards is so compelling that schools and districts will implement standards-based school reform even in the absence of federal or state mandates or incentives" (Marzano & Kendall, 1996).

Regardless of your point of view, nearly everyone sees the logic behind having a certain level of achievement in mind when undertaking any enterprise. If a hostess is planning a dinner and decides to make a lemon meringue pie for dessert, she has a certain ideal in mind for what the pie should look like. There should be exactly the right amount and consistency of sunshine yellow filling in a tan crust. Two inches of firmly swirled white meringue on top should have peaks toasted golden brown with at least a half dozen or more crystal pearls of moisture adding the final touch. The end result is beautiful to look at and delicious to eat—and anything below that standard just won't do. Students are not pies, but their fillings should meet equally high standards and teachers who plan for and prepare their lessons to fill students' minds should be well aware of the role standards play in promoting success in student learning.

Focus QUESTIONS

After reading this chapter you should be able to answer the following questions:

1 Why are there standards for student learning? Who establishes these standards?

2 Why is it important for a teacher to become familiar with standards and benchmarks and incorporate them into lesson plans? Why would meeting standards and benchmarks be critical to a student's performance?

3 Does focusing on the results of student learning improve teaching practices? Discuss some of the ways your teachers' focus on student learning helped you meet local, state, and national standards.

4 Effective teachers must also meet standards for teaching by reflecting on their practice and the behavior of their students in order to improve their instructional practices and student achievement. Name some of the ways in which focusing on teacher standards can affect student learning.

5 How were the results of your learning when you were a K–12 student evidence that you were meeting certain standards and achievement-specific benchmarks?

How Do Teachers Focus on Learning?

Nathan's major concern as a high school English teacher and as chair of the English department at Liberty High School is that all of the students pass the state proficiency exam required for a high school diploma. One of the principles that guides Nathan's teaching is based on something he learned in a time-management course: "If you fail to plan, you plan to fail." So Nathan begins each year reviewing his major goals and outlining a yearly plan that sets the framework for the unit and lesson plans he will use throughout the year. The focus on what the students in his classes at Liberty High School will learn in English and be able to demonstrate through the state proficiency test is evident in each lesson plan Nathan writes and in the ways he evaluates the students' progress over time. Nathan uses a specific lesson-plan format that he believes helps him focus his instructional practices on the knowledge students need to acquire and the standards they are expected to meet. It is important to Nathan that the little time he has for instruction with his students is used in a purposeful manner.

Teachers focus on learning through planning and organizing instruction. Planning lessons that assure the best possible opportunities for students to learn what they need to know is a major responsibility of teaching. All teachers bring multiple and interactive layers of experience, knowledge, and skills to the process of planning for instruction. Beginning teachers' knowledge of content and methods of teaching has been mostly learned through college and university classes and their initial attempts to plan lessons can be somewhat rigid, following a predetermined set of criteria. Over time and through experience, teachers gain what Canning (1991) terms **tacit knowledge** that helps them understand what works in a specific context and with a specific group of students. The tacit knowledge teachers develop helps make their planning less rigid, more creative, and ultimately reflects their individual teaching styles. Most teachers engage in a form of **preplanning** long before they begin to write any formal lesson plans. This preplanning stage, identified by Freiberg and Driscoll (1992), allows teachers to play with ideas, collect resources that might be used during the actual lesson, and to run an imaginary virtual lesson through their minds, mentally assessing the benefits and pitfalls that might result.

Nathan knows his high school students will be required to write a personal essay on what democracy means to them. One day, he is in the post office mailing a letter to his brother in the Marine Corps when he notices a poster announcing a series of stamps commemorating Black History Month. He begins to think of other artifacts of democracy at work that he can put on the walls of his classroom to prompt his students' thinking about the ways democracy affects their lives. He thinks of activities the students can engage in that will connect the democratic ideals of freedom and suffrage and how his lesson can be tied to the state and district standards for English and history. His mind takes off at high speed, planning a weeklong unit that involves his students reading essays by Frederick Douglass and Sojourner Truth and writing and delivering speeches on freedom and

Tacit knowledge. Knowledge that is implied, not stated; happening almost automatically.

Preplanning. The thinking that takes place ahead of making an actual plan.

democracy. Planning should be fun. It should be as engaging for a teacher to plan a lesson as it is for the students to participate in it.

Lesson Structure

"Planning is the systematic process of deciding what and how your students should learn" (Borich, 2004, 123). Teachers must make numerous decisions and possess considerable knowledge to be able to plan effective lessons. Teachers must make decisions about the design of the lesson in general and how each element of any lesson is to be translated into instruction that will result in student learning. They have to be well versed in the content and the way the content is organized; what concepts come first and which follow. They have to know what their students already know, how the students learn best, and how quickly the students grasp new concepts. They have to know a range of teaching methods. In addition, they have to have knowledge of the goals of the school district, the standards and benchmarks in the district curriculum guides, and the state and national standards for student achievement.

Teachers also have to know how to organize lessons so that the content is presented in an orderly and comprehensive manner so that each element of a lesson is in some logical way related to the elements that come before and that follow. Before a plan is set for any specific lesson, teachers must make decisions about the content that will be taught, the students' ability levels, and target objectives.

Your lesson plan book is an essential tool in the planning process.

Madeline Hunter's Plan   Madeline Hunter, one of the 10 most influential women in education of the twentieth century and a former professor at the University of California at Los Angeles, found that no matter what the teacher's style, grade level, subject matter, or the economic background of the students, a properly taught lesson contained seven elements that enhanced and maximized learning (see Table 8.1). According to Hunter "elements in a planning sequence are necessary for every mode of learning, no matter how the plan is implemented, i.e., by direct input from the teacher, by materials, by computer, or by the students in discovery or cooperative learning" (1994, 88).

Planning as a Means of Focusing on Results

Through planning, teachers are able to emphasize the connections between ideas and help students recognize relationships between topics (Rosenshine & Stevens, 1986). Without well-laid plans, instruction becomes happenstance and some of the pieces of information necessary for the next level of learning are left behind. If an 8th grader is learning about changes in indigenous societies in the Americas prior to the Columbian voyages, it will be useful for the student to

Table 8.1 Elements in a Planning Sequence

Element	Example
Anticipatory Set: Develops readiness to learn	Teacher introduces topic/content through a demonstration, a story, a picture, a song, etc., to focus student attention and heighten student interest.
Instructional Objective: Provides rationale for learning; value to learners	Teacher explains to students what they are to accomplish and the purpose for the activity. Objective may be written on the board.
Instructional Input: Identifies source and type of information	Teacher decides which teaching strategy to use, whether students will read, listen, watch, work in groups, or conduct research.
Example/Model of Intended Learning: Provides criteria for meeting objective	Teacher shows students what their work is to look like and provides them with a rubric for self-assessment.
Check Learner Understanding of Objective: Offers opportunity for questioning and class discussion	Teacher pauses during instructional input to review previous information or steps and to answer students' questions.
Guided/Monitored Practice: Allows students to practice knowledge or skill while teacher observes and corrects	Teacher has students work math problems on the board, make grammatical, spelling, and punctuation corrections to sentences or phrases.
Independent Practice: Helps students develop fluency and retain information	Teacher gives assignments for students to complete on their own, praises their achievements and reminds students of how much they are learning.

know something about tribal cultures, their technologies, and their social practices. For example, a talented and well-educated teacher will, through careful planning, be able to weave together multiple pieces of the rise and decline of the society of the Native American Mound Builders of the upper Mississippi River region in order for the student to analyze reasons for change in indigenous societies in the Americas. In addition, a highly qualified teacher is able to tie the lesson to the National History Standards for grades 7–12. The structure of the plan from general information to a specific example helps the students make generalizations and use data to predict and analyze outcomes. The Connecting to the Classroom on page 303 will give you the opportunity to consider ways to enhance lessons.

Lesson Plan Formats

Many teacher education candidates become overwhelmed by the number of lesson plans they are expected to write during their methods courses. One college instructor may require a specific format be used while another prefers a different sort of lesson plan altogether. For the beginning student of teaching, this focus on planning may seem unreasonable and time consuming. Knowing the elements of a lesson that should be included in each plan and being able to organize those elements in the most judicious way to optimize student learning is one of the most important tools you will have as you begin your teaching career. Two lesson-plan formats are provided in Tables 8.2 and 8.3 to give an idea of the detail required in planning for lessons and demonstrating your competence in organizing meaningful lessons for your students. Naturally, the teaching strategy used for delivering a lesson as well as the grade level and subject for which a specific plan is written will influence to some degree the final version. Planning can be a creative and exciting process when teachers possess the knowledge and skills necessary to make their own plans come alive. The two lesson-plan formats in the tables are summarized from the Field Experiences Handbooks for elementary and secondary education majors at the University of Nevada, Las Vegas.

Revisiting Nathan's Plan to Focus on Learning

As Nathan reviews his major teaching goals for the year, he is ever mindful of the progress his students must make in order to be successful on the state proficiency test. His lesson plans, the strategies he intends to use to teach the content, and the materials he will use to extend student learning are all incor-

Table 8.2 Elementary Lesson-Plan Format

Basic Information	Context of the lesson including date, length of lesson, subject, grade level, and other information that may influence student performance
Objectives	Indicate what students will learn; describe learning outcomes that are observable, not the activity the students will perform
Materials	List resources to be prepared and used during the lesson; describe how materials will be distributed to students
Procedure	Indicate steps to be followed to introduce, develop, and close the lesson; include a. motivational introduction b. developmental activity c. culminating activity d. extension Also describe how technology will be used if appropriate; identify tools of inquiry that will be used as students examine/explore the content and expand their knowledge
Student Assessment/Evaluation	Describe how students will be evaluated and how this information will be recorded
Teacher (Self) Assessment/ Evaluation and Student Work Sample	List strengths, concerns, and insights

Connecting
TO THE CLASSROOM

Although you may not be a teacher yet, you are probably planning to be one someday soon. It is never too early to begin collecting ideas and resources that will help you create outstanding lessons. When you observe and practice teach in classrooms, be aware of the unusual ways teachers use resources to enhance their lessons.

With one of your classmates, brainstorm ideas that you think would make the following lessons highly motivating. Share your ideas with other teacher education candidates in your program.

- A 4th grade math lesson on fractions
- An 11th grade literature lesson on story elements
- A 9th grade science lesson on the muscle system of frogs
- A 1st grade lesson on vocabulary building
- A 7th grade lesson on the statues of Easter Island

aim of Satan was to keep men from knowledge of the Scriptures. Every township of 50 or more families was ordered to appoint someone within the town to provide all children with an elementary education so they could read the Scriptures. Benjamin Franklin's 1749 *Proposal Relating to the Education of Youth in Pensilvania* [*sic*] was intended to make English the standard of instruction rather than Latin and to establish a curriculum that was both scientific and practical. Thomas Jefferson's 1779 Bill for the More General Diffusion of Knowledge planned to establish cumulative and consecutive levels of education from elementary schools to secondary schools and then possibly on to college. It also called for states rather than the church or the federal government to control the schools. The curriculum of the Common School Movement of the 1800s outlined the skills needed for everyday life, for ethical behavior, and for responsible citizenship (Cremin, 1951, 62). George W. Bush's No Child Left Behind (NCLB) act of 2001 supports reading instruction that will ensure that every child in public schools reads at or above grade level by 3rd grade. The No Child Left Behind act also strives to strengthen teacher quality for public schools by investing in training and retention of high-quality teachers. Each of these efforts, in addition to a multitude of other proposals, bills, and plans, to establish standards and improve U.S. education have contributed to and continue to contribute to setting criteria for a cumulative and consecutive system of universal public education for all children who attend the nation's schools.

Although the establishment of standards may appear to be the purview of lawmakers, politicians, and educators, parents also have major concerns

Ed Lines

"**Skill in planning is acknowledged to be one of the most influential factors in successful teaching.**" *Madeline Hunter*

Experienced teachers prepare for the National Board for Professional Teaching Standards Exam.

about what schools will expect of their children. Parents want their children to succeed in school and to have rewarding and enriching experiences there. Some standards are easy for parents to understand—for example, "all children will learn to read"—while some standards are less clear—"children will be ready to learn." Readiness for elementary school is an implicit standard for beginning formal schooling in the United States. Although school attendance is not mandatory in most states until 1st grade, national surveys of parents of early elementary pupils show that a large majority of primary school children attended kindergarten before entering 1st grade. Such reports provide evidence that parents are concerned that their sons and daughters begin school well prepared to meet the standards. The Teachers and the Law on page 305 provides an example of ways states set standards for student achievement.

The Many Characteristics of Standards

There are standards for content, for teachers, and for teacher education. In Chapter 1, you learned about the Interstate New Teacher Assessment Support Consortium (INTASC) standards stated as principles and about national certification for teachers by the National Board for Professional Teaching Standards (NBPTS). You can learn more about the purposes of each of these organizations by visiting their respective websites at www.ccsso.org/intascst.html and www.nbpts.org. You will become very familiar with the INTASC standards during your teacher-education coursework and with the NBPTS later in your career. Each chapter in this text deals in some way with one or more of the INTASC standards providing you the opportunity to see how these standards are played out in the life of a teacher education candidate and a teacher.

▶ **National K–12 Standards for Student Learning.** A compilation of statements of expectations for learning outcomes to be used across the country.

A more recent set of standards, the **National K–12 Standards for Student Learning** developed by the Committee on Undergraduate Science Education in collaboration with the Center for Science, Mathematics, and Engineering Education and the National Research Council addresses the teaching of science, mathematics, engineering, and technology at the college level in an attempt to provide potential teachers with the best undergraduate education possible. The primary goal of this committee is that "institutions of higher education provide diverse opportunities for all undergraduates to study science, mathematics, engi-

Teachers and the Law

The federal No Child Left Behind (NCLB) Act of 2001 requires each state to provide a school accountability system. School districts in a state that receive federal dollars based on the percentage of students who live in poverty must compile annual accountability reports. In Connecticut, student performance is reported in mathematics and reading on the Connecticut Mastery Test (CMT) and the Connecticut Academic Performance Test (CAPT). There are five levels of achievement for these tests: Advanced, Mastery, Proficient, Basic, or Below Basic. Standards in the federal NCLB accountability act are based on the percentage of students scoring at the Proficient level or higher. States are required to determine annually if every district and school is making adequate yearly progress (AYP) toward a predetermined goal.

Can states set their own goals for meeting federal requirements?

Yes. Connecticut has set a goal, by 2014, of having 100 percent of its student population scoring at or above the Proficient level in mathematics and reading on the CMT and CAPT. For a school or district to have made AYP in Connecticut, all students in the district and each subgroup (major racial and ethnic groups, students in poverty, students with disabilities, and English language learners) must meet the following criteria: (1) 95 percent participation on both the mathematics

and reading on the CMT and CAPT; (2) achievement of the AYP target percentage at or above Proficient on the two tests; and (3) achievement of the AYP target for an additional academic indicator: 70 percent at or above Basic on the writing subtest of the CMT or improvement from the previous year for elementary and middle schools and 70 percent graduate rate or improvement from the previous year for high schools. Keeping track of student progress and seeing that students are in school and taking required tests have become something of a monster to deal with. In Connecticut, if a district does not make AYP for two consecutive years, it will be identified as "in need of improvement."

Can teachers be held responsible for their students not meeting federal standards?

Yes. The consequences of not meeting the standards set by NCLB are up close and personal. The goals and benchmarks states and school districts set for meeting NCLB standards are similar in nature given the overarching goals of national standards and federal mandates. It is probably pretty well understood that no school district wants to be classified as "in need of improvement," and that teachers do not want to be working at a "school on watch." Teachers are expected to assume their portion of the responsibility for seeing that student achievement at the schools where they teach meets the standards.

Source: Connecticut Technical High School System No Child Left Behind (NCLB) District Report: 2004–05 School Year, p. 2. Retrieved August, 2006 from www.cttech.org/WHITNEY/nclb/0900_Districtv4.pdf.

neering, and technology as practiced by scientists and engineers, and as early in their academic careers as possible" (Executive Summary, 1999, 1). The committee recognizes that achievement of this goal relies in part on precollege experiences that include quality instruction in standards-based classrooms and a clear awareness that achievement in science, mathematics, and technology become prerequisites for admission to college. Standards are woven through the education process in an attempt to articulate the connections among all levels of learning.

During the 1990s, the use of standardized high-stakes achievement tests for certification of beginning teachers became prevalent. In 1998, the reauthorization of Title II of the Higher Education Act (ESEA) mandated that institutions report pass rates of teacher education program completers on teacher tests. Nearly 80 percent of states that include tests as part of their teacher licensure process rely on The PRAXIS Series, a set of rigorous and carefully validated assessments that provide accurate, reliable information. The thread of standards that weaves through the education process appears solidly connected at all levels.

Standards for Teacher Education Candidates

Table 8.4 is an overview of the standards-based examinations you will face as a teacher education candidate. Results from such tests help state departments of education and colleges of education determine whether a student is qualified to be admitted to and matriculate through a teacher education program. Teacher education programs across the nation are either requiring candidates pass the PRAXIS II prior to graduation or recommending that it be taken soon after graduation. Upon graduation from an approved program, test results can help determine whether candidates meet state criteria for licensing. "In Spring 2003, 16 states and the Department of Defense Dependents Schools required that teacher-education candidates pass PRAXIS II: PLT to obtain a license" (Sutton, 2004, 464).

An example of how standards have become a standard fixture of the professional scene is the way in which the INTASC standards were conceived, constituted, and connected to every aspect of teacher preparation and performance. The standards were originally created to promote in-district professional development of beginning teachers, but have evolved into a system for evaluating teaching performance at all levels. There is no question that standards and accountability will be in your teaching future.

Teacher education candidates should be aware that state departments of education can establish their own pedagogical standards for beginning teachers. The state of Iowa has identified eight standards for beginning teachers who have earned a two-year initial license. These standards can be found at www.state.ia.us/boee/stndrds.html. To receive a standard Iowa state teaching license, teachers must be approved by their building principal as passing the Iowa state teaching standards. In the future, all Iowa teachers, not just beginning teachers, will be evaluated using the Iowa teaching standards. You need to become knowledgeable about how the state where you want to teach assesses beginning teachers.

All teacher education candidates must complete the PRAXIS II exam or some other mandated test to become fully certified.

Table 8.4 Standards-Based Examinations for Teacher Education Candidates

Basic Academic Skills	Subject and Pedagogy	Multiple Subject	Final Licensure
Assessment: Mathematics, reading comprehension, writing	Assessments: Principles of learning and teaching	Assessment: Specialty area tests	Classroom performance assessment
Colleges and universities may use results of these tests to qualify individuals for entry into teacher-education programs.	Commonly takes place at the end of an undergraduate teacher preparation program.	Commonly takes place at the end of an undergraduate teacher-preparation program.	Takes place during the first year of teaching.
Three tests, one in each academic area	Assessments generally divided into grades K–6, 5–9, and 7–12.	Over 100 subject areas in grades K–12; tied to areas of teacher certification	Assesses individual performance in an actual classroom setting.
States set individual passing scores for each test	Assess candidate knowledge of • students as learners • instructional strategies • communication skills • profession and community	Typical content tests include: Early childhood education, biology, physics, business education, general science, English language literature and composition, physical education, social studies, and art.	

To learn more about professional assessments for beginning teachers, visit www.ets.org/praxis/index.html.

Standards for Teachers

Standards for teaching and for learning to become a teacher are not a new phenomenon. Teachers have always been held to some form of standards and accountability. Even before a degree and graduation from an accredited institution was mandatory, school boards or directors of schools demanded a level of respectability demonstrated by social status, family background, or gender. A list of 26 suggestions for what a teacher should do offered in 1867 included the following:

- Labor diligently for self-improvement
- Thoroughly understand [what] he attempts to teach
- Prepare himself for each lesson assigned
- Ask two questions out of the book for every one in it
- Be courteous in language and action
- Insist upon attention from the whole class
- Avoid governing too much

- Visit the parents of his pupils
- Subscribe to some education journal
- Teach the subject, not mere words
- Dignify and elevate his profession by his personal worth as well as by his skill and scholarship

Perhaps the male reference in this list implies that most of the teachers at that time were men. Even today, regardless of gender, what a teacher knows and what a teacher knows how to do are fundamental to being employed. They are also keys to success in one's identity as a teacher and level of confidence in teaching. However, what a teacher does with this know-how is far more important to the achievement and success of students than simply having the knowledge.

Charlotte Danielson's Four Domains of Teaching Responsibility   In *Enhancing Professional Practice: A Framework for Teaching* (1996), Danielson describes the elements of a teacher's responsibilities that promote student learning. The elements of her framework are derived from the findings of research studies on the connection between teaching behavior and student learning. Danielson's framework delineates the complex act of teaching into four domains of teaching responsibility.

> Domain 1: Planning and preparation
>
> Domain 2: Classroom environment
>
> Domain 3: Instruction
>
> Domain 4: Professional responsibilities

Distinct features of each domain are further defined by five to six components, and each component is comprised of two to five elements. For example, Domain 3: Instruction has five components:

1. Communicating clearly and accurately
2. Using questioning and discussion techniques
3. Engaging students in learning
4. Providing feedback to students
5. Demonstrating flexibility and responsiveness

Elements under the component *Providing feedback to students* are quality and timeliness. Quality is defined as "accurate, substantive, constructive and specific." You can no doubt recall a teacher whose feedback to you was both timely and constructive. On the other hand, you may recall a teacher whose feedback was not specific enough to be helpful or was not given in a time frame that helped you learn. The manner in which teachers provide feedback to students can affect student achievement.

Ed Lines

"The standard for a home run is a fair ball in the stands or out of the park. But this standard is not the same in all ball parks." *M. T. Temple*

Danielson's framework provides teachers and the administrators who evaluate them a standard for determining individual levels of performance by means of a series of rubrics identifying performance as being either distinguished, proficient, basic, or unsatisfactory. In Danielson's own words, "the framework for professional practice can be used for a wide range of purposes, from meeting novices' needs to enhancing veterans' skill. Because teaching is complex, it is helpful to have a road map through the territory, structured around a shared understanding of teaching" (Danielson, 1996, 2). Danielson's framework does not prescribe the only way to reach a goal, but it does offer meaningful mileposts to guide teachers on their professional journey.

Standards for Content

Professional associations have established groups to create standards to guide curriculum development in specific disciplines. These associations include:

- National Council of Teachers of Mathematics
- National Council of Teachers of English
- National Geographic Society
- National Council on Economic Education
- National Council for Social Studies
- Center for Civic Education
- Consortium of National Arts Education Associations
- National Center for History in the Schools
- International Society for Technology in Education
- National Academies of Science

National standards in the arts, behavioral studies, civics, economics, foreign language, geography, health, history, language arts, life skills, mathematics, physical education, science, and technology have also been developed. Some professional associations list standards for K–12, while others divide the standards into grade-level groups (e.g., K–4, 5–8, 9–12). Visit the text website (www.ablongman.com/hall1e) to view a table that provides examples of how national standards from content areas are interpreted at a specific grade level of student performance, and how standards might be stated as learning objectives for students at designated grade levels.

State departments of education and some school districts have also created separate sets of content standards. While states strive to meet the needs of their specific residents when establishing standards, they also make every effort to align their state standards with national standards in order to meet the mandates of the ESEA. Standards can be viewed by state at www.education-world.com/standards/national/index.shtml. Iowa is the only state in the union that does not have official state-mandated curriculum. Therefore, school districts establish their own content standards. State curriculum guides suggest ways that districts can formulate their standards, but in reality most districts adapt the national content area standards.

Ed Lines

"The best defense against tyranny is to 'illuminate as far as practicable, the minds of the people at large.' " *Thomas Jefferson*

Understanding
USING EVIDENCE

ARE STANDARDS FOR AMERICAN STUDENTS SET TOO LOW?

The National Center for Education Statistics (NCES) collects and reports reliable data on student assessments in the United States and other nations in its ongoing examination of education systems around the world. One report, the Program for International Student Assessment (PISA) that was conducted in 2003, focused on 15-year-olds' capabilities in reading literacy, mathematics literacy, and science literacy. The data presented here represents the combined mathematical literacy scores for each country.

Country	Mathematical Literacy Scores	Country	Mathematical Literacy Scores
Finland	544	Germany	503
Korea	540	Ireland	503
Netherlands	538	Slovak Republic	498
Japan	534	Norway	495
Canada	532	Luxembourg	493
Belgium	529	Poland	490
Switzerland	527	Hungary	490
New Zealand	526	Spain	485
Australia	524	United States	483
Czech Republic	516	Portugal	466
Iceland	515	Italy	466
Denmark	514	Greece	445
France	511	Turkey	423
Sweden	509	Mexico	385
Austria	506		

Your Task: Using the list of combined mathematics literacy scores from the 29 member countries of the Organization for Economic Cooperation Development (OECD), discuss why you think U.S. standards for student achievement in mathematics literacy might or might not need to be revised.

Refer to the **Understanding & Using Evidence Appendix** *at the end of the text for answers and information related to these activities.*

Standards and Accountability One of the paradoxes of the performance-based movement in U.S. education is that we know from experience, from psychology, and from human learning and development courses that not all of us fit the standards in the same way, learn at the same pace, or reach certain standards at the same time—if we reach them at all. This dilemma poses a great challenge to teachers who are expected to bring all students up to a specific standard within a designated period of time, as well as grow in skill themselves. At the outset, it seems an impossible task. Amazingly, however, at the end of each school year, millions of students meet and in many cases exceed standards that have been set for them by departments of education, by school districts, and by their teachers, while their teachers also improve their own effectiveness.

When comparing the achievement of students in the United States with students from other countries, some people might say U.S. standards are too low. Consider the data in the Understanding and Using Evidence on page 310 to help you form an opinion about the state of U.S. standards.

Revisiting Charles's Understanding of Standards

Charles learned about standards in his teacher preparation program and he plans the lessons he teaches around the standards set by Texas. He has become proficient in talking about these standards with his fellow teachers though he sometimes struggles over ways to incorporate the standards into engaging activities for his students. He knows that the concept of standards has been evident in the field of education for some time. He knows how standards are developed and that there are standards for students, for teachers, and for teacher education candidates. He is beginning to see the connection between his knowledge of standards and his effectiveness as a teacher. The purpose of standards in education is no longer a mystery to Charles.

Why Are Standards Necessary?

Andrew has had extensive experience working with other educators to develop standards. His experience began when he was invited by the National Council of Teachers of Mathematics (NCTM) to join one of the first committees established to develop standards in mathematics. Each person joining the math standards development committee was asked to make a commitment to serve on a specific grade-band team for 2 years. Initially, the committees met for one full week during the summer and for shorter periods during the academic year. The 15-member team, later divided into three subgroups of 5 members each, was comprised of elementary, middle, and high school math teachers, university professors, school principals, department chairs, and a district superintendent who had a degree in mathematics. Andrew was a member of the team charged with writing standards for grades 9–12. The first draft of the standards was sent to 10,000 members of the NCTM for feedback. Following 2 years of revising the original draft based on comments and suggestions from NCTM members, a final version of the NCTM standards was published. However, Andrew's commitment to his profession did not end once the standards were published. He has been involved in subsequent revisions and editions of the math standards. More recently, he has helped develop a set of national standards for the teaching of mathematics to complement the national standards for mathematics.

Andrew has also served on a committee to write standards for the college boards. His participation in both processes has made him aware that standards are written for different reasons and for different audiences. One set of standards was written to describe what knowledge and skills were necessary to successfully complete high school; one set was written to describe the knowledge and skills necessary to be successful in a university program. As students move through the

*ranks of formal education, the standards they are to achieve must naturally
change to demonstrate the increased expectations they will face.*

In considering the question, "Why do we need standards?" Marzano and Kendall
(1996) provide five reasons elementary to the establishment of standards. First,
standards provide a starting point from which to articulate goals for student
achievement and performance. Without this starting point, goals can become
idiosyncratic and develop through some untested assumption or poorly articulated observation. Disassociation with other elements of the educational enterprise can result and confusion reign. Secondly, standards provide a basis for
developing curriculum benchmarks that will help students meet specific levels
of content knowledge. If a standard is "All students will demonstrate improvement in reading throughout their attendance in school," then the curriculum
must be written and benchmarks must be established to assure that all students
have the opportunity to reach this standard and that schools, teachers, and students are held accountable as students progress toward it. Thirdly, standards
should be written in such a way that they include both content knowledge and
the skills necessary to apply that knowledge. Knowing is not sufficient. How to
use the knowledge is equally important. Fourthly, because standards and assessments are inexplicably connected, standards naturally form the basis for developing assessments to measure whether they have been met. Finally, standards should
present a recognizable progression from one level to another. Standards should
build on one another. Achievement of one standard should prepare learners for
subsequent standards. In essence, standards clarify and raise expectations and provide a common set of expectations.

In her book, *National Standards in American Education: A Citizen's Guide* (1995),
Diane Ravitch provides a commonsense rationale for standards:

> Americans . . . expect strict standards to govern construction of buildings,
> bridges, highways, and tunnels; shoddy work would put lives at risk. They
> expect stringent standards to protect their drinking water, the food they eat,
> and the air they breathe. . . . Standards are created because they improve the
> activity of life. (8–9)

Standards are developed by real people who have both practical and theoretical knowledge of their discipline. People who are educators concerned with student learning and the quality of instruction that will assure student achievement
help write standards. People who develop standards teach in P–12 classrooms,
serve as school administrators, work for state and national departments of education, and teach in colleges and universities. They donate their time and effort to
the national goal of assuring all students an equal and excellent opportunity to acquire the knowledge and skills expected of citizens in a democracy.

Developing Standards in the Content Areas

National standards for content areas have been previously introduced in this
chapter. However, in order to help you understand the scope and design of the
standards movement, it seems wise to provide a brief history of the activity to
standardize content goals and establish assessments that are intended to provide

Teachers' Lounge

What Alvin Taught Me

It was my first year as a reading recovery teacher at P.S. 75, the Bronx, New York. Working with the 20 percent of the lowest-functioning 1st grade students, my role was to teach them to read and write at grade level within 20 weeks: Quite a task for a novice reading recovery teacher!

After careful screening of all eligible students, Alvin was chosen to be one of four students I was to teach in a one-on-one "behind-the-glass" lesson, wherein the student would not be aware that he or she was being observed. Alvin's mother was allowed to observe the lesson as well. Alvin and I worked very hard, and after 20 weeks, he successfully completed the program.

Several months later, our school had a fire drill. While I was outside with my class, Alvin's mom came up to me. She told me that she was so happy that Alvin was doing well in school. She went on to tell me that she was going to school for her GED, and that Alvin was helping *her*! That summer, I received a letter from Alvin, telling me that his little sister would be entering the 1st grade in the fall, and could I please help her to be a good reader and writer, too?

- Audrey Yuster
  Teacher for the New York
  City Board of Education

accurate data on student performance. The amount of time invested, the personnel needed to staff the numerous committees that were created, and the funding from tax dollars over a 15-year time period should make it crystal clear that the establishment of national standards in education was not a frivolous endeavor.

At the beginning of 1990s, a National Council on Education Standards and Testing (NCEST) was created to make recommendations regarding voluntary national standards. The NCEST in turn proposed an oversight board to establish guidelines for standards setting and assessment development. This board became the National Education Standards and Assessment Council (NESAC) to review and evaluate content standards and assessments proposed by specialized professional associations. Of course, before all these councils and boards were created by the federal government, the National Council for Teachers of Mathematics (NCTM) published *Curriculum and Evaluation Standards for School Mathematics* (1989) blazing the trail for other content areas to follow (Marzano & Kendall, 1996).

Many content standards were drafted and finalized during the last decade of the twentieth century. Part of the Goals 2000: Educate America Act, signed into law by President Bill Clinton, created the National Education Standards and Improvement Council (NESIC) to certify national and state content and performance standards. Federal funding was made available to support other content area organizations in creating standards. Creating standards for each content area in school was often a controversial task and garnering few rewards for the initial designers. For example, the National Endowment for the Humanities and the National Geographic Society worked together on a first draft of geography standards. When the standards for U.S. and World History, Civics and Government and Geography were released, the history standards were denounced by the U.S. Senate as being unacceptable. It was back to the drawing board for this group.

314

NON SEQUITUR © 1996 Wiley Miller. Dist. by UNIVERSAL PRESS SYNDICATE. Reprinted with permission. All rights reserved.

Other groups had more success. For example, in 1992, the Committee for National Health Education Standards was funded by the American Cancer Society (Marzano & Kendall, 1996). The Consortium of National Arts Education Associations published the arts standards (dance, music, theatre, and the visual arts). National standards for sports and physical education were published, standards for foreign language learning were published, national science education standards, the national council of teachers of English and the International Reading Association published standards.

Standards for each content area have seen much revision since the first installments. They have undergone strict scrutiny from peers and from the general public for their cost, their ability to truly reform education, their content, and their voluminous size. Through a decade of lively discussion, the current standards and assessment criteria have survived and are rapidly becoming a permanent pillar of the education panorama.

For most taxpayers, it often seems the federal government only takes money away. However, in the case of creating national standards for education, the federal government established grants to support the process of designing standards and it also withdrew funding for certain organizations when controversy over the standards ran counter to national goals.

A rich source for learning more about standards can be found on the Education World website at www.education-world.com/standards/national/index. shtml. Navigating the ocean of standards can sometimes seem like an impossible task for teachers and teacher education candidates, but the thread of content standards in education is strong and easy to follow. The manner in which national standards are articulated can help teachers understand the ways in which courses and subjects are defined. Standards help describe levels of student performance and help determine how student performance is graded and reported. Visit the text website (www.ablongman.com/hall1e) to view a table that offers a snapshot of how specific overarching concepts in five different disciplines are categorized in the standards movement.

National standards do not define a national curriculum per se. They do, however, specify broad areas of agreement on content to which all students are expected to be exposed. Some national standards are divided into grade-level bands to further articulate content deemed especially relevant to particular grade levels. For instance, the National Standards for Social Studies are divided into sets of standards for civics, economics, geography, U.S. history, and world history. Each professional association determines the range of its standards and the exact number of standards that will cover the structure of each discipline.

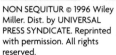

Ed Lines

"The act of teaching includes students' learning." *Michael Scott Cain*

The purposes behind each set of national standards are explained in detail and explanations are provided for developing student abilities and understandings. Examples are provided in the content standards documents illustrating how intermediate objectives might be achieved. State department of education and district curriculum committees establish subsets of objectives and classroom teachers deliver these objectives through instructional practices. The route from the overarching concepts embedded in national standards to a specific objective may be long, but it is clear and at the end of the journey, it is the teacher who conveys all of the standards to the students.

Education without Standards

Because the content of education is of extreme importance to the future of society, the absence of standards would leave society vulnerable to all manner of misfortune. Beginning teachers use published standards as a guide for what they can and should do and as a caution against things they shouldn't do. New teachers also depend in some ways on the advice of others who are experienced with the actual ways standards are enforced and assessed. Teachers, both new and experienced, rely on established guidelines and standards to help them navigate the educational sea without going astray. There are guidelines for professional behavior and for professional relationships between students and teachers. There are curriculum guides that set benchmarks for student achievement. There are standards for attendance, for grading, for discipline, and for dress. There are even standards for textbooks and protocols for the ways states and districts adopt one textbook over others.

Accreditation Standards   There are also standards for school districts, universities, and colleges of education. Such institutions are expected to meet these standards as approved by state and federal departments of education. This is another reason why standards are so important to teachers and to teacher education candidates. Teacher-education programs at accredited institutions have been approved by the specialized professional associations and by state departments of education. Candidates at these institutions must pass standardized tests and maintain a required grade point average. Most states with institutions who have received national accreditation have reciprocal agreements with other states for licensure. This means if you get your degree in New York and want to be licensed to teach in Indiana, the Indiana State Board of Education will consider whether you graduated from an accredited institution. If so, your chances of being granted a license to teach in Indiana will be better than if you graduated from an institution that has not achieved national, regional, or state accreditation. It is in your best interests to become aware of the standards underpinning your teacher education program and do your best to exceed these standards at every opportunity. The following Challenging Assumptions feature demonstrates the importance of you meeting the standards set for teachers.

Ed Lines

"I am always ready to learn although I do not always like being taught." _Winston Churchill_

Revisiting Andrew's Knowledge of Standards

Andrew works diligently for his profession in helping to develop standards that will improve student achievement and teaching practices. His membership on various committees has provided him firsthand understanding of the process of drafting and revising standards to achieve a final version that will meet approval by members of the profession.

Challenging Assumptions
FINDINGS FROM RESEARCH

Does setting standards automatically result in increased student academic achievement?

The Assumption: The idea behind the NCLB initiative was that if there are specific standards for student achievement and if the students' abilities to meet such standards are assessed over time in standardized and organized procedures, then teachers and school districts will be held accountable and will make the necessary adjustments to practice and organization to assure that all students have equal opportunity to meet the national standards.

Study Design and Method: Not all school districts have the wherewithal to make the necessary changes to meet the mandates of NCLB. Some large school districts continue to struggle to fill each classroom with a teacher who meets the qualifications of the High Objective Uniform State Standard of Evaluation (HOUSSE) rules that each state must determine in order to show that teachers in all classrooms are highly qualified. Some school districts lack the funding to adjust class size and or to provide each classroom with the materials and technology that are viewed as necessary support for students to meet mandated standards. Schools that are classified as "in need for improvement" often find themselves in an untenable position to demonstrate how they have improved to meet standards when they had not been able to meet them in the first place. However, increased funding for schools has not always provided a better learning environment for students. What is to be done?

Study Findings: In May 2006, the U.S. House of Representatives began a hearing related to NCLB to examine how the federal government can help states reach the goal to have all students proficient in reading and math by the year 2014. One way some public organizations are beginning to approach this problem is to demand that school districts allow students zoned for a school categorized as "in need for improvement" to go to another school which is not. A class action suit against the New Jersey schools is demanding that students in low-performing schools receive vouchers to attend a public or private school of their choice. Clint Bolick, the president and general counsel of the Alliance for School Choice, vows that such measures would provide educational relief for the 60,000 students attending the 97 New Jersey schools cited as failing. Approximately half of the students in these schools have failed to meet state standards in language arts and mathematics.

Implications: The school of choice movement has been around for some time now and the voucher system has been in place for students; however, the mandates of NCLB have placed a greater emphasis on the potential for parents to demand that their children have an equal opportunity for an education in a high-quality school with a highly qualified teacher. As a candidate in a teacher education program, you should know about the voucher programs in your state and the status of the schools in the area where you wish to teach.

Source: Hoff, David J. (2006). Choice advocates seek vouchers as remedy for N.J. students in low-performing schools. *EdWeek*. Retrieved July 13, 2006 from www.edweek.org/er/articles/2006/07/13/.

It would be unnatural if parents and teachers alike didn't question the validity of the increase in testing or ask "What's the point?" or "When will I have time to teach?" Testing is part of what you must contend with as a teacher. Think of it as a challenge, not as an unsettling catastrophe. Tests can provide teachers useful data. They can be used for improvement, not just to condemn. As a new teacher, you will have to understand that testing is a large part of the education scene. Reconcile yourself to that fact and do what you can to make certain it doesn't cause harm. Your response to the testing of your students is of extreme value to your students' success, to your peace of mind, and to the overall standing of your school.

Revisiting Carla's Knowledge of Expectations for Teachers

Carla approaches planning strategically. She is well organized and accesses necessary resources to make certain her students have every opportunity to learn. Teachers like Carla are constantly collecting data to keep track of student progress. When teachers know the standards and benchmarks their students are expected to achieve and what their students will be expected to demonstrate in assessments and in future classes, they are better prepared to help students reach higher levels of achievement.

Chapter Summary

This chapter has provided a very broad picture of the influence of standards and benchmarks in educational practices. Everyone involved in education is concerned with standards, with the steps to achieving them, and with how standards will be assessed. Teachers may find it difficult at times to translate national standards and school district curriculum benchmarks into lesson objectives that can lead to observable student performance. However, because teachers are the people who make standards come alive in classrooms, they must never cease to improve their own teaching practices so they can, in turn, improve the learning of their students. The thread of standards creates a teaching/learning loop in education. Teachers must make sure that the thread runs true, that it does not unravel or knot, and that the results of the enormous effort to establish high standards in education is always focused on student learning.

How do teachers focus on learning? The focus teachers bring to learning begins with their own skills and knowledge of the content they are teaching. It has been said that you can't teach what you don't know, so when teachers want their students to learn something, the teachers themselves must first assess their understanding of what they intend to teach. Teachers have to be skillful in planning lessons that focus student attention toward accomplishing specific objectives and that will help students recognize the connections between ideas and concepts. Teachers understand the importance of prerequisite student knowledge to the success of any lesson. This helps teachers zero in on what students need to know before they can learn new material. Teachers are aware of a range of materials and resources that interest students and that will help them learn. Teachers gather such resources and organize them in meaningful ways before the lesson begins. Teachers collect data from ongoing assessments of student learning and through results from standardized tests. They use this information to plan subsequent lessons directed toward improving student performance and increasing the likelihood that students will achieve school district, state, and national standards.

What are standards? Standards provide a generalized picture of the expectations for professional institutions and for student performance while attending these institutions. Standards provide a measure of learning that occurs in different places and under differing conditions. Standards in education explain a level of performance that is expected at transition points in student learning. Standards assure the public and the profession that proper steps are being taken to educate citizens for participation in a democracy. Standards come in all shapes and forms and have permeated the educational landscape since the first schools opened in the United States. Becoming a licensed teacher depends on one's ability to meet standards for basic skills, for principles of learning and teaching, and for specialty areas. Standards are used to assess teacher performance and guarantee that every child in every classroom has a highly qualified teacher. Standards offer a framework for providing evidence of accountability in teaching practices and in student learning.

Why are standards necessary? Standards provide coherence in education. They express what knowledge and skills all students should possess. A set of standards can be the scaffolding that supports the construction of a well-planned education. Standards form the basis for creating evaluation tools to measure progress. The time and effort of educators from all areas of education have been necessary to the establishment of a feasible set of national standards. Without national standards, state, district, or school guidelines for curriculum could become idiosyncratic, and a general picture of the performance of students in the United States would be vague and unfocused. Standards are used to evaluate the effectiveness of teacher preparation programs and in turn help to assure graduates of such programs will be well prepared to teach all children.

How are standards and benchmarks related? Think of benchmarks as landmarks on the way to a final destination. Scouts in the Old West used landmarks to check their progress across uncharted territory. They knew whether they were headed for the silver mines of Nevada, the missions of Los Angeles, or even the dense forests of Oregon. There were no white and green signposts to guide their way. There were not even roads for that matter, but they had descriptions of the landmarks they would pass along the way from scouts who had gone before—and they had courage. Someone, or a group of folks, with the dream of a final destination lodged firmly in their minds, charted the steps necessary to reach that final destination safely. Standards provided the incentive, the fire of desire to keep one moving along the route. Benchmarks made it possible to evaluate progress; to offer encouragement of an intermediate achievement when the final goal seemed too remote or at times impossible to attain. Of course, many scouts and westward travelers were so awed by landmarks along the way, places that called to their hearts and minds, that they settled down before they reached the places that had been their initial goals. (Do students do that?) Students, teachers, and administrators approach benchmarks and standards from differing perspectives and may interpret them in different ways. Regardless, the benchmarks and standards remain as tangible representations of where we might travel on our journey to becoming more knowledgeable, wiser, and better educated.

How do teachers implement benchmarks and standards? In the same way that scouts may have kept journals or made sketches of the landmarks they were passing, teachers keep records of lesson they have taught. They keep artifacts, samples of student work to share with future students, lists of resources, and their own comments on the success or failure of a particular lesson. They take note of the ways in which curricular objectives must be adapted to meet the unique abilities and learning styles of the students. Teachers understand the structure of the disciplines they teach and they know what comes before and what follows. They make reference to district curriculum guidelines in their lesson plans and know that these guidelines are tied to state and national standards. They assess students frequently and use the results from these assessments to determine if it is necessary to reteach a particular concept or move ahead.

What do teachers do after they have been successful and effective, helping students reach benchmarks and standards along the way to becoming educated? Some keep up the good work. Others consider the options available and decide to serve the profession outside the classroom. Merrie

Schroeder, the teacher you met at the beginning of this chapter, left classroom teaching to become a university administrator. She suggests that anyone interested in becoming a teacher has a world of opportunities before them.

Being a successful educator requires having had a successful teaching experience. After that, there is yet another world of opportunity in education that affects students more indirectly. Those opportunities are most often thought of as school administration or counseling, but that is just the tip of the iceberg. I have been a regional consultant to schools, a district curriculum coordinator, and a university professional development coordinator and administrator. Critical work to be done outside of classrooms also exists in test/assessment programs, national curriculum writing organizations, textbook development, and governmental agencies that address education policy.

Equally important is the work of professional organization leadership. Whether one is a K–12 classroom teacher/administrator or a university professor, content-area organizations demonstrate profound leadership in the profession. People are needed to serve on committees and task forces and to hold leadership positions in the organizations. Major organizations also have a complete staff of people who work in a variety of capacities to serve their memberships. Some of these positions open doors to work in other organizations and governmental agencies. The education profession has a vast array of important jobs that allow former teachers to continue to affect the lives of children.

Class Discussion Questions

1. School districts are setting goals for student achievement in order to comply with mandates embedded in the No Child Left Behind Act. These goals may cause difficulty for teachers if their students do not score at or above the 75th percentile on required standardized tests. What can teachers do to make certain that the goals set by the district are realistic for the student population and reasonable given the resources of their district?

2. Do state requirements for teacher licensure assure that all teachers will be highly qualified?

3. What can teachers do to improve their own status as qualified members of the profession?

4. What role should teachers play in the development of standards for student performance and for their own?

5. Will the stipulation by school districts that instruction at specific grade levels is standardized through identical lesson objectives increase student achievement?

Field Guide for School Observations

Read a set of standards from a specialized professional association (NCTM, NCTE, NCSS, ACEI, or ISTE) for a specific grade level. Make a list of some of the learning activities recommended by the organization to help students achieve the organization's established standards. The next time you are in a classroom, take note of the instruction and student tasks that are taking place. Compare what is taking place in the classroom to activities suggested by the standards. Talk to the teacher about how he or she decides which activities to use to match standards.

Ask a Teacher

Teachers plan every day. They know that at the end of the day, at the end of the quarter (or semester), and at the end of the year, they will be held accountable for the learning their students have achieved. Benchmarks to mark progress and standards and to set goals are helpful tools in the planning process. Ask a teacher how they incorporate standards in lesson plans and how they use benchmarks to make sure their students are headed toward meeting the standards.

Journaling — Becoming a Thoughtful Teacher

You have met many standards on your journey to becoming a teacher. There are standards for performance on standardized tests such as PRAXIS and CBST. There are standards for performance in each one of the courses you have had to complete. You have no doubt had to demonstrate your understanding of the INTASC principles and provide evidence that you have met at least one of them as a teacher education candidate. How will your own personal involvement with standards help you recognize the importance of standards in K–12 classrooms? How has achieving certain standards been helpful to you in your journey to becoming a teacher?

Portfolio Tasks

Collect one artifact from your college coursework. It might be your college transcripts, your score on a standardized test, a paper you wrote, or a lesson you planned and taught to a small group of your peers, or even some feedback you received from your university supervisor or cooperating teacher. Reflect on how this artifact demonstrates your professional growth as a teacher. Explain why the artifact is important to you and why you decided to use it as evidence.

Self-Assessment — What Am I Learning?

In what ways does Charlotte Danielson's framework apply to you as a teacher education candidate? Evaluate your level of content and pedagogical knowledge using Danielson's initial rubric for Domain 1: Planning and Preparation on page 308. Given the outcome of your self-evaluation, describe a goal you will set for yourself to improve your practice in planning and preparing for teaching. Record this goal in your teaching portfolio.

Using the Web

1. Conduct a search of the Oregon Department of Education website. Select a subject standard and a strand and search for an instructional resource matching your selected standard. Discuss ways teachers in Oregon might use the website to inform their practice.

2. Visit the InTime website at **www.uni.edu** and view a lesson. Are the standards the lesson is expected to meet identified? Why is it important to relate lesson objectives to established standards?

Your Professional Library

The National Council of Teachers of Mathematics (2000). *Principles and standards for school mathematics: An overview*. Reston, VA: National Council of Teachers of Mathematics.

Why, you might ask, should I purchase a book about mathematics standards when I don't intend to teach mathematics? The reason is quite simple. Every teacher should be familiar with the way standards are written and the way each subsequent performance standard in a content area is designed to build on previous knowledge and skills. Members of NCTM have been writing standards since 1989, so they are very good at it. This easy-to-read summary is an excellent tool for introducing you to the comprehensive ideas contained in the NCTM set of standards.

Sarason, Seymour B. (1993). *You are thinking of teaching? Opportunities, problems, realities.* San Francisco, CA: Jossey Bass.

Since you are reading this textbook, you have probably already decided to become a teacher. Reading Sarason's book will help you be sure that you made the right choice.

To access chapter objectives, practice tests, weblinks, and flashcards, visit the Companion Website at **www.ablongman.com/hall1e**

Go to Allyn & Bacon's MyLabSchool (**www.mylabschool.com**). Enter Assignment ID **PRXL** in the **Assignment Finder**. Read the *Guide to Licensure* document. Read the sample case study and answer the questions at the end of the study. Check your accuracy. Nothing prepares you for success like knowing what to expect. The Careers section in MLS provides a variety of PRAXIS-related materials (Assignment ID **PRX**), video case studies and practice tests (**PRXE, PRXP**) for your benefit. Select one of the video case studies and respond to the questions at the end of the video. Consider the information in this chapter and the PRAXIS information to answer the following questions.

1. Why is it important to demonstrate your knowledge as a teacher by successfully completing the PRAXIS exams?
2. Is successfully completing PRAXIS II a requirement for licensure in the state in which you plan to teach?
3. How might preparing for the PRAXIS II exam help you become a better teacher?

Teaching Strategies

Educators in Real Schools

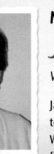

M E E T

Janet Stramel

Wamego Middle School

Janet Stramel has been a junior high/middle school mathematics teacher for 21 years and has taught 8th grade mathematics at WMS for the past 5 years. She recently earned national board certification in early adolescence mathematics. As a national board-certified teacher, Janet is committed to her students and their learning, knows her subject and how to teach it to students, is responsible for managing and monitoring student learning, thinks systematically about her practice, and is a member of the National Council of Teachers of Mathematics.

Wamego Middle School (WMS) is one of four schools in the Wamego Unified School District. At WMS, approximately 325 "Red Raiders" reap the benefits of an average class size of 16 and a pupil to teacher ratio of 14 to 1. Located in the small city of Wamego, Kansas, just 34 miles west of the state capital in Topeka, students at WMS are part of a vibrant community offering historical sites, museums, parks, and the most comprehensive collection of Oz memorabilia ever collected and displayed. The WMS mission statement describes the school as a learning community that develops confident and capable students growing toward responsible citizenship. Teacher teams at WMS plan integrated units that capitalize on learning across content areas, with reading, writing, and problem solving emphasized in every classroom.

❖ *Why did you become a teacher?*

I don't really remember ever making a conscious decision to become a teacher. I believe that I AM a teacher. Teaching is what I do; what I have always done. I do remember after that first day of kindergarten, I came home ready to teach my dolls and my sister. My

kindergarten teacher, Mrs. Dorothy Smith, was kind, gentle, and soft-spoken and had a love for students and learning. I wanted to be like her. She made learning fun.

❖ *What do you see/expect when you see excellence in teaching?*

When I see excellence in teaching, I expect the teacher to have enthusiasm for the subject they teach and to convey that enthusiasm to the students. Teachers can also display their own enthusiasm by actively listening to students' stories, ideas, suggestions, and thoughts. Personally, I show my own enthusiasm in several ways; through the tone of my voice expressing excitement and interest, greeting students by name as they enter the classroom, and by always being on time to class. When a teacher is on time, ready to start class at the first bell, it conveys to the students that they are excited to begin the day's lessons.

A teacher must also be interested in the students outside of the classroom. Teachers should attend football or basketball games or be present at band or choir concerts. When students notice that you are interested in their lives, they will do more for you in the classroom. An excellent teacher also keeps in constant contact with parents. My goal every year is to make positive contacts with parents. Some students don't start out by loving or even enjoying algebra (or any subject), but they can learn to love the class and love the teacher. I also believe that any time you can relate the subject to "real life" situations it makes the lesson more meaningful for the students. A teacher must make learning interesting, and make the students believe that knowledge is important, not just for a test, but for their lives.

❖ *How do you know when you have made a difference in student learning?*

Sometimes a teacher does not know they made a difference in a student's learning until later. Often it is when you see a former student's name on a scholarship list after they have graduated from high school, or when you see a former student who totally surprises you by telling you how much they enjoyed your class and how much they remember! The most obvious way a teacher knows they have made a difference in student learning is when a student does well on a test, but other behaviors can also be observed. When a student gets that "I understand" look on his face, you know you have made a difference, for that student, on that day.

❖ What brings joy to your work as a teacher?

Joy comes from knowing you made a difference in a student's life. Joy also comes from teaching the subject that you love and teaching students to love and appreciate it, too. I love teaching students mathematics. It doesn't feel like a job at all. In fact, I never say, "I'm going to work." I say, "I am going to school." Teachers must be continual learners. You can learn from your students, your colleagues, and your parents. Teaching is exciting! There is an element of surprise any time you are working with children or teenagers. Every day is a new day!

❖ What are the teaching strategies beginning teachers are most likely to be successful with? Why?

One teaching strategy that beginning teachers are most likely to be successful with is to be overprepared for every class every day. When a teacher is more than prepared for each class, there are fewer surprises. When some students finish an assignment early, the teacher can then go on to the next lesson, or have a set of questions to reinforce that day's lesson. Students always seem to recognize when a teacher is not totally prepared, and they may use that as an opportunity to get the teacher off task.

The use of "bell work" is the teaching strategy that has been the most helpful to me. Bell work is not a new concept, and it is one that I have used for most of my career, although Harry Wong made it popular in his book *The First Day of School*. A teacher should have work for students to do as soon as they enter the classroom. This is for two reasons. First, the students are actively engaged in the subject as soon as class begins. Students should be doing something useful, something purposeful that will help them practice and perfect a particular skill. The bell work I use is always a review, although there may be a few questions about how to do a particular problem. This gives me the perfect opportunity to reteach and reinforce a particular skill.

Another teaching strategy that I use is devoting individual attention to every student every day. If a student knows that you care about him or her, that you are truly interested in their questions, they will do anything for you. My goal is to at least talk with or help every student every hour every day. It is easy to get off track or lose time during the class period. What I continue to do every day is decide, as I am making out my lesson plans, how much time I want to devote to each activity. Then I write down the actual time that I want to be at a particular point in my lesson.

❖ What influence has the present emphasis on student performance had on the type of teaching strategies teachers currently use?

Effective teachers are finding good and creative ways to teach the curriculum and make it applicable to the students and their learning. For example, one of our state standards in mathematics is "The student uses the coordinate plane to list several ordered pairs on the graph of a line and find the slope of the line." The day before I am to begin the discussion of slope, I ask my students to notice the stairs in their homes, in the school, or other buildings. We then talk about the steepness of stairs and if the steepness is the same between any two consecutive steps in the set of stairs. The day of the lesson, I take the students to our school gym and ask them to measure the rise and the run of at least two different sets of stairs. They then explore the ratio of the vertical rise to the horizontal run between the two steps. Then they can compute the rise and run of the set of stairs to the vertical and horizontal change between any two points on a line. I also ask students if they have a family member who is a carpenter. Every year, I have at least one student who is willing to ask their family members about the carpenter's guidelines for stairs and share those guidelines with the class. If possible, that person is invited to our class to talk about the mathematics involved in their work.

❖ *What is the best way for teachers to increase their skill at using a variety of teaching strategies and why is this important?*

The best way for teachers to increase their skill at using a variety of teaching strategies is through practice. A mentor can also help new teachers learn different teaching strategies. A mentor could be someone assigned by the school district or it could be the teacher next door. I had several mentors when I started teaching. Joyce Hladik was the "teacher next door" who guided me and helped me as a beginning teacher. She was there when I had questions about curriculum, school rules and regulations, and classroom management. She was also willing to listen to me when I had problems with a particular student or just needed some ideas for teaching a particular skill. Hobart Jones was my "assigned" mentor. He had been a math teacher, a principal, and an assistant superintendent. He chose to return to the classroom and teach junior high mathematics. He was respected and admired by the whole community. Because Mr. Jones had served in many roles in the school system, he had insights into the workings of the school, and he shared those insights with me.

Questions to Consider

1. Do you believe most people who chose teaching as a career decide early in their lives that teaching is what they want to do?

2. Can you recall a specific instance when a teacher made you feel excited about learning?

3. What teaching strategies do you recognize when your teachers use them?

4. Who have you turned to for support in your journey to become a teacher? For what purpose?

Teaching has been described as both an art and a science. Teaching as an art requires a level of intuition seldom demanded of other professionals. The intuition aspect of teaching develops through a process of reflection that is automatic, continuous, and that draws on all manner of visual and sensory awareness of the multitude of stimuli emanating from learner-teacher interactions in a specific context. As teachers practice their art and reflect on the outcomes of that practice, they construct a framework for intuitive and spontaneous actions that promote student learning. Although it may seem that way, intuition and spontaneity in teaching are not random. Some beginning teachers walk into the classroom with a well-developed sense of intuition. They already possess some of the experiences necessary to the development of the intuitive aspect of teaching. However, for most teachers, their intuition grows through experience and develops over time.

Teaching as a science is evident in the strategies that teachers learn to use to achieve desired results in student learning. Strategies are used to capture and hold student attention, to direct that attention to a specific detail of knowledge, or to develop a skill the students will begin to incorporate into their own framework for learning. Other strategies help students exercise, practice, and connect new bits of information to what they already know and to what they will be expected to know in the future. These and other strategies are all part of the science of teaching.

▶ **Learning cycle.** A five-phase research-supported method for education, especially in science.

The science of teaching is concerned with keeping track of where students are in the **learning cycle**, who has just fallen off the cart and who has already made a leap of learning to dimensions beyond the scope of the lesson. The science of teaching is in the planning, the tactical adjustments teachers make in action, and in documenting their own progress and performance and that of the students.

When you ask your instructor for a definitive answer about what particular strategy will work in a classroom and the instructor answers, "Well, it depends," your frustration at such an equivocal answer may not be entirely warranted. What your instructor knows is that intuition is developed through experience and because nearly every day in the classroom represents a different set of experiences, how a teacher might respond in any given situation depends often on an unpredictable set of conditions. Your instructor also knows that the science of teaching can be learned and what will work for you in a classroom will depend on how well you learn to use a range of teaching strategies and how well you monitor the effects of the applied science of your teaching.

You have probably heard the comment that teachers are born, not made. The truth is that some people are born to be teachers with all the natural talents necessary to produce excellent results in student achievement. However, most must learn and practice the science of teaching skills that comprise the characteristics of excellent teachers. Teachers also learn through persistence, practice, and patience to develop the art of teaching talent that others may be born with.

This chapter will introduce a variety of teaching strategies that work in classrooms and will help you understand a scientific approach to teaching. You will also learn ways specific strategies can be used to meet the learning needs of the range of student abilities and learning styles most commonly found in a single classroom. The art of teaching will emerge as you begin to practice these skills in classrooms.

Focus QUESTIONS

After reading this chapter you should be able to answer the following questions:

1. What are some teaching strategies commonly used in classrooms?

2. Why are some teaching strategies used more frequently than others?

3. Some teaching strategies appear to work better with one content area than another. For example, using discussions to introduce books may help facilitate reading readiness, but an experiment or demonstration might be best to begin a lesson in chemistry. Why is this so?

4. In what ways can different teaching strategies be used for different purposes?

5. How important is it for teachers to develop detailed lesson plans prior to actually teaching a lesson? How might this help a teacher decide which strategy to use?

6. Why should teachers develop skill in using a variety of teaching strategies?

What Is a Teaching Strategy?

*It seems like yesterday that as a student, I joined my classmates to crowd around a table in **Mrs. Fuqua**'s Algebra I class as she used different-size containers of water to demonstrate the ways in which algebraic equations could be reorganized to solve for a specific factor. She used a question-and-answer approach as she guided us in discovering how many of one of the smaller containers was held in the largest vessel. The containers were marked with letters (X, Y, and Z) and they were of unfamiliar sizes and shapes. She was trying to get us to see how many "X" size containers filled a "Y"; how many "Y" size containers filled a "Z," and so forth, so that we could eventually use equivalency to figure out that if, for example, it took 3 Xs to fill the Y container, and it took 2 Y containers to fill the Z container, then 3X = Y, and 2Y = Z, then 6X = Z, and 4Y = 2Z, and so forth. Mrs. Fuqua was extremely patient. Some students drew pictures to illustrate the process; others kept tally sheets as water was poured back and forth from container to container. Once we solved how many smaller containers were held in the largest container, we were called on one by one to replicate and explain the process.*

We worked at this single task all period. No formal pencil-and-paper work was done. Our homework assignment was to show the folks at home how the process worked. For most of us, it was a new experience in math class and we didn't associate the fun we were having with learning. However, the next day, few of us had any difficulty with the equations we were given to solve from the text. Mrs. Fuqua even encouraged us to talk about how what we had done the day before helped us understand how to do the problems. She had a strategy, a purpose. The lesson was well planned and thought out, and many of us were tricked into learning to love algebra.

Doing math is different from teaching math. Teaching math, as well as other subjects, is as much an art as it is a science. Teachers must train themselves to think like artists at times. They must constantly draw on creativity in their approach to teaching. If you approach teaching strictly from an **empirical** perspective you're painting by the numbers. Art is a creative way of organizing reality. The logic of teaching is the logic of the well-organized artist whose palette is arranged methodically so that his or her creativity can have full rein.

We all remember clearly the teachers we had who were able to help us see and understand concepts that were new to us or difficult for us to grasp; teachers who used all manner of paraphernalia to help us connect what we already knew about the world in general to what we had to learn specifically. These were the teachers who carried bags full of objects they had collected to school so that we could hold and manipulate them while they talked us through ideas, lessons, and experiments.

Generic Teaching Strategies

The word **strategy** is defined by the *American Heritage Dictionary* (2000) as the science or art of military command as applied to the overall planning and conduct of combat operations, a plan of action resulting from the practice of this science. *Webster* Online (2006) expands on this definition to include the "science and art of employing the political, economic, psychological, and military forces of a nation or group of nations to afford the maximum support to adopted policies in peace or war—a careful plan or method, a clever stratagem, the art of devising or employing plans or stratagems toward a goal." Any teaching strategy certainly falls into the category of something that is carefully planned, a method, or a stratagem for reaching a desired goal. The word *stratagem* has a somewhat negative connotation, defined as being a cleverly contrived trick or scheme for gaining a desired end, but effective teachers know they have to invent all manner of activities to encourage their students to drink from the fountain of knowledge. Consider the admonition, "You can lead a horse to water, but you can't make it drink." Well, it's a smart farmer who sprinkled alfalfa sprouts in the watering trough or a Mary Poppins who figures out a clever way to get the "medicine to go down." Teaching strategies properly used make it possible for teachers to help students acquire useful and necessary information, sometimes contrary to a student's desire.

There are as many ways to teach as there are teachers. Since human societies first emerged, knowledge and skills have been handed down from one generation to another through the use of specific teaching strategies. The apprentice model has worked in the past and even today some aspiring potters spend weeks, months, or even years, carrying the master teacher's clay from the source to the wheel to the kiln. In Iran, students learn the Persian alphabet through repetition and spend hours each day at a table writing a single Arabic symbol over and over until it is so etched in the mind that only an act of Allah could erase it. Children

Empirical. Depending on experimentation and observation.

Strategy. In teaching, any one of a multitude of plans for conducting instruction or an activity.

Ed Lines

Every day in a classroom can be like Spring; something new is always popping up.

These Japanese students demonstrate that repetition and drill is a powerful teaching method still utilized in many cultures.

in school in China or Japan must learn over 8,000 symbols to properly communicate in an educated society; they copy these symbols until every individual brush stroke becomes as natural as taking a breath.

A Continuum of Generic Teaching Strategies

In their framework of universal teaching strategies, Freiberg and Driscoll (1992) list seven generic instructional strategies along a continuum that ranges from a teacher-focused or teacher-centered perspective to a student-focused or student-centered perspective. The strategies are (a) lecture, (b) questioning and discussion, (c) interactive practice, (d) grouping, (e) reflective learning, (f) role play, simulation, and drama, and (g) resources, audiovisual, and computers. The most teacher-centered teaching strategy is the lecture. It is the strategy used most often in classrooms and provides the teacher with the most immediate control over what content the students are exposed to, the expected behavior of the students, and the valuable commodity, time. When teachers are expected to cover a set amount of curriculum in a specified period of time, the lecture is often the favored strategy. David Ausubel, an educational psychologist, argues that lectures provide the most efficient use of time when trying to impart large amounts of information to a group of students (1963). Since teachers and students have the gift of language, Ausubel's contention was that teachers should use language to impart knowledge.

At the resource end of the continuum, students interact with books, audio- and videotapes, computer programs, and the **Internet**. Students use these resources to

Internet. A worldwide decentralized association of networked computers using a common working protocol.

Ed Lines

"The only questions that really matter are the ones you ask youself." *Ursula K. LeGuin*

Figure 9.1 A continuum of teaching strategies

Teacher Focus			Student Focus
Lecture	Question/Discussion	Group Work	Reflective Learning/Inquiry
Demonstration		Guided Practice	Role Play/Simulation

investigate topics assigned by the teacher or topics that they are interested in and are highly motivated to learn. Use of resources as a teaching strategy requires a high level of teacher competence and knowledge of a range of subjects and of what resources are available. The teacher must be able to guide students to resources that will give them adequate, useful and accurate information. Figure 9.1 shows the relationship of a variety of strategies along the continuum.

There is a logical organization to the strategies. Because students can't be expected to discuss what they know nothing about, inputting information is important, usually done most efficiently through lecture or presentation. Group work also requires that the students know how to ask questions of one another and discuss topics in a civilized manner. Role playing and drama require students to demonstrate their knowledge of a subject using higher-level thinking skills. Students who engage in inquiry need to know how to access information, what to do with it, and how to synthesize it. All learning has to begin with some level of knowledge. As you progress through your teacher education program, you will learn more details of a range of teaching strategies and the optimum application of each for specific content areas. The website www.aea267.k12.ia.us/cia/framework/strategies offers over 30 teaching strategies and suggestions on how each might be implemented in kindergarten through high school classrooms.

Lecture We've all had the experience of being "talked to." Sometimes it was inspirational; sometimes we struggled to suppress yawns. There were probably even times when we had no idea what the lecturer was talking about. Fortunately or unfortunately, the lecture-teaching strategy has survived for over 2,000 years and is used in all content areas and at all grade levels. While the lecture may not always enjoy a favorable reputation, it can be effective in both elementary and secondary settings. To gain information from a lecture, listeners must attend to what the speaker is saying and in the case of a presentation, be able to see what the lecturer is talking about. Al Capp, the creator of the Li'l Abner comic strip, once said in an interview that the length of time a person could attend to a lecture was equal to their age: 1 minute for every year. He then qualified his statement by adding that once a person reaches the age of 13, this rule does not apply and that most people despite their age can seldom listen for more than 20 minutes. Sometimes the main problem with lectures is that some people just never know when to stop talking.

Perhaps the unfavorable reputation the lecture might have as a teaching strategy could be, in part, a result of the failure of teachers to recognize and use the guidelines that help make this teaching strategy effective. The research on effective instruction provides guidelines for effective delivery of lectures and presentations (Rosenshine, 1983). For the teacher education candidate or beginning teacher who is just becoming familiar with delivering a lecture or presentation, these guidelines can be summarized into five major elements essential for planning and delivering an effective lecture. Table 9.1 organizes these guidelines for easy reference.

The lecture strategy can be a very effective teaching tool. Using a lecture makes it possible for teachers to present the most information in the least amount of time. All members of the class as well as the teacher hear the same information at the same time. A lecture can also be a perfect beginning to a unit or to introducing a new concept. However, when using the lecture strategy, it is difficult to address individual needs because the information is presented to all students in the same mode.

Questioning and Discussion

We all learn from the questions we ask and from the questions others ask us. We have questions we want answered, we have questions we are sometimes afraid to ask, and sometimes people ask us questions for which we have no answers. There are probably plenty of questions we hope

A lecture must stimulate students in order to be an effective instructional method.

Table 9.1	Know Your Students
Audience	Know what is developmentally appropriate for them—be aware of their interests, their abilities, and what prerequisite skills and knowledge they need to have to understand what you are talking about.
Focus	Know your subject, be enthusiastic about it and stick to it. We all can be seduced into talking about things we really don't know much about. Everyone wants to have an opinion, but an educative lecture should be a learning experience for the listener, not just an opportunity for the speaker to spout their opinion. Present ideas in small chunks, one idea at a time. Make sure your students are with you; keep their attention.
Organization	Know how to introduce the topic, to expand on it, and to summarize what has been talked about. Know when to change pace and when to stop.
Clarity	Know how to present an idea from the listeners' perspective. Provide examples that are relevant; make the subject come alive through explanations that are colorful, unusual, or startling.
Pacing	Know when to shift gears, check for understanding, and bring an idea to its logical conclusion. Make students think about what you are saying by having them take notes and write down the names of important people or important dates. Provide students with an outline of your lecture before beginning so that they can make notations.

Source: Adapted from Rosenshine, 1983.

Questions that elicit eager student responses are a gateway to learning.

no one will ask us, and there are questions we know we shouldn't ask of others but do anyway because humans basically want to be in the know. People ask questions to gain information, to increase understanding, and even to draw attention. Some of the questions people ask are silly, some are shocking, and some are just downright wrong. Sometimes teachers are so concerned with answers that they miss the importance of questions; of asking the right questions and of listening to and learning from the questions their students ask of them.

Teachers ask questions of their students for many reasons. Questions such as "Have you ever had an alligator nibble at your toes?" are asked to generate interest and gain student attention. Teachers ask questions to check for student understanding, to encourage student thinking, and to structure and redirect learning. Questioning is used by teachers as a diagnostic tool in determining the level of instruction at which students need to begin learning. Questions asked to manage student behavior or classroom organization are usually intended to help students remember rules, while some questions allow students to express their own feelings and opinions. Questioning is the predominant method of checking for student understanding. Questions can be delivered in a rapid sequence for review of content or used as final evaluations of student learning. Learning the art of asking the right question at the right time and in the right way can be one of the most challenging aspects of teaching.

Guidelines have been created to help teachers with this task. Decades ago, John Dewey developed an "Art of Questioning Guide" (1934) that still holds true today:

- Questions should not elicit fact upon fact, but should be asked in such a way as to delve deeply into the subject (i.e., to develop an overall concept of the selection).
- Questions should emphasize personal interpretations rather than literal and direct responses.
- Questions should not be asked randomly so that each is an end in itself, but should be planned so that one leads into the next throughout a continuous discussion.
- Teachers should periodically review important points so that old, previously discussed material can be placed into perspective with that which is presently being studied.

Ed Lines

"**Books not discussed lose their value.**" *Mortimer Adler*

- The end of the question-asking sequence should leave the children with a sense of accomplishment and build a desire for that which is yet to come.

Other classification systems, **taxonomies**, have been created to aid teachers in developing questions for multiple purposes. The Gallagher-Aschner System for analyzing and controlling classroom questioning behavior has four categories of questions (Gallagher & Aschner, 1963):

Taxonomies. Organizational structures for classifying objects or ideas.

1. Cognitive memory
2. Convergent
3. Divergent
4. Evaluative

The Norris Sanders Taxonomy of Questions (1966) has seven levels:

1. Memory
2. Translation
3. Interpretation
4. Application
5. Analysis
6. Synthesis
7. Evaluation

Benjamin Bloom's (1956) taxonomy of educational objectives is perhaps the most widely used to provide a framework for classifying questions into types that elicit lower-level thinking skills and types that require higher-level thinking skills. The six levels of questioning identified by Bloom are knowledge, comprehension, application, analysis, synthesis, and evaluation. (See Table 9.2.) This table shows the types of questions that elicit different responses from students and that require differing types of cognitive activity.

Wassermann (1992) identifies both unproductive questions and less-than-productive questions that teachers ask. In her unproductive category, she lists "stupid" questions, too-complex questions, teacher-answered questions, trick questions, and questions that humiliate. An example in the stupid question category is:

Student: "I want to learn more about the aurora borealis."

Teacher: "Have you got a library card?"

A too-complex question is usually impossible to answer intelligently in a short answer. For example, "What were the causes of the American Revolution?" Such a question could be reworded or narrowed in focus to make it more manageable and

Ed Lines

"Never underestimate the power of heterogeneous cooperative learning to promote high quality, involved learning." *David & Roger Johnson*

338

Table 9.2 Bloom's Taxonomy of Question Types

Question Type	Student Performance	Examples
Knowledge	tell, list, describe, recall, identify, what, when, where, which	How many queens have ruled Great Britain?
Comprehension	summarize, compare, contrast, explain, define, make comparisons	What happened in the experiment?
Application	demonstrate, use prescribed methods, restate, transfer	Using the population grid, which of the three cities has the largest population?
Analysis	list why, make inferences, generalize, categorize, break into parts	When did you know that Goldilocks was tired?
Synthesis	create, suppose, make predictions, write an essay	What is the best air route to take from Tokyo, Japan, to Disney World in Orlando, Florida? Why?
Evaluation	judge, evaluate, rate, prove, give opinions about issues	Should world governments control population growth?

therefore more answerable. A better question might be, "What were some of the conditions that led to the colonists' discontent with British rule?"

Teacher-answered questions need no explanation. Those who have seen the movie *Ferris Bueller's Day Off* watch with humor as the high school social studies teacher asks, "Anybody? Anybody?" and then either answers his or her own question or goes on to the next. Once a teacher starts answering his or her own questions, the students soon learn to wait the teacher out; that's exactly why teachers have to learn to use **Wait Time** and **Wait Time II** during questioning and group discussions. Teachers who consistently use Wait Time II are helping their students learn the fine art of discussion.

Trick questions are designed to stump students so that the teacher can appear incredibly smart and/or the students overwhelmingly uninformed. Teachers who frequently use trick questions to demonstrate their own knowledge or berate students should be taught the art of asking the right questions. The effect of trick questions on students is demeaning and deserves no further comment here.

Questions that humiliate are even worse than trick questions. There is no trick involved and they are simply mean and inappropriate to use in a classroom. There is absolutely no productive outcome possible to a question given to a high schooler such as, "How come you can't do this? It is so easy a 10-year-old could do it."

Wasserman's less-than-productive questions category includes questions that don't require students to examine their own responses. They often fall short because they deal with trivia, are too difficult for the students, or because their wording is ambiguous (Wasserman, 1992, 15). With a little thought about the types of questions they are asking, teachers can modify less-than-productive questions to make them productive. Wasserman suggests that instead of asking a ques-

Wait-time I. The time a teacher waits after asking a question before calling on a student to answer it.

Wait-time II. The time a teacher waits after a student has answered a question to give other students the opportunity to consider the response and perhaps add comments.

tion like "Why do people litter?" ask, "What can you tell me about how all the candy wrappers and orange peels end up in our schoolyard?"

One purpose of asking questions is to promote thought. When teachers ask questions that promote thoughtful responses, the students are encouraged to develop the habit of thinking. For every unit Ms. Fuqua (the teacher at the beginning of this section) teaches, she first considers the essential questions that her students will need to answer in order to understand the content of her algebra classes. She makes a rough draft of the questions and imagines the type of responses her students will give. She may ask the questions of one class and then modify them for another. Every question she asks takes into consideration the content, the context, and the learners. She might instead use questions to stimulate discussions.

A lot of talk goes on in classrooms. Productive talk is structured by the teacher and engaged in by the students. Teachers who understand the art of questioning teach their students how to answer and ask questions and prepare them to engage in discussions. Questioning is more teacher centered than discussions. Discussions are designed to get students actively engaged in the content. Through discussion, students can learn to think and value their own ideas as well as those of others. Discussion can help students solve problems, attain goals, and develop concepts. Effective teachers prepare their students for their role in discussions. They teach students how to carry on a discussion before they put them in cooperative learning groups.

Students may find it difficult to work productively in groups if they do not understand that discussions require (1) active listening, (2) respect for the ideas of others, and (3) noninterference when others are speaking. When introducing a group of students to new instructional strategies, a useful rule of thumb is never to teach a new strategy with new content. Teachers who want their students to engage in meaningful discussions let them practice the discussion skills. Teachers make certain all students understand the skills they have been practicing by asking the following questions:

1. Were your comments relevant to the current discussion?
2. Were your comments supported by facts?
3. Did you consider the importance of your comment before you made it?
4. Did your comment broaden the discussion or clarify a point being discussed?
5. Were your comments complete and concise?

Find out more about the art of asking good questions at www.youthlearn.org/learning/teaching/questions.asp and at http://questioning.org.

Grouping Humans are not born with the ability to collaborate, though learning to cooperate has been a major factor in the survival of the species. However, learning how to work with others takes much energy and patience. Parents remind their children to share, to take turns, and to let someone else be first. Teachers organize classroom activities and playtime so that students have opportunities to practice behaviors necessary for life in a community and in a democracy. Henry Ford developed a model of teamwork for mass production of cars. His motto was simple: "Coming

Learning to work together takes guidance and patience.

▶ **Cooperative learning groups.** Learners who work together to help one another learn a task, skill, or concept.

together is a beginning; keeping together is progress; working together is success" (www.quotedb. com/quotes/2096). Working together may not come naturally for everyone, but through every step of formal education, students are prompted to develop greater and greater skills at becoming productive members of a group. Johnson and Johnson (1990) emphasize that the skills needed to interact effectively with others need to be taught just as systematically as math or social studies.

Formal group work has been a teaching strategy used in schools since the early 1800s. Grouping students for instruction usually involves grouping students by age to form grade-level classes and then within-class grouping by ability. (Remember the reading group you were in during elementary school?) Students can be grouped to study specific subjects, for tutoring purposes, and in **cooperative learning groups**. When teachers think of grouping students, it is usually to accomplish a specific goal and provide students increased opportunity to learn both academic content and group participation skills. Johnson and Johnson (1999) define cooperative learning as the instructional use of small groups so students work together to maximize their own and each other's learning. Slavin (1983) provides an organizational structure for managing cooperative learning in the classroom.

Early socializing activities can begin by teachers handing out cards with numbers or symbols. Students find the classmates with the same number or symbol, form groups, and start to get to know one another. An "In the Bag" activity has small groups of students working together to blow a paper cup into bags taped at the edge of their desks or tables. In a strategy called "Number Heads Together," each student in the group has a number. The teacher asks a question, then says, "Put your heads together and made sure everyone knows the answer." Students discuss the answer, then the teacher calls a number, and that student answers.

In high school classes, students are often given the task of working together to solve problems or complete experiments. Group activities of this nature can provide a virtual experience for students' future roles as citizens in the larger community of their city, state, or country. Such activities also make learning fun. When students learn the strategies and skills necessary to work together in productive groups, the end result can be enjoyable and intrinsically rewarding. Initial group activities should be short and simple and should concentrate on positive social interaction. Academic emphasis in group work can be addressed once students have learned to successfully interact with one another (Ellis & Whalen, 1992).

When teachers place students in group they have much to consider—the Understanding & Using Evidence demonstrates one way teacher use student performance scales to group students.

Understanding
& USING EVIDENCE

USING 3RD GRADE MATH SCORES ON A UNIT TEST TO CREATE COOPERATIVE LEARNING GROUPS

The following data provide the individual scores of 3rd grade students on an end-of-unit test. It has been determined by the teacher that a majority of the students could benefit from review work on regrouping when subtracting three-digit numbers. The teacher has decided to place the students in heterogeneous groups for cooperative group work. The purpose of the group work will be to provide students with the opportunity to ask questions of one another and to practice and develop skill in regrouping.

End-of-Unit Test Scores on Regrouping during Subtraction of Three-Digit Numbers

Student Name	Test Score (highest possible score 100)
Carl Adams	96
Garcia Bloom	60
Caitlin Broker	100
Tiffany Brown	40
Carla Castenada	88
Nita Chang	24
Neil Fox	76
Pete Lowinsky	68
Ahmad Mesgari	84
Timette McKay	74
Richard Power	72
Jaylynn Price	88
Patrick Quest	28
Stacy Romano	68
Kenneth Sharp	80
Angelica Spooner	64
Jacko Tanaka	52
Susan White	48

Refer to the **Understanding & Using Evidence Appendix** *at the end of the text for answers and information related to these activities.*

Your Task: Establish cooperative learning groups of three or four students. Establish heterogeneous groups including high- and low-performing students and gender difference.

Before groups of students can work together successfully, they must learn the skills of cooperative work, communication, and division of labor. Before teachers can implement cooperative learning strategies effectively, they must know how to organize materials, equipment, and workspace. Teachers must carefully plan and schedule group work. For your benefit, Eric Hsu, a math teacher, asks and answers questions on teaching with group work at http://math.sfsu.edu/hsu/talks/asilo-groupthoughts.html. David and Roger Johnson

Table 9.3 Common Characteristics of Cooperative Learning

Heterogeneous groups	These groups are a mixture of gender, ethnicity, and ability.
Positive interdependence	Everyone in the group has a meaningful task to complete.
Verbal face-to-face interaction	Students engage in purposeful discussion.
Individual accountability	Each member must complete an assessment appropriate to the group goal.
Social and academic goals identified	Guidelines for group work have been explained and practiced.
Group processing conducted	During group work, the instructor monitors student involvement; at the close of group work, the level of success of the group is assessed.

provide a wealth of information on cooperative groups at www.co-operation .org/pages/cl.html. Descriptions of the characteristic of cooperative learning are provided in Table 9.3.

Reflective Learning/Inquiry Discovering something for yourself is intrinsically rewarding because you are actively involved in exploring and manipulating your environment. Most people love a well-planned scavenger hunt and movies that have the hero fight nature, the forces of evil, and doubting Thomases to finally discover some wondrous prize. It's the reason scientists of all kinds spend long hours laboring over test tubes, ancient texts, or computer programs to finally solve a puzzling piece of nature, history, or engineering, to say "I did it." Reflective-learning strategies deal with a problem or problems the students must solve. In reflective learning, students are often asked to contend with circumstances that lay outside the range of what is commonplace and normal to them. Students involved in reflective learning must discover facts and concepts and knowledge that are new to them. They also have to compile evidence to support or refute a solution. Students must develop hypotheses.

One well-known reflective-learning teaching strategy is the social inquiry model described by Joyce and Weil (1986). It was specifically developed for the social studies curriculum and has six phases. It offers the benefit of helping students develop cooperation and collaboration skills in addition to the cognitive benefits of the inquiry process. The six phases are:

1. Orientation: Presentation and clarification of a puzzling situation
2. Hypothesis: Development of an hypothesis to structure an exploration or solution to the problem
3. Definition: Process of defining, clarifying, and understanding the hypothesis
4. Exploration: Looking for the assumptions, implications, and logical validity of the hypothesis

Challenging Assumptions
FINDINGS FROM RESEARCH

Is cooperative group work beneficial to high-performing students?

The Assumption: High-performing students do not benefit from working cooperatively on group projects with students who are achieving at lower levels. Students, and occasionally their parents, may complain that by being placed in groups with lower achieving students they simply end up doing the work for others and are not challenged to learn at the high levels of which they are capable.

Study Design and Method: The benefits of cooperative learning have been extolled through extensive research. It has been claimed that cooperative learning is one of the best researched of all teaching strategies. The research indicates that cooperative learning consistently improves achievement and that students who learn cooperatively have greater retention of the information learned. Working in cooperative learning groups has been shown to encourage positive relationships among all students, improved relations among different ethnic groups, and improved relationships between mainstreaming students with learning disabilities and others. Cooperative learning groups also promote positive feelings about learning and about one's own abilities. Higher-level thinking is promoted through cooperative group learning.

Implications: While the reasons to use cooperative learning groups in a classroom are clear, the potential for individual student success of any cooperative learning group often rests directly on a teacher's ability to plan tasks that require input from each student and address individual needs. In addition to planning appropriate tasks, a teacher must also make certain that all students have the opportunity to stretch their learning and reach ever-increasing levels of achievement.

Sources: King, A. (2002). Structuring peer interactions to promote high-level cognitive processing. *Theory Into Practice, 41*, 31–39; Johnson, D. W., & Johnson, R. (1999). *Learning together and alone: Cooperation, competition, and individualization* (5th ed.). Boston: Allyn & Bacon.

5. Evidence: Assembling facts and evidence to support or refute each hypothesis
6. Generalizations: Arriving at an acceptable solution based on evidence

Adams and Hamm (1996) ask, "What good are critical-thinking, reasoning, and problem-solving skills if your learners cannot apply them in interaction with others?" Marzano, Pickering, and Pollack (2001) say that cooperative learning activities instill in learners important behaviors that prepare them to reason and perform in an adult world. Teachers are expected to pose problems for students to solve. When students can work together to find solutions to posed problems and also to problems that may emerge through other sources, they are using critical-thinking skills in interaction with others. The Challenging Assumptions above offers additional perspectives on grouping students.

Role Play, Simulation, and Drama   Teaching strategies that involve students in acting a part or responding to a specific set of circumstances are perhaps the most emotionally charged of all teaching strategies. Role playing, simulations, and drama allow students to experience tough, real-life problems in a controlled

Encouraging the sharing of ideas should be a focus in every classroom.

environment. Students in a first-aid class learn to resuscitate drowning victims and administer CPR with the assistance of lifelike dummies whose touch and response is similar to that of a living person. Second graders learn to "drop and roll" to extinguish flames and to crawl along the floor of an escape route to exit a burning building. We learn how to act in places we have never been and how to negotiate unknown territory. Simulations can help students learn empathy, to understand the predicaments life creates for others, and to learn how to negotiate unknown territory. In simulations, students are faced with dilemmas. They must make choices, take action, and then experience the consequences of their actions. Training for medical triage groups and rescue teams relies heavily on simulation and role playing. Role play, simulation, and drama can help students learn by doing, thinking, feeling, or responding. It allows students to have vicarious experiences that can substitute for first-hand experiences and also to develop their own knowledge, skills, and dispositions.

Role play, simulation, and drama all create experiences that help students learn by doing something, thinking about what they are doing, having certain feelings about their actions, or responding to stimuli from someone else or some other thing. Experiences provided through role play, simulation, and drama can take the place of firsthand experiences that may be impossible to achieve. Role play, simulation, and drama can aid students in development of content understanding, skills, and attitudes. Teacher education candidates often cite field experience as the most informative and influential part of teacher-education coursework. Perhaps that's because fieldwork puts them in the "role" of teacher.

The Powerful Effect of Role Play and Simulation   An infamous simulation exercise, "Blue-eyed/Brown-eyed," had its birth in 1968, in Jane Elliott's 4th grade classroom in Riceville, Iowa. Following the assassination of Martin Luther King Jr., when one of her students asked why this had happened, Elliott decided to provide her students with firsthand knowledge of racial discrimination. Because Jane Elliott's students lived and attended school in an all-white community, she had to create a hypothetical situation that would demonstrate to her students what racial discrimination looked and felt like and the demoralizing effects it could have on individuals. Students in her classroom were assigned to either a blue-eyed or brown-eyed group, though not according to the actual color of their eyes. One group was not allowed to enjoy the benefits enjoyed by others in the classroom;

Ed Lines

"We don't have to think alike, but we do have to think together." *Marzella Brown*

one group enjoyed all of the benefits plus special considerations. After a time of being in one group, students switched roles. Elliott's Blue-eyed/Brown-eyed simulation exercise is a classic in teaching about racial discrimination and is a perfect example of the impact a well-planned teaching strategy can have on students. Elliott's simulation was such a powerful piece of teaching that her students still remember it today. Read more about Jane Elliott's lesson at www.horizonmag.com/4/jane-elliott.asp or find copies of Jane Elliott's videos, *The Angry Eye, The Eye of the Storm*, and *The Stolen Eye*.

The website www.simulations.com offers educators and students a wide range of well-planned simulations to explore. The website www.sciencesimulations.com offers simulations in chemistry, biology, and physics that combined create a complete classical lab for experimentation.

Viewing Teaching Strategies as Direct or Indirect Instruction

Teaching strategies can also be grouped into two overarching categories of **direct** or **indirect** instruction sometimes referred to as **explicit** and **implicit** instruction. Explicit instruction can be viewed as instruction that helps students increase and broaden their existing knowledge. Teaching strategies that are explicit or direct are successful in helping students acquire information that is highly structured (Rosenshine & Stevens, 1986). Implicit teaching strategies are intended to assist students to consider their own thinking. This is called **metacognition**, deciding on a specific choice or solution and acting on its decisions. Each area of instruction requires different behaviors from teachers and responses from students.

Direct instruction/explicit. Providing clear and distinct information for students.

Indirect instruction/implicit. Providing information that requires students to problem solve and question in order to uncover the essence of the information.

Metacognition. Thinking about the ways that we think.

Direct instruction represents a teacher-centered approach with the teacher providing the instructional input. The teacher's role in direct instruction is to pass facts, rules, or action sequences on to students in the most direct way possible (Borich, 2004). Direct instruction has been shown to correlate highest with student achievement as measured by standardized tests emphasizing facts, rules, and sequences (Anderson, Evertson, & Brophy, 1982; Walberg, 1991). Direct-instruction strategies make it possible for teachers to serve up information in chunks palatable to students; to make dry, boring information interesting; and to help students master content. We all know how tedious it is to memorize rules and facts.

Indirect teaching strategies encourage students to think beyond the facts given, to draw conclusions, or make generalizations. Teachers who use direct instruction focus learner attention on a problem and then provide students with background information (Woolfolk, 2004). This approach activates the cognitive processes required to form concepts and to recognize patterns and abstractions. Borich and Tombari (2003) suggest that indirect teaching functions are most useful in providing behaviors that students will use in their adult lives. Reaction to the world outside the classroom requires students to be able to analyze situations, make decisions, organize information, and adapt. These skills are not learned through

Ed Lines

"We cannot help people if we have no faith in their ability to solve their own problems."
George Gazda

Effective teachers use demonstration and experiment to pique student curiosity.

memorization of rules and facts, but must be constructed through experiences demanding higher-level thinking. They are using information to draw conclusions and they are thinking. When students think well while learning, they learn well.

A Constructivist Approach to Teaching Constructivist approaches to teaching are built on the concept that each student actively creates, interprets, and reorganizes information in ways that are unique to them. Present knowledge is used to achieve predetermined educational goals. Students engage in **problem-based learning**, inquiry activities, and dialogues with others to connect elements in the learning environment. They come together in communities of learners with an opportunity to think critically by challenging and explaining their thinking to one another. Students experience the ideas, phenomena, and artifacts of the discipline before having formal explanations of them. In a constructivist environment, teachers do not prescribe, but instead are more likely to respond to the needs of the learners, the content, and the context. The teacher's role is that of a facilitator of learning; one who responds to the students' needs in a flexible manner. By allowing students to construct knowledge as learners, teachers help them to think critically about concepts (Goldin, 1990). In a constructivist classroom, the teacher designs and sequences lessons that encourage learners to use their own experiences to actively construct meaning and acquire understanding that makes sense to them (Richardson, 1997).

There are many constructivist strategies that a teacher might employ when teaching a particular content area. Two are scaffolding, which allows the learner to make sense of a complex task and modeling, which requires the teacher to think aloud about problem solving. Teachers probe students' thinking through coaching, guiding, and advising. To create a constructivist-learning environment, teachers must clearly understand how the theory of constructivism translates into practice (Windschitl, 1999). Read more about the application of constructivist

▶ **Problem-based learning (PBL).** An approach to learning that requires students to solve problems, draw conclusions, and make inferences.

teaching strategies from Dr. Savannah Young at www.fergflor.org/Curriculum/constructivists.html.

Activity Learning   Simply put, the **activity approach** to teaching is exactly what it implies. Students develop understanding of the link between the conscious and the objective world by engaging in activities. Through the manipulation of objects and tools, students can gain knowledge in a variety of domains. Piaget (1985) proposed that individuals gain knowledge through active exploration in which they form schemes, cognitive structures that help them organize patterns or thoughts to interpret their experiences. A teacher might allow a student to choose either a pictorial or concrete representation to solve the math problem, 2×3. The student then can either make two groups with three cubes in each group or draw two circles with three boxes in each, thus concluding the answer is six. The objective of the activity is achieved through a physical or mental product.

> **Activity approach.** An approach to learning that engages students in activities that will instruct and help the students construct their own knowledge.

When teachers plan activities for their students to engage in, they consider the curricular objectives for that activity, what resources should be available, and what prerequisite knowledge the students have. Teachers take into account the context in which the activity will take place; they know that as students engage in the activity things will happen that may change the intended outcome, and that sometimes students will come up with solutions or answers that may not have been considered before. Teachers using constructivist and activity teaching strategies must be both well prepared and flexible. That is not a contradiction; it is just one of the phenomena (characteristics) of teaching.

Never Just One

It would be nearly impossible to use only one teaching strategy in a single lesson. Even lectures usually include some questions. Discussions are loaded with questions. When students work together in groups, they share information with one another, ask questions, and carry on discussions. Inquiry whether done individually or in groups depends on questioning and working through hypotheses and sometimes acting out a problem. Role playing, simulations, and drama draw on any number of teaching strategies to achieve desired results. When students are using resources, audiovisual equipment, computers, and the Internet, they are receiving lectures of sorts from books and videos, asking and answering questions, and sharing their information through discussions and presentations with their classmates. Teachers who use a variety of strategies have a high degree of instructional success (Cruickshank, 1990). Selecting the best teaching strategy to match students with subject matter is a teaching skill not always easy to master, but it can be accomplished when a teacher keeps in mind the needs and abilities of the learners, the content goals to be achieved, and the time and resources allowed by the context.

Revisiting Mrs. Fuqua's Strategy for Teaching Algebra

Mrs. Fuqua, the math teacher at the beginning of this section, might have decided to use a presentation/lecture teaching strategy to introduce the lesson on reorganizing algebraic equations to solve for a specific factor. Students would have

Teachers' Lounge

"Her Did It!"

During my first year as a speech/language pathologist, I was full of fear yet anxious to utilize what I had just learned in graduate school.

One of my students, a 3rd grader named Sarah, had a problem with confusing "her" with "she" in her sentences. "Her did that" or "When her goes . . . ". I tried to model the correct usage of the pronouns by casually repeating Sarah's sentences when she misused them, replacing "her" with "she": "Yes," I'd say, "*she* did that!"

Day after day, I monotonously repeated these corrections, wondering if they were having any effect. Finally, around mid-year: the ah-ha moment!

As I repeated yet another correction, Sarah stood up and smiled broadly. She said, "Oh, I get it! I know what you're doing. You're fixing my 'hers'." I smiled just as broadly back at Sarah. Modeling works! It was a memorable first reward as a new speech/language pathologist!

● Kate Ross, MS, CCC-SLP
  Middlesex, Vermont

watched her as she talked through the process and made notations of her examples. Her reasons for choosing one strategy over another were probably defined by a variety of factors including the size of her class, the amount of time allotted for the period, and the materials she had available. Her knowledge of the learners may have indicated that a brief lecture and presentation would be sufficient for them to grasp the concept. Her choice of teaching strategy didn't change the objective of the lesson; it only affected her teaching behavior and the actions of her students. The choice was hers to make. Teachers must make hundreds of decisions a day regarding what they are going to teach and how they are going to teach it. Teacher knowledge of the best uses for a particular teaching strategy, how to most effectively implement the strategy, and the learner response to a particular approach are the key ingredients in any instruction.

What Makes Teaching Strategies Work?

*The curriculum guide in the district in which **Tracy** teaches requires that 2nd grade students be introduced to the concept of community and be able to explain how people in their own community interact and depend on one another. Students are expected to know the services that are provided in their community and how* *these services help the people who live in the area. Tracy does not live in the area where she works and she realizes that before she can teach a lesson on the local community, she needs to learn more about it. She makes choices about the strategies she will use to help students connect with the content as she drives around the neighborhood, visiting the fire station, the post office, the police department, and interviewing the school crosswalk guard who is on duty every morning and afternoon at J. Carson Elementary School.*

She collects materials and discovers resources that will make the lesson about the community highly motivating to the students. She even visits the site of a large supermarket that is being built and that has stirred much controversy in the neighborhood. She uses a map of the area to mark where her students live and she interviews her students to find out how they get to school each day. By the time Tracy is ready to begin the lesson, she is very knowledgeable about the area and has also learned a great deal more about the learners in her classroom. She decides to begin the lesson with a picture book about The Firefighters' Thanksgiving at Station #1. *The telling of this story will give the English language learners in her classroom opportunity to participate, and she will be able to learn more of her students' experiences with the firefighters in the area through their responses to her questions and through their own stories.*

Teacher knowledge, skill, dedication, disposition, enthusiasm for helping students learn, and the ability to assess student learning are the catalysts that can bring any teaching strategy to its full potential. Teachers who can motivate students to learn by making the content engaging and meaningful, who can use the context in which the students must learn to best advantage, and who understand the needs of the students use a variety of teaching strategies. Knowing a variety of instructional strategies and having the flexibility to change them both within and among lessons are two of the greatest assets a teacher can have (Emmer, Evertson, & Worsham, 2003). Without variety and flexibility to capture the interest and attention of students, it is unlikely that any other key behavior, however well executed, will have the desired effect (Borich, 2004).

During your first attempts at teaching a small group of students or an entire class, it may be that you will feel more confident and competent with only one teaching strategy. The fear of losing control, that the students won't pay attention to you, or that they won't learn what you need to teach them may keep you locked within the parameters of this one teaching strategy. That's natural. We begin learning in small chunks and we feel very comfortable when we know how to do something so we practice it and get better at it and feel even more confident as we continue to practice that particular skill. However, the research base in education tells us that teachers who use a range of teaching strategies have a greater chance of meeting the learning needs of their students and of helping students develop academically. Therefore, it becomes every teacher's responsibility to develop skill in using a variety of strategies to help students connect with the content. Over time, effective teachers learn to make any teaching strategy work for them. Observe some of the ways effective teachers use different strategies to engage students in learning in the Connecting to the Classroom on page 350.

Connecting
TO THE CLASSROOM

This chapter introduces you to some of the teaching strategies that teachers employ in the classroom. There are many reasons teachers use a variety of teaching strategies to help students access information. As you visit classrooms for observation and practice, be alert to the rationale a teacher might have for using one strategy over another. Here are some ideas to help focus your observations.

- Not all students learn in the same manner.
- Learning skills and facts are more easily facilitated by some strategies.
- Space and time have a major influence on the strategies teachers can use.
- Materials and resources my influence the strategies teachers use.
- Most effective lessons utilize more than one teaching strategy.
- A teaching strategy should always match the method by which students will be assessed.

The Importance of Planning Revisited

Planning is of the utmost importance in making a variety of teaching strategies work for you and the students. Some types of plans work better with some types of teaching strategies. You have read about planning in Chapter 8 of this text. You will hear and read about the importance of planning in nearly all of your teacher-education coursework. In your personal life, you have no doubt had much opportunity to plan, but as a student you have been mainly concerned with enacting the plans of others. Your teachers have told you what they expect you to do and, in best-case scenarios, have provided you with examples, directions, and a time-line for achieving the objective. In becoming a teacher, it is necessary to make the shift from enacting the plans of others to creating plans for others to follow.

Plans need to be detailed, thorough, and doable. Plans must be based on accurate content information, a comprehensive understanding of the context, and both theoretical and practical knowledge of learner capabilities and potential. Plans must include objectives that will meet established curricular goals. In other words, they must make sense across many dimensions.

Instructional Theory Into Practice   Madeline Hunter's (1994) seven basic elements of an effective lesson, (1) anticipatory set, (2) instructional objective, (3) instructional input, (4) example of intended learning outcome, (5) check for understanding, (6) guided practice, and (7) independent practice (developed by example in Table 8.1), help form the foundation for any plan involving any teaching strategy. These elements might not be arranged in the same order and some of the elements might not be shared with the students to encourage discovery or inquiry learning. Whether all elements of Hunter's seven basic elements of an effective lesson are shared with the student, they should be part of the instructional plan in one form or another.

Jarolimek, Foster, and Kellough (2005) define a lesson plan as a step-by-step plan of action or a trip map through the lesson that can be followed easily while the lesson is being taught. Beginning teachers and teachers in training need to keep their plans close by for easy reference. We have all had the experience of driving to a new destination, map on the car seat next to us, checking reference points, and trying to read street signs. Plans help teachers reach goals and bring the students along with them. It is not an easy task to write a lesson plan; it, is complex and time consuming. One reason for developing the skill of writing effective lesson plans early in your career is so that once you do write a plan, use it, and judge it as topnotch, you won't have to write the whole plan over again and again.

The MyLabSchool (MLS) feature, a resource for this textbook, provides you the opportunity to develop your skill at creating lesson plans and then share them with others. The Internet is a rich source of lesson plans. Start your search for lesson plans at http://teachers.net/lessons/.

The Planning Cycle Effective teachers are always planning. They think through the design and implementation of lessons long before it is time to actually teach them. They collect artifacts, talk to other teachers and friends about what they want to do, and maybe even try out a plan for a lesson on an unsuspecting family member. Freiberg and Driscoll (1992) explain teacher planning through four phases of a planning cycle as illustrated in Figure 9.2.

Figure 9.2 A lesson-planning cycle

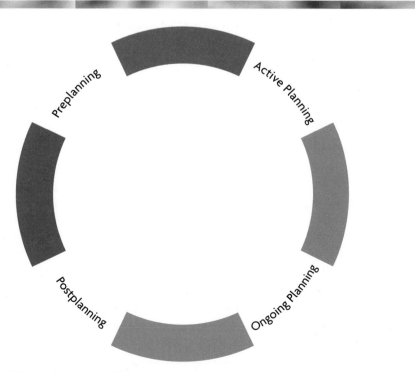

Source: Adapted from Freiberg & Driscoll (1992).

The first phase may find a teacher sitting quietly in a backyard swing looking at a sky full of clouds and listening to the sound of the wind in the trees. Ways to teach a unit on weather to next year's 3rd graders come to mind. Questions pop up. What do 8-year-olds need to know about weather? What would they find most interesting about weather? How would it be possible for them to experience weather conditions in other parts of the world? How many children's books does the school library have on weather? Questions come together in ideas, and ideas spur teachers to action. Resources are collected and organized. Before you know it, it is fall, the school year has begun, and it is time to teach a lesson on weather.

The active planning phase of Freiberg and Driscoll's cycle is when the teacher actually writes the lesson plan they intend to teach. The teacher opens the mental box of weather lessons where all the ideas collected during the preplanning stage have been stored and begins to write the actual plan. Ongoing planning takes place while the teacher is actually teaching the lesson. A student's question may prompt the teacher to include a bit of information that wasn't in the original plan, a fantastic book recommended by the school librarian may be read, or an unbelievable weather pattern develops outside that the children simply must see. The world is full of reasons teachers need to be ready to include ongoing planning in their teaching strategies repertoire. Postplanning is what teachers do when the lesson is over, the school is quiet, and most everyone has gone home for the day. In postplanning, the teacher asks if the goals of the lesson were achieved, if student learning met expectations, and if there are changes that should be made the next time the lesson is taught. Quite naturally, postplanning goes right into preplanning and the cycle begins again.

At the beginning of this chapter, Janet Stramel suggested that teachers should always plan more than they expect the students to do. Teachers should also let the students know the plan. No one likes to be kept in the dark. In explaining the plan with the students, the teacher may become aware of an approach or idea that the students or a particular student may be interested in that the teacher had not included. Through interactions with students about plans, an opportunity to uncover the curriculum may present itself.

Getting Students Ready to Learn

One of the most critical parts of any teaching strategy is how it is applied in the beginning of the lesson. How do your university instructors begin their lectures? With stories? With anecdotes? By directing your attention to a picture or a chart? Did math classes you attended begin with a "stumper" problem on the board for you to try to solve in the first few minutes of class? When you entered your psychology class was there a sealed envelope on each desk with instructions not to open it until an exact moment in time? Such simple devices can capture attention. They are often mysterious and frequently so compelling that we don't need to be reminded to pay attention. We already are! Our own internal monitoring devices are turned on and learning has us in its grasp. Attention-getting activities

Ed Lines

During instructional time, talk less so that students think more.

may include a quick demonstration with an unexpected outcome or asking students to close their eyes and visualize an unlikely event. Riner (2000) says that gaining attention need not be elaborate but the event should cause all students to be involved.

Bracketing or Let's See. Where was I?   **Bracketing** is a strategy that teachers can use at the beginning of a lesson or at the end of the lesson. Teachers talk the students though the process of bracketing what happened between yesterday's lesson and today's lesson and setting it aside so that the ideas from content studied previously can be easily associated with the ones they are about to learn. For example, a teacher reminds students of the class discussion on magnets held the previous day. She acknowledges that after class the students were engaged in activities unrelated to the discussion and that pieces and particles of information from other experiences may have gotten mixed in with the information the students were carrying around about magnets. Then she tells the students it is time to organize the information and ideas surging around in their thinking. Find all the information about magnets, focus on it, and attempt to set aside unrelated information to access at a later time. Bracketing used often becomes a habit of mind and can aid considerably in focusing attention on instruction.

Sponges   Another simple yet effective technique used by teachers to gain student attention at the beginning of a lesson or to keep student attention during the lesson is the **sponge**. This term coined by Hunter (1985, p. 93) describes review or extension activities that help to keep learning on track. Sponges can also be used effectively to summarize a lesson through an enjoyable activity. For example, at the end of a lesson on parts of speech or sentence construction, have students in the classroom call out four letters as you write them on the board or overhead projector. Then ask the students to come up with a four-word sentence in which each word in the sentence begins with the letters written on the board. It may take a few seconds for the first sentence to be formed but once you have written two or three sentences on the board the students ideas will come at you like wildfire. Such an activity could be used to introduce a lesson or as a wrap-up. For additional ideas on sponge activities, visit www.atozteacherstuff.com/Tips/Sponge_and_Transition_Activities.

Bracketing. A teaching method that asks students to isolate a specific period of time or an experience to be able to consider it separately from an ongoing chain of events.

Sponge. Short, motivating activities that focus students on a learning task.

Evaluating Learning

The purpose of assessment is to measure student learning. Because different teaching strategies tend to stimulate different types of learning, it is important for teachers to learn about and be able to use a wide variety of assessment strategies. It would be illogical to evaluate student learning following a role-play situation with a multiple-choice test—and a test on the facts and rules of one content area would not work for a classroom of students who were researching different subjects. Assessment should become a part of every teacher's repertoire of teaching

Ed Lines

"**Learning is enhanced by challenge and inhibited by threat.**" *Renate Nummela Caine & Geoffrey Caine*

strategies so that knowledge of assessment is applied in planning, in decision making, and in communicating with students.

Knowledge about learners is gained through interactions with and observations of the students. Teachers need to observe students, to record their observations, and to seek information about students from outside the classroom. Teachers also need to be clear about the methods of assessment they are using and to what end they are using them. Young (2000) provides guidelines for collecting information about students:

1. Incorporate time to observe students, and record these observations using anecdotal records

2. Have daily conversations with students, learning about their interests and events important in their lives

3. Include many of these findings in your daily teaching.

4. Provide opportunities for students to work together and then observe these interactions with their peers.

You will learn more about assessing student learning in Chapter 11 of this text, and as you do, keep in mind the connection between the content, the context, the learner, and assessment and teaching strategies.

Teacher Work Sample   Teachers can also document student work and their own effectiveness as teachers by a process of work samples. Perhaps you have already been introduced to Teacher Work Samples (TWS) in your teacher education program. Teacher work samples are exhibits of teaching performance that offer evidence of your ability to design and implement standards-based instruction, assess student learning, and reflect on the teaching and learning process. They also provide credible evidence of your ability to facilitate learning of all students. Teacher work samples are one source of evidence your instructors and supervisors use along with classroom observations and other measures to assess your performance as a teacher relative to national and state teaching standards. TWSs require teacher candidates to focus their efforts on standards-based instruction and preK–12 student achievement of state and local content standards. Also, TWS requires new teachers to reflect on and evaluate teaching and learning processes.

Understanding the Connection between Teaching Strategies and Curriculum

In Chapter 5 of this text, you were introduced to the role curriculum plays in instruction and learning. What we immediately discover in learning about teaching strategies is that they share a symbiosis with curriculum. Teaching strategies cannot really exist without curriculum and vice versa. They rely on one another for successful delivery. Of what use would a teaching strategy be if there were no pur-

Ed Lines

"Children that learn together, learn to live together." *David & Roger Johnson*

pose for using it? Curriculum supplies the purpose. Curriculum is what we teach. Instruction is how we teach the curriculum.

In many ways, the teacher is in control of the curriculum, though sometimes it may seem otherwise, given the heft of district curriculum guides and state and federal curriculum policies. Curriculum materials can be used in different ways. Teachers use curriculum materials according to their own personal practical knowledge. They consider how curriculum can be applied in the context and best meet the needs of the students. Teachers use different approaches to teaching to make the relevance and significance of curriculum apparent to the students. Teachers have to be able to visualize what written curriculum looks like in action. The talent it takes to make the transition from text to action is much greater than the talent it takes to recognize it once it occurs, but a teacher must possess both talents.

Revisiting Tracy's Plan

Tracy, the teacher at the beginning of this section, is well prepared to teach the unit on community to her class. She has checked the district curriculum guide to make certain of the content her 2nd graders are required to learn. She has selected goals for the unit and has decided which teaching strategies she will use. Her pre-planning has been comprehensive. She considered the abilities of her students. She is ready to teach the curriculum on community and make it come to life for her students. Tracy will have no difficulty making the teaching strategies she uses work for her.

How Are Different Strategies Used for Different Purposes?

André knows from his courses in general psychology and educational psychology that all of his students share universal needs inherent in human life; the need to know how to do things that will achieve desired outcomes, the need to belong, and the need to have control over one's own actions. As André plans lessons and decides on the strategies he will use to implement them, he considers the behaviors of his 11th grade students in different circumstances, how they perform on academic tasks, how they interact with other students and with himself, and how willingly they seem to participate in lessons. Naturally, André wants to provide the best opportunities for his students to be successful and he knows that in order to do this, he must meet the basic psychological needs of all of them. André knows from experience and from his education that the greater the range of approaches to teaching, the greater the potential for all students to learn. He understands their development as learners and as people, and he uses this knowledge to plan lessons. Consequently, every time he plans a lesson, he makes certain that he asks

Ed Lines

"Hope is not a strategy." *Rick Page*

a variety of questions and allows his students to ask questions, that he always has more than one example of a concept or idea, and that he allows students to interact with the content on their own. During a unit on Victor Hugo's Les Misérables, *André incorporates a range of strategies from lecture, to cooperative learning, to research, to art and music, and student-generated reports that include writing, technology, and student performance. He also provides the students with current popular texts that deal with the problem of social injustice to encourage discussion about Jean Valjean's persecution. André is helping his students find new interests and express themselves as well as learn required content.*

Culturally Relevant Teaching Strategies

Culturally relevant teaching strategies refer to the ways generic strategies are modified or implemented to address the fact that students' orientations to learning may be influenced by their cultural backgrounds. The ways in which students interact with one another and with the teacher also may be influenced by their cultural background (Irvine & York, 2001; Putman, 1997). Students who live in an Italian or Jewish neighborhood in New York City, students from a fishing town in Florida, students who attend an inner-city school in Chicago or Los Angeles, and students from a small mining town in a remote area of northern Nevada will bring different backgrounds to school and have different orientations to learning. Teaching strategies that accommodate learning styles influenced by culture have a greater chance of matching students' varying orientations to learning. You read in Chapter 1 of this text that the greater the range of approaches to teaching, the greater the potential for all students to learn (Sanders & Rivers, 1996). Teachers have to be aware of the range of culture differences in their classroom in order to adjust instruction for the benefit of all. When content is presented to students so that they have the option of using their preferred learning style, they are likely to accept it more readily and connect it to what they already know. Some students need more structure. Some students require less structure and want to solve problems on their own with a minimum of teacher help. Planning lessons that provide opportunities for students to learn within differently structured contexts is part of what makes teaching such an interesting and engaging profession. Visit the website at www.lab.brown.edu/tdl/tl-strategies/crt-research.shtml to learn more about culturally responsive teaching through reviews related to learning styles, culture, and research on effective teaching strategies.

Multiple Intelligences   Learners view the world from different perspectives and react to it with differing abilities. Gardner (1999) believes children develop abilities, "intelligences," by their own spontaneous interaction with the world in which they live. According to Gardner, curriculum and teaching strategies should respond to the individual differences in intellectual potential related to eight intelligences: (a) linguistic, (b) musical, (c) logical-mathematical, (d) spatial, (e) bodily kinesthetic, (f) interpersonal understanding, (g) intrapersonal understanding, and (h) naturalistic intelligence. People generally possess all eight intelligences, and these intelligences interact with one another—yet individuals are likely to be more highly developed in some of the intelligences than others. Some students perform well on standardized tests; some don't. Students who have not yet mastered computation skills but perform well on story problems may be using their ability to understand the meaning and order of words to solve problems rather than mathematical skills.

Inclusion Strategies: Least Restrictive Environment (LRE)   As a teacher, you will be expected to create a classroom environment that provides all students equal access to learning. An intended goal of federal and state special education requirements has been to afford opportunities for students with disabilities, to the maximum extent possible, to interact with their nondisabled peers. The Individuals with Disabilities Education Act (IDEA) presumes that all children with disabilities are, to some extent, educated in regular classes. Special education and related services provided to special needs students are to be in addition to and affected by the general education curriculum, not separate from it. Research supports the idea that students with exceptionalities benefit from time in inclusive environments (Hardman, Drew, & Egan, 1996). As teachers create an all-inclusive learning environment, they need to focus on good teaching for each and every child in their classroom.

- Have students create the structure of the classroom. (If they build it, they will learn!)
- Design learning situations in which students are responsible for tracking their own achievements. (A visual reminder of the growth students are making is a great motivator.)
- Maintain high expectations for all students. (Remember how the turtle won the race.)
- Involve families. (Family involvement expands the boundaries of the classroom.)
- Incorporate curriculum that focuses on individual worth. (Learn about what matters in your students' lives by having them tell their own stories.)
- Create curriculum that involves students and their interests. (Can a single worksheet or a basal reader address the interests and needs of all the learners in your classroom?)

Because not all students learn the same, the federal government has established guidelines for providing optimal learning environments for students with exceptional needs. See the Teachers and the Law on page 358.

Strategies for English Language Learners (ELL)   Many students in your future classrooms will have limited or no English-language capacity. You will be responsible for helping these students learn the content. Because the role of language has a strong influence on student learning and may place students who do not speak, read, or understand English at a disadvantage, you will be expected to implement strategies that diminish this disadvantage. Some schools may use a "pullout" approach, allowing limited English proficient (LEP) students to spend part of the day in a special bilingual class. However, chances are that all teachers will need to possess some skill in using strategies to help LEP students learn. Teachers should incorporate the following strategies in

Not all students have common capabilities for learning. Some students may need more time to learn a concept or skill that will lead to meeting academic standards. Some students may need special instruction or materials and resources to help them process instruction. Laws have been established to regulate and determine the placement of such students in schools. The Individuals with Disabilities Education Act (IDEA) is the federal law governing the education of children with disabilities. IDEA and its regulations define the least restrictive environment (LRE) and require that all states demonstrate they have policies and procedures in place to guarantee they meet the federal LRE requirements.

INCLUSION AND LEAST RESTRICTIVE ENVIRONMENT

Is inclusion a right?

No. People often assume that IDEA regulations require schools to practice inclusion. However, the term *inclusion* is not included in the IDEA statutes. The terms **mainstreaming** and **least restrictive environment** are included in the IDEA regulations. These terms require school districts to educate students with disabilities in regular classrooms with their nondisabled classmates in the school they would attend to the maximum extent appropriate. According to the definition of least restrictive environment, a child with a disability may only be removed from the regular classroom when the nature or severity of the disability is such that the education in regular classes cannot be achieved satisfactorily, even with the use of supplementary aids and services. Students with disabilities may at times be removed from the regular classroom to work in a small group or in one-on-one situations designed to provide them with additional education in a specific academic area.

Do parents of students with disabilities have to pay for the special services provided by the school?

No. Reauthorization of the IDEA in 1997 extended federal funding for special education services to assure that all children with disabilities were provided with a free appropriate public education (FAPE), and that the student's placement and the services he or she receives depend on the student's individual needs, not on administrative convenience.

Is there a test to determine a student's eligibility for IDEA services?

Yes. In a two-part test, a student's disability must fit within one of the categories of eligibility and then it must be proven that the child needs special services because of this disability. Not all children with physical or mental impairments will satisfy the IDEA's two-part eligibility test and so will not be eligible for IDEA services.

Does the individual education program (IEP) of a student with disabilities indicate what the extent of their least restrictive environment should be?

Yes. The 1997 amendments to IDEA require that in a situation in which a child will not participate fully with peers without disabilities, the IEP must include an explanation of why and to what extent the child will not be included.

Are there special requirements for classroom teachers who will teach students with disabilities in the least restricted environment?

Yes. All general and special education teachers responsible for providing services to students with disabilities must receive appropriate training, resources, and support necessary to help such students achieve academic goals. Specifications for a teaching certificate require that some college coursework related to the special needs of students with disabilities is included on a licensure applicant's transcript.

teaching English language learners
(Walling, 1993).

1. Extend the time allowed for learning activities.

2. Use students as translators and spend more time on discussions.

3. Use straightforward language and avoid jargon or language that can be easily misunderstood.

4. Read written instructions aloud pointing out key words.

5. Use multiple examples.

6. Give directions in a variety of ways.

Simple modifications to instruction can make a world of difference for LEP students. However, the first step should always be to show respect for students' cultural backgrounds. It doesn't take much energy for a teacher to learn how to pronounce a student's name correctly, but the effort will make a world of difference in the student's attitude toward the teacher and consequently toward learning.

Homework as a Teaching Strategy

One of the best pieces of advice I received from an experienced teacher when I began my professional career was to never have students do homework that they had not started in class or that they weren't sure how to complete. No teacher wants a student to go home and report, "I don't know why I'm doing this and I don't understand it at all." Homework is a form of interactive practice in which the learner is interacting with the content. However, when the teacher is not present to mediate this interaction, the student had better be absolutely clear about what needs to be done and why. Homework is an extension of classroom learning and when planned carefully can assist student achievement, but like every other strategy a teacher uses, homework should fit the content, the context, and the learner. If practice makes perfect, then it becomes a teacher's responsibility to somehow monitor the practice that occurs during homework so that it will not become imperfect practice. An adaptation of a list of appropriate and inappropriate uses of homework developed by the U.S. Department of Education is presented in Table 9.4.

Revisiting André's Students

Andre does his best to make learning relevant to the students in his charge. He considers their talents, abilities, and orientations to learning and attempts to introduce the curriculum in ways that will motivate the students and encourage their participation. Students choose how to show they learned the content. Some

Mainstreaming. Integration of students with disabilities into regular classrooms.

Least restrictive environment (LRE). To the maximum extent appropriate, children with disabilities should be educated with children who are not disabled.

Table 9.4 Appropriate and Inappropriate Uses of Homework

Use Homework	Do Not Use Homework
To expand learning opportunities	To punish students
To use devices and materials found at home	To substitute for guided practice
To involve parents in enjoyable learning activities	To introduce a new content or a new skill
To review or practice mastered material	When too much time is required
To stimulate or satisfy intellectual curiosity	When there is no clear purpose or benefit to the student
To attend to individual needs	
To provide a worthwhile experience	

Source: Adapted from the U.S. Department of Education (1986).

students in his class ask if they can draw a mural representing the characters in *Les Misérables*. Another group wants to act out a scene from the story. One student chooses to compare the difficulties his own family has faced immigrating to the United States to the problems and dilemmas Jean Valjean encounters.

Chapter Summary

Understanding that instruction is the systematic delivery of content to a unique set of individuals in a specified context is part of the specialized knowledge of a professional teacher. Learning how to use particular strategies effectively comes with practice over time. Learning about different approaches to teaching can begin the first day you decide to enroll in teacher-education coursework. Connecting your own experiences as a student to the information you acquire about different teaching strategies and having the opportunity to glean some knowledge and skill from your own practice will set you on the path to becoming a competent and confident professional.

What is a teaching strategy? A teaching strategy is the yeast in the lesson that makes it rise to meet students' interests and abilities. Teaching strategies provide the pedagogical framework around which the professional teacher builds instruction and activities. In many ways, teachers are

architects of learning. Teaching strategies are the blueprints that help teachers and students construct meaning, build concepts, and integrate ideas. Without a well-defined approach to teaching a specific lesson or content, instruction is just an action with no connection to theory, research, or outcomes. Time is precious. Understanding the role teaching strategies play in the gestalt of instruction helps teachers make productive use of whatever time they have. Teaching strategies come in all shapes and sizes and often produce different types of student performance. The ability to apply and integrate a range of teaching strategies is the mark of a true professional.

What makes teaching strategies work? When we're watching a movie, if the directing is superb and the production flawless, we don't pay much attention to the camera angle, the lighting, the details of the way the actors move, or even the transitions from one scene to another. We become lost in the story, the lives of the characters, and go home with memories and experiences we are eager to share. We learn something from an excellent production whether it be a movie or a lesson. Teachers are constantly setting the stage for learning. In order to do this well, they have to plan extensively, they have to know their audience, and they have to know how one chunk of content relates to another. Teachers have to be able to get students ready to learn and to help students focus when their attention wanders. Part of making teaching strategies work is being able to assess their impact on student learning, so teachers have to collect data and use that data to guide future practice. Teaching strategies used correctly have the power to transform a ripple on a pond to wave length and frequency in a student's mind.

How are different strategies used for different purposes? We're not the same as people or as learn-ers. Each of us sees the world from a single perspective born of a million different influences and effects. Not all students discover the same bit of information simultaneously, if at all. One particular teaching strategy may be more likely to trigger a learning response from one student than from another. If a teacher used a single teaching strategy in every context and with every group of students, it would be easy to see how some students would be at a disadvantage and would not have as much access to information as others. We all remember our favorite teacher; the one who taught the way we learned. We understood every lesson and caught every nuance. Being in school was fun. However, we struggled to learn during the year we had a teacher who was somewhat global in lesson structure when we required a more linear, step-by-step approach or vice versa. Teachers must always look through the eyes of their students to see where learning connects for each of them.

Class Discussion Questions

1. It would be unreasonable to expect a novice practitioner to enter the classroom highly knowledgeable of and skilled in the use of multiple approaches to teaching. Which teaching strategy would you like to learn first? What advice is of most worth in this process? How might you practice a teaching strategy even before you have a classroom of your own?

2. Resources are like advice; they fall into categories of useful and not so useful. What types of resources are most likely to help teacher education candidates increase their knowledge of teaching strategies? What are some ways to store and organize resources so they will be readily available when needed?

3. The diversity of student characteristics in a classroom can make some teachers lack confidence in their ability to meet the learning needs of all students. What examples have you seen when the strategy clearly matched the students' backgrounds?

4. Helping students identify and build on their strengths is an often underemphasized tenet of teaching. Recognizing one's own strengths can lead to confidence. Feeling confident when teaching a group of students leads to competence. Consider your strengths. How will these help you in teaching? Which strategies do you believe will benefit most from the strengths you possess?

Field Guide for School Observations

Plan a short lecture on a subject you feel will be of interest to students at a specific grade level. Be sure to follow the five guidelines discussed in the chapter (audience, focus, organization, clarity, and pacing). Make an outline of your lecture. Visit a classroom when the teacher is delivering a lecture. Compare your lecture structure to the one the teacher used. If the teacher used a lecture structure different from the one you outlined, ask why.

Ask a Teacher
Ask a teacher what their favorite teaching strategy is and why they prefer it over others. Have them tell you how they learned and developed skill in using it. Also, ask the teacher if the strategy is most effective with any particular content area.

Journaling *Becoming a Thoughtful Teacher*

Think of something you learned and who taught it to you. For example, how did you learn to tie your shoes, scramble an egg, play a musical instrument, dance, or wash a load of clothes so all the clothes didn't come out some shade of pink or dusty brown? Describe the process. How did the person who helped you learn teach you? What strategy(ies) did they use? Was there repetition, written instructions, or a demonstration? Did you have to practice on your own or did the teacher work through the process with you? Write a brief description of the learning process you went through. What teaching strategies work best for you?

Portfolio Tasks

Teachers who continue to grow and learn access the resources available to them, work with other professionals, and collect data representing their teaching performance and the performance of their students. You have no doubt already begun a professional development portfolio. This is a perfect place to keep a record of your growth in understanding and using an array of teaching strategies. Make a list of the key components of one teaching strategy you have observed and understand. Describe how you might have used it in one of your practicum experiences.

Self-Assessment *What Am I Learning?*

Select a content area (i.e., reading, math, science, social studies, art, music, etc.) that you are interested in teaching. Write six questions you could ask the students that would be designed to elicit differing levels of student thinking. Make certain the questions you write will help the students achieve the objective of a particular lesson. Write one question for each of the levels in Bloom's Taxonomy.

Using the Web

You were directed to the InTime website at www.uni.edu in Chapter 8 to see examples of the ways teachers incorporate standards into lesson plans. Visit the website again. Download two lesson plans using different teaching strategies and write a one-page paper comparing the elements and style of the two lessons. Focus on teacher behaviors and expected student behaviors as you consider the content, the context, and the learners.

Your Professional Library

Hunter, Madeline (1994). *Enhancing teaching*. New York: Macmillan.

Everyone who teaches should read this book. It is easy to read, addresses many aspects of designing instruction to help students achieve success in school, and is written from the personal perspective of an educator who understands the teacher's role.

Liberman, Ann, & Miller, Lynne. (1984). *Teachers, their world, and their work*. Alexandria, VA: Association for Supervision and Curriculum Development.

Ann Liberman and Lynne Miller write about the world of teachers with honest and inspiring voices. They present all aspects of the teaching/learning/school world in ways that make the reader nod in agreement and smile to find out that their experiences in teaching are shared by many.

Wright, Esther (1999). *Why I teach*. Rocklin, CA: Prima Publishing.

This text is a delightful compilation of teachers' personal experiences of the ways they helped their students learn and managed to connect with their students and their students' parents. The stories in the text demonstrate that teachers must use a variety of strategies in meeting the needs of all students.

To access chapter objectives, practice tests, weblinks, and flashcards, visit the Companion Website at **www.ablongman.com/hall1e**

mylabschool
Where the classroom comes to life!

Go to Allyn & Bacon's MyLabSchool (**www.mylabschool.com**). Enter Assignment ID **GMV5** in the **Assignment Finder**. View the clip, *Multiple Intelligences in the Classroom*. The team teachers in this segment attentively plan learning center activities related to Gardner's multiple intelligences. As the teachers contemplate various aspects of tracking student progress and student choice of centers, they work collaboratively to create meaningful learning experiences for the students. Next view the video clip, *Strategies for Teaching Diverse Learners* (also within Assignment ID **GMV5**), also provides examples of ways teachers use different instructional strategies to help students learn. Consider the information in this chapter and the examples provided in these video clips to respond to the following questions.

1. Students who have the same learning styles as their teachers usually find school a satisfying and rewarding experience. Recall one learning situation your teacher created that you believe was identical to your personal learning style. Did completing the tasks required of this learning situation seem easy for you? Explain.

2. How did the detailed planning by the teaching team in the *Strategies for Teaching Diverse Learners* clip help make the learning centers successful for both teachers and learners.

Return to General Methods home page and click on the Research Navigator link. In Research Navigator scroll down to the Link Library subject box. Enter Education—Educational Psychology. Click on "C" and then the Cooperative Learning link. Read *Teaching Models*.

List the major strength of each of the three teaching strategies discussed.

Integrating Technology and Teaching

Educators in Real Schools

M E E T

Dave V. Jones

King Kamehameha III Elementary School

King Kamehameha III Elementary School is located in the small
town of Lahaina on the western side of the island of Maui in Hawaii.
The schools on Maui are organized into complexes. A complex consists of a high school and all of the intermediate/middle and elementary schools that flow into it. Kamehameha III Elementary
School is part of the Lahainaluna complex. The Lahainaluna complex is comprised of two elementary schools, one intermediate
school and one high school. There are 38 teachers at Kamehameha:
five in kindergarten, three in 1st grade, five in 2nd grade, six in 3rd
grade, five in 4th grade, and four in 5th grade. There are four special
education teachers, two counselors, a librarian, an ESLL Coordinator, a teacher for the gifted
and talented program and a technology specialist. Six hundred eighty-five students are enrolled
at the school, making the average student teacher ratio 18 to 1. A principal and vice-principal
administer the school with the support of five office staff members.

Teachers take part in workshops to become more knowledgeable of new programs and
to improve home/school/community communications. Students who attend Kamehameha
have experiences that are designed to establish a desire for lifelong learning. They are prepared to respond to the challenges of the future and grow to become productive, contributing citizens of a global community. The vision statement for Kamehameha is "Cherish the
past; Explore the present; Embrace the future."

Dave V. Jones is someone who was considered a "nontraditional" teacher education
candidate. He earned his teaching degree at a large research institution in the Southwest.
While enrolled in the elementary teacher education program, he became part of a special

369

What Should Every
Teacher Know about
Integrating Technology
into Teaching?

What Should Every Teacher Know about Integrating Technology into Teaching?

*As each student enter **Jesus**'s classroom, they approach the classroom computer console and click on the square after their name to mark their attendance in class. The time and date are registered automatically in Jesus's electronic grade book and in the central office of the school. When the students take their seats, homework assignments are scanned and evaluated on their individual desk consoles by programs designed to recognize correct responses. Within minutes of the first bell, Jesus receives a printout showing him who has done what and how well. From his technology station at the front of the room, Jesus can post grades and send private messages to students who might need clarification of the grade. He can also schedule times when he would like to visit privately with individual students about their work and attendance. While these messages are being sent, Jesus has directed the students to a National Geographic website where they are to read about the Alashan Plateau section of the Gobi Desert as an introduction to the unit on natural deserts. Questions for discussion are listed on the board. Little time is wasted. The students are engaged in learning and soon a lively, thoughtful, and informed discussion is taking place about barren landscapes, fragile soils, and scarce water sources. When the alarm clock rings and Jesus wakes up, the first thought that crosses his mind is, "Why not?"*

Today, students have access to wonders around the world and can take virtual tours of many of them. For example, go to the IBM website www.eternalegypt.org and explore the culture of Egypt through virtual visits to famous sites and museums. It is only one of many sites available to help teachers and students increase their knowledge and understanding of the world, its past, and its peoples. The Internet provides a wealth of information for teachers to create unusual learning opportunities for students, to manage student work, to develop presentations for introducing and investigating topics, to plan virtual field trips, find games students can play with other students across the nation to improve skills, or even to get help in creating their own games. Integrating technology into instruction is not a difficult task, but it is up to the teacher to decide when and how such integration will take place. In addition to knowing what materials to use, teachers must also be knowledgeable about legal issues of such material. See the Teachers and the Law on page 370.

In addition to the decisions teachers make about students, curriculum, and instructional strategies, they have to now make decisions about the purposes of technology in their teaching, quality software, and equal access for students. Visit a classroom at any grade level and look around the room to see what technology tools are available for teacher and student use. You may find these tools more obvious in elementary classrooms where one group of students uses the space throughout the year. Technology tools may be less visible in junior high or high school classrooms where student traffic is high and changing groups of students and teachers may make it difficult to keep track of pricey hardware. Even when technology may not be obvious to the casual observer, it

Searching for and finding a juicy piece of information to complement any work in progress is a satisfying process. The accessibility of the Web even makes it convenient. What is not so clear given the ease of downloading artifacts or evidence from the Web is just how closely protected Web-based sources are, and what the requirements are for using such sources in your own work.

Is all information on the Internet considered public domain?

No.   A handful of federal, state, and international laws govern copyright practice. In general, they are designed to protect the rights of scholars and artists while preserving the public's right to benefit from the works of those same creators. Copyrights protect the imagination of individuals. Federal law protects copyright owners from the unauthorized reproduction, adaptation, performance, display, or distribution of copyright protected works. Penalties for copyright infringement differ in civil and criminal cases. Civil remedies are generally available for any act of infringement without regard to the intention or knowledge of the defendant or harm to the copyright owner. Criminal penalties are available for intentional acts undertaken for purposes of "commercial advantage" or "private financial gain." Private financial gain includes the possibility of financial loss to the copyright holder as well as traditional "gain" by the defendant.

Is there some information for teachers regarding copyright information on the Web?

Yes.   The Recording Industry Association of America (RIAA) website at www.riaa.com/issues/education offers numerous links to sites that will help teachers, children, and parents gain knowledge of cyberspace copyright laws. At *Cyberethics for Kids* (www.cybercrime.gov/rules/kidinternet.htm), the U.S. Department of Justice offers teachers a lesson plan outline and exercises for K–8. CyberSpacers (www.cyberspacers.org/) provides activities for kids to learn about cybercrime. Play It Cybersafe (www.playitcybersafe.com/) is dedicated to helping students learn how to use the Internet safely and responsibly. The site was created by the Business Software Alliance and the Hamilton Fish Institute at George Washington University. It represents a cyber crime and intellectual property theft prevention and education project funded by the U.S. Department of Justice. The Netmonkey website at

may be under lock and key nearby and quickly available or in a technology center. Ask the teachers you know or work with what technology tools they use and how they gain access to them.

Technology Tools for Teaching

Think of the technology tools you commonly use. These probably include a camera of some sort—digital, cellular, or film; maybe a video- or audiotape recorder; certainly a video player or DVD player. Technology is all around and we use it for our personal pleasure and business without giving a moment's thought to how or why it works. In fact, the only time we really think about it is when it doesn't do what we want it to. Digital media in our homes comes at us constantly through music, voice, data, and video. The digital generation of today's youth has no problem watching TV, listening to music, e-mailing friends, or surfing the Internet to see what's happening, all at the same time. **Multitasking** is a new vocabulary word and for many has become habitual. It is not always safe and it sometimes causes important pieces of information to be missed, but it is a part of today's culture. Switching perspectives from using technology for personal need or plea-

► Multitasking. The ability to perform more than one task at a time.

www.netmonkey.info/ is designed to educate young people about the risks of online piracy. It's fun and loaded with information.

Are there some exceptions to copyright laws on the Internet?

Yes. Fair use criteria can create some exceptions to copyright laws for teachers and students; however, there are no absolute guidelines for fair use in educational settings. According to the Stanford University Libraries website at http://fairuse.stanford.edu/, the only way to get a definitive answer on whether a particular use is a fair use is to have it resolved in federal court. Judges use four factors to resolve fair-use disputes:

1. the purpose and character of your use
2. the nature of the copyrighted work
3. the amount and substantiality of the portion taken
4. the effect of the use upon the potential market

Additionally, guidelines have also been established for uses and copying information in educational settings. These guidelines are not part of the Copyright Act, but should be studied carefully before embarking on any major use of copyrighted material.

According to a Smartype.com info sheet, "many newcomers to the Internet may perceive it as a lawless space where communication is ungoverned and anything goes." Not necessarily so. Internet users are accountable to copyright laws in the same way that they are when accessing and using information in the real world. Since April 1, 1989, every communication (words, photos, music, or art) produced on the Internet is copyrighted by default. It's also not true that as long as you don't use the material for commercial purposes you are not breaking any laws. Be safe. Ask for permission when using any material produced by anyone else.

You may not be in the habit of scrolling down to the bottom of any web page that you access, but in the future click on the disclaimer and copyright information posted at the bottom of nearly every Web page. You'll find out quickly how much of the information on that website is available for public use. In most cases it's zilch, but there is usually a place where you can contact the designers or owners of the website to see if they will let you use some of the information they have organized. Most would be more than happy to give permission to educators.

Sources: Recording Industry Association of America. Retrieved May 24, 2005 at www.riaa.com/issues/copyright.laws.asp; Smartype info sheet 09: Internet Copyright laws. Retrieved June 2006 at www.smartype.com.au/info/txt/09_Internet_Copyright.asp.

sure and using it in a classroom to augment student learning requires a focus of attention on what the technology does and what it can be used for. A beginning teacher who is digitally oriented may need to change their mind-set toward technology tools. Here are some examples of ways teachers could use common technology tools such as cameras, video- and audiotape recorders, and learning games in instruction and management.

Fair use. An exemption to the U.S. Copyright Law created to allow education, news reporting, commentary, research, and parody about copyrighted material without the permission of the author.

The Camera Will Weber, a professor in the College of Education at University of Houston, tells his college classroom management students to catch students being good. He says that positive reinforcement is the most powerful management tool in a teacher's possession. Take pictures of your students being wonderful and load the pictures on the computer. When things get a little out of hand in the classroom, run the photos as a slide show. Soon all students will get the "picture" and order will be restored without you having to say a word. A picture really is worth a thousand words.

An opposite approach would be to take a series of pictures of a classroom out of control, put them on a computer monitor, and ask the students to explain what's happening. Then ask what can be done so this does not happen again.

The use of appropriate technologies enhances student involvement in classroom projects.

Students sometimes think they are invisible to the all-seeing eyes of a teacher. They're wrong, of course, but the difference between having a teacher tell students what they see and showing the students what is seen can be a mighty behavior management tool.

Digital pictures can be used to show student progress and what it looks like when students are learning and growing. Mrs. Katts took pictures of her class's DARE graduation. She made a slide show out of it and showed it to the kids; they were immensely and rightly proud of themselves. A copy of the slide show became each child's record of their achievement.

Pictures can provide background for a story or lesson. Mr. Shoemaker was teaching a story set in Yosemite National Park. He created a slide show of pictures of Yosemite so the students had a visual image during the reading of the story and afterwards during questions about Yosemite. Only one person in the whole class had actually been to Yosemite, but after the story with accompanying slide presentation, every student in the class had a virtual trip there.

The Videotape Recorder   Video cameras are a little harder to manipulate than single-shot cameras. It's difficult to tape and teach at the same time. Teachers can help one another videotape lessons or with a little training and preplanning, students can become expert camera people. Videotaping an environment or event enables viewers to react to the information on the tape at a later time. Filming lessons can make learning entertaining. Imagine the titles; "Kate Learns to Add," "Shannon and Sean Build an Ant Farm," "Room 68 Crosses the Potomac," "Terry Totally Rocks at Soccer." The possibilities are endless and the learning potential through technology is exceptional.

Learning Games   When something is fun, we want to do it again and again. Children learning a new game that they enjoy are very persistent. Persistence is one of the prerequisites to learning. According to Jenn Shreve, "A good game can motivate students to understand things they couldn't or wouldn't learn before" (Shreve, 2005, 30). As a student, did you ever encounter the video games "Oregon Trail" (1974) or "Where in the World Is Carmen Sandiego" (1985)? If so, you know exactly what's happening with game machines. Game machines blend a range of digital media into one hub making possible things that traditional teaching cannot. Sid Meier's "Civilization III" computer game has moti-

Ed Lines

"**Any sufficiently advanced technology . . . is indistinguishable from magic.**" *Arthur C. Clarke*

vated failing middle and high school students to high levels of involvement and achievement. Students who design their own games have additional opportunities to connect content to other skills and ideas. Games and simulations are also used to train teachers. A Vermont-based SimSchool **PT3 Project** is developing a game that will give preservice teachers "a chance to try out their lesson plans before subjecting an entire classroom to them" (Shreve, 2005, 30). The world of technology is making possible amazing opportunities.

Audiotapes are a great aid for progress in learning to read.

Audiotape Recordings   Often, audiotape recordings can be used to augment single pictures. Audiotapes are great for feedback on progress in learning to read or explaining how to compute a math problem. Students read stories into a tape recorder, read the story again as they listen to their own words, and begin to make self-corrections all the while learning to monitor their own learning. Students who record their thinking processes are often able to recognize where they may have gone astray without having someone else point out their mistakes. Go to www.stg.brown,edu/projects/WWII_Women/tocCS.html for an example of an oral history project. Students in the honors English program at South Kingstown High School interviewed 26 Rhode Island women to create photos, audiotapes, and essays about women and World War II.

PT3 Project. An initiative of the U.S. Department of Education to Prepare Tomorrow's Teachers to use Technology by funding technology for teacher education programs.

Using Technology Effectively

Think about the fact that computers don't teach people; people teach people. People design programs and tell the programs how to run. Lousy instruction whether it is backed up with technology or not is still lousy instruction. The teacher's task is to determine the purpose and effect of the benefit of technology in any given situation. Teachers need to focus on what they want the students to learn and then consider how the use of technology can help them achieve their goals. They have to modify all of the technology tools available to them to fit their needs as teachers, the needs of the learners, and how effectively the curriculum can be augmented through the use of any specific technology tool. The combination of technology and effective teaching can be a powerful motivation for student achievement. See the Challenging Assumptions on page 374.

Ed Lines

The joy of teaching isn't found in a book; it's found in the hearts and minds of teachers.

Challenging Assumptions
FINDINGS FROM RESEARCH

Does access to technology necessarily translate into increased student achievement?

The Assumption: Much attention has been directed toward preparing schools and teachers for the technological age of the twenty-first century. Elementary and secondary schools have rapidly become "wired" to the Internet. Hasselbring and Bausch (2005–2006) reported that in 2004, virtually all public schools in the United States had Internet access. Teachers and teacher education candidates have received training through support from the Department of Education's Preparing Tomorrow's Teachers to Use Technology (PT3) program. Over 400 PT3 grants have been funded in the belief that projects directed at faculty development, course restructuring, and new and better uses of electronic formats will transform teaching and learning. Private companies such as IBM Corporation and Microsoft have provided funding to school districts and individual schools in the belief that the presence of technology and technological expertise will support and encourage student learning. There is an extremely strong assumption in education today that in order for each student to have an equal opportunity to learn they must have access to technology.

Study Design and Methods: Researchers who seek to accurately identify the effect of the use of technology in student achievement will have to design studies that take into account both the technology in use and teacher expertise in understanding and using the technology to help students learn. The study cited here examined the relationship between computer use and 4th and 8th grade students' mathematics achievement. The findings indicate that higher mathematics scores were related to adequate access to computer technology and access to a teacher who knew how to apply the technology to help the students learn higher-order concepts. It was also pointed out in the study that the most pronounced inequities in computer use and teacher training were across socioeconomic status, race, and geographic locale. It appears that technology does help students learn, but a knowledgeable teacher is still key to the process.

Implications: This study provides one example of the interaction necessary between teacher expertise and available resources to increase the potential for student learning. Sometimes a knowledgeable and effective teacher can be all the enticement a student needs to excel in any given subject. However, the availability of up-to-date equipment coupled with teacher expertise in specialized uses of the technology can sometimes increase student performance. According to the study, computer use was associated with increased performance when the following conditions were met:

- adequate access to up-to-date computer technology
- computers used specifically to help students learn higher-order concepts
- well-trained teachers who are capable of assisting students in using the technology for specific purposes

Sources: Wenglinsky, H. (1998). *Does it compute? The relationship between educational technology and student achievement in mathematics.* Princeton, NJ: Educational Testing Services (ETS); Hasselbring, T. S., & Bausch, M. E. (2005–2006). Assistive technology for reading. *Educational Leadership* 63(4), 72–75.

Your first classroom may be equipped with less-than-brand-new technology. The fact is that even computers that cannot run the latest software programs or at the fastest speeds can still be used for word processing and for students to practice and improve skills. Some older games with fewer graphics can be run effectively on older model computers, and, in fact, many older games do not run (or run well) on new machines. Regardless of the age of the available technology or what it can do,

375

What Should Every
Teacher Know about
Integrating Technology
into Teaching?

there are guidelines for using technology for instructional purposes that every teacher should follow. The following checklist will help any teacher make integrating technology in instruction a plus and not a frustrating, time-wasting experience.

- Is the equipment ready to be used? (Have you tried it yourself to make certain it is in good working order and that it will not break down in the middle of the lesson?)

- Are directions for student use of the equipment available? (Are they posted near the equipment? Have you gone over them with the students?)

- Does the program to be run fit within the time limit you have set for the lesson? (Have you previewed the program from start to finish?)

- Will students be able to run the program without assistance? (If not, who will assist them?)

- If you are planning to access the Internet, do you know the content of the Web page?

- Are you sure all of the links you plan to use are available?

- Do all the students who need it have visual or physical access to the technology?

- Are follow-up activities to the lesson communicated to the students?

Involving Students in the Use of Technology

Using technology in the classroom is a team sport. No member of the class should be only a spectator. Students may be more capable of coping with the technology in the classroom than you yourself are. In the same ways that a smart teacher shares power with the students through designating student helpers and leaders, students can be given responsibility for the use and care of classroom technology tools. Students can prove extremely resourceful in straightening out glitches in computer use. Your future students will truly be children of the computer age and they may have a better understanding of the technological revolution than you do. It is always important for teachers to listen to their students, and no less so regarding to the uses to which technology can be put in the classroom.

Research and Presentations You have certainly used technology for research and presentations. Developing presentation skills helps students to focus on the critical details of a topic, to present a solid argument, and to summarize information in concise forms. Students should be constantly involved in collecting and organizing information, accessing and compiling lists of resources, or even making video clips to illustrate details of their chosen

topics. Evaluation of student work should also emphasize these details; otherwise the student research presentation can become a cut and paste exercise. Even very young students can prepare digital presentations to share with their classmates. In order for students to think about technology as a learning tool and not just one to use for personal pleasure, they will have to use the technology to learn, not just watch the teacher use it to teach.

Student Work Samples   How did you keep track of your progress through your teacher education coursework? Formerly, cumbersome, paper portfolios were required as summative evidence of a teacher education candidate's achievement. Most likely you are now expected to keep an electronic record of meeting each standard and goal set forth by your college and state licensing agency. There is a variety of e-portfolio programs available for organizing, assessing, and presenting work. Nuventive's iwebfolio at www.nuventive.com and Chalk and Wire's e-portfolio at www.chalkandwire.com allow students to create, maintain, and showcase their work. FolioLive hosted by McGraw-Hill at www.foliolive.com provides a simple framework for creating Web-based portfolios. Folio by ePortaro at www.eportaro.com is advertised as a cradle-to-career portfolio tool—TaskStream's Web folio builder at www.taskstream.com is geared toward teachers.

Maybe, at the time you compiled your e-portfolio you considered the activity of keeping a record of your progress just one more hurdle to leap before graduation with the thought that once you'd done it you could put it behind you. Not so. Your skill in establishing a personal electronic record will be put to use in helping your own students set up electronic folios of their assignments and assessments over time. Many examples of student work websites can be viewed at www.lasw.org/resources_stuwork.html. The Electronic Learning Marketplace at www.elm.main.edu/index.asp provides teachers with the opportunity to exchange ideas and gives examples of student work and teacher-developed assessments. When students know their work will be published in a public venue, they are inclined to take greater pains in making certain it is correct. Look at the math graphing projects of the 6th graders at Kamiloiki Elementary School in Honolulu at www.kwe.hi.us/%7Emarcworng/work/work.htm to see a colorful example of student work samples.

Technology for Managing the Classroom

In Jesus' dream, technology makes managing the classroom a breeze. Paperwork is kept to a minimum and information is processed and stored without the teacher having to worry about losing data that is supposed to make its way to the central office. While Jesus' dream may not be a reality for him, it could be for you. Even without all the bells and whistles that Jesus imagined, any teacher can begin to develop an electronic format for keeping track of student information. Spreadsheets can be filled out by students at the beginning of the day and entered into a data base by an aide, a parent helper, or even a student helper. Teachers and students can keep in touch during the day through e-mail. Don't laugh; e-mail communication may cut down on interruptions from students when the teacher is working with a small group or with a single student. Teachers often have students

377

What Should Every
Teacher Know about
Integrating Technology
into Teaching?

There is a variety of
ePortfolio programs
available for organiz-
ing, assessing, and
presenting student
work.

with burning questions ask them of other students in the classroom before they ask the teacher. Putting the question on e-mail would be one additional step in thinking through the question and perhaps coming up with an answer before requiring the teacher's assistance.

Teachers have to keep track of books, supplies, borrowed resources, and schedules. Amazingly, teachers have the capacity to keep all of that information stored in a special part of the brain teachers have for miscellaneous information. Even though teachers can come up with all the right answers at the right times, it would be comforting to know that the information was stored somewhere else and that it could be accessed by other people without the teacher having to stop what they were doing or thinking about how to find a specific piece of information within their hugely cognitive framework. Computer programs provide great storage places for docuemnts and information—and, when they are connected to a printer, a clean copy of any document can be produced even if the first one had someone's lunch spilled on it.

Revisiting Jesus's Plans to Make His Dream a Reality

Jesus plans to make his dream a reality. He has considered following Bill Gates's model for creating a technology-rich environment. After taking a virtual tour of Gates's home in Seattle, Washington, at www.usnews.com/gates, Jesus knows he must create spaces that are rich in sound and visual experiences. He begins to organize his room around the few technology tools that he does have. He uses a laptop to run a screensaver showing exotic fish in one corner of his classroom. He finds a famous manuscript online and runs this program in the reading corner. He occasionally calms his class with soft music played on his SIRIUS satellite radio. He has a camera available for students to take pictures of meaningful moments. There are areas in his room for play, for meetings, and areas for contemplation. With a little imagination and help from technology, Jesus creates a productive learning space for all of the students.

How Has Technology Changed Approaches to Teaching and Learning?

As **Anton** looks over the state goals and objectives for the advanced placement (AP) junior and senior courses in English he teaches at Yates High, he makes notes of the works of playwrights and poets his students will be expected to read. He also checks the annual school calendar to block out periods of time for the units he hopes to cover. The assignments the students in his classes have to complete are often in direct competition with football and basketball seasons. Anton knows that feelings about sports run high where he teaches and he must prepare motivating lessons to draw his students into the subject and acquire the knowledge they will need when they attend college.

Fortunately Yates High is part of a Federal Title II D Technology grant with a local university and the students and faculty at Yates enjoy an environment rich with technology. So, Anton quite naturally uses technology to find ways to increase the learning potential for his students. He downloads scenes from Shakespeare that involve physical interactions, he chooses a scene from Chekhov's Cherry Orchard that he hopes will make his students laugh, and he downloads a clip from Death of a Salesman in which Dustin Hoffman's small-man version of Willie Loman explains to his football-playing son how to take life by the throat and make good things happen.

He also considers a clip of the fight scene at the beginning of The Invisible Man. Anton is an excellent teacher. He loves his subject and he knows how to use sounds and images to bring the power of different genres of literature to his students and to excite and familiarize them with the ways literature displays the human soul. His laptop, the Internet, and student access to technology make implementing his plans a breeze and teaching electrifying.

Some people can remember the first time they saw a television set, some can remember the first time they saw a computer, a remote control, a calculator, a cell phone (or better yet, a cell phone with a camera), a blue tooth, a digital camera, an iPod, a handheld computer, a video game system, or computerized navigation systems. What type of technology will your students remember seeing for the first time?

A major challenge in teaching is that what a teacher learned in order to be able to be successful in the world and the way the teacher learned it may be quite different from how their students will learn and what their students will need to

Ed Lines

"Just having technology in the classroom will not necessarily promote learning. It is what the teacher does with the technology that counts." *Richard Clark & Gabriel Salomon*

Teachers' Lounge

Mixed Signals

A few years ago, when I first started teaching an ESL class of students, I learned quickly that subtle gestures sometimes have completely different meanings across cultures. At the end of one day early in the year, I waved good-bye to Addis, one of my new students, as she was getting ready to board her school bus. Addis whirled around and ran toward me as her bus drove away. She noticed how confused I looked; I couldn't figure out why she decided to miss her bus and instead come running to me. What I didn't realize at the time—and what Addis was unable to articulate in English—was that in Ethiopia, the gesture that Americans use to wave good-bye means "come here."

● Paul Dragin
East High School
Columbus, Ohio

know to be successful. Teachers are constantly in the mode of retooling, learning new programs, and adjusting to and adopting new methods of delivering content. The requirement of teachers to learn new things certainly applies to technology. Learning new technology should be as much a part of a teacher's life as learning the behavioral and learning styles of a new group of students. Nearly everyone born after 1950 knows how to use a computer for some purpose. The challenge for beginning teachers is to know how to use technology to help someone learn.

When you begin teaching, your students will come from a generation of learners for whom technology and the Internet are as commonplace as Starbucks. They have been "surfing the Web" and downloading music, videos, and using PlayStations maybe even before they attend school for the first time. Your students will have high expectations for visually stimulating interactive learning. How you satisfy that expectation will depend to a large extent on your own abilities in using technology. Teachers have to meet this challenge head on by integrating the technology students are familiar and comfortable with into lessons and the classroom environment.

A teacher's comfort level using technology may not always match the students' ability to use the same technology. Many teachers are trying to close that gap. Unfortunately, some have given up. Your potential for being on the same technological page as your students is excellent. You represent a generation of teachers for whom many forms of technology have always been an integral part of your life and learning. Driving along the information highway is something you do on a daily basis. That may not necessarily make integrating technology into your

"The immediate feedback you get from computer programs is something you don't get from many other things." *Bill Gates*

The Internet provides a worldwide, decentralized association of net-worked computers using a common working protocol. What that means to most of us is a world of information at our fingertips.

teaching easier, but you enjoy the benefit of having a greater range of knowledge of technology than teachers from earlier generations.

The Information Highway

Technology is the infrastructure of the digital information age. It has drawn people from the youngest PlayStation addict to the most experienced graphic artist into a high-speed, often psychedelic environment of digital images designed to instruct, entertain, and con. The Internet and the World Wide Web (WWW) are intricately linked. The Internet represents a worldwide decentralized association of networked computers using a common working protocol. The WWW provides a way of creating a geographically distributed pool of information by marrying technological **hypermedia**, hypertext that can include graphics, video, and sound, for **nonlinear access** to multimedia information. From Wikipedia, "The World Wide Web (WWW, W3, or simply Web) is an information space in which the items of interest, referred to as resources, are identified by global identifiers called Uniform Resource Identifiers (URLs). The term is often mistakenly used as a synonym for the Internet but the Web is actually a service that operates over the Internet." It is a **hypertext** information-retrieval system that represents an entirely new form of mass communication that has emerged largely from the users themselves in a spontaneous outgrowth of information (Burstein & Kline, 1995). What that means to most of us is that we can access information anywhere and at any time.

> ▶ **Hypermedia.** Hypertext that includes graphics, video, and sound.

> ▶ **Nonlinear access.** Access to the Internet is not through a straight line; it is weblike.

> ▶ **Hypertext.** A database format in which information related to that on a display can be accessed directly from the display.

Free Rides and Tolls

Search Engines   Wow, what a switch from having to check out 50 pounds of books for a report or presentation. For the most part, search engines are free, they are fast, and, in the right hands, foolproof. Search engines are Web based and can be accessed from any place the user has Internet access. Search engines such as www.google.com, www.yahoo.com, www.msn.com, or ask.com have become as much a boon to learning as librarians and books. Like knowledgeable librarians, search engines provide users with advanced links that display a menu of choices to aid in the quest for information. Sometimes surfers pay a small fee for search engine access that offer help with creating categories and refining searches. Copernicus is one such search engine.

Web Browsers   Web browser–based applications such as an approach dubbed "Ajax" may be of particular interest for language-learning professionals. The open-source Firefox Web browser from Mozilla is attracting much interest with claims to allow users to browse faster, more safely, and more efficiently than with any other browser. Google, AOL, Internet Explorer, Safari, and Opera are other popular Web browsers. Ask.com is rapidly becoming a favorite with technophiles.

Websites   Teachers have a wealth of entertaining resources at their fingertips through websites. Some are free; some are not. Once you start to visit different sites, you'll become a regular, looking for new interactive content and resources. You have probably been directed to conduct a Web quest in one of your college classes. If you haven't been on a Web quest before, now is a good time to get started. First explore a topic that interests you and then one that might interest students from a range of grade levels. Refer to Table 10.1 for a list of websites and topics to explore.

Two outstanding features of the Internet are that it is constantly growing and changing with some new surprise around the next click, and that your travel itinerary is determined by your own personal sense of delight. Remember that links get old just like everything else and they can die, so check out websites before you send students to them. Teacher enthusiasm, knowledge, and preparedness are qualities of effective teaching. They are no less important in implementing the use of technology.

Learning My Way on My Time

Does the opportunity to access information 24 hours a day improve student learning? Of course, it depends. Accessing information and learning from the

Table 10.1 Starting Your Own Web Quest

Duke University Library	http://library.duke.edu/	Tour exhibit of early newspaper comic strips (1899–1916)
Kidsmart Guide to Early Learning and Technology	www.kidsmartearlylearning.org	Find out how to make computers a regular part of any childhood program
Froguts	www.froguts.com	A virtual dissection service—science with no smell
National Library of Virtual Manipulatives	http://nlvm.usu.edu/en/nav/vlibrary.html	K–12 emphasis in mathematics instruction
Try Science	www.tryscience.org	Contemporary science and technology through on- and offline interactivity with science and technology centers worldwide
National Geographic	www.nationalgeographic.com/education/	Find ways to help students learn more about geography

information are not always inevitable. The core skills students need today are not just to locate data, but to filter a plethora of information that results in a pattern of knowledge (Dede, 1997). Without an expert teacher's guidance, learners may be confounded by the morass of unstructured data. Students who are not capable of finding a synonym in a thesaurus are certainly not going to achieve wisdom on the WWW. The skills students must acquire to use information on the Internet for their own learning are, in fact, the same skills teachers should know how to use and teach students to use.

Teachers must prepare students to learn on their own both during school years and after graduation. Because individuals engaged in lifelong learning will be best positioned to survive cultural, technological, and thought transitions and to actively and intelligently interact in a global arena, teachers must become facilitators and guides in technology's learner-centered classrooms. They must use technology to show students what can be learned from the past, to understand current information, and to adapt presently acquired knowledge to tomorrow's ideas. Teachers need to help their students understand the **BEAR** fundamentals of self-directed learning.

Base intelligent decisions on accurate and comprehensive information.

Evaluate information critically.

Access reliable information.

Recognize inaccurate and misleading information.

When teachers use successful strategies for locating reliable information sources, they can help their students do the same. Kathy Schrock at http://discoveryschool.com/schrockguide/eval.html has designed a series of evaluation surveys to help students learn to critically evaluate a Web page for authenticity, applicability, authorship, bias, and usability. Visit the Discovery School website and check out one of Kathy Schrock's surveys.

Virtual and Online Learning Opportunities   Technology is making it possible for students at all levels to be able to go to school without ever leaving home. No more waiting for the bus. No traffic jams to blame for tardiness. No more stress over bad hair or what to wear. For some online students, it's roll out of bed and turn on the computer. For example, U.S. education is experiencing a fast growing trend in high school online education. Education World's website, www. educationworld.com, offers a detailed look at four virtual high schools: The Electronic High School, Utah, The Virtual High School, Concord Consortium; The Florida High School; and The Virtual High School, Ontario, Canada. Suggestions for making a virtual high school successful for administrators, teachers, and students include leaving the heavy technology task of maintaining servers to another company, carrying out continuous evaluations of programs and progress, offering interactive courses that are easy for both instructors and students to negotiate, and

Ed Lines

The U.S. Department of Education reported that in 2003 90 percent of public 4-year institutions offered Internet courses.

Understanding & USING EVIDENCE

THINKING ABOUT THE IMPACT OF INCREASED COMPUTER USE IN CLASSROOMS

The December/January issue of *Educational Leadership* was devoted to an examination of learning in the digital age. Numerous statistic sources cited in this issue provide evidence of the increase of student access to and use of computers in classrooms. According to Monke (2005/2006) the National Center for Education Statistics offered the following percentages of U.S. students who used computers in school in 2003:

- 97% of high school students
- 95% of middle school students
- 91% of students in grades 1–5
- 80% of kindergarten students
- 67% of nursery school students

In this same issue of *Educational Leadership*, the South Central Regional Technology in Education Consortium reported frequency of classroom technology use by percentage.

Electronic presentation	81%
Word processing	68%
Internet	50%
Publishing	40%
Web editors	36%
Spreadsheets	6%
Databases	<1%
E-mail	<1%

The data are based on observations and teacher self-reports in 10 low-income middle and high schools (Burns, 2005/2006).

Information in Burns (2005/2006) indicates that in 2005, schools spent an average of $103 per pupil for educational technology. Richardson (2005/2006) reports from eSchool News that fifty-one teachers surveyed say that the ideal ratio of students to computers is one to one, but only 10 percent say that their schools have a one-to-one ratio of computers to students.

Your Task: So what's happening here? Are today's schools well equipped to educate students for success in the digital age? Do you see any problems that might be lurking in the data? Is the focus on computer use in schools the direction educators should be headed as they prepare students for the future?

Refer to the **Understanding & Using Evidence Appendix** *at the end of the text for answers and information related to these activities.*

Sources: Educational Leadership: *Learning in the digital age.* Vol. 63, No. 4. Alexandria, VA: Association for Supervision and Curriculum Development; Monke, L. W. (2005/2006). The overdominance of computers. *Educational Leadership, 63*(4), 20–23; Burns, M. (2005/2006). Tools for the mind. *Educational Leadership, 63*(4), 48–53; Richardson, W. (2005/2006). The educator's guide to the read/write web. *Educational Leadership, 63*(4), 24–27.

Progress Portfolio at www.progressportfolio.northwestern.edu. Technology will help you quickly find many ways to enhance student achievement. The HP New Education Center, a mobile classroom by Hewlett Packard, is a computer-assisted education system that connects a teacher and up to 20 students to the Internet, a projector, and a laser printer. Imagine the possibilities.

At the surprising young age of less than 50 years, computers and the Internet have begun to revolutionize education mainly because of their interactive capabilities. Even more surprising might be the advent of the WWW/HTML in 1993. The Internet, although in existence since the 1970s, really had very limited value before Tim Berners-Lee developed the HTML model and Mosaic, later to become Netscape, and disseminated the first graphical browser. Thus, for all practical purposes, a truly usable Internet is only slightly more than 10 years old.

Revisiting Anton's Integration of Technology and Teaching

Anton understands the ways in which technology has changed the teaching and learning landscape. He has never been afraid to attempt a new approach to his teaching. In fact, he doesn't want to be one of those teachers who teaches the same way for 30 years and then retires. When Yates High School became part of a large technology project, Anton attended the workshops provided by the district and learned to take advantage of the help desk support for the software and tools he was learning to use. He recognizes that technology has the power to transform teaching and when it does, he wants to be in the forward guard, not struggling to keep up. Because he was eager to incorporate technology into his classroom, he was immediately viewed by many of the other teachers at his school as an exemplar of ways learning could be improved through the use of technology tools.

Why Can It Be Difficult to Integrate Technology into Teaching?

Randy fears change. Nothing is like it was when he began teaching 20 years ago. Although he understands that progress is a natural human phenomenon, he is concerned about some of the changes taking place in his profession. Randy understands the need to cite standards in his lesson plans and make sure the assessments in his lessons are tied to the instructional goals. After all, he is a professional. However, yesterday there was a sign in the teachers' lounge that said "Integrate Technology or Die" and he thought for the first time in his career that it might just be time for him to look for another job. Randy loves books. His home is full of hardbound copies of books on every subject. Randy owns a computer, and his family is connected to the Internet through a local cable company, but he only uses the computer for word processing, writing lesson plans, the annual Christmas letter, and

Ed Lines

Learning to teach is a never-ending journey. Even when you think you've arrived, there's always another website to explore.

387

Why Can It Be Difficult
to Integrate
Technology into
Teaching?

answering e-mails. He has accessed the Abebooks website looking for a particular out-of-print book but he has never really considered the ways technology might be used for instruction. At the last faculty meeting, it was made quite clear that one of the requirements of satisfactory teaching at his school was that teachers would integrate technology into their teaching. Randy's technology anxiety is at an all-time high. So Randy talks to Ken, a second-year teacher. Ken is passionate about what technology brings to teaching and Randy asks if he can visit Ken's classroom during his planning period. Ken is actually excited to have Randy's company, and so begins a professional friendship carved out of necessity, interest, technology, and kindness.

By this time, you should be well aware that teaching requires no small amount of knowledge and skill. Integrating technology in teaching certainly demands time and effort beyond what has formerly been expected of teachers. Each new generation of teachers, since the first American public schools were established, has had to adapt in some way to meet new and unexpected demands on their practice. This will be no less true for you. Teachers who lack necessary technological skill, have received little or no training, or have limited support are bound to be anxious about integrating technology in their instruction.

Time for Technology

Learning to integrate technology in teaching can place a considerable strain on a teacher's established organization of time. Visit any school and talk to any group of teachers and you are likely to hear that they haven't enough time; time to teach the approved curriculum, to talk with one another, to plan together, and to learn the new skills necessary to their success as teachers—and all the while they must spend more and more time assessing student achievement. Integrating technology in teaching can certainly create an additional challenge to a teacher's use of time. As a result, teachers' views on the use of technology can be less than positive. Learning new programs or checking out websites for their appropriateness to the curriculum and for the students requires a large investment of time—time taken away from tasks that may be considered more pressing. The introduction of technology into classrooms also presents a challenge to administrators to arrange time for teachers to learn. Teachers should look for payoffs in time invested. While it may take a significant amount of time to learn a school's grading program, the payoff in saved time come report card time could be substantial.

Software Programs   Sometimes it seems like there are just too many different computer software programs available for each teacher to learn each new one that is adopted by a school or district. When there is a technology specialist on the staff, they can help teachers incorporate programs into lessons. Teachers are more likely to use technology when it is user friendly and intuitive and when the design of the software proves useful to the teacher's instructional purpose. When students see teachers use a range of technology tools, they are encouraged to try them. It doesn't always work the other way around. Teachers need more support and encouragement than students to try something new. It doesn't always seem that way, but it's true. Companies that vie for consumer markets through fancy bells and whistles found only on their software might be wise to focus on commonalities across programs. Consumers would like this. All programs would have similar features and would be easy to use.

Time for Training

Change in practice precedes change in beliefs. A teacher is not going to integrate technology into their teaching if they don't know how to do it and if they don't believe that the benefits gained from using technology will outweigh the effort to learn how to use it effectively. To counter teachers' questioning of the value of integrating technology in instruction, a well-organized structure for training and support must exist. Teacher education programs have been redesigned to prepare candidates to incorporate technology in teaching. What happens all too often, though, is that once in the classroom, even a freshly and adequately trained new teacher, faced with moving against the established norms and traditional ways of conducting business found in every school setting, suffers setbacks.

There is little time left over from the business of teaching for teachers to engage in training. Some districts provide training during summer break with financial incentives and technology products for use during the school year. Teachers also need support during actual teaching time in the form of an expert coach. Having students be adroit with technology has little or no effect on a teacher's practice. The teacher must become highly capable in using technology in order to integrate it in instruction. The individual must be totally engaged with the tool to make it work for them.

When you take your first teaching job, you should be well prepared to integrate technology into your classroom. You may even be considered an expert by the more seasoned teachers in the school. They will look to you for example and guidance. Consider that making inroads into established norms cannot be achieved without support from colleagues and backing from the central administration. We mentioned earlier that integrating technology in instruction is a team sport. Certainly that applies to teachers working together to support one another in the use of technology. Don't be afraid to assume a leadership role in helping your colleagues use technology. Remember, you are a child of the digital age.

Observing teachers' use of technology can help you become more knowledgeable in this area. Consider how other teachers address the major points outlined in the Connecting to the Classroom.

Revisiting Randy's Efforts to Integrate Technology into Teaching

Even though Randy, the teacher at the beginning of this section, may not be of the "digital" generation, he believes in lifelong learning and is going to do his best to develop new skills in the use of technology. Randy is experienced. He knows

389

How Can Teachers
Integrate Technology
into Their Own
Professional
Development?

Connecting

— TO THE CLASSROOM —

Using technology in teaching is not necessarily a new idea. What is novel to many teachers though is making a transition from telling, explaining, and demonstrating to helping students find information on their own from a worldwide resource pool, and then assisting the students in explaining and demonstrating what they have learned. This requires a huge shift in defining one's purpose as a teacher in a classroom of the twenty-first century. For some it is a slow, often painful process. Here are three major points to think about when establishing your own personal-professional philosophy of becoming an effective teacher in the information age.

1. Learn to ask divergent questions that will encourage students to consider possibilities rather than pat answers.

2. Listen to the questions that students ask and extend those questions rather than provide answers.

3. Teach as though tomorrow is a mystery and the students are as much a part of solving the mystery as you are. Be like Watson and Sherlock Holmes. Search for clues and rely on one another.

that success requires effort and he is determined to make whatever efforts he does expend to integrate technology into his teaching pay off. So, he is putting in the time to learn. Ken helped him learn an assessment program for monitoring student progress and as Randy becomes more proficient, his confidence grows. Randy was also able to purchase a digital camera with school funds and is working with his students to create a pictorial history of their school. It has been a pleasant surprise for Randy to discover that he is no technophobe after all.

How Can Teachers Integrate Technology into Their Own Professional Development?

Tiffany *has just started her second year of teaching. Another teacher at her school is working toward national board certification and Tiffany is interested in following the same path. Tiffany's colleague directed her to the National Board for Professional Teacher Standards website at www.NBPTS.org to learn more about the organization and the process she will have to complete to achieve her goal. At the website, she discovers that there are low-interest loans available to help defray the expense of the fees associated with certification. There is also an application form she can complete when she is ready to enroll. After perusing the website, she has a better idea of what will be expected of her once she starts the journey toward national board certification. She is a bit overwhelmed at the prospect of following the NBPTS guidelines, but she has ready access to the website and she can refer to it when she feels it is time for her to begin. In the meantime, she wants to begin by building a web-based professional portfolio where she can keep a record of her accomplishments during her first 3 years of teaching.*

It is not uncommon for first-year teachers to spend most of their efforts managing the day-to-day duties of teaching. Ideas for professional development or keeping a record of professional accomplishments take a back seat to learning curriculum standards and helping students raise their achievement to meet district and state criteria. Dave, the teacher at King Kamehameha III Elementary School introduced at the beginning of this chapter, is so overwhelmed by the press of responsibilities of a first-year teacher that he has not yet taken the time to create a professional development portfolio. If you are in the process of constructing a professional portfolio, you already have a start toward using technology for your own professional development. Your next steps should be directed toward meeting specific criteria for teacher performance.

Educational Technology Standards for Teachers

According to the ISTE National Educational Technology Standards for Teachers (NETS*T) website:

> The NETS*T focus on preservice teacher education and define the fundamental concepts, knowledge, skills, and attitudes for applying technology in educational settings. All candidates seeking certification or endorsements in teacher preparation should meet these educational technology standards. (www.iste .org/inhouse/nets/cnets/teachers/t_stands.html)

The instructors at your institution are responsible for making sure that you have had the opportunity to meet the six NETS*T standards. Figure 10.1 lists NETS*T six standards' areas with performance indicators. The standards are specific enough to define the broad goals of using technology in educational settings, yet general enough to allow for a comfortable fit with local circumstances.

Visit the NETS for Teachers website at http://cnets.iste.org/teachers/t_stands. html to learn more about the performance indicators for teachers. These performance indicators will give you a better understanding of what will be expected of you once you begin teaching.

Twenty-First Century Skills   The North Central Regional Educational Laboratory has identified specific skills needed by citizens in the digital age. See Figure 10.2 and visit www.ncrel.org/engauge/skills/skill21.htm. Teachers in the twenty-first century should possess these skills and be able to document the ways in which the skills are translated into professional practice. Comparing your behaviors to those expected of citizens in the digital age will provide a useful framework in developing a professional portfolio and in choosing avenues for professional development. Staying current with trends and issues in education is a full-time endeavor. Staying ahead of current issues and trends is nothing short of miraculous. However, when teachers engage in the pursuit of genuine questions, problems,

Figure 10.1 Educational technology standards and performance indicators for all teachers

1. Technology Operations and Concepts

   Teachers demonstrate a sound understanding of technology operations and concepts. Teachers:

   - Demonstrate introductory knowledge, skills, and understanding of concepts related to technology (as described in the ISTE National Educational Technology Standards for Students).
   - Demonstrate continual growth in technology knowledge and skill to stay abreast of current and emerging technologies.

2. Planning and Designing Learning Environments and Experiences

   Teachers plan and design effective learning environments and experiences supported by technology. Teachers:

   - Design developmentally appropriate learning opportunities that apply technology-enhanced instructional strategies to support the diverse needs of learners.
   - Apply current research on teaching and learning with technology when planning learning environments and experiences.
   - Identify and locate technology resources and evaluate them for accuracy and suitability.
   - Plan for the management of technology resources within the context of learning activities. plan strategies to manage student learning in a technology-enhanced environment.

3. Teaching, Learning, and the Curriculum

   Teachers implement curriculum plans that include methods and strategies for applying technology to maximize student learning. Teachers:

   - Facilitate technology-enhanced experiences that address content standards and student technology standards.
   - Use technology to support learner-centered strategies that address the diverse need of students.
   - Apply technology to develop students' higher order skills and creativity.
   - Manage student learning activities in a technology-enhanced environment.

4. Assessment and Evaluation

   Teachers apply technology to facilitate a variety of effective assessment and evaluation strategies. Teachers:

   - Apply technology in assessing student learning of subject matter using a variety of assessment techniques.
   - Use technology resources to collect and analyze data, interpret results, communicate finding to improve instructional practice, and maximize student learning.
   - Apply multiple methods of evaluation to determine students' appropriate use of technology resources for learning, communication, and productivity.

5. Productivity and Professional Practice

   Teachers use technology to enhance their productivity and professional practice. Teachers:

   - Use technology resources to engage in ongoing professional development and lifelong learning.
   - Continually evaluate and reflect on professional practice to make informed decisions regarding the use of technology in support of student learning.
   - Apply technology to increase productivity.
   - Use technology to communicate and collaborate with peers, parents, and the larger community in order to nurture student learning.

6. Social, Ethical, Legal, and Human Issues

   Teachers understand the social, ethical, legal, and human issues surrounding the use of technology in preK–12 schools and apply that understanding in practice. Teachers:

   - Model and teach legal and ethical practice related to technology use.
   - Apply technology resources to enable and empower learners with diverse backgrounds, characteristics, and abilities.
   - Identify and use technology resources that affirm diversity.
   - Promote safe and healthy use of technology resources.
   - Facilitate equitable access to technology resources for all students.

Source: Reprinted with permission from *National Educational Technology Standards: Preparing Teachers to Use Technology.* © 2002, ISTE® (International Society for Technology in Education), iste@iste.org, www.iste.org. All rights reserved.

Figure 10.2 The enGauge twenty-first century skills

Digital-Age Literacy

- Basic, scientific, economic, and technological literacies
- Visual and information literacies
- Multicultural literacy and global awareness

Inventive Thinking

- Adaptability and managing complexity
- Self-direction
- Curiosity, creativity, and risk taking
- Higher-order thinking and sound reasoning

Effective Communication

- Teaming, collaboration, and interpersonal skills
- Personal, social, and civic responsibility
- Interactive communication

High Productivity

- Prioritizing, planning, and managing for results
- Effective use of real-world tools
- Ability to produce relevant, high-quality products

Source: Learning Point Associates www.ncrel.org/engauge/skills/skill21.html. Reprinted with permission.

and curiosities through reflection and discussions with colleagues, they are capable of creating their own futures.

Using the Internet for Professional Development

You know that everyone learns at a different pace and through different stimuli. Your development as a teacher will also take its own path and move forward at a pace that you choose and with which you are comfortable. The online learning opportunities for professional development will allow you to choose when and what you learn. When you do choose an online learning environment, Sandra Levin and associates (2001) suggest you look for (1) relevant and challenging assignments, (2) coordinated learning environments, (3) adequate and timely feedback from instructors, (4) rich environments for student-to-student interaction, and (5) flexibility in teaching and learning. It's no surprise that these are the same characteristics you should strive for in any lesson you plan to teach.

Most education websites contain professional development links. The professional development link on the Education World website at www.educationworld.com/ is a rich source of opportunities to manage your own professional development. Many school districts also offer online professional development sites to aid teachers in learning new skills and improving the ones they already possess. One example of an online professional development site is the "lifelong learning" website of Jefferson County Public Schools. As you get closer to the end of your teacher education coursework, check out the website of the school districts you intend to apply to and see what offerings are available for professional development.

Using Technology for Self-Improvement Everyone has a blind spot—even teachers! There is something they don't see about themselves, something in their manner of teaching that they are not aware of, content that they do not properly or adequately present, and comments that they make that are unnecessarily harsh. Who will point out your flaws? Someone not afraid to tell you the truth might be hard to find. Technology is your answer. The hard truth of a videotape viewed in solitude can help you see the changes you need to make, the habits you need to break, and the outstanding acts you need to repeat. Watching yourself teach can be a startling and educative experience—but you won't be able to do it without the use of technology.

Revisiting Tiffany: Technology and Professional Growth

In her quest for national board certification, Tiffany, the teacher at the beginning of this section, will have to do more than just videotape herself teaching. She will have to critique the videotapes with a critical eye explaining every minute detail of her lesson presentation, interaction with students, and assessment of student learning. The national board considers such activity the sign of an expert teacher. Every child deserves an excellent teacher. If you already are using technology to improve your teaching practices, keep it up. If you aren't, get started. Technology can transform teaching and learning, but you have to use it before it can.

Chapter Summary

Integrating technology into teaching requires knowledge and skill. It also requires that teachers who wish to integrate technology into teaching possess a curiosity about new ways of doing things and a willingness to learn how to do something they haven't done before. Teachers may find success and joy in the amazing technology tools available to them.

What should every teacher know about integrating technology into teaching? In order for technology to be integrated into instruction, the teacher must grasp the meaning of it and how it can be purposefully applied. As John Dewey put it, "To grasp the meaning of a thing, an event, or situation is to see it in its relations to other things; to note how it operates or functions; what consequences follow from it; what causes it, what uses it can be put to" (Dewey, 1910). John Dewey described the process of learning with understanding as a process in which the individual develops a well-

differentiated, elaborated mental representation of the topic. Teachers develop an elaborate mental picture of technology by using it in a number of ways. Each new tool that is used to augment instruction becomes a meaningful extension of what a teacher knows and does. Without the tool, the teacher is unable to discover the meaningful uses it can be put to. Teachers should use technology (1) to enhance instruction in the classroom and beyond, (2) for presentations, (3) to encourage student use of technology, (4) for managing student achievement, and (5) for their own professional development.

How has technology changed approaches to teaching and learning? The introduction of any content can begin dramatically with pictures, music, video, or an Internet presentation. A social studies unit in anthropology on the peoples of the Tigris Euphrates cradle of civilization can begin with a Web quest to set up a data retrieval chart à la Hilda Taba. Technology can motivate and excite students to become interested in something they may not have considered before. Moving images draw attention and watching a snake shed its skin or a cactus blossom can generate curiosity. Technology provides opportunities for teachers and students to collaborate on problems with people beyond the normal reach of a single classroom or school. In addition to the Internet, fiber and coaxial networks form fast, wide-bandwidth connections that make possible networks of knowledge and information relevant to state and district standards and goals. Students can use technology to practice a skill on their own and receive reinforcement on their progress via the technology. Technology can assist teachers and students in reviews of content and also when summarizing lessons learned. Once you incorporate technology into your teaching and learning, you'll wonder how anyone ever taught without it.

Why can it be difficult to integrate technology in teaching? Learning anything new takes time, effort, and motivation. Teachers represent a range of interests and abilities not unlike those they encounter among their own students. Implementing the optimum training strategy at the precise moment in time when it will have the most effect on teacher learning is an elusive prospect. Even when new teachers with highly developed skill in using technology join existing teaching faculties, they are often overwhelmed by the status quo and are likely to adopt the practice of the more experienced teach-

ers than to use what they have learned in their teacher education programs.

All schools do not have access to the latest technology. Teachers become frustrated when they plan to integrate technology in a lesson only to discover that the equipment is faulty or not available. Schools may not be able to provide the necessary training or support for teachers to effectively integrate technology into their teaching. Teachers have a limited number of minutes in a school day to help students meet required standards and when time for teaching is lessened, teachers are not happy.

How can teachers integrate technology into their own professional development? Teachers spend their lives helping other people's children become educated. Teaching is a sacrifice. Sacrifice is heroic; it is noble. Millions of teachers every day are engaged in heroic and noble acts. They do not spend a great deal of time thinking about how they can grow professionally because they are more concerned with helping someone else learn and grow. Many teachers feel isolated within the four walls of a classroom and prevented from continuing their own learning. Technology gives teachers the power to communicate with educators across that nation and the world to inform their practice and encourage their professional development. Technology makes it possible for teachers to attend workshops and classes at times convenient to their hectic schedules. Technology provides teachers an array of learning opportunities around their specific interests and needs, making learning relevant and useful.

Class Discussion Questions

1. Is it possible that anyone beginning a teaching career in the twenty-first century would not have some skills in using technology? Why would this be possible? Why not?

2. In what ways might a beginning teacher help create technology-rich learning environments in a school setting where there is little use of technology?

3. How can students support teacher integration of technology in instruction?

4. What are some ways students could help make technology an integral part of every student's learning in the classroom?

5. Why should every teacher commit to using technology for their own professional development from their first day as a new teacher?

Field Guide for School Observations

Classrooms usually contain a variety of technology for teacher use. Make a list of the technology tools in two classrooms. Remember to include all types of technology (e.g., listening station, tape recorder, TV, metronome, overhead projector, computer, record player). Indicate whether the technology is being used by the teacher, the students, or by no one. After comparing your two lists, make an inference about each teacher's comfort level with technology. What conditions that you observed in the classrooms might either facilitate or inhibit the use of technology?

Ask a Teacher

Teachers have different learning styles and preferences just as their students do. Ask a teacher what technology they use on a regular basis and why. Ask her or him when they were introduced to the technology and to explain how they learned it. Do teachers at the school where they teach share their expertise in the use of technology?

Journaling Becoming a Thoughtful Teacher

Refer to the "Using the Web" feature for this chapter. Write a short journal entry on how viewing the ways other teachers integrate technology into their teaching might give you ideas for integrating technology into your own future lessons.

Portfolio Tasks

Take three pictures of a child or young person engaged in some activity. This could be your own child or the child of a friend. Remember to get their permission and tell them what your intentions are. Show the pictures to the individual and ask them to tell you what they are doing or thinking. Develop a PowerPoint presentation of the pictures with excerpts from the person's comments. Summarize the PowerPoint by reflecting on what the pictures may have helped the person notice about their actions and thoughts and what you learned about the person through the process. Comment on the ways this reflection provides evidence of your understanding of the Interstate New Teachers Assessment and Support Consortium (INTASC) Principles 3 and 4 introduced in Chapter 1 of this text.

Self-Assessment *What Am I Learning?*

Check Your Technology Skills

Complete the following survey. Rate yourself on a Likert Scale from 1 to 5, with a score of 1 indicating a high level of disagreement and a score of 5 indicating a high level of agreement. A score of 28 would indicate you are well on the way to being a technology-savvy teacher. A score of less than 18 would indicate you have some work ahead.

1. I feel confident in using a wide range of technologies.
2. I am not the least bit apprehensive about using technology in teaching.
3. I believe that using technology in teaching can help students have learning experiences beyond the classroom walls.
4. I am willing to explore and use new technologies for learning.
5. There are many advantages to integrating technology into teaching.
6. Teachers should take risks and attempt to incorporate technology in teaching even before they are entirely competent with the technology themselves.

Using the Web

The website www.netc.org/classrooms@work, maintained by the Northwest Educational Technology Consortium, provides four examples of ways teachers have successfully integrated technology into teaching. The examples range from applications in 1st grade to a 9th grade research-and-analysis project. Visit this website. Review the ways these four teachers have integrated technology into their teaching. Note any of the common uses of technology across the grade levels.

Your Professional Library

Lessig, Lawrence. (2001). *The future of ideas: The fate of the commons in a connected world*. New York: Random House.

This book proves a provocative look at the impact connectivity through the Internet will have on society, learning, and creativity. This interesting text covers a range of topics related to control of intellectual property.

To access chapter objectives, practice tests, weblinks, and flashcards, visit the Companion Website at **www.ablongman.com/hall1e**

Go to Allyn & Bacon's MyLabSchool (**www .mylabschool.com**). Enter Assignment ID **CMV2** in the **Assignment Finder**. View the video clip, *Technology*. Then consider what you have seen along with what you've read in Chapter 10 to answer the following questions.

1. Does the content of the video clip confirm the ideas expressed in Chapter 10? In what ways? Provide an example.

2. Integrating technology into teaching can provide students a rich resource for learning, but according to the information in the video clip, should technology necessarily be a component of every lesson?

Read question #4 at the end of the *Technology* video clip and answer part B of that question.

In your opinion, will the role of technology in teaching ever be more important than the teacher? Provide evidence for your opinion.

Assessing Student Learning and Results

Educators in Real Schools

M E E T

Dr. Elliott Asp

*Assistant Superintendent in the
Cherry Creek (Colorado) School District*

Dr. Asp has an unusual title: Assistant Superintendent for Performance Improvement. Usually assistant superintendents will be responsible for administration, curriculum and instruction, facilities, or finance. Dr. Asp's title reflects the high priority that his school district is placing on student learning. In fact, in his school district there are two Assistant Superintendents for Performance Improvement! He is in charge of curriculum, assessment, staff development, and instructional technology. The other assistant superintendent is in charge of supervision and evaluation of principals and teachers. Together these two leaders are responsible for leading the districtwide effort to assess and increase student performance.

Dr. Asp also is a nationally recognized expert in assessment of student learning. He has published many papers and is regularly sought after to assist school districts engaged in improving the assessment of student performance.

❖ *What do you expect when you are looking for excellence in teaching?*

I am looking for a teacher who is very well grounded in understanding learning goals and is clear about what is essential versus nice to know. I also am looking for somebody who has some understanding of how to create evidence of student learning. They understand the role of assessment in guiding instruction and serving as a model for teaching and for kids.

Chapter 11

❖ *How do you know that a teacher has made a difference in student learning?*

Certainly I would know by looking at the assessment data for each standard. There are a couple of other ways. One is that a teacher can talk about what students have learned and he or she can talk about a sample from 2 weeks ago and what has changed since then. I also could ask students. I would be very impressed if the students could say, well I started here and now I am here, and here's where I want to go from here.

❖ *How do you see joy in teaching?*

I see joy if the teacher is a learner along with the students. They are showing in authentic ways that learning is a lifetime process that they enjoy; for example, a teacher who shares his or her writing with students and allows them to give feedback. You also see joy when teachers and students develop a partnership around learning. It is you and the students together enjoying the excitement of watching them improve. There also is joy in watching students grow in their life and a relationship that is caring and respectful.

❖ *What do you expect a first-year teacher to know and be able to do?*

I want them to understand this generalized model of assessment. This doesn't mean that they can do all of it now, but that they understand the goal and expect themselves to improve over the next 3 or 4 years. I want them to know the components of quality instruction and that they are working to achieve a high level of performance. Our job is to provide them with experiences to help them get better, not to have to teach them the components of high-quality instruction.

✤ *In what ways have you seen teachers think differently as they have learned more about high-quality instruction and the importance of assessing student learning?*

Sometimes it pushes them into places they do not want to be. For example, they now know what their students can and cannot do, but they do not know what to do about it. It is a frustrating place that can lead to greater teacher learning. They start to have some "ah ha's" about the role of assessment in guiding their instructional practices. The clearer they are that the summative assessments are the evidence that students have learned what is really important, the more they will teach across time, rather than day to day.

✤ *What differences do you see in teaching and in student learning as a result of the assessment push?*

In this whole standards-based movement, there are some best hopes and worst fears. The worst fear is that we will have a very narrow and sterile curriculum. There are assessments that mimic the state tests and the focus is on improving test scores, rather than on improving student learning. In this situation, teachers see their whole job being to get students ready to take the state tests. Our best hopes are that we have a coherent instructional program. We are clear about the performance requirements in the outside measures and we know what they look like in everyday practice; my push is for students to really experience authentic learning and apply skills and knowledge in different settings. I know then that they will be able to demonstrate what they have learned in the summative setting. I have seen teachers become more in touch with the unique needs of students and that instruction is motivating and has a point. The job is for kids to learn, not for teachers to be assessing them all the time.

Questions to Consider

1. If you were being interviewed for a teaching position by Dr. Asp, what questions would you expect him to ask?

2. What do you think he means when he says he expects teachers to "understand the role of assessment in guiding instruction"?

3. How will you feel about his suggestion that as a teacher you should share with students what you are learning?

4. What do you think he means when he talked about authentic learning?

Today's teachers cannot escape hearing, talking, and reading about testing and assessing. Teachers are told that assessing is a key component of all lesson plans. School districts, state policy makers, and the federal government have mandated annual testing of students and licensing tests for teachers. Curriculum and instruction experts constantly talk about assessing student learning. Teacher educators, as well as school district administrators like Dr. Asp, are constantly pointing out that good instruction and high-quality teachers are continually assessing their students. Policy makers and the media focus intently on test results and use the scores to rank schools, school districts, and states.

So, what's all the fuss about? Teachers continually observe their students, evaluate their homework, give tests, and assign grades. Why is there so much interest in testing? Also, why do some people talk about "testing" and others seem to prefer the term "assessing"? Other important question for aspiring teacher candidates include: What are different methods for assessing student work?; how do I determine grades and prepare report cards? Some educators are beginning to ask another question: Doesn't it seem that too much time—and money—are going into testing? The topics in this chapter examine these questions and provide examples of different ways teachers can assess student learning.

Focus QUESTIONS

After reading this chapter, you should be able to answer the following questions:

1 What are the purposes and characteristics of good assessments?

2 What are different ways to test student learning?

3 How can test results be turned into an assessment?

4 What are keys to developing final grades and reporting annual progress?

5 How do the critical issues around testing relate to the classroom teacher?

Why Is Assessing So Important?

Allison Johnson was very excited about this day, the second Monday in August. Today she would attend her very first staff meeting as a teacher. Dr. Young, the principal, stressed how important it was for all teachers to be there and be ready to begin the new school year.

The morning topics included presentation of final class schedules, reviewing school rules, and filling out new health insurance forms; Dr. Young emphasized several times that the budget would be tight, "so be very careful about making unnecessary copies." Molly Schneider, an enthusiastic department chair, organized the social events for the year. Allison signed up for the Holiday Party Committee.

Things got confusing for Allison right after lunch. Dr. Young spent a long time talking about the state testing that would take place next April. This was not confusing, but what was confusing was all of the chatter between teachers and the principal that followed: "Will we be using the same CRTs as last year?" "What about the NRTs that the district had us doing in January?" "You know, that is the real problem, the CRTs are performance based, while the NRTs are multiple choice. No wonder our test scores are not improving."

NRTs? CRTs? Performance based? Allison had no idea what they were talking about!

▶ **Tests.** Structured opportunities to measure how much a test taker knows and can do.

▶ **Assessing.** The process of using testing and other evidence to plan a course of action.

▶ **Formative evaluation.** Using information in ways to improve a process or procedure.

▶ **Summative evaluation.** Using information to make a judgment about the merit or worth of an effort.

Allison's experience is regularly repeated across the United States. Teachers, administrators, policy makers, and parents talk a lot about testing and assessing, but it is not always clear that they are talking about the same things. There are very important differences to keep in mind. **Tests** are structured opportunities to measure how much the test taker knows and can do. The test conditions should be consistent for all test takers and there is an expectation that each individual will make a maximum effort. **Assessing** is the process that includes testing, determining the value of the test, interpreting test results, and developing a plan for what will be done next.

A metaphor to illustrate these two important concepts is how property tax rates are determined. Every 2 or 3 years, the value of your home, rental unit, or office building is reexamined. The potential sale price is estimated by comparing its value to like properties that had been sold recently. That price is similar to a student's score on a test. The tax assessor examines the property and its likely sale price and sets the amount of tax to be paid accordingly. Determining the final tax amount requires some interpretation and judgment. The tax bill is not a simple calculation, rather the assessor takes into consideration a number of factors such as condition, trends in the neighborhood, and the amount of taxes paid for like properties. A parallel process takes place in assessing student learning. The test score has little meaning until the assessor interprets it, compares the results to that obtained by students in similar and different situations, and takes into consideration the special needs of each student. The assessor then develops recommendations and plans for next steps for instruction.

An expert assessor also keeps in mind how the test results will be used. If the purpose is purely to provide feedback on student progress and to guide preparation of tomorrow's lessons, which is called **formative evaluation**, then there will be less concern about the rigor of the testing. When test results are used to make conclusions about how much a student has learned or to decide whether a student is ready to move to the next grade level, which is called **summative evaluation**, then the assessor must be much more careful in considering the adequacy of the test and the consequences of the final decision. Teachers make formative decisions about student learning continually within each lesson and throughout the day. They also make summative decisions when they assign report card grades and at the end of the school year recommend promotion—or not. In most states, the results of mandated testing are used to make summative judgments about high school graduation, the ranking of schools, and teacher licensure.

Within these two general ways of thinking about testing and assessing are a number of different purposes. For each purpose, the design of tests is different, but each must have an acceptable level of quality, given an understanding of how the results will be used. Also, the type of learning being assessed is associated with certain kinds of tests being more appropriate. An additional important consideration is taking into account the characteristics of the students being assessed. For example, there is an obvious mismatch when English language learners are given a mathematics word-problem test in English and their scores are treated the same as for those students whose native language is English.

Different Purposes for Assessing

Teachers need to keep in mind why they are assessing. Just because it is Friday does not necessarily mean that it is time for a test. There should be a clear understanding about the purpose of all assessment efforts. There are a number of reasons for assessing that will be of help to the teacher. Often forgotten is that there are a number of purposes for assessing that are of direct benefit to the students. Teachers need to think carefully about why they are assessing, and they need to pay particular attention to how the assessment activity will contribute to increasing student learning.

Diagnosing Readiness for Learning This purpose is obvious. One reason for assessing students is to find out what they already know, don't know, and whether they have the prerequisite knowledge and skills for an upcoming lesson. Another reason to assess diagnostically is to find out if students have certain learning difficulties or skill deficiencies. For example, a diagnosis might indicate that students are not writing introductory sentences for paragraphs, or that when given a table of numbers, most students cannot construct bar graphs correctly. Diagnostic information is extremely important for teachers in preparing lessons. It also is important for teachers to be on the lookout for deficient knowledge and skills during a lesson.

Checking for Understanding As each lesson unfolds, it is important for the teacher to be continually checking for understanding. Checking for understanding is one of the reasons that once a week, or more often, teachers insert "pop quizzes" and other tasks that provide a quick check on current student understanding. Homework assignments are another useful way to check for understanding. This part of teaching is equally important for the high school algebra teacher and the 1st grade reading teacher. The teacher-question–student-answer strategy during a lesson, having students do a sample problem and having one or more

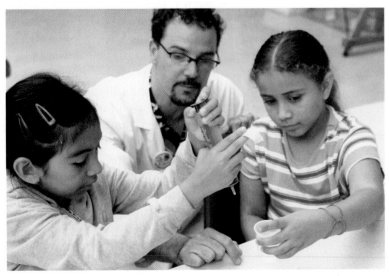

Good teachers are always checking for student understanding of the content, as well as monitoring for safety.

students solve an example in front of the class can be used as unobtrusive ways to see if there is understanding.

Improving Instruction   The first two purposes for assessing, diagnosing, and checking for understanding are obvious teacher responsibilities. That assessment information can be used for improving instruction is not as commonly considered. Using assessment information to improve instruction happens every day for secondary school teachers who teach more than one class. They have the opportunity to reflect on what occurred in the first class and make refinements for what they do in the second or third class. Elementary school teachers also can use assessment information for improving instruction, but the time frame is more likely to be in preparing for tomorrow's lesson or making notes for how to approach the same lesson next year. Regardless of the time frame, a critical component of assessing for teachers is self-reflection, thinking about what can be done with the current students to improve their learning, and what might be tried with the next group of students, whenever that will be.

Assessing Student Learning   Yes, the primary purpose for assessing is to determine the extent of student learning. The more subtle part is adjusting the rigor in the testing to the weight of the decision making. Assessing learning at the end of a unit requires more rigor than daily checking for understanding. Assessing learning for a semester or year is an even larger responsibility requiring much more careful construction of the test and extensive consideration of how to interpret and report the results. Teachers also need to make sure that the tests that they construct are well grounded in the curriculum standards and benchmarks. Students doing well on a teacher-made test that has little correlation with the district and state standards will not be as helpful to the students or the teacher as will the test that has a clear relationship to the standards and benchmarks.

Reporting Progress   Careful and through assessment work is absolutely necessary when it is time to report progress. Providing students with feedback on a teacher-made quiz is not likely to be challenged. However, as the consequences of the progress report increase, so do the expectations for quality in the assessment work. For example, students and parents will want to know what test information was used in deriving the final grade. They also will want to hear what the reasoning was behind interpretation of the test scores and the evaluations of student work. Rarely will they challenge the details of test construction or the teacher's "judgment," unless the teacher has concluded that the student is "failing." In those situations, the assessor needs to be able to explain the quality of the **assessments** (each testing with its interpretation) and the composite reasoning that led to the summative conclusion. The quality of assessments becomes even more important at the end of the school year when the teacher makes a recommendation about each student's promotion or graduation status.

▶ Assessment. Formal
and/or informal collection
of evidence along with its
interpretation.

Gatekeeping   Even though talking about it makes us feel uncomfortable, a reality today is that much of the testing that is being done by school districts, states, schools and teachers is for the purpose of sorting students. Students are not being allowed to advance to the next level of schooling (e.g., middle school to high school) unless they "pass" a test. No-pass no-play policies prohibit students from participating in sports and band unless they maintain a certain grade point average. In addition, teacher-education candidates cannot become licensed to teach unless they pass a state-mandated licensure exam. When tests are used to gatekeep, there is likely to be little room for interpretation or accommodation of special situations or unique individual differences. Instead there is **high-stakes testing**, where the score on the test is the determinant for passage to the next level.

High-stakes testing. Tests that are used to make decisions with significant consequences.

Comparing Purposes and Expectations for Assessing   One way to think about testing and assessing that was noted here is to ask whether it is to be used for formative (quality improvement) or summative (final judgments) decisions. A more refined way is to describe specific purposes for assessment work. Figure 11.1 presents a summary of these purposes in graphic form. The left-hand side of the continuum signifies major teacher responsibility for the design of tests and the interpretation of the results. As your eyes move across the continuum from left to right, the role of the teacher as test maker decreases, while expectations for test quality increase. A teacher-made test should not be used to make a high-stakes grade promotion or graduation decision. Note, also, that there should be multiple assessments employed for all purposes, especially in making gatekeeping decisions. This is one of the hotly debated issues in today's state and federal education policy environment where frequently the score on a single test is used to make a high-stakes decision.

Figure 11.1 Comparing purposes and quality of assessments

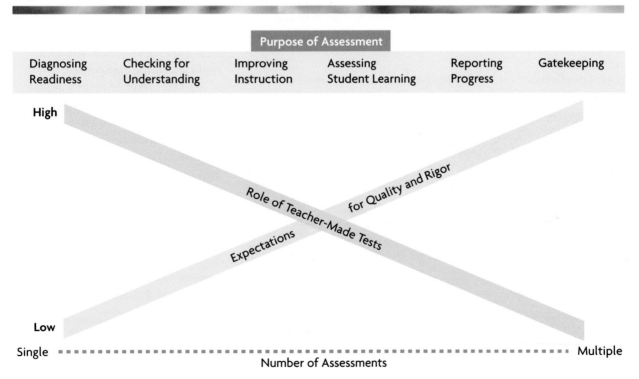

One important caution for teachers to keep in mind is that all of their assessments can face close scrutiny if someone initiates legal action. The legal action could come from a number of fronts. For example, a suit could be filed on behalf of a student where there is an indication of discrimination or where there is parent disagreement about promotion. Another possibility for legal action arises when there is a belief that a particular test was not scored correctly or that the test used was not an appropriate estimate of the amount of student learning. In summary, it is important for teachers to think carefully about each assessment activity and its purpose and to keep careful documentation of all assessments.

Two Very Different Kinds of Tests

Whenever testing is done, one of the most critical decisions relates to how the resulting test scores will be compared. A test score by itself has no meaning. A student could have a test score of 33, or 5, or 357. The score does not make any sense until it is compared to something. One of the interesting and important parts of testing is determining which comparison to make. In today's schools, two very different ways of comparing test scores are being used. One way to interpret the test score is to compare it to how other students did on the same test. The other way is to compare the score to a certain level of performance. Teachers need to understand these two extremely different ways of interpreting test results. Unfortunately, there is a great deal of confusion and misunderstanding about the two ways of thinking and their consequences.

▶ **Norm-referenced tests (NRTs).** Tests where an individual's score is compared to an established distribution of scores by an earlier sample of test takers.

Norm-Referenced Tests   The most widely used and well-understood approach to comparing test scores is when the test score of one student is compared to the scores of other students. This is called a **norm-referenced test (NRT)**. The comparison group for teacher-made tests is typically the other students in the class. For high-stakes tests and in the ideal application, the comparison group of test takers will represent a large sample of like students. The sample could be all other 3rd graders in the state or a national sample of like students. When all of these students take a well-designed test, the distribution of their scores will form a "normal" curve. If a perfect test score were one hundred, then the scores for all students would be distributed across the total possible range of test scores as is illustrated in Figure 11.2. Very few students would have extremely low or extremely high scores and the one test score received by the highest number of students would be fifty.

Criterion-referenced tests (CRTs) compare each student's level of performance to a particular level of accomplishment.

Figure 11.2 The normal curve: a statistical description of the chance distribution of test scores for a theoretical population

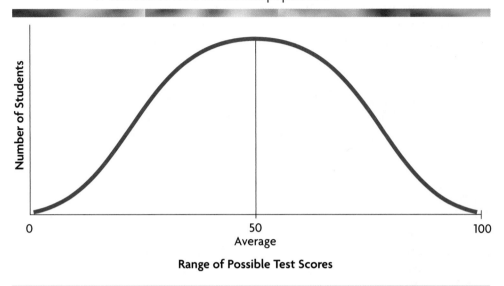

The average, or "mean," test score for all students would be fifty. Regardless of how the comparison group is assembled, in norm-referenced testing, one student's test score is compared to the scores of other students.

Criterion-Referenced Tests   An important alternative way to compare test scores is to identify a level of performance, a *criterion*, and then check to see if a particular student's score is above or below that level. As the name implies, with a **criterion-referenced test (CRT)**, a student's test score comparison is to a level of performance, rather than to how other students have done. This approach is particularly useful when student learning is being defined in terms of standards and benchmarks. The formative, and summative, question is, has the student attained the desired benchmark? Rather than comparing the student's level of learning to how well a comparison group of students has done, the test results are compared to the level of learning stated in the benchmark and standard.

Comparing NRT and CRT Test Scores   Teachers, school leaders, and policy makers often confuse the two ways of thinking about test results. Some simple examples can be helpful in clarifying the differences between NRTs and CRTs. In high school track meets, one of the standard events is the high bar. Athletes run up to a horizontal bar and attempt to roll their body over the bar without knocking it off its brackets. In a norm-referenced view, the height that one athlete is able to clear would be compared to the heights reached by a sample of other students. If the average 10th grade girl can clear 48 inches and Rowanda cleared 60 inches, her performance is far above average. In the criterion-referenced view, a certain height would be set as the benchmark and if the student cleared that height that would be seen as success. Ralph cleared 5 feet, which was the minimum level of performance set for his age group. This example is not used here to identify the

Criterion-referenced tests (CRTs). Tests where an individual's score is compared to a specified level of performance.

Authentic performance tasks are related to standards and benchmarks, and to real-world applications.

▶ Authentic assessment. Assessment tasks that are similar to real-world applications of the related knowledge and skills.

"winner"; instead, this is a visual example to illustrate the different comparisons that are made in norm-referenced and criterion-referenced testing.

Performance Tasks Another characteristic of good assessments is asking for student performance, in other words, doing an activity rather than only a mental exercise. When the assessment is based in students applying their learning through accomplishing an activity, there is greater certainty that they really have learned the benchmark and standard. This emphasis on performance is built in to the descriptions of most standards and benchmarks. Actually, these descriptions can be extremely helpful to teachers who are constructing their own assessments. Visualizing the actions that students can do when they have learned the material can lead to assessment tasks that require the students to demonstrate through action what they have learned.

Authentic Assessment tasks that are clearly related to the benchmarks and standards, as well as to real-world applications are called **authentic**. It is much easier for students to demonstrate what they have learned when the tasks are related to the student's background and world experiences. There are many disturbing examples of assessments that were not authentic such as asking low-income students in the desert southwest to write about a white Christmas. Teachers, as well as commercial test makers, must be extremely careful in constructing assessment tasks to make sure that they are not assuming background and context that has not been a part of the knowledge and experience of the students being assessed.

Assessing for Different Types of Learning

Up to this point, the discussion of testing and assessing has addressed the different purposes, two ways of thinking, and some of the characteristics of good assessments including asking for performance and using authentic tasks. What hasn't been addressed is the type of learning being assessed. There are a number of useful models that teachers can use for organizing and sorting the level and extent of student learning. One of the most widely used is from *Bloom's Taxonomy of Educational Objectives: Cognitive Domain* (Bloom, 1956). This taxonomy was developed as a way to describe different levels of learning.

Bloom's Taxonomy (see Figure 11.3) provides a useful set of categories for gauging the type of learning that is expected in assessment tasks. The taxonomy is equally useful for teachers, and other test makers, as they think about the type of learning they want students to demonstrate when tests are being constructed. Asking students to provide facts and figures (Level 1 Knowledge) is very different from asking students to use their knowledge of certain facts to solve a problem (Level 3 Application). An even higher level of learning is required to provide rea-

Figure 11.3 The six levels of Bloom's Taxonomy of the Cognitive Domain

Level VI: Evaluation—Making judgments about the quality of a solution or solution to an issue or problem.

Level V: Synthesis—Using original thinking to develop a communication, make predictions, and solve problems for which there is no single correct answer.

Level IV: Analysis—Identifying causes, reasons, or motives; analyzing information to reach a generalization or conclusion; finding evidence to support a specific opinion, event, or situation.

Level III: Application—Applying previously learned information to answer a problem. Using a rule, a definition, a classification system, or directions to solve a specific problem that has a correct answer.

Level II: Comprehension—Going beyond simple recall and demonstrating the ability to arrange and organize information mentally. Putting previously learned information into one's own words.

Level I: Knowledge—Using memory or senses to recall or reorganize information.

Source: Bloom, B. S. (Ed.) (1956). *Taxonomy of educational objectives handbook I: Cognitive domain.* New York: David McKay Co.

soned judgment about the strengths and weaknesses associated with certain phenomena (Level 6 Evaluation). Of course Bloom's Taxonomy has to be adjusted for the grade level and subject area being assessed. What would represent analysis at 7th grade would not be the same for high school seniors or 2nd graders. Still, within each class all levels of Bloom's Taxonomy can be applied to the construction of assessments, and making clear the expectations in objectives.

Accommodating Different Types of Learners

The final assessment topic to be introduced has to do with accommodating different types of learners and special needs students. An assessment that is perfect for middle-class suburban students may not be appropriate for urban poor students. The reverse may also be true; an assessment that worked well with an urban high school English class may not be make sense with a rural high school English class. Consideration of the exceptional learners must be considered in all assessment work. Two particularly important student learner populations that all teachers must consider are English language learners (ELL) and special needs students.

Accommodating Special Needs Students   A particularly challenging problem for teachers as well as for professional test makers, is developing assessments that are appropriate for special needs students. Each student is unique and is likely to have a tendency to do better with certain types of test situations. However, there is a legal distinction for students that have been formerly identified as having special needs. Students with *recognized* learning disabilities, physical handicaps, and other special needs will have an assigned school district team, including the parents, and an individual education program (IEP). A key component of each student's IEP will be information related to any **accommodations** that must be made in assessments. Accommodations are those adjustments that are made in

Accommodations. Adjustments that can be made in order to ensure that a student with special needs is not placed in an unfair or disadvantageous situation for instruction or testing.

order to ensure that a student with special needs is not placed in an unfair or disadvantageous situation for instruction or testing. In developing tests and with other assessments, the classroom teacher has a responsibility to be knowledgeable about any and all accommodations that have been specified in student IEPs.

In addition to whatever accommodation information is provided in a student's IEP, another readily accessible resource is each state's department of education website. A federal requirement is that each state provide a list of acceptable accommodations. Some of the examples from Pennsylvania are presented as Figure 11.4.

Figure 11.4 Examples of appropriate testing accommodations for special needs and English language learner students

Test Preparation

- Read directions to the student (reread as necessary).
- Use sign language or the student's native language to give directions or to simplify the directions. This may include American Sign Language or spoken English with sign support.
- Provide audiotape directions verbatim.

Test Administration

- Prompt the student to remain on task.
- Read test items (for mathematics or writing items only; do not read reading test items).
- Check periodically to make sure the student is marking in correct spaces.
- Provide materials to the students to mask portions of the test to direct the student's attention to specific areas.
- Provide materials to the student to use colored stickers or highlighters for visual cues.

Test Response

- Allow the student to answer questions orally (mathematics and reading only).
- Use enlarged answer sheets.
- Allow the student to point to the response.
- Allow the student to answer on a typewriter or computer (turn off spelling, grammar checker, and thesaurus).

Timing/Scheduling

- Increase or decrease opportunity for movement.
- Permit additional breaks or extended rest breaks for student during testing session.
- Increase the test time.

Setting

- Allow the student to use adaptive or special furniture, such as a study carrel.
- Test in a separate room or in a small group to reduce distractions.
- Test in a special education or bilingual classroom, if appropriate.
- Reduce stimuli (e.g., limit the number of items on the desk).
- Provide for reduced acoustical distraction.

Assistive Devices

- Allow augmentative communication systems or strategies, including letter boards, picture communication systems, and voice output systems (no voice output for writing).
- Provide a magnifier or large-print or Braille materials.
- Provide pencil grips.

Other Options

- Provide a sign language interpreter, if necessary (mathematics and reading only; no sign language output for writing).

Source: Testing Accommodations for the Pennsylvania System of School Assessment 2002–2003.

Challenging Assumptions
FINDINGS FROM RESEARCH

In small-group instruction, should teachers call on students randomly or in turn?

The Assumption: A frequently used teaching tactic is to organize students in small groups for instruction. This tactic is used heavily for reading and mathematics instruction in elementary schools. Researchers have identified a number of principles that make for success including: (a) the difficulty of teacher questions should be such that the lesson can move right along; (b) the teacher should aim for 80 percent of student answers being correct; (c) students should have frequent opportunity to respond; and (d) the teacher should provide clear feedback about the correctness of student responses. A critical assumption has to do with whether the teacher should call on the students in small-group instruction randomly or in turn.

Study Design and Methods: One of the early major studies that examined teacher behaviors in relation to student achievement was the Texas Teacher Effectiveness Study. In this study, 4 years of student achievement data were available for 165 2nd and 3rd grade teachers. A sample of these teachers (n = 31) were observed for 10 hours in the first year of the study and 30 hours in the second year of the study. Their teaching behaviors were correlated with student achievement. Much to the researcher's surprise, "patterned turns" in small groups was positively correlated with student achievement. In other words, teachers who called on students in sequence had greater gains than those who called on students randomly or called on students who volunteered.

Implications: Contrary to the logic that calling on students randomly will keep them attending to the lesson, the findings from this research indicates that calling on students in turn ensures that all students participate and in equal proportions. The study findings apply to high- as well as low-SES classes. In high-SES classes, it helps students focus on the content of the lesson, rather than trying to get the teacher to call on them. In low-SES classes, it provides a structure and predictability that may help more anxious students participate.

With the findings from this research in mind, in your next practicum experiences, observe small-group instruction. Find situations where students are called on in turn and where they are called on randomly. What differences do you see in terms of student participation and achievement?

Source: Brophy, J., & Evertson, C. (1976). *Learning from teaching: A developmental perspective.* Boston: Allyn and Bacon.

Teacher Initiative   Always keep in mind that teacher initiative is an important element in student success. Teacher initiative is important to student success in testing, too. For example, one high school teacher had a student who did well with all assignments, but failed every test. The teacher reflected on this discrepancy between consistent indications of achievement during instruction and the string of F's on tests. The teacher called a parent to help in understanding what was happening. It seems that the student would freeze and not be able to read the test questions during formal test-taking situations. The teacher then adjusted the test setting by presenting the test questions on audiotape and allowing the student extra time. From then on the student passed the tests.

Accommodating ELL Students   The accommodation examples presented in Figure 11.4 also can be appropriate for ELL students. There is additional pressure on schools and school districts to do all that they can to assure a fair opportunity for ELL students to demonstrate what they have learned. Under the No Child Left Behind (NCLB) Act, 95 percent of all students, including ELL and those with special needs, must take the annual state tests. Much of the reasoning that states use in setting accommodations for ELL students is applicable in the classroom as well. For example, the New Mexico State Department of Education has identified a useful list of guidelines for making accommodations as long as they:

- Do not change the intent of the test
- Do not change the purpose of the test
- Do not change the content of the test
- Do not provide the student with an unfair advantage
- Continue to allow the testing contractor to be able to score the test
- Do not violate test security
- Do not change the focus of what is being assessed

Each of these points is important for teachers to keep in mind as they develop their own assessments. Teachers have the responsibility of providing all students with the opportunity to fairly demonstrate that they have learned.

Revisiting Allison Johnson's Staff Meeting Concerns

Allison's confusion about CRTs and NRTs should now be clear. NRTs are tests designed to compare a student's test score to a comparison group of students, while CRTs report whether a student has met a particular level of performance. A bigger set of implications were embedded in the discussion that took place in that opening faculty meeting. Although the district and state testing will not come until later in the school year, Allison and her colleagues will be assessing student learning throughout the year. Every formative and summative assessment that Allison does with her students will be laying the foundation for her students doing well on the major district and state tests. If Allison pays close attention to the curriculum standards and benchmarks in her assessment activities, then her students' scores on tests she has made should turn out to predict very closely how well the students will do on the "big" tests.

What Are Some Ways to Test Student Learning?

Harold Pratt, a high school science teacher, is deciding what kind of test he will construct to assess his students' learning about cell division. "There are a number

Ed Lines

In a 2004 survey of 12,000 high school students, 62 percent admitted cheating on an exam at least once in the previous year. *(Josephson Institute of Ethics, 2004)*

of scientific terms that they need to know. These are bound to be on the state test. They need to be able to describe the basic processes that take place, and the differences in plant and animal cell division, which will be on the state test. I also would like them to be thinking more about some of the implications for current medical research," he mused.

In the end Harold developed a two-part test. The first part consisted of 10 objective test items, and the second part was one open-ended question.

Testing has become a very important component of the work of teachers and students. Teachers must continually assess developing student understanding, and each year school districts and the state are testing students learning in several subjects. An important message for beginning teachers is that from the very first day in the classroom, they must have expertise in developing different types of tests. From the first day onward, each of the purposes for assessing must be addressed. Within each lesson and across the school day, teachers are engaged in informal assessing of each student. Across the weeks and semesters, teachers must develop tests and report student grades. All of these classroom activities are done in anticipation of the testing that the school district and state will require toward the end of the school year. See the Teachers and the Law on page 414 for more on testing.

Informal Testing within Lessons

When the term *testing* is used, don't think only of paper-and-pencil exams. There are a number of other ways to probe and examine student understanding and the extent of their learning. Expert teachers continually assess by using a variety of informal ways before, during, and in follow-up to each lesson. For example, when teachers employ the all-too-familiar "Q&A" tactic during a lesson, their intent is to use short questions that require lower-level (Bloom's Taxonomy Levels 1 and 2) student responses as a way to spot-check understanding across a number of students.

Teacher Observation   Quite naturally the most prevalent concern for beginning teachers is classroom management. Their concerns tend to focus first on preparing each lesson, managing student activities, and keeping on top of the paperwork. When teachers have these concerns, their observations of students focus on whether all students are attentive, they are not misbehaving, and they are not creating distractions. Observing student behavior in order to assess classroom management is a necessary first step for all teachers. However, one significant reason for student misbehavior is their not understanding what they are supposed to be doing.

The critical difference between novice teachers and expert teachers is found in the extent to which the purpose for a teacher's observations of students extends beyond a focus on classroom management. Expert teachers go further by continually observing students in order to pick up clues about their extent of understanding and engagement with learning the material. For example, by looking around the class-

Interpretation of any measure requires a comparison.

Teachers and the Law

Testing and using the results of tests are important tasks and responsibilities for teachers, schools, and school districts. Test scores are just one of the many forms of data and information that teachers and schools collect about their students. Teachers must be particularly careful in compiling information about student performance and fully understand who can, and who should not, have access to these records. Past court decisions and related laws provide the foundation for what teachers and schools can and should not do. For example, federal statutes have addressed the important question of who should be able to see student records. A clear message for teachers is that they must keep accurate records for each student and be very careful about who gains access. Although the trend toward high-stakes testing is recent, there are many past laws and statutes that are applicable. An emerging topic for the courts and legislative bodies is the extent to which test scores can be used alone to make high-stakes decisions for students and schools. It seems likely that in the near future there will be more questions about the role of testing in determining the quality of teachers.

PROTECTION OF THE PRIVACY OF STUDENT RECORDS

Do parents have the right to see all of the school records kept on their child?

Yes. Concern about parents not having access to student records led Congress to pass the Family Educational Rights and Privacy Act of 1974—P.L. 93-

380, also known as FERPA and generally referred to as the Buckley Amendment. This statute makes clear that schools can not deny parents "the right to inspect and review any and all official records, files, and data directly related to their children, including all material that is incorporated into each student's cumulative record folder, and intended for school use . . . (including) identifying data, academic work completed, level of achievement (grades, standardized achievement test scores, attendance data, scores on standardized intelligence, aptitude and psychological tests."

Can parents challenge the accuracy of the school's records about their children?

Yes. FERPA makes it clear that parents must be provided an opportunity for a hearing to challenge the content of their child's school records in order to ensure accuracy and that they are not misleading.

Can schools and colleges release personal information about their students?

No. No state or local educational agency can permit "the release of personally identifiable records or files (or personal information contained therein) of students without the written consent of their parents to an individual, agency, or organization. . . ." Teachers need to keep in mind that they are likely to have children in their classes with divorced parents and/or court orders that will specify who can, as well as some who cannot, have access to individual student records.

STUDENT PAPER SWAPPING

Is it legal to have students grade each other's work?

Yes. The likely immediate reaction to this question is, "Of course. Students grading each other's work goes

room, teachers can immediately see if students are reading or writing or calculating. During group work, expert teachers are monitoring to see that all students are participating. In lab work, teachers check to see if each student has set up the equipment properly and it is working safely. By walking around the classroom, teachers can look over the shoulder at student work and listen in on student-to-student talk. Some teachers walk around the classroom primarily to monitor for misbehavior. Expert teachers have a higher level purpose; they are checking for student learning and understanding. It is disappointing to note that in some classrooms, teachers do not walk around the classroom and monitor closely what students are doing. They sit at

on all the time." Teachers regularly ask their students to swap and grade each other's homework assignments, quizzes, and other products. The teacher may report the correct answers or have one or more students present the answer at the board or with the use of a projection device. However, the legality of this practice was challenged and the case went all the way to the U.S. Supreme Court.

The case began when a mother, Kristja Falvo, was upset that her learning-disabled son was ridiculed as a "dummy" when his low grade was read aloud. In 1998, she sued the Owasso, Oklahoma, school district claiming that paper swapping violated students' civil rights and the right to privacy of student records. The appeals court agreed. However, when appealed, the U.S. Supreme Court in a unanimous (9–0) decision in 2002 ruled that prohibiting this practice would overly involve the federal government to "exercise minute control over specific teaching methods and instructional dynamics in classrooms throughout the country." The Court also saw the educational importance of this activity because it provides an additional opportunity for instruction.

(*Source: Owasso Independent School District No. 1-001 et al. vs. Falvo et al.*)

HIGH-STAKES TESTING OF STUDENTS WITH DISABILITIES

Can students identified to have disabilities be required to take and pass high-stakes tests?

Yes. There have been legal challenges using Section 504, IDEA and the 14th Amendment of the U.S. Constitution. The courts have said that the due-process conditions are met if students with disabilities have had adequate notice of the requirement (e.g., passing a test to graduate, sufficient time to prepare, and that the school curriculum adequately presented the content). The 1997 Amendment to IDEA requires states and school districts to develop guidelines that enable children with disabilities to participate in district and state testing. When there is need, each student's IEP must describe any modifications that are needed and appropriate. If the IEP team decides that a student should not participate, then they must state reasons and specify how the student will be assessed.

Is it legal to have teacher licensure based on the results of a single test?

Yes. As problematic as this may be, the highly qualified teacher component of the No Child Left Behind Act (2001) makes clear that a high-stakes test may be used to determine teacher qualifications. Of course the due-process condition of reasonable time to prepare must be met. The test has to be a valid measure of job-related skills and knowledge, and it must not discriminate on the basis of race, national origin, religion, or gender. Also, accommodations must be made for teachers with recognized handicaps.

Will high-stakes test continue to be the sole measure used to make gatekeeping decisions?

Unlikely. Given the significance of decisions being made from high-stakes testing, it seems very likely that in the near future there will be new court challenges especially related to the potential for bias and the narrowness of knowledge and skills being assessed with any single measure. Regardless of the outcome in court and statute, there will continue to be needs to find better ways to evaluate the extent of student learning and the quality of teachers.

the teacher's desk, doing some other task, and only occasionally look up to see what students are doing. *Do not become this type of teacher!*

Teacher Questioning   Of course teacher questioning is a very useful way to check on student understanding. Teachers are always asking **closed questions** that ask for specific information about procedures and facts. With closed questions, student answers are brief so many students can be spot-checked in a few minutes. Another type of teacher questioning uses **open-ended questions** that require students to provide an explanation, interpretation, or elaboration.

Closed questions. Questions that require a short phrase or fact answer.

Open-ended questions. Questions that require interpretation, elaboration, and thought.

FOXTROT BILL AMEND

Open-ended questions require higher-level student thinking (Bloom's Taxonomy Levels 4 Analysis, 5 Synthesis, and 6 Evaluation). Open-ended questions also require more time for the teacher to ask and for students to construct their response. One way to save time and take advantage of open-ended questions is to pose a single well-thought-out open-ended question and then allow several students to present their responses. The teacher may ask closed questions for clarification purposes as each student responds. This way more students are able to construct a thoughtful response. With both types of questions the teacher is listening for the extent and depth of student understanding and learning. Read the Challenging Assumptions on page 411 for another perspective on questioning.

Student Self-Reflection   Teacher questioning is used continually to check on student understanding and learning; in fact, it is overused in most classrooms. There are some other ways to check on student progress during lessons. One tactic that is underused is student self-reflection. Instead of the teacher assuming all of the responsibility for determining where students are, place some of the responsibility on the students. After all, it is the students who have to do the learning. Asking students to talk or write about what they know or don't know is an important activity. This type of self-reflection should be tied to the curriculum standards and benchmarks. In today's environment of high accountability, it is especially important for students to be assessing themselves in terms of the extent of their current understanding and learning in relation to how they will be tested. Ask them to describe their current level of understanding in relation to a specific benchmark and its standard.

Pop Quizzes   All of us have experienced the dreaded pop quiz. Teachers always seem to know when students will be less well prepared and need to be reminded of the importance of doing each day's assignments. The unannounced short test where students need to respond to a few questions can be useful. The pop quiz not only serves as a stimulus, it also provides evidence about the extent of student understanding and learning. A related activity is to have some students solve problems or present their answers on the white board, overhead, or with PowerPoint. Then all students can share in the discussion of the response.

Ed Lines

To be "authentic" requires real-world application of what has been learned.

Formal testing of stu-
dent learning, espe-
cially for high-stakes
decisions, must be
done in secure and
closely monitored
settings.

Homework   Homework can be a very useful way to check on student understanding and learning. Do not think about homework simply as another way to
have scores to compile and use in determining the final course grade. Instead, use
homework assignments as another way to check on student understanding and
learning. Of course homework also is a form of instruction and in and of itself can
be used to help students learn the material. Student reporting on their homework
and guided class discussions around the homework become additional ways to
check on student progress. In other words, don't simply collect homework and
grade it after class. Use homework as a way to diagnose learning difficulties and
engage all students in further learning.

Objective Tests

The more formal tests that teachers develop frequently use test items that are called
objective. **Objective test items** get their name from the characteristic that the answers are either right or wrong. There is no gray area in scoring well-constructed objective test items. Everyone who scores the test items will agree on which of the
possible student responses is correct. One advantage of using objective test items is
that scoring the student responses can be done quite quickly. Another advantage is
that a wide range of student knowledge can be assessed relatively quickly, because
answering objective test items takes less time than items that require students to
construct an original response. A disadvantage is that constructing good objective
test items is not as easy as it seems and takes considerable time.

Objective test items.
Items that can be scored
clearly as either correct or
incorrect.

Ed Lines

Performance tasks do not have to be authentic.

Different types of objective test items range from true-false to fill-in to multiple choice. Each format is particularly good at testing a certain type of learning and each has certain keys to construction that teachers need to keep in mind. Regardless of the item format, it is important to be sure that there is a clear relationship to the learning objective(s), benchmark(s), and standard(s).

True-False Items DIRECTIONS: Place a T in front of those items that are true and place an F in front of those items that are false.

___ 1. NRTs are very useful to teachers in planning daily lessons.

___ 2. With CRTs, students either pass or fail.

___ 3. The use of objectives tests is not unsatisfactory since more areas of student learning can be sampled in a short time.

True-false test items appear to be easy to write, however, writing items that are clear requires careful work. For example, items 1 and 2 are clear and should be easy to answer correctly. One of the keys to good true-false items is that they are clearly either true or false, at least to those respondents who have learned the material. Items 1 and 2 address a single idea and are clearly worded. Item 3 is problematic. It is convoluted and includes the *double negative* "not unsatisfactory." Therefore, which is the correct response: T since objective tests are good at sampling a range or F since objective tests are satisfactory? Another important consideration with true-false items is that there are only two possible responses: true or false. Thus students can guess with a 50 percent chance of being correct.

Matching Items DIRECTIONS: Column A contains the levels of Bloom's Taxonomy and Column B short definitions. Match the level in column A with the correct definition in column B by writing the correct letter in front of the correct numeral.

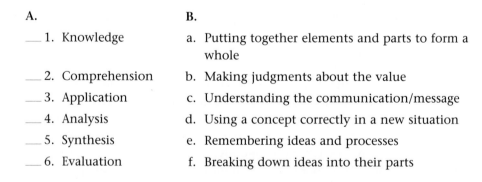

A.	B.
___ 1. Knowledge	a. Putting together elements and parts to form a whole
___ 2. Comprehension	b. Making judgments about the value
___ 3. Application	c. Understanding the communication/message
___ 4. Analysis	d. Using a concept correctly in a new situation
___ 5. Synthesis	e. Remembering ideas and processes
___ 6. Evaluation	f. Breaking down ideas into their parts

As with all objective test item formats, writing good matching test items takes time. Teachers need to be careful to keep all of the items similar. One useful tip is to have a name or title for the list of items. In the example here, it could be "definitions for Bloom's Taxonomy." Items related to other types and categories of objectives would not be included. A mistake in the design of this example is that the shortest list is placed on the left. Ideally the column with the longest list should be placed on the left. This will save student time because they will only need to read each definition once and then look for the correct single word classification. When the list with the shortest number of words is at the left, students can read the name quickly but have to re-read the longer phrases in the second column each time. One of the inherent weaknesses in matching items is that there is a chance to guess correctly, especially if the student knows all but one of the correct responses. A way to avoid this problem is to include one or two extra response options.

Multiple-Choice Items   DIRECTIONS: Circle the letter of the correct answer for each of the following questions.

1. One reason that true-false test items are useful is that
   a. They are easy to write.
   b. Students have only a 50 percent chance of responding correctly.
   c. So many things are 100 percent true or false.
   d. They are easy to score.

2. In writing matching test items, be sure to
   a. Include some phrases that are longer than others.
   b. Make sure all of the descriptions are equally plausible.
   c. Place the list of descriptions to the right.
   d. Place the list of options to the left.

3. Multiple-choice test items can be written to measure student learning at the higher levels of Bloom's Taxonomy. In writing higher-level items, it is important to
   a. Pose a problem clearly and without extraneous information.
   b. Have each of the response options clearly distinct.
   c. Include new terms and facts from the out-of-class assignments.
   d. Have long response items as a way to incorporate the higher level thinking.
   e. Have more response options.

With the possible exception of primary grade students, all students and their teachers are familiar with the multiple-choice test item format. One of the strengths of this format is that items can be constructed to assess learning for each of the levels in Bloom's Taxonomy. Simple recall-type items indicative of the knowledge level can be written. Items also can pose complex problems that address higher-level thinking. Writing good multiple-choice test items is hard work. In part this is due to the extensive experience that students have gained as test takers. They become expert at eliminating answer options based on structural clues such as verb and article mismatches, as well as items that address "all" or "never." Another clue is that quite often the correct response will have more words than those that are incorrect. Test making experts advise that "none of the above" be used very sparingly. Students tend to expect it to be the correct response. "All of the above" should not be used. Students are quick to guess that it is the correct answer.

Using multiple-choice items to test higher-level thinking is not only possible but regularly done. Aspiring teachers have experienced this test item format on the SAT and ACT tests and will again with the state licensure exam. The item format begins with posing a problem. Students may need to read a paragraph or more or study a chart or map. On teachers licensure exams, one or more of the items will present a sample of student work, which is to be analyzed and a plan for instruction developed. A number of test items can be presented in relation to a single posed problem. The higher-level item responses need to include one clearly best answer, and the others need to be plausible. One way to increase the difficulty is to make each of the responses more similar.

Fill-in-the-Blank Items   DIRECTIONS: Complete each sentence by inserting the best word in the blank.

1. _____ is the title in Bloom's Taxonomy for being able to recall names, concepts, facts, and dates.

2. Multiple-choice test items can be used to assess _____ and _____ levels of learning.

3. One of the purposes of assessment is for _____ _____ _____.

Another test item format is fill-in-the-blank. As these examples illustrate, fill-in-the-blank items can require one or two words or a short phrase response. It is best to ask for one word. If there is a numerical response that represents the amount of something such as miles per hour, or pounds, be sure to include the label. Fill-in-the blank items need to be written very clearly. If not, students are likely to insert words and phrases that the teacher was not expecting. The Item 3 example illustrates this problem. The desired response is "student self-reflection," but a number of other response options such as "student gatekeeping" or "teacher grade reporting" could be inserted and are equally appropriate.

Watch Out for Bias in Test Items   No matter the test-item format, an important responsibility for teachers is to make sure that each item does not unwittingly include some form of bias. It is all too easy to accidentally write a test item that includes a sexual, racial, or cultural bias. There also is risk of including a socio-economic status (SES) bias. SES refers to the level of wealth, education, social class, and range of experiences that a teachers and students bring to the classroom. Check all test items for the following:

1. Overuse of "he" or "she" or stereotyping of boys and girls

2. The use of terms that may be offensive to certain ethnic and cultural groups

3. Using examples from a middle-class experience that poor children may not have had, for example, travel to Disneyland

Ed Lines

Assessments that are connected to the world of students will be of more interest.

4. Selecting content and examples that will have different meanings to students from different parts of the country; for example, a "blizzard" for students from New England will likely mean a heavy snowstorm while for students in Arizona, it is a special type of milkshake from Dairy Queen

5. Built-in implicit expectations that "some" (boys, girls, ELL, special needs, the "brightest") will do better or worse on the test item than others

Subjective Tests

Objective test items take time to write, provide students with a limited number of response options, and can be scored quickly. An alternative test-item format is called **subjective**. Subjective test items pose a problem or task and students must construct an original response, which must be scored individually. Subjective test items are easier to write, more challenging for students to answer, and require judgment and interpretation by the teacher in scoring each response. A very important strength of subjective test items is that each student's response is their own work and usually requires higher-order thinking.

Subjective test items. Test items that require interpretation and judgment in order to score them.

Short-Answer Items   DIRECTIONS: If you were writing objective test items for 7th grade students in an inner city school, what are three elements of good test items that you would want to be sure to attend to? Be sure to explain your reasoning.

_____

_____

_____

Short-answer test items are an effective way to test for student use of vocabulary, their ability to think using key concepts, and to construct a brief narrative response. Another advantage of short-answer items is that several of them can be presented within a typical class period. A challenge is that each student's response will be unique and open to interpretation. Variations in interpretation can come from the students as some interpret the test item in different ways. There also can be variation in how the teacher interprets what students have written. This challenge of interpretation is a component of all subjective test items, thus the name.

A number of techniques can reduce the subjectivity, while still requiring originality in the student response. For example, in the test item just presented the number of elements is specified (three). This removes any debate about whether a response that only provides one or two elements is sufficient. Without adding the request for the response to include the reasons, there could be debate about the need to provide more in the response than the number of elements. The challenge in writing subjective test items is to reduce the unnecessary ambiguity in what is

Ed Lines

Students learn more when teachers do more interim assessing.

expected while at the same time delimiting what the student is to demonstrate based on what they have learned.

Essay Test Items   DIRECTIONS: A very important skill for teachers to develop is writing good test items. In this chapter, you have been reading about different test item formats. Each format is particularly useful for testing certain levels of learning and understanding, and each has particular technical elements that must be addressed. Teachers must understand when to use each test item format. For a subject area that you will be teaching, describe the types of test items that you would use in writing an end of unit one class period test. Use at least three test-item formats and include an example test item for each. Be sure to describe your reasoning. Use five to eight pages to write your answer. Organization, composition, and spelling will count.

One of the most useful ways to test higher-order student thinking is the essay. They can require students to organize complex ideas and to use what they have learned in new ways. Essay test items present a situation or problem and each student must construct his or her own response. Essay test responses are expected to be long, well organized, and to include detail as well as analysis, synthesis, and evaluation. Essay test items are relatively easy to construct. The challenge in writing essay test items is to circumscribe the topic without making the item so prescriptive that students do not have to think long and hard in composing their essay. We all have experienced essay test items that were so open and vague that we had no clear idea of what a good response would include.

The major challenge for the teacher comes when it is time to score an essay test. First of all, the ease with which an essay test item can be constructed is out of balance with the time it takes to read each student's multipage response. It takes extended time to read each paper and to decipher student penmanship. Another challenge is deciding which components will be scored. How much weight will be given to the quantity of facts and terms that are used? Will there be a clear distinction between lower-level and higher-level thinking? Will grammar and spelling be counted? Will there be one composite score or will each of these questions result in a separate score? An additional challenge with older students is judging whether a particular response really reflects understanding or is bluffing.

Open-Ended Formats   DIRECTIONS: By the end of this semester, you should have in place the foundations for what will become your professional portfolio. This foundation should include: (a) summary of your education and work experience, (b) description of your academic record, (c) documentation that you have passed all entry tests and requirements, (d) artifacts that indicate the type of product you produce, and (e) the first draft of your education philosophy statement.

There are a number of other formats that teachers can use to assess the extent of student learning and especially their higher-order thinking. These various formats are open ended. They require students to organize and construct their response in creative and unique ways. Open-ended formats include portfolios, exhibits, group projects, investigations, creative works and performances, presentations, panels, and juries. Student work in response to an open-ended format task will take extended time and should be based in a number of weeks of cumulative class work. Don't forget that open-ended format items can be structured for students working in groups or as teams.

Group projects add a challenge for the teacher when it comes to evaluating the contributions of each student individually. One way to accommodate this challenge is to assign each student an individual grade and each student a grade for the group. Another approach is to have each student grade the other members of the group in terms of the effort and/or the extent of their contributions to the group's product.

Teacher supervision during the time period when students are constructing their open-ended response can be tricky. Beyond monitoring student engagement and the effort of each student, there is the need to not provide too many suggestions and hints while at the same time facilitating having all students succeed with producing a final product.

Open-ended formats require extended time for students to produce the final product. One way to maximize student learning is to build in time for students to report, share, present, or exhibit their product. This can become a major celebration and highly visible way for students and teachers from across the school to see what has been going on in your classroom.

Which Format Is Best?   Deciding on which test-item format to use, as with so much of teaching, comes back to consideration of the expected learner outcomes. What are the most important facts, concepts, and understanding that students should be acquiring? These are the elements that should be tested. Some of the test-item formats can be fun for students to do, especially the open-ended ones, but teachers must always keep in mind that testing in the classroom must be grounded in state and district standards and benchmarks. Also continue to think about the level of thinking, learning, and understanding that is expected. Bloom's Taxonomy (see Figure 11.3) has been used in this chapter because it is such a useful way to think about the level of learning and understanding that is being tested. Fill-in-the-blank test items work well for recall of vocabulary, but are not useful for testing application. Table 11.1 provides a number of tips to use in writing test items. For every test item that teachers develop, one final check should be made for any sort of bias or discrimination. It is surprisingly easy to accidentally build into a test item favoritism for certain students or an unfair disadvantage for certain students. Teachers must be careful in constructing test items to ensure that all students have an equal opportunity to show what they have learned.

Scoring Tests and Assignments

Once students have completed and turned in their test or assignment, the teacher has to evaluate them. Evaluation begins with reading, observing, and/or listening to each student's work. The teacher then must make a judgment about the quality of the work and assign a grade. Experienced teachers have worked out a number

Table 11.1 Test Item Formats and Writing Tips

Objective Test Item Format	Tips to Writing Good Items
True-False	• Write items that are clearly true or false.
	• Avoid using absolute terms such as always, never, and only.
	• Avoid double negatives.
	• Don't include two ideas/parts in a single item.
Matching Items	• Provide a title for the list of items.
	• Place the longest list on the left.
	• Consider having one or two extra response options.
Fill-in-the-Blank	• It is best to require one-word responses.
	• Include the label for an amount of something.
	• Write clear statements.
Essay	• Be careful to circumscribe the topic without being too prescriptive.
	• Decide in advance which items will be scored.
	• Decide if spelling and grammar will count.
Open-Ended	• Determine whether there will be group or individual responses.
	• Establish in advance the criteria for evaluating group work.
	• Plan to monitor student work during the response construction process.
	• Consider ways for students to share/publish their works.

of systems for doing this work. In large part, learning the best ways to evaluate student work comes through experience. Still, there are a number of suggestions and tips that can make the task easier and more helpful.

Numerical Scoring   One of the advantages of objective test items is that they are easy to score. The answer is either right or wrong. Correct answers are assigned a numerical value and wrong answers are given zeros. Of course the scoring can become a little more complex when partial credit is given. Partial credit is used regularly in mathematics and science classes where students have correctly completed a number of steps to solve a problem.

Grading with Letters   In many ways using numerical test scores to grade makes the teacher's job easier. As just noted, writing good test items is hard work. However, scoring objective test items is easy. Determining the grade for an objective test is easy, too; just add up the score for each correct item and refer to the cut score(s). Grading test items and assignments that require students to construct their own response places a heavier scoring burden on the

Ed Lines

Student teaching is an authentic performance activity with multiple assessments.

teacher. First each student's work has to be read/observed/experienced, then an analysis has to be made of the quality of the work. Finally, a grade can be assigned. However, each of these steps can be very subjective. The evaluative judgments are made by the teacher, but what criteria were used? Is each student's work treated the same or was there some sort of favoritism given some students?

A useful approach to subjective grading is for the teacher to identify a list of example elements of student work that are indicative of each grade. For example: C work includes correct use of vocabulary, B work also includes application of one of the principles, and A work includes application of several principles. Ideally, students should share in the development of these elements and examples of each level are displayed in the classroom.

In standards-based education it is important that students understand how their current work compares to key benchmarks. A 3rd grade student explains to her teacher what she will do next to improve her writing.

Rubrics: Important and Useful Evaluation Tool   A useful tool for evaluating student work is the **rubric**. Rubrics are multiple point continua that describe different levels or degrees of quality of work or a product. An example of a rubric for assessing student writing that is used in the Fairfax County, Virginia, Public Schools is presented in Figure 11.5. With rubrics of this type, a large part of the mystery is taken out of subjective evaluation. Each of the points in the rubric describe a level of performance that can be observed and that is distinguishable from other levels.

The beginning point for developing a rubric is writing down observable descriptions of different levels of quality. The suggestion just made that teachers (and their students) note example elements for each letter grade is a good beginning step for developing rubrics. Rubrics can be **holistic** for evaluating the total effort. Rubrics also can be used to evaluate subparts or components of the effort. For example, one rubric could be used to assess the overall level of thinking (Bloom's Taxonomy) that was used in a student report, while another rubric could be used to evaluate the quality of grammar and spelling. A fun and informative activity is to involve students in the development of rubrics.

Rubric. Criteria for judging a person's performance against standards that include descriptions of performance at levels such as inadequate, proficient, and beyond expectations

Holistic. Viewing the whole as a product or response to a whole.

Turning Test and Evaluation Information into Assessments

Once student projects and tests are evaluated and scored, the information can be used for the various purposes described at the beginning of this chapter. The teacher needs to be reviewing the information to see if students have achieved the

Ed Lines

In 2003–2004, nearly 6.6 million children received services related to a disability.
(National Center for Education Statistics)

Figure 11.5 Rubric for analyzing writing tasks

Task Completion

1. Minimal completion of the task; content is extremely superficial; ideas are repetitive and/or irrelevant; paragraphing is haphazard

2–3. Partial completion of the task; content is superficial; ideas are sometimes repetitive and/or irrelevant; paragraphing is generally inappropriate

4–5. Completion of the task; content is appropriate; ideas are relevant; paragraphing is appropriate

6. Superior completion of the task; content is appropriate; ideas are well-developed and well-organized

Comprehensibility

1. Text barely comprehensible, requiring frequent interpretation on the part of the reader

2. Text mostly comprehensible, requiring some interpretation on the part of the reader

3. Text comprehensible, requiring minimal interpretation on the part of the reader

4. Text readily comprehensible, requiring no interpretation on the part of the reader

Level of Discourse

1. Predominant use of single-clause sentences with a few multiclause sentences; little or no linkage between sentences

2. Blend of single-clause and multiclause sentences with mostly coordinating clauses and an occasional subordinating clause, limited use of cohesive devises

3. Adequate blend of single-clause and multiclause sentences with some coordinating clauses and a few subordinating clauses; appropriate use and range of cohesive devices

4. Variety of single-clause and frequent multiclause sentences with some coordinating and several subordinating clauses; appropriate use and wide range of cohesive devices

Vocabulary

1. Inadequate range and use of vocabulary

2–3. Limited range of vocabulary; use sometimes inaccurate and/or inappropriate

4–5. Varied range of vocabulary; use generally accurate and appropriate; a few idiomatic expressions

6. Wide range of vocabulary; use mainly accurate and appropriate, including some idiomatic expressions

Grammar

1. Emerging use of basic language structures and minimal or no use of advanced language structures

2–3. Emerging control of basic language structures with some advanced language structures

4–5. Control of basic language structures and emerging use of advanced language structures

6. Control of basic language structures and emerging control of advanced language structures

Source: Foreign language teachers, Fairfax County (VA) public schools.

benchmarks and are ready to move ahead. This also is a time to reflect on how effective the lessons were and what should be done the same, and differently, next time. Two important related tasks are to examine how each student is doing and to plan for feedback.

Disaggregating the Data An important task that must be done for every test and assignment is to compare the evaluation results for different kinds of students. Rather than simply accepting the results for each class of students as a

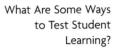

Teachers' Lounge

Zoo Vocabulary

One of the hallmarks of kindergartners is their effervescent love of learning. Concepts and vocabulary expand at an exponential rate. They work to make sense of their world, linking what they already know with new information they're learning about; the familiar with the unfamiliar. Every year, our kindergarten visits the San Francisco Zoo. Before the trip, we take time to study the names and characteristics of wild animals such as lions, bears, zebras, giraffes, and antelopes. On one trip, one of my students ran up to me, yelling at the top of his voice, "Hey! I just saw a cantaloupe!"

● Kim Sakamoto Steidl
Kindergarten teacher and community
college instructor, Cabrillo College,
Aptos, California

whole group, it is important to examine the results for various subgroups of students. The test scores need to be broken out for each type of student. This is called **disaggregation**. In most cases, the spread of data for the whole class will look pretty good. However, beneath the surface it is quite likely that some subgroups of students did not do as well as others. Teachers need to find out if this is the case. One of the first breakdowns of test or project grades should be to see if boys and girls scored differently. Other ways to disaggregate the data should include examining potential differences between students of different cultural and ethnic backgrounds. The relative success of special need and ELL students should be examined as well.

> Disaggregation. To analyze test data by breaking out the scoring patterns for various subgroups.

Providing Students with Evaluation Feedback

By this point in the assessment process, the test/project was specified, students completed their work, the teacher evaluated the work, grades have been assigned, and the results have been examined for any differences across subgroups. Along the way the teacher will have been reflecting on how the process has gone and what has been learned for next time. The remaining step is to provide feedback to the students.

Some teachers simply return the product to the student with a numerical or letter grade circled at the top. Returning quiz, test, and other student products is a key opportunity to further learning. At the very minimum, there should be discussion of the correct answers and examples of the various ways that the work could be done. An important additional step is to link the feedback to the benchmarks and standards. Students, as well as the teacher, need to keep the benchmarks and standards in mind. This is true for elementary students as well as high school students. The feedback session is a time for students to reflect on what they did well, what they still need to learn, and where they need clarification. For the teacher and the students, feedback sessions on the evaluation of tests and projects needs to be a time for reflection and further learning, not just a time to tally the grade.

Preparing Report Cards and End-of-Year Recommendations   All of the evaluation activities should be seen as accumulating across each grading period and the entire school year. The work of the whole year culminates in the teacher making the recommendation for promotion, graduation, or retention. This is a major decision point for each student and one that teachers need to take seriously. Teachers need to have clear and continuing documentation of the accumulating learning of each student. The report card grades and accompanying written descriptions need to be to the point. They need to be supportive of the student and they also need to identify areas of accomplishments, and areas of need.

Revisiting Harold Pratt's Concerns about the Science Test

Harold developed 10 objective test items and made sure that some were at each of the levels described in Bloom's Taxonomy. Five of the items were fill-in-the-blank that required knowing key vocabulary, one was matching of the different steps in the cell-division process, three were multiple choice dealing with comprehension and application, and one was multiple choice that required higher-level thinking. The open-ended question required students to write a two- to three-page essay in which they were to apply their understanding of cell division and to include brief discussion of implications for medical research.

What Are the Critical Issues in Assessing Student Learning?

In this chapter basic concepts and procedures for assessing student learning are described. There are a number of purposes for assessing and many methods for testing what students have learned. Scoring and interpreting test results needs to be done carefully by the teacher, as does making feedback to students meaningful. Testing in and of itself has become a major component of schooling. School districts, states, and now with the No Child Left Behind act, the federal government all have become preoccupied with testing. The larger goal of assessing—using information from tests to inform instruction and improve learning—is being lost. There are many issues to consider. Some of those that press directly on teachers are addressed.

Standardized Tests

▶ Standardized tests. Tests that have been developed to rigorous standards and are used to make high-stakes decisions.

Until this point in this chapter, the discussion has focused on teacher-made tests. The formal testing that is directed by the school district and state use **standardized tests**. These tests have been developed by commercial corporations and are sold to school districts and states. Standardized tests are devel-

Connecting
TO THE CLASSROOM

This chapter first introduced seven purposes for assessment. Then different approaches to testing, including CRTs and NRTs, and the construction of different types of test items were described. Teacher-made tests, standardized tests, and a number of issues, such as high-stakes testing, were described. The following summary points should be kept in mind as you engage in assessing student learning.

1. The primary purpose for assessment should be to help students learn, which means that teachers must be continually using a variety of methods to assess the extent to which each student's understanding is increasing.

2. Don't forget that students have a responsibility to self-assess and to use the results of tests and other assessments to reflect about and to improve their learning.

3. Norm-referenced tests (NRTs) compare one's student achievement to how other students have done.

4. Criterion-referenced tests (CRTs) compare student achievement to a particular level of proficiency or performance.

5. Bloom's Taxonomy is a useful tool for classifying test items and teacher questions. Low-level questions seek recall of facts and procedures. High-level questions ask students to analyze, synthesize, and evaluate using what they know and understand.

6. Objective test items take more time to write and are quick to score. Subjective test items may take less time to construct, but require extended time to score.

7. For all assessment activities, teachers should disaggregate the data. Teachers need to be constantly checking for biases that inhibit certain students from having optimal opportunities to learn.

8. High-stakes testing is a major issue for students and teachers. Multiple assessments should be used when making any major decision.

- Simple steps need to be taken such as making sure desktops are clear and that the teacher has not left up classroom displays with relevant information.

- Student handwriting can be compared with previous samples and students can be asked to provide the reasoning for their answer.

- With objective tests ask students to turn in their worksheets so that you can see if they actually did the necessary steps.

Testing Is a Means for Sorting Students

The last issue to be introduced has to do with a basic consequence of all testing activity, which is the sorting of the test takers. At the beginning of this chapter, we talked about gatekeeping. A more direct way of raising this issue is to use the word *sorting*. Some students "pass," some receive "A's" while others receive "B's" or "C's." One of the functions and consequences of grading is sorting students. Being this direct about this issue should make you more sensitive of the need to be careful and responsible. Teachers need to be careful that there is not a built-in bias to the sorting. Boys, girls, rich, poor, black, white, and brown all need to have an equal opportunity to succeed. Teachers are responsible for providing instruction in ways that all students have the opportunity to learn. When this is the case, there will not be an achievement gap.

Chapter Summary

In this chapter, testing and the use of those test results (assessing student learning) has been the topic. Teachers need to understand the differences between norm-referenced and criterion-referenced testing. They also need to become skilled at constructing different types of objective and subjective test items. Further, teachers should continually be looking for any biases in their instruction and assessments. Disaggregating the data is an important step for ensuring that all students are learning.

Why is assessing so important? The whole purpose of schooling is to provide opportunities for students to learn. Assessing student learning is important for the student and the teacher as the way to gauge progress. Assessing also is important in determining the steps in instruction and as a means of accountability in reporting to parents and the public. Norm-referenced tests (NRTs) compare the performance of one student to the performance of a comparison group of students. Criterion-referenced tests (CRTs) compare the performance of each student to a particular level of accomplishment.

What are some of the ways to test student learning? The many ways to test student learning range from teacher observation to commercially developed standardized tests. Each form of test item is particularly good for measuring certain types of learning. Also, as the decision to be made with the test results become more high stakes, the quality of the tests and the use of multiple measures becomes increasingly important.

What are some of the critical issues in assessing student learning? A number of issues directly affect teachers. Certainly the current emphasis on high-stakes testing being applied not only to students, but to teacher licensure is an issue. The overpreoccupation of some teachers and schools with test preparation is leading to other areas of the curriculum being neglected. Other issues include the importance of making sure tests are not biased and that multiple measures are used in making judgments.

Class Discussion Questions

1. High-stakes testing is being used to decide which students will receive a high school diploma and which teacher education candidates will be licensed by the state to teach. What do you think about this practice? It can be argued that it is fair; everyone takes the

same test and has the same chance. Others will argue that the test is better than trusting the (professional) judgment of administrators. What are some of the intended and unintended consequences of high-stakes testing?

2. One of the purposes for assessment that was introduced in this chapter is for student self-reflection about their learning. What can teachers do to help students use tests for self-reflection? At what grade level are students ready to self-assess? In other words, do you think that it would be useful for primary grade teachers to work with their students on self-assessment? Or in elementary school is this really only the teacher's job?

Field Guide for School Observations

Find a rubric for some component of student learning for a subject that you plan to teach. When you next visit a classroom where that subject is being taught, use the rubric to score examples of student work. Compare your scoring with that of the teacher. Did the teacher use a rubric or some other scoring system? If possible, check with some students about how they have assessed their learning. See if the rubric makes sense to them.

Ask a Teacher

Look over the various assessments that a teacher has used across a term to evaluate student work. Ask the teacher to explain the reasoning for the different forms of assessment that have been used. How did he or she derive the final grade? Also, ask if the teacher detected any differences in student learning that might be indicative of an achievement gap.

Journaling Becoming a Thoughtful Teacher

One of the biggest concerns for all teachers, not just beginning teachers, is wading through all of the paperwork. Every time teachers give an assignment, there is likely to be a student product that has to be reviewed and graded. Take a few minutes to think about the business of testing and assessment. Write down some of your current ideas for how the testing you will do can be made most efficient. Which forms of testing will be most useful for you as a teacher? How can you reduce the amount of time that is spent in dealing with assessment work? Be sure to record your notes from observations of expert teachers managing this work efficiently. How do they do it?

Portfolio Task

It is never too soon to start drafting test items that you could use in the classroom. For a subject that you plan to teach, select a unit, chapter, or week's worth of lessons and construct a set of test items. Be sure to develop a combination of objective and subjective items. Use Bloom's Taxonomy (Figure 11.3) as a guide for developing items that will assess different levels of student learning. Also be sure to include your plan for scoring and grading. Once you have the test drafted, have a colleague take the test and give you feedback on what made sense and where they had questions.

Self-Assessments What Am I Learning?

In this chapter, each of the test-item format examples dealt with teacher education content. Go back through these items and record your answers and compile your grade. Which test-item format are you most comfortable with? As you worked through the items, how did you deal with the poor design of some of them?

Using the Web

The Web represents a powerful resource for obtaining information about any of the public schools in the country. However, there always has to be caution in assuming that all of the information is accurate. Exploring and comparing information about student performance in different schools and school districts can be informative. For example, go to www.greatschools.net and search for high schools in the Cherry Creek, Colorado, school district. This is the district where Dr. Elliott Asp, the Educator in Real Schools interviewed for this chapter, is an assistant superintendent. You can see and compare information about each school in terms of academic performance rating, the ratio of full time equivalent (FTE), and other factors. Then search for where you went to high school. Develop a table that compares high schools in the two districts. What inferences would you make?

Your Professional Library

Benn, John J. (2004). *Assessing students with special needs*. Upper Saddle River, NJ: Pearson.

Assessing learning progress with special needs students can be a challenge for teacher-education candidates and beginning teachers. This text addresses the issues and makes clear what teachers can do to assess general performance and academic achievement. Each chapter offers many concrete ways for teachers and their students to be successful. For example, Chapter 3 includes a description of a dozen approaches to alternative grading including contracts, level, and IEP grading.

Trumbull, Elise, & Farr, Beverly (Eds.) (2000). *Grading and Reporting Student Progress in an Age of Standards*. Norwood, MA: Christopher-Gordon.

Each of the nine chapters is written by an expert who has carefully considered the challenges and approaches to grading in a standards-based environment. Topics covered include different grading methods, avoiding bias, special populations, and reporting to parents. Examples of report cards and strategies for addressing standards are presented throughout each chapter.

Wiggins, G., & McTighe, J. (1998). *Understanding by design*. Alexandria, VA: Association for Supervision and Curriculum Development.

This book is one of the classic references for developing understanding of the relationships between learning outcomes, assessment, and the design of curriculum. The authors walk the reader through each topic and than draw implications for the design of instruction, including an examination of how the way teachers teach is linked to how and what students learn.

To access chapter objectives, practice tests, weblinks, and flashcards, visit the Companion Website at **www.ablongman.com/hall1e**

mylabschool
Where the classroom comes to life!

Go to Allyn & Bacon's MyLabSchool (**www.mylabschool.com**). Enter Assignment ID **EPV8** in the **Assignment Finder** and view video clip, *Forms of Assessment*. The educators in this clip discuss a variety of methods for assessing student learning and emphasize the importance of matching the assessment method to the learning task. As stated in clip 12, teachers are constantly assessing student learning. Using the information in the video and the information in this chapter, list at least 5 methods of assessing student learning available to teachers. Describe one way that assessments of student learning can create a vehicle for communicating with students and with their parents.

Now enter Assignment ID **CS25** and read Case 2: *Putting Yourself in the Picture*. All teachers have exceptional learners in their classrooms. Determining the most productive course of action to provide the optimum learning opportunities for each student requires that teachers develop skill at assessing behavior patterns and deciding on which intervention strategies to implement.

1. How might you decide what to do about the situation in Case 2?
2. What knowledge about assessment would help you make the best decision?

Managing the Classroom and Student Behavior

Educators in Real Schools

M E E T

Teressa Colbrook

Ullom Elementary School

Teressa Colbrook has been a teacher at Ullom for 7 years. In addition to her teaching responsibilities, Teressa teaches part-time for the university, is enrolled in a teacher education doctoral program, and conducts mentoring seminars for the cooperating teachers at her school. Teressa is an excellent manager of her time and enthusiastic about her choice of career. She exudes pride in her profession. The joy she brings to interactions with her students is emphasized by a quick, bright smile and the ability to listen with uninterrupted concern and thoughtfulness. Teressa strives for excellence in teaching and is well aware of the responsibilities she must fulfill as a teacher.

Ullom Elementary School is a Title I K–5 school in the Clark County School District in Las Vegas, Nevada, the fastest growing metropolitan area in the United States. There are 35 teachers and 750 students in 45 classrooms and portable classrooms at Ullom. Built in an open-air style popular in the Southwest in the 1970s, each classroom door opens to the outdoors along a covered walkway. There is a library, a technology room, and a courtyard where students plant vegetables and flowers. Thirty-two percent of the teachers at Ullom hold advanced degrees; some are just beginning their careers as teachers and others have been teaching for more than 20 years. Grades one through three have less than 20 students per class due to Nevada's reduced class-load ruling. Grades four and five have over 30 students in a class. Sixty-five percent of the students at Ullom are Hispanic, 6 percent are African American, 24 percent are White, and 5 percent are of Asian or other ethnic groups.

Chapter 12

❖ *Why did you choose to become a teacher?*

I hadn't always planned to be a teacher. In fact, I planned to be a pediatrician and got a bachelor's degree in biology. However, I guess I'm one of those people who have teaching in the blood because both of my parents were teachers. After I graduated with my B.S. in biology, I went back to the university to earn a master's degree and obtain a teaching license and I've never looked back. Teaching is the absolute perfect career for me.

❖ *What do you expect when you see excellence in teaching?*

Excellence in teaching means that the teacher is learning right along with the students; that both parties are enjoying themselves and are able to articulate the processes and the products of the learning. It means so much more than test scores or adequate yearly progress. It means students look forward to the adventure of learning and the teacher looks forward to facilitating that adventure. It means taking seriously the questions and concerns of the young people who are to become avid learners and teachers in the future. It means sharing literature, experiments, discoveries, and intelligent failures.

❖ *How do you know when you have made a difference in student learning?*

The only way to truly know that students have learned is to see the application of skills in another context. When we've discussed writing traits and my students are able to identify those in authentic text, I know they've learned what the writing traits are. When we identify metaphors in literature and I see them being used in students' writing, I know they've learned what a metaphor is. Application is the true assessment of learning.

✤ What brings you joy in teaching?

The joy of teaching occurs when a student gasps and says, "Oh! I get it!" It occurs when I overhear students explaining to one another the way numbers can be taken apart and put back together, when students rush to the classroom library simply to read a book we've read together the day before. Joy in teaching occurs when I say it's time to stop writing and the students beg for 10 more minutes. There's joy in teaching when a student relates that she's never liked writing before, but she does now. The joy comes in those tiny moments we take for granted.

✤ How would you define classroom management?

Classroom management is the orchestration of innumerable components to ensure a safe and comfortable learning environment. It is the reason students feel secure enough to share their thoughts, written or otherwise. Classroom management means specific routines and procedures developed deliberately and collaboratively. Classroom management is a part of teaching that is never perfected because it must always be adapted to fit the needs of the students and the teacher. It is the reason students know learning is important. It is the reason teachers can teach and students can learn.

✤ How do you prepare to manage a classroom?

The first day of school always makes me nervous. I feel like a child the night before Christmas. Being on a 9-month schedule, I usually am able to put school out of my mind for the first several weeks of summer break, but as soon as August arrives, it's as if a switch goes off, and I am immediately thinking (obsessing) about school and how things will/could/should be. I think much of that has to do with the fact that I am always changing things. I have never taught one year the same as another year. I am always reflecting on and revising my strategies and programs. The best way to prepare to manage a classroom is just that—PREPARE. Have your strategies in mind before the students walk into the room. Be prepared to revise the strategies if they don't fit—but be prepared.

✤ To you, what is the most important aspect of managing student behavior?

The most important aspect would have to be respect: respect for and from the students. Often, teachers expect respect, but do little to earn it. To develop trust, students must see that teachers are real people who make mistakes and fail. Teachers must be willing and able to admit wrongs and apologize. Modeling this life skill for students begins a relationship of trust and respect, which leads to a community of learners who are able to respect one another.

✤ What advice about managing a classroom and student behavior would you give to a beginning teacher?

Beware of being a friend too soon. I failed miserably at classroom management my first year because I was very concerned about my students LIKING me. I forgot that I wasn't there to be their friend; I was there to be their teacher. This doesn't mean you shouldn't get to know your students on a personal level. It means there are times you have to be strict and hold extremely high expectations for behavior . . . and be prepared to implement consequences when those expectations aren't met. If your students see you as a friend only and not a teacher, they are apt to disregard your requests because the requests are coming from a friend. This can make classroom management difficult, if not impossible.

Questions to Consider

1. Think back to your days as an elementary, middle school, or high school student and how one of your classrooms was arranged. What was it about the classroom that was most appealing to you? Why?

2. What does the phrase, *a friend to my students*, mean to you?

3. What concerns you most about managing a classroom?

4. Do you think students can be comfortable in a highly organized, tightly structured environment?

5. What is involved in managing someone else's behavior?

6. How did one of the teachers you had manage student misbehavior?

All schools, classrooms, students, and teachers are not the same. What works in one setting or for one group of learners may not work for another. School days begin and end on different notes and the times in between are strung together by such a variety of events that even the most experienced teachers can be perplexed by unexpected outcomes. Individual teachers must develop personal systems for classroom management that are comfortable to work in, that allow for professional choice, and yet are acceptable within a given school culture.

Any classroom management system must support teaching and learning, recognize individual needs and desires among students, and encourage growth of acceptable behaviors. Every teacher holds an ideal classroom in mind. The challenge is to make that classroom come to life through knowledge of oneself, through an awareness of the wide range of techniques and strategies available for building a management plan, and through communicating with students to inform them of that vision. Winston Churchill once said, "We shape our dwellings, then our dwellings shape us." It is also likely that teachers shape their classrooms and then the classrooms they have created shape the learning that occurs there as well as the behavior of the learners. What every teacher wants is a classroom of students who want to learn, who feel good about being in school, and about what they do when they are there. Expert classroom management can make that desire become a reality.

What Is Classroom Management?

*The procedure for students to follow when they want the teacher's attention in **Lucy**'s classroom works perfectly for her and her 4th graders. If a student holds up one finger, they are asking for permission to get a drink of water, two fingers indicate a need to use the restroom, a raised pencil is a request to use the pencil sharpener, and a raised hand indicates the student either has a question to ask or would like to say something. Simple, yes, but Lucy believe this quiet management strategy she has taught her students to use for communicating needs does not interrupt other students' concentration or focus and it saves valuable minutes of time that can be spent in instruction and learning.*

Classroom management involves all of the tasks that teachers and students perform in any given day covering a wide range of actions and attitudes associated with teaching and learning. Educators discuss classroom management from differing perspectives, but these different perspectives all take into consideration the interaction among students, teachers, and the content to be taught in an effective learning environment. McEwan (2000) views classroom management as "the ways in which rules are established and reinforced, how consequences are enacted or exacted, how frequently communication with parents takes place, the physical setup of the room, the ready availability of materials, the methods used for resolving conflicts, and the verbal interactions with students."

Weber (1994) defines classroom management as "that complex set of strategies that a teacher uses to establish and maintain the conditions that will enable students to learn" (p. 234). Wong (1998) views classroom management as "all the things that a teacher does to organize students, space, time, and materials so that instruction and student learning can take place" (p. 84). Iverson (2003) defines classroom management as "the act of supervising relationships, behaviors, and instructional settings and lessons for communities of learners" (p. 4) and views management as separate from discipline in that discipline refers to "teaching students how to behave appropriately." To Emmer, Evertson, and Worsham (2000), classroom management involves a series of decisions teachers make to assure "smoothly running classroom communities where students are highly involved in worthwhile activities that support their learning" (xiii).

If one considers the alternative to managing a classroom (which is chaos), effective classroom management can be viewed as central to all that is good and right about teaching. Because the responsibility for managing a classroom rests almost entirely on the teacher's shoulders, this is perhaps the main reason that managing a classroom is often cited as the number one concern of beginning teachers. Such concern is not just a recent phenomenon in education. Consider the following excerpt from D. H. Lawrence's 1915 novel, *Rainbow*, in which Ursula Brangwen begins her teaching career and is faced with the daunting task of managing the behavior of her students.

> The day passed incredibly slowly. She never knew what to do. There came horrible gaps, when she was merely exposed to the children. . . . Before this inhuman number of children she was always at bay. She could not get away from it. There it was. This class of fifty collective children, depending on her for command, for command it hated and resented. It made her feel she could not breathe: she must suffocate, it was so inhuman. They were so many, that they were not children. They were a squadron. She could not speak as she would to a child, because they were not individual children, they were a collective, inhuman thing. (pp. 355–356)

Ursula's experience may seem a bit extreme and out of the ordinary, but it is a rare teacher indeed who has never felt outnumbered or outmaneuvered by an unmanageable group of students. Teacher education candidates can take comfort in the fact that a modicum of knowledge about human behavior and skill in implementing management strategies can provide even a novice teacher some degree of self-confidence and competence in managing a classroom. It is a huge undertaking, but it does not have to be overwhelming.

Establishing and maintaining an effective learning environment through management of space, time, instruction, and behavior requires a teacher to have expert knowledge of the learners, the content, and the context. A teacher's ideas about classroom management often go through a series of transformations as they observe, learn, and reflect on the success of the management plans they have enacted. The way a particular teacher chooses to manage a classroom also derives from a specific system of values and priorities for attending to a range of educational functions. As you develop your personal professional philosophy of teaching introduced in Chapter 7, you will most likely include some of the ideas you have for managing a classroom.

Using What You Already Know about Classroom Management

In learning theory, the technique of **activation** or the use of **advance organizers** helps bring a student's full attention to what they are about to study. For example, if a teacher wants to teach a science lesson about weather, he might ask the

Activation. Beginning, being made aware of something, being ready to learn.

Advance organizers. Organizing frameworks that provide an overview for content to be studied.

▶ Cognitive framework. The arrangement of what is known and perceived and how this information is organized through the process of learning.

students to recall a time they experienced stormy weather. He will talk about the sound of the wind moving objects around or the sound of rain and the smell of ozone or dust in the air. These are all things students would be familiar with and recalling the memory of them will help students build a **cognitive framework** to connect additional information about weather to.

Likewise, we've all had some experience with management. If you've ever packed a suitcase, loaded the car, decorated a house or a room, planned a wedding or birthday party, or been shopping, you probably already have a good idea about the importance of organization, time management, and access to resources. If you have spent any time at all working with young children, you no doubt know quite a bit about behavior management. You've also spent considerable time in classrooms observing how other teachers organize tasks and activities and manage the behavior of their students.

The fascinating thing about becoming a student of teaching is that you have had so much practice being in classrooms. People often choose to enter the teaching profession because the years they spent in school were enjoyable for them. They had pleasant experiences that they are eager to recreate. However, one of the difficult things about learning to teach is that most of the years you've spent in classrooms were as a student. So naturally, learning to teach requires a shift in perspective. Danielson (1996) suggests that what students recall about their favorite teachers is usually related to the teacher's skill in creating a businesslike environment, with routines and procedures that directed student behavior in positive ways and supported instruction.

Frameworks for Learning about Classroom Management

Performance in managing a classroom does not rest entirely on rules, routines, rewards, and reprimands, but is a far more complex combination of all that a teacher is, knows, and does. As an aspiring teacher education candidate, you need to recognize the relationships between teacher dispositions, teacher knowledge, pedagogical and management skills, and the level at which a teacher performs. The Venn diagram created from the framework of good teachers and good teaching (Figure 12.1) is an example of the skills expert teachers exhibit.

Froyen and Iverson (1999) categorize effective classroom management into three distinct areas of content management, conduct management, and covenant management. Each area of management requires a specific set of teacher knowledge, skills, and dispositions, and each area contributes to and is influenced by the effectiveness of the others.

Three Areas of Classroom Management

Content management includes planning (1) the use of the physical environment, (2) procedures that occur during the instructional day, and (3) instruction (Froyen and Iverson, 1999, 49). Planning is the key. Remember, if you fail to plan, you plan to fail. Teachers plan during the summer break for the coming school year. They plan on weekends. They plan before and after school and during free periods. The planning that teachers do has a profound effect on instruction, student behavior, and the relationships that are formed with their students.

Figure 12.1 Venn diagram: good teachers; good teaching

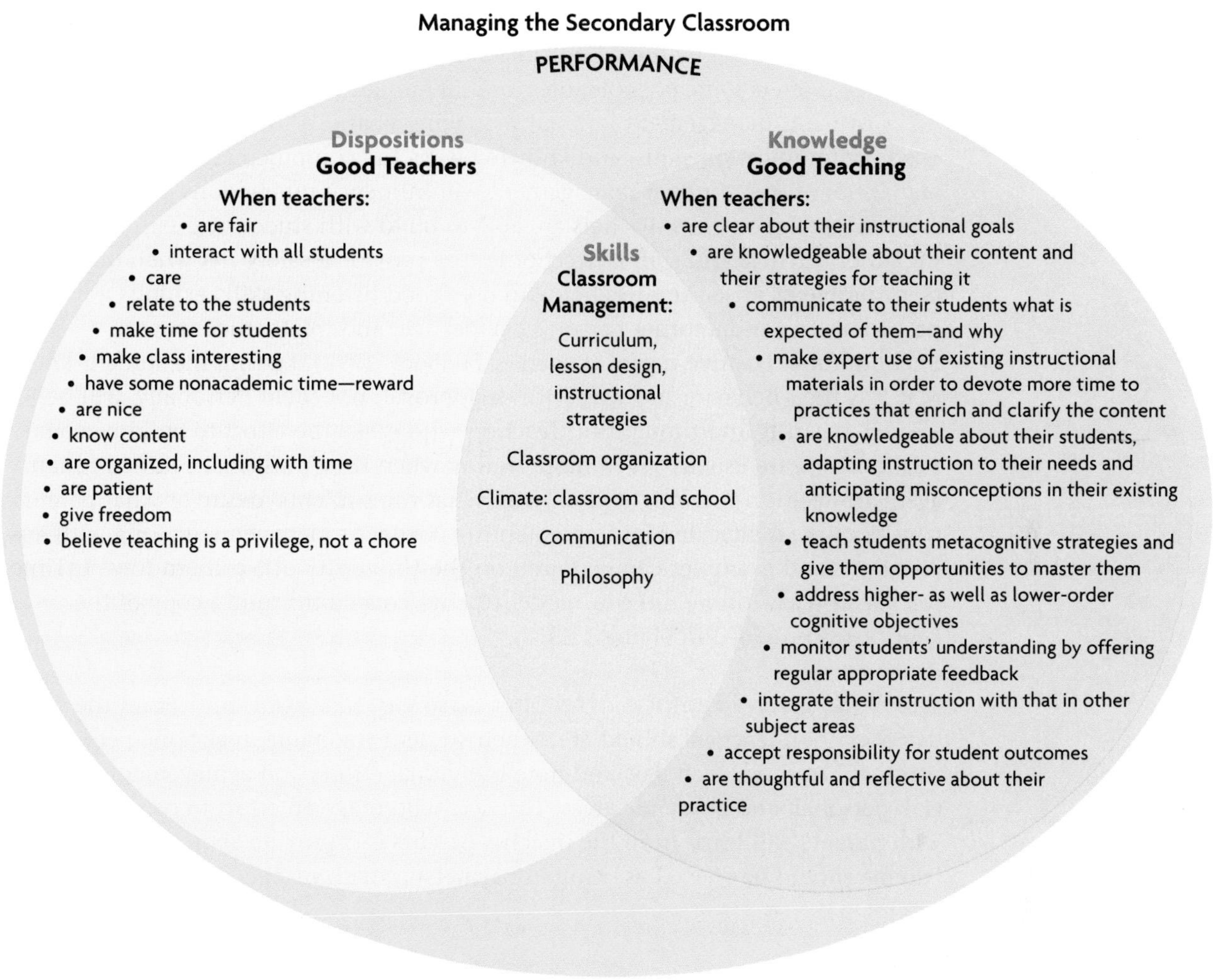

Managing the Secondary Classroom
PERFORMANCE

Dispositions
Good Teachers

When teachers:
- are fair
- interact with all students
- care
- relate to the students
- make time for students
- make class interesting
- have some nonacademic time—reward
- are nice
- know content
- are organized, including with time
- are patient
- give freedom
- believe teaching is a privilege, not a chore

Skills
Classroom Management:

Curriculum, lesson design, instructional strategies

Classroom organization

Climate: classroom and school

Communication

Philosophy

Knowledge
Good Teaching

When teachers:
- are clear about their instructional goals
- are knowledgeable about their content and their strategies for teaching it
- communicate to their students what is expected of them—and why
- make expert use of existing instructional materials in order to devote more time to practices that enrich and clarify the content
- are knowledgeable about their students, adapting instruction to their needs and anticipating misconceptions in their existing knowledge
- teach students metacognitive strategies and give them opportunities to master them
- address higher- as well as lower-order cognitive objectives
- monitor students' understanding by offering regular appropriate feedback
- integrate their instruction with that in other subject areas
- accept responsibility for student outcomes
- are thoughtful and reflective about their practice

Source: Schroeder, M. L. (2002). Adapted from Porter and Brophy.

Conduct management is maintained through the establishment of rules and guidelines of behavior. Three to five rules for appropriate behavior seem to be the ideal numbers. How these rules are established depends on grade level, the teacher's philosophy of classroom management, and what is considered acceptable behavior in the school. "Be nice" is a little vague for a rule. A 5th grader might interpret "be nice" as an invitation to chat with whoever is in earshot, while a high school senior might choose to "be nice" by doing a friend's homework. Rules and procedures must be taught so that students know how to succeed in the classroom. Children in different grade levels react in different ways to rules, regulations, and procedures so naturally what works in a kindergarten class to get students' attention may not work in a middle school class. Experienced teachers have learned that each developmental level has a set of typical behaviors that help determine which strategies teachers can use to best advantage. Third graders tattle. Fourth graders will do everything the teacher does. Middle school students will do whatever their friends do, and high school students usually make behavior choices based on a combination of the norms set by the school administration and the norms of their peers. Figure 12.2 offers some possible rules for different grade levels.

Covenant management is about managing relationships, having highly developed communication skills, and knowing ways the combined effects of content management and conduct management will influence interactions in the classroom. The relationships teachers are able to build with students, their parents, and the other teachers and staff in a school often provide a safety net when management problems arise. Any teacher who uses good listening skills exhibits a willingness to understand another person's perspective, and treats students with unconditional positive regard (Rogers & Freiberg, 1994). Letting the student know that it is their behavior meeting with disapproval, not them personally, will be viewed as caring and thoughtful. Teachers who make the effort to build personal relationships are usually given more leeway when they must make difficult management decision that might clash with what the students' desire or what parents consider just. A checklist for implementing covenant management along with applications and examples can be found on the University of Northern Iowa InTime website at www.intime.uni.edu/model/teacher/covenant.html. A copy of the checklist is provided in Figure 12.3.

The Personal and Parental Affect in Classroom Management   From the first day of school, teachers should greet their students by name, make one personal comment to them each day, and note individual efforts and achievements in social, personal, and academic areas. Teachers who make an effort to communicate with parents will learn from the insights parents can provide about their children. Parents should be viewed as being in partnership with teachers in the education of

Figure 12.2 Examples of classroom rules (elementary, middle, and high school)

Some rules of conduct are appropriate for all grade levels (i.e., *Treat other students the way you would like to be treated*).

Some variations are required to address the specific behaviors and attitudes of different age groups.

Elementary Classroom Rules

Try Hard.
Speak Softly.
Ask Before You Act.
Clean Up After Yourself.

Middle School Classroom Rules

Respect Other People's Property.
Keep a Tidy Workspace.
Keep Your Hands to Yourself.
Act as if Your Mother Is Watching.

High School Classroom Rules

Express Yourself Appropriately.
Straighten Up Your Area Before You Leave the Room.
Respect the Rights of Others.
Turn Off Cell Phones, Beepers, and Other
    Communication Devices.

447

How Do You Build
a Personal Philosophy
of Classroom
Management?

ier to learn from your own experience, to learn first hand with the support of a mentor or expert guide. Think about this: When you give a speech in your own words, it's pretty easy. When you use someone else's words, you have to memorize them. The value of experiential learning is something beginning teachers come to understand in very short order.

Revisiting Lucy's System for Uninterrupted Instructional Time

At the beginning of this section, Lucy uses a very simple management strategy that allows for silent communication in her classroom. Lucy had an objective in mind when she decided to use this system. She wanted to have less interruptions of instructional time. She put her plan in place by teaching her students some ways to let her know what they needed without disturbing the other students or interrupting her. It is clear that Lucy understands the value of classroom management to create a productive learning environment.

How Do You Build a Personal Philosophy of Classroom Management?

Belinda is completing her student teaching in a high school on the Navaho Reservation in Piñon, Arizona. Her first teaching unit was to have the students write personal essays because she thought that would be an excellent way to get to know the students. She created lessons that involved reading essays, writing prompts, and intensive, vocabulary work. She taught the students how to create vocabulary sheets using a technique she learned in her methods course at the university. She sectioned off part of the room as the word wall where the students can see what other students are writing.

Belinda wants her students to read the essays they are writing out loud. The first time Belinda asked her students to read out loud resulted in a chain reaction of "no!" Now she knows the students' names and has taken a personal interest in them, and the last time she called their names and asked them to read out loud, only one student said "no." No one in her class makes fun of another person for being a poor reader or writer. Instead, some of the more advanced students are helping the ones who have more difficulty with reading and writing.

Establishing a personal philosophy of classroom management must naturally begin with knowledge of some of the common models and theories in the field. With an understanding of the basic tenets of numerous models, any teacher education candidate can begin to incorporate specific strategies and key elements from each model into a personalized perspective. Most of us try out new skills beginning with what feels comfortable or with what we think might work given past experiences and personal attributes. In that respect, learning how to manage a classroom is not much different from learning how to snowboard. There are certain things you should know before starting out and there are many things you will learn along the way. Attempting to learn either can meet with resistance and cause stress, but both should be fun. Here are some of the theories you should be familiar with when learning about classroom management.

Theorists, Theories, and Models

Teachers as well as teacher education candidates have access to a wide range of approaches to classroom management. While having so many choices is nice, making the right ones in a highly charged classroom situation presents a challenge. The best prepared teachers become familiar with many approaches and are ready to act effectively when called upon to do so. Each theory or model of classroom management discussed in this section can serve as an advance organizer for a set of strategies and teacher behaviors. You may be learning or have learned some of the philosophical and psychological underpinnings of the theories in coursework associated with human learning and development and psychology. As you read about these models, make notes on which strategies you would most like to incorporate into your own personalized classroom management style. As Madeline Hunter (1994) wrote in response to criticism of her Instructional Theory into Practice model, "Models are judged on their ability to guide behavior, predict outcomes, and stimulate research, not on being the final answer to the establishment of any one method of classroom management" (p. 36).

Behavior Modification   Behavioral psychology tells us that behavior is learned and can be modified through positive reinforcement, punishment, extinction, and negative reinforcement. Burrhus Frederic Skinner, as discussed by Wattenberg (1967), is most often associated with the ideas of behavior modification in classrooms. His theories related to behavioral psychology have been applied in numerous ways to help teachers change student behavior. The most common use of Skinner's theories is the idea of positive reinforcement, providing students with tangible rewards or praise for completing work or demonstrating acceptable behavior. The expected outcome is that when children are rewarded for acceptable behavior, they will continue to exhibit that behavior and nonproductive behavior will be "extinguished." Positive reinforcement can be a powerful classroom management tool, however, there is disagreement in the professional community about the effect continued use of extrinsic rewards will have on self-motivation.

One of the most common mistakes in the use of behavior modification strategies by teachers is the practice of taking back a reward once it has been earned. For example, if a teacher distributes "behavior bucks" to students who are following directions and then demands that they are paid back to the teacher when directions aren't being followed, a reward that has been earned is being taken away. This practice only serves to reinforce in students a negative attitude toward work-

Ed Lines

"**Effective teachers manage their classrooms. Ineffective teachers discipline their classrooms.**" *Harry Wong*

449

How Do You Build
a Personal Philosophy
of Classroom
Management?

ing for a goal. If the goal might be moved or removed entirely, the uncertainy of attaining it would negate even trying for it in the first place. Consider how many of us would run a race without a clear understanding of the finish line. Even a race car driver going around and around the track knows how many laps to the checkered flag.

Assertive Discipline   Lee and Marlene Canter (1992) established a system to manage behavior that relies, in part, on a set of hierarchical consequences. In their **assertive discipline** model, teachers must insist upon responsible behavior from students. The most easily recognized example of assertive discipline in elementary classrooms is the use of a set of colored cards for each student, usually kept in individually named pockets on a wall chart. When a student displays irresponsible behavior, he or she is directed to rearrange their individual cards from green, to yellow, or to red. Each colored card represents a corresponding consequence. Ask any student in any classroom in the United States and they have probably had some experience with the Canter model of behavior management. You can learn more about Lee and Marlene Canter's views at www.canter.net.

In middle schools and high schools, students are often directed to write their names on the board if misbehavior occurs and to place tally marks after the name if the misbehavior continues. This method makes it easier for middle and secondary teachers to keep track of student behavior over time given the frequent change in class venue. Keeping track of student behavior is a prerequisite to changing it. Tracking behavior and the effectiveness of interventions to improve behavior is a critical aspect of any kind of classroom management plan. In addition, it is one of the most difficult things for teachers to stay on top of in light of their already taxing schedules.

Social-Emotional and Group Dynamics Management Approaches   Classroom management methods based on the theories of group dynamics, social psychology, and **judicious discipline**, a philosophy that creates an environment respectful of the citizenship rights of students (Gathercoal, 1997), focus on the importance of membership in a group, the need for individuals to control their own behavior, and for teachers to provide guidance and create environments conducive to a candid exchange of ideas. William Glasser's (1997) choice theory model calls for teachers to help students satisfy their five psychological needs (the need for survival, the need to belong, the need for power, the need for freedom, and the need for fun), so that students can choose appropriate behavior individually and as a group. Glasser believes that performance is raised by doing what's real, responsible, and right.

Quay and Quaglia (2004) suggest providing opportunities for students to be leaders in the classroom and to take responsibility for their choices. For example, when students feel that they are an important part of the classroom, that their opinions matter, that they have the chance to lead, and that they are held

Assertive discipline. A discipline model that demands responsible behavior from students.

Judicious discipline. Classroom management that is based on an understanding of respect for the rights of the students.

Ed Lines

"**The conventional wisdom about good classroom management is that no one notices it unless it's missing.**" *Carolyn Evertson*

accountable for their decisions, increased enthusiasm for learning can be the result. The research of Fritz Redl and Wattenberg (1959) provides a framework for understanding ways individual behavior affects group behavior and vice versa, as well as the importance of teaching students to exert self-control and monitor their own behavior.

▶ **Democratic classroom.** Classroom management method based on shared decision making and responsibility.

The **democratic classroom** of Dreikurs and Grey (1968) uses class meeting to engage students in shared decision making and in taking responsibility for building a democratic learning environment. Democratic classrooms depend on a teacher who recognizes the worth and dignity of every person, can build a sense of community within the classroom, and who has the ability to build positive relationships with students, parents, and members of the professional community. Visit the website of the Adler-Dreikurs Institute at www.bowiestate.edu/academics/profess/adi/ to learn more about the democratic classroom.

Teachers employing democratic classroom strategies view students as social beings who want to be accepted into the group and use encouragement rather than praise to direct student behavior. Robert Sylwester (2000) argues that a democratic classroom provides an excellent venue for brain maturation. To enact a democratic classroom Digna Artiles, a teacher at Hudtloff Middle School in the State of Washington establishes a court process to monitor discipline. She holds court once every 2 weeks to involve the students in the process and to satisfy the students' need for justice. The teaching personal and social responsibility model (Hellison, 1995) designed to be used in physical education classes has many implications for regular classrooms. The model emphasizes the importance of involving students in decision making for personal and social responsibility and outlines four levels of responsibility (self-control, involvement, self-responsibility, and caring) that teachers should help students attain.

Instruction and Communication Approaches to Classroom Management

Additional models of classroom management rely on the teacher's ability to provide effective instruction and to shape the classroom environment to facilitate positive behavior. Ginott (1972) views the teacher as a sort of central command fostering harmony and cooperation through effective communication. For a summary of Ginott's ideas, visit www.chaminade.org/inspire/i_am.htm. In a Ginott classroom, teachers talk to their students like the sensitive, intelligent individuals they are. Teachers refrain from threatening comments and sarcasm, they guide rather than criticize, and they learn to let some misbehavior slip by. When teachers learn to use Gordon's (1989) I-messages, which avoid any nega-

Class meetings provide an opportunity for shared decision making and responsibility.

tive or neutral use of the word *you* and instead use the principles of active listening by intentionally focusing on who they are listening to, they show respect for students' needs, interests, and abilities.

Johnson and Johnson (1999) advocate cooperation as the key to promoting a well-managed classroom, and propose the three C's (cooperating, conflict resolution, and civic values) as the basis for effective learning environments. Visit the website of the Cooperative Learning Center at the University of Minnesota at www.co-operation.org to learn more about the three C's of school and classroom management.

For Evertson, Emmer, and Worsham (2000) classroom management becomes routine once rules and expectations are made clear and instruction is well managed and related to the individual needs and talents of the students. In this well-managed classroom, it is vital that teachers recognize the relationship between their own behavior and that of their students and understand the support classroom management provides for instruction. Carolyn Evertson and Alene Harris describe ways to manage learning-centered classrooms at http://peabody.vanderbilt.edu/faculty/tl/evertson.htm.

Kohn (1996) invites teachers to move beyond rules; to understand the needs of children and how these needs can be met. This seems a reasonable challenge given the diversity of culture and backgrounds represented by students in classrooms today. Visit Alfie Kohn's home page at www.alfiekohn.org for a better understanding of the ideas in his book.

Revisiting Belinda's Philosophy of Classroom Management

Every day of her student teaching on the Navajo reservation, Belinda learns useful lessons and gains experience necessary to becoming an effective teacher. Her cooperating teacher and other teachers in the school offer advice and provide resources for her to use. The students she interacts with provide her with insights into the minds and behaviors of high school students. Because she spends so many evenings back at school for sporting events and other functions, she is learning valuable information about her students and their families. She is beginning to incorporate some of the theories and strategies you've read about in this section into her own theory of classroom management.

What Constitutes a Well-Managed Classroom?

Janet, a first-year teacher, was assigned a room in the basement wing of a rather large, rambling older building. Janet's classroom was actually a storage space down a narrow hall. There were no windows and the space was marred by six large pillars that held up the floor of the classrooms above. Janet had a desk. New florescent lights had been installed. A blackboard had been hung, there were student desks, two bookcases, one table, and one storage cabinet to complete the suite of furniture Janet had to work with. Janet began the year with the positive attitude so characteristic of beginning teachers. Janet tried to create an intriguing learning environment within the physical circumstances afforded her. She added color and light. She decorated the six pillars as different content areas (math, science, social studies, reading, writing, and health), and organized centers around each of the pillars. It was a work of desperate genius. Her efforts at room arrangement made an unattractive physical space an intriguing learning environment.

William Morris could have said that décor is what makes a home a thing of beauty and a joy forever. While students spend almost as much time in school as they do at home, schools are built from a utilitarian viewpoint with maintenance and durability the determining factors of what goes where. Nearly all classrooms are rectangular shape. Most have windows, though it is cheaper to build schools without windows. The desks, bookcases, shelves, and tables in classrooms are institutional in style and by themselves don't offer much in the way of décor. Teachers are wonderfully creative people, however, and have the power to turn a somewhat bland environment into a scintillating palace of learning. Wise teachers let the students help build the environment that is the most comfortable for their needs and expressive of their individual and group personalities while the teacher keeps in mind simply that room arrangement should promote learning in every nook and cranny.

Room Arrangement

The arrangement of a classroom can contribute to the responsibility students may feel toward a specific classroom. If it is a pleasant place to be, a place the teacher seems happy in, a place to be proud of, a place where significant things happen, then students are likely to perform in ways conducive to learning. The placement of furniture and materials in a classroom can also contribute significantly to instruction. Jones (2003) discusses the "interior loop" of a classroom and describes the ways in which room arrangement relates directly to time on task and fewer behavior issues. Find out more about Jones's model at www.educationwork.com/a-curr/jones/Jones001/shtml.

In order for classroom arrangement to support learning, students need to have a clear view of the focal point for instruction. The teacher must be able to move easily around the classroom to monitor students' work, and materials and resources should be easily available to keep lessons moving. Teachers need to identify traffic routes and be ever on the lookout for obstacles that would impede movement or create a management problem.

Evertson et al. offer four key elements to good room arrangement (2006):

1. Keep high-traffic areas free of congestion.
2. Be sure students can be easily seen by the teachers (and vice versa).
3. Keep frequently used teaching materials and student supplies readily accessible.
4. Be certain students can easily see instructional presentations and displays. (p. 4)

Classroom arrangements are dictated by the size of the classroom, the number of students, and the types of furniture in the room. The Teach-nology website at www.teach-nology.com/ideas/ provides a seating arrangement section as well as diagrams of different types of arrangements.

Classrooms U, V, and W   The three classroom arrangements presented here in Figures 12.4 through 12.6 all begin with identical floor space. The furniture and the desks in the rooms have been arranged to accommodate the plans individual teachers have for instruction, their expectations for individual and group work, and to accommodate the ways they plan to manage student movement and available resources. The arrangement of furniture in each classroom is determined somewhat by the location of windows and the door to the classroom. Work space is provided for group work and for teacher-directed instruction. The pencil sharpener is near a wastebasket in every case but not necessary near the teacher's desk. Each classroom presents a particular challenge and also some benefits. It will definitely be more difficult for the teacher in room U to move from one side of the room to the other, and if there is a behavior problem that needs quick attention, the teacher will probably have to use verbal commands rather than proximity control. The research of Bennet and Blundell (1983) found that there was an increase of work completion in classrooms with row and column seating; however, the quality of the work did not necessarily change.

Figure 12.4 Classroom arrangement for classroom U

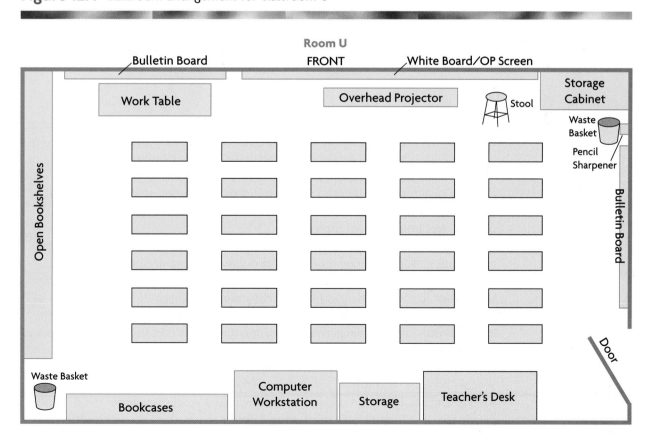

Figure 12.5 Classroom arrangement for classroom V

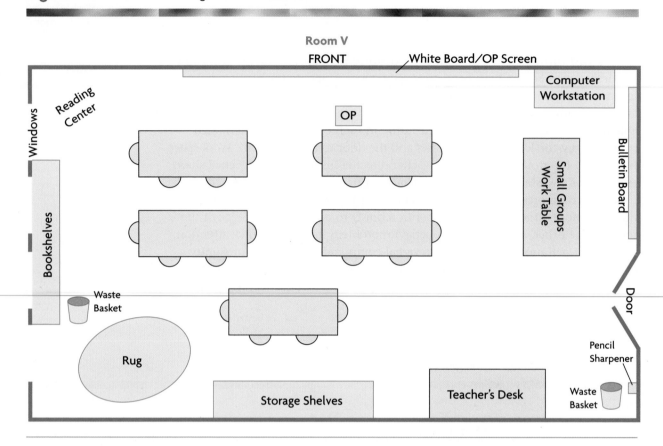

In classroom V with students sitting around a table and sharing a workspace, there may be more talking and students may be more easily distracted by one another. However, such an arrangement facilitates the distribution and collection of materials and the use of group work as an instructional strategy. Classroom W makes it easy for the teacher to walk around the horseshoe-shape arrangement of desks and check independent work, but the arrangement could encourage students to feel isolated from the group.

Arranging a room for optimal student participation and effective classroom management does not happen easily. On occasion, the space provided for a classroom can pose extreme problems to classroom management. As school populations bulge, trailers serving as portable classrooms are often brought onto school grounds. These portable classrooms, separate from the main school building, may be highly susceptible to negative environmental conditions and to noise from outside. Student movement to and from a portable classroom might necessarily need to be more tightly controlled than student movement within the main building. Teacher access to assistance from other teachers is more constrained, and use of resources and materials not normally found within a single classroom must be prudently planned for and organized. In real estate, the bottom line is "location,

Figure 12.6 Classroom arrangement for classroom W

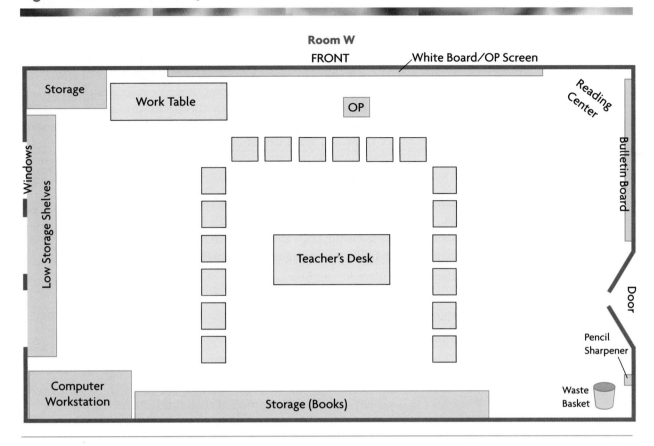

location, location." In the classroom management, "arrangement, arrangement, arrangement" may be the most powerful determinant. Try your hand at arranging a classroom following the guidelines provided in the Connecting to the Classroom on page 456.

Helping Students Be Comfortable in the Room You Have Arranged

Students need to know what is expected of them; how to act in certain situations and what instructional purposes are assigned to different spaces in the classroom. Everyone wants to know what is theirs. Therefore, helping students find their own space and becoming comfortable in it might be one of the first orders of building a productive teacher/learner relationship. Students should be taught everything from how to enter the classroom, to where personal possessions should be kept, to how materials should be passed out and collected, to rules regarding the teacher's personal space. For students to feel comfortable in the space you have arranged, they need to know the procedures for success in the classroom. When students understand what they must do and why they must do a certain thing a certain way, they have a tendency to do what is expected.

Connecting

TO THE CLASSROOM

Try the visualization exercise (described here) from the Stallings (1990) Effective Use of Time program to create a personalized mental image of a classroom. When you have finished creating a mental image of your classroom, draw a picture of it. Then think about how your choices for placement of desks and other furniture match Evertson, Emmer, and Worsham's (2000) guidelines for effective use of classroom space described earlier in this chapter.

Visualize Your Classroom

- With your eyes closed, visualize an empty classroom.
- In your mind's eye, look carefully at the space you have to work with.
- Imagine a space for the large group, a space for small-group learning, and a space for individual learning (a space where a student can be alone).
- Decide on a place for your desk.
- Think about sound—quiet places—noisy places.
- Consider storage.
- Think about what will be on the walls.
- Think about putting some color in the room (red and orange for energy, blue and green for quiet, purple for deep thought).

Remember that people space is more important than furniture space.

Sources: Stallings, J. A. (1990). *Effective use of time program*. Houston, TX: University of Houston; Evertson, C., Emmer, E. T., & Worsham, M. E. (2000). *Classroom management for elementary teachers* (5th ed.). Boston: Allyn and Bacon.

Hardly anyone learns a thing perfectly the first time it is taught. Rules and regulations that are taught and learned on the first day of school or during the first week will no doubt have to be reviewed from time to time to reinforce students' comfort in your classroom. Reteaching can take the form of gentle reminders or practice accompanied by a clarification of the goals and intended outcomes for the procedure. Certainly some things that were stressed at the beginning of the year may change, but once a teacher has established a process for learning a procedure, future changes to procedure will be simplified.

Storage Space and the Backpack Phenomenon   Thirty-five years ago, backpacks were carried mainly by campers and hikers. Today, it would be unusual to see anyone going to school without a backpack stuffed to overflowing. No longer do teachers have to contend with merely brown paper lunch bags and cartoon lunchboxes. Huge packs are coming to school on the backs of tiny kindergarten children and high school seniors. It's almost frightening. What in the world do they contain? You can see them under desks, jammed in bookcases and cubbyholes, and hanging under jackets and coats and in lockers. The backpack phenomenon is simply amazing. Some students are pulling those wheeled briefcases frequently seen in airports to school. One might wonder where these semisuitcases will be stored in classrooms and what management problems they might cause.

Managing Paperwork

Have you ever stood in a post office and watched folks empty out their mailboxes? There is usually someone standing near a huge waste basket throwing away what is commonly referred to as junk mail. Even the advent of the digital age and e-mail has not appeared to reduce the amount of paperwork that floods our lives. As a student, you have more than enough experience dealing with paperwork. Mostly you learn to organize paperwork in files, notebooks, or stacks. Dealing with paperwork can seem like a never-ending job.

Teachers have to take care of a torrent of paperwork that appears in their mailboxes at school (e.g., administrative policy statements, requests, reminders, meeting agendas). Teachers must also create paperwork and then keep track of it. Teachers are required to maintain paper trails of student academic progress, attendance, and behavior. Teachers have to communicate with parents and guardians through newsletters and schedules and written reminders of field trips, school events, and individual student needs. Elementary teachers manage book clubs and holiday gift clubs to augment supply funds. Secondary teachers write letters of support for students who are applying for college or jobs. Managing paperwork is a full-time job and is cited as the number one concern of first-year teachers along with behavior management (Quinn, 1991).

Developing a plan or system for handling the huge amount of documents and other paper forms associated with teaching is absolutely necessary in order for the management of paperwork not to interfere with effective instruction. The first step in dealing with documents, records, reports, and resources is to create one or more filing systems. Efficient filing systems provide ways of tracking individual student performance and progress, organizing forms and letters that are used on a regular basis, organizing lesson materials (plans, assessment criteria, teacher reflections on success or shortcomings of lessons, student evaluations of lessons, and resources), dating entries, and keeping track of schedules. Teachers often organize student daily work, weekly assignments, and projects in folders. How the folders will be stored and organized must also be taken into consideration.

© Martha Campbell.

"This backpack thing is getting completely out of hand."

Scan, Sort, Discard, Record, and File   When dealing with the paper in your mailbox at school, use the scan, sort, discard, record, and file method. Scan everything you receive in your mailbox before leaving the teacher's room. Sort the mail to decide what you should keep and what you can discard. If there is anything you can get rid of immediately, do so. Don't take unnecessary paperwork back to your classroom. Important dates in mail should be recorded on your desk calendar. No need to keep the piece of paper if you have recorded pertinent information and a date. Finally, you should be left with a few items that should be filed. Develop a habit of going through your mail in the morning and after lunch. Don't take your mail out of the mailbox at the end of the day. It will become mixed with student work and all the other things you have jammed in your briefcase to take care of later.

Managing Classroom Paperwork   In the classroom, teach students to manage some of the paperwork. Even first graders can keep a folder of the week's work in their desks. Teach them to arrange items chronologically. Secondary students can learn to pick up and return daily assignments from a designated spot when entering and leaving the classroom. Students can be held responsible for making entries in a homework log to assist the teacher in keeping track of individual student progress.

Some teachers provide space in the classroom for student mailboxes. The flow of assignments and communication between student and student, between student and teacher, and between teacher and parent flows through these mailboxes. Strategically positioned mailboxes make it possible for a teacher to see at a glance, who has checked their mailbox, who has returned work, and who, given the clutter in their mailbox, might need a reminder about the routine of checking their own paperwork. Storage space is always a problem in classrooms as well as at home. Your task as a teacher is to determine which paperwork needs to be dealt with on a daily basis and which can be stored away for less-frequent access. Once you have established a routine for handling paperwork, you will have more time for instruction and the students will have more time for learning.

A Multidimensional Look at Classroom Management

Walter Doyle (1986) described five dimensions of classroom life that provide a framework for theorists, researchers, and practitioners to study the myriad events and interactions that can occur in any given time span in classrooms. Doyle's five dimensions (multidimensionality, simultaneity, immediacy, unpredictable and public, and history) can serve as a guide for teachers to develop and organize a range of management strategies that will address the activities they must orchestrate in any given day.

Multidimensionality   Classrooms are complex, tightly populated social structures. Many events take place and every single action can result in multiple ef-

Ed Lines

"All battles are won before they are fought." *Sun Tzu*

fects. This variety of events with multiple effects that occur in a classroom can challenge a teacher's ability to keep student attention focused and to manage student behavior. For example, the domino effect of one student reaching down to get something out of a backpack may disturb another student with the result of an exchange of words that causes a student across the room to stand up to see what is going on. Which action is the teacher to respond to, if at all? Or enthusiastic comments from students working on a group project may create a wave of excitement that draws other students to see what all the talk is about. How does a teacher manage such a situation and keep learning at a peak?

Simultaneity   Many actions occur at the same time in a classroom. Like the captain of a ship at full sail who knows exactly when to turn the wheel to keep the ship on an even keel as he watches all hands on deck performing a variety of duties, a teacher also observes many actions occurring in the classroom and processes information on student behavior or idleness to adjust the lesson pace, input, and interest to keep all students onboard. Students are also aware of the teacher's response to them. Students make their own adjustments to the events occurring around them and these adjustments may give rise to additional actions. An effective classroom manager must be aware of what students are paying attention to and constantly be aware of the impact the simultaneousness of events will have on the learning environment.

Immediacy   Life in classrooms is fast paced and up close and some events must be taken care of immediately. The movement in a classroom is perpetual; some students move at a faster pace than others, but no one really stands still. Immediacy in the classroom can come in the form of a call over the intercom asking a student to report to the office or students leaving the classroom at odd times for special programs; something is misplaced, a necessary book can't be found, a pencil is broken, or someone gets sick. Each day a teacher must respond to a hundred such interactions that often require immediate attention. Having routines and contingency plans in place can help both teacher and students adjust smoothly to some of the immediacy of the classroom.

Unpredictable and Public   Everything that happens in a classroom is public and many of the events that occur are unexpected. An experienced teacher once explained to her practicum students that the first time she meets with parents she tells them that she won't believe anything the children tell her about what happens at home if the parents won't believe anything the children tell them about what happens in the classroom. She was joking, of course, but her humor did illustrate the fact that everything that goes on in a classroom is very public and can be unpredictable. A teacher in a sour mood can overreact to a minor problem and every student within earshot can hear and be ready to spread the word. Teachers have been know to discuss their personal lives as well as the lives of their students in hallways overflowing with "big ears" that may misunderstand what

Ed Lines

Movement is management: An effective classroom manager hardly ever sits down.

Teachers' Lounge

The First Day: The Horror . . . the Absolute Horror

When I began student teaching, I worshipped my cooperating teacher, Bob: How did he make it look so easy? I observed his wonderful methods of teaching; I vigorously took notes. Then I took over my first class.

I knew. I knew they were all going to be my friends. They were going to love me and learn from me as they never had. I had my lesson plan, materials, and all the stuff I was told to have in my preservice training. Bob left the room. I stood up, smiling, and told the class exactly what we were going to do, gave them my life story, and just when I was about to ask them about themselves, they, like sharks, smelled blood in the water. They began ignoring me and started talking to each other. The talking grew into shouting. Then it escalated alarmingly into throwing things around the classroom: pencils, books, and chairs (yes, chairs!). I almost started crying—I wanted to curl up under the desk. Bob met me after my hooligans had left. "So, John, how were the little dar-

lings?" I told him what had happened. I also told him I should quit and that I was a horrible teacher. He reassured me: "John, don't worry about a thing. I'll take their next class today. You come in tomorrow and they'll be like kittens with milk on their whiskers."

The next day while driving to the school, I practiced my speech to Bob about why I was going to give up teaching and pursue a career at Starbucks. They must take teachers with master's degrees in English education, right? I wanted to tell him in person, but he wasn't around when the first-period class of these kids met, so I had no choice but to walk in solo. I'll never know exactly how Bob did it, but these boys and girls all had their hands folded on their desks and politely said, "Good morning, Mr. Gibney. What will we be learning today?"

That is the day I figured out classroom politics, and the day I began loving . . . loving! . . . teaching.

● John Gibney
University of
Massachusetts–Amherst

---

they are hearing. Even the way a teacher responds to different students is viewed by many pairs of eyes. The teacher may smile and listen to one student, but turn away from another student in mid-sentence. Teacher behavior is always public and can have lasting effects on students and their ability to learn.

Unpredictable events come in a variety of shapes and sizes. An administrator can drop in unexpectedly to observe a teacher or simply to deliver a message. How the students and the teacher react to such unexpected visits has much to say about how well prepared they are for interruptions and how they perceive visitors. University supervisors have reported walking into classrooms and having a student come up and say, "May I help you?" When the supervisors explain that they are there to observe, the student points out a place for them to sit and then goes back to what she were doing before the supervisors came into the room. While such supervisory visits may not be entirely unpredictable, they can be handled in a way for which the students have been prepared.

History   History is a powerful force constantly in the making. It takes a strong will and much determination to live down past mistakes or to change direction once a particular path has been chosen. Classroom histories are created as norms and common understandings develop in a single class over a single year. What happens in the very beginning when a class is formed can have long-lasting consequences. The history of each classroom is often being constructed even before the school year begins. Parents will swap details of the teachers their children had the previous year and the classrooms these teachers managed. Judgments are being formed that will either be confirmed or dismissed as the year gets under way. The manner in which each teacher begins the year, how well they have planned for the multitude of activities that will take place within the first week, how well organized resources and materials are, and how the teachers deal with minor upsets or behavior malfunctions start a classroom's history ball rolling. Each day in a classroom can be a positive addition to the weekly, monthly, or yearly history, or it can detract from the good that has happened before and will happen again. The way a teacher manages a classroom is often a strong predictor of the history of that class. You all shared in the history of the classrooms you attended, but the teacher set the tone and designed the space in which the history would occur.

Management of Movement on School Grounds and in Hallways

Movement in schools is almost constant. Students are moving between their own classrooms and other rooms in the school at regular and irregular intervals. Some schools do not allow students to move around in the school alone or unsupervised while other schools may leave student movement outside of the classroom up to the discretion of individual teachers. The advent of school violence and dangerous weapons in the hands of elementary and secondary students has given rise to stricter rules governing student movement outside classrooms and to the utilization of metal detectors to assure that harmful instruments will not be available to students on school property.

While lock-down situations do not exist in most schools (such restrictions are usually reserved for detention centers or correctional centers), the freedom to move around in the school environment is carefully managed by administrators and teachers in the form of bells and hall passes. In high schools and middle schools, short periods of time are allocated for students to go from one class to another.

Rules are central to all human activities and are essential especially in classrooms.

Taking the time to understand the concerns of individual students is every teacher's responsibility.

Teachers or hall guards stand watch at strategic locations throughout the building during the break between classes. In elementary schools, teachers generally lead students to special classes such as music, art, or technology. Growing concern for the safety of students has changed school landscapes.

Teacher responsibilities include duties assigned by the administration to supervise large groups of students at recess or during lunch. As a teacher, you will spend many hours on the playground, watching students interact and play games. You may learn to play 4-square and tether ball with students from your own classroom and from other classrooms. It is educational to observe the ways students behave outside of the classroom and to have conversations with students in a relaxed atmosphere. Playground, lunch, or hall duty should not be seen as drudgery or a responsibility to avoid, but welcomed as an opportunity to learn more about the students.

Routines, Rules, and Schedules

Routines, rules, and schedules provide the framework in which actions take place. When a routine is established, some of the uncertainty of life is laid to rest. Rules provide security. Rules and schedules relieve stress. They also encourage responsibility. Routines, rules, and schedules do not discourage spontaneity or creativity. The self-discipline that they encourage can give rise to disciplined expressions of creativity.

Routines   Routines help teachers keep track of student academic and personal progress. Teressa, the teacher at the beginning of this chapter, uses routines, in part, to manage her classroom at Ullom. At the beginning of the year, she assigns every student a number for the year in much the same way that U.S. citizens are assigned Social Security numbers. The numbers students in Teressa's class are assigned are used to take attendance, lunch count, and even to hand back student work. This use of numbers allows other students to participate in the management of the classroom. The numbers even allow for flexible grouping and lining-up strategies. Teressa believes there are far more uses for the numbers than she has yet discovered. A simple strategy or routine can offer many benefits.

Rules   Rules provide guidance and clarity to routines. Who makes the rules should be determined for the most part by the person or people who are going to enforce them or monitor students' response to them. Keep in mind that any rule that is set forth may be scrutinized by students, parents, other teachers, and the school administration, and that the First and Fourteenth Amendments of the U.S. Constitution address students' and teachers' rights and responsibilities related to the establishment and enforcement of rules.

Some rules are predetermined and everyone at school is expected to follow them. Some rules are determined by space and school structure. Smart teachers seek cooperation from the students so in most classrooms rules are determined by the teacher with input from the students; the smartest teachers allow the students to believe they are the ones who determine the rules. The possibilities for establishing and implementing classroom rules are endless, and result from variables such as standards, student needs, and expectations. See Figure 12.7 for a list of key components crucial to the constitutionality and perhaps success of any rule (Reutter, 1975).

Schedules Schedules form a framework for routines. Imagine getting through a day or a day at school without at least the semblance of a schedule. In fact, when schedules at school are interrupted, it doesn't take long for disorder to ensue. Getting from point A to point B in a timely manner depends mightily on a schedule.

Schedules are usually set by school administrators and to some extent determine ways routines will be enacted in individual classrooms. For example, in a high school with block scheduling, or an A/B class schedule, routines take on quite a different shape than if classes meet every day for 55 minutes. A block schedule also provides extended class time and opportunities to enhance instruction through project work and role playing experiences, thereby dictating the need for routines governing such activities. See the Understanding & Using Evidence on page 464 to discover how much a few interruptions can take from learning time.

Figure 12.7 Key components of classroom rules

1. The rule must be publicized to students. Whether it is issued orally or in writing, school authorities must take reasonable steps to bring the rule to the attention of students.

2. The rule must have a legitimate educational purpose.

3. The rule must have a rational relationship to the achievement of the stated educational purpose.

4. The meaning of the rule must be reasonably clear.

5. The rule must be sufficiently narrow in scope so as not to encompass constitutionally protected activities along with those that constitutionally may be proscribed in the school setting.

6. If the rule infringes a fundamental constitutional right of students, a compelling interest of the school (state) in the enforcement of the rule must be shown.

Source: Reutter, E. E. (1975). *The courts and student conduct*. Topeka, KS: National Organization on Legal Problems of Education.

Understanding & USING EVIDENCE

REVIEWING DATA ON TIME SPENT ON MANAGEMENT TASKS AND ON CLASSROOM INTERRUPTIONS

Teachers have to plan and implement strategies for starting each day, and maintaining a purposeful pace throughout the day that keeps students focused on learning and completing required tasks. The Stallings (1990) Time Spent on Organizing and on Classroom Interruption checklist provides teachers with a snapshot of the time that it actually takes to complete certain management tasks as well as track instructional time that is lost during interruptions. The checklist is easy to complete and summarize, and analysis of the data provides instant information about events which are, to some extent, out of the classroom teacher's control but which influence instructional activities.

Tracking the rate at with instructional time is diminished through poor classroom management can help a teacher gain a greater awareness of the value of efficient and effective routines. Actions or behaviors that infringe on the finite amount of time for teaching and learning in any given school day can have an accumulative effect of student opportunity to learn. An average school day at Ullom begins at 8:55 and ends at 3:06. With time reserved for lunch and transition between specialists, the amount of time for classroom instruction is roughly 5 hours a day.

Time Spent on Organizing and on Classroom Interruptions

School:	Teacher:	Observer:	Time Started	Time Stopped
Observation of Classroom Organizing				
Taking Attendance			8:57	8:58
Collecting Lunch Money			8:57	9:00
Collecting Homework or Seatwork			8:57	8:58
Making Assignments for Seatwork			9:50	9:54
Making Assignments for Homework			2:55	3:05

The Characteristics of a Well-Managed Classroom

The characteristics of a well-managed classroom as identified by Wong (1998) are:

- Students involved with academic work and instruction.
- Students know what is expected of them and are generally successful.
- Time is used wisely; students are not confused and do not disrupt one another.
- Work is being done in a purposeful manner in a comfortable environment (p. 86).

While the elements of a well-managed classroom are easy to understand, translating these characteristics into purposeful actions is a major undertaking for teachers. Just as important as laying the groundwork for a great beginning to the

School:	Teacher:	Observer:	Time Started	Time Stopped
Distributing Books and Materials			9:05	9:07
Explaining Activities and Procedures			9:00	9:05
Organizing Groups			1:15	1:18
Shifting from One Activity to Another			10:20	10:22
Disciplining Students			9:45	9:46

Observation of Classroom Interruptions

Students Enter Late			9:10	9:12
Students Leave Early			2:30	
Parents Enter			2:27	2:30
Administrator Enters			11:10	11:15
Other Visitors Enter		Observer	8:55	
Loudspeaker Announcements			9:00	9:05
Special Sales		5th graders selling tickets to drama extravaganza	2:15	2:25
School Events				
Outside Noise				

Your Task: Use the data on the following Time Spent on Organizing and on Classroom Interruptions checklist to analyze approximately how much time can be consumed by management in an average school day. What conclusions can you draw from the data? Is the teacher represented on this checklist an effective classroom manager?

Refer to the **Understanding & Using Evidence Appendix** *at the end of the text for answers and information related to these activities.*

Source: Stallings, J. A. (1990). *Effective use of time program.* Houston, TX: University of Houston.

year, teachers have to plan and implement strategies for starting each day and maintaining a purposeful pace that keeps students focused on learning and completing required tasks. Maintaining on-task behavior when students are actively engaged in learning is one of the most important responsibilities of a teacher. The more time students have to learn, the more chances they have for success. Many events can interfere with students' time to learn and it is a teacher's job to anticipate and eliminate distractions that interfere with learning time. In order to accomplish this responsibility, teachers must possess knowledge of classroom management strategies and be able to implement procedures in an efficient and timely manner.

Students are compelled by law to attend public school whether they want to be there or not. While at school, the U.S. Constitution's Fourteenth Amendment of due process and equal protection under the law protects students in the classroom and ensures their rights to a full range of opportunities. Given that all students must be provided an equal and full range of opportunities to learn, a well-managed classroom may be the first step in making this goal attainable.

Janet Revisits Her Management Plan

Janet, the teacher at the beginning of this section, was determined not to let the physical structure of her classroom inhibit her lack of success as a teacher. She arranged the space she was given in creative ways that would contribute to her ability to help the students learn the content. She helped the students learn how to navigate the unusual classroom space. Each child had a colorful plastic box for storing personal items, and a mailbox for handing in and receiving homework assignments. Special areas in the classroom were designated as meeting spaces where directions and whole group instruction could be available for all of the students to see. As the students worked with Janet to develop the classroom rules, they took into account their location in the school and the unusual arrangement of the classroom. Janet had done her best and now she and the students were beginning to build a positive history of their 4th grade year.

What Is the Difference between Discipline and Management?

Marjorie often complains to the other teachers in the teachers' lounge that her students always seem to be out of order and misbehaving. They can't walk to the library in a quiet and orderly manner, they talk constantly during times when she is trying to deliver instruction, and they leave the room in a mess at the end of the day in a flurry of push and shove to get their assignments in their backpacks and to get out the door. There are frequent altercations among students and she suspects that some students are bullying others. She pleads with the more experienced teachers to tell her discipline methods that might work best for the unruly group of students she has this year. When Carl, an experienced teacher of 10 years, asked Marjorie what expectations were in place for student behavior in her classroom, Marjorie responded that she just expected them all to act like decent children. Over the next couple of months, Carl helped Marjorie establish routines, create classroom rules, and devise natural consequences students could expect if any of the rules were broken.

A common view of discipline is gaining control by enforcing obedience or order. In this view, teachers are seen as enforcers or controllers. Another view of discipline sees teachers as the trainers or guides that help mold and develop student

Ed Lines

"Never give up. Never surrender." *Tim Allen in* Galaxy Quest

behavior. Discipline can also be viewed as a way to get students to change their misbehavior. When students misbehave, teachers must make decisions about how to manage the misbehavior. Managing furniture and classroom space is much easier than managing students' behavior. Students talk back. They disagree. They have their own ideas about what should be done and how it should be done. Managing behavior or disciplining students who have misbehaved requires communication and effective interpersonal skills.

Discipline problems do pop up in even well-managed classrooms, and when they do, it is the knowledgeable teacher who has the best chance of coming up with fair and just solutions. The classroom discipline landscape changes constantly throughout a school year. The Teachers and the Law on page 468 shows which discipline measures are acceptable and which ones are not.

Four Stages of Classroom Life that Influence Behavior

Within the framework of content, conduct, and covenant management described earlier in this chapter, Froyen and Iverson (1999) describe four stages that can influence management and discipline in a classroom: (1) forming, (2) storming, (3) norming, and (4) performing (p. 227). Two effects can disrupt these clearly delineated stages of behavior. One effect results from the rapidly changing demographics in U.S. schools. The other effect is the result of the rapid pace at which human bodies grow and change. In the first effect, cultural differences and shifts in dominant groups in classrooms can present new structures and stages causing teachers to readjust management and behavior practices. In addition to the stages, human growth phases also present changing climates in classrooms. Fourth grade students who begin the year as gentle beings may soon begin to show signs of the exuberance and impatience of 5th graders. Likewise, seemingly out-of-touch sophomores can become mature, thoughtful seniors. Little ever stays the same in elementary or secondary classrooms and the more prepared teachers are to respond to the changing environments they will experience, the more competent they will become at exhibiting best practices.

Forming At the beginning of the year, students learn information about their new surroundings as roles and procedures are established. They compare the ways they were required to conduct themselves last year with what is being expected of them this year. In some instances, this first stage presents a sort of "honeymoon" period, when for the most part, everyone is trying to put their best foot forward. The more effective the teacher is in content management at the beginning of the year, the longer the honeymoon period can last.

Storming As the year progresses, students may begin to test the limits that have been outlined and through peer pressure or for some other reason begin to distance themselves from established norms of behavior.

Ed Lines

"One of the nice things about problems is that a good many of them don't exist except in our imaginations." *Steve Allen*

Teachers and the Law

Administrators, teachers, and parents are concerned about students behaving appropriately. Debates on ways to discipline students who do not behave according to guidelines established by the teacher and the school have often had to be settled in the courts. While the idea of punishing a student for their uncivil behavior by the use of force might seem counterproductive, such measures are possible in some school districts.

CORPORAL PUNISHMENT

Are there statutory provisions designed to protect teachers and administrators from suits resulting from their administration of corporal punishment?

Yes. According to La Morte (1999, 130–131), the use of corporal punishment in this country as a means of disciplining school children dates back to the colonial period. It has survived the transformation of primary and secondary education from the colonials' reliance on optional private arrangements to our present system of compulsory education and dependence on public schools. The practice continues to play a role in the public education of schoolchildren in most parts of the country.

In 1977, the U.S. Supreme Court upheld the practice of corporal punishment. The law was chal-lenged in *Ingraham v. Wright* with Justice Powell delivering the opinion of the court. Two issues were raised during the court case: (1) does the punishment represent cruel and unusual punishment in violation of the Eighth Amendment of the U.S. Constitution, and (2) whether prior notice and the opportunity to be heard were required. According to the court, three categories of corporal punishment exist.

> Punishments that do not exceed the traditional common law standard of reasonableness are not actionable; punishments that exceed the common law standard without adequate state remedies violate procedural due process rights; and finally, punishments that are so grossly excessive as to be shocking to the conscience, violate substantive due process rights, without regard to the adequacy of state remedies. (p. 135)

More than half of the states do not allow the practice of corporal punishment. In some instances, local school boards, in states that allow corporal punishment, have banned or curtailed the practice. Such is the case in Clark County School District where Teressa, the teacher at the beginning of this chapter, teaches. Teachers must be aware of any statutory provisions pertaining to corporal punishment in the state where they teach and if practices within a school district are in conformance with state and local provisions.

Norming Somewhere around the middle of the year, nearly all behavioral and management struggles have been reconciled and the content and conduct standards have been accepted. There are few reasons for behavior problems to interrupt opportunities for students to learn, and both teacher and students feel a sense of accomplishment.

Performing During the performing stage, students exhibit self-reliance and self-discipline. They have formed close relationships with their classmates and with the teacher and can rely on support from them when needed. With expert teacher management, it is possible for behaviors associated with the performing stage to be evident throughout the school year. When teachers understand these stages, there is less opportunity to be caught off guard or frustrated by the changing climate of the classroom.

STUDENT SEARCH

Is searching a student or student's personal belongings lawful?

Yes. It is not uncommon for school administrators to be placed in the unfavorable position of having to search students or student lockers when there is a suspicion that a student or students may possess some illegal substance, a weapon, or property that is not rightly theirs. When such searches are deemed necessary by administrators or teachers, it is possible that students will complain that their rights according to the Fourth Amendment of the U.S. Constitution have been violated. Courts must then come to a decision about an individual student's rights versus the responsibility of the school administration to maintain a safe and secure school environment for all students.

In the 1985 *New Jersey v. T.L.O.* case, the courts concluded that a search of a student's belongings for evidence of cigarettes that further turned up evidence of drug dealing did not violate the Fourth Amendment. According to the courts, the search was reasonable, but only because there was evidence that provided a substantial suspicion that the student was indeed in possession of an illegal substance.

LOCKER SEARCH

Can a student's locker be searched without a warrant?

Yes. Courts allow locker searches on the grounds that schools ultimately retain control over lockers as school property. Schools are also held responsible for protecting the educational function of the school and students' welfare. Lockers can be searched to prevent their illicit use.

TEACHERS AND LAWSUITS

Are teachers protected by the district they work for from being sued by their students and parents of their students?

No. In the May 3, 2004, issue of *Time* magazine, a feature story titled "See You In Court, Teach" focused on the concern teachers and school officials feel over being the target of lawsuits arising from their actions in disciplining students. According to the article, teachers worry as much about being sued as about low test results for their students. Some recent school-related cases cited in the article included a teacher's use of duct tape to quiet a chatty 6-year-old, a student injured while jumping from a moving bus in order to avoid being disciplined, a principal pointing a toy gun at a student, and a coach's verbal abuse and comments about a student's weight. It is not necessarily the case that anything a teacher does can result in a lawsuit, but foolish behavior on the part of teachers can possibly lead to unpleasantness in court. Teachers' organizations work to protect teachers from unreasonable and irresponsible claims against their behavior. However, the best protection is to be aware of district, state, and national statues regarding what is considered reasonable in managing student behavior.

Sources: La Morte, M. W. (1999). *School law: Cases and concepts* (6th ed.). Boston: Allyn and Bacon; Caplan, J. (2004). See you in court, teach. *Time*, May 3, p. 19.

Managing Student Behavior Proactively

Kounin (1970) identified eight different ways that teachers can proactively manage the group behavior of students. Each group management strategy does not necessarily occur in isolation and may influence the implementation of additional interventions.

1. *With-itness:* Teachers anticipate what is going to happen. A teacher may see a student start to get out of his seat with a pencil in hand and quietly remind him that he will be able to sharpen his pencil when math instruction is over.

2. *Overlappingness:* Teachers take care of problems without disrupting instruction. A student cannot find the correct textbook. The teacher hands the student a

textbook from the bookshelf, opens it to the correct page, and points to the item being discussed, all the while directing the discussion by other students.

3. *Smoothness:* Teachers make certain that instructional focus is maintained. If the teacher is guiding students to make generalizations from a data retrieval chart and a disruptive comment is made by a student, the teacher quickly redirects the students thinking to the focus of the lesson.

4. *Momentum:* Teachers do not allow disruptions to interfere with the pace of the lesson. Disruptions can be handled by proximity control, by quietly moving a student from one location to another, or by increasing or decreasing the pace of the lesson.

5. *Group alerting:* Teachers do not allow students to be uninvolved in instruction. If it appears that students are becoming inattentive or distracted, the teacher utilizes some device to alert students to the task at hand.

6. *Accountability:* Teachers do not allow students to slide in the classroom. Students are reminded of their responsibility for completing tasks and for their performance. Students may be reminded of next steps and the effect completion of one task will have on their ability to complete the next.

7. *Challenge arousal:* Teachers use questioning strategies and directives to make certain that all students are involved. Students are asked to restate a previously stated answer to a problem, to give an explanation of how a specific solution was arrived at, or to share a problem they just completed with the class.

8. *Variety:* Teachers avoid monotony in instruction. Teachers implement a variety of approaches to encourage student interest and involvement during instruction.

A wide range of resources are available to teachers seeking solutions to behavior problems in the classroom. A problem may involve only one student or a misbehavior could involve a group of students. Whichever strategy or method is used to correct the misbehavior, the teacher must take into account the cultural background of the student or students involved, the expectations and norms for student behavior that have been shared among the group, and outside influences that may have influenced the misbehavior.

The Importance of Communication in Behavior Management

Most forms of management begin with talk. Teachers explain rules, they correct behavior, they give directions, and they issue orders. The manner in which teachers conduct their communication with students can have an enormous influence on the ways their students behave. *Star Trek's* Dr. Spock's trademark salutation of "Live long and prosper" conveys an emotional message full of kindness and hope. Teachers should emulate Spock in the ways they communicate their desires and expectations to students.

Ed Lines

"Memories of our lives, of our works, and of our deeds will continue in others." *Rosa Parks*

Large class sizes, the number of details to keep track of, and so little time all contribute to decreasing the amount of friendly and polite conversation a high school teacher can have with students. Because some high schools are as large as small villages, once teachers leave their familiar section of the school, they may seldom meet anyone they know. Knowing the names of the students they teach is a challenge in itself, and knowing the names and faces of the other 3000 students in the school is close to impossible. A former student of mine who was a high school nurse indicated the number of traumas in any given day in her school far exceeded those cases that show up at the quick care medical facility in the neighborhood. Having the skills to communicate in positive and productive ways becomes exceedingly important in such environments.

All talk contains some type of emotional content. Imagine how boring communication would be if there was never any emotion in what people had to say. When teachers talk to students, when students talk to teachers, when students talk to one another, the resultant messages are likely to contain emotional content that has the ability to shade the actual meaning of the words being expressed. Certainly a pouting child or teenager can be intimidated into saying what a parent wants to hear, but the emotional overtones in such a forced message can speak volumes in resentment and anger. Every communication you have with your students is filtered through personal sieves woven together of hopes, fears, needs, and intellectual potential. When you talk to students or when you ask them to do something or to behave in a particular way, you must always be aware of the emotional impact your words will have. Learn how to handle student's personal issues and learn how to prioritize your own personal concerns.

Garrett, Sadker, and Sadker (1994) offer a taxonomy of interpersonal communication skills (p. 193) for understanding the types of listening and questioning skills teachers can use to encourage interpersonal communication in the classroom. The skills are grouped in three clusters, each representing two dimensions of student process and teaching skills. Cluster III (adapted from the trumpet model of Weinstein and Fantini, 1970), focuses on encouraging alternative behaviors and includes

a. generating alternative behaviors
b. practicing them and sensing how they feel
c. receiving feedback from others
d. predicting short-term and long-term consequences
e. choosing which patterns of behavior seem most congruent with personal needs

The skills in Cluster III form a logical next step after the skills of attending, active listening, reflecting, and inventory questioning have been mastered (Garret et al., 1994, 194). It should be noted that at the root of any communication should be sincere unconditional positive regard for the worth of an individual and a commitment to their potential to learn.

Ed Lines

"In a truly national society, the best of us would be teachers, and the rest would have to settle for something else." *Lee Iaccoca*

Challenging Assumptions
FINDINGS FROM RESEARCH

What matters most in classroom management?

The Assumption: Many beginning teachers worry most about their ability to manage the movement and behavior of their students. They have heard horror stories and observed unfortunate examples of teachers who have little or no effect on getting students ready for learning. Having no control over a classroom is a frequent concern of teacher education candidates. Cooperating teachers who work with practicum or student teachers may advise them to begin the year with a stern and strict attitude and to reserve smiles for later in the year. Teressa, the teacher at the beginning of this chapter, advises new teachers not to become a friend too soon. So what really works in classroom management and how is a new teacher to approach this aspect of teaching?

Study Design and Method: There are probably as many approaches to managing a classroom as there are teachers who implement one course of action or another. What approach works for each teacher really does depend on individual attitudes and capabilities. Certainly having a high level of self-efficacy is important. Teachers who view themselves as capable of managing a classroom are more likely to be successful doing so than a teacher who is unsure. One way researchers have approached the study of effective classroom management is to observe teacher behaviors and document those behaviors that result in positive student actions and attitudes.

The study cited here looked at two teachers who represented contrasting styles of classroom management. One teacher used an authoritarian style of classroom management and the other used a style that encouraged students to take responsibility for their own behavior. Three variables—(1) student interactions (behaviors), (2) teacher questioning, and (3) quality of teaching—were used to analyze the effectiveness of the teacher's management styles. Both teachers used lower-level questioning skills and it was determined in the study that the overall quality of instruction was poor. The study found that neither of these two teachers' classroom management styles affected "consistent positive student interactions." The study concluded that the "quality of instruction is central to the interplay between student interactions and teacher's classroom management practices."

Implications: While this study is of a very small scope, and perhaps the teachers who participated in the study did not employ the most effective instructional strategies, it does provide a small piece of evidence regarding the connection between management style and instructional practices. When students are engaged in learning they are more likely to exhibit positive behaviors. The success of the approach a teacher uses for classroom management may be highly influenced by the instructional practices that are in place. Teachers who teach well usually have little problems with classroom management.

Source: Jeanpierre, B. J. (2005). Two urban elementary science classrooms: The interplay between student interactions and classroom management practices. *Education, 124*(4), 664–676.

Basic Rules of Engagement Listen, listen, and listen: Otherwise you might not hear what your students are saying. Two students come in from the playground or hallway, yelling and pushing one another, followed by a growing number of spectators. The great lesson you are ready to start will have to be postponed until tempers cool and you defuse the anger. What do you do? First, take charge. Give some orders in a low, clear voice. Send students from other classes back to their rooms. Tell your own students to go to their desks. If you are in an elementary grade, you might hold the hands of the two students who created the disturbance, keeping them near you. In high school, you might ask the students to remain standing by the door until you are ready to listen to them. State some rules. For example:

- Each of you will be able to tell me in your own words what happened.
- NO ONE will be allowed to interrupt.
- I will talk when you are finished.

Then you magically pull out the small circular disk you have in your pocket (one side heads, one tails), ask one of the students to choose heads or tails, and flip the disk. In a flash, what has happened on the playground or in the hallway becomes of lesser interest to most of the students than what is about to happen in the classroom. The key is that you have made decisions, the students know what to do, and you have not added to either student's frustration or humiliation.

When teachers listen actively to what the students have to say, they use a variety of response strategies. They make eye contact. They nod or make sounds indicating that they are taking in every word. They encourage students

Fun and games build trust and friendship between students and teachers beyond the confines of the classroom.

having difficulty expressing their thoughts to "tell me more" or "go on." Teachers who listen well don't interpret but try to identify with honest labeling the feelings and attitudes they are hearing. Teachers who are good listeners help students recognize how they feel and the ramifications of these feelings for themselves and for others.

Revisiting Marjorie as She Learns the Difference between Management and Discipline

Marjorie, the teacher at the beginning of this section who couldn't understand the reasons behind her students' misbehavior has learned, with the help of Carl, the difference between management and discipline. She has explained to her students what appropriate behavior is in her classroom and in the school and has set consequences for inappropriate behavior. Her students are responding to her systematic discipline strategies and lately Marjorie has found fewer reasons to complain and more reasons to compliment her students on their fine behavior. Research can help you learn about what is important in classroom management. See the Challenging Assumptions on page 472.

Chapter Summary

This chapter on classroom management addresses a range of models and approaches to creating and maintaining an effective learning environment. Teacher behaviors that are conducive to creating a well-managed, highly productive environment for learning are discussed. An overarching theme of this chapter is that classroom management is the responsibility of the teacher. Classroom management does not occur through happenstance. It requires teacher knowledge, skill, and a particular set of dispositions that recognize the individual worth of students and their right to an effective learning environment. Classroom management is also dependent on specific actions by teachers to communicate expectations to students and to enlist student acceptance of these ex-

pectations. Life in classrooms is complex and changeable. Developing the ability to manage such a dynamic environment is an essential function of learning to teach.

What is classroom management? Classroom management encompasses a wide range of complex behaviors resulting from the interaction between intellectual, physical, psychological, and personal dimensions. The concept of classroom management can at times be paradoxical. The challenge in classroom management is to not lose sight of the fact that classroom management must be present for effective instruction to take place. It does not exist in isolation, but it does precede all that will be educative in a classroom. Effective classroom management requires teachers to make numerous thoughtful and knowledgeable decisions each day. The best part about classroom management for teachers is that there are many models to follow or borrow from, and the teacher usually has the final word on which particular strategies or model to implement.

How do you build a personal philosophy of classroom management?   As you progress through your teacher education program, you will hopefully have opportunities to observe a variety of classrooms. You will watch experienced teachers interact with students, guiding and correcting their actions. Each teacher and each classroom setting can provide examples of differing levels and styles of classroom management. You will learn by example. Keeping track of specific models and techniques that you see being implemented is up to you. You will also have time to review established models of classroom management and to acquire an understanding of the basic tenets of these models through discussions with colleagues and your instructors. You will begin to develop a personal philosophy of classroom management based on what you have observed and what you learn from theories and leading researchers in the field. In trying out various approaches to classroom management, you will identify with those that seem most comfortable to you. Keep in mind, however, that classroom situations change and the greater your knowledge of classroom management practices, the greater the likelihood that you will be ready to cope with any management problem that arises.

What constitutes a well-managed classroom? A well-managed classroom can be demonstrated in a variety of ways. The dynamic aspects of a classroom (multidimensionality, simultaneity, immediacy, public and unpredictable, and history) dictate that no two classrooms will be managed in exactly the same way or produce the same results even if similar methods of management are applied. Well-managed classrooms can be buzzing hives of activity or as quiet as library reading rooms. It is the student learning that results from the organization of a classroom that best determines the effectiveness of any management plan. The establishment of routines, rules, and schedules contributes to successful classroom management as well as procedures for paperwork, storage, and student movement.

What is the connection between discipline and management?   Discipline can be viewed as one of the many components of classroom management. Discipline can be a response to student misbehavior, to the breaking of a rule, or to a student's disregard of the rights of others. Discipline can be a way to guide students toward acceptable behaviors. It is expected that teachers who have a well-managed classroom are able to manage student behavior as well. In order to do this, teachers must possess highly developed communication skills. They must be able to establish reasonable consequences for misbehavior and dispense discipline justly, without infringing on student rights. The Internet provides a wealth of resources and tips to help teachers with effective discipline strategies. It is the wise teacher who accesses these resources and begins to build a repertoire of humane and informed management techniques that will aid in the effective modification of student behavior.

Class Discussion Questions

1. We have all had the experience of managing something. We have organized our personal space and time and have arranged furniture to suit our tastes. Recall a time when you were required to manage something. How successful were you? What do you consider your strengths in making arrangements and in organization?

2. When you have had to include others in your plans, how did you convince them to go along with your ideas? What did you do to enlist their support? If someone disagreed with your plans, what did you do to change their minds? How did you make them comfortable with your expectations?

3. Teachers are required to manage the behavior of students so that everyone in the group has the greatest opportunity to learn. When teachers are faced with difficult behavior issues that infringe on the rights of other students in the class, they must often enforce consequences that might seem harsh and unreasonable to the unpracticed eye. Think about a time when you observed a child or youth being disciplined that made you uncomfortable. How might you have handled the situation differently? What about the situation might have been unknown to you?

Field Guide for School Observations

Use the following grid to document the ways that the teacher you are observing manages different events during the day. Some, but not all, management concerns are listed on the grid. You may need to add some others that you observe. Choose one of the management strategies the teacher exhibits and ask how they learned and decided to use it.

Events to Manage and How to Manage Them	
Students entering classroom	
Beginning instruction/Focusing attention	
Distributing materials/resources	
Monitoring students during guided practice	
Responding to individual requests	
Getting students ready to leave classroom	
Providing individual attention	

Ask a Teacher

Chances are that teachers in most schools lean toward different strategies for handling similar problems. Ask six teachers for advice on how to cope with a specific management problem, and you'll more than likely receive six or seven different responses. This can be somewhat confusing for a beginning teacher or for someone who has not yet developed a personal classroom management game plan, system, or approach.

In the 1995 film *Dangerous Minds*, the protagonist, Lou Anne Johnson, is desperately seeking ways to connect with her inner-city students. One scene shows Lou Anne sitting in her apartment, taking notes from a classroom management book, and then wadding up her notes and throwing them across the room. This scene could leave viewers with the impression that there was nothing in the book that was going to help Lou Ann succeed as a teacher. However, in finally gaining the attention and respect of her high school students, she employed the techniques and strategies research has shown to be effective in managing student behavior.

- She made her lessons relevant to the students' lives.
- She piqued their interest so they became engaged in learning.
- She rewarded their efforts.
- She showed them the respect she herself so desperately sought.

Ask the teacher you are observing or practice teaching with, how they address the four strategies just mentioned in their daily management of the classroom and student behavior.

Ask a Student and a Teacher

The next time you're in a classroom, ask one of the students if you can make a list of what is in their backpack. What you find may amaze you. Write a report on the contents of student backpacks as a sign of the times. Ask the teachers how they handle the advent of 30 backpacks in a room.

Journaling *Becoming a Thoughtful Teacher*

Learn what experts or researchers have determined are important things to know and to know how to do in regard to classroom management. Keep a journal or scrapbook of ideas, actual events, and observations in classrooms. Mark down what happened, how the teacher handled it, and the ways a particular student or many students reacted. There is no lack of information about classroom management strategies available. The teacher's task is to learn enough to know which of the multitude of strategies is worth testing or adapting.

Portfolio Task

What did the classrooms you most enjoyed as a student look like? What kinds of things happened during the day that made these classrooms comfortable places for you to be? Do you remember a teacher who seemed to take care of problems with little effort or without disrupting your learning? Did you have a teacher who made you laugh; made you look forward to each school day?

Reflect on your responses to these questions and then describe how your ideal classroom might be managed. How might your classroom be arranged? What type of learning activities might take place? How might you interact with each of your students? Give reasons from your personal experiences and from what you have read about classroom management to support your rationale for the classroom you have described.

Self-Assessment *What Am I Learning?*

Two Examples of Classroom Management and Opportunity to Learn

Consider the following two examples of management in classrooms. Which of the two classrooms might provide students more opportunity to learn? Why? What actions and teacher behaviors in Classroom Z might lead to student confusion or to extra time spent in managing the classroom?

Classroom X	Classroom Z
Rules and routines are posted for easy referral by teachers and students	No evidence in classroom of rules and routines students are expected to follow
Clearly marked space for students to hand in completed work	Teacher collects completed student work when time permits
Daily schedule posted and reviewed at the beginning of each day or class period	Schedule determined by teacher on a daily basis; teacher informs students of daily events
Students have assigned responsibilities in completing classroom tasks	Teacher calls on individual students when tasks need to be performed
Materials and resources are clearly marked so that students can access them when necessary	Teacher distributes materials as needed; resources kept in a locked cabinet
Students receive daily oral or written feedback on their academic progress	Students receive a report card once every 9 weeks; teacher derides students when they are behind in their work
Free-time activities, based on a variety of student developmental levels and interests are well organized	Teacher chooses when free-time activities will occur and usually involve one activity for the entire class
Transition time between subject instruction and movement between classroom are rehearsed and maintained	Teacher says, "Get out your math books," we're finished with social studies." Or, stops instruction to remind a student it is time for them to go to the specialist
Technology is readily available, software maintained, schedules for student use are clearly posted; teacher has clear view of all monitors	There is a computer in the classroom but it is covered with a sheet so students won't be distracted
Time is set aside at the end of the day or class period for summarization of events and activities	Students pick up backpacks and leave when the bell rings as teacher shouts out reminders

It's not too difficult to see what is good about one classroom and not so good about the other. Which classroom more closely aligns with Wong's characteristics of a well-managed classroom?

Using the Web

The Internet is loaded with sites for teachers seeking information on classroom management and discipline. Conduct a Web search to locate at least two sites that have information on different aspects of classroom management that interest you. Briefly describe what information on the sites you think might be of value to you in the future. Include the descriptions of the two sites in your portfolio. For example, you could visit **www.teacher-institute.com** for newsletters on a variety of subjects, or you could visit **www.pecentral.org** to find out how to create a positive learning environment. Using the Internet as a resource should become one of your professional habits as a teacher.

Your Professional Library

Holloway, J. H. (2003). Managing culturally diverse classrooms. *Educational Leadership, 61*(1), 1–3.

This book offers teachers an informative and refreshing perspective on the productive interactions possible among teachers and learners in a democratic classroom.

Glasser, W. (1998). *Choice theory: A new psychology of personal freedom*. New York: Harper Collins.

This article clarifies how recognizing the differences among cultures can help teachers understand some of the root causes of perceived misbehavior.

Movie

Simpson, D., Bruckheimer, J., Robins, S., Foster, L. (Producers), & Smith, J. (Director). (1995). *Dangerous minds*. Hollywood, CA Hollywood Pictures, Via Rose Productions, Simpson-Bruckheimer Productions.

If you haven't seen it already, you should watch it. Just remember that it is a Hollywood perspective. Some events in the film must be taken with a grain of salt, though overall it does a good job showing some of the management problems teachers might face in inner-city high schools.

 To access chapter objectives, practice tests, weblinks, and flashcards, visit the Companion Website at **www.ablongman.com/hall1e**

mylabschool

Go to Allyn & Bacon's MyLabSchool (**www.mylabschool.com**). Enter Assignment ID **CS01** in the **Assignment Finder** and read Case Study Level A, Case Two under *Effective Room Arrangement*. Consider what you have read about room arrangement in this chapter along with the teacher's goals in this MLS case to maximize ease of movement for a particular student.

Decide which of the three seating locations suggested on page 3 (A, B, or C) is most suitable to maximize access and ease of movement for Cheri, the student in this case. Support your selection with rationale from the Star sheet at the end of the Case Unit and from Chapter 12.

Of the three examples of room arrangements offered in Chapter 12 (U, V, or W), which would be most appropriate for Cheri's needs?

Improving Teachers and Schools, and School Reform

Educators in Real Schools

M E E T
Rocio Jimenez
Santa Ana Partnership

One powerful example of a communitywide approach to improving student success is the Santa Ana Partnership in Santa Ana, California (CA).

This partnership, conceived in the early 1980s, is an institutionalized ongoing communitywide effort to "to jointly analyze barriers to student success in the Santa Ana area" and to increase the success of all children. The partnership has programs, projects, and activities that address the entire range from early childhood readiness for school, to Saturday academic programs for high school students, to mentoring and financial support for high school graduates who are entering one of the postsecondary institutions. One of the partnership's key messages to the families of young children, which is continually repeated as they progress through schooling, is that *you/your child can go to college.*

Rocio Jimenez is living proof of the success of the Santa Ana Partnership. *We came from Mexico because my dad wanted us to get an education.* She came to Santa Ana with her family, speaking no English. *We knew we had to study because my dad was going to provide.* She entered junior high school and took advantage of the programs and activities offered through the partnership. *In high school, I started doing programs at UC Irvine. I remember going during the summer and learning more about math, chemistry, and physics, and we had to do a research paper. So that is how I started, even before I finished high school.*

Following graduation from high school she then earned her bachelor's degree at UCI, and then earned her teaching credentials. *I also participated in a project that helped me pre-*

Chapter

pare for the CBEST (the California teacher licensing test). Now she is a mathematics teacher in Julia C. Lathrop Middle School, teaching Algebra 1, Transition Algebra, and Support Math. There are some 1500 6th, 7th, and 8th graders in her school. The Santa Ana school district is the fifth largest in California with 91.6 percent of the students identifying themselves as Latino and 66.7 percent being English Language Learners. *Support Math is for the same kids who are in my Algebra 1 class and they are learning English.* She also teaches in the UCI professional development programs for math teachers.

❖ *What do you expect when you are looking for excellence in teaching?*

One of the things that I expect is that teachers will have high expectations for themselves and for their students. They need to know their students' strengths and help bring out the best in them. They have to have knowledge in their content area so that they can teach it in different ways. Instead of just covering the subject, they need to be able to uncover it. They need to be willing to teach it in more than one way, do experiments, and bring people to talk with their students. And, they need to have care and compassion.

If you don't know, ask. I always like talking with high school teachers and elementary school teachers. If I can see what they are doing and how they are teaching, then maybe I can do the same things in teaching my students algebra. Knowing math, I can tell my students where the subject is going.

❖ *How do you know that a teacher has made a difference in student learning?*

I had to think about this question. One of the things that I have noticed in my own classes is that when they start picking up the book on their own and trying to learn more about something—or they bring something they found on the Internet or they learned

somewhere else; when they start to make connections. Also, when they start questioning; what would happen when we do this? They are not just taking information from me; they are starting to make connections. Also, when they start giving me their own examples, I know they are learning.

❖ *What brings you joy in teaching?*

Being a positive role model; I believe that I am a hard worker and I work at things because I enjoy them. I wanted to be in this school because I think they need an advocate. They need someone to be telling them, "Yes, you can do it." They can become English proficient, because I didn't know English until I was 11 or 12. I see myself as a bridge between the education system and the parents. I can talk with the parents about the expectations, and I can do it in Spanish. I also get joy from learning from my students. It makes me a better person and a better teacher. For example, when a student gives a criticism, I tell them they are allowed to do that because it just makes me better. Last year one of the classes was not behaving very well, so I asked, "What do you need?" They made a suggestion and we tried it, and it worked.

❖ *What do you expect a first-year teacher to know and be able to do?*

They should be able to be flexible and to try different things. Not to try everything at once, just try one or two things. When they are comfortable, try more. Usually first-year teachers just follow the script. I think they need to try to put in their own ideas. They should also understand that the standards are the guide. So whenever they are designing assessments or activities, they are not to do them just because they like the subject. They are supposed to do activities that teach the standards. Eventually that is what the kids are going to be tested on.

❖ *In your time as a teacher, what education reforms have you had to implement? What have you learned through these experiences?*

In one of the schools where I taught, the whole school was based on students doing a lot of projects. There was not a lot of reading or vocabulary development and no textbooks were available. I was saying that there is a hole here; some of the kids are not getting it. In other schools, all they do is the textbook. Doing just projects is not good enough and only doing a textbook is not good enough. So one of the things I do is have both. Students learn differently. They have to be able to read the textbook, because that is how they will be tested, and they have to do projects so that they can see how it is applied.

I am also getting involved in writing for reading comprehension in the content areas. Once you do this, their behavior totally changes. They are able to play with the content. Their behaviors change; they seem more calm.

❖ *What advice would you have for a first-year teacher about what they should know and be able to do about the various efforts to reform schools, curriculum, and teachers?*

They have to be aware of what NCLB really means. Parents, students, teachers, and districts are being held accountable. Schools have to hire teachers with the appropriate credentials and teachers have to teach to the standards. Otherwise, the students are not going to score very high. Teachers have to get together and plan as a team; we have to be willing to work with each other and make changes. I have ELL students and when I was a student some teachers watered down the curriculum. Instead of giving us a truthful mathematics, they made it easy. It wasn't the real thing, so they were shortchanging us. We were not learning what we were supposed to. I teach the concepts in Spanish to the same high level that I do in English. If they don't speak the language, it doesn't mean they don't know, it just means they speak a different language.

One of the things that is important for teachers to do every day is to clarify your values; why are you teaching? Is it because of the paycheck? It is because of the students? Clarify your values. That is what is going to make you wake up and go to school every morning with a smile. Find one thing that you really believe in and try everything to make it happen. For example, in my school some students were not being allowed to take Algebra 1, because they didn't speak English. I am really against this because I was one of those students who was going to be denied. However, I had one teacher who said, "No, you are going to be there." So my vision is that I am not going to let it go. I am going to get parents involved. That's what I am talking about, something that is not happening but you want it to. If we don't, someone can come and say "don't do it" and we will say "OK, you are right." You have to be willing to risk something for the betterment of the kids.

Questions to Consider

1. Rocio Jimenez talks about teachers having high expectations for students and themselves. How can you tell when a teacher has high expectations?
2. What kind of role model do you want to be?
3. How can teachers help ELL students learn the content vocabulary?
4. What are your reasons for wanting to become a teacher?

Americans always have had a strong interest in and concern about the quality of education. One consequence, as was described in Chapter 5, is that since colonial times there have been many changes in schools and ever-increasing expectations. Today there is widespread belief and commitment to the ideal that all citizens should have access to public schools. For example, one hundred years ago, the commitment was for all children to have an elementary school education. Following World War II, the commitment was elevated to all students graduating from high school. Now there is the growing expectation that early childhood and postsecondary education are important to success.

Over the years there have been criticisms too. However, in the last 25 years, criticism has been incessant: "Public schools are failing," "students are not as well prepared," and "teachers are of poor quality." Most beginning teachers today have grown up in this time of sustained criticism of schools, teachers, and students. Rarely in the last 25 years have there been positive statements about schools, teachers, and students. In this environment of constant criticism, it is easy to have doubts. However, the reality is that today's teachers are better prepared than ever before and today's schools are serving more and more diverse students than ever before. In addition, there are continuous efforts to change and improve schools and the quality of teachers. All of this is being done with the explicit expectation that there need to be continuing increases in learning by all students.

The trigger that started the current phase of criticizing schools is generally acknowledged to be a small report, *A Nation at Risk*, published in 1983. This report opened by stating:

> Our nation is at risk. Our once unchallenged preeminence in commerce, industry, science, and technological innovation is being overtaken by competitors throughout the world. This report is concerned with only one of the many causes and dimensions of the problem, but it is the one that undergirds American prosperity, security, and civility. We report to the American people that while we can take justifiable pride in what our schools and colleges have historically accomplished and contributed to the United States and the well-being of its people, the educational foundations of our society are presently being eroded by a rising tide of mediocrity that threatens our very future as a Nation and a people. What was unimaginable a generation ago has begun to occur—others are matching and surpassing our educational attainments. (p. 1)

Since the publication of *A Nation at Risk*, there have been literally thousands of commissions and reports about the current state of public education. Few of these reports have pointed out any of the many successes of today's schools. As Bracy (2003) observed: "Good news about public schools serves no one's political education reform agenda even if it makes teachers, kids, parents, and administrators feel better" (p. 59).

The *Nation at Risk* report was short on recommendations for fixing schooling. The few suggestions in that report were not innovative or new. In the intervening years, other critics have offered other solutions. The various solutions proposed can be seen as directed toward fixing students, fixing the curriculum, fixing the teachers, fixing schools, and a few have recommended fixing teacher education. The key word being used when talking about improving schools is **reform**. All of the initiatives whether directed at the curriculum, teachers, students, schools, or states are encompassed under the label of reform. Ironically, 60 years ago, reform schools were state-operated schools for juvenile delinquents. Now the term is being applied to all public schools with the connotation that they have been "bad" and need to be fixed.

There are good news stories coming out of the last 25 years of school reform. One is that a large number of positive, exciting, and innovative approaches have been developed to help teachers and schools better serve today's highly diverse students. Some of these reforms are directed at improving the curricula. Other reforms are intended to increase the quality of teachers and teaching, while others are intended to improve schools, school districts, and entire states. Today's teacher education candidates will be able to observe many of these reforms as they participate in practicum, student teaching, and other field experiences. As a teacher edu-

▶ **Reform.** Initiatives to improve student learning by implementing specific approaches to teaching, curriculum, and school organization and processes.

cation candidate and in the future as a beginning teacher, you will be an active participant in implementing many of these reforms.

Focus QUESTIONS

After reading this chapter you should be able to answer the following questions:

1 Why has there been so much talk and so many efforts to reform schools?

2 What strategies are being used to improve the quality of teachers?

3 What kinds of innovations are being introduced to improve classrooms?

4 What is being done to reform whole schools?

5 Instead of making changes in the subparts, what efforts are being initiated to improve the whole system of education?

6 What kinds of issues and consequences are being discovered as the reform movement continues?

What Are Strategies for Improving and Rewarding Teacher Quality?

> *Judy Berg really was enjoying her first year as a high school English teacher. She had two composition classes with a large number of kids who were just learning English. It was hard to communicate with them, but they helped each other and all were making progress. Judy also had a literature class and was coadvisor of the yearbook.*
>
> *In talks with her mentor teacher, and in the English department meetings, Judy kept hearing about "performance pay." Teachers talked about "skills blocks," "high performing teacher," and "group incentive" pay. She wasn't sure what they were talking about, but there seemed to be several ways that teachers could earn extra pay. Some of the pay seemed to be tied to what teachers did in their class-rooms and other parts were tied to student achievement. This pay was different from the stipends that coaches received. Her mentor observed, "The whole plan is part of the school board's efforts to recognize and keep high-quality teachers."*

Special pay is just one of many ways that are being devised to identify, recognize, and support high-quality teachers. As is summarized in Figure 13.1, a number of mechanisms are being used currently to increase the quality of teachers. Researchers have compared the knowledge and skills of novice and expert teachers. States and Congress have mandated teacher testing, and in a few states such as Tennessee, student test scores are being followed from year to year and related back to which schools and teachers they had. The research

Figure 13.1 Mechanisms for improving teacher quality

findings clearly document that high-quality teachers have particular knowledge and skill.

Using Research to Define Teacher Quality

A basic assumption throughout history has been that teachers make a difference in student learning. As obvious as this assumption is, it has not been easy for researchers to clearly document differences in effects that can be associated with how teachers teach. There are several parts to this research problem: Student learning has to be assessed; teacher performance has to be measured. Differences in effects of "high" and "low" have to be identified. Finally relationships between what teachers did and what students learned have to be drawn. In addition, there is the awkward challenge of conducting the study and reporting the findings while preserving confidentiality.

▶ Teacher effectiveness
studies. Systematic re-
search on the relation-
ships between teacher
behaviors and student
achievement on standard-
ized tests.

Finding Correlations between Student Achievement and Teacher Effects   The pioneering set of **teacher effectiveness studies** was done by Brophy and Everston (1976). Their studies began with having several years of elementary and junior high schools test scores where they also knew which classrooms the students had attended. The first significant study finding was that there was a correlation between student test score gains and which teachers they had. Even more significant was the finding that regardless of test scores at the beginning of the school year, in some classrooms, students gained more than did comparable students in other classrooms. In other words, no matter the entering level of the students, there was a teacher effect with some teachers being associated with higher student gains each year. This finding strongly indicated that teachers make a difference, but did not inform at all about what teachers were doing that made the difference. Brophy and Everston then conducted a series of observational studies where there were high student gains and classrooms where each year students achieved less. (see Figure 13.2).

In the 1970s and 1980s, other classroom researchers were uncovering other behaviors and characteristics of more effective teachers and classrooms. For example, Emmer and Evertson (1980, 1981) focused on classroom management. Good, Grouws, and Ebmeier (1983) studied the teaching of mathematics. These early studies were important because they were based on systematic observation of classroom behaviors and correlations were drawn with student achievement. As is illustrated in the tips offered in Figure 13.2, the studies resulted in a great deal of useful information and suggestions for becoming an effective teacher.

Comparing Novice and Expert Teachers   Shulman (1987), Berliner (1994, 2001), and other researchers took a different approach to discovering differences teachers make. Where the teacher-effectiveness researcher's methods were highly **quantitative**, using objective measures and counting the frequency of particular classroom behaviors, these researchers used **qualitative** methods. In a qualitative

Quantitative. The use of counts and numbers as data.

Qualitative. The use of descriptions and narratives as data.

Systematic observation of classrooms by researchers is an important source of information about the ways students learn and effective teaching strategies.

Figure 13.2 Guidelines from teacher effectiveness research

Principles for Small-Group Instruction in Beginning Reading

1. Reading groups should be organized for efficient, sustained focus on the content.

2. All students should be not merely attentive but actively involved in the lesson.

3. The difficulty level of questions and tasks should be easy enough to allow the lesson to move along at a brisk pace and the students to experience consistent success.

4. Students should receive frequent opportunities to read and respond to questions and should get clear feedback about the correctness of their performance.

5. Skills should be mastered to overlearning, with new ones gradually phased in while old ones are being mastered.

6. Although instruction takes place in the group setting, each individual should be monitored and provided with whatever instruction, feedback, or opportunities to practice that he or she requires.

Principles of Direct Instruction

1. Instruction begins with an advance organizer who poses the problem or task.

2. Teacher-directed instruction occurs more than 50 percent of the time.

3. Active presentation of information by the teacher or student(s) or through technology.

4. Presentations are well-organized and clear.

5. Build understanding step by step.

6. Use many examples.

7. Pacing of instruction is based on assessments of student understanding.

Keys to Effective Classroom Management

1. Conduct lessons with few interruptions.

2. Establish and use automatic mechanisms for taking care of students' procedural and personal needs.

3. Make sure that students know what to do upon completion of assignments.

4. Establish relatively few rules and teach them.

5. The rules should be somewhat general and well-explicated at the beginning of the year.

6. Use the board to communicate assignments to students.

7. Have students involved in the management of housekeeping tasks.

8. Have clearly laid out expectations from the first day.

9. Give feedback promptly.

10. Have smooth and short transitions.

Sources: Anderson, L., Evertson, C., & Brophy, J. (1982). Principles of small-group instruction in elementary reading (Occasional Paper No. 58). East Lansing: Michigan State University, Institute for Research on Teaching; Emmer, E. T., & Evertson, C. M. (1981). Synthesis of research on classroom management. *Educational Leadership* 38(4), 342–343, 345–347; Evertson, C. M., Emmer, E. T., Sanford, J. P., & Clements, B. S. (1982). Improving classroom management: An experiment in elementary school classrooms. *Elementary School Journal* (2), 172–188.

approach, observers develop narrative descriptions of all that they see in the classroom. Then these descriptions are analyzed to see what types of patterns and themes can be detected.

The other significant difference in research method was that teachers were selected based on their reputation as expert or novice. In teacher effectiveness studies, teachers were sampled based on correlations with student test scores. In the expert/novice studies, teachers were selected based on the professional judgments of colleagues and supervisors. Findings from these studies reinforced the findings from the earlier quantitative studies, and they offered important new insights about differences in teacher knowledge, skill, and beliefs. As a result of the expert/novice studies, today six domains (see Figure 13.3) of teacher knowledge, skill, and attitudes have been identified as keys to teacher quality. Each of these domains should be addressed in teacher preparation programs and is likely to be assessed in determining the quality of teachers.

Increasing Qualifications for Teacher Licensure

Another strategy for education reform is to address the qualifications of teachers. In recent years, state policy makers, and most recently with the No Child Left Behind (NCLB) act, the federal government has increased the reliance on various forms of inspection to ensure that teachers are qualified. In colonial times, teachers were selected and employed based on the recommendations of their pastor and

Figure 13.3 Domains of expert teacher knowledge and skill

1. **Content Knowledge** Expert teachers know their subject matter. They not only know the basic facts and constructs, they have in-depth understanding of how these combine to make the big ideas and themes of the discipline. They can provide examples of how the discipline develops and what today's cutting-edge questions and debates are about. Expert teachers can predict the typical mistakes and misunderstandings students will make as they are learning the content. Expert teachers also can describe how topics and lessons will unfold over the course of the term.

2. **Pedagogical Knowledge** Expert teachers know concepts, theories, and research about curriculum and instruction. They can describe the findings from research on best practice and the characteristics of different models of teaching. They also are knowledgeable about approaches that will be effective with different kinds of students. They can identify and describe characteristics, strengths, and weaknesses of different teaching strategies.

3. **Professional Knowledge** Expert teachers are knowledgeable about the foundations of education: history, sociology, educational psychology, philosophy, administration, and law. They know about issues of diversity and other policy matters. They also have knowledge about ethical practice.

4. **Pedagogical Skills** Expert teachers not only know about pedagogy, they can perform in classrooms in ways that are consistent with what is known from research and theory about best practice. They can model a number of teaching strategies and manage their classrooms with a minimum of off-task student behavior.

5. **Dispositions** Expert teachers hold positive beliefs and attitudes about students, teaching, their subjects, the school, and the families of their students. They truly believe that they can make a positive difference for all of their students. They treat boys, girls, slow learners, fast learners, poor and rich, with respect and set high expectations for all. They are excited about the subjects they teach and share their enthusiasm with their students.

6. **Pedagogical Content Knowledge** Expert teachers are able to combine and apply what they know about the subject, teaching strategies, and their beliefs in ways that serve the unique needs of a particular class of students. They select examples for illustrating concepts that are related to the background and experiences of the students they teach. They anticipate the typical mistakes that students might make and adjust their teaching accordingly. They are able to integrate their content knowledge, pedagogical skill and knowledge, and professional knowledge with a deep understanding of their students' current understanding and prior experience. The result is lessons that make sense to students and have all students engaged, understanding, and learning.

having completed a certain number of years of education. In the nineteenth century, elementary school teachers would only have needed to complete high school. In that time, most teachers were unmarried women and their employment contract likely prohibited their dating or becoming married. As recently as the 1950s, it was possible to become a teacher with as few as 2 years of college coursework. Today, completion of a bachelor degree is only one of many requirements. Teacher candidates must fulfill an increasing number of requirements and are closely and continuously inspected as a means for ensuring quality.

Teacher Background Checks   State and school district requirements for becoming a teacher have become much more rigorous. Requirements go way beyond the completion of a bachelor's degree. As was noted in Chapter 1, one requirement is that the bachelor's degree comes from an accredited institution and an approved program. A recently established requirement is that teacher education candidates be fingerprinted one or more times during the completion of their teacher preparation program. The fingerprints are used to check if there is any form of criminal record in the person's past. Becoming a teacher is a major responsibility and the public has the right to expect that children will be protected from individuals with past criminal convictions whether they be for drug possession, theft, or child abuse. U.S. citizenship must be verified and foreign nationals must have the appropriate visa. Don't forget that an original Social Security card and perhaps a birth certificate will be required at the time that your first teacher contract is being approved.

Teacher Testing and Evaluation   Another near universal requirement to become a teacher today is passing one or more standardized tests. In different states, the form and number of tests will vary, but most states require a certain level of test score in order to become licensed. Two-thirds of the states use one or more of the Educational Testing Service (ETS)-developed PRAXIS series of tests. Several states, such as New York, Ohio, California, and Texas, have established their own tests. These standardized tests are being required at one or more of the following points:

- **Entry into a teacher education program.** At the beginning of a teacher education program, candidates will be required to pass a basic skills test, such as PRAXIS I. This will be an assessment of knowledge, understanding, and skill in English and mathematics. Typically, these tests are designed at the 8th grade level, which means that the expectation is that at the time of entry into a teacher education program, the candidate should be able to write and compute at the level of 8th grade students. Each teacher education program will have additional admission requirements such as a certain minimum grade point average in content courses. The assumption is that grades are an indicator of the candidate having an acceptable level of content knowledge.

- **Student teaching.** Arguably the most critical component of a teacher education program is student teaching. In recent years a number of checks on

Ed Lines

"A child cannot be taught by anyone who despises him, and a child cannot afford to be fooled." *James Baldwin*

developing teacher quality have been established as screening for entry into student teaching and to evaluate performance during student teaching. Candidate interviews and prestudent teaching portfolios may be required. During student teaching, many programs are requiring candidates to develop teacher work samples (TWS) (see Chapter 9), which requires student teachers to teach a group of students and provide through pre- and postassessments evidence about student learning.

- **Program exit.** Teacher testing at the time of completion of the preparation program is required in most states. In most states, there will be a test of content knowledge, professional knowledge, and pedagogical knowledge. In most states, achieving a passing score on this program exit test is a requirement to begin teaching. Check the requirements carefully in the state where you plan to teach because there may be limits to how many times this licensure test can be taken.

Assessing Beginning Teacher Performance   In most states, there are additional requirements for induction-year teachers. For example, Florida specifies a number of classroom observations that principals must complete with beginning teachers. In Ohio, teachers must take a third test that includes documentation of classroom performance and student learning. Oregon requires submission of a teacher work sample that includes lesson plans, examples of student work, pre- and posttest results as evidence of learning, and a teacher reflection piece. Connecticut's Beginning Educator Support and Training (BEST) program requires beginning teachers to address a set of standards by submitting a portfolio that includes a video of their teaching, samples of student work, and information about the teacher's efforts to improve. This portfolio is then judged by trained assessors.

Shared Standards of Expectations for Beginning Teachers   As each state has increased the licensing requirements for teachers, there has been increasing dialogue between the states and the development of a shared set of standards for beginning teachers. These are referred to as the Interstate New Teacher Assessment and Support Consortium (INTASC) standards. It is extremely important for you to become knowledgeable about the INTASC standards. In most states, the teacher licensure tests and related requirements are based on these.

Teacher Continuing Professional Development

Determining teacher quality and increasing teacher quality can be defined in terms of research findings and can be set through licensure requirements. However, for the most part, both of these mechanisms are external to the teacher. Research findings are based on the work of other teachers. Tests and other requirements apply to all teachers in the same way. They may be reasonable parameters for describing teacher quality in general. However, individual teachers have a professional responsibility to be investing in their own efforts to become high quality. Becoming a

Ed Lines

High school grade students in high-minority and high-poverty public schools are more often taught English, science, and mathematics by out-of-field teachers than their peers in low-minority and low-poverty public schools.

Novice and expert
teachers take advan-
tage of every oppor-
tunity to learn.

high-quality teacher is not going to happen by simply passing a state-required test or completing all of the necessary licensure requirements. High-quality teachers continually are looking for ways to learn and to continually improve. This is an indicator of a professional disposition.

Teacher Training Completion of a teacher preparation program only certifies that a candidate is ready to begin practice as a teacher. No teacher education program is going to guarantee that their graduates have the knowledge and skills to be highly effective teachers. The expectation is that beginning teachers are ready to continue their learning and safe to begin practice. One of the best ways to increase expertise is to attend and actively engage with the teacher workshops offered by the school district and perhaps by the school staff where the beginning teacher is assigned. Workshops that are intended to provide teachers with specific knowledge and skills that they are expected to use in their classrooms are called **training** sessions.

    Teachers have plenty of other opportunities for learning. Many of these include speakers, readings, media-based seminars, Web courses, and working on a master's degree. All of these are **professional development** (PD) opportunities. Each is not intended to provide the teacher with specific knowledge and skill, but rather to introduce new ideas and different perspectives.

Action Research Another form of professional development that is completely in the hands of teachers is **action research**. All of the research in classrooms does not have to be done by outside researchers. In action research, teachers become the researchers. The process begins with one or more teachers having a question about which they are curious. Questions might be related to behavior of students,

▶ Training. Formal sessions
and materials to teach a
specific set of knowledge
and skills.

▶ Professional development.
Sessions and materials
intended to advance
one's general knowledge
and skills.

▶ Action research. Studies
that are designed and
conducted by teachers in
their classrooms.

495

What Kinds of
Innovations Are Being
Used to Improve
Classrooms?

formance pay. In addition to learning about the different possibilities for obtaining additional pay, she also needs to check on her eligibility. Probably some of the options are not available to beginning teachers. Even so, Judy should start preparing whatever materials and documentation are required, because in subsequent years, she most assuredly will want to apply as one way of showing that she is becoming a high-quality teacher.

What Kinds of Innovations Are Being Used to Improve Classrooms?

Mary Beth Nowinski was talking with her grandmother who had been a teacher for many years about what it was like to be student teaching. "Today's classrooms seem so busy! The children are not sitting straight and quiet. There is so much clutter and mess! There is so much talking, how can anyone learn?" her grandmother asked.

Mary Beth explained that in today's classrooms, "It is important for students to be interacting with each other and using manipulative materials. Also, classes are much more diverse than they used to be. Students have very different backgrounds and all of them don't come to school ready to learn."

Her grandmother then said, "Well, what about their parents? Didn't they teach them the alphabet and read to them every night?"

"This is a problem. Did you know that one in four children lives with only one parent, and that one in three is born to unmarried parents? Even worse, one in 24 children lives with neither parent. Teachers must use everything in their classroom to help all of them learn," Mary Beth answered.

Two key targets for reform have been students and classrooms. Addressing early childhood education has become the priority area for improving student's readiness to begin school. Today's classrooms are busy places. Of course teachers teach, but so do many other classroom resources. A large variety of reform strategies has been developed to improve teaching and learning in the classroom. Some of the strategies are organizational. Others are based in new understandings of how children learn.

Having Children Ready for School

The statistics are cause for concern. In addition to those cited by Mary Beth, consider the following (Children's Defense Fund, 2002):

- One child in three is behind a year or more in school.
- One child in five is born to a mother who did not graduate from high school.
- One child in eight never graduates from high school.
- One child in twelve has a disability.

Clearly all of today's students are not fully ready to learn when they enter the classroom.

Teachers' Lounge

How I Learned to Love Crayfish

As a new teacher, I was often learning the curriculum along with the students in my classroom. For instance, in science class, we were to use crayfish to teach the students about the cycle and structures of life. I discovered that it was difficult to keep the crayfish alive, because the temperatures in our classrooms were extremely warm. Despite the fact that I really didn't want to touch them, I was determined to take good care of them so that none of them would meet an untimely end on my watch!

Things went smoothly enough the first week that I had them. I would come into my classroom in the morning, excited to see how they were doing. However, one morning I was horrified when I saw two of "my" crayfish lying huddled together in a lifeless heap in the corner of the tank. I nudged them carefully, my hands shaking, but they did not move.

I solemnly asked the curriculum specialist to come in to help me remove "the dead." When she came in, she started laughing. I regarded her quizzically, not understanding what could possibly be so humorous about the situation. (I guess I must have grown attached to the little critters!) She turned to me and said, "You *have* taken good care of them. They are not dead; they are mating!"

● Kristen Liporto
4th grade teacher,
Spring Street School,
Shrewsbury, Massachusetts

Increasingly, policy makers, educators, and researchers are focusing on the importance of early childhood as the key to student readiness. Normally it is more effective to prevent problems than to have to invest in remediation. This certainly is the case with children coming to school ready to learn. As was stated in a WestEd Policy Brief (2002), "Most educators agree that by age 8 a typically developing child should be able to read, write, add, subtract, pursue a line of inquiry, function within the classroom environment, listen to and follow instructions, and avoid aggressive action through negotiation" (p. 1).

Child Care Research findings from a number of disciplines are documenting the critical importance of early childhood development. Panels have examined cognitive, social, emotional, and neurophysiological research and there is a consensus about how young children learn (Bowman, Donovan, & Burns, 2001). Young children don't learn through isolated skills but rather through integration. Their cognitive learning is integrated with the social and emotional. For example, learning the alphabet in isolation is not as effective as having the letters and words associated with sitting on the lap of a parent who is reading a book aloud. Expensive toys are less important than having continuing interactions with adults who are interested in supporting the child learning. Active participation is important.

497

What Kinds of
Innovations Are Being
Used to Improve
Classrooms?

Another implication of the research findings is that development in early childhood is the key to readiness for school and ultimate success in school. In addition to the role of parents, for infants and toddlers (birth to age 3), child care is a significant factor. Child care must be attentive, safe, and interesting. At this early age, infants are learning security, predictability, language, ways to structure new knowledge, and rules for appropriate behavior. A crying child who receives prompt soothing attention from a caregiver is learning to persist with a difficult task, while a child whose crying is ignored or is punished is more likely to be anxious and have difficulty focusing outward.

Readiness for school is highly dependent on the quality of parenting and child care in the early years. This point is made graphically clear in studies that compare children of low-income families who have received Early Head Start (EHS) services with those who did not. EHS is a child care program funded by the U.S. Department of Health and Human Services. Children receiving EHS services did better on tests of cognitive, language, and social development and their parents read more to them, spanked them less, and were more likely to provide support for literacy and learning at home (U.S. Department of Health and Human Services, 2002). The EHS program is having positive impact on children and parents. Unfortunately, there is not sufficient funding so that all eligible children can receive EHS or other child care services. In many ways, the achievement gap is born through the experiences of infants and toddlers.

Preschool As more attention is placed on the early years, the more interest there is in having 3- to 5-year-olds attend preschool. To be ready for school, children need command of language, preliteracy skills, the ability to think abstractly, social and emotional skills, and the motivation to learn and get along with others. Addressing

Early childhood education, preschool programs, and all day kindergartens are important foundations for future student learning.

the development of these school readiness skills is increasingly being seen as the role of preschools. However, parents must be careful in selecting a preschool, because there are different philosophies and, most important, different emphases, on child care versus preparing for school. Quality preschool programs will address cognitive, social-emotional, and physical development. The adult-child ratio will be small and there will be little staff turnover. The curriculum should encourage children to reflect, predict, and question. In addition, the approach to teaching and learning needs to build on children's existing understandings (WestEd Policy Brief , 2002).

Improving Classroom Structures and Processes

Efforts to reform classrooms have been less dramatic and more subtle. Curiously, the basic design of the classroom has not changed in the last 100 years. This is true around the world. The basic plan places the teacher at the front, students at desks or tables, chalkboards, bulletin boards, and storage. In the 1960s, some schools were constructed with open classrooms. These were "pods" equivalent in size to three regular classrooms. Typically, three teachers, an aide, and 100-plus students would work in this open space. Teachers and parents were not fully accepting of this more public approach, and there was more noise. By now, walls have been placed in the open spaces and the traditional classroom returned. The one noticeable change in the last 100 years would be the introduction of technology ranging from radio to television, movie projectors to VCRs, overhead projectors to video projection, and laptops with LCD projectors. Still, reform of the classroom begins with the teacher and a class of students.

Class-Size Reduction   One target for classroom reform that is regularly considered is class size. Teachers advocate for smaller classes so that they can give students more individual attention. Parents are supportive, believing that their children will learn more. Many school boards and state legislatures are interested too. However, reducing class size is costly. Reducing the average class size from 25 to 15 would mean that for every three classes, an additional teacher would need to be hired. The additional class would need a classroom too. Research findings are generally supportive of reducing class size to around 15 to 18 in the primary grades. However, there is no clear support for reducing class size in the upper grades. Legislatures in several states, including California and Nevada, have supported class-size reduction. However, the costs sets limits on how much can be done.

Infusion of Technology   Educational applications of technology are not only the most visible innovation in classrooms, they have the potential for significantly changing instruction and increasing student learning. An unusual characteristic of educational technology as an innovation is that it is continually changing. Most educational reforms, such as curriculum materials and teaching strategies, do not

Ed Lines

The teacher signing bonus program established by the Nevada legislature in 2001 pays a $2,000 bonus to newly hired teachers.

499

What Kinds of
Innovations Are Being
Used to Improve
Classrooms?

change drastically over time. With technology, there are new tools and applications each year! Technology has become so important to teaching that in this book an entire chapter (Chapter 10) is devoted to descriptions of the many exciting tools and applications.

Classroom Climate

An entirely different form of classroom reform is to examine elements of classroom climate. **Classroom climate** refers to the social and physical environment and the ways that these can influence teaching and learning. Think about schools and classrooms where you have been a student and others that you have visited. Each has its own "feel." Some classrooms are busy, others highly organized, some are welcoming, some are cheerful. Each classroom will have a unique climate. In recent years, more attention has been given to classroom climate. As the cultural diversity of students has increased, there have been concerted efforts to make sure that all students are welcomed and treated with respect. For example, the inclusion in regular classrooms of special needs students has required teachers and students to create a welcoming and supportive atmosphere that accommodates everyone. The extent to which students feel comfortable to make mistakes and to express divergent ideas is a direct consequence of classroom climate.

> Classroom climate. Social and physical characteristics of the classroom.

Staffing Patterns

As was described in Chapter 4, the worldwide image of a classroom is one teacher and 20 to 50 students. However, other staffing patterns are possible. A common practice in elementary schools is to have a paraprofessional or classroom aide assigned to each classroom for part of the day. Parent volunteers are another strategy for adding adult help. Another widely used staffing strategy is some form of team teaching. Teachers can team only for shared planning, to specialize in teaching certain subjects, or to teach interdisciplinary units.

Standards-Based Education

Across the United States, the one universal reform has been the establishment of standards and related testing. This reform reflects everything that has been presented in the last three chapters. In the "old days," the curriculum was organized around topics; teachers devised their own lessons and preferred ways to engage the students. The students read the text, wrote reports, and completed "cookbook" laboratory experiments. Success was defined by the teacher and supervisors in terms of the extent to which students completed the tasks and enjoyed the lesson.

Today, high-quality teaching is defined in terms of the extent to which students can demonstrate that they are making progress toward learning the identified outcomes as stated in the standards. Teachers are to teach to the standards and students are assessed in terms of the standards. Teacher planning begins and ends with analysis of the expectations for student learning. Instead of prescribing the one right way to solve a problem, teachers now are expected to pose

Ed Lines

Private schools and schools with high minority enrollments are more likely to employ teachers with 3 or fewer years of teaching experience than are public schools and schools with low minority enrollments. *(National Center for Education Statistics)*

open-ended tasks and problems. Students are expected to derive solutions in their own way(s) and be able to explain their reasoning.

Figure 13.4 presents a prototypical outline for a unit plan that is standards based. In this example, a 3rd-grade teacher has outlined the plan for a unit on

Figure 13.4 Unit plan outline for teaching 3rd graders to write a report of information

Unit Plan—Report of Information

Prerequisite Learning Experiences

- Distinguish fiction and nonfiction.
- Read several examples of nonfiction/reports.

Standards to Be Assessed

- Create a single paragraph.
- Develop a topic sentence.
- Include simple facts and supporting details.
- Write descriptions that use concrete sensory details to present and support unified impressions of people, places, or things.
- Indent paragraphs and use appropriate punctuation and capitalization of simple sentences.

Standards to Be Practiced

- Distinguish common forms of literature (e.g., fiction, nonfiction).
- Use titles, tables of contents, chapter headings, glossaries, and indexes to locate information in text.
- Demonstrate comprehension by answering questions from text.

Assessment

Students will independently write a multiparagraph report on animals using information gathered from various text and other resources.

Criteria for Success

- Gather facts from at least one source.

- Organize writing in paragraphs/topic sentences.

- Use sensory details to describe.

- Use appropriate conventions.

Requisite Opportunities to Learn

Lessons and Practice:
- Identifying sources of information
- Using structural features of text, titles, subtitles, index, etc.
- Identifying relevant types of information about animals
- Concept of paragraph/ purpose for reader

- Identifying topic sentences
- Grouping sentences on same topic
- Ordering sentences and paragraphs
- Composing topic sentences to indicate main idea and transitions for reader

- Identifying descriptive words
- Writing "showing" not "telling" sentences

- Norms for indentation
- Punctuation/capitalization of simple sentences
- Sentence construction

Source: Copyright © 2002 by WestEd. From *Isolation Is the Enemy of Improvement: Instructional Leadership to Support Standard-Based Practice* by Kate Jamentz. Reprinted by permission of WestEd : www.wested.org.

writing a report of information. For any other standard(s), the same type of advance analysis and planning would be needed. Note that the majority of the work in the unit has to do with learning and assessing learning. Only after the left-hand side and the center columns are completed is the question of "what to teach" examined. Standards now drive reform in the classroom and schoolwide.

Revisiting Mary Beth's Talk with Her Grandmother

Mary Beth's grandmother was a teacher in a very different time. In her time, teachers were judged on the orderliness of their classroom and the quality of their presentations. Today, teachers are judged in terms of their impact on student learning. Unfortunately, today more children are coming to school who are not fully ready to learn. This need certainly makes the job of teaching much more challenging. We also know from research that interacting with the subject, both mentally and interpersonally, are important strategies for optimizing learning. Therefore, today's classrooms are more noisy and messy. Standards-based education has been developed as the way to bring together the targets of learning, what is known about how students learn, and key elements of instruction. Today's teachers and students are expected to keep the learning targets in mind, not just the instructional activities that are employed.

How Can the Whole School Be Improved?

Emmy Lou Chin now was experiencing the feelings that she had heard so much about from friends who had student taught last semester. She was swamped and she did not understand what she was expected to do! She knew her subject—after all, she had earned mostly A's in her English composition and literature courses and Dr. Young was very encouraging about her small ratio teaching in the English methods class. As Emmy Lou thought it through, the biggest challenge seemed to be with her student teaching placement in Northwest High School.

Northwest High School was an award-winning school with a diverse student population. What had come as a surprise was that she was not expected to teach English in isolation and she did not have the typical 150 students each day. Instead, the schedule was "blocked"! She was teaching with a social studies teacher and their lessons were based in interdisciplinary themes. In addition, she was expected to get to know each of her students and mentor them.

As she reflected at the end of the second week of student teaching, she became clear about one of the sources of her discomfort. There was no way at the pace they were going that she could cover all that was listed in the state curriculum. When she mentioned this concern to her social studies colleague, Harry reminded her that Northwest was a Coalition of Essential Schools school and a key principle was that "less is more." He told her, "Instead of skipping across the surface of many topics, in this school we teach deep. That is why the school uses a block schedule, and why we have students develop portfolios instead of our issuing the usual report cards."

The many efforts to improve the quality of individual teachers and classrooms and to have students ready to learn when they arrive at school have had limited success. In some places, there have been modest gains in student achievement, while in other settings, no changes have been detected. Gradually, reformers have come to see that the school as a whole needs to be the primary unit for change. Asking teachers to change one at a time fails to acknowledge the important influence of other teachers and, most importantly, the principal. Individual teachers can launch innovative efforts, but without the support of the whole school, it is very difficult to sustain initiatives over time.

Today there are many innovative strategies designed to be used schoolwide. Some of these target variations in the organization of the adults and students. Others aim to redistribute power and involve more of the adults in decision making. A number of reform strategies are intended to provide consistency in approaches to teaching and classroom management. There also is set of whole school reform models where curriculum, instruction, governance and staffing patterns are changed, all at the same time.

Staffing Patterns and Processes

The regular ways for organizing adults and children as "workers" were described in Chapter 4. Here, several alternative approaches are introduced. A useful question to keep in mind while reading these is to ask, To what extent would you expect each of these reforms to result in increases in student learning?

▶ Site-based decision making (SBDM). A school organizational structure that involves teachers and parents to a greater degree in the running of the school.

Site-Based Decision Making   One of the problems in schools today is that so many of the decisions about curriculum, budgets, staffing, and even student schedules are made without input from teachers. The decision-making power is concentrated at the district, school board, and state and federal levels of government. Once this problem was identified, the reform proposal that emerged was to move the power for decision making closer to those who have to implement the decisions; in other words, schools, teachers, and parents. This is called **site-based decision making (SBDM)**.

The core structural piece with SBDM is establishment of an added governance structure—the SBDM council. This is a committee composed of teachers, the principal, parents, and possibly some students. The council can be responsible for making decisions in the following areas:

Schools do not have to look the same, or be organized and staffed in the same way.

Budget: All schools typically have some discretionary funds. In regular schools, teachers may not know how much money is there or have much say in how the funds are spent. The principal decides. In SBDM schools, decisions about how the funds will be spent are made by the SBDM council. For example, purchasing technology and curriculum materials may be decided by the council.

Staffing: In some school districts, the council only makes decisions about supplemental materials. In some districts, councils decide how many teachers will be employed and whether the school will have an assistant principal. They interview teacher applicants and in some districts select the principal.

Curriculum: Councils may have responsibility for developing the school's philosophy, selecting textbooks, and deciding instructional strategies that will be used. They also will have a say in which, if any, of the whole school reform models will be adopted.

Communication: Sharing of information within the school, with parents, and the larger community may be a responsibility of the SBDM council. The council members also must develop knowledge about the whole school and strategic directions of the school district.

As with other reforms, there are points of tension in having a SBDM council. One is that no matter what the council may decide, the final legal authority for the school is the principal. If anything goes wrong, it will be the principal who is held accountable. Therefore, the willingness of the principal to share authority with the council has to be earned and respected.

School Improvement Process   Most school districts and states have implemented formalized approaches for schools to use in reviewing student test scores and developing plans for improving them. The general approach is called **school improvement process (SIP)** and a key document is the **school improvement plan**. The SIP plan lays out the specific steps that will be taken across a school year that are intended to increase student learning in targeted areas. Typical steps in the SIP plan are outlined in Figure 13.5. The process begins with establishing a school improvement committee that works with the principal to review data about student achievement. Typically this work is done in the spring and the committee develops a school improvement plan. The plan reports on the data analysis, identifies specific needs, and proposes steps the school will take over the next 12 months with the intention of increasing student achievement. Ideally the next spring the SIP team will review the new data, be able to report gains, and propose new steps that will be taken over the following 12 months. Also see the Understanding & Using Evidence on page 505.

High School Reform Strategies   The general stereotype of high schools is that they are the most resistant to change, least student centered, and in many ways unresponsive. However, there are a number of interesting reform strategies being applied in high schools. One that received a great deal of attention in the last 10 years is **block scheduling**, which combines two, or sometimes more, of the regular 50-minute class periods. The longer block of time provides uninterrupted

School improvement process (SIP). A systematic set of steps that a school takes to review student data and plan for changes in curriculum, instruction, and other arrangements for the purpose of increasing student achievement.

School improvement plan. The written plan of action that is produced as part of the school improvement process.

Block scheduling. Combining two or more 50-minute class periods into one period.

Figure 13.5 Steps in the school improvement process plan

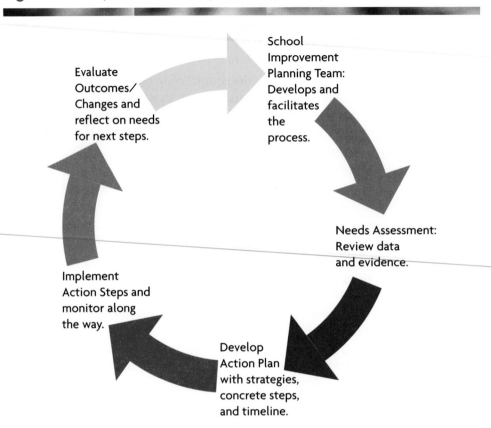

opportunity to develop and follow though to completion a science lab investigation or the presentation of a panel with discussion. This relatively simple structural change has had a mixed reception. Some teachers have celebrated having more time while some, such as math teachers, have found the extended time less useful. One clear finding is that simply changing the schedule is not sufficient. Teachers need professional development and training in how to make best use of the expanded time blocks.

Another high school reform strategy that is receiving a great deal of attention at this time is **small learning communities**. Everyone knows about the very large— too large—high schools that attempt to serve thousands of students. Too many students are not served well in these large "factories." Small learning communities is a reform strategy based on the assumption that the ideal size for a high school is somewhere between 400 and 600 students. At that size, students do not become lost, there is a sufficient number of teachers to offer a full curriculum, and the principal can know the staff and the students. The Bill and Linda Gates Foundation is investing millions of dollars with different school districts engaged with implementing this reform strategy (see www.gatesfoundation.org). Also, the U.S. Department of Education has funded a number of school districts to implement small learning communities.

▶ Small learning communities. Organizing high school students in groups of four to six hundred for all of their classes.

Understanding & USING EVIDENCE

USING 6TH GRADE MATH DATA IN AN SIP-NEEDS ASSESSMENT

The following table is a summary of 6th grade student performance on the selected subparts of the annual state testing. These data are the annual results over 5 school years. The school improvement team for the school used these data to develop action steps for the next year. What do you see in these data? As a member of the SIP team, what would you recommend be reported to the full staff and what steps should be included in the action plan?

State Test Scores 6th Grade Math Percent of Students at Mastery

	1998	1999	2000	2001	2002
Concepts					
1. extends pattern & states rules	53	74	77	77	93
2. id. alt. forms w/expanded notation	93	96	94	97	97
3. id. alt. forms using regrouping	24	41	46	61	59
Facts & Computation					
10. add/sub 2–3 & 4 digit whole no.'s & $'s	80	90	89	88	90
11. mult/div mults of 10 7 100 by same	56	63	67	79	77
12. mult/div fractions	99	97	97	97	94
14. add/sub fracts mixed (no.'s like denoms)	46	69	70	81	67
Problem Solving/Application					
17. solve prob: order/mag of whole no.'s	94	96	94	95	99
19. draw conclusion from graph/table/charts	84	86	80	81	90
20. create graphs from data	90	94	94	96	97
21. id. operation to solve story problem	69	81	76	81	74
26. est reasonable ans. fractions	56	63	58	69	62
Measurement/Geometry					
32. id/draw/describe/classify geo shapes	73	63	81	88	70
33. measure/determine perimeter & area	44	36	31	59	51
34. estimate length & area	30	47	57	65	57

Your Task Examine this set of data.

1. What do you see in these data?

2. In what areas are students doing well?

3. Where are the problem spots?

4. As a member of the SIP team what would you be recommending for Targets and Action Steps?

*Refer to the **Understanding & Using Evidence Appendix** at the end of the text for answers and information related to these activities.*

▶ Parent coordinator.
School staff professional
role that serves as liaison
with parents.

▶ Community school. A
school that houses social,
health, and other services
for adults.

Parent Involvement   Making connections with parents and reaching out to the community is very important to school success. As parents have become busy with both working, as well as there being a greater number of single parents, the challenge of getting them involved in schools has become more difficult. Further complicating this problem is that many non-English speaking parents and poverty-level parents can be intimated by teachers. Given these factors, schools have become more systematic and innovative as they seek effective ways to involve parents and gain community support.

A key new and important member of the school staff is the **parent coordinator**. These professionals are skilled at working with parents of diverse cultures. They facilitate communication between teachers and parents in relation to student successes and problems. They also offer information programs and training sessions for parents on how to support their child's school learning. Topics include emphasizing the importance of attendance, reinforcing the child completing homework, and activities that parents can do that will increase literacy.

Some schools are offering special evening programs to draw in parents, such as Family Literacy Night, or providing free breakfast to the parents as well as the children. The school may offer "Moms & Muffins" or "Dads & Donuts" as a way of reaching out to parents.

The goal of many schools is to be seen as a **community school** (see www. communityschools.org), also called a coordinated service school or full-service school. These schools are open from early in the morning until late at night, and in some cases 365 days a year. They not only partner with the various social service agencies but will provide office space for them within the school. As a result, the school site might include medical, dental, and social service agencies; college classes; after-school youth development organizations such as the Boys and Girls Club of America (www.bgca.org); a reading room for senior citizens; computer classes for adults; and after-school sports programs. The goal is to have the school become the center of community activity.

Community Partnerships   Today, educators fully understand the importance of having close links and partnerships with the community. Parent involvement is only one component. Business owners, religious leaders, local political leaders, senior citizens, and other members of the community are seen as important resources and potential partners for the school. The police and social service agencies are fully understanding of the importance of working with schools. In addition, service organizations, such as Rotary Clubs, are willing partners to help students and schools. An exciting example of a community-wide reform effort is the Santa Ana Partnership, which is described in the introductory educator interview for this chapter.

One of the challenges for schools is to somehow coordinate and effectively develop partnerships with so many individuals and organizations. One national resource that can help is called Communities in Schools (CIS) (see www.cisnet .org). The CIS mission is "to champion the connection of needed community

Ed Lines

Georgia was the first state to fund "universal" voluntary pre-K for all 4-year-olds.

509

Instead of Changing Pieces, How Can the Education System Be Improved?

Figure 13.6 Efforts to reform schooling and improve student learning are coming from all parts of the system

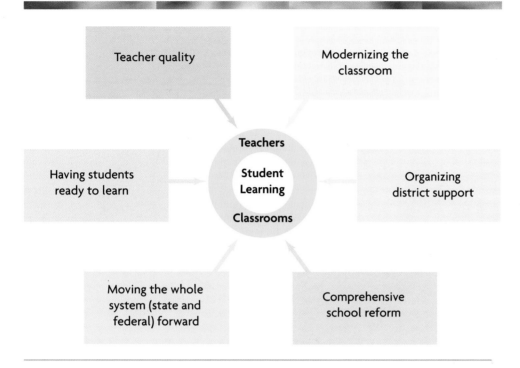

School District Reforms

The organization and financing of school districts was described in Chapter 4. Those descriptions were structural and related to governance and addressing accountability for the spending of public dollars and supervision of employees. However, many of the structural representations of school districts do not have a clear and direct focus on accountability for student learning. Several of the proposals for school district reform address this end.

Elements of School Districts that Are Accountable for Results   School districts have been recognized for helping the majority of their schools improve. In a recent study, nine of these districts were studied in order to see how they were able to make a difference in school and student success. The districts ranged from small suburban to one of the largest school districts in the country. Although their context varied, the researchers discovered underlying consistencies in their approaches. All had documentable gains on standardized tests (Improving districts, 2002).

The researchers found that each district was a "well-functioning system"; the entire district was thinking and working as whole. Leadership, decision making, and communication had student learning as the focus. Figure 13.7 is a graphic representation of the system elements in school districts where accountability for student learning is at the center of action. This way of viewing a school district is in sharp contrast to the structural descriptions presented in Chapter 4. In this

Figure 13.7 Elements of the school district system for improving learning

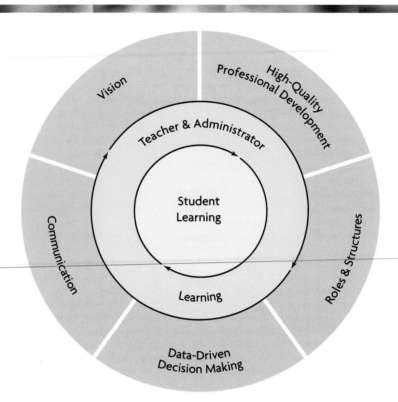

Source: *Improving districts: Systems that support learning.* Copyright 2002 by WestEd. Reprinted by permission of WestEd : www.wested.org.

view, student learning is at the center; teachers and administrators surround this focus. Note that "learning" also is an element with the teacher and administrator circle. In these school districts, there is a organization cultural norm that the adults are learners, too. The outer elements again reflect shared systemwide ways of working and thinking. Communication is not simply a structural task of the superintendent or the district public relations staff, it is a part of everyone's effort. With each of these elements there is a structural side; the district evaluation office is responsible for compiling and reporting data. There also is an organizational culture side; schools uses the data to make instructional decisions. This type of district is a good place to be a teacher.

Grouping Schools   Another example of rethinking the organization of school districts is the way schools are grouped on the organizational chart. In the traditional organization arrangement as is reflected in Chapter 4 (Figure 4.1), each school is in a "line" relationship with a district office administrator, typically an assistant superintendent or director. In larger school districts, there will be separate district office administrators for elementary and secondary. In even larger districts, there will be "area" administrators responsible for all of the schools in a geographic region of the community. In these organizational arrangements, each school "reports" directly to someone in the central office.

they be able to speak out freely on such questions without fear of retaliatory dismissal.

Keep in mind that teachers do not have carte blanche. They have the right to discuss matters of public concern, but not to unveil student or personnel matters or to make unsubstantiated personal attacks.

Can a teacher refuse to use the district curriculum or substitute their own materials?

No. Although the U.S. Supreme Court has not addressed this question, it has been answered in state and district courts. The states have granted authority for selecting curriculum materials to school boards. The only way a teacher can substitute materials is with prior approval of the appropriate administrator. Also teacher presentations in class must be balanced. They cannot present one-sided views without providing the opposing view.

SCHOOL SAFETY

In response to growing concerns about violence and school safety, state legislatures and school boards have established new statutes and policies. Some of these have set uniform rules and procedures; for example, no-pass no-play, while others have specified consequences. For example, zero tolerance policies have been established in relation to actions such as bringing a weapon to school. In these situations, school officials have no choice but automatic suspension (10 days or less) or more likely expulsion (a quarter, semester, or full academic year).

Can school officials search students and their lockers?

Yes. This might be seen as a violation of protection against unreasonable search as addressed in the Fourth Amendment in the Bill of Rights. The historical view was that school administrators were acting as in loco parentis, and as such could search students at will. In *New Jersey v. T.L.O.* (1985), the Court mandated a balance:

> Today's public school officials do not merely exercise authority voluntarily conferred on them by individual parents; rather, they act in furtherance of publicly mandated educational and disciplinary policies. . . . In carrying out searches and other disciplinary functions pursuant to such policies, school officials act as representatives of the State, not merely as surrogates for the parents, and they cannot claim the parents' immunity from the structures of the Fourth Amendment.

However, the Court went on to say:

> Although this Court may take notice of the difficulty of maintaining discipline in the public schools today, the situation is not so dire that students in the schools may claim no legitimate expectations of privacy.

The court then established a two-prong test for determining the reasonableness of a search. First was the search "justified at its inception" and second was the search, "as actually conducted," reasonable.

STUDENT RIGHTS

With the increase in gangs, school official now have concerns about clothing and other items that might have symbolic meaning, which could lead to violence. In the past, court cases about student dress tended to side with the student.

Can schools regulate what students wear?

Yes. Although schools can have dress codes, they must be careful to not violate students' First Amendment right to freedom of expression. The critical criteria for school officials and the courts is where there is reason to see certain dress as having the potential to contribute to substantial disruption and threats to safety.

How far do students free speech rights go? Can they be insolent, disrespectful, and curse?

No. In *Tinker v. Des Moines Independent Community School District* (1969), the Court ruled that there are limits on student expression. However, "undifferentiated fear or apprehension of disturbance is not enough to overcome the right of freedom of expression." Some disruption has to be accepted. Only when their actions would "materially and substantially interfere" with the requirements of appropriate discipline in the operation of the school may officials prohibit the behavior.

replaced, and outside experts are brought in to accomplish a district turnaround.

- **Reconstitution:** An extreme form of reform is for the state to declare that a school has failed to the point where there needs to be a complete replacement of staff. This is one of the final steps mandated in NCLB.
- **School closure:** The final step can be to completely close a school due to its failure to increase student test scores.

Competition Is "Good" for Schools

An entirely different set of strategies for reforming the education system is being championed by those who believe that competition is good. They compare the "closed market" of public schools to the "open markets" in business. They believe that teachers will work harder and do better if they know that they are in a competition. A related theme is that services offered by public sector employees cost more and are of less quality than when the service is offered by a private sector company as the result of competitive bidding.

Rankings Are "Good"   Students, schools, and states are now being compared and ranked on a large number of factors. In addition to test scores, states are regularly compared and ranked by per-pupil expenditure (see Figure 4.6), high school graduation rates, and many other factors. Student performance in each state is compared regularly with the National Assessment of Educational Progress (NAEP). NAEP uses a set of standardized tests to compare student performance in the basic subjects state-by-state.

In addition, the nation's performance is being compared and ranked internationally. One informative summary of the various international comparisons has been reported by Boe and Shin (2005). As can be seen in Figure 13.8, U.S. students do well in the elementary grades, but are more middle of the pack in the middle grades and high school. These comparisons are used by those who champion competition to point out how poorly U.S. students do when compared to the performance of students in other countries. The critics of the champions (Gerald Bracey, 2003; Berliner & Biddle, 1995; Berliner, 2004) regularly present counterarguments about the problems with these comparisons and how that in many ways U.S. students are doing as well as, or better, than their peers in other countries. They add in other rankings that document how U.S. teachers spend more hours in front of the class, have less time for planning, and fewer professional development days than their counterparts in countries such as Japan. Neither side is swayed by the statistics of the other; so the rankings debate continues.

Choice Is "Good"   The advocates of competition point out that in most neighborhoods and school districts, parents have no choice in the selection of the pub-

Ed Lines

Beginning in 1984, Texas has required pre-K in school districts with at least 15 4-year-olds who are poor, homeless, or don't speak English.

515

Instead of Changing
Pieces, How Can the
Education System Be
Improved?

Figure 13.8 International comparisons of student performance across subjects

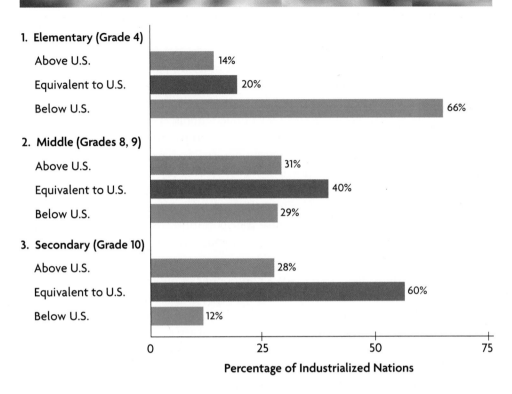

* Results for each grade level were aggregated across reading, mathematics, science, and civics.

Source: Boe, E. E., & Shin, S. (May 2005). Is the United States really losing the international horse race in academic achievement? *Phi Delta Kappan, 86*(9), 688–695.

lic school their child will attend. Historically, this decision was made by setting the geographic boundary, or **attendance area**, for each school. Children who live inside that area attend the school designated to serve that attendance area. Increasingly school districts are opening up this restriction and permitting parents to choose the school, as long as that school has room to add students.

Three other mechanisms are being used to increase choice:

1. **Magnet schools** became an effective strategy to increase school integration. Magnet schools do not restrict their attendance area. Instead, the intent is to draw students from all over so that the result is a diverse student body. Magnet schools draw students by having a specially developed curriculum based around a theme. Themes could be health/science related or based on technology, the performing arts, sports, or some other multidisciplinary set of topics.

Attendance area. The geographic area within which students are assigned to a specific school.

The number of charter schools across the United States was above 2,700 for the 2002–2003 school year.

In many cities such as Kansas City, Missouri, new school facilities have been constructed that reflect and support the unique theme of each magnet school.

2. **Vouchers** represent another approach to providing parents with choice and increasing competition. With a voucher program, instead of the public dollars for each pupil being distributed to the school district and used to pay for each school, parents receive a credit that they can use to pay to whatever school their child attends. There is heavy debate about the desirability and constitutionality of vouchers. Teacher unions and others oppose vouchers, seeing this as a strategy to undercut support for public schools. A problem with vouchers is that the amount of money is not sufficient to pay the full cost of a year of school. Therefore, parents—or the school district—have to make up the difference. Thus, another concern with vouchers is that poor families still do not really have choice, because they cannot afford to supplement the voucher. They also may not be able to afford the transportation costs for their child to attend a particular school. Of course transportation costs can also be a limiting factor with magnet schools. However, most school districts offer school busing for attendance at magnet schools.

3. **Charter schools** have been made a component of public education in many states. The full definition of what is a charter school varies by state, but in general, they are public schools that receive public school funds and are able to operate largely independent of the school district and school board. Charter schools will have their own governing board, their own facility, and will develop their own vision, philosophy, and curriculum approaches. The funding made available to each charter school does not cover all of the costs associated with staffing and operating a school facility. To fill in the shortages requires additional fund-raising activity by the school community.

▶ **Privatizing.** Contracting to an outside organization for a service or product that historically had been done internally.

▶ **Education management organizations (EMOs).** For-profit companies that assume responsibility for operating a school.

Outsourcing and Privatizing Are "Good"   In response to the criticism that the private sector can do things at less cost than can public schools, two strategies have been used with mixed results over the last decade. **Privatizing** entails contracting for an outside company to do a service that traditionally had been done by school district employees. For example, some school districts have privatized building custodial and transportation services. The service is put out to bid and when a contract is accepted, the school district is able to terminate the employees who had provided that service. Ideally the contracted service costs are less than were the costs associated with having permanent employees do the work. The downside can be less quality and commitment to the quality of service provided.

Education management organizations (EMOs) are for-profit companies that take over the operation of a school or a school district. Throughout the 1990s, a number of organizations were established to take over the running of individual schools and whole school districts. These newly formed businesses, such as Edison Schools, Advantage

Joel Pett, Lexington Herald-Leader, Cartoon Arts International

517

Instead of Changing
Pieces, How Can the
Education System Be
Improved?

Connecting

TO THE CLASSROOM

This chapter introduced various strategies and initiatives to reform schooling. Some are ways to improve teaching, others are designed to reform whole schools, and some are intended to change school districts and states. Behind all of these efforts is the expressed intention of increasing student learning. The following are suggestions for how you can use the ideas presented in this chapter.

1. Teachers are expected to continually be looking for and testing new approaches.

2. Today's teachers are part of the whole school and cannot simply stay in their classroom and "teach."

3. School improvement processes (SIP) and other strategies for reform depend heavily on teacher participation.

4. Comprehensive school reform (CSR) models provide consistency in classroom approaches for all teachers and students.

5. Many policy makers, critics, and educators see competition as being good for public schools.

6. Reducing the achievement gap continues to be the biggest challenge for all teachers and schools.

Schools, the Leona Group, and the National Heritage Academies, openly express their intentions of increasing student success and turning a profit. The EMOs represent another form of competition for public schools, and, at the same time, they are partnering with public schools. In most cases, extra public dollars are invested in tooling up the launch of each EMO school. The educational philosophy of most EMOs is toward having more tightly structured expectations for student behavior, including uniforms, and having students in school for longer days and longer school years. There also is a tendency to employ more inexperienced teachers, because they have lower salaries. To date none of the EMOs has shown a clear profit and there is little evident to suggest that across a number of schools and years that students are more successful.

The Achievement Gap Is Still There   One of the primary reasons for establishing the reform movement has been the glaring differences in student learning for white and nonwhites. Addressing this achievement gap is a major component of most reform proposals and programs. Unfortunately, the evidence is not encouraging; the gap continues. For example, in California, the state tests are organized so that each school receives an academic performance index (API). The schools are then ranked into one of 10 levels. Most of the schools with over 50 percent economically disadvantaged students are in the bottom half of the API ranking. These data clearly document why the 30-plus–year press to find and implement school reforms that work and the need to have high-quality teachers in every classroom must continue.

Revisiting Joan Rodman and the Desert Palm Charter School

Joan's school illustrates how a number of the themes in the reform movement can become operational. Charter schools offer choice. Parents choose to send their children to Desert Palm with its strong discipline and predominant use of direct instruction. Joan obviously likes the structure and orderliness. Each charter school is unique. Another charter school could be open ended and use inquiry teaching strategies. These are choices that parents and school staff make in forming a charter school. Desert Palm is unusual in that it is operated by an EMO. More typical is for charter schools to be self-managed and funded using a combination of public dollars and fund-raising.

Chapter Summary

To paraphrase an ancient Chinese saying, today's educators are living in interesting times. This is a very interesting, exciting, and challenging time to become a teacher. The one clear certainty is that the work of teachers, the organization of schools, and the operation of the education system is changing. There are many pressures in support of change including the increasing diversity of students, the low performance of some students on high-stakes tests, international comparisons, and the globalization of the world. As is illustrated in Figure 13.6, there are many efforts to bring about reforms at all levels of the education system. Whichever reform strategy is selected, teachers are at the center of action and the single most important factor for improving the education system and its effects on student learning.

How can teacher quality be improved? Policy maker concern about the quality of teachers has contributed to the development of new requirements for teacher licensure, especially the use of high-stakes test. Researchers have developed clear understanding of the differences in knowledge, skill, and dispositions of novice and expert teachers. Other researchers have examined the classroom behaviors of more- and less-effective teachers. Related efforts have included development of the INTASC standards as a way of describing performance expectations for beginning teachers. New strategies to support high-quality experienced teachers include performance pay plans and national board certification.

What types of initiatives are being proposed and used to improve what goes on in classrooms? A beginning target for improving classrooms is to have students coming to school ready to learn. Early childhood care and education programs are being seen as important to achieving this goal. Strategies for improving what goes on in the classroom include structural innovations, such as class-size reduction and the infusion of technology, as well as increasing teacher collaboration through teaming. An array of innovative instructional strategies is being introduced such as constructive teaching and standards-based education to change classroom processes.

What is being done to reform the whole school? Many see whole school reform as the key to improving learning for all students. Several strategies are being used to increase the involvement of teachers and parents in schoolwide decision making. School improvement processes and site-based decision making are becoming regular ways of working. There also are a number of comprehensive school reform models, each of which is supported by university-based scholars, training, and networks of participating schools.

Instead of focusing on individual teachers and schools, what is being done to change the education system? There are efforts to reform school districts by organizing feeder schools and examining the role and authority of school boards. Many critics believe that introducing different forms of competition is a good idea. Magnet schools, vouchers, and charter schools, as well as outsourcing some services, are attempts to increase competition and productivity. At the national level, strategies such as the No Child Left Behind act are being established to force improvement of all schools, districts, and states.

Class Discussion Questions

1. There are many ideas and initiatives for "reforming" education. Some target teachers, others classrooms or schools, and still others are intended to impact the system. Which of these targets do you think should be the priority? In other words, how can the greatest impact be made?

2. Which of the reforms would you personally support and which do you think are bad ideas? Which of your ideas about quality teachers are consistent with these reforms? Also, if you had to implement one of the reforms, which would you find the most interesting to do?

Field Guide for School Observations

Schools in your community will be engaged with many of the reforms described in this chapter. There may not be many schools implementing whole school reform models but all are having to implement some of the strategies such as high-stakes testing and a school improvement process. Without becoming a nuisance, obtain a copy of a school's school improvement plan. (Some schools and districts will have these published on their website.) Study all that is required to develop the plan. Review the SIP and pay particular attention to the needs assessment, which is the part where the data about student learning should be examined. Also review the part of the plan that lays out the action steps that are being implemented this school year. Then interview someone from the school to find out how the SIP is working. See if there are checkpoints where new data are being reviewed and the plan is being adjusted. To what extent are the staff in the school aware of the SIP and seeing connections between their work and achieving the SIP targets?

Ask a Teacher or Principal

1. One of the reform themes has been efforts to define the criteria for being a highly qualified teacher. Some observers have pointed out that being highly qualified and high quality are not necessarily the same. Seek out a teacher who is known for being high quality. Ask that teacher what their thoughts are about the various reforms that have been introduced in the last 10 years. How have these reforms contributed to this teacher being high quality?

2. Using Research Findings—review the standards for NBPTS certification. Then talk with a board-certified teacher. Ask him or her what it was like to prepare the application. Be sure to ask about the kinds of learning the teacher experienced as a result of engaging in the process. Identify three steps you should take in your teacher-preparation program that will move you toward being ready to apply for NBPTS certification.

Journaling Becoming a Thoughtful Teacher

At this point in your becoming a teacher, there is a lot about education reform that is new to you. That is to be expected. Items for you to think about at this time are: 1) How do you feel about the reform movement in general? 2) Are you comfortable with becoming a teacher in this time where there are very high expectations? 3) What do you see being the most important tasks and responsibilities of teachers in this time of reform?

Portfolio Task

It is highly likely that the schools where you participate in field experiences and where you ultimately accept a teaching position will have a school improvement process. The steps and vocabulary may be different, but the overall process and plan will be the same. Review a school improvement plan and make notes about the possible role of teachers in each step. Which steps would you be ready to contribute to now? Where do you see that you need to know more before you could be a high-quality contributor?

Self-Assessments *What Am I Learning?*

Write an outline for a three- to five-page essay that responds to the question: What do you know and understand about the education reform movement?

Once you have developed the outline, use the following rubric to assess your performance.

Incomplete	Novice	Proficient	Professional
Presents a few of the approaches without elaboration; some of the descriptions are inaccurate.	Names some basic approaches and identifies consequences in general ways.	Describes different approaches, explains related pressures, and points out consequences.	Uses descriptions of reform strategies to illustrate differences in expectations and consequences for schools, teachers, and students.

Using the Web

One of the key strategies for improving student learning is comprehensive school reform. Select one of the CSR strategies identified in Appendix 13.A and go to the website concerning it. Think about what it would be like to be a teacher in a school that was using that CSR strategy. Using the website information, develop a description of the key tasks and activities that you as a teacher would be expected to know and be able to accomplish. Also, what would students be expected to know and be able to do? Prepare a table that compares the regular roles of teachers and students with what would be expected for the selected CSR.

Your Professional Library

School reform continues to be the theme in the writings of several prominent scholars. Each of the following books addresses current needs, aspirations, and issues related to school reform. An important strength of both authors is their placing schools within the larger context of communities and society in general.

Elmore, Richard F. (2004). *School reform from the inside out: Policy, practice and performance.* Cambridge, MA: Harvard Education Press.

In order for schools, teachers, and student learning to improve more than testing is required. In this book, the author examines the challenges of policy makers making external demands on schools, while the arguing that

successful school reform happens "from the inside out."

Rothstein, Richard. (2004). *Class and schools: Using social, economic, and educational reform to close the black-white achievement gap.* New York: Teachers College Press.

This book begins with a review of the historical problems and studies that contributed to today's problems. The Coleman report and other precursors of how the achievement gap is viewed today are described. The author moves on to addressing different policies and strategies that are being attempted today in efforts to reduce the gap.

To access chapter objectives, practice tests, weblinks, and flashcards, visit the Companion Website at **www.ablongman.com/hall1e**

Log on to Allyn & Bacon's MyLabSchool (**www.mylabschool.com**). Enter Assignment ID **ELV3** in the **Assignment Finder**. View the video clip, *Peer Observation and Feedback*. Consider what you read in this chapter and what you observed in the clip and then answer the following questions.

1. Do you believe that peer observation is a viable professional development process for teachers? Explain.

2. Would you be willing to participate in peer observation? Why or why not?

As directed at the end of the clip, go to **www.houstonaplus.org/criticalfriends.htm** and explore the Critical Friends Groups Protocols as well as the links to the Annenberg Institute for School Reform.

What impact do you feel these philosophies have on teachers and their professional development?

Succeeding in Your Teacher Education Program—and Beyond

Educators in Real Schools

M E E T
Karen Faiman

Public School District, Hartford, Connecticut

Hartford, Connecticut, is a historic New England city located at the intersection of two interstate highways along the west side of the Connecticut River. The Hartford Public School system serves 24,000+ students in 33 schools. The student population is over 95 percent minority (compared with 25 percent for the state) and over 50 percent of the students do not speak English at home. More than 95 percent of the students are eligible for free and reduced lunch.

One of the school reform strategies in Hartford was developed through funding from the Wallace Foundation. It is a Leader Succession Model, or career path for the development of today's and tomorrow's school leaders. A particularly innovative level in this model is that of School Turnaround Specialist.

During her initial teacher education program at the University of Connecticut, Karen had clinical experiences at all elementary school grade levels and did her student teaching in 4th grade. She knew that she wanted to teach in an urban setting, so when she heard that the Hartford Public School District had an opening for a 1st grade teacher, she applied. She taught 1st grade for 2 years and when a 6th grade position opened up, she asked her principal if she could have it. *I learned a lot from the 1st graders. I am glad that I had that experience, because when I did jump (to 6th grade), I had the basis for understanding what goes on in the younger grades.* For the next 3 years she taught 6th grade and then was asked by district office administrators to consider applying for a School Turnaround Specialist position.

As a Turnaround Specialist, my position includes not only dealing directly with the children but going into the schools to which I am assigned and assisting the administration and

Chapter 14

teachers in their efforts to improve student learning. On a day-to-day basis, I go into classrooms to model, teach, and observe and then conference with teachers about what went on. Teachers call me saying that they need a little help or guidance. Also, an administrator will suggest that I visit a certain classroom to assist instructionally. Good teaching is good teaching, so I help teachers in all subject areas.

❖ *What do you expect to see when you are looking for excellence in teaching?*

I like to see students who are excited, talking, motivated, being creative, and are asking questions of each other and the teacher. In regard to teachers, I like to see them asking questions and being responsible for their own learning as an educator. It is okay to say, I don't know and I need to go find the answer, or that I need help. Or, that I am really good at this, do you want me to share and help you? I want to see creativity and imagination, and students who are engaged in projects, not just textbooks. I want to see instruction that is not just lecture, children in small groups and large groups, and different activities across the room. I see students who are in charge of their own learning and having the freedom to learn in different ways.

❖ *How do you know that a teacher has made a difference in student learning?*

When students say "Hey, I got it!" or they ask the next question. When they go out on their own and bring back more information, then I know they have absorbed it and it was not just a paper-and-pencil activity. They have the skill and can apply it. When they come back and say they have talked with their parents about what they learned in class today lets me know that a teacher has made a difference in student learning. Learning is being able to take it outside the four walls and into real life.

❖ What brings you joy in teaching?

I like when the kids get excited to learn. They are anxious to get started on a unit or to continue one, and when you hear them talking about the lesson in the hallway—all brings me joy. When kids ask questions, which I may or may not know the answer to, and they want to know more. It is kind of hard to put into words what about teaching brings me happiness. It is just a really unbelievable feeling.

I appreciate the joy of teaching children more now that I am not in the classroom. How to explain it . . . I did not recognize the joy I had until I was out of the situation. I recognized on a day-to-day or lesson-to-lesson basis, but now I can look back and think, "Hey, being in the classroom was a good feeling." It took me a while as a beginning teacher to be sure to recognize the joy that you get every day. It is easy to get caught up in "I had a tough class today, my lesson didn't go well, I don't feel good, I'm tired, I don't want to go back tomorrow." We really have to push those thoughts aside and say, I touched one kid or I know that kid got it, or I know he is going home better because I shared one idea with that child.

❖ What do you expect a first-year teacher to know and be able to do?

The obvious is to be able to present a lesson from beginning to end, how to initiate and follow it through to the closure. More importantly, teaching can be a lonely profession if you don't go outside your door. You need to make conversations with other teachers in the lunch room, the hallway, and be able to call them at home. Be willing to ask even another first-year teacher "How did you do it today?" It is really important for first-year teachers to be willing to ask questions.

❖ In your first several years of teaching, what kinds of leadership opportunities became available to you?

My first year I was assigned to be the grade level team leader for science, which meant that I went to the district in-services and came back to the school to share with the other teachers. The next year that turned into my becoming the lead science teacher for the school, which meant that I went to the district professional development sessions and brought the information back to the school. It progressed into being a participant in the Institute for Learning (IFL). I kind of gathered my 6th grade team together and said we are going to do this. We are going to be the team from our school to attend the professional developments from IFL and bring it back. From this experience, more leadership opportunities appeared from attending workshops, to presenting, to being paired off with another teacher to share. Some of these opportunities came to me but, in some cases, I reached out to participate. I want to learn. I want to know what is going on. I want to know how to get the answer. I saw it as an honor as a first- or second-year teacher to be asked to go to a workshop and then come back and share what I had learned.

❖ What leadership advice would you give to teacher education candidates?

My theme is: Ask questions. Ask what's going on. Nobody is going to be hesitant to answer you or to direct you in the right direction. If you see an opportunity, ask about it. You need to be observant; have your ears open about what's going on so that you know what's going on around the district and the school. Seek out leadership opportunities in your teacher education classes, volunteer to help in class. I held positions in my sorority as well as vice president of my dorm council. Seek out opportunities and ask questions.

Whether I was at the university or in my school, making sure that my team worked well together has always been important to me. For example, before I came to my 6th grade team, it was very much closed doors and nobody talked to each other. The idea of planning together was foreign from what I heard when I got there. I started knocking on doors and saying, "I want to go to this, and I want you to go with me." I like that feeling of gathering people together and working toward one goal. You definitely have to want to learn. When I was going to be out of the classroom, I would tell my kids where I was going, and when I came back I would tell them what I had learned.

I like the feeling of people coming together around a common mission. Although I have only done it in a small way, it would be nice to take an entire staff with tons of students and make a difference.

Questions to Consider

1. Karen Faiman seemed to have moved quickly into a teacher-leader role. What do you think were the keys to her advancement?

2. Does the idea of beginning teachers being leaders sound strange to you?

3. What kinds of leadership activities have you done in the past? What leadership activities are you involved in now? What leadership activities are possible for you to be involved in between now and the completion of your initial teacher education program?

T eaching is one of the most important professions. Now, more than at any other time in history, students, parents, communities, and the nation need outstanding teachers. As was described in Chapters 1 and 13 because the need is so great and their efforts so important, the preparation to become a teacher is more rigorous than ever before. The expectations for beginning teachers are higher, too. For all of these reasons it is extremely important for you to take advantage of every opportunity presented throughout your teacher preparation program. Now is the time to begin anticipating what you will need to know, be able to do, and have on record as you seek and obtain your first full-time teaching position. Failure to be thinking ahead could result in not obtaining your most preferred beginning teaching position.

This chapter begins with recommendations for succeeding in your teacher-education program. The remainder of the chapter describes themes, offers recommendations, and identifies issues related to being a successful and influential beginning teacher. Again, it is not too early for you to begin thinking about, preparing for, and anticipating what you will need to have and be able to do to be a successful beginning teacher. How will you apply for a teaching position? What kinds of documentation will you need to have and how can you prepare for the position interview? If you start anticipating and planning now, you will see how much of what you do in the remainder of your preparation program will be useful to you in seeking, applying for, and obtaining the perfect teaching position.

Focus QUESTIONS

After reading this chapter you should be able to answer the following questions:

1 By the end of a teacher education program, what should be the accomplishments of high-quality teacher education candidates?

2 How do successful applicants get their first teaching position?

3 As the first year of teaching unfolds, how do beginning teachers learn the job and their school?

4 In what ways can teacher education candidates and beginning teachers be leaders?

5 What are keys to seeing the joy in teaching?

What Are Keys to Succeeding in Your Teacher Education Program?

*As **Mark Mercer** moved further into his teacher education program, the more intense were his concerns. He had many concerns about getting everything done, because he couldn't afford to give up his delivery job and he now had to find time during the day to observe in schools. To make things worse, the school where the observations were scheduled was across town. He also had continuing doubts about whether he was going to be good enough. He was more excited than ever about becoming a teacher, but could he really do it?*

Two things he was finding useful, he had picked up in his Intro to Teaching class. First of all, he now understood that his "Self" and "Task" concerns were natural but he sure wished they would go away. Second, the Generic Teaching Model that seemed so theoretical at the time really helped! He could see parts of it in action during every observation. It saved him in that low-ratio teaching lesson with the two physical science students that he did yesterday. If he had not started with "Judges Prior Learning," it would have been a disaster. Now, if he can find time to write that up and get the reading done for tomorrow's ed psych class.

Ed Lines

Two-thirds of student teacher concerns about teaching will typically be in the self and task areas. *(Fuller, 1969)*

As you continue with your preparations to become a teacher, you will take a number of professional education courses and have a variety of clinical and field experiences. As you will have heard already from your fellow candidates, some courses and experience are perceived as being "better" than others. What you will discover is that, regardless of the perceived quality of the course or experience, the really good candidates use them to advantage. They use every assignment and activity as an opportunity to learn more about teaching, student learning, and what classrooms and schools are like. Regardless of the

A very useful strategy for teacher reflection and self-assessment is occasionally to take time to share current concerns about teaching with a colleague.

situation, the high-quality candidates learn and contribute to the learning of others. They are able to do this because they understand themselves, what teaching is about, and the importance of using every experience and opportunity to learn more. They also collect evidence to document their efforts, what they have learned, and artifacts that indicate the differences they make. They do all of this in spite of their feelings of not knowing it all and being very busy.

Understanding Your Concerns

In order to understand their students, teachers must first understand themselves. This does not require a complex psychological analysis; however, each of us will have certain feelings and perceptions about every situation. In addition, each of us may perceive the same situation differently. Depending upon our own perceptions, we construct our personal interpretations of what each situation means. Teachers do this all the time when talking with students and colleagues and when thinking about what they and others are doing. Teacher education candidates worry about getting good grades and wondering what it will feel like to be in front of a whole class of students. Understanding that all of us filter and ascribe personal meaning to events and actions is very important, especially for teachers. This is a component of the personal side of teaching; understanding our **concerns**; one's feelings, perceptions, worries, and preoccupations about teaching.

Concerns. A combination of feelings, preoccupation, worry, and attitude.

Ed Lines

It is OK to have personal concerns. They are a very real part of any change process, including becoming a teacher.

Writing Your Own Concerns   To illustrate how easy it is to examine your concerns, take a minute to respond to the following:

> **Open-Ended Concerns Statement**
> As you think about becoming a teacher, what are your concerns? Don't say what others are concerned about, what are *your* concerns? (Write your concerns using complete sentences.)
>
> Don't read any further until you have written your response.

The activity of writing your concerns is easy. Developing an understanding of what you have written is guided by 40-plus years of research. Researchers have documented that the concerns of teacher education candidates can be placed in categories and used by candidates and the program faculty to improve learning. In the end, teachers who understand their own concerns are better able to understand the concerns of their students and colleagues.

It turns out that our concerns can be sorted into a set of easy-to-understand categories. The original research on teacher concerns was pioneered by Frances Fuller (1969), a professor at The University of Texas at Austin. Since then, the analysis of concerns has expanded beyond teachers and now includes understanding the concerns of people involved in change (Hall & Hord, 2006). Now, the Concerns Model is applied regularly to the design of teacher education programs around the world.

The Concerns Model   Teacher education candidates, teachers, and others will typically have concerns in one of four areas: Unconcerned, Self, Task, and Impact. Researchers have divided these major areas of concern into a set of **Stages of Concern** that people may move through as they experience any type of change. Since becoming a teacher represents a major change process the concerns model certainly applies. The following are general descriptions of each of these areas of concern:

▶ Stages of Concern. Seven types or categories of concern about a change, innovation, or practice.

> **Unconcerned** There is little or no concern about teaching. Instead, the concerns are about other topics such as work, a family problem, getting along with a roommate, or an upcoming event such as getting tickets for a concert.
>
> **Self** Having enough information and wanting to know more are of concern as well as concerns about one's adequacy and ability to be a successful teacher. Doubt might be about knowing enough content, controlling the class, knowing how to teach a particular lesson, or being uncomfortable when standing in front of the class.
>
> **Task** Finding the time to fit everything in, getting all the materials organized, preparing lesson plans, and grading papers are likely topics of concern. Learning the how-to-do-its of teaching and coordinating schedules are other indicators of Task concerns.
>
> **Impact** Having ideas about what could be done to further improve one's effectiveness and student learning are indicators of Impact concern. Increasing all students' learning, improving one's effectiveness as a teacher, and getting

529

What Are Keys to
Succeeding in Your
Teacher Education
Program?

the last two students to understand are clear indicators of Impact concern. Another concern could be about working with one or more fellow teachers so that *together* they can have a greater effect on student learning.

Assessing Your Concerns   Assessing one's concerns is easy to do. Once there is an understanding of the four areas of concern and the more specific Stages of Concern, as outlined in Table 14.1, a person's concerns can be analyzed. Whether written or spoken, most concerns can be sorted into one of the four areas and then the specific stage identified.

As a first example of how to assess an Open-Ended Concerns Statement, read what you wrote in response to the question. Do the following:

1. *Which area of concern (Unconcerned, Self, Task, or Impact) is most present? Which area(s) of concern was not reflected in your statement? Were your concerns about teaching or other things? Were your concerns centered mainly on your ability to succeed, the management of teaching, or what your students are learning?*

Table 14.1 Stages of Concern

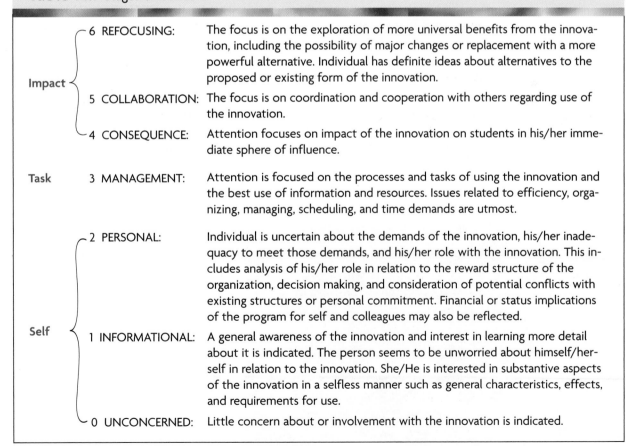

Impact	6 REFOCUSING:	The focus is on the exploration of more universal benefits from the innovation, including the possibility of major changes or replacement with a more powerful alternative. Individual has definite ideas about alternatives to the proposed or existing form of the innovation.
	5 COLLABORATION:	The focus is on coordination and cooperation with others regarding use of the innovation.
	4 CONSEQUENCE:	Attention focuses on impact of the innovation on students in his/her immediate sphere of influence.
Task	3 MANAGEMENT:	Attention is focused on the processes and tasks of using the innovation and the best use of information and resources. Issues related to efficiency, organizing, managing, scheduling, and time demands are utmost.
Self	2 PERSONAL:	Individual is uncertain about the demands of the innovation, his/her inadequacy to meet those demands, and his/her role with the innovation. This includes analysis of his/her role in relation to the reward structure of the organization, decision making, and consideration of potential conflicts with existing structures or personal commitment. Financial or status implications of the program for self and colleagues may also be reflected.
	1 INFORMATIONAL:	A general awareness of the innovation and interest in learning more detail about it is indicated. The person seems to be unworried about himself/herself in relation to the innovation. She/He is interested in substantive aspects of the innovation in a selfless manner such as general characteristics, effects, and requirements for use.
	0 UNCONCERNED:	Little concern about or involvement with the innovation is indicated.

Source: Hall, G. E., & Hord, S. M. (2006). *Implementing change: Patterns, principles and potholes* (2nd ed.). Boston: Allyn and Bacon.

2. *Which Stage(s) of Concern was most present?* Use the paragraph definitions presented in Table 14.1 as the guide for determining which Stage of Concerns is most reflected in the statement. Sometimes this will not be as easy to figure out, but with a little practice it can become easier.

3. Keep this analysis of your concerns in mind as you read the following.

Implications of the Concerns Model for Teacher Education Candidates

Once a teacher's concerns have been analyzed, the important follow-up question should be: What needs to be done to address the concerns and to facilitate the teacher continuing to improve? This question is what makes the concerns model so important for teacher education candidates and in-service teachers. When you understand your concerns, you can do something about them. Effective teacher-education programs are designed with candidate concerns in mind. For example, candidates have concerns about managing the classroom (Task Concerns), so many preparation programs include a course on classroom management. Another important component of effective teacher education programs is assessment of student learning (Impact Concerns). Candidates that understand their concerns can do many things on their own to help them develop further. For example, this chapter's Educator in Real Classrooms, Karen Faiman, emphasized being willing to ask questions. Candidates with Self concerns will be more hesitant to ask questions of others: "What if they think my question is stupid?" However, Karen pointed out that people are willing to answer questions and that getting those questions answered is a way to improve.

It is very important to keep in mind that there are no "bad" areas of concern; all areas of concern are possible. In fact, there are some general trends to teacher concerns. For example, teacher education candidates have more Self and Task concerns, while experienced teachers have more Impact concerns. If you think about it, this difference in the distribution of concerns makes sense. Beginners are more likely to have doubts about their ability to do something (Self concerns) and to be more preoccupied with logistics and getting everything done (Task concerns). These areas of concern are also characteristic of first-year teachers.

Impact concerns are more likely to be present with those who are comfortable and confident with what they are doing. This is the time when teacher concerns can truly focus on improving student learning. For example, Impact concerns were reflected throughout the interview with Karen Faiman.

Charting Your Concerns What will be important for you to document as you move through your teacher preparation program is the

Teachers have many concerns about teaching and are always wondering what they can do to further help each student succeed.

531

What Are Keys to
Succeeding in Your
Teacher Education
Program?

Understanding & USING EVIDENCE

TELLING STORIES WITH DATA/EVIDENCE

Analyzing Teachers' Concerns about Teaching

In most of the chapters in this text the Understanding & Using Evidence box has required you to work with quantitative data. The task required working with numbers or graphic representations and developing an interpretation. In addition, each of these activities was based in data about students or schools. The task for this chapter is different in two ways. First, the subject is teachers and aspiring teachers like you. Second, the data are qualitative instead of quantitative.

Open-Ended Concerns Statements from Three Student Teachers

The following paragraphs were written by student teachers.

JoAnne

Yesterday, right in the middle of my lesson one of my students raised his hand and asked me who I went out with Saturday night! I said that we were in the midst of the lesson now. I just went on with the lesson. It really shook me. I don't really mind saying whatever I was doing because they really did see me Saturday night. Should I have had him stay after school for asking? I felt like ignoring it; it was the only thing I could do. But I'm not sure if I was losing control. Will they disrespect me for it? I don't know how to react to it.

> *Refer to the* **Understanding & Using Evidence Appendix** *at the end of the text for answers and information related to these activities.*

Greg

Now, I am less concerned about their learning the facts and more interested in their seeing the general patterns and understanding the concepts. If there is a word or concept they don't understand, we stop and go over it. I realize more clearly now how little they know and how lacking their background is. When I can help them make the connections, they really get it.

Sue Lee

My father wants me to get a teaching certificate. Right now I am most concerned about getting married. We have booked the hotel and have the photographer too, but there is so much to do in the next 2 months!!!

Your Task: Analyzing Concerns Statements: Use the descriptions of the four areas of concern presented in Table 14.1 to assess each of the concerns statements. What areas and stages of concern are represented in each statement? First reread each concerns statement and determine its overall flavor. Does it sound most like unconcerned, self, task, or impact? Then read each sentence and assign a specific stage of concern to it. How could you summarize your analysis?

Addressing Teacher Concerns: Understanding teacher concerns can be a helpful tool for self-reflection and for considering what steps can be taken to resolve concerns. What steps could be taken by each of these student teachers and their supervisors to address their concerns?

proportion of concerns you have in each area. Ideally, by the end of student teaching, you will have fewer Self and Task concerns and more Impact concerns. As you become a first-year teacher, what do think will happen to your concerns? It is likely that you will return to having more Self and Task concerns. This is OK. It is what happens when any of us are experiencing change (Hall & Hord, 2006).

Strive for Quality in Your Teaching

In everything that you do in your preparation program, strive for quality. If an instructor makes an assignment that is confusing, ask for clarification. If you are not fully satisfied with a field placement, think through what you can do to learn from the experience. Use every assignment and experience as opportunities to learn more about teaching. In every situation, there is the potential to find an idea that can help you become a better teacher. Finding these ideas is your responsibility. Three particularly useful strategies are:

1. Have in mind a generic teaching model that can be used to examine any teaching situation.
2. Take advantage of every field experience to learn something.
3. Whenever possible, collect samples of teacher and student work.

Emerson Elliott's General Unit of Instruction   Throughout this text, the importance of teachers focusing on student learning (back to Impact concerns) has been emphasized. A broad array of contextual factors (e.g., student diversity, special needs, and ELL) were described and several instructional strategies (e.g., Direct Instruction) introduced. The importance of assessing student learning and methods for doing so (e.g., rubrics) has been emphasized. Given the large number of methods, strategies, and factors that have been introduced, it now should be helpful to offer a general model that can serve as an organizer, reminder, and guide for what teachers need to do to have high-quality teaching that results in all student learning.

One such model has been proposed by Emerson Elliott (2005) (see Figure 14.1), who is a national expert on accreditation of teacher education and assessing high-quality teaching. His model "defines appropriate expectations for evidence that P–12 student learning has occurred, constructed around a core of activities in which the candidate *takes responsibility for a significant unit of instruction*" (p. 1). This model is generic; it can be applied to all levels of schooling, different kinds of students, and all subject areas. Each of the core activities is basic to effective and high-quality teaching. The elements outlined in Figure 14.1 have been introduced and emphasized throughout this textbook.

One of your major responsibilities as you complete your preparation program is to become knowledgeable and skilled at doing each of the activities outlined in this model. By the end of your program, you will need to have artifacts in your portfolio that document your capabilities to do each part of this model. Be sure to collect specific examples and artifacts related to each component of the model. One useful approach that addresses each of the activities of this generic model is the teacher work sample (TWS) methodology that was described in Chapter 9.

Challenging Assumptions
FINDINGS FROM RESEARCH

Is the teacher shortage due to limited supply or is it a problem of teacher retention?

As each summer unfolds newspapers and television programs in some parts of the United States report that once again school districts have a number of open teaching positions and are having difficulty finding qualified applicants. Shortages of mathematics, special education, and ELL teachers will be true nearly everywhere, while shortages of all teachers will be likely in the rapidly growing school districts of the Southwest. Why do these shortages continue to exist? Is the number of teacher-education graduates insufficient? Is this simply a result of the demand for more teachers as communities continue to grow? What about teacher retirements? Is this the reason? Or, do too many teachers leave? Why do teachers leave teaching? Are salaries the big reason?

Study Design and Method: One important source of data is the Schools and Staffing Survey (SASS) that is conducted by the National Center for Education Statistics (NCES). The SASS includes a 1-year follow-up questionnaire to 8400 teachers. "The purpose of the Teacher Follow-up Survey is to provide information about teacher mobility and attrition" (p. 1). Researchers, such as Ingersoll (2001), have used the data from these surveys to more closely examine the teacher-shortage problem. The first step was to classify teachers as "stayers" who remained in the same school; "leavers" who left the teaching profession; or "movers," who moved to another school.

Study Findings: As can be seen in the pie chart, by far the majority of teachers remained in their same school. Curiously, a regular

finding in these data is that a higher proportion (13%) of private school teachers leave teaching. Another regularly found pattern is that the distribution of leavers forms a U-shaped curve. Those early in their careers and those with the most years of experience leave in higher proportions.

In his analyses, Ingersoll determined that the problem is less one of a teacher shortage and more a problem of teacher retention; in other words, if fewer teachers left their school, there would be less need to hire new teachers. Further, "the amount of turnover accounted for by retirement is relatively minor when compared to that associated with other factors, such as teacher job dissatisfaction and teachers pursuing other jobs" (Ingersoll, 2001, p. 499). Ingersoll concludes "that improvements in organizational conditions, such as increased support from the school administration, reduction of student discipline problems, and enhanced faculty input into school decision-making and increased salaries, would all contribute to lower rates of turnover" (p. 525).

Implications: If the reasons for some teachers moving and others leaving the teaching profession are those identified by Ingersoll (2001), what are implications for you and other aspiring teachers? Although salary is a factor, it appears that work conditions are more significant. One implication is for you to be observant of conditions in your various field experiences. What factors do teachers in those settings see as important to their staying? What factors seem to be related to high levels of teacher turnover? Another set of implications are related to your seeking a teaching position. Be sure to check out the factors identified by Ingersoll as well as others that are important to you and your being successful as a beginning teacher. Teacher success depends on more than their individual effort.

Sources: Tabs, E. D. (August, 2004). *Teacher attrition and mobility results from the Teacher Follow-up Survey, 2000–01*. Washington, DC: National Center for Education Statistics; Ingersoll, R. M. (2001). Teacher turnover and teacher shortages: An organizational analysis. *American Educational Research Journal, 38*(3), 499–534.

85% stay in same school · 8% move to a different school · 7% leave the profession

Figure 14.1 Elliott's Generic Unit of Instruction: Core activities for a significant unit of instruction that leads to P–12 student learning

Setting appropriate expectations for evidence that P–12 student learning has occurred, constructed around a core of activities in which the candidate *takes responsibility for a significant unit of instruction*, and:

- JUDGES PRIOR LEARNING—undertakes a systematic assessment (based in standards and benchmarks) to understand the prior P–12 student learning in the area he or she will teach

- PLANS INSTRUCTION—plans an appropriate sequence of instruction to advance P–12 student learning, based on the prior assessment

- TEACHES—teaches P–12 students to acquire and use content knowledge in meaningful ways, en-gaging those who bring differing background knowledge and learning needs, and providing students opportunities to demonstrate the use of critical and creative thinking skills

- ASSESSES—conducts a concluding objective test or alternative assessment(s)

- ANALYSES—analyzes the results of the concluding assessment(s), documenting the student learning that occurred at individual and group levels, including explanations of results form students who learned more or less than expected, an results form each subgroup of students

- REFLECTS—reflects on changes in teaching that could improve results

Source: Elliott, E. (2005). *Student learning in NCATE accreditation.* Washington, DC: National Council for the Accreditation of Teacher Education.

The Importance of Each and Every Field Experience Striving for quality in field experiences is extremely important for aspiring teachers. Candidates consistently report that the most important part of their preparation program was student teaching. This is the capstone experience where everything that has been introduced, studied, and dissected is brought together in the "real" world. This is the time when each candidate is expected to teach and to be able to show that their students are learning.

As important and significant as student teaching is, do not underestimate the important learning opportunities that come with every other clinical activity and field experience. Whether it is observing a lesson or monitoring student behavior on the playground or in the cafeteria, there are opportunities to learn. Your learning will not always be about teaching; it might be about characteristics of students, classrooms, or school procedures. The Impact-concerned candidate always takes advantage of every activity as an opportunity to learn something new. One way to do this is to set a personal objective: In every experience, I will seek to learn at least one new thing. When you engage each experience with the expressed intention of learning something new, you will!

Be sure to express your appreciation to the teacher(s) who permitted you to be there. They did not have to open the door. Teachers are under tremendous pressure to make every minute count. Many are self-conscious (self con-

Ed Lines

3.1 percent of all teachers hired in 2001–2002 were first-time teachers.

cerns?) about letting anyone observe them. Without their openness, you would be having to learn the basics of teaching OJT (on the job); be sure to say "thank you."

Revisiting Mark Mercer's Concerns

It sure was good that I hung on to that Generic Teaching Model. If I had not started with *Judges Prior Learning*, I would have wasted the students' time. In planning, I figured that I would be given two students who did not understand the assignment, but instead, both of them were really sharp! If I had not reviewed the standard and specific benchmarks that the teacher had been addressing and done the quick check for current understanding at the beginning, I would not have helped these students at all. As it turned out, I was able to expand their understanding and get them ready for learning the next benchmark. (Hey, in rereading this journaling I see hints of my having Impact concerns!)

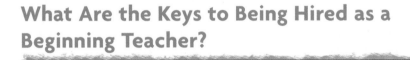

YOUR CHILD IS AN 'A' STUDENT BECAUSE I'M THE TEACHER

David Quintanar

What Are the Keys to Being Hired as a Beginning Teacher?

Juanita Ramirez was really nervous. As she sat outside the school district office meeting room and thought about the interview that would begin any minute now, her stomach was in knots! *What questions will they ask me? I know that I have the required qualifications for the position. In addition, I speak Spanish and I have a major in the subject. But what if they ask me something I don't know? I have brought my portfolio just in case there is something there I can pull out. What if . . . ?*

"Ms. Ramirez? Will you please come in."

It is not too early to be thinking about what will be needed and what it will be like to seek and get your first teaching position. There will be a number of applicants competing for most positions. This is especially true for low-need areas such as elementary, social studies, and physical education. As was introduced in Chapter 1, a number of steps and requirements must be completed to become a fully qualified teacher. Now is the time to begin anticipating and preparing what you will need to have accomplished and be able to demonstrate so that you are the one who will be hired for the teaching position you would most like to have.

Ed Lines

"The quality of teachers keeps going up. In 1961, 23 percent of teachers held an advanced degree and 15 percent lacked a bachelor's degree. In 2001, 57 percent held an advanced degree and zero percent had not completed a bachelor's degree." *(NEA Status of the American Public School Teacher 2000–2001: Highlights, 2003.)*

Requirements for Obtaining a Teacher License

The licensing requirements for public school teachers are set by each state. In addition, the federal No Child Left Behind legislation has required each state to establish requirements for teachers that are "highly qualified." The following are typical basic requirements for obtaining a teaching license.

Typical Requirements for a Teaching License   Although there will be some differences by state, the basic requirements for obtaining a license to teach include:

- Successful completion of a state approved preparation program. Programs may be offered by a higher education institution, a school district, or other agency.

- **Criminal background check**, including fingerprinting. No one with a criminal record may teach.

- Passing state required tests, typically of content and pedagogical knowledge. In some states examples of teaching performance such as a portfolio or teacher work sample may be required.

- Having a major, or advanced study, in the subjects you plan to teach.

> **Criminal background check.** Review of police records to determine if a candidate has a past that would prohibit them from receiving a teacher's license.

In addition to state requirements each school district may have additional requirements. If you have not already done so, check both state and specific school district websites for the specific requirements you must meet in order to be eligible to apply for a teaching position.

Ideas for Your Professional Résumé   A useful resource, that you can begin preparing now, is a professional résumé (see Figure 14.2). This is a one- (no more than two-) page summary of your qualifications and related experiences. Although most of the categories seem obvious, preparing a strong resume will take some time and thought. Your portfolio tasks and artifacts will be a useful resource. Keep in mind that employers are looking for teachers who not only have good grades, but ones who will be a resource to the school and contribute to the community. They also will be interested in your past work experiences, even if they were not in education. Your résumé provides the opportunity to document that not only do you meet the basic requirements for the position but that you bring additional related expertise and valuable experience.

Teacher Dispositions Are Important   As necessary as meeting the licensure requirements and completing program requirements are, the most important criterion for becoming a teacher is dispositions. The attitudes, beliefs, and values that teachers hold about students, the subjects they teach, their colleagues, parents, and the school are critical. Teachers who are not excited about the subjects they teach cannot develop enthusiasm for the subject in their students. Teachers who do not believe that certain students (boys/girls, poor, brown, special needs, or ELL) can learn cannot help those students learn. Teachers who do not see value in their colleagues, parents, and the school cannot help the school be successful. Reflect back on the interview with Karen Faiman at the beginning of this chapter. There

Figure 14.2 Professional résumé: suggestions for topics and elements

Select, organize, and present these in a format that matches you to the position requirements.

Name

Address

Phone number

E-mail

Philosophy/Bio Paragraph: In one paragraph, describe who you are and why you want to be a teacher. What do you believe about teaching and students? Why are schools important?

Qualifications:

Education: List education, degrees, and any specialized certificates. Don't forget to name the institution(s) and the dates for each. You might want to include GPA or other indicators of strength and quality.

Licensure: Name the license and areas of certification.

Special Certifications/Recognitions: List honors, awards, and other forms of recognition.

Outside Interests: Perhaps you will want to list hobbies or other activities that are an important part of your life. These can be especially useful for high school teachers who are expected to work with cocurricula activities.

Work Experience: List past work experience. These may include nonschool work. List those that demonstrate that you are reliable, can hold a job over time, and that you will bring a range of experiences to the classroom.

Community Service: Describe ways that you have been or are involved in giving back through volunteer activities, or in other ways, providing service to one or more parts of your community.

Special Skills: Do you have areas of expertise or special skills, such as speaking a second language? Have you lived in different places or abroad? Have you had leadership experiences in work, your community, or church?

was nothing negative or undercutting about anything that she said. She was enthusiastic, reflecting a belief that all students can learn, and that she can be a positive influence on students and colleagues. Everything that she said had to do with opportunities and possibilities, not barriers. High-quality teachers always think, teach, and lead with a view that the glass is half full, not half empty.

Revisiting Juanita Ramirez's Job Interview

This was Juanita's first interview for a teaching position. She did not expect that the superintendent would be there, but he was. Also on the interview committee were two teachers, the principal of the school where the teaching position was located, a parent, and a woman from the human resources office. Upon reflection, she thought that she had done well. The questions, especially those from the superintendent, were exactly what her favorite teacher education professor had predicted:

What do you know about interim assessment of student learning? (*I sure am glad that I had reviewed the standards last night and was able to quickly pull out of my portfolio the assessment I developed for the teacher work sample project.*)

Teachers' Lounge

On-the-Job Training

I did my first year of teaching without benefit of methods courses, student teaching, an entry-year program, or an assigned mentor. I was hired because I "looked like someone who could teach middle school students." I was assigned a class of speech and drama, a class of remedial reading, four classes of 8th grade social studies, and given a coaching assignment. I did not have 1 credit hour of training in any of those courses. The teacher I replaced quit because the students had been so difficult to manage. I remember writing "firm and fair" on the back of my left hand.

Thirty-seven years later, I answered a knock at my door and it was a man with his son. The man had been a student in my first social studies class. He reintroduced himself to me and said he wanted his son to meet the best teacher he ever had. We talked for hours like class had just ended. You never know whom you are going to impact—or how long that impact will last.

● Douglas Brooks, Ph.D.
Professor, Miami University,
Oxford, Ohio

When you don't know what to do, how will you find out? (*My example of asking my student teacher supervisor for ideas, and also one of my classmates, indicated that I will actively seek information.*)

What will you do when one of your students is failing? (*It seemed obvious to me, but I guess some of the other applicants had not done so well on this one. You contact the parents, and as I did for John during student teaching, you schedule a meeting with the parents and student and develop a plan.*)

As Juanita's interview illustrates, having clear examples of what you have done, and would do, in different teaching situations is important to answering those "what-if" questions that are a part of most job interviews.

In What Ways Can Candidates and Teachers Be Leaders?

"Gulp!" This was the first reaction when Joe Rice thought about what had just happened in the school staff meeting. His second thought was: "I don't want to be a leader; I just want to teach." There were the usual items on the agenda for the

*monthly school staff meeting. When the principal came to the agenda item, "Task
Force for Teaching Literacy in the Subject Areas," **Joe** assumed that this was something that senior teachers and department chairs would handle. Wrong! The principal presented a list of names of staff whom he wanted to lead this major
initiative. "We clearly need to work together to see that all of our students do better on the literacy parts of the SAT, and that our ELL students learn the basic
terms in each subject lesson. I am asking the people on this list to develop a plan
that all of us will implement in the fall. This needs to be a schoolwide effort." Yes,
Joe's name was on the list—and as* cochair!

$\mathcal{C}$ontrary to what you may be thinking, leadership is not reserved to the principal
or the superintendent. All members of an organization have a leadership responsibility. This is true for schools, businesses, church groups, and families. Unfortunately, too many teacher education candidates and teachers assume that they
have no leadership responsibilities. In fact the opposite is true; every member of
the school staff, including those who refuse to participate, affect potential progress
and success. Leadership skills and functions can be learned and participating in
different ways can be informative, influential, interesting, and even fun. There are
many unofficial and informal ways to contribute to leadership, and there are formal leader positions and career paths for those who are motivated to make a difference in what the whole school/district accomplishes.

Different Ways Teachers Can Lead

Teachers tend to first think about leadership as something that administrators do.
In this way of thinking, the only people who are leaders are those who have official titles and responsibilities such as the principal, department chair, vice principal, and superintendent. However, scholars make a careful distinction between
leaders and **leadership**. Leaders are
those with formal, and informal, roles
and responsibilities related to a group
or the whole school accomplishing its
objectives. Leadership encompasses the
actions of leading. All members of the
school staff have a leadership responsibility. You cannot escape this responsibility; you either help or hinder the
attainment of the desired ends. Teacher
leadership is accomplished through a
number of ways.

Leaders. Those with formal, or in some cases in-
formal, responsibility to
lead a group in accom-
plishing a task(s).

Leadership. Leading in
ways that develop the ca-
pacity of the whole group.

Beginning teachers will have many opportunities to share with colleagues and to contribute within their school, across the district and
state, and through professional associations.

Formal Teacher Leadership   There
are many opportunities for teacher
education candidates and beginning
teachers to have formal leader responsibilities. Karen Faiman, the educator in
the Real Schools interview for this chapter, described a number of ways that as a

Teachers and the Law[1]

*T*eacher education candidates must consider legal aspects of their activities every time they are in field settings and whenever they are in contact with students. They also need to learn about the responsibilities, liabilities, and protections accorded to beginning/probationary teachers. Although first-year teachers have the same professional responsibilities as tenured teachers, they do not have all of the same protections, especially for nonrenewal and dismissal.

BEGINNING TEACHER NONRENEWAL AND DISMISSAL

Do administrators have to provide reasons for dismissal of a nontenured teacher?

No. School administrators have the responsibility for evaluating the fitness of teachers and determining whether their level of performance is satisfactory. They must follow the provisions outlined in state statutes; however, the U.S. Supreme Court in *Board of Regents of State Colleges v. Roth* (1972) decided that nontenured teachers need not be given reasons for nonrenewal. Note that this case addressed the dismissal of a college faculty member. As with many other cases, court decisions that have addressed questions related to higher education have been interpreted as applying to public school teachers as well. Each state has statutes that address the dis-

[1]Two useful resources for learning more about teachers and the law are: LaMorte, M. W. (2005). *School law cases and concepts* (8th Ed.). Boston: Allyn and Bacon; Essex, N. L. (2002.). *School law and the public schools*. Boston: Allyn and Bacon.

missal of tenured teachers or ones under a continuing contract. These provisions lay out the due-process requirements. Grounds for dismissal, such as insubordination, incompetency, failure to comply with reasonable orders, and conviction of crimes involving moral turpitude are addressed.

TEACHER FREEDOM OF PUBLIC EXPRESSION

Do teachers have freedom of public expression?

Yes, but there are limits. In Chapter 13's Teachers and the Law feature the case of a teacher (Pickering) writing a letter was described. Historically, teachers were seen as government employees and therefore had less freedom of public expression. This view was formalized at the federal level in the Hatch Act. However, this view has been questioned in the last 50 years. In *Pickering v. Board of Education Township High School District 205* (1968), a teacher (Pickering) was dismissed for writing a letter to the newspaper that was critical of actions taken by his school board. He challenged in court his loss of First Amendment rights as a citizen. The Court stated in part:

> The problem in any case is to arrive at a balance between the interests of the teacher, as a citizen, in commenting upon matters of public concerns and the interest of the state, as an employer, in promoting the efficiency of the public services it performs through its employees.

However, *Pickering* does not mean that teachers can say anything they want and not have it lead to employment consequences. For example, in *Mt. Healthy City School District Board of Education v. Doyle* (1977), a nontenured teacher, Doyle, had an altercation with a colleague, argued with cafeteria employees, swore at students, and called a radio station. He was dismissed.

beginning teacher she had leader responsibilities. Every time she represented the school at a district in-service session and brought the information back to the school, she was acting as a leader. Other ways that a beginning teacher can lead include chairing school committees, serving as grade-level team leader, being the coordinator of a cocurricula such as the pep squad, yearbook, or assistant coach.

During the remainder of your teacher education program, there will be a number of opportunities to be a formal leader. These include serving as the representative to organize candidates for an accreditation visit, chairing the student education association or honor society, and serving on the student advisory board. During stu-

He then alleged that his not being rehired was in conflict with his First Amendment rights. The Court ruled that the school board would not have rehired him, regardless of his "protected conduct."

What about teacher dress, can school districts impose dress standards?

Yes. For example, a high school English teacher in East Hartford refused to wear a tie. In court, he argued that requiring him to wear a tie would deprive him of his right to free speech. The courts in *East Hartford Education Association v. Board of Education of Town of East Hartford* (1977) had to balance the policy of the school board, which required teachers to dress more formally with the teacher's (Brimley) individual rights. In these cases, the courts have weighed heavily the community standards and values as reflected through the school board's policies and procedures. In this case, and others, the courts have supported the school board's interest in requiring a degree of uniformity.

DRUG TESTING OF TEACHERS

Can teachers be screened for use of drugs?

Yes. As drug use has become widespread among students and adults, some school districts have implemented policies related to teacher use of drugs. When teachers have challenged these policies, the courts have to balance the interests of schools in having a drug-free environment with the Fourth Amendment privacy interests of the teacher. Considerations include: How extensive is the drug problem? How intrusive is the search? How significant is the action that led to the search? In *Knox County Education Association v. Knox County Board of Education* (1999), the 6th Circuit Court ruled that the Fourth Amendment was not violated. The school district had a two part policy: (1) Suspicionless drug testing of all candidates for "safety sensitive" positions (e.g., teacher and principal) and (2) "reasonable suspicion" drug testing of individual employees.

TEACHER LIABILITY

Can teachers as individuals be sued?

Yes. Teachers must constantly be aware of the potential of being personally liable for damages as result of what they do or don't do. They must always act in ways that are seen as reasonable and prudent. Wrongful actions can result in their being sued, which deals with tort law. This area of law deals with civil wrongs instead of criminal wrongs, although there may also be a criminal component. The plaintiff is seeking compensation for a loss or damages. Liability for alleged injury, death, malpractice, or depriving someone of his or her constitutional rights, while under the teacher's or school's supervision can lead to legal action.

Negligence that leads to a student being injured, within a classroom, on the school grounds or on a field trip can lead to questions of teacher liability. Assault and battery is another area of torts. Threatening a child in anger, even without striking them, can be interpreted as assault. Striking someone, even without harming them, can be interpreted as battery. Teachers can only use sufficient force for self-protection when attempting to restrain a student.

To protect oneself from monetary loss, it is possible for teachers to obtain liability insurance. Typically, coverage is included as part of membership in the union and sometimes as part of membership in professional organizations. Individual liability insurance also is available.

---

dent teaching, there may be opportunities to assume some responsibility within the school. The basic message is that rather than avoiding leader assignments, take them on. This is the best way to learn more about being a leader. Do it!

Informal Teacher Leadership As important as formal leader roles can be, the informal roles are important also. One of the least understood is that of **followership**. As good as the formal leader may be, he or she will accomplish little unless the members of the group/team/committee/staff do their parts. Being a constructive member of the group, offering to help, contributing positively to the

Followership. When members of a group or organization assume responsibility for helping the group succeed.

discussions, and being sure to complete assigned tasks with quality and on time are important skills for all followers. Each of us has experienced the colleague who sits in meetings with folded arms or the one who grades papers, rather than contributing to the discussion. We also have experienced the team member who promises to do a task and then doesn't deliver. Effective followership entails participating and helping the team to accomplish its objectives.

A related concept is that of **distributed leadership**. The primary assumption in this model of leadership is that rather than leadership being the sole responsibility of the formal leader at the top of the organization (in other words, the principal), leadership should be distributed to many people and be seen as a shared responsibility. Distributed leadership is particularly useful in schools where teachers are seen as professionals whose work is not to be closely supervised. As professionals, teachers are expected to assume and share responsibilities for leadership.

> **Distributed leadership.**
> Involving a number of individuals with responsibility for leading the school, rather than relying on the principal for everything.

Revisiting Joe Rice's New Assignment as Cochair of the Task Force

Just as with Karen Faiman, Joe was identified as being a developing leader early in his teaching career. If we were to learn more about Joe's experiences, we would likely see that earlier he had initiated a number of informal leadership efforts and that he was seen as credible and proactive to his colleagues. Of course, Joe would have some self concerns about being cochair of the task force. However, the principal wisely made him cochair, rather than giving him the full responsibility. Assuming that the other cochair was experienced as a teacher and skilled as a leader, cochairing the task force would be a good learning experience for Joe. He would be able to learn about the formal role and tasks of chairing a committee. He would be able to observe the extent of followership of the task force members and the creation of the task force certainly demonstrated the principal's intentions to have distributed leadership in the school.

How Does a Master Teacher Think about the Joy of Teaching?

Beginning with the title and embedded in each chapter of this text in the theme, *joy of teaching*. This theme was selected because having joy in what you do as a teacher is so important to you and to the students and adults with whom you work. Joy is about emotions. It is seeing success in each student; taking delight in their learning and how the class is growing. Joy includes the great pleasure that comes from making a difference in each and every student. It comes in the satisfaction of having a lesson go well. It also comes in grap-

Ed Lines

> "All practical teachers know that education is a patient process of mastery of details, minute by minute, hour by hour, day by day." *Alfred North Whitehead*

pling with the major challenges in teaching and schooling and knowing that being a teacher is important.

People in business gain a great deal of their satisfaction through their efforts to grow a business and from the amount of money they make. Teachers most certainly are not joyful when they see the size of their paychecks. For teachers, the joy comes from the difference they make in the lives of their students. There is joy in seeing the lightbulb come on for a student who has been struggling to understand a concept. There is joy in seeing the whole class work together to share strategies for solving a puzzling problem. Teachers have enormous responsibilities. Almost completely by themselves, elementary teachers are responsible for the care and learning of 30 students for an entire school year. Secondary teachers will be responsible for 150 students each day! There is satisfaction and purpose in this level of responsibility and in making a positive difference.

Teaching is a significant and special profession that most people do not get the opportunity to do. Most adults never have the opportunity to teach. Yet, nearly every adult can readily name one, two, or even three teachers who made all the difference to them and what they have become. This is another of the many ways that teachers experience joy in teaching. When one of their former students returns and describes the difference the teacher made in their lives and how successful they are now, their teacher will be delighted.

The inclusion of less-obvious elements of joy has been intentional. Seeing the joy in teaching is in large part the responsibility of the observer. Some teachers can list everything that is wrong with teaching and have to think hard to remember the good parts. Other teachers see only the joy in their students, themselves, and their school. This difference in teachers is not simply a matter of how old they are or how long they have been teaching; it is a part of one's spirit. There are really "old" teachers who are still enthusiastic and looking for opportunities to learn new things. Some teacher education candidates already are grumps, while others are laughing at themselves and overflowing with excitement about learning to teach. In many ways, experiencing the joy in teaching is *your* responsibility.

Joyce Schneider

Mrs. Schneider, a Master Teacher

To illustrate the joy of teaching and how master teachers never lose this perspective this text ends with an interview with Mrs. Joyce Schneider. She recently retired after 42—yes, 42 years—of teaching! Parents would press the principal to have their children assigned to Mrs. Schneider's classroom. She was known across the entire school district as a phenomenal teacher. As a result of her status as a master teacher, she was asked to serve on district and state committees, to lead teacher workshops, and to teach teacher education courses. She worked with the local university student teaching supervisors to develop their student-teaching handbook. She is known by all as a master teacher who always sees the joy in teaching.

Ed Lines

"Despite Long Hours, Low Pay, Teachers Love Their Profession." (NEA's *Status of the American Public School Teacher 2000–2001*)

As you will see in the interview excerpts, she continues to have high enthusiasm about teaching and continues to be involved. As a result, the interview wandered over many topics and experiences and concluded with one of those unplanned happenings that so clearly illustrates the joy of teaching.

❖ *"First of All, I Love Kids."*

I love kids. That's the key. When I walked into the classroom, I wanted everyone to feel valued. They have to feel that they are a very important part of the family that I was working with as my classroom. I never looked at my class as a class. I looked at them as individuals who came together.

Every year as I got to know them as completely as I could, and then say: How can I help that person be the best he or she can be? It was fun. I would do a lot of activities to get them to empower themselves.

For example, at the start of every year, I would watch them. I would greet them at the door, welcoming them to my room, and saying, "I am so happy you are here." We would exchange smiles and positive things. If they were working on something, I would make sure that I asked, "How did you do on your writing last night?" "Did you finish that chapter in the book that you were enjoying?" There was that positive connection and it was individual. I was never a phony; kids pick up on that real quick.

I did the same thing when they left: "OK now, I know that you are going to work on your 5s in multiplication tonight. Which ones are you still struggling with? Which ones are you good at?" I would be specific and always focus on the positives. "I see you improving in your sentence structure and here's why." Those kids would skip out of the room. Do you think they wanted to come back on Monday? Absolutely.

I am a positive person. I taught the whole class to focus on the positives. As they saw me do it, they would begin to see the same things I saw. They would see that this kid improved on his writing, or reading, or became a much better thinker.

❖ *"I Saw that I Was Making a Difference."*

I stayed in teaching because I saw that I was making a difference. I love talking with kids. I love building and empowering people. I was not always a strong person. I was very quiet. I had to build positiveness in me first, and then I could build it in others. Not only did it work in the classroom, but parents would come to me and say, "Whatever you are doing is making a huge difference in our family." It's the same in business and elsewhere; if you value that human being, the results are magnificent and the joy is there.

How adults think and how kids think are so different. Kids are so literal. One time we were selling something for PTA. It was chocolate or something. There also was a coupon that the buyer could exchange for something. I

Ed Lines

"**The road to happiness lies in two simple principles: find what it is that interests you and that you can do well, and when you find it, put your whole soul into it—every bit of energy and ambition and natural ability you have.**" *John D. Rockefeller*

The most important thing on entering the classroom is that you have a positive outlook on life. I never allowed things to not be a joy.

I know that people keep saying that "kids are different today" but I didn't see that difference. I always taught the child. . . . I taught kids to love to learn.'
—Joyce Schneider

Serendipity Occurs As We Are Concluding the Interview with Mrs. Schneider

The interview with Mrs. Schneider took place in a neighborhood coffee shop. Just as the interview was concluding, a middle-aged woman approached. Mrs. Schneider stood up and they greeted each other with smiles and a hug. The woman's son had been in Mrs. Schneider's classroom, and he now was a senior in college. The mother proudly reported on how he was doing and acknowledged the important contributions Mrs. Schneider had made. Mrs. Schneider smiled and showed great interest in her former student's successes. What a wonderful anecdote to illustrate the joy of teaching!

An Epilogue

Mrs. Schneider can't stay away from teaching. In 2006, she called a principal and volunteered to serve as the mentor for all the new teachers in that school.

Connecting
TO THE CLASSROOM

Key themes in this chapter have been related to your being successful in your teacher education program and being successful in your first year of teaching. Two important additional themes addressed the importance of teacher leadership and looking for the joy in teaching. The following suggestions will help you apply these themes as you advance through your teacher education program and anticipate your first year as a teacher.

1. Understanding your concerns is as important as understanding the concerns of your students. No one has Impact concerns all of the time. For example, teacher education candidates have many Self and Task concerns, which is understandable given all that they have to learn and be able to do.

2. The Generic Teaching Model outlines the basic tasks and steps that should be a part of planning, presenting, and evaluating each lesson. Keep these components in mind when observing others teacher and in reflecting on your own teaching. The model also can be a guide for reflecting on a whole day or week of instruction.

3. As you move through your teacher preparation program, check carefully and make sure that each course you take will count in two ways: (1) toward program completion and (2) toward obtaining a teaching license from the state. All too often candidates get to what they think is the end of their program and then discover that a course did not count or they have not taken one that is required.

4. Approach every field and clinical experience as an opportunity to learn. Make it a personal challenge to identify one learning about teaching from every assignment.

5. Make a personal commitment to not just participating but leading some type of activity or effort each term.

6. Schedule a 15-minute period each week where you stop doing and reflect on the question: What was joyful about the things I did this week?

Chapter Summary

Becoming a teacher is an exciting, intense, and time-consuming process. Teachers are dedicated professionals who have to learn a lot in order to help all of their students learn a lot. There are going to be many new experiences, challenges and, yes, concerns along the way. As busy as you will be, be sure to still take time to reflect and to enjoy the many opportunities that are presented.

What are the keys to being successful in your teacher education program? Certainly seeing every course and field experience as opportunities to learn is a key. Understanding your concerns and seeing how they develop as you become more knowledgeable and experienced is another key. Always striving for quality in what you do and setting high, but realistic, expectations for your students are keys. Using the Generic Teaching Model as guide for planning your lessons and observing the instructional practices of others will be a useful key.

What are keys to obtaining your first real teaching position? Although over 300,000 first-time teachers are hired every year, this does not mean that the teaching position you would most like to have will be available or easy to get. An important prior step is to complete an approved program. Another key is to keep in mind what you will want to be able to include in your professional portfolio and on your résumé. It will be easier and more useful to be collecting and compiling as you continue through your program. Waiting to the last minute is bound to result in a lower quality application. Also, begin searching and checking out the posted openings now. Having in mind what a hir-

ing school district expects will help you to be ready to show them you are the one.

How can you be a leader now? There are many ways, both formal and informal, for teacher education candidates to have leadership experiences. Volunteer to be a group discussion leader in class. Join the student education association and be willing to help with projects. Volunteer time as an aide in a school. If you live on campus, become involved in leadership in your dorm and/or with your sorority or fraternity. Don't forget to see opportunities with your church, and if you have a part-time job, there may be possibilities there. There are opportunities every day to practice the other part of leadership; being an effective follower. Help others with completing tasks and be sure to deliver on your commitments on time and with quality.

What can be learned from master teachers? You might have been thinking that retired teachers have nothing to offer: "After all, today's schools and students are different." Hopefully, the interview with Mrs. Schneider demonstrated how much experienced teachers have to offer beginning teachers. Their joy in teaching should be catching. As far as today's students being different, what did Mrs. Schnider say about that?

Class Discussion Questions

1. Teacher leadership was a major theme in this chapter. How do you feel about this idea? Do you see yourself as a leader? What opportunities do you have at this time to experience being a leader?

2. What tips did you pick up about steps you should take in the remainder of your teacher education program that will help you obtain your desired teaching job?

3. Karen Faiman, the educator interviewed at the beginning of this chapter, moved into leadership roles at every turn. What about Karen would you think made her available for each opportunity?

Field Guide for School Observations

There are many indicators of joy in teaching. Walk around your college classroom and building or a school's classroom and building. Take field notes on the activities and indicators of joy. Which students and which teachers seem to be enjoying what they are doing? Which seem to not be joyful? What explains the differences?

Ask a Teacher or Principal

As was described in the first section of this chapter, all of us have concerns. Ask a teacher or principal about their concerns. As they describe them, what Stages of Concern do you hear? What could be done to address their concerns? Are their concerns affecting their work? Is so, in what way?

Journaling *Becoming a Thoughtful Teacher*

The journaling task for each chapter has asked you to think more deeply about an aspect of becoming a teacher. Take a look at what you have written following the study of each chapter. In a similar way to the task described in the Understanding & Using Evidence, use the Stages of Concern (Table 14.1) to analyze your concerns statements. What kind of pattern has there been to your Stages of Concern? What would you predict will happen next for you and your Stages of Concern?

Portfolio Tasks

1. Start a folder for storing each of the open-ended concerns statements that you write. By the end of your program, you should have 6 to 10 of these. Develop a table or graph to illustrate how your concerns have changed over time in your teacher education program.

2. Review the list of suggested items for a professional résumé outlined in Figure 14.2 on page 537. Start now collecting documents, artifacts, and the records that you will need to have to prepare your résumé. When the time comes to apply for your first full-time teaching position, you will find it being very helpful to have collected materials and examples along the way.

3. At various times as you have been reading this text, you have probably thought about one or more of your teachers who made a significant difference in your life, and perhaps in your decision to become a teacher. Now is the time to write a letter to that teacher. Tell him or her what you are doing now and describe the way(s) that teacher impacted you. The following is what one aspiring teacher wrote to one of her teachers. In your teaching career, hopefully some of your students will take the time to write similar letters to you.

Letter to a Teacher

Dear Mrs. Griggs,

I am writing you a letter to thank you for influencing my life. When I came into your class my senior year in high school, I had no idea what I was going to do with my life. With graduation just around the corner, I was just taking your class for an easy A.

But being a teacher's aide in your class changed my life. I realized that teaching could be such a rewarding job. I immediately fell in love with all the kids and the whole classroom environment. Some days when I would help out in the reading center, I would think, "Wow . . . this would be such a cool job." I loved the idea of being able to come to work every day to a room full of eager children and to teach them something. Whether it be teaching them how to read, write, do math problems, or just learn the different days of the week, I am looking forward to having a class of my own.

Sometimes I could see that you were stressed out, but then somebody would say something funny or sweet to you and it would just wash away all the stress. While in your class, I learned that children could be so honest, like the time when I walked into the class on a windy day and the kids started giggling at me and said, "Whoa, Erica, you have rock star hair!" Children could also be so loving like the time when Alex was walking out of the class and he turned back and said, "I love you, teacher!"

These are just some of the reasons that I want to be a teacher. Well, Mrs. Griggs, I was just writing you a letter to say, "Thanks for changing my life." You are the person who inspired me to become a teacher!

Sincerely,

Erica Nuñez
Student Teacher

Self-Assessments *What Am I Learning?*

This self-assessment is in the form of a "pop quiz."

1. Name the four areas of Concerns about Teaching.

2. Name and describe what is entailed within each of the six core activities identified in Elliott's generic model for a unit of instruction.

3. Three key pieces you already have in your professional portfolio are:

4. Do you already have information, such as addresses and websites, about position openings where you want most to teach?

5. In her interview, Mrs. Schneider recommended that you know what you want your classroom to be like before you get there. What are three features you plan to have in place in your first classroom?

6. Three things that brought you joy during this term were:

Using the Web

Surf the Web using the term "teacher leadership." You may be surprised at the number of resources and efforts to support teacher leaders, their professional development, and ways to network. For example, the Center for Teacher Quality (**www.teacherleaders.org**) has organized the Teacher Leaders Network. They offer a free newsletter, provide information about teacher leaders and facilitate conversations through listserv discussions.

Virginia Commonwealth University has a Center for Teacher Leadership (**www.ctl.vcu.edu**) that has been established to promote and support teacher leadership to improve teaching and learning.

Explore several of these websites and contact one or two to learn more about the ways that teacher education candidates and beginning teachers can learn about and serve in leadership roles.

Your Professional Library

Bolman, L. G., & Deal, T. E. (2003). *Reframing organizations: Artistry, choice, and leadership*, 3rd ed. San Francisco, CA: Jossey-Bass.

There are many theories of leadership and extensive research on the characteristics of organizations. Bolman and Deal have developed an interesting and useful way to understand organizations and leadership. In their book, they have identified four frames or ways of thinking about organizations. Each of these frames is instructive and represents a useful tool for teachers and others who want

to understand why things are done the way they are.

Lieberman, A., & Miller, L. (2004). *Teacher leadership*. San Francisco, CA: Jossey-Bass.

The authors are nationally recognized professional development experts and have championed teachers being leaders for many years. In this book, they describe why teacher leadership is important, summarize the research, and present case studies of teacher leaders who have made a difference.

mylabschool
Where the classroom comes to life!

Log on to Allyn & Bacon's MyLabSchool (**www.mylabschool.com**). Enter Assignment ID **JOBRES** in the **Assignment Finder** and read *What Makes a Good Résumé*. You may be at the beginning of your teacher education program and think it is too soon to be concerned about creating a résumé. But time has a way of slipping away and what you've accomplished this year may be forgotten if you don't document it. A résumé is an evolving document and when you keep track of each year's accomplishments as a teacher education candidate you can select the most stellar evidence that you are highly qualified and have the potential to become an effective teacher.

Using what you have read in this chapter and in *What Makes a Good Résumé*, create a résumé document and include at least one professional growth experience you have had as a teacher education candidate.

It is also a good idea to be well prepared for the time your résumé leads to a job interview. A favorable face-to-face meeting with a prospective employer is perhaps the most crucial element in getting the job you want. Enter Assignment ID **JOBINT** in the **Assignment Finder** and look for *Preparing for an Interview*. Click on the link to commonly asked interview questions and think through how you would answer each question.

1. Write down three questions that you might ask a potential employer.

A Final Note from the Authors of this Text

There is an enormous need for outstanding teachers who are real people. This is your time.

- Be relentless in your pursuit to become an exceptional teacher.
- Envision what you want your classroom to be like.
- Enjoy your students.
- Laugh with your students and about yourself.
- Share with your colleagues.
- Be sure to make time for your loved ones.
- Take vacations.
- Take advantage of every opportunity to learn more, and **have joy in your teaching!**

Your authors:

Gene E. Hall, husband, father, scholar (road racing and snow skiing)

Linda F. Quinn, wife, mother, grandmother (fishing, hiking, and sporting clays)

Donna Gollnick, mother, administrator, scholar (tennis and golf)

APPENDIX

Understanding & Using Evidence

CHAPTER 1

UNDERSTANDING & USING EVIDENCE: LICENSURE TEST SCORES

One way to analyze test scores across states is to look for patterns. In the following table, the yellow highlights indicate the state(s) with the highest qualifying score and the blue highlights indicate the state with the lowest qualifying score. In some cases, states have qualifying scores that are close, but the range between high and low scores can be as much as 33 for elementary education for the states shown.

Test	AR	CT	LA	MS	NV	OH	PA	VA
Biology: Content Knowledge		152	150	135	154	148	147	155
Elementary Education: Curriculum, Instruction, & Assessment	—	163	—	135	158	—	168	—
Elementary Education: Content Knowledge	—	—	150	—	—	—	—	143
English Language, Literature, & Composition: Content Knowledge	159	172	160	157	150	167	160	172
Mathematics: Content Knowledge	116	137	125	123	144	139	136	147
Social Studies: Content Knowledge	155	162	149	143	152	157	157	161

CHAPTER 2

UNDERSTANDING & USING EVIDENCE: MAKING A CHOICE ABOUT DIVERSITY

No matter in which area of the country you would like to work, you can find schools with either limited or great student diversity. As you look at the table on Understanding & Using Evidence, you see that African Americans are more likely to be found in urban areas in the Mid-Atlantic, Midwest, and South. Larger numbers of Hispanic students are in the cities of the Southwest, South Central, Northeast, and West. You also see that urban cities have large percentages of students from low-income families. Many schools have webpages that indicate the diversity of their student populations that you may want to check when you are considering a specific school. For more information on schools in large cities, visit the website of the Council of Great City Schools at www.cgcs.org/pdfs/citybycity03.pdf.

CHAPTER 3

UNDERSTANDING & USING EVIDENCE: PARENTAL INVOLVEMENT IN HOMEWORK

The data in the Public Agenda surveys indicate that parents and teachers have different perceptions of the support parents provide to their children to get them to complete their homework. The difference in perceptions is clear when you compare the teachers' responses to whether parents are involved in helping students with their homework; teachers report that only 6 percent of the parents are involved. Half of the parents, on the other hand, indicate that they are involved, often resulting in arguments with their children about doing their homework. These differences in perceptions could suggest to a teacher that they need to provide more assistance to parents in how to help their children with their homework, rather than assuming that the parents do not care and are not involved with their children's homework. To review the analysis of these tables by Public Agenda go to www.publicagenda.org/research/pdfs/playing_their_parts.pdf.

CHAPTER 4

UNDERSTANDING & USING EVIDENCE: SCHOOL FINANCING

Tables of numbers are easily understandable for some people. For others, it is easier to understand a summary number, such as a ratio. An even easier way to understand numbers (for those who are visual) is to present the same information in a graph.

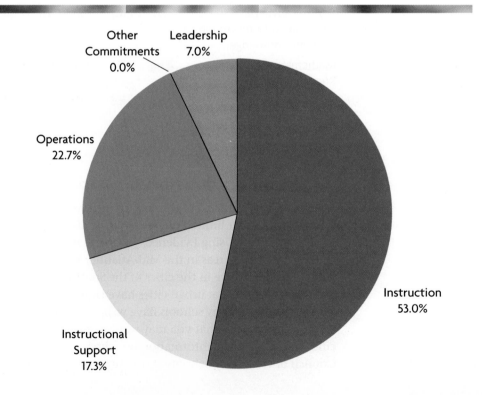

The data point out a discouraging fact and one could quickly jump to the conclusion that, yes, standards for U.S. students are set too low.

Teachers are often presented with data that provide an overall picture of the state of the profession or the achievement of students. Sometimes such data can be encouraging and sometimes it can leave one in a state of wondering how things could have gone so poorly. Data presented in a simple format like the one provided require that teachers take a critical look at what important information might be missing. Ask questions about the missing information. For example, what are the requirements for a teaching license in mathematics in each country listed? How does the elementary and secondary school curriculum in mathematics in each country compare with that in the United States? What is the diversity of the students tested in each country? What cultural and linguistic advantages might each country listed have over any of the others?

While the showing of U.S. 15-year-olds is nothing to be proud of, the idea of raising standards to improve these scores does not take into account other variables that might have as great an impact. Teacher excellence is undeniably one of the key components of student success. While standards provide a goal, excellent teaching is the path to that goal.

CHAPTER 9

UNDERSTANDING & USING EVIDENCE: USING 3RD GRADE MATH SCORES ON A UNIT TEST TO CREATE COOPERATIVE LEARNING GROUPS

Teachers must constantly assess student learning through reflection on data and then organize that data in useful ways. The teacher of this class has decided to put the students into cooperative learning groups so that the students can have more practice in using regrouping strategies. Teachers always know, or should know, more about their students than just raw data can show, and so they may make decisions based on personal experience rather than what the raw data indicate. This is a teacher's professional right and one that all effective teachers exercise from time to time.

End-of-Unit Test Scores on Regrouping during Subtraction of 3-Digit Numbers

Student Name	Test Score (highest possible score 100)
Carl Adams	96
Garcia Bloom	60
Caitlin Broker	100
Tiffany Brown	40
Carla Castenada	88
Nita Chang	24
Neil Fox	76
Pete Lowinsky	68
Ahmad Mesgari	84
Timette McKay	74
Richard Power	72
Jaylynn Price	88
Patrick Quest	28
Stacy Romano	68

Student Name	Test Score (highest possible score 100)
Kenneth Sharp	80
Angelica Spooner	64
Taeko Ono	52
Susan White	48

The teacher has decided to put one high-performing student in each group. There were 25 items on the test and the teacher also considers the number of questions missed along with the raw score.

Group 1. Caitlin missed no problems and works well with all other students in the class, even with Neil who can sometimes be a behavior problem, so the teacher has placed Caitlin, Neil, and Nita in one group. The teacher wants Nita to have as much practice as possible during the group work time and so has decided that a smaller group will be better suited to Nita's needs. Also, a smaller group may give Neil less of an opportunity to act out.

Group 2. Carl is also an excellent student though sometimes he disregards others' feelings. The teacher is placing him with Timette who has a calming personality and with Patrick who is Carl's friend and with Susan. The teacher believes a larger group with numerous interactions will engage Carl's helper potential.

Group 3. Carla and Kenneth scored very close in their performance on the test and have often helped one another in the past. The teacher is placing Taeko and Tiffany in this group because all of these students are hard workers and have demonstrated their ability to cooperate during group work in the past.

Group 4. Jaylynn and Ahmad performed very close on the test and the teacher feels they will provide great assistance to Angelica and Garcia. Jaylynn also speaks Spanish and will be able to help with translation of any terms that may be unfamiliar to Garcia.

Group 5. Pete, Stacy, and Richard will form a group. Richard scored in the middle range on the test but he is very thoughtful and patient. The teacher feels that she will be able to spend some extra time with this group if her calculations about the other groups are correct.

CHAPTER 10

UNDERSTANDING & USING EVIDENCE: THINKING ABOUT THE IMPACT OF INCREASED COMPUTER USE IN CLASSROOMS

Educators are inundated with bytes of information regarding the state of teaching and learning. Most of these bytes are designed to alert and amaze the reader and often to prompt some sort of action that will respond to the information. The evidence that can be gleaned from the data presented in Chapter 10 could lead a person to presume that all is quite well and good with the use of technology in today's classrooms. There are, however, some questions that you should consider from a review of the three sets of data.

1. U.S. students who used computers in school in 2003:
   - 97% of high school students
   - 95% of middle school students

- 91% of students in grades 1–5
- 80% of kindergarten students
- 67% of nursery school students

2. Frequency of classroom technology use by percentage:

   - Electronic presentation: 81%
   - Word processing: 68%
   - Internet: 50%
   - Publishing: 40%
   - Web editors: 36%
   - Spreadsheets: 6%
   - Databases: <1%
   - E-mail: <1%

3. Average expenditure of $103 per pupil for educational technology.

   Is it more important for high school students to use technology than elementary school students?

   Should the use of word processing in classrooms be higher than 68%?

   Why is use of the Internet at a low 50%? Is it possible that teachers do not include the resources on the Internet in lessons?

   What benefit do students receive from the $103 spent on educational technology?

   What other technology tools besides computers and the accompanying software should schools be investing in for student learning?

   Marc Prensky (2005) says that "one of the most important tools for 21st century students is not the computer that we educators are trying so hard to integrate, but the cell phone that so many of our schools currently ban." Students already know this.

   Data provide us with starting points to think about teaching and learning. Data should never be taken as the final word.

Source: Prensky, M. (2005). Listen to the natives. *Educational Leadership, 63*(4), 12.

CHAPTER 11

UNDERSTANDING & USING EVIDENCE: TELLING STORIES WITH DATA/EVIDENCE: LOOKING FOR AN ACHIEVEMENT GAP

Rarely will trend data be a perfect straight line from low to high or high to low. The data presented for the White and Asian 5th grade mathematics scores is quite typical. From year to year, the means vary but there is no clear direction other than each year being about the same. However, there is a clear pattern for the test score means with nonwhite 5th graders. The average test score increases each year after the 2000–2001 school year. However, this trend by itself does not tell us if the achievement gap is shrinking. A comparison has to be made of the differences in means with the White and Asian test takers.

One interesting way to illustrate the size of the achievement gap is to determine its size each year by subtracting the nonwhite mean from the mean for the White and Asian mean. When a bar graph is constructed using these differences, the decreasing achievement gap is readily seen. Note that the significant drop took place in the most recent 2 years. Why do you suppose this pattern occurred?

Size of Achievement Gap in One Elementary School (5th grade mathematics)

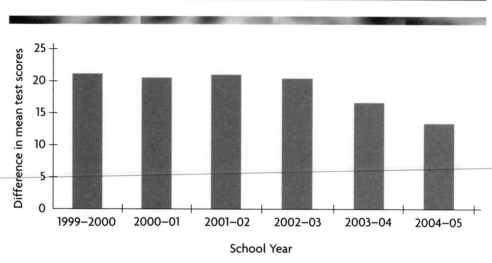

Achievement gap = White and Asian mean minus nonwhite mean

CHAPTER 12

UNDERSTANDING & USING EVIDENCE: REVIEWING DATA ON TIME SPENT ON MANAGEMENT TASKS AND ON CLASSROOM INTERRUPTIONS

This teacher has spent approximately 30 minutes of the day managing class activities and getting ready for instruction. The short times spent for each management routine add up and at the end of a week 2.5 hours of instructional time have been lost.

Time Spent on Organizing and on Classroom Interruptions

School:	Teacher:	Observer:	Time Started	Time Stopped
Observation of Classroom Organizing				
Taking Attendance			8:57	8:58
Collecting Lunch Money			8:57	9:00
Collecting Homework or Seatwork			8:57	8:58
Making Assignments for Seatwork			9:50	9:54
Making Assignments for Homework			2:55	3:05
Distributing Books and Materials			9:05	9:07
Explaining Activities and Procedures			9:00	9:05
Organizing Groups			1:15	1:18
Shifting from One Activity to Another			10:20	10:22
Disciplining Students			9:45	9:46

School:	Teacher:	Observer:	Time Started	Time Stopped
Observation of Classroom Interruptions				
Students Enter Late			9:10	9:12
Students Leave Early			2:30	
Parents Enter			2:27	2:30
Administrator Enters			11:10	11:15
Other Visitors Enter		Observer	8:55	8:57
Loudspeaker Announcements			9:00	9:05
Special Sales		5th graders selling tickets to drama extravaganza	2:15	2:25
School Events				
Outside Noise				

Your first question after considering the data could have been, why does it take the teacher a minute to take attendance? Good question. Establishing a routine that has students entering the room for the first time in the morning and moving a tag with their name or picture on it to a designated slot would make it possible for a teacher to take attendance in a glance. Homework should also be placed in a designated folder at the same time that each student marks their attendance.

A second question about the amount of time spent making assignments is certainly called for. Assignments for seatwork can be on the board or in folders located at centers around the room; the same goes for homework assignments. Time at the end of the day should be spent summarizing what was learned during the day while homework assignments should be given immediately following the related instructional episode.

Too much time seems to be consumed when moving from one activity to another or getting students ready for group work in this example. Time can be saved here by well-established routines and procedures. When students know what they are supposed to do if they enter the classroom, then arriving late should not cause an interruption, and students who have been taught how to get ready for group work can certainly do so in less than 3 minutes. Teachers may have little control over the interruptions that come from outside the classroom; however, there is no crime in placing a "Do Not Disturb" sign or a "Testing" sign outside the door when the teacher feels any interruption would be detrimental to student learning.

The teacher represented on this checklist is no doubt conscientious and aware of the benefits of a well-managed classroom. Collecting data that would indicate the time actually spent in organizing and in interruptions can only serve to help her improve her professional practice.

CHAPTER 13

UNDERSTANDING & USING EVIDENCE: USING 6TH GRADE MATH DATA IN AN SIP-NEEDS ASSESSMENT

Schools are often presented with computer printouts of tables with abbreviated language and lots of numbers. It is the responsibility of the principal, SIP team, and the entire staff to make sense out of these printouts. They usually contain important information.

1. In this case, your very first question should have been, what type of testing is represented here: NRT or CRT? The data are percentages of students who have reached mastery on the various subparts of the state CRT. There is valuable diagnostic information in this table. It provides clear evidence about where the school's students are doing well and where they are not.

2. The table provides 5 years of scores so it is possible to look at trends. There are a number of trends. In identifying these, it always is a good idea to start with the positives. All of us like to know that we are doing some things well; then identify the areas that seem to be problematic. What trends did you see across the school years?

State Test Scores 6th Grade Math Percent of Students at Mastery

	1998	1999	2000	2001	2002	
Concepts						Notes
1. extends pattern & states rules	53	74	77	77	93	Last year, big jump! Why?
2. id. alt. forms w/expanded notation	93	96	94	97	97	Do well each year
3. id. alt. forms using regrouping	24	41	46	61	59	Improvement in last 2 years. Why?
Facts & Computation						
10. add/sub 2–3 & 4 digit whole no.'s & $'s	80	90	89	88	90	Most students do well each year
11. mult/div mults of 10 & 100 by same	56	63	67	79	77	Problem here
12. mult/div fractions	99	97	97	97	94	Strong here
14. add/sub fracts mixed no.'s like denoms)	46	69	70	81	67	Need work here
Problem Solving/Application						
17. solve prob: order/mag of whole no.'s	94	96	94	95	99	Superb!
19. draw conclusion from graph/table/charts	84	86	80	81	90	Last year was better
20. create graphs from data	90	94	94	96	97	They can do this!
21. id. operation to solve story problem	69	81	76	81	74	Needs attention
26. est reasonable ans. fractions	56	63	58	69	62	Fractions again
Measurement/Geometry						
32. id/draw/describe/classify geo shapes	73	63	81	88	70	This area is being missed. Why?
33. measure/determine perimeter & area	44	36	31	59	51	
34. estimate length & area	30	47	57	65	57	

The notes to the right of the table point out some of the trends.

1. If you were a member of the SIP team, which elements would you want to address? Remember that teachers need to know where they have been successful, as well as being guided to areas where they need to improve. Clearly, student learning in the areas of fractions and measurement/geometry is not as high as for the other areas.

2. In the SIP, what action steps would you recommend? The areas where students have been doing well should be identified. Perhaps the whole staff should join in a review of what they have done in past years that seems to be working. The problem areas of fractions and measurement/geometry are in need of targeted improvement. This is the type of target in a SIP that could be addressed through teacher training, involving a mathematics education consultant—perhaps purchasing some additional curriculum materials, and a different approach to instruction.

CHAPTER 14

UNDERSTANDING & USING EVIDENCE: TELLING STORIES WITH DATA/EVIDENCE

The three open-ended concerns statements reflect different stages of concern (see Table 14.1). One way to summarize each teacher's concerns would be to construct a table.

Student Teacher	Overall Area of Concern	Stage(s) of Concern
JoAnne	Self	Stage 2 Personal
Greg	Impact	Stage 4 Consequence
Sue Lee	Unconcerned (about teaching)	Stage 0 Unconcerned

Addressing Their Concerns

Given how different each student teacher's concerns are, probably each person should be supported individually.

JoAnne's concerns could be addressed through a talk with her cooperating teacher or student-teacher supervisor. There will definitely be times when students ask inappropriate questions or ask them at the wrong time. JoAnne's not letting the question disrupt the flow of the lesson certainly made sense. In this particular case, JoAnne might also consider not going to certain places on the weekend where her students will see her.

Greg clearly has Impact concerns at Stage 4 Consequence. He is focused on how well his students are learning. He also is discovering how important it is to be knowledgeable about the learning background and experiences students bring to his classes. Now his challenge is in helping students build a bridge/scaffold from where they are to understanding the concepts that Greg is teaching. He might want to read more about informal ways to assess student understanding and learn more about his students' background of out-of-school experiences that could used to help them understand in-class content.

Sue Lee doesn't seem to have teaching-related concerns. Although each of us will have personal things going on in our lives, when it comes to being a successful teacher, the nonteaching concerns need to be set aside. Someone needs to help Sue Lee focus on her responsibilities as a teacher. She also should seriously consider the question, do you *really* want to be a teacher?

Glossary

Accommodations (p. 409). Adjustments that can be made in order to ensure that a student with special needs is not placed in an unfair or disadvantageous situation for instruction or testing.

Accreditation (p. 9). Recognition by members of a profession that an educational institution meets standards.

Achievement gap (p. 429). The difference in test scores between majority and minority students.

Action research (p. 492). Studies that are designed and conducted by teachers in their classrooms.

Activation (p. 441). Beginning, being made aware of something, being ready to learn.

Activity approach (p. 347). An approach to learning that engages students in activities that will instruct and help the students construct their own knowledge.

Administrative law (p. 154). Rules and procedures developed by the executive branch of government that have the authority of law.

Advance organizers (p. 441). Organizing frameworks that provide an overview for content to be studied.

Afrocentric curriculum (p. 226). A curriculum that is centered in African history, culture, and experiences.

Agnostic (p. 75). A person who is not sure of the existence of a god, and does not commit to believing that God exists or not.

Analytic-pluralistic classroom management (p. 445). A process of planning for classroom management that is identical to planning for instruction; stating objectives, providing instructional input, allowing for guided practice, and then assessing results.

Artifacts (p. 35). The documents and presentations included in a teacher's portfolio.

Assertive discipline (p. 449). A discipline model that demands responsible behavior from students.

Assessing (p. 402). The process of using testing and other evidence to plan a course of action.

Assessment (p. 404). Formal and/or informal collection of evidence along with its interpretation.

Assimilation (p. 56). Process by which groups adopt or change the dominant culture.

Asynchronous communication (p. 384). Digital communication that has no time requirement for transmission of comments.

Atheist (p. 75). A person who does not believe in the existence of a god.

Attendance area (p. 515). The geographic area within which students are assigned to a specific school.

Authentic assessment (p. 408). Assessment tasks that are similar to real world applications of the related knowledge and skills.

Authenticity tests (p. 60). Tests often applied to biracial students by their peers to authenticate the real racial identification of biracial students. They often marginalize the dual identity of these students.

Authoritarian (p. 177). Leadership that requires blind submission to the rule of a teacher or another person.

Authorizing legislation (p. 154). Legislative acts that grant authority for a certain activity.

Axiology (p. 270). The branch of philosophy that examines values and ethics.

Benchmarks (p. 8). A description of performances required to meet a standard at an expected level (for example, unacceptable, acceptable, and target).

Bilingual education (p. 20). An education strategy that uses both English and the native language of students in classroom instruction.

Block scheduling (p. 503). Combining two or more fifty-minute class periods into one period.

Born-again (p. 76). Individuals who have had a religious experience that led them to recommit themselves to God and Jesus Christ as an evangelic.

Bracketing (p. 353). A teaching method that asks students to isolate a specific period of time or an experience to be able to consider it separately from an ongoing chain of events.

Budget legislation (p. 154). Statutes that provide for an authorized activity.

Bullying (p. 507). Teasing, threatening, hitting, stealing, or intentionally excluding fellow students.

Catechism (p. 181). Series of questions and answers, usually on religious doctrine..

Chain of command (p. 136). The uninterrupted linkage of line positions from top to bottom in an organization chart.

Class (p. 231). Group of people, such as working class, who share the same social status based on socioeconomic status (SES).

Classroom climate (p. 499). Social and physical characteristics of the classroom.

Closed questions (p. 415). Questions that require a short phrase or fact answer.

Cognitive framework (p. 442). The arrangement of what is known and perceived and how this information is organized through the process of learning.

Color-blind (p. 104). A teacher's belief that race makes no difference in the lives of students and that the teacher treats all students alike regardless of their race.

Common schools (p. 180). Eighteenth-century schools that mixed students from different socioeconomic levels in the same classes and taught the same curriculum to all students.

Community school (p. 506). A school that houses social, health, and other services for adults.

Comprehensive school reform (CSR) (p. 507). The use of multiple reform strategies in an integrated and coordinated effort to improve student learning.

Compulsory attendance (p. 177). Required attendance at school until an age (now 16) set by state legislatures.

Concerns (p. 527). A combination of feelings, preoccupation, worry, and attitudes.

Cooperative learning groups (p. 340). Learners who work together to help one another learn a task, skill, or concept.

Corporate income tax (p. 159). Taxes paid by businesses based on their income.

Criminal background check (p. 536). Review of police records to determine if a candidate has a past that would prohibit them from receiving a teacher's license.

Criterion-referenced tests (CRTs) (p. 407). Tests where an individual's score is compared to a specified level of performance.

Cultural borders (p. 102). A social construct based on cultural membership that is political and involves differences in power.

Cultural capital (p. 72). Endowments such as academic competence, language competence, and wealth that provide an advantage to an individual, family, or group.

Cultural relativism (p. 102). Judging other cultural groups through the lens of members of that culture rather applying the standards of one's own culture.

Culturally responsive teaching (p. 229). An educational strategy that affirms the cultures of students, views the cultures and experiences of students as strengths, and reflects the students' cultures in the curriculum.

Cultures (p. 47). Socially transmitted ways of thinking, believing, feeling, and acting within a group. These patterns are transmitted from one generation to the next.

Current expenditures (p. 163). Funds spent in the current budget year.

Cut-off scores/cut scores (p. 156). The raw score on a test or performance measure that is set as the minimum necessary to be judged as a pass.

Deductive (p. 68). A way of thinking and reasoning that begins with the general and moves to the details.

***De facto* segregation (p. 200).** The voluntary separation or isolation of racial, ethnic, or socioeconomic groups in a community, leading to neighborhood schools attended by students from one group.

De jure segregation (p. 204). State policies or laws that separate or isolate racial, ethnic, or socioeconomic groups in a community, requiring students of one group to attend the same school.

Democratic classroom (p. 450). Classroom management method based on shared decision making and responsibility.

Direct instruction/explicit (p. 345). Providing clear and distinct information for students.

Disability (p. 46). A long-standing physical, mental, or emotional condition that can make it difficult for a person to do activities such as walking, climbing stairs, dressing, bathing, learning, or remembering.

Disaggregation (p. 427). To analyze test data by breaking out the scoring patterns for various subgroups.

Discovery method (p. 268). A method of teaching that introduces a general concept through questioning and problem solving.

Dispositions (p. 8). The values, commitments, professional ethics, and behaviors that influence beliefs, attitudes, and behaviors.

Distributed leadership (p. 542). Involving a number of individuals with responsibility for leading the school, rather than relying on the principal for everything.

Dominant group (p. 51). The group with power in society. In the United States the group with the most power is white, heterosexual, Christian, English speaking, middle class, able-bodied, and male.

Education management organizations (EMOs) (p. 516). For-profit companies that assume responsibility for operating a school.

Emotionally literate (p. 69). The ability to read and understand our emotions and those of others (Klindlon & Thompson, 2000, 4).

Empirical (p. 332). Depending on experimentation and observation.

Empowering policy (p. 146). Formal statements that set targets for action but leave open who personnel are to approach achieving the end.

Enculturation (p. 101). The process of learning your culture's expectations for behavior, communications, and ways of knowing.

English as a Second Language (ESL) (p. 20). An education strategy for teaching English to speakers of other languages without the use of the native language for instruction.

Epistemology (p. 270). The branch of philosophy that seeks to explain knowledge and knowing.

Equal educational opportunity (p. 220). Access to similar education for all students regardless of their cultural background or family circumstances.

Equity (p. 222). The state of fairness and justice across individuals and groups; it does not mean the same educational strategies across groups, but does expect equal results.

Essentialism (p. 276). A philosophical belief that for any specific entity it is theoretically possible to specify a finite list of characteristics.

Ethnic studies (p. 226). A curriculum or courses that focus on the history, contributions, and conditions of a specific ethnic group (for example, Asian American studies or American Indian studies).

Ethnicity (p. 47). Membership based on one's national origin or the national origin of one's ancestors when they immigrated to the United States.

Ethnocentric curriculum (p. 226). A curriculum that is centered in the ethnic roots of an ethnic group.

Evangelical (p. 76). Identification with Christian groups who believe the Bible is the actual word of God.

Existentialism (p. 277). A school of philosophy that stresses the free will of individuals.

Fair use (p. 371). An exemption to the U.S. Copyright Law created to allow education, news reporting, commentary, research, and parody about copyrighted material without the permission of the author.

Feeder school grouping (p. 511). Organizing as a unit the set of elementary and middle schools that send their students to a particular high school.

Feminism (p. 69). Movement that actively supports the rights of women.

Field-based supervisors (p. 27). The teacher or other professional school personnel who provide support for teacher candidates when they observe and work in schools.

Followership (p. 541). When members of a group or organization assume responsibility for helping the group succeed.

Formative evaluation (p. 402). Using information in ways to improve a process or procedure.

Free and universal education (p. 176). Public education for all children and youth.

Funding formula (p. 165). The use of selected factors and characteristics of schools and school districts to determine the relative amount of state funding.

Gender (p. 67). The behavioral, cultural, or psychological traits typically associated with one sex.

Hidden curriculum (p. 103). The norms and values that define expectations for student behavior and attitudes and that undergrid the curriculum and operations of schools.

High-stakes testing (p. 405). Tests that are used to make decisions with significant consequences.

Holistic (p. 425). Viewing the whole as a product or response to a whole.

Horizontal communication (p. 135). Passing information to others at the same level in the organization chart.

Hypermedia (p. 380). Hypertext that includes graphics, video, and sound.

Hypertext (p. 380). A database format in which information related to that on a display can be accessed directly from the display.

Idealism (p. 275). A school of philosophy that holds ideas as the only true reality.

Inclusion (p. 82). The integration of all students, regardless of their background or abilities, in all aspects of the educational process.

Indigenous (p. 52). Population that is native to a country or region. In the United States, Native Americans, Hawaiians, and Alaska Natives are the indigenous populations.

Indirect instruction/implicit (p. 345). Providing information that requires students to problem solve and question in order to uncover the essence of the information.

Individual Education Program (IEP) (p. 79). A document that describes the classroom accommodations and activities needed to meet the unique needs of a student with disabilities.

Induction (p. 23). School district and state programs designed to provide support for new teachers throughout the first one or two years of practice.

Inductive (p. 68). A way of thinking and reasoning that begins with the details to figure out the general.

Institutional discrimination (p. 199). Policies and practices that give advantages to one group over another.

Intelligent design (p. 107). The belief that an intelligent being (for example, God) influenced the development of living things.

Internet (p. 333). A world-wide decentralized association of networked computers using a common working protocol.

Intrinsic rewards (p. 8). Importance due to internal satisfaction such as helping a child learn rather than external incentives such as salary or prestige.

Journals (p. 37). Documents in which teacher candidates record their thoughts about a topic or their reflections on the teaching of a lesson, student behavior, and other classroom events.

Judicious discipline (p. 449). Classroom management that is based on an understanding of respect for the rights of the students.

Leaders (p. 539). Those with formal, or in some cases informal, responsibility to lead a group in accomplishing a task(s).

Leadership (p. 539). Leading in ways that develop the capacity of the whole group.

Learning cycle (p. 330). A five-phase research-supported method for education, especially in science.

Least restrictive environment (LRE) (p. 359). To the maximum extent appropriate, children with disabilities should be educated with children who are not disabled.

Lesson plans (p. 8). A teacher's detailed guide for classroom instruction.

Line relationship (p. 134). Where one position in an organization has direct supervisory authority over another.

struction, and other arrangements for the purpose of increasing student achievement

Schools of philosophy (p. 275). Groups of philosophical thought that provide frameworks for categorizing an array of ideas.

Schoolwide behavioral management system (p. 507). Having a consistent set of rules for behavior and sanctions that all teachers and site administrators use.

Secular (p. 107). Not religious in nature; sometimes identified as based on science rather than religion.

Self-contained classroom (p. 138). An assignment where a teacher is responsible for a class of students for the whole day.

Self-fulfilling prophecy (p. 234). Teacher's expectations for student achievement at the beginning of the year being realized by the end of the year.

Service learning (p. 97). Learning that requires students to work with members of the community.

Sexual orientation (p. 47). One's sexual attraction to persons of the same or opposite sex or both.

Site-based decision making (SBDM) (p. 502). A school organizational structure that involves teachers and parents to a greater degree in the running of the school.

Small learning communities (p. 504). Organizing high school students in groups of four to six hundred for all of their classes.

Social justice (p. 189). A philosophy or program promoting equality especially for children and adults who are economically disadvantaged or have been marginalized in society.

Social stratification (p. 233). Levels of social class ranking based on income, education, occupation, wealth, and power in society.

Socialization (p. 68). Process of learning the social norms and expectations of the culture.

Sociobiology (p. 233). The belief that intelligence and achievement are based almost solely on genetics or heredity.

Socioeconomic status (SES) (p. 46). Composite of the economic status of families or persons on the basis of occupation, educational attainment, and income.

Sociology (p. 218). The science of society, its members, and their interactions.

Socratic method (p. 264). A method of teaching or discussion in which the teacher asks a series of questions that lead the answerer to a logical conclusion.

Sponge (p. 353). Short, motivating activities that focus students on a learning task.

Staff relationships (p. 134). When one position does not have direct supervisory authority over another but there is an expectation that the two will communicate, coordinate, and work together.

Stages of Concern (p. 528). Seven types or categories of concern about a change, innovation, or practice.

Standardized tests (p. 428). Test that have been developed to rigorous standards and are used to make high-stakes decisions.

Standards (p. 302). Guidelines for student achievement set by national, state, and local educational institutions.

Standards-based curriculum (p. 25). A course of study designed to help students meet the proficiencies identified in standards adopted by a school or state.

State education agency (SEA) (p. 142). Each state's department of education.

Stereotype (p. 50). Exaggerated, and usually biased views about a group.

Strategy (p. 332). In teaching, any one of a multitude of plans for conducting instruction or an activity.

Subjective test items (p. 421). Test items that require interpretation and judgment in order to score them.

Substantive due process (p. 153). Constitutional protection against the loss of rights guaranteed in the U.S. Constitution.

Summative evaluation (p. 402). Using information to make a judgment about the merit or worth of an effort.

Superintendent (p. 145). The top executive who has overall line authority and responsibility for a school district.

Symbolic ethnicity (p. 57). Conscious identification with one's ethnic group through ethnic clubs or celebrations rather than primary relationships with other members of the ethnic group.

Symbolic race (p. 61). Identity of multiracial persona with one racial group while accepting their multiracial heritage and not denigrating the second racial group.

Synchronous communication (p. 384). Digital communication that happens in the same time period.

Tacit knowledge (p. 297). Knowledge that is implied, not stated; happening almost automatically.

Taxonomies (p. 337). Organizational structures for classifying objects or ideas.

Teacher effectiveness studies (p. 486). Systematic research on the relationships between teacher behaviors and student achievement on standardized tests.

Team teaching (p. 138). A staffing pattern in which two or more teachers jointly plan and teach a group of students.

Tests (p. 402). Structured opportunities to measure how much a test taker knows and can do.

Tracking (p. 235). The practice of separating students based on their academic abilities to receive instruction that is most appropriate for their abilities.

Training (p. 492). Formal sessions and materials to teach a specific set of knowledge and skills.

Underground economy (p. 161). The practice of barter, work exchange, and sale of products and services between individuals that is not reported to any of the taxing agencies.

Values (p. 100). The ideals or morals that we believe are important.

Vertical communication (p. 135). The passing of information up and down the organization chart.

Wait-time I (p. 338). The time a teacher waits after asking a question before calling on a student to answer it.

Wait-time II (p. 338). The time a teacher waits after a student has answered a question to give other students the opportunity to consider the response and perhaps add comments.

Bibliography

Abercrombie, N., Hill, S., & Turner, B. S. (2000). *The Penguin dictionary of sociology* (4th ed.). New York: Penguin.

Acs, G., & Koball, H. (2003). TANF and the status of teen mothers under age 18. Washington, DC: The Urban Institute.

Adams, D., & Hamm, M. (1996). *Cooperative learning: Critical thinking and collaboration across the curriculum.* Springfield, IL: C. C. Thomas.

Albert, B., Brown, S., and Glanigan, C. M. (2003). *14 and younger: The sexual behavior of young adolescents.* Washington, DC: National Campaign to Prevent Teen Pregnancy.

Alexander, K., & Alexander, M. D. (2001). *American public school law* (5th ed.). Belmont, CA: Wadsworth/Thomas Learning.

Alexander, W. M. (1968). *A survey of organizational patterns of reorganized middle schools.* Washington, DC: U.S. Department of Health, Education, and Welfare.

American Academy of Pediatrics. (2003, August). Prevention of pediatric overweight and obesity. *Pediatrics, 112*(2), 424–430 [online], retrieved March 12, 2005, from http://aappolicy. aappublications.org/cgi/reprint/pediatrics;112/2/424.pdf.

American Heritage® Dictionary of the English Language, 4th ed. (2000). Boston: Houghton Mifflin.

American Library Association. (2006). Banned Books Week 2006: More than a book a day challenged in U.S. schools. Retrieved September 5, 2006, from www.ala.org/-ala/pio/presscentera/piopresskits/bannedbooksweek2006/bbwpk06.htm.

Anderson, J. (1988). *The education of blacks in the south, 1860–1935.* Chapel Hill, NC: The University of North Carolina Press.

Anderson, L., Everton, C., & Brophy, J. (1982). *Principles of small group instruction in elementary reading.* East Lansing: Michigan State University, Institute for Research on Teaching.

Annie E. Casey Foundation. (2003). *Kids count data book 2003.* Baltimore, MD: Author.

Annie E. Casey Foundation. (1998). *What teens have sex: Issues and trends.* Washington, DC: Author.

Apple, M. (2004). *Ideology and curriculum.* New York: Taylor & Francis.

Aron, L. Y., & Mears, D. P. (2003, May 22). *Disability law and juvenile justice.* Washington, DC: The Urban Institute.

Ausubel, D. (1967). *Learning theory and classroom practice.* Toronto: The Ontario Institute for Studies in Education.

Ausubel, D. (1963). *The psychology of meaningful verbal learning.* New York: Grune & Stratton.

Bailey, M. (2006) Learning, technology and educational transformation: From philosophy to pedagogy. Berglund Center Summer Institute http://education.edu.pacificu.edu/bcis/workshop/philosophy.html.

Ball, S. J. (2003). *Class strategies and the education market: The middle classes and social advantage.* New York: RoutledgeFalmer.

Ballantine, J. H., & Spade, J. Z. (Eds.). (2004). *Schools and society: A sociological approach to education* (2nd ed.). Belmont, CA: Wadsworth/Thomson.

Beane, J. A. (2001). Introduction: Reform and reinvention. In T. S. Dickinson (Ed.), *Reinventing the middle school.* New York: RoutledgeFalmer.

Bedley, G. (2001). *Values in action.* Rancho Santa Margarita, CA: People-Wise Publications.

Bennet, N., & Blundell, D. (1983). Quantity and quality of work in rows and classroom groups. *Educational Psychology, 3*, 93–105.

Berliner, D. C. (2004). If the underlying premise for no child left behind is false, how can that act solve our problems? In K. Goodman, P. Shannon, Y. Goodman, & R. Rapoport (Eds.), *Saving our schools: The case for public education in America.* Oakland, CA: RDR Books.

Berliner, D. C. (2001). Learning about and learning from expert teachers. *International Journal of Educational Research, 35*(5), 463–483.

Berliner, D. C. (1994). Expertise: The wonders of exemplary performance. In John N. Mangieri & Cathy Collins Block (Eds.), *Creating powerful thinking in teachers and students* (pp. 141–186). Ft. Worth, TX: Holt, Rinehart and Winston.

Berliner, D. C., & Biddle, B. J. (1995). *The manufactured crisis: Myths, fraud, and the attack on America's public schools.* Reading, MA: Addison-Wesley.

Bethel School District v. Fraser, 478 U.S. 675, 106 S.Ct. 3159, 93 L. Ed. 2d 549 (1986).

Black America's Political Action Committee. (2004). 2004 National survey of African American registered voters. Retrieved July 1, 2005, from www.bampac.org/opinion_polls.asp.

Blank, Martin J. (2004). How community schools make a difference. *Educational Leadership, 61*(8), 62–65.

Bloom, B. S. (Ed.). (1956). *Taxonomy of educational objectives handbook I: Cognitive domain.* New York: David McKay Co.

Board of Education v. Pico, 457 U.S. 853 (1982).

Boe, E. E., & Shin, S. (2005). Is the United States really losing the international horse race in academic achievement? *Phi Delta Kappan, 86*(9), 688–695.

Bolling v. Sharpe, 347 U.S. 497 (1954).

Books, S., Polakow, V. (2001, Fall). Introduction to special issue: Poverty and schooling. *Educational Studies, 32*(3), 259–263.

Borich, G. D. (2004). *Effective teaching methods,* 5th ed. Upper Saddle River, NJ: Pearson Prentice Hall.

Bourdieu, P. (1990). *Reproduction in education, society and culture.* Thousand Oaks, CA: Sage.

Bowles, S., & Gintis, H. (1976). *Schooling in capitalist America.* New York: Basic Books.

Bowman, B. T., Donovan, M. S., & Burns, M. S. (2001). *Eager to learn: Educating our preschoolers.* Washington, DC: National Academy Press.

Bracey, Gerald W. (2003). *On the death of childhood and the destruction of public schools.* Portsmouth, NH: Heinemann.

Brantlinger, E. (2003). *Dividing classes: How the middle class negotiates and rationalizes school advantage.* New York: RoutledgeFalmer.

Briggs v. Elliot, 98 F. Supp. 529 (E.D.S.C. 1951), *vacated and remanded,* 342 U.S. 350 (1952), *on remand,* 103 F. Supp. 920 (E.D.S.C. 1952).

Briggs, V. M., Jr. (2000). Immigration policy and the U.S. economy: An institutional perspective. In S. Steinberg (Ed.), *Race and ethnicity in the United States: Issues and debates.* Malden, MA: Blackwell, pp. 253–266.

Brophy, J., & Evertson, C. (1976). *Learning from teaching: A developmental perspective.* Boston: Allyn and Bacon.

Brown v. Board of Education, 98 F. Supp. 797 (D. Kan. 1951).

Bureau of Indian Affairs. (2005). Retrieved January 30, 2005, at www.doi.gov/bureau-indian-affairs.html.

Burns, M. (2005/2006). Tools for the mind. *Educational Leadership, 63*(4), 50.

Burstein, D., & Kline, K. (1995). *Road warriors: Dreams and nightmares along the information highway.* New York: A Dutton Book.

Cain, M. S. (2001) Ten qualities of the renewed teacher. *Phi Delta Kappan, 82*(9), 702–705.

Cambron-McCabe, N. H., McCarthy, M. M., & Thomas, S. B. (2004). *Public school law: Teachers' and students' rights* (5th ed.). Boston: Allyn and Bacon.

Canter, L., & Canter, M. (1992). *Assertive discipline: Positive behavior management for today's classrooms.* Santa Monica, CA: Lee Canter & Associates.

Cavanagh, S. (2005a, December 20). U.S. judge rules intelligent design has no place in science classrooms. *Education Week.* Retrieved September 5, 2006, from www.edweek.org/ew/-articles/2005/12/20/16dover_web.h25.html?qs=intelligent+design.

Cavanagh, S. (2005b, February 2). Teachers torn over religion, evolution. *Education Week, 24*(21), 1, 18.

Center for Science, Mathematics, and Engineering Education National Research Council. (1999). *Transforming undergraduate, education in science, mathematics, engineering, and technology.* Executive Summary. Retrieved August, 2005, from www.nap.edu/html/transund/es.html.

Children for Exceptional Children. (2006). Mental retardation. Retrieved September 3, 2006, from www.cec.sped.org/AM/Template.cfm?Section=Mental_Retardation&Template=/TaggedPage/TaggedPageDisplay.cfm&TPLID=37&ContentID=5630.

Churchill, Winston S., 28 October 1943 to the House of Commons (meeting in the House of Lords). Retrieved August 2006 from info@winstonchurchill.org.

Clark, C.M., & Peterson, P.L. (1986). Teachers' thought processes. In M.C. Wittrock (Ed.), *Handbook of research on teaching* (pp. 255–314). New York: Macmillan.

Cochran-Smith, M. (2004). *Walking the road: Race, diversity, and social justice in teacher education.* New York: Teachers College Press.

Coles, R. (1989). *The call of stories: Teaching and the moral imagination.* Boston: Houghton Mifflin.

College participation rates for students from low income families by state: 1992 to 2002. (2004, December). *Postsecondary Education Opportunity*, 150.

Connelly, F.M., & and Clandinin, D.J. (1988). *Teachers as curriculum planners: Narratives of experience.* New York: Teachers College Press.

Cordier, M. H. (1992). *Schoolwomen of the prairies and plains.* Albuquerque: University of New Mexico Press.

Council of Chief State School Officers (CCSSO). (2006). National Teachers of the Year. Retrieved August 31, 2006, from www.ccsso.org/projects/National_Teacher_of_the_Year/National_Teachers/.

Council of Chief State School Officers (1992). *Model standards for beginning teacher licensing, assessment, and development: A resource for state dialogue.* Washington, DC: Author. Available at www.ccsso.org/content/pdfs/corestrd_pdf.

Council of Great City Schools. (2006). City-by-city statistics: 2001–2003. Retrieved September 2, 2006, from www.cgcs.org/pdfs/citybycity03.pdf.

Cremin, L. A. (1951). *The American common school: An historical conception.* New York: Teachers College Press.

Cross, W. E., Jr. (1992). *Shades of black: Diversity in African American identity.* Philadelphia: Temple University Press.

Cruickshank, D. (1990). *Research that informs teachers and teacher educators.* Bloomington, IN: Phi Delta Kappa.

Cutler, William W., III. (2000). *Parents and schools: The 150-year struggle for control in American education.* Chicago: University of Chicago Press.

Danielson, C. (1996). *Enhancing professional practice: A framework for teaching.* Alexandria, VA: Association for Supervision & Curriculum Development.

Darling-Hammond, L. (1999). *Teacher quality and student achievement: A review of state policy evidence.* Seattle, WA: Center for the Study of Teaching and Policy, University of Washington.

Darling-Hammond, L., French, J., and García-Lopez, S. P. (2002). *Learning to teach for social justice.* New York: Teachers College Press.

Davis v. County School Board of Prince Edward County School Board, 103 F. Supp. 337 (E.D. Va. 1952).

Dede, C. (1997). The evolution of learning devices: Smart object, information infrastructures and shared synthetic experiments. Retrieved June 2006 from www.ed.gov/technology/futures/ded.html.

Dewey, J. (1997). *Democracy and education.* Detroit, MI: Free Press.

Dewey, J. (1974). *The child and the curriculum: And the school and society.* Chicago: University of Chicago Press.

Dewey, J. (1963). *Experiences in education.* New York: Collier Books.

Dewey, J. (1943). *The school and society.* Chicago: University of Chicago Press.

Dewey, J. (1934). *Art as experience.* New York: Minton, Balch & Co.

Dewey, J. (1910). *How we think.* Lexington, MA: D.C. Heath.

Diversity data. (2000). *Principal, 79*(5), 18.

Donohue v. Copiague Union Free Schs., 391 N.W.2d 1352 (N.Y. 1979).

Downey, L. W. (1988). *Policy analysis in education.* Alberta, Calgary: Detselig Enterprises.

Doyle, W. (1986). Classroom organization and management. In M. Wittrock (Ed.), *Handbook of research on teaching* (3rd ed., pp. 392–431). New York: Macmillan.

Dreikurs, R., & Grey, L. G. (1968). *Logical consequences: A new approach to discipline.* New York: Dutton.

Du Bois, W. E. B. (1989). *The souls of black folks* (pp. 54–56). New York: Penguin.

Ducasse, C.J. (1958). What can philosophy contribute to educational theory? *Harvard Educational Review, 28*(4), 285–297.

Duckworth, E. (1996). *The having of wonderful ideas and other essays on teaching and learning* (2nd ed.). New York: Teachers College Press.

Edley, C., & Swanson, C. (2004). *Losing our future: How minority youth are being left behind by the graduation rate crisis*. Cambridge, MA: The Civil Rights Project at Harvard and Urban Institute.

Education Trust. (2002–2003, Winter). Education Watch: The nation: Key education facts and figures: Achievement, attainment and opportunity from elementary school to college. Washington, DC: Author.

Educational Testing Service. (2002). *A national priority: Americans speak on teacher quality.* Princeton, NJ: Author.

Egley, A., Jr., & Ritz, C. E. (2006, April). Highlights of the 2002 national youth gang survey. *OJJDP Fact Sheet*, #01. Washington, DC: U.S. Department of Justice, Office of Juvenile Justice and Delinquency Prevention. Retrieved September 8, 2006, from www.ncjrs.gov/pdffiles1/ojjdp/fs200601.pdf.

Elliott, E. (2005). *Student learning in NCATE accreditation.* Washington, DC: National Council for the Accreditation of Teacher Education.

Ellis, S. S. & Whalen, S. F. (1992). Keys to cooperative learning. *Instructor, 101*(6), 34–37.

Emmer, E., & Evertson, C. (1981). Synthesis of research on classroom management. *Educational Leadership, 38*(4), 342–347.

Emmer, E., & Evertson, C. (1980). Effective management at the beginning of the school year. *The Elementary School Journal, 80*, 219–231.

Emmer, E. T., Evertson, C., & Worsham, M. E. (2003). *Classroom management for secondary teachers* (6th ed.). Boston: Allyn and Bacon.

Evertson, C. M., Edmund, T. E., & Worsham, M. E. (2006). *Classroom management for elementary teachers* (7th ed.). Boston: Pearson/Allyn and Bacon.

Family Income and Higher Education Opportunity: 1970 to 2002. (2004, May). *Postsecondary Education Opportunity*, 143.

Farkas, S., Johnson, J., & Duffett, A. (1999). *Playing their parts: What parents and teachers really mean by parental involvement.* New York: Public Agenda.

Farkas, S., Johnson, J., & Foleno, T. (2000). *A sense of calling: Who teaches and why.* New York: Public Agenda.

Federal Interagency Forum on Child and Family Statistics. (2004). *America's children in brief: Key national indicators of well-being, 2004.* Retrieved June 27, 2005, from http://childstats.gov/americaschildren/pdf/ac04brief.pdf.

Ferdman, B. M., & Gallegos, P. I. (2001). Racial identity development and Latinos in the United States. In C. L. Wijeyesinghe & B. W. Jackson III (Eds.), *New perspectives on racial identity development: A theoretical and practical anthology* (pp. 32–66). New York: New York University Press.

Finkelhor, D., & Ormrod, R. (2000, June). *Characteristics of crimes against juveniles.* [online] Retrieved from www.ncjrs.org/html/ojjdp/2000_6_4/contents.html. Washington, DC: U.S. Department of Justice, Office of Juvenile Justice and Delinquency.

Flood, C. (2001). Schools fail boys too: Exposing the con of traditional masculinity. In H. Rousso & M. L. Wehmeyer (Eds.), *Double jeopardy: Addressing gender equity in special education* (pp. 207–236). Albany: State University of New York Press.

Ford, J.E. (1995). *Teaching the research paper.* Metuchen: The Scarecrow Press Inc.

Fox, J. A., & Zawitz, M. W. (2002). *Homicide trends in the United States.* Washington, DC: U.S. Department of Justice, Bureau of Justice Statistics.

Frankenberg, E., Lee, C., & Orfield, G. (2003). *A multiracial society with segregated schools: Are we losing the dream?* Cambridge, MA: The Civil Rights Project, Harvard University.

Freiberg, H. J., & Driscoll, A. (1992). *Universal teaching strategies.* Boston: Allyn and Bacon.

Froyen, L. A., & Iverson, A. M. (1999). *Schoolwide and classroom management: The reflective educator-leader* (3rd ed.). Upper Saddle River, NJ: Prentice-Hall.

Fuller, F. (1969). Concerns of teachers: A developmental conceptualization. *American Educational Research Journal, 6*(2), 207–226.

Furstenberg, F. F., Jr. (1999). Family change and family diversity. In N. J. Smelser and J. C. Alexander (Eds.), *Diversity and its discontents: Cultural conflict and common ground in contemporary American society* (pp. 147–165). Princeton, NJ: Princeton University Press.

Gallagher, J., & Aschner, M. (1963). A preliminary report on analyses of classroom interaction. *Merrill-Palmer Quarterly, 9*, 183–194.

The Gallup Poll. (2005). Religion. Retrieved September 3, 2006, from www.galluppoll.com/content/?CI=1690.

Gamoran, A. (2004). American schooling and educational inequality: A forecast for the 21st century. In J. H. Ballantine & J. Z. Spade, *Schools and society: A sociological approach to education* (2nd ed.) (pp. 7–26). Belmont, CA: Wadsworth/Thomson.

Gardner, H. (1999). *Intelligence reframed: Multiple intelligences for the 21st century*. New York: Basic Books.

Garrett, S. S., Sadker, M., & Sadker, D. (1994). Interpersonal communication skills. In J. M. Cooper (Ed.), *Classroom teaching skills* (5th ed. p. 234). Lexington, MA: D.C. Heath.

Gates, B. (1995). *The road ahead*. New York: Viking Penquin.

Gathercoal, F. (1997). *Judicious discipline* (4th ed.). San Francisco: Caddo Gap Press.

Gay, Geneva. (2000). *Culturally responsive teaching: Theory, research, & practice*. New York: Teachers College Press.

Gebhart v. Belton, 87 A.2d 862, aff'd, 91 A.2d 137 (Del. 1952).

Genesee, F. (Ed.) (1999). *Program alternatives for linguistically diverse students*. Washington, DC: Center for Research on Education, Diversity and Excellence.

Ginott, H. (1972). *Teacher and child*. New York: Macmillan.

Glasser, W. (1997). A new look at school failure and school success. *Phi Delta Kappan, 78*(8), 597–602.

Goldhaber, D. D., & Anthony, E. (2004). *Can teacher quality be effectively assessed?* Seattle, WA: Center on Reinventing Public Policy, University of Washington.

Goldin, G. A. (1990). Epistemology, constructivism, and discovery learning in mathematics. *Journal for Research in Mathematics Education, 4*, 31–47.

Gollnick, D. M., & Chinn, P. C. (2006). *Multicultural education in a pluralistic society*. Columbus, OH: Merrill.

Good, T., Grouws, D., & Ebmeier, H. (1983). *Active mathematics teaching*. New York: Longman.

Gopal, A. (2004). Managing an economy of emotion, not reason. Retrieved from http://gmj.gallup.com.

Gordon, T. (1989). *Teaching children self-discipline: Promoting self-discipline in children*. New York: Penguin.

Grant, G., & Murray, C. E. (1999). *Teaching in America: The slow revolution*. Cambridge, MA: Harvard University Press.

Greene, M, (1988). *The dialectic of freedom*. New York: Teachers College Press.

Gurian, M. (2001). *Boys and girls learn differently!: A guide for teachers and parents*. San Francisco: Jossey-Bass.

Hall, G. E., & Hord, S. M. (2006). *Implementing change: Patterns, principles and potholes* (2nd ed.). Boston: Allyn and Bacon.

Haque, A. (2004). Islamophobia in North America: Confronting the menace. In B. van Driel (Ed.), *Confronting Islamophobia in educational practice*. London: Trentham.

Harassment-free hallways: How to stop sexual harassment in schools: A guide for students, parents, and teachers, section III for schools. (2002). Washington, DC: American Association of University Women Educational Foundation.

HarrisInteractive. (2004a, May 4). The Harris Poll #32: Opinions regarding the condition of public education is split down racial lines. Retrieved June 26, 2005, from www.harrisinteractive.com/harris_poll/index.asp?PID=461.

HarrisInteractive. (2004b, September 15). The Harris Poll #65: Doctors, scientists, firemen, teachers and military officers top list as "most prestigious occupations." Retrieved June 26, 2005, from www.harrisinteractive.com/harris_poll/index.asp?PID=494.

Hawkes, M. (2001). Variables of interest in exploring the reflective outcomes of network-based communication. *Journal of Research on Computing in Education, 33*(3), 299–315.

Hellison, D. (1995). *Teaching responsibility through physical activity*. Champaign, IL: Human Kinetics.

Helms, J. E. (1995). An update of Helms's white and people of color racial identity models. In J. G. Ponterotto, J. M. Casas, L. A. Suzuki, & C. M. Alexander (Eds.), *Handbook of multicultural counseling* (pp. 181–198). Thousand Oaks, CA: Sage.

Hendrie, C. (2000). In black and white. In *Education Week*, Lessons of a century: A nation's schools come of age. Bethesda, MD: Editorial Projects in Education.

Hewes, D. W. (2001). NAEYC's first half century: 1926–1976. In National Association for the Education of Young Children, *NAEYC at 75 (1926–2001): Reflections on the past: Challenges for the future*. Washington, DC: Author.

Hirsch, Jr., E.D. (1987). *Cultural literacy: What every American needs to know*. Boston: Houghton Mifflin.

Hobson v. Hansen, 267 F. Supp. 401 (D.D.C. 1967).

Hord, Shirley M. (2004). Professional learning communities: An overview. In Shirley M. Hord (Ed.), *Learning together, leading together, changing schools through professional learning communities*. New York: Teachers College Press.

Horse, P. G. (2001). *Reflections on American Indian identity*. In C. L. Wijeyesinghe & B. W. Jackson III (Eds.), *New perspectives on racial identity development: A theoretical and practical anthology* (pp. 91–107). New York: New York University Press.

Hunter, M. (1994). *Enhancing teaching*. New York: Macmillan College Publishing Co.

Hunter, M. (1985). Standards in elementary education. In W. J. Johnston (Ed.), *Education on trial: Strategies for the future*. San Francisco: Institute for Contemporary Studies.

Hutchison, W. R. (2003). *Religious pluralism in America: The contentious history of a founding ideal*. New Haven, CT: Yale University Press.

Immerwahr, J. (2003, June). *With diploma in hand: Hispanic high school seniors talk about their future* (National Center Report #03-2). San Jose, CA: National Center for Public Policy and Higher Education and Public Agenda.

Immerwahr, J., & Foleno, T. (2000). *Great expectations: How the public and parents—white, African American and Hispanic—view higher education*. New York: Public Agenda.

Ingersoll, R. M. (2003). *Is there really a teacher shortage?* Seattle, WA: Center for the Study of Teaching and Policy, University of Washington.

International Society for Technology in Education (ISTE) National Educational Technology Standards for Teachers (NETST). *Education Technology Standards and Performance Indicators for All Teachers* at www.iste.org/inhouse/nets/chets/teacher/t_stands.html.

Interstate New Teacher Assessment and Support Consortium. (1992). *Model standards for beginning teacher licensing, assessment, and development: A resource for state dialogue*. Washington, DC: Council of Chief States School Officers.

Irvine, J., & York, D. (2001). Learning styles and culturally diverse students: A literature review. In J. Banks & C. Banks (Eds.), *Handbook of research on multicultural education* (pp. 484–497). San Francisco: Jossey-Bass.

Iverson, A. M. (2003). *Building competence in classroom management and discipline* (4th ed.). Columbus, Ohio: Merrill/Prentice Hall.

Jackson, B. W., III. (2001). Black identity development: Further analysis and elaboration. In C. L. Wijeyesinghe & B. W. Jackson III (Eds.), *New perspectives on racial identity development: A theoretical and practical anthology* (pp. 8–31). New York: New York University Press.

Jamentz, K. (2002). *Isolation is the enemy of improvement: Instructional leadership to support standards-based practice*. San Francisco: WestEd.

James, W. (1975). *Pragmatism*. Cambridge, MA: Harvard University Press..

Jarolimek, J., Foster, Sr., C. D., & Kellough, R. D. (2005). *Teaching and learning in the elementary school* (8th ed.). Upper Saddle River, NJ: Pearson.

Jefferson, T. (1820, September). Letter to William C. Jarvis. Retrieved September 8, 2006, from http://etext.virginia.edu/jefferson/quotations/jeff1350.htm.

Jefferson, T. (1813). Letter to John Adams. Retrieved September 8, 2006, from http://etext.virginia.edu/jefferson/quotations/jeff1370.htm.

Johnson, D., & Johnson, R. (1999). The three C's of school and classroom management. In H. Jerome Freiberg (Ed.), *Beyond behaviorism: Changing the classroom management paradigm* (pp. 119–144). Boston: Allyn and Bacon.

Johnson, D. W., & Johnson, R. T. (1999). *Learning together and alone: Cooperative, competitive and individualistic learning* (5th ed.). Boston: Allyn and Bacon.

Johnson, D. W., & Johnson, R. T. (1990). Social skills for successful group work. *Educational Leadership, 47*(4), 30–32.

Johnson, J., & Duffett, A. (2003a). *An assessment of survey data on attitudes about teaching including the views of parents, administrators, teachers, and the general public.* New York: Public Agenda.

Johnson, J., & Duffett, A. (2003b). *Where we are now: 12 things you need to know about public opinion and public schools.* New York: Public Agenda.

Johnson, J., Duffett, A., Farkas, S., & Wilson, L. (2002). *When it's your own child: A report on special education from the families who use it.* New York: Public Agenda.

Johnson, J.A., Dupuis, V.L., Musial, D., Hall, G.E., & Gollnick, D.M. (2005). *Foundations of American education,* (13th ed.). Boston: Allyn and Bacon.

Johnson, K. (2004, Summer). Confronting child labor. *Rethinking Schools, 18*(4), 26–30.

Jones, F. (2003). More time on task, less goofing off. Retrieved from www.educationworld.com/ a_curr/jones/jones001.shtml.

Joyce, B., & Weil, M. (2000). *Models of teaching.* Boston: Allyn and Bacon.

Joyce, B., & Weil, M. (1986). *Model of teaching.* Englewood Cliffs, NJ: Prentice Hall.

Kaestle, C. F. (1983). *Pillars of the republic: Common schools and American society, 1780–1860.* New York: Hill & Wang.

Kagan, J. (1998). *Three seductive ideas.* Cambridge, MA: Harvard University Press.

Kaiser, R. G. (2005, August 7). In Finland's footsteps: If we're so rich and smart, why aren't we more like them? *The Washington Post, 128*(170), B1–B2.

Kauchak, D. & Eggen, P. (2005). *Introduction to teaching: Becoming a professional* (2nd ed.) Upper Saddle River, NJ: Merrill Prentice Hall.

Keeping Current (2003). *Increasing parent involvement. Research-based ideas for teachers from the editors of Better Teaching.* Fairfax Station, VA: The Teacher Institute.

Kim, J. (2001). Asian American identity development theory. In C. L. Wijeyesinghe & B. W. Jackson III (Eds.), *New perspectives on racial identity development: A theoretical and practical anthology* (pp. 67–90). New York: New York University Press.

Kindlon, D., & Thompson, M. (2000). *Raising Cain: Protecting the emotional life of boys.* New York: Ballantine Books.

Kohn, A. (1996). *Beyond discipline: From compliance to community.* Alexandria, VA: Association of Supervision and Curriculum Development.

Kounin, J. S. (1970). *Discipline and group management in classrooms.* New York: Holt, Rinehart, and Winston.

Kreeft, P. (1988). The pillars of unbelief—Sartre. *The National Catholic Register,* Jan-Feb. www .catholiceducation.org.

Lareau, A., & Horvat, E. M. (2004). Moments of social inclusion and exclusion: Race, class, and cultural capital in family-school relationships. In J. H. Ballantine & J. Z. Spade (Eds.), *Schools and society: A sociological approach to education* (2nd ed.). Belmont, CA: Wadsworth/Thomson.

Latino Coalition. (2004). 2004 national survey of Hispanic adults. Retrieved July 1, 2005, from www.thelatinocoalition.com/news/pdf/ 2004NationalHispanicSurveyTopline.pdf.

Lau v. Nichols, 414 U.S., 563–572 (Jan. 21, 1974). Retrieved February 10, 2006, from www.nabe.org/ documents/policy_legislation/LauvNichols.pdf.

Lawrence, D. H. (1915). *The Rainbow.* New York: Random House.

Lee, J., & Zhou, M. (2004). *Asian American youth: Culture, identity, and ethnicity.* New York: Routledge.

Legal Information Institute. (2006). United States Constitution: Amendment XIV. Retrieved February 10, 2006, from www.law.cornell.edu/ constitution/constitution.amendmentxiv .html.

Levin, S. R., Waddoups, G. L., Levin, J., & Buell, J. (2001). Highly interactive and effective online learning environments for teacher professional development. *International Journal of Educational Technology,* January, 2001.

Lieberman, A., & Miller, L. (1984). *Teachers, their world, and their work: Implication for school improvement.* Alexandria, Va.: Association for Supervision and Curriculum Development.

Linder, D. (2000). The Scopes Trial: A final word. Text of speech on the 75th anniversary of the Scopes Trial, July 10. Retrieved July 7, 2006 from www.law.umkc.edu/faculty/projects/ftrials/ scopes/evolut.htm.

Lipsky, D. K., & Gartner, A. (1996, Winter). Inclusion, school restructuring, and the remaking of American society. *Harvard Educational Review, 66*(4), 762–796.

Lorti, D.C. (1977). *Schoolteacher: A sociological study.* Chicago: University of Chicago Press.

Lyons, L. (2004, December 14). Teens: Sex can wait. Princeton, NJ: The Gallup Organization. Retrieved on December 19, 2004, from www.gallup.com/poll/content/?ci=14341.

Males, M. A. (1996). *The scapegoat generation: America's war on adolescents*. Monroe, ME: Common Courage Press.

Martin, J. (2002). *The education of John Dewey: A biography*. New York: Columbia University Press.

Marzano, R., Pickering, J., & Pollack, J. (2001). *Classroom instruction that works: Research-based strategies for increasing student achievement*. Alexandria, VA: Association for Supervision and Curriculum Development.

Marzano, R. J., & Kendall, J. S. (1996). *A comprehensive guide to designing standards-based districts, schools, and classrooms*. Alexandria, VA: Association for Supervision & Curriculum Development.

McCarty, D. (2004). A literacy luncheon. Retrieved from www.TeachingK-8.com.

McCarty, D. (1997). The great bike ride across Iowa. *Teaching Pre K-8*, September, 72–74.

McCarty, D. (1994). Kids writing for kids. *Teaching Pre K-8*, November/December, 67–69.

McCarty, D. (1993). Travelmates: Geography for kids (and stuffed pets). *Teaching Pre K-8*, April, 32–35.

McCaslin, M., & Good, T. L. (1992). Compliant cognition: The misalliance of management and instructional goals in current school reform. *Educational Researcher, 21*(3), 4–17.

McEwan, B. (2000). *The art of classroom management: Effective practices for building equitable learning communities*. Columbus, OH: Merrill/Prentice Hall.

McEwin, C. K., Dickinson, T. S., & Jenkins, D. M. (2003). *America's middle schools in the new century: Status and progress*. Westerville, OH: National Middle School Association.

McGraw, P. (2004). *Family First*. New York: Free Press.

Merriam-Webster OnLine. (2006). www.m-w.com.

MetLife, Inc. (2005). *The MetLife survey of the American teacher: Transitions and the role of supportive relationships*. Retrieved June 26, 2005, from www.metlife.com/WPSAssets/34996838801118758796V1FATS_2004.pdf.

MetLife, Inc. (2003). *The MetLife survey of the American teacher: An examination of school leadership*. Retrieved June 26, 2005, from www.metlife.com/WPSAssets/20781259951075837470V1F2003%20Survey.pdf.

Mid-continent Research for Education and Learning. (2002). Retrieved August 2005 from www.mcrel.org.

Minority undergraduate enrollments at leading public and private colleges and universities. (2005, August). *Postsecondary Education Opportunity*, 153.

Mosier, R. (1965). *Making the American mind: Social and moral ideas in the* McGuffey Readers. New York: Russell & Russell.

Nansel, T. R., Overpeck, M. D., Haynie, D. L., Ruan, J., & Scheidt, P. C. (2003, April). Relationships between bullying and violence among U.S. youth. *Archives of Pediatrics and Adolescent Medicine, 157*(4), 348–357.

National and state-specific pregnancy rates among adolescents—United States, 1995–1997. (2000, July 14). *Morbidity and Mortality Weekly Report, 49*(27), 605–611.

National Association for the Education of Homeless Children and Youth. (2004). Homeless education: An introduction to the issues. Retrieved September 15, 2004, from www.naehcy.org/introtoissues.pdf.

National Board for Professional Teaching Standards (NBPTS). (1987). *What teachers should know and be able to do*. Arlington, VA: Author.

National Center for Education Statistics. (2004). *Digest of Education Statistics, 2004*. Washington, DC: Author.

National Center for Health Statistics. (2003, June 25). U.S. birth rate reaches record low. Retrieved June 27, 2005, from www.cdc.gov/nchs/pressroom/03news/lowbirth.htm.

National Center for Public Policy Research. *Brown v. Board of Education*, 347 U.S. 483 (1954). Retrieved February 10, 2006, from the Constitution and the Courts Archive at www.nationalcenter.org/brown.html.

National Commission on Excellence in Education (1983). *A nation at risk: The imperative for educational reform*. Washington, DC: Department of Education.

National Commission on Teaching and America's Future. (2003). *No dream denied: A pledge to America's children*. Washington, DC: Author.

National Education Association. (2004). *Estimates databank: NEA rankings and estimates. Fall 2003 update*, Table 1. Washington, DC: Author.

National Education Association. (2003). *Status of the American public school teacher 2000–2001*. Washington, DC: Author.

National PTA. (2005a). Our history. Retrieved on July 2, 2005, from www.pta.org/ap_our_history.html.

National PTA. (2005b). Questions to ask during the conference. Retrieved July 2, 2005, from www.pta.org/documents/Questions%20to%20ask%20during%20the%20conference.doc.

National PTA. (1998). *National standards for parent/family involvement programs*. Chicago: Author.

Netterville, C. (2002). Sample portfolio contents. *2002 AAEE job search handbook*. Columbus, OH: American Association for Employment in Education, Inc.

Nichols, S. L., & Good, T. L. (2004). *America's teenagers—Myths and realities: Media images, schooling, and the social costs of careless indifference*. Mahwah, NJ: Lawrence Erlbaum.

Noguera, P. (2003). *City schools and the American dream: Reclaiming the promise of public education*. New York: Teachers College Press.

North Central Regional Laboratory. www.ncrel.org/tech/netc/2004/blue.htm.

O'Grady, M. (1999). *Why I teach: Inspirational true stories from teachers who make a difference*. Esther Wright (Ed.). Rocklin: Pima Publishing.

Oliva, P.F. (2005). *Developing the curriculum*. Boston: Allyn and Bacon.

Olson, L. (2004, January 8). Enveloping expectations: Federal law demands that schools teach the same content to children they wrote off a quarter-century ago. *Quality counts 2004: Count me in* (pp. 8–20). Washington, DC: Education Week.

Olson, L. (2000, September 27). Mixed needs of immigrants pose challenges for schools. *Education Week, XX*(4), 38–39.

Olson, L. (2000a). The common good. In *Education Week*, Lessons of a century: A nation's schools come of age. Bethesda, MD: Editorial Projects in Education.

Olson, L. (2000b). Tugging at tradition. In *Education Week*, Lessons of a century: A nation's schools come of age. Bethesda, MD: Editorial Projects in Education.

Orfield, G., & Frankenberg, E. (2004, Spring). Where are we now? *Teaching Tolerance, 25*, 57–59.

Orfield, G., & Lebowitz, H. L. (Eds.) (1999). *Religion, race and justice in a changing America*. New York: Century Foundation.

Partridge, C. (Ed.). (2005). *Introduction to world religions*. Minneapolis, MN: Fortress Press.

Pesce v. J. Sterling Morton High School District 201, Cook County, Ill., 830 F.2d 789 (7th Cir. 1987).

Peter W. v. San Francisco Unified School District, 131 Cal. Rptr. 854 (Ct. App. 1976).

Piaget, J. (1985). *The equilibrium of cognitive structures: The central problem of intellectual development* (T. Brown & K. L. Thampy, Trans.). Chicago: University of Chicago Press.

Pierce v. Society of Sisters, 268 U.S. 510, 45 S.Ct. 571, 69 L. Ed. 1080 (1925).

Pinar, W., Reynolds, W., Slattery, P., and Taubman, P. (Eds.) (1995). *Understanding Curriculum*. New York: Peter Lang.

Plessy v. Ferguson, 163 U.S. 537 (1891).

Plyer v. Doe, 457 U.S. 202 (1982).

Portes, A., & Rumbaut, R. G. (2001). *Legacies: The story of the immigrant second generation*. Berkeley: University of California Press.

Public Agenda. (2005). Education: Quick takes. Retrieved June 26, 2005, from www.publicagenda.org/research/pdfs/religion_2005_questions.pdf.

Purrington, C. (2006). Textbook disclaimer stickers. Retrieved September 5, 2006, from www.swarthmore.edu/NatSci/cpurrin1/textbook disclaimers/.

Putman, J. (1997). *Cooperative learning in diverse classroom*. Upper Saddle River, NJ: Merrill/Prentice Hall.

Quay, S. E., & Quaglia, R. J. (2004). Creating a classroom culture that inspires student learning. *The Teaching Professor, 18*(2), 1.

Quinn, L. F. (1991). Mentor teacher/first-year teacher interactions: A case study. Unpublished dissertation research. University of Houston.

Ranck, E., & NAEYC's History & Archives Panel. (2001). Timeline of early care and education. In National Association for the Education of Young Children, *NAEYC at 75 (1926–2001): Reflections on the past: Challenges for the future*. Washington, DC: Author.

Ravitch, D. (1995). *National standards in American education: A citizens guide*. Washington, DC: Brookings Institution.

Recruiting New Teachers, Inc. (2003a). *The essential profession: American education at the crossroads*. Belmont, MA: Author.

Recruiting New Teachers. (2003b). *The urban teacher challenge: Teacher demand and supply in the great city schools*. Belmont, MA: Author.

Redl, F., & Watternberg, W. W. (1959). *Mental hygiene in teaching* (2nd ed.). New York: Harcourt, Brace, and World.

Reese, W. (1995). *The origins of the American high school*. New Haven, CT: Yale University Press.

Reutter, E. E. (1975). *The courts and student conduct*. Topeka, KS: National Organization on Legal Problems of Education.

Richardson, V. (1997). Constructivist teaching and teacher education: Theory and practice. In V. Richardson (Ed.), *Constructivist teacher education: Building new understanding* (pp. 3–14). Washington, DC: Falmer Press.

Riner, P. S. (2000). *Successful teaching in the elementary classroom*. Upper Saddle River, NJ: Merrill/Prentice-Hall.

Rivkin, S. G., Hanushek, E. A., & Kain, J. F. (1998). *Teachers, schools and academic achievement*. (Working Paper No. 6691.) Washington, DC: National Bureau of Economic Research.

Robertson, C. (2004). *Understanding comprehensive reform: Component four: Measurable goals and benchmarks*. Retrieved August 2005 from www.serve.org/UCR/UCRCompFour.html.

Rodriguez v. San Antonio Independent School, 411 U.S. 1 (1973).

Roffman, D. M. (2004, February 25). Separation of church and school: The broader moral dimensions of our approach to gay students and parents. *Education Week, 23*(24), 34–35.

Rogers, C., & Freiberg, H. J. (1994). *Freedom to learn*. Upper Saddle River, NJ: Prentice-Hall.

Root, M. P. P. (2004). Multiracial families and children: Implications for educational research and practice. In J. A. Banks & C. A. M. Banks (Eds.), *Handbook of research on multicultural education* (2nd ed.) (pp. 110–122). San Francisco: Jossey-Bass.

Rose, L. C., & Gallup, A. M. (2005, September). The 37th annual Phi Delta Kappa/Gallup Poll of the public's attitudes toward the public schools. *Phi Delta Kappan, 87*(1), 41–54.

Rose, L. C., & Gallup, A. M. (2004, September). The 36th annual Phi Delta Kappa/Gallup Poll of the public's attitudes toward the public schools. *Phi Delta Kappan, 86*(1), 41–52.

Rose, S. J. (2000). *Social stratification in the United States*. New York: New Press.

Rosenshine, B. (1983). Teaching functions in instructional programs. *The Elementary School Journal, 83*, 335–351.

Rosenshine, B., & Stevens, R. (1986). Teaching functions. In M. C. Wittrock (Ed.), *Handbook of research on teaching*, 3rd ed., (pp. 376–391). Upper Saddle River, NJ: Merrill/Prentice-Hall.

Rothstein, R. (2004). *Class and schools: Using social, economic, and educational reform to close the black-white achievement gap*. New York: Economic Policy Institute and Teachers College, Columbia University.

Rumbaut, R. G., & Portes, A. (2001). *Ethnicities: Children of immigrants in America*. Berkeley, CA: University of California Press.

Sadaker, M.P. & Sadaker, D.M. (2000). *Teachers, schools, and society*. New York: McGraw Hill.

Sadovnik, A. R. (2004). Theories in the sociology of education. In J. H. Ballantine & J. Z. Spade, *Schools and society: A sociological approach to education* (2nd ed.) (pp. 7–26). Belmont, CA: Wadsworth/Thomson.

Salpeter, J. (2003). Professional development: Twenty-first century models. *Technology and Learning*, 24. Retrieved June 2006 from www.techlearning.com/story/showArticle.jhtml?articleID=13000492.

Samuels, C. A. (2005, February 2). Advanced placement participation grows. *Education Week, 24*(21), 3.

Sanders, N. (1966). *Classroom questions: What kinds?* New York: Harper & Row.

Sanders, W. L., & Rivers, J. C. (1996). *Cumulative and residual effects of teachers on future acade-mic achievement*. Knoxville: University of Tennessee Value-Added Research and Assessment Center.

Sartre, J.P. (1948). *The emotions, outline of a theory*. Tr. from the French by Bernard Frechtman. New York: Philosophical Library.

Segregation of higher education enrollment by family income and race/ethnicity 1980 to 2004.

U.S. Department of Health and Human Services, The Administration for Children and Families. (2002). *Early Head Start research: Making a difference in the lives of infants and toddlers and their families; The impacts of Early Head Start.* Washington, DC: Author.

U.S. Department of Health and Human Services. (1996). *Physical activity and health: A report of the Surgeon General at-a-glance.* [online] Retrieved from www.governmentguide.com/govsite .adp?bread=*Main&url=http%3A//www .governmentguide.com/ams/clickThruRedirect. adp%3F55076483%2C16920155%2Chttp%3A// www.dhhs.gov. Washington, DC: Author.

U.S. Department of Justice, Office of Juvenile Justice and Delinquency Prevention. Retrieved September 8, 2006, from www.ncjrs.gov/ pdffiles1/ojjdp/fs200601.pdf.

United Nations. (2002, May). Backgrounder: First meeting of permanent forum high point of UN decade. Retrieved March 19, 2005, from www.un.org/rights/indigenous/backgrounder1 .htm.

Urban Institute. (2000). *America's homeless II: Populations and services.* Washington, DC: Author.

Viadero, D. (2004). Disparately disabled. *Quality counts 2004: Count me in* (pp. 22–26). Washington, DC: *Education Week.*

Wahl, L., & Duffield, J. (2005). Using flexible technology to meet the needs of diverse learners: What teachers can do. *WestEd Knowledge Brief.* San Francisco: WestEd.

Walberg, H. (1991). Productive teaching and instruction: Assessing the knowledge base. In H. Waxman & H. Walbert (Eds.), *Effective teaching: Current research.* Berkeley, CA: McCuchan.

Wallheiser, M. (2005, June 8). Keeping in touch. *Education Week, 24*(39), 30–33.

Walling, D. R. (1993). *English as a Second Language: 25 Questions and Answers.* Bloomington, IN: Phi Delta Kappa Educational Foundations.

Walton, J., & Adamson, E. (2000). *Labrador retrievers for dummies.* New York: John Wiley & Sons.

Wassermann, S. (1992). *Asking the right question.* Bloomington, IN: Phi Delta Kappa.

Watternberg, W. (1967). *All men are created equal.* Detroit, MI: Wayne State University Press.

Weber, B. (2005, June 2). A town's struggle in the culture war. *The New York Times.* Retrieved June 29, 2005, from www.nytimes.com/2005/ 06/02/books/02ban.html?oref=login.

Weber, W. A. (1994). Classroom management. In J. M. Cooper (Ed.). *Classroom teaching skills* (5th ed.) (pp. 234–279). Lexington: D.C. Heath.

Weinstein, G. A., & Fantini, M. F. (1970). *Toward humanistic education: A curriculum of affect.* New York: Praeger.

Weiss, D. (2004). Unwrapping the holidays: Reflections on a difficult first year. *The new teacher book: Finding purpose, balance, and hope during your first years in the classroom* (pp. 202–209). Milwaukee, WI: Rethinking Schools.

Welner, K. G. (2001). *Legal rights, local wrongs: When community control collides with educational equity.* Albany: State University of New York Press.

West Virginia State Board of Education v. Barnette, 319 U.S. 624, 63 S.Ct. 1178 (1943).

WestEd Policy Brief. (2002, Winter). *Urgency Rises for Quality of Child Care.* San Francisco, CA: WestEd.

WestEd. (2002). *Improving districts: Systems that support learning.* San Francisco: WestEd.

Who should teach? The states decide. *Education Week, XIX*(18), January 13, 2000.

Windschitl, M. (1999). The challenges of sustaining a constructivist classroom culture. *Phi Delta Kappa, 80,* 751–755.

Wisconsin v. Yoder, 406 U.S. 205 (1972).

Wong, H. K. (1998). *The first days of school.* Mountain View, CA: Harry K. Wong Publication.

Woodhead, L. (2005). Secularization and sacralization. In C. Partridge (Ed.), *Introduction to world religions* (pp. 445–448). Minneapolis, MN: Fortress Press.

Woodward, C. V. (1971). *Origins of the New South, 1877–1913.* Baton Rouge: Louisiana State University Press, pp. 416–417.

Woolfolk, A. (2004). *Educational psychology* (9th ed.). Boston: Allyn and Bacon.

Young, J. (2000). Guidelines for collecting information about student learning. *New Teacher Advocate,* Fall, 2.

Young, R. L., & Pang, V. O. (1995, Winter). Asian Pacific American students: A rainbow of dreams. *Multicultural Education, 3*(2), 4–7.

Zehr, M. A. (2005, May 4). Newcomers bring change, challenge to region. *Education Week, 24*(34), 1, 18–19.

Subject Index

Photo Credits

Chapter opening pages photos, Corbis; Page 2–3, Courtesy of Michelle Clark, Pointers Run Elementary School, Howard County, Maryland; 6, Topham/The Image Works; 16, Jim West/The Image Works; 21, Rachel Epstein/The Image Works; 23, Jonathan Nourok/PhotoEdit; 26, Bob Daemmrich/The Image Works; 35, Frank Siteman/PhotoEdit; 44–45, Courtesy of Katherine Wright Knight, Parkview Magnet School, Little Rock, Arkansas; 58, David McNew/Getty Images; 65, Bob Daemmrich/The Image Works; 68, Comstock; 72, Gabe Palmer/Creative Eye/MIRA.com; 77, Ellen B. Senisi/The Image Works; 79, Ellen Senisi/The Image Works; 90–91, Courtesy of Blanca Estela Carbajal Rodriguez, Frederick Elementary School, Colorado; 96, Mark Richards/PhotoEdit; 99, John Birdsall/The Image Works ; 103, Steve Warmowski/ Journal-Courier/The Image Works; 119, Ellen B. Senisi/The Image Works; 128–129, Courtesy of Lucy Diaz Duncan, McBee Elementary School, Austin, Texas; 137, Dennis MacDonald/PhotoEdit; 141, Michael Newman/PhotoEdit; 145, Clayton Statler/ Jacksonville-Courier/The Image Works; 149, Steven E. Frischling/Corbis; 165, Frank Ordorez/Syracuse Newspapers/The Image Works; 172–173, Courtesy of Verena Jessen, Sand Springs Elementary School, Montana; 181, Image Works/Mary Evans Picture Library; 186, Image Works/Mary Evans Picture Library; 189, Courtesy of Library of Congress; 195, John N. Choate/Liaison/Getty Images; 200, Bettmann/ Corbis; 206, Courtesy of Library of Congress; 216–217, Courtesy of Les Nakasaki, Rosemead, California; 223, Michael Newman/PhotoEdit; 230, David Lassman/ Syracuse Newspapers/The Image Works; 236, Frank Siteman; 241, Frank Siteman; 245, Dennis MacDonald/Alamy Images; 247, Will Hart/PhotoEdit; 258–259, Courtesy of Lisa A. Mason Sykes, George H. Corliss High School, Chicago, Illinois; 265, Chris Kirzedar/University of Chicago Laboratory Schools; 270, Courtesy of www.statute.com. Reprinted with permission; 275, Courtesy of Joseph Adler, www.aarweb.org. Reprinted with permission; 292–293, Courtesy of Merrie Schroeder, Malcolm Price Laboratory School, Iowa; 298, Bill Aron/PhotoEdit; 304, Michael Newman/PhotoEdit; 306, Corbis; 318, Duomo/Corbis; 320, Courtesy of Aitken Thompson, Taskstream, Inc. Reprinted with permission; 326–327, Courtesy of Janet Stramel, Waumego Middle School, Waumego, Kansas; 333, Cary WolinskyAurora & Quanta Productions; 335, Billy E. Barnes/PhotoEdit; 336, Peter Hvizdak/The Image Works; 340, Mary Kate Denny/PhotoEdit; 344, Eric Fowke/PhotoEdit; 346, Ellen Senisi/The Image Works; 364–365, Courtesy of Dave V. Jones, King Kamehameta Elementary School, Lahaina, Maui, Hawaii; 372, Bob Daemmrich/The Image Works; 373, Tony Freeman/PhotoEdit; 380, Bob Daemmrich/PhotoEdit 398–399, Courtesy of Dr. Elliott Asp, Superintendent, Cherry Creek School District, Colorado; 403, Michael Newman/PhotoEdit; 406, Dennis MacDonald/PhotoEdit; 408, Joel Rafkin/PhotoEdit; 417, Michael Newman/PhotoEdit; 425, Courtesy of Jocelyne Villafane, student, and Alexandra Reub, teacher, at Paradise Professional Development School, Las Vegas,